ALSO BY NICHOLAS FOX WEBER

The Drawings of Josef Albers

The Woven and Graphic Art of Anni Albers

Leland Bell

Warren Brandt

Josef Albers: A Retrospective

The Art of Babar

Patron Saints

Cleve Gray

Anni Albers

Balthus: A Biography

Marc Klionsky

Josef & Anni Albers / Designs for Living

The Clarks of Cooperstown

LE CORBUSIER

Le Corbusier

A Life

Nicholas Fox Weber

Alfred A. Knopf
NEW YORK
2008

THIS IS A BORZOI BOOK PUBLISHED BY ALFRED A. KNOPF

www.aaknopf.com

Knopf, Borzoi Books, and the colophon are registered trademarks of Random House, Inc.

The author gratefully acknowledges the support he received from the Furthermore Foundation, a program of the J. M. Kaplan Fund.

Translations of Le Corbusier's letters by Richard Howard

Library of Congress Cataloging-in-Publication Data
Weber, Nicholas Fox, {date}
Le Corbusier : a life / by Nicholas Fox Weber. — 1st ed.
p. cm.
"A Borzoi book."
Includes bibliographical references.
ISBN 978-0-375-41043-7
1. *Le Corbusier, 1887–1965.* 2. *Architects — France — Biography.* I. *Title.*
NA1053.J4W39 2008
720.92 — *dc22*
{B} 2008032654

Manufactured in the United States of America

FIRST EDITION

For Nancy

In his highest flights, musical and architectural above all,
for they are one, man gives the illusion of rivalling the order,
the majesty and the splendor of the heavens.

HENRY MILLER, *The Colossus of Maroussi*

CONTENTS

ILLUSTRATIONS

ILLUSTRATIONS

ILLUSTRATIONS

ILLUSTRATIONS

COLOR INSERT I

COLOR INSERT II

PREFACE

Cézanne at the Lefèvre

> But these . . . qualities (of "varied and inimitable" colour and his handling) do not account for the look of hard and unrelenting authenticity that distinguishes his work from that of lesser men. It is Cézanne's peculiar determination to pin down his sensation, and the exactness and intensity of notation resulting from this, that made Cézanne pre-eminent. . . . In a Cézanne there can be no question of juggling with the elements of design, no possibility of glossing over difficulties, no equivocation. With Cézanne integrity was the thing, and integrity never allowed him to become fixed at any one point in his development, but sent him onward toward new discoveries of technique, new realisations of the motive.
>
> —Graham Bell, *The New Statesman and Nation*

I note the above both for itself and because it adds to subject and manner the thing that is incessantly overlooked: the artist, the presence of the determining personality. Without that reality no amount of other things matters much.

— WALLACE STEVENS

Until now, there has been no substantial biography of Le Corbusier. There are nearly four hundred monographs devoted to his work, among them detailed accounts of his early years and some excellent books on specific aspects of his career. There are fascinating volumes on his architecture, several written by people who had the good fortune to know Le Corbusier and had considerable insight into his character. But no single book has given primary focus to Le Corbusier as a human being and provided a comprehensive account of his entire life.

While I subscribe to Mark Twain's dictum that a person's "real life is led in his head, and is known to none but himself,"[1] I have made it my goal to understand and reveal what this extraordinary architect was like inside, as well as in the eyes of others. In my attempt to gain access to the feelings and desires of Charles-Edouard Jeanneret, our subject's name before he recreated himself as Le Corbusier, I have benefited from access to his copious correspondence with his mentor and confidant, William Ritter. He wrote to Ritter about his fluctuating humors and about everything he saw and did. Jeanneret freely focused on his own sexual obsessions; at about the age of thirty, he directly associated the vigor of his erections (mostly had in solitude) with creative power and the ability to build. Ritter was an intensely passionate novelist and music critic. Overtly homosexual, devoutly Catholic, he lived outside the strictures of Jeanneret's Swiss background. Ritter exemplified the courage to seek extremes, the independence from Calvinism that Jeanneret craved, which is why Jeanneret opened himself up to him.

I have been even more fortunate in having unprecedented access to the letters Jeanneret wrote to his parents and, following his father's death, to his mother alone. Marie Charlotte Amélie Jeanneret-Perret lived to the age of one hundred—or so Le Corbusier, with his passion for round numbers, made it seem to journalists and the public by moving her birth date back a full year. She was alive for all but the last five years of Le Corbusier's life, and he revealed himself to her more truthfully than to anyone else, as if he were confiding in a private diary more than to a person with emotions or reactions. The intimacy with which Le Corbusier wrote to her about his taste in women is extraordinary. The intensity of his program to change the world, the leaps and plunges of his spirit, the rapidity of his mood swings, and the relentlessness of his emotional needs and professional ambition: all these emerge unmasked.

I have, in addition, enjoyed the rare opportunity to read letters between Le Corbusier and his wife and have been allowed to see documents—usually off-limits—that recount a love affair of thirty years' duration between the architect and an American woman. That epistolary narrative, while touching and charmingly erotic, is evidence both of Le Corbusier's tenderness, a trait he generally concealed, and of his relentless solitude. By compulsively charting the workings of his mind—with an astounding absence of screening, exposing thoughts that most people would keep within—Le Corbusier came close in these various letters to revealing Twain's "real life." In public, he propagated his myths, but in private he knew himself well.

Marie Charlotte Amélie Jeanneret-Perret, Le Corbusier's mother, at about the age of ninety-eight

WITH HIS PERPETUAL AWARENESS of the elemental—both in his individual being and in every aspect of the universe—Le Corbusier consciously credited his mother for his existence. He never fully separated from her; nor did he ever have what he wanted from her. He fought, relentlessly and unsuccessfully, to garner the approval she gave mainly to his older brother.

At Ronchamp—the masterful country church of 1955 with which Le Corbusier burst the boundaries of architecture by composing with light and color and by animating a small space so that it is a vessel of both ceaseless motion and ineffable calm—he dedicated one of the three side chapels to the woman who bore him. While Ronchamp is officially a shrine to the Holy Virgin, the brilliant stained-glass window that bears, in exuberant script, the message "Marie shining like the sun" closely echoes the way Le Corbusier often flattered his mother, then in her nineties, in that time period. A triumphant work of pure sculpture, a celebration of red and yellow and blue and white so vibrant as to become audible, a shelter as protective as Noah's ark and as modern and functional as a spaceship, Ronchamp is a temple to femininity in general and, very specifically, to the person who created him, much as he created it. Le Corbusier revered the sun as the source of all life; Marie was the origin of his Ronchamp, with its womblike hidden chambers, so rich and nurturing, and its organic form and pulsating surfaces. It was, even more than a fabulous homage to the Holy Mother of Christianity, a hymn to the more universal idea of women as givers of life—and to Marie Charlotte Amélie Jeanneret-Perret. It is not surprising to discover, half a century after its completion, that its essentially secretive and private maker poured out his soul to his inspiration.

IT IS LE CORBUSIER in his own voice who has been my primary quarry. With that objective, I have visited almost every extant building he designed. I have also drawn on testimony from anyone I could find whose path the architect crossed—the waitress at a seafood restaurant in Roquebrune-Cap-Martin who remembered him from frequent encounters in her childhood, the architects who served in his office, his doctor, his banker's daughter.

Le Corbusier said that his biography could be written only after his death. He would have been dismayed to have it written by an American. At sixty-three, when he felt burned by events concerning the design of the new United Nations headquarters in New York and betrayed by the architect Wallace Harrison, he declared to Marie Jeanneret—in surprising words to address to a ninety-year-old Calvinist lady—

No head
No heart = Harrison
No balls = American[2]

He considered the United States "a titanic machine out of control: a runaway horse. Dangerous."[3] I will show why he came to feel that way—while demonstrating, I hope, that not all Americans were or are against him.

OFTEN ANGUISHED or furious, Le Corbusier was equally given to ecstasy. When he was not despondent, he had an unequivocal confidence that he knew solutions to some of the gravest issues of human existence. He felt he could serve mankind even in its most dire moments—and that through architecture he could counter all evil.

In March 1942, when freedom itself was at the brink of extinction in Europe, Le Corbusier wrote his mother from Vichy that she must share his joy because, having navigated within the cabinet of Maréchal Pétain, he had finally triumphed after twenty years of battle. Seemingly impervious to the realities of current events, he believed that with that alliance he would solve all the problems of Paris—the place he alternately loved and loathed, both paradise and inferno, the center of his universe—and, then, of every other city in France. While free France was shrinking, Le Corbusier was mentally rebuilding the entire empire from his new power base in a hotel room in the former spa town where Pétain's government held its seat. He

Photo taken by Robert Doisneau in 1944

had no qualms about being there—so long as he would succeed in "focusing the problem of Paris, the city, and its region. To study, to make propositions, to outline the possibility of major operations under the aegis of the president of the Municipal Council (who is a firm ally) and of the director of the Maréchal's Cabinet (who has become a great partisan). From Paris our mission will fan out over the other cities and the countryside of France and over the empire."[4]

During the previous world war, he had likened neutral Switzerland to a eunuch. He left it to start a factory for concrete blocks in a Paris suburb while the center of the city was being regularly bombed. In the thirties, he allied himself with the Soviet authorities and built in Moscow. He also tried to work with Mussolini, and with two American presidents. His goal was to build—no matter what.

What concerned him was design: of our surroundings—whether the immediate room or the larger city—and of gardens and paintings, the sights of which would penetrate our psyches. Nothing else counted. But if we agree, as Bertrand Russell observed, that "fanatics are seldom genuinely humane, and those who sincerely dread cruelty will be slow to adopt a fanatical creed,"[5] we need to ask if Le Corbusier was primarily fanatical or humane—or if he was the rare person who could combine both traits.

Le Corbusier took a definitive stance about every person, street corner, plant specimen, and idea. He readily unleashed his wrath. He could also express, although less frequently and rarely in public, immense warmth and sweetness. When he let down his guard to verbalize the depths of joy that are so gloriously manifest in the colors and angles and textures of his architecture, he was capable of a subsuming generosity of spirit. Nothing was in half measures: his lust for voluptuous women or his miserable loneliness; his passion for great paintings or his rage at public blindness; his admiration for honest naïve art or his disgust with the academies. When he was not elated, he was pulverized by a sense of failure.

Compassionate, arrogant, generous, selfish, Calvinist, hedonistic, proud, enraged, ecstatic, sad, Le Corbusier the man was as provocative, and unique, as the buildings with which he changed the visible world.

LE CORBUSIER

I

If personality is an unbroken series of successful gestures, then there was something gorgeous about him, some heightened sensitivity to the promises of life, as if he were related to one of those intricate machines that registers earthquakes ten thousand miles away. The responsiveness had nothing to do with that flabby impressionability which is dignified under the name of the "creative temperament"—it was an extraordinary gift for hope, a romantic readiness such as I have never found in any other person and which it is not likely I shall ever find again.

—F. SCOTT FITZGERALD, *The Great Gatsby*

1

SEPTEMBER 2, 1965

How ironic that the funeral of the man who had purified architecture and erased history from building facades should take place at the Cour Carrée du Louvre. Le Corbusier had constructed brazen forms of rough concrete in lieu of the fluted columns and ornate medallions that now surrounded his casket, draped with the French flag. He prized boulders and beach pebbles, not pomp.

But the setting fit. Le Corbusier had always sought entry to the palace, even when its ruler was a despot. He had worked with many of the most powerful leaders of the twentieth century, regardless of their values or politics, so long as he might build their monuments. He mocked them, but craved their complicity—provided that they served his purpose. He would have scoffed at the spectacle with which a society that had often attacked him and thwarted his dreams now bade him a lavish public farewell, but it fulfilled his ambitions.

The ceremony was high theatre. The weather helped make it so. A strong wind was buffeting fluffy cumulus clouds that late-summer evening. Their rapid flight beyond the roof balustrades and pediments was illuminated by powerful beams from two light projectors below. More than three thousand people braved the unseasonable cold as they waited for the arrival of Le Corbusier's remains. Then, at 7:40 p.m., all heads turned. Carried on the shoulders of a retinue of undertakers, the coffin slowly penetrated the crowd. A detachment of twenty young soldiers, "in bright-colored uniforms bearing torches, surrounded it." To the lugubrious beat of Beethoven's Funeral March, the convoy passed "in front of the four squadrons of the Republican Guard presenting arms." As the clouds began to give way to a clear and starry sky, the coffin was placed on trestles "at the top of a huge inclined plane" covered with grass. "In the rear, six guards in full-dress uniform with drawn swords were silhouetted against a background of columns."[1] A couple of minutes later, the wind lifted the covering off the casket, but no act of nature could deflect the order and majesty of the precisely orchestrated proceedings. Often accused of wanting to destroy Paris, Le Corbusier was now being honored with the ultimate symbols of the tradition he had threatened.

THE BUILDING WITH which Le Corbusier had liberated the idea of home—much as Coco Chanel had freed women by letting them wear pants—contained, on a modest scale, a space similar to this vast paved garden within the Louvre. His 1929 Villa Savoye also encased raw nature within man-made walls. Its forms were clear and spartan in contrast to all this Baroque excess, but it, too, showed the wish to worship, and to tame, the elements of the universe. Like the architects who at the bidding of Henri II, Richelieu, Louis XIV, and Napoleon had made the Cour Carrée, Le

Military honor guard at Le Corbusier's funeral service in the Cour Carrée du Louvre, September 2, 1965

Corbusier had framed the sky and exercised quiet control over the outdoors, rather than submit to them. The result was a staged ambience that steadies the breath.

Le Corbusier knew that well-placed walls could alter our mental states, that through measure and proportion one might bring calm to the human soul. The style of the Villa Savoye was as restrained as the Louvre was lavish, but a consciousness of visual effects was everywhere. Human beings must cultivate their environment to the fullest extent possible.

IN THIS COURTYARD where the kings of France had once strolled with minions vying for their attention, the assembled coterie now consisted mainly of government officials, young architects, and Le Corbusier's work associates. There were few relatives or friends among the hordes who had just returned to Paris from their summer vacations.

Le Corbusier, too, had been on holiday. Four days earlier, his body had been spotted floating about fifty meters from the shore at Roquebrune-Cap-Martin on the Côte d'Azur. Since the tenth of August, he had been staying alone in his small, square *cabanon,* nestled into a rocky slope overlooking the Mediterranean. Accessible only by a foot path, the *cabanon* was surrounded by a panoply of cacti, lilacs, honeysuckles, and lemon and orange trees. The only sounds were the constant lapping of the Mediterranean surf on the shore below and the rumbling of the occasional local train on the tracks just behind the uphill wall. The rugged simplicity of the one-room house was strident next to the neighbors' Italianate villas and the high style of Monte Carlo, within walking distance along the coast.

Sheathed in rough pine logs, this modest dwelling was like the Alpine mountain huts of Le Corbusier's childhood. The bare-bones furniture comprised a single table, a couple of simple wooden stools, and the bunk bed that had been his wife's. Before her death seven years earlier, Le Corbusier had slept on the floor; since then, his mattress was where hers had been. There was a small, train-style industrial sink near the table. The conspicuous toilet—separated from the headboard of the bunk bed by only a flimsy curtain—testified to Le Corbusier's belief that a water closet was the most beautiful thing in the world.

The sparse and minimal *cabanon* had its aesthetic distinction. Its measurements of 3.66 by 3.66 meters, and 2.26 meters for the height, were inspired by his "Modulor" device, the invention with which he made human scale the determining factor of his architecture. The multipurposed table, constructed from handsomely grained blocks of olive wood, was angled under the one picture window so that the plane of its top penetrated the tiny space with a strong beat. Le Corbusier had painted vibrant, sexy murals on the wooden window shutters and the entrance wall. These erotic celebrations counteracted the austerity of the rest. The hardworking man who rose at six every morning to do his gymnastics and start his day's work loved physical pleasure unabashedly.

AMONG THE FEW PEOPLE who had seen the architect since he had arrived in Roquebrune-Cap-Martin were the Rebutato family, the proprietors of the small restaurant that abutted the *cabanon.* Their lives were entwined with his. The Rebutatos' "police dog" was waiting for Le Corbusier on the corrugated iron roof of the *cabanon* during his final swim and was falsely assumed to be the architect's own pet when its photo appeared in the Parisian newspapers in the following days.

For three weeks, the Rebutatos had delivered Le Corbusier the meals he ate in solitude. They were concerned about his condition. But when the local doctor visited two days before Le Corbusier died, he assured them that, while the architect was far from strong, there was no need for alarm.

Robert Rebutato, the son of the restaurateurs, was an architect in Le Corbusier's Paris studio. For many summers, he had been Le Corbusier's constant companion for the vacation routine of two swims a day, one at the end of the morning, the next in the late afternoon, each followed by an aperitif. Over ritual drinks, Le Corbusier would hold forth to his acolyte about architecture, nature, color, or whatever the passionate theme of the day was.

Robert had been troubled by a conversation with Le Corbusier the day after the doctor's visit, when the junior architect was about to head off to Venice, to work on the hospital Le Corbusier was designing there. Le Corbusier asked his young friend to take a manuscript edited by Jean Petit—a publisher and loyal devotee of the master—for the book *Corbusier Himself.*[2] Le Corbusier had marked his self-propagandizing text with corrections and changes and asked Robert to give it to the editor in Paris. Robert said that since Le Corbusier would be returning to Paris himself at the start of September, he would most likely get there before Robert arrived from Venice. For Le Corbusier to hand over such an important document was completely out of character; he always dealt with such things on his own.

But Le Corbusier insisted. Reluctantly, Robert took the envelope. It made him uneasy: "It shocked me. I found it bizarre," he said later.[3]

Robert recognized that the world-renowned architect who liked to present himself as a straight shooter, resolute in his convictions, with a bawdy, friendly wife, had his mysterious sides. But like most everyone else, Robert had no idea of the extent to which Le Corbusier was morbid and plagued by demons. The celebrant of life who exalted nature in his sun-infused murals and tapestries often experienced moments of crushing darkness.

7

THE FOLLOWING DAY, Simon Ozieblo and Jean Deschamps, two fellow vacationers, found Le Corbusier floating dead near the shore. His head was turned "toward the bottom." They brought his body onto the beach at about 10:00 on that sunny August morning.

Roughly an hour earlier, Ozieblo and Deschamps had seen him swimming with great difficulty. "Each time he returned to the edge, he experienced the greatest difficulty climbing the boulders separating him from the path along the creek," they said.[4] But when they had offered to help him, which they did a number of times, he had refused with a smile.

For much of Le Corbusier's life, swimming had been his way of bringing himself to his preferred mental state. Almost forty years earlier, when he was anxiously awaiting the results of the competition for the Palais des Nations in Geneva and was feeling highly impatient toward his cousin Pierre Jeanneret, with whom he was collaborating, he had vigorously stroked his way toward equilibrium. From the small house he had built for his parents in Vevey on the shore of Lac Leman, Le Corbusier wrote to his "little Vonvon"—Yvonne Gallis, the Monegasque woman whom he was to marry three years later—"If I hadn't had the chance to get into the water (and I swim amazingly well) I would have been completely disgusted."[5] Having grown up landlocked and taught himself to swim in his twenties, he had discovered that moving weightlessly through water under the open sky was his salvation.

Entering the sea at Roquebrune-Cap-Martin, August 1965

Ozieblo tried mouth-to-mouth resuscitation for three quarters of an hour. "There was still a pulse, the heartbeats were irregular, but I already knew that death would do its work: a thread of blood was running down from the victim's mouth," he said.[6] He and Deschamps learned the identity of the old swimmer only after the local firemen arrived. For another half hour, the firemen continued to attempt artificial respiration with oxygen and "shots of solucamphire," but to no avail. In the previous months, Le Corbusier had been rereading his well-worn, marked-up copy of *Don Quixote,* a favorite book of his youth.[7] He had bound it with a piece of coarse-haired hide from a beloved dog. Now, like Cervantes's hero, he seemed to have picked the time, and way, to die.

LE CORBUSIER'S LIFELONG task had been to exercise control, corral his emotions, determine the appearance of buildings, and promulgate his gospel. Death was an inalienable part of nature; so as not to fail in relationship to it, one must work with it intelligently. In a private letter to his mother in January 1927, a year after his father's death, he referred to "the injection he had been given which allowed him to leave this earth without being buried in it. Hour by hour, I kept seeing dear papa in his bed: sunset. His beloved voice, his last words."[8] It was euthanasia with poetry.

Le Corbusier once asked his Parisian doctor, Jacques Hindermeyer, his closest confidant late in life, what he would do if he was an architect. The doctor replied that he would build houses upside down. Le Corbusier was puzzled. "What do you mean?" he asked.

Hindermeyer explained, "Since you celebrate sun, space, and greenery, I would build them like pyramids to let the most in."

"That's not bad," Le Corbusier said, approving with a smile. He then answered Hindermeyer's inquiry as to what he would do as a doctor. "I wouldn't do anything. I would just let people die peacefully."[9]

Death, like architecture, is ideally in accord with the inescapable cycles of the universe and should have grace and proportion. Like the terraces and roof gardens of Le Corbusier's houses, one's way of dying should provide a direct connection to the cosmos. "How nice it would be to die swimming toward the sun," Le Corbusier had been quoted as saying on two different occasions.[10]

DR. HINDERMEYER had last seen Le Corbusier at the end of July, at lunch in the doctor's sprawling apartment on the boulevard Saint-Germain. For years, they had maintained the habit of dining together shortly before embarking on their summer holidays. With their strong and trim physiques, neat haircuts, and immaculate suits, the two dignified professionals could readily have been taken for a father and son in business together, perhaps industrialists or merchants.

Hindermeyer felt that Le Corbusier looked fatigued, which he attributed to the architect having worked especially hard of late. But he was surprised when, after having been summoned from the table for a phone call, he returned to the dining room to find his guest standing up, with his shirt off. He asked what was going on. "I don't feel well, it's as if there were rats in the plumbing," said Le Corbusier.[11]

The rough terminology from the building trade amused the doctor, but its message concerned him. He quickly retrieved his stethoscope and was distressed to discover Le Corbusier's "heart in complete arrhythmia." But there was no getting him to abandon his plan to leave for Roquebrune-Cap-Martin the next day. When Hindermeyer warned Le Corbusier of the severity of his health situation, his patient and friend answered—in his usual way of looking at himself as if he were his own astute observer—"You know me well, and you know that I don't want to suffer physical diminution. Imagine the scene: Le Corbusier in the wheelchair and you pushing. No, not that, never."[12]

But then Le Corbusier quickly added, "I'm not ready to go, I still have so much to do."[13]

Hindermeyer phoned Le Corbusier's cardiologist and arranged for his patient to be seen that afternoon. In the evening, Hindermeyer went to Le Corbusier's apartment. The setting was a different world from the doctor's own flat, with its paneled walls and mélange of family antiques evoking previous centuries in a grand Haussmannian building in the elegant faubourg St. Germain. In Le Corbusier's stark, if spacious, digs on the outskirts of the sixteenth arrondissement, there was no molding; the furniture was streamlined; and industrial windows looked over modern Paris and the new suburbs beyond the city limits. The two-story nest had changed little since Le Corbusier had designed it, at the top of a boxlike apartment building of his own making, more than thirty years earlier.

Le Corbusier was lying on his high-legged, platform-style bed, which was positioned near the open cylindrical shower. The doctor made some recommendations for the holiday. Unable to persuade Le Corbusier to give up swimming completely, Hindermeyer insisted that the septuagenarian not dive into the Mediterranean too early in the day. Le Corbusier consented to the doctor's further advice that he not swim too hard and confine himself to one swim a day, at noon.

Toward the end of August, Hindermeyer was pleased to learn from the Rebutatos—such loyal, devoted guardians and protectors—that they were giving Le Corbusier all of the requisite pills and injections and that the architect was taking only short swims. But on August 25, the day before he was to return to Paris, Le Corbusier disobeyed all the advice. He had plunged in shortly after 8:00 a.m. By the time Ozieblo and Deschamps saw him, he had been swimming for nearly an hour.

AS WORD OF Le Corbusier's death spread all over the world, it was said only that he had drowned—startling enough for a man of his age. But the doctor whose advice Le Corbusier had deliberately spurned, and the young colleague to whom the architect had implied he would not return to Paris, could not help wondering if it was an elegantly orchestrated suicide.

2

The setting of Le Corbusier's funeral had its irony; so did the presence of all those people. He had devoted his life to trying to build spaces to accommodate the physical and emotional requirements he considered inherent in all human beings, especially the poorer masses, but he disdained "bourgeois" taste and would have distrusted many of the individuals who came to pay him their last respects, for he knew that they did not really grasp or advocate what mattered to him.

Few among the shivering crowd felt any intimacy with the man they had come to honor. Most deplored his wish to raze large parts of existing cities, to eradicate the old and replace it with startling new vertical communities, and they were relieved that so few of his concepts had become reality. But most everyone recognized his relentless devotion to his beliefs. He was convinced that the buildings we inhabit in our private lives, and those where we pray and learn and run our governments, are key determinants to the thoughts and emotions that occur within them. By re-forming our physical surroundings, he had tried to alter our existence irrevocably. Even if people debated the success of his buildings, no one doubted that he had permanently changed the visible world.

To the public, however, Le Corbusier's personality and ways were elusive. He offered no images of café life with glamorous friends. The man himself seemed more remote than Sartre, Picasso, Freud, and other great pioneers of change in the twentieth century—although he, too, had initiated a radical alteration of thought and was recognized for his impact on civilization.

Even his name had violated custom and shown the triumph of imagination. At age thirty-three, Charles-Edouard Jeanneret had transformed himself from an ordinary person into an institution. His sobriquet echoed the "Le C." of "Le Christus"—"Jesus Christ" in French. Additionally, with its sequence of syllables like four right angles making a square, "Corbusier" had a built, structured ring to it. It resembled a bare-bones building free of ornament and clear in structure. The "Le," further, objectified it. Especially in its shortened form, "Corbu," the name was also kin to "corbeau"—the French word for raven, the powerful bird of death. Like another twentieth-century linguistic invention, "Bauhaus," it had come to symbolize modernism, in all its effrontery as well as its brave elegance. It was no surprise that Le Corbusier was the first artist ever to be honored by these obsequies before a vast audience at the Cour Carrée of the Louvre, previously reserved, on the rarest occasions, for military or government leaders.

The Parisian newspapers called him, unequivocally, "the greatest architect in the world." He had "achieved control of the sun."[14] Even though "in 1925 he wanted to raze half of Paris,"[15] he "has liberated us from a tyrannical past."[16]

For three days following his death, Le Corbusier's body had been lying in state in the town hall of Menton, near where it had been swept ashore. Then, on a route prepared by the police forces, it went to the monastery the architect had built near Lyon, at La Tourette, where it was displayed ceremonially throughout the night of August 31. During the afternoon prior to the ceremony at the Louvre on September 1, the casket had been in Le Corbusier's office on the rue de Sèvres, for more intimate viewing by his friends and colleagues. It was all part of "the carnival" the architect had predicted. Referring to the way, when he built his great Unité d'Habitation in the early fifties, he was labeled with the term that in Provençale dialect means "inhabited by a fairy," implying that he was a madman, he told Jacques Hindermeyer, "My whole life, they made fun of me and criticized me. They called Marseille 'La Maison de Fada.' You wait: after my death, they'll use me for themselves. I'll become a great man. That's why I am telling you not to go to my funeral. It will be a masquerade."[17] In an autobiographical essay, *Put into Focus,* completed shortly before his death, he said that the speakers would be more interested in themselves than in the one who died.[18] Someone as privy as Hindermeyer to the truths of human behavior should not have to suffer such hypocrisy.

Two weeks before he died, Le Corbusier saw a man smashing against a rock an octopus he had just harpooned. The architect compared himself to the sea creature. "For most of my life, I have simply been smashed down. Many people were so jealous, they wanted to destroy me, to crush my head just like that octopus."[19] He never tired of finding analogies to vivify his tortured martyrdom. "They grilled me over a slow fire: grotesque!!" he cried after one failed collaboration.[20] In 1953, at the ceremony in London where he was presented with the Royal Gold Medal recommended by the Royal Institute of British Architects and approved by the queen—an occasion when one glowing tribute followed another—he chose, rather than to bask in the pleasure, to declare, "If tonight I am wearing this magnificent medal, it is because I was a cab-horse for more than forty years. . . . I received, like a true cab-horse, many blows with a whip."[21] He was, chronically, the victim of merciless critics and bureaucratic corruption; as a result, he had not built a fraction of what he hoped to build. Nor had he been credited adequately for whatever little he had done. Unlike Don Quixote, he had never had illusions to the contrary, but, like Cervantes's knight, he had awoken to the hard truth of a lifetime of being pummeled.

Now, in the Cour Carrée of the Louvre, he was only a hero. Following Beethoven's solemn dirge and the impeccable staging of the entrances and the exits of the uniformed honor guard, the casket made its journey forward on that rolling sea of shoulders with magisterial choreography. In addition to the crowd packed into the vast courtyard, hundreds of thousands of Parisians, tuned in to the ceremony on their radios or televisions, heard the single, memorable eulogy that followed. The enthralling speaker with his deep, tremulous voice was Charles de Gaulle's minister of culture, André Malraux.

Malraux had been a champion of Le Corbusier's work and had recently commissioned the architect to design a major new museum of modern art on the outskirts of Paris, although Le Corbusier had rejected the site. Other people in power had disdained Le Corbusier's modernism or faulted his politics. Some had declared him pro-Soviet; others thought him fascist. There

Le Corbusier's casket entering the Cour Carrée du Louvre, September 2, 1965

were rumblings that he had collaborated with Vichy. But Malraux was one of the few people who considered Le Corbusier's genius more important than anything else about him, and he had been consistently loyal.

At precisely 10:00 p.m., Malraux faced the clustered microphones. Ambassadors stood at attention, and young architects fought back tears. The broad-shouldered culture minister stood with one foot slightly twisted as he leaned on the lectern, stared downward through his black-framed glasses, and began his homily. His straight, dark hair was swept back; a white pocket handkerchief provided the only relief against his somber double-breasted suit. With gravelly timbre and priestlike cadences that imparted portent to each word, Malraux announced that a Greek delegate would deposit a portion of earth from the Acropolis on Le Corbusier's grave and that a representative from India would pour water from the Ganges over the architect's remains in honor of his creation of the territorial capital of Chandigarh.

Then this most intellectual of public figures shifted tone. Malraux had no intention of letting people forget the ignominy suffered by creative geniuses. "Le Corbusier has had great rivals, several of whom still honor us with their presence; the others are dead. But no one else has so forcefully signified the architectural revolution, for no one else has been so long and so patiently insulted. It is through disparagement that his glory has attained its ultimate luster." Malraux touched on Le Corbusier's achievements in painting, sculpture, and poetry. Those were the calmer realms. Le Corbusier's battles were confined to issues of building and to urban design. "Only for architecture has he done combat—with a vehemence he has shown for nothing else, since only architecture awakened his impassioned

André Malraux giving his homily at Le Corbusier's funeral service

Le Corbusier and André Malraux laying the cornerstone for the Assembly Building in Chandigarh in 1952

hope for what might be achieved for mankind."[22] Le Corbusier had to stay the course like a solitary crusader and had encountered infinitely more obstacles than accolades, yet his accomplishments were such that now the minister could proudly read tributes from the presidents of the United States and Brazil, from the esteemed architects Alvar Aalto and Richard Neutra, from colleagues in the Soviet Union.

There was one moment above all when Malraux homed in on the real work of the controversial pioneer whose body rested at his side. This was when, early in his eulogy, he quoted Le Corbusier's own declaration of his lifelong goals: "I have worked for what mankind needs most today: silence and peace."[23]

LE CORBUSIER'S warnings of false theatricality, however, were more warranted than anyone in the funeral audience could have imagined.

The day before the ceremony, Malraux had telephoned a demand to the Indian ambassador to France, Rajeshwar Dayal: "You have to come with some water from the Ganges." Dayal had replied that he didn't have any, to which the culture minister responded, "Somebody at your embassy must have some."[24] When the ambassador arrived at the Cour Carrée with a silver vial allegedly containing water from the sacred river in the country where Le Corbusier had made his greatest work, the only people who knew it was merely Parisian tap water were the great orator and the Indian ambassador. When Le Corbusier had counseled Jacques Hindermeyer to boycott what the architect knew would be "a masquerade," he had used the perfect word.

3

When André Malraux was done with his homily, drumrolls began from the honor guard. Delegates from all over the world heaped floral tributes on Le Corbusier's casket. The man who had always admired soldiers in full uniform would have been pleased with the military parade that followed. Then the crowd, like a flood tide, forced its way past the police barriers and surrounded the stand on which the casket was resting, as if it were their last chance to approach a deity.

The following day, *Le Monde* reported the details: "Toward midnight the coffin was placed in a hearse which, preceded by motorcycle escort, crossed sleeping Paris along the banks of the Seine."[25] Few in that honor guard would have known that they were passing the tiny attic apartment where Charles-Edouard Jeanneret, a young man just arrived from Switzerland fifty-eight years earlier, had regularly climbed eight flights of stairs. But all knew they were honoring someone who was credited with having changed the look of the world, if not always for the better.

It was a stark contrast to Yvonne's funeral eight years earlier. The handful of people in the Cour Carrée who were personally close enough to have been there noted the difference. Yvonne, to whom Le Corbusier had by then been married for nearly thirty years and with whom he had lived for the previous decade, had died on the day before the architect's seventieth birthday. She had scarcely been known to the public at large. Le Corbusier, himself so visible, had always managed to keep his intimate side private.

Some people said Le Corbusier had met Yvonne Gallis in a bordello, a rumor that the salty Mediterranean woman, her deep red lipstick painted in the form of a heart, did little to dispel. When Walter Gropius, the architect who had founded the Bauhaus, and his wife were dining in Le Corbusier's apartment in the 1930s, Yvonne, after being silent through most of dinner, suddenly asked Gropius, "Have you seen it?" The ambiguous question puzzled Gropius, whose demeanor reflected his military training. She clarified: "*Mon cul*"—"my ass."[26] Twenty-five years later, when a young messenger boy went to the same apartment to deliver art supplies, she posed the identical question, again with a wink. It was her everyday line.

The architects in Le Corbusier's office knew that, whatever work was on the master's agenda, he had to be home by 5:30 p.m. each day for the first pastis of the evening—*his* first one, anyway.[27] When Le Corbusier was traveling, as was often the case, there were strict instructions for his young associates to phone Yvonne regularly and call on her frequently. If one was privileged enough to be invited to dinner, one knew that there were certain rules to follow in Yvonne's presence. Work, or architecture in any aspect, was forbidden as a topic of conversation. The talk would mainly be gossip—Yvonne would report on the other inhabitants of the building.

A former beauty, Yvonne had begun to look gaunt and dissipated in the 1940s. She used a cane and had a pronounced limp. But among Le Corbusier's younger cohorts, who during the war generally got nothing more than the slim pickings of the cafeteria at architecture school, Yvonne's cooking was legend, in particular her spicy aioli and other Mediterranean specialities.[28]

Insiders knew that her situation was a tragedy that on some level must have torn her husband apart. Besides osteoporosis and gastritis, the primary cause of Yvonne's health problems in the last years of her life was her severe alcoholism. Le Corbusier had always done his best to keep this problem, as well as her many other maladies and the rages as intense as her joking, secret from his friends. It was the reason he rarely attended openings, even of exhibitions of his own work. For years, Le Corbusier had taken her to the best doctors, but no one could persuade Yvonne to give up the bottle.

Ever since the end of the war, Yvonne had been in the care of Jacques Hindermeyer. By that time, she was already noticeably debilitated. The reason was a complete loss of sensibility in the legs, a by-product of intense alcohol consumption.

When he wasn't denying or avoiding it, Le Corbusier partially blamed himself. The architect would often discuss the problem with Hindermeyer, the one person in whom he was comfortable confiding. He told the doctor how sorry he was not to have known earlier in the marriage that Yvonne was addicted to pastis. At the beginning, she rarely drank in front of him. She was by nature so funny and gay that he had failed to recognize her symptoms of drunkenness—or so he claimed. Now that he accepted that she was suffering from something other than the sort of nervous disorder that might be remedied by the right vitamin regime or another of the many solutions he had proffered when he thought there was hope, all that he tried to do was take care of her as best he could.

On one occasion in the midfifties when Le Corbusier went to Baghdad for work and needed to go next to Chandigarh, he returned to Paris first. Hindermeyer asked him why he had not gone straight from Iraq to India. Le Corbusier replied that he could keep only one project in his head at a time and had to return to the office in between. Hindermeyer knew this was a cover-up; the truth was that Le Corbusier hated to leave Yvonne alone for long periods of time and always felt he had to look in on her. To the doctor, "his love for his wife, and his tenderness," were unlike anything he had ever seen.

Yvonne, late 1920s

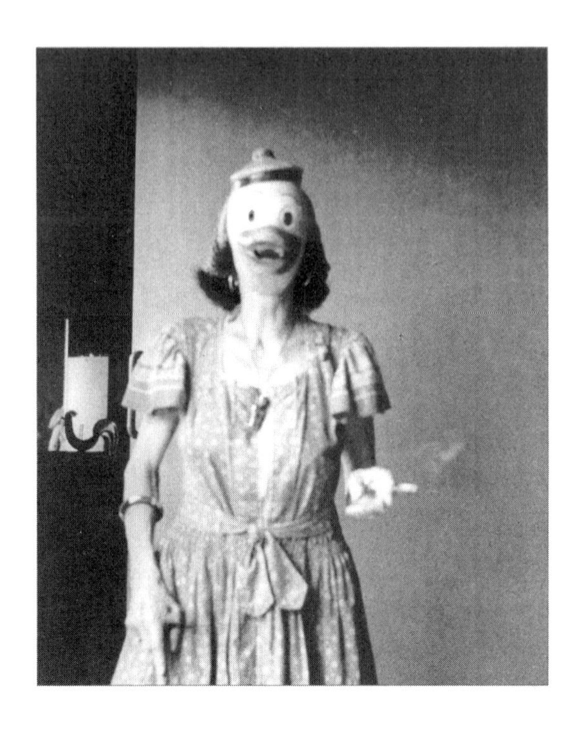

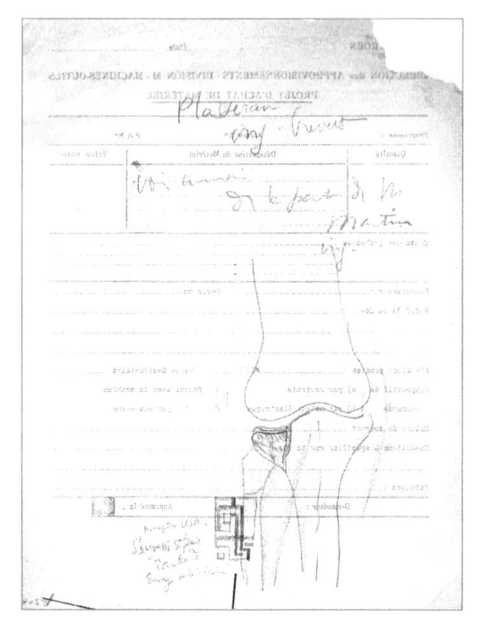

Sketch of a femur by Le Corbusier

Yvonne by that time was so unhappy about the way she looked that she kept the apartment dark. "It was horrible for a man who had searched for sunlight his whole life to live in the dark," his doctor observed.[29] Then Yvonne developed a cancer of the anus. Hindermeyer proposed that she see a specialist who could treat her with radium. When the specialist told her to remove her clothes, she delivered a revised version of her famous line, but with none of the old coquetry. "You want me to show the world my ass?" she asked in a rage.[30]

Yvonne often shouted obscenities and abused and humiliated her husband in front of anyone who happened to be present. Whatever toll he was paying inside, Le Corbusier responded to her wrath by smiling benevolently and caring for her patiently. At one point, Hindermeyer asked Le Corbusier why he never protested when Yvonne said insane things. He told the doctor, "I think only of my happy memories of our youth."[31]

THE DAY YVONNE DIED, Le Corbusier had his wife's emaciated corpse brought home from the clinic and placed in a small room on the upper floor of the apartment. When Charlotte Perriand, his collaborator of many years, came to call, he took her to see it. "Look how lovely she is," he said to his horrified visitor.[32] He was convinced that Yvonne had the purest heart of anyone he knew.

Yvonne's modest rites took place in the crematorium of the prestigious Père Lachaise cemetery, on the other side of Paris from the apartment. Entering the august cemetery grounds, on their verdant hilltop overlooking the city, and following the road upward to the section for those whose bodies would be turned to ashes, Le Corbusier took in the eerie rows of temple-like stone mausoleums at the burying place of some of the most powerful families in France, as well as of Balzac and Proust and Oscar Wilde. His eye appraised the weighty pediments and ornate carving intended to house the dead for eternity. The crematorium chapel itself was everything Le Corbusier loathed in a building: a ponderous compendium of ill-matched historical references, with a scale that bore no relationship to actual human beings. Only the rows of pines and the deciduous trees, whose leaves were showing the first tinge and withering of autumn, offered some connection with what he knew to be the reality and poetry of life.

Just as Yvonne's body slid from public view to be incinerated, Le Corbusier rose from the front row of the small chapel. Strong and fit, impeccably dressed in one of his well-tailored dark suits, he bolted forward and disappeared behind the curtain in front of the room. A moment later, the bereaved husband returned, holding a cone of newspaper. "This is all I have left of my dear Yvonne," Le Corbusier exclaimed to Denise René, his longtime friend and gallerist, and Perriand. He had one of Yvonne's bones in the rolled-up paper. Among his wife's ashes, he had found "a tiny cervical vertebra" that was perfectly intact. Cremation in that period was not as thorough as it is now, and this bone, from the top of the neck, had remained.[33] René and Perriand gripped one another's hands in terror. "It was a hellish business, perfectly dreadful," according to René, on whom the scene made such a gruesome impression that years later she maintained with absolute conviction that the bone had been one of Yvonne's femurs.[34]

Le Corbusier walked among the assembled group displaying this remainder of his wife. He continued to clutch it as he followed the urn containing Yvonne's ashes. The vertebra had a gruesome truth to it that was totally lacking in the monumental neo-Classical and Renaissance-revival style of every surface and object in these oppressive surroundings. The architect took the bone back to his apartment on the rue Nungesser-et-Coli.[35] For the rest of his life, he kept it in his pants pocket, like a talisman, occasionally placing it on his drafting table when he was working.

"HE WAS A MAN who loved reality," observed Jacques Hindermeyer, who often saw Le Corbusier touching the small vertebra. Clinging to his relic, he was rooting himself in a kernel of his wife's existence, with which he could counteract the vagaries of his feelings.

Le Corbusier's own bones became relics as well. The day after the public ceremony in La Cour Carrée, the architect's body was also cremated at Père Lachaise. Deliberately echoing what Le Corbusier had done following Yvonne's death, his older brother, Albert, the only surviving blood relative, gathered up some of the bone fragments and distributed them. Robert Rebutato's father, Albert himself, and other intimates always prized their small Plexiglas boxes of Le Corbusier's remains. They were honored to possess the physical reality of someone whose personality and emotional character were so much harder to grasp.

4

The man whose coffin stood before the mob in La Cour Carrée had been preoccupied by death throughout his adult life. Le Corbusier viewed mortality as an integral part of the grand scheme of human existence, like the skulls that sit amid ripe lemons and velvety flowers in Cézanne's still lifes. When the mother of one of the most important architects in Le Corbusier's office, André Wogenscky, died, Le Corbusier had written a condolence letter that treated death as the key element of a building plan: "Death is the exit for each of us. I can't see why it should be regarded as cruel and hideous. It is the horizontal of the vertical: complementary and natural."[36]

Le Corbusier was forty years old when his father died at age seventy-one. He remarked at the time, "I'm well aware now that one is born, grows up, creates, and dies. I am past the growing season. Beside Pierre [his cousin], who is dancing through his thirties, I'm already an old man, a producer certainly, though for some already a hoary traditionalist. One shinnies up one's trajectory until—when?—it falls back to Earth?"[37]

On the Monday morning the week after his father's death at La Chaux-de-Fonds, the mountain town where Le Corbusier had grown up, he wrote to his mother, "I often think of dear papa's serene death, that winter Sunday so full of sunlight and so magnificently solemn. How pure papa's image remains—so correct, so attached to things of the spirit. He always fixed his eyes on the horizon of an ideal, chimerical country."[38] Georges Jeanneret, an enameler of watch faces, had been a practical man, skillful of hand, but at the end he was above all a poet and spiritual voyager who had found tranquility.

Another week after his father's death, Le Corbusier wrote his mother again, this time about the death of one of his and Yvonne's two pet parakeets: "Saturday. Yesterday we found Pilette lying quite peacefully in the middle of the nest. Pitou had been chirping for a whole day, terrified by this emptiness. Believe me, the death of a little bird has something quite mournful about it, awaking ideas related to other deaths, and the coldness of the little bird's head was the same as the coldness of our dear Papa's forehead."[39]

ON JANUARY 11, 1926, at 4:00 a.m., Le Corbusier made a drawing of his stone-cold father annotated in the manner of a death certificate. The open mouth and closed eyes on the gaunt head are almost unbearable to look at.

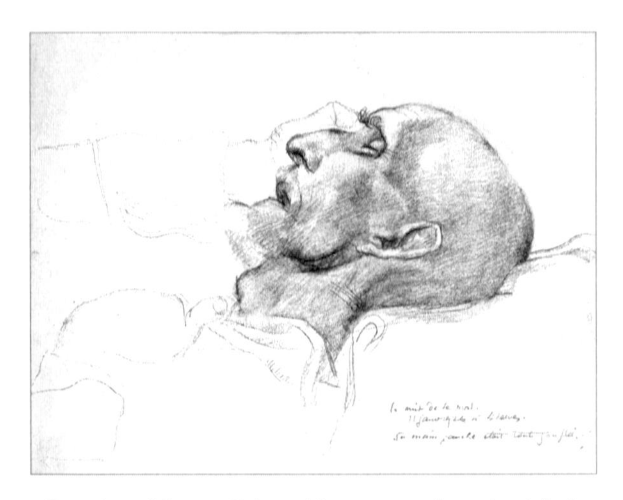

Drawing of Georges-Edouard Jeanneret made on the night he died. The caption reads: "La nuit de sa mort. 11 janvier 1926 à 4 heures. Sa main gauche était toute gonflée." ["The night of his death. January 11, 1926, at 4 a.m. His left hand was completely swollen."]

In 1957, he made four drawings of the dead Yvonne. They are like torrid images of the afterlife in a northern Renaissance depiction of the Last Judgment. The bonne vivante who had used lipstick to form her mouth like a movie star's has no lips whatsoever; she has a lifeless slit sunk within a sharply concave face. Her nose is like the bony beak of a small bird. Her head is wrapped tightly in a bandage that seems to hold it together.

The portrait Le Corbusier drew of his mother on February 15, 1960, just after she died at the age of ninety-nine and to which he attached a lock of her hair, is, if possible, even more horrific. The old woman's head is thrown back as if it had snapped at the neck. Her tiny pointed chin juts forward. Le Corbusier did not dissemble about the ultimate destiny of the woman whose youthfulness he had exalted only a few days earlier. The truth had to be met squarely.

II

1

Georges Edouard Jeanneret-Gris and Marie Charlotte Amélie Perret—both Swiss Calvinists, both natives of La Chaux-de-Fonds, a center of the watchmaking industry high in the Alps—were married in 1883. Their first son, Jacques-Henri Albert, was born February 6, 1886. Charles-Edouard came along twenty months later, on October 6, 1887. Marie was then twenty-seven, Georges thirty-two.

Jeanneret-Gris's meticulous journal reported that, once his wife's "labor pains announced the imminent arrival of the expected child," he "went back to work." The doctor "anticipated the birth would be at 9 o'clock in the evening. As 9 sounded, the child was there. . . . All went well, he was put immediately on cows' milk and he drinks his bottle like a man."[1]

Some five years later, Marie miscarried; she bore no further children. The mother and father and two boys were a close-knit unit. Their disputes as well as the siblings' rivalry were often intense, but the importance of the core family to each of its members never wavered.

The family lived at 38 rue de la Serre, a few blocks from the main thoroughfare of La Chaux-de-Fonds. It was an unprepossessing apartment in a nondescript five-story structure of reddish-brown stone, pressed against similarly monotonous buildings. The city, in spite of its location, had no Alpine charm. Relentlessly grim, it was composed on a regular grid, with street after street of blank-faced building facades climbing its tedious slopes. Having been destroyed by a fire in 1794, La Chaux-de-Fonds was rebuilt in the nineteenth century in a taciturn architectural style. Laid out as if with a watchmaker's tools, its sad and weighty rows of shops and apartment houses had none of the magic or complexity of clockworks, only their precision and insistent order. In 1910, when he was twenty-three years old and imagining his return to his natal city while working in Berlin, Charles-Edouard Jeanneret wrote William Ritter, "La Chaux-de-Fonds is indeed a leprous place. You found the right term for this incoherent agglomeration of eyesores. Yet through it blows a wind of living idealism which is quite

Charles-Edouard Jeanneret (on pedestal) with his family, taken two months after his second birthday (December 1889)

remarkable and fills you with hope. . . . Since the old farms of the 18th century, there has been no art tradition."[2] The next year, having returned home, he told Ritter, "But I feel I'm a stranger here, and I still can't get it through my head that I would always feel that way."[3] On the back side of an envelope, he noted his birthplace as "La Chaux-de-Fonds of shit."[4] After another year had passed, he wrote Ritter: "I've already told you how agonizing I find the notion of ending my days here."[5]

Later in his life as his own propaganda machine, Le Corbusier insistently presented his birthplace as a rich wellspring. Determined that his youth and education be seen as a progression of successes in a well-organized milieu, he summarized a childhood in which he took to the mountains to study the workings of nature, applied pencil and watercolor to paper with the genius of a prodigy, and acquired the education necessary to make buildings and plan cities of unprecedented harmoniousness. He let it be known that his father instructed him about plant life and birds and led him on rigorous hikes, and that his mother taught him music. But he carefully cast aside his Swissness.

When World War II was raging and Le Corbusier had spare time because of a lull in his practice, he collaborated with Maximilien Gauthier on a mid-career biography, *Le Corbusier; or, Architecture in the Service of Mankind.*[6] Hitler had given unprecedented significance to national identity and genetic heritage, an emphasis supported by France's leadership in Vichy. While the first sentence of Gauthier's book gives Charles-Edouard Jeanneret's place of birth as La Chaux-de-Fonds, it leaves out that this is in Switzerland, while stating that Le Corbusier was "naturalized French in 1930, or rather reintegrated within French nationality."[7] In 1964, in *Corbusier Himself,* the architect amplifies his French roots. He explains that in about 1350, the French of the north massacred the French of the south because the southerners held libertarian ideas about various points of religious doctrine; some of these southern rebels fled to the mountains of Neuchâtel, then primarily inhabited by wolves. Le Corbusier's ancestors were among the French rebels. "Why these indications of origins?" asks the book. "In a spirit of honesty, to help others understand the rationale of the movement of ideas. Le Corbusier is not 'Schweiz.' "[8]

2

As long as the name of the country could be skirted, Le Corbusier emphasized that he came from a mountain paradise inhabited by strong individuals. Three wooden farmhouses built by his ancestors and still called "Les Jeanneret" embodied that fine tradition. As a boy, Charles-Edouard often opted to stay in these rugged dwellings rather than his parents' apartment. Dated 1626, they bore the family's name and coat of arms. The future architect credited his distinguished ancestors with having brought to the high Jura region the "*style languedocian*" they had known in southern France. It showed up especially in the overpowering sloped roofs of these chalets. Their disproportionate scale and profound pitch—they resembled giant, wide-brimmed hats—served effectively to shed snow and assure warmth inside.

The three farmhouses were destroyed by fire in 1910, but Le Corbusier often voiced pride in the role of his relatives in developing such splendid domestic architecture. He also emphasized, in various statements and texts, that the Jeannerets in Languedoc descended from the Albigenses—those Cathars who came from the south of France, primarily the Languedoc and Provence. The Cathars were a heretic religious sect who demanded that the pope and the archbishops forsake all worldly riches, and who were therefore vilified by the Catholic Church for six centuries. They favored an austere and humble way of life; the simplicity of their rites eliminated the need for elaborate churches, liturgical vestments, and all manifestations of ceremonial pomp. Le Corbusier was proud to claim them as his spiritual ancestors.

IN A HISTORY of La Chaux-de-Fonds published in 1894, which Le Corbusier kept in his personal library years after he escaped Switzerland and had achieved international importance, he annotated various passages and drew arrows to others.[9] He fastened on to every hint of passion and rebellion. In feverish pencil strokes, he called attention to a maternal great-grandfather who had died in prison for his role in the unsuccessful Swiss revolution of 1831. The architect's paternal grandfather did even better seventeen years later by descending from La Chaux-de-Fonds on foot to help take the château of Neuchâtel. Le Corbusier bragged, "In 1848, the revolution succeeded. My grandfather was one of the leaders . . . there is nothing to blush for or to hide about bearing this past of freedom, ingenuity, free will, stubbornness, and guts in one's own blood."[10]

The toughness and willpower Le Corbusier acquired from the milieu of his youth were at his core. At an altitude of one thousand meters, La Chaux-de-Fonds had a rough climate that taxed all who lived there. In the course of a year, there was an average of only five hours of sunshine a day; 173 days had some form of precipitation, 65 of them with snow. One learned to endure. For all the misery Le Corbusier would suffer as an architect, he had the strength to withstand the most challenging conditions. Nothing ever prevented him from taking the next step—even if it was toward his own death.

3

Charles-Edouard Jeanneret's education at home and school emphasized solitude and observation. Drudgery was prized; so was the search for higher spiritual truths. The motto of the Jeanneret-Gris family was

Though silver I possess and gold,
Convinced that this life is a fever,
To my God and his Heaven I pray
The whole thing will last forever.[11]

Le Corbusier remained faithful to his ancestors' skepticism about the value of money and focus on that universal timeless sky that precedes and outlives us all.

He also took pride in the qualities he felt he inherited from the competent craftsmen, skillful businessmen, and noblemen from whom he descended. Le Corbusier made much of the qualities that endowed him with intrinsic abilities and reflected favorably on his own endeavors. His father and grandfather had been "skillful enamellists of watch-dials and clock-faces," while his mother's family included successful merchants.[12]

Among his few truly prosperous ancestors was a Monsieur Lecorbesier, a Belgian wed to a Spaniard, whose daughter, Caroline Marie Josephine Lecorbesier, married Louis Perret, a Swiss seller of bed linens who lived in Brussels. M. Lecorbesier's portrait had been painted by Victor Darjou, a court painter of the Empress Eugénie's. That cachet inspired Charles-Edouard Jeanneret ultimately to give himself a variation of the man's name.

Le Corbusier also let it be known that Marie de Nemours "has accorded patents of nobility to Jonas Jeanneret," while another branch of the family was "confirmed in its nobility by Friedrich Wilhelm II of Prussia."[13] He did not value anyone more or less because of family background—he married the daughter of a gardener and a flower seller—but he gladly stressed his ancestors' prestige in the belief that any sort of connection with the people who ran the world might help him achieve his goal of making invigorating architecture for all humankind.

Edouard, age three, and Albert, five (1890)

4

The meaninglessness of artistic phenomena obsessed the minds of our fathers.

—LE CORBUSIER, *The Decorative Art of Today,* 1925

The prosperous merchants, titled noblemen, religious heretics, and political radicals in the family's past had little to do with the reality of life in the three small, cluttered, overstuffed apartments in which Charles-Edouard Jeanneret's family lived during the future architect's first fifteen years.

Georges Jeanneret-Gris was a competent craftsman, clear thinker, and true devotee of the great outdoors. Marie was sufficiently talented at the piano to teach it. They both esteemed artistry and diligence. But they were above all hardworking middle-class people who had no interest in budging from the society they knew or in transforming it. We can find hints of what seeded Le Corbusier's mind, but he was one of those rare people whose fire and genius developed inexplicably. How did he emerge from a morose and stultifying milieu with the lust to reshape the world, a generous instinct to improve all human lives, and the creativity to take color and form in unprecedented directions?

Marie Charlotte and Georges-Edouard Jeanneret, ca. 1900

Marie Jeanneret, who ran the household competently, often repeated the motto of the Gallet family (her mother's side): "What you do—do."[14] Never procrastinate, even for a second. Although the message eluded Albert, Le Corbusier periodically reminded his mother that these words were his constant gospel. Georges embodied that same principle of concentrated labor. He worked long, hard days, enameling watchcases, writing in his diary with the same order and discipline he applied to his profession. He was so frugal that he recorded the slightest fluctuation in cheese prices in his daily journal. His only break from routine came on weekends when he headed off mountaineering with the Alpine Adventurers' Club, or took day trips and summer vacations when he led his family on hikes.

Albert and Edouard spent their free time practicing music or drawing or reading. Birthdays and holidays were celebrated as orderly rites.

Jeanneret-Gris's unmarried older sister, the very pious "Tante Pauline," lived with the family of four, making the ambience all the more sober. She credited God for everything that happened in people's lives. But the solitary spinster offered rare playfulness as well, teasing the boys with nicknames they relished. Edouard was delighted with the terms that likened him and Albert to characters from Rabelais. To be a "braggart," "slattern," "saber rattler," "boaster," "rogue," "dandy," "runt," or "loser" certainly beat being anyone's idea of an angel.[15]

FROM THE TIME Edouard was six until he was nineteen, the family lived in a fifth-floor attic apartment at 46 rue Léopold-Robert. The street's only charm was its name, which was for an early-nineteenth-century painter, Louis-Léopold Robert, who had demonstrated the possibilities of leaving La Chaux-de-Fonds; Robert became a student of David's in Paris and gained renown all over Europe for his highly colored mythological scenes. One of the main thoroughfares of the city, the avenue was a divided boulevard that, like a river, ran through the base of the valley in which brick buildings and cross streets had been built, sloping upward from it in both directions. Number 46 was pressed between two other identical structures and did not have much of a garden in the back. The Jeannerets' windows overlooked their neighbors' massive rooftops.

Inside, the apartment was comfortable enough, cluttered with the trappings of bourgeois life. A fringed valance hung over the dark and lugubrious draperies that were pulled back by ornate cords with large tassels to frame the living-room windows. Lacey casement material muted whatever sunlight might find its way in. The heavy, carved furniture was stained dark brown. Plants in ornate pots crowded the metronome on top of a flower-patterned cloth on the upright piano. Wall hangings flanked Darjou's portrait of Marie's grandfather alongside narrow shelves packed with curios. What was absent was any place to rest the eye.

The only weightless aspect of Charles-Edouard Jeanneret's childhood was music. The piano was almost constantly being played. Marie gave lessons to her students at it, and, starting at a young age, Albert began practicing intensely. Edouard himself began to play the piano at age seven, although he was not nearly as serious about it as his older brother was. The sound of

Mozart, universal, light of foot, may have been the first hint of an alternative to the dreariness of the family's apartment.

Part of what made Le Corbusier extraordinary is that all that he later designed for himself and others provided what his childhood home lacked: visual lightness, playful rhythms, the proximity to nature. Greenery and the sky would be brought into settings full of whiteness, light, and visual calm that would be the antithesis of that hodgepodge of ornament and antimacassars. Once Le Corbusier took charge, the gloom and clutter of 46 rue Léopold-Robert would be eradicated.

5

> Study your Physics well, and you'll be shown
> In not too many pages that your art's good
> Is to follow Nature insofar as it can,
> As a pupil emulates his master.
>
> —DANTE, *The Inferno,* CANTO XI

The young family escaped the dark domestic clutter on their Sunday expeditions to the open spaces and uninterrupted whiteness of the high Alps. On hikes that tested Marie and the boys to the maximum, Georges brought them to ravishing vistas. Shouldering backpacks, the family explored the gorges of the Doubs and ascended to marvelous views of the Tyrol and Mont Blanc.[16] The devoted father taught his sons rudimentary facts about flowers, trees, ice, clouds, and other aspects of the natural world. Years afterward, Le Corbusier fondly recalled that these lessons in botany and geology were followed by "calm discourse, more abstract but no less respectfully heeded, for favoring one's neighbor as well as for justice."[17]

In adulthood, once he became an avid painter and designer, Le Corbusier considered knowledge and appreciation of nature to be indispensable. In his 1925 *The Decorative Art of Today,* he wrote, "I knew flowers inside and out, birds of every shape and color. I understood how a tree grows and why it remains standing, even in the midst of a storm. . . . My father, moreover, had a passionate love of the mountains and the river which formed our landscape."[18] He discoursed romantically on the process of plant growth: "In slow motion, you have observed the poignant, hasty, irresistible drama of buds which unfold, twist with passion, frenziedly gesture toward the light, a veritable rut of plant life, a mystery hitherto sealed which the impassive eye of the lens and inexorable machinery of time-exposure have revealed."[19] When, after World War II, Le Corbusier developed his concept of the Modulor—an organizing unit for all of architecture—he included in his explanatory text one of the drawings of a young pine tree he had made as a child. Like the Modulor, the well-structured tree offered an antidote to disorder. It embodied regularity, a system of governance, and an organizational scheme with the logic of its patterns; nature was a source of balance and control.

On those Alpine outings, Charles-Edouard Jeanneret had felt pure elation: "We were constantly on the peaks; accustomed to the enormous horizon. When the sea of fog stretched to infinity, it was like the real sea (which I had never seen). It was the ultimate spectacle."[20] That attraction to the larger vista later inspired architecture that insists that you know where you are on the planet and guides you to feel the orientation to the sun. Le Corbusier configured the outdoor pulpit at Ronchamp to face the hillside and devised the vast terrace at the Villa Savoye as a command post of the surrounding fields.

Young Edouard watched with fascination when his father went off in climbing clothes to ascend treacherous rock faces on Mont Blanc and sleep in natural enclosures formed by boulders. These rudimentary mountaintop shelters, open to infinity, were lifelong models.

The mundane had its impact as well. Edouard's grandfather made "dials covered with painted flowers or wisps of golden straw" while his father, "under the buyer's imperious pressure, found himself obliged to make an entirely new effort: to achieve the impeccable enamels, their background of a perfect whiteness."[21] The need to conform to the latest trend in taste bothered Edouard, but he considered craftsmanship and diligence as vital as the freedom of the Alpine crags. Necessity, skill, and the sense of wonder could all function in tandem.

6

It was, for the most part, a predictable Calvinist childhood, except for one unusual element of Edouard's early education. When he started school at the end of August 1891, more than a month before his fourth birthday, he attended, as did Albert, a private kindergarten that based its methods on the ideas of the early-nineteenth-century German educator Friedrich Wilhelm August Froebel. Froebel had invented special wooden bricks and balls, as well as prescribed activities, to encourage playfulness and practical knowledge of materials. His objective was for children at this vital moment of their psychological formation to acquire skills and a way of life in harmony with the larger world and with God. Froebel's methods may be among the origins of the seemingly carefree arrangements of brightly colored forms with which Le Corbusier would invigorate and give spiritual life to his chapels at Ronchamp and La Tourette.

In 1893, after two years at the Froebel kindergarten, Edouard switched to more humdrum learning at the primary school, where he remained for the next six years. His life took on a clockwork order except that it was often interrupted by bouts of sickness. Edouard was of frailer constitution than Albert and notably thinner. Aside from the usual measles and chicken pox, he had long-lasting head colds and chronic coughs. His parents tried to keep these at bay with cod-liver oil, but the health problems persisted throughout Le Corbusier's life, with his search for cold remedies obsessing him almost as much as his quest for clients.

At Le Corbusier's beckoning, Maximilien Gauthier wrapped up his description of Edouard's ten years at primary and high school by saying that the boy was "noted as a hard-working and talented student."[22] These are the exact adjectives that Le Corbusier repeats in the first person in *Corbusier Himself.* It was not so. When nine-year-old Albert delighted his parents by passing his spring exams with flying colors, Georges Jeanneret-Gris wrote in his journal, "The boy gives us much pleasure. His brother is less conscientious."[23] In spite of such a crippling stutter that made it difficult for even his parents to understand him, Albert was considered the easier brother. At age thirteen, now playing the violin, he publicly performed a Mozart trio with his mother and his music teacher. Jeanneret-Gris reported, "The dear child gives us great pleasure, whether in his musical or his scholarly studies. . . . His brother is usually a good child, but has a difficult character, susceptible, quick-tempered, and rebellious; at times he gives us reason for anxiety."[24]

Initially, Edouard had regularly been one of the top three students in the class, and, like Albert, often ended his school year by taking first prize, but the problems began in secondary school, where he began to slack off in general studies, while doing well in languages and the arts. In this French-speaking school, he succeeded in both German and English; in math, however, he never progressed beyond algebra, where his grade was 4½ out of a possible 6—or a flat C.

As reported by Gauthier, though, he was diligent with all his schoolwork; beyond that, "after class and on Sundays, his lessons learned and his homework done, he drew passionately for his own pleasure."[25] His family often found him drawing at the dining table in his spare time. Sometimes he copied illustrations from children's books. Rodolphe Töpffer's *Travels in Zigzag,* an 1846 account of a walking trip in Switzerland, was a favorite, imprinting notions that affected his subsequent ideas of urban design. He was also a voracious reader, enthusiastic about Old French and passionate about Rabelais, as well as Cervantes, whom he read in translation.

Regardless, it was Albert who won his parents' approval for pushing himself hardest. While the fifteen-year-old practiced the violin for up to six hours a day, Edouard disappointed his father by making "much less effort than his brother."[26] Le Corbusier never succeeded in dispelling that impression; for the rest of his mother's life, whenever she was congratulated on the achievements of her son, she purportedly thought that it was Albert to whom the speaker was referring.

IN THE SPRING OF 1900, when Albert and his mother were playing in the orchestra of a local production of *Snow White,* Edouard took the role of the gnome Sarcasm. His father, unsettled that his son would voluntarily assume a character trait he disdained, accused Edouard of sending everyone into a tailspin. But the part suited the contrary teenager who had dropped down to the lower half of the class and begun to be absent from school without explanation. His algebra teacher in 1901 reported, "Student careless and negligent"; his French teacher complained that he talked in class and dropped things on the floor. In history class, the naughty lad "left his seat in an unwarranted and noisy manner."[27] Required to write a three-page essay on the proper behavior of a student, he made matters worse by failing to do so.

At age thirteen, however, Edouard had started taking courses at the local art school, an establishment founded in the nineteenth century to train engravers who specialized in watch decoration. Then, at age fourteen and a half, he left the traditional secondary school—he would have needed to stay for two more years to graduate—to go to the School of Applied and Industrial Arts, a tuition-free institution funded and run by the local commune. Claiming he wanted to follow his father's footsteps as a designer and engraver of watchcases, for sixty hours a week he studied engraving, design, and artistic drawing in an Art Nouveau style.

Young Sarcasm, however, quickly deemed the family profession "a useless *métier,* a wretched and outdated *métier.* . . . This was how Charles-Edouard Jeanneret learned quite early that the practice of decoration for decoration's sake is absurd, and the worker who persists in it may well die of it: a severe lesson not easily forgotten when as a young person one has learned it at one's own expense. . . . Moreover, it had never occurred to the boy Jeanneret to be engraving flourishes on watch-cases all his days, all his entire life. Without saying a word, he waited for the first occasion to break his apprentice's contract."[28] So Le Corbusier later explained, through his mouthpiece Gauthier, his pivotal decision not to emulate his father as expected.

While decoration disgusted him, he was becoming a proficient watercolorist, patiently and systematically recording the visual world before his eyes: chalets, trees, flowers, fields, as well as simple interiors. He regularly hung out his neatly executed watercolors to dry on his mother's clothesline. In their remarkable legibility and graceful application of color, these gentle responses to the local scenery reflect exceptional discipline and control.

They also reveal the obsession Edouard shared with his father over weather conditions and seasonal change. In 1933, Le Corbusier wrote, "Over civilizations, as over trees and animals, passes the play of seasons. . . . There is winter when only dead wood is visible. . . . There is spring when the squat buds break out, where the direction of stems and branches appears, where the explosion is universal, life itself! What movement all of a sudden! How joyous it is."[29] The fluctuation between the darkness of winter and the flush of spring and between dark rainy days and bright sunny ones—evident in his early paintings—was increasingly echoed in his psyche.

7

Into his twenties, Charles-Edouard Jeanneret was so determined to escape his stultifying milieu that he fastened zealously onto individuals who offered hope. The first of these hero figures was Charles L'Eplattenier, who taught at l'Ecole d'Art.

Charles L'Eplattenier, ca. 1905

Born in 1874, the son of Swiss peasants from a village between La Chaux-de-Fonds and Neuchâtel, L'Eplattenier demonstrated an alternative to life and death in the world of Swiss watchmakers. Attracted to the visual arts early on, he had taken off first for l'Ecole des Arts Appliqués in Budapest and from there had gone to Paris to study painting, sculpture, and architecture at l'Ecole des Arts Décoratifs and then at l'Ecole des Beaux-Arts. With fourteen-year-old Edouard Jeanneret, he continued the education Georges Jeanneret had begun by teaching that the technical perfection as well as the aesthetic charms of trees, plants, and the larger landscape could be the models of all creativity. In turn, art based on nature could exceed nature itself with certain attributes.

Le Corbusier later wrote, "My master, an excellent teacher, free of all routine, a true man of the forests, made us men of the forests as well. . . . My master had said, Only nature inspires, nature alone is true and capable of supporting human endeavor."[30] That insight changed him forever. Even in his purest and most rational architecture, Le Corbusier invoked the givens of the universe as the ruling force. He invited the natural world inside and made growth and change central to his design. L'Eplattenier also gave his student the initial push to design buildings. "I had a horror of architecture and of architects," Le Corbusier later recalled, but "I accepted the verdict and I obeyed; I committed myself to architecture."[31]

8

Certain books that L'Eplattenier put in the art-school library took hold of Jeanneret. One was *The Grammar of Ornament,* a historical anthology of decorative design motifs, written by the Englishman Owen Jones in 1856.[32] Jones's premise was consistent with the beliefs already burgeoning in the young man: "Beauty arises naturally from the law of the growth of each plant. The life-blood—the sap, as it leaves the stem, takes the readiest way of reaching the confines of the surface, however varied that surface might be; the greater the distance it has to travel, or the weight it has to support, the thicker will be its substance."[33] This sense that a physical structure, be it a plant or a building, gains its proportions and skeletal organization in response to the life that occurs within it is at the essence of Le Corbusier's greatest achievements.

During the long hours he spent exploring Jones's compendium, Jeanneret's mind exploded with a new faith in human capability. "The plates in the book paraded past us the pure ornaments which man has created entirely out of his head," he wrote. "Ah, but it was here that we found, to even greater degree, the natural man, for if nature was omnipresent, man himself was there in his entirety with his faculties of crystallization, his geometric formation. From nature we passed to man. From imitation to creation. This book was beautiful and true, for everything in it was the summary of what had been created, profoundly created: the decoration of savages, Romans, Chinese, Indians, Greeks, Assyrians, Egyptians. . . . With this book we discovered the problem: man creates an *oeuvre* capable of affect."[34] Jeanneret was developing his breathtaking receptivity to visible beauty, natural or man-made, in any form and epoch.

At the same time, with L'Eplattenier's tutelage, he was acquiring an ability to work with the tools of his trade, as well as a steadfastness that was to stay with him forever. Le Corbusier later reflected, "At fifteen, I held the burin in my hand. A tool more than fierce. The tool of the straight path. Impossible to turn right or left. A path of loyalty, of honesty. My watch from La Chaux-de-Fonds is its symbol." In 1962, after spending two weeks near an oven heated at eight hundred degrees Centigrade to make 110 enamel panels for great entrance doors in Chandigarh, he connected his own standards to the rigors of that early training: "If I call yesterday's work into question, it is because it had left the right path. That is what the watch signified to me. If difficult problems arise, one must press on in spite of everything, straight ahead on the narrow path. If I am a possible architect today, it is because my training was not that of an architect. I have learned to see, with difficulty sometimes. You know, perhaps, that without the somewhat absurd and antiquated watch I had when I was 15, Le Corbusier would not be what he is so modestly now."[35]

JEANNERET ACQUIRED DISCIPLINE and skill, but he was not yet remarkable. A table clock and watchcases he designed and a wooden pencil box he carved at age fifteen, as well as an elaborate silver cane handle that he gave to his father and a wrought-iron gas chandelier for his parents' dining room, were executed capably but without distinction. At the end of his third year at l'Ecole d'Art, he hammered and embossed a repoussé copper relief, a portrait of Dante, which won the highest prize in the school, but it, too, did not show genius.

Then, when Jeanneret's fourth year at art school began in April 1904, his father requested that he be exempted from engraving. Georges Jeanneret produced a certificate from a local eye specialist showing that Edouard was suffering from significant difficulties with his vision. The school administration accordingly reduced Edouard's weekly hours of engraving and had him concentrate instead on interior decoration and furniture design. His physical liability pushed him in the direction of his true vocation.

L'Eplattenier obtained authorization to start a new and independent branch of the school, open exclusively to students in their last year who wanted to specialize in a program of art and decoration geared for architects, painters, sculptors, and jewelry designers. Following a summer when he had six weeks of religious instruction at l'Eglise Protestante Indépendante and his confirmation at the end of August, Charles-Edouard Jeanneret joined "the New Section." A revolution—within himself and in the local community—was in the making.

9

At the same time that Charles-Edouard was breaking out of the family mold, Georges developed a serious case of pneumonia. It was the beginning of a decline, and he was forced to retire from the Alpine Adventurers' Club. Now selling his watchcases through Longines, he was often in a rage at the great watch company with its cumbersome and demanding administration. Georges fumed, "Little by little I retire from civic life in order to become more and more cloistered and ignored. Will I soon disappear completely!"[36] Struck by his father's glumness, intense worries about money, and struggle to validate himself, Edouard became all the more determined not to take the same path.

Within a year, Charles-Edouard Jeanneret was, without any official credentials, practicing architecture. In 1905, the seventeen-year-old designed his first building. Construction began in the spring of 1906 and took two years. Commissioned for l'Ecole d'Art and called the Villa Fallet, it was on the outskirts of La Chaux-de-Fonds.

In later life, Le Corbusier often boasted that he had designed his first building at that young age, while declaring, "The house itself is probably dreadful."[37] In fact, the Villa Fallet has an impressive energy. Naturalistic ornament animates its surface with an abandon and spirit absent in the other houses of La Chaux-de-Fonds. The house is distinguished by its young designer's instinct to impart movement and by his drive toward organic form. A happier structure than its neighbors, it enjoys a rare liaison with its bucolic surroundings. Unlike most of the turgid, weighty domestic architecture of La Chaux-de-Fonds, the inventive form of the Villa Fallet resembles the chalets that dot the nearby countryside, and its surfaces echo the local trees and indigenous plant life. Vividly colored leaves and stems adorn the exterior walls. Inside, Jeanneret used three different blends of mortar to create lively murals in the salon and dining room, depicting the flora and fauna of the Jura.

The columns that support the pediment of the roof of the Villa Fallet are topped with edgy, geometric capitals that are variations of cubes. Sharply angled, with bold flat surfaces, these capitals betray an unexpected dash of modernism. In their stark whiteness and rhythmic charge, they are like a sudden explosion into free verse on the part of a young poet who until this moment has adhered diligently to the expected traditions of his trade. Breaking the rules, he had invented something new and exuberant.

Jeanneret gleaned essential lessons for his future from the work on the Villa Fallet. He came to recognize that two important elements in any building project are the materials and the workers who handle them. He also realized that, obvious though the point seems, the plan and its execution determine the success or failure of a project. Seeing the Villa Fallet come to life, he developed a terror of traditional teaching and formulas, while feeling a faith in his own on-the-spot judgment. He knew he must listen more to stone and mortar and his own instincts than to any rule book of architecture.

10

> As he saw it, every moment that he tarried he was cheating
> the world and the needy ones in it of his favor and assistance.
>
> — CERVANTES, *Don Quixote*

Jeanneret was suffocating amid the tasseled curtains and antimacassars. The hideousness of La Chaux-de-Fonds, he believed, stemmed from an economy

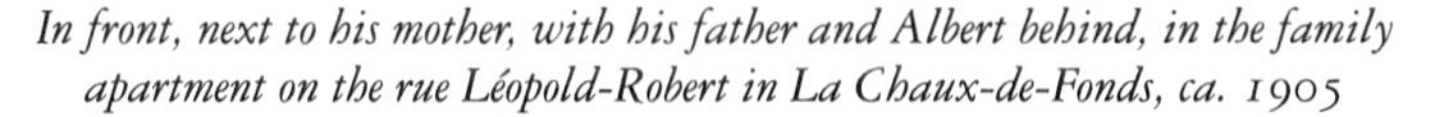

In front, next to his mother, with his father and Albert behind, in the family apartment on the rue Léopold-Robert in La Chaux-de-Fonds, ca. 1905

centered on mordant mechanization. The systematically processed pettiness of the watchmaking industry penetrated the lives of the local citizenry.

John Ruskin's *The Seven Lamps of Architecture,* another life-changing book for him, justified and soothed his rage at his surroundings and became his torch. Le Corbusier later recalled, "The times were intolerable: it could not last. We were surrounded by a crushing stupid bourgeoisism, drowned in materialism, garlanded with idiotic and machine-made decoration which, without our knowing how to stop it, produced all that pasteboard and cast-iron scroll-work for the delectation of Monsieur Homais. It was of spirituality that Ruskin spoke. . . . To this swollen mass of the elementary saturations of a dawning machine-age, he offered the testimony of honesty."[38]

"The blasphemies of the earth are sounding louder, and its miseries heaped heavier every day," Ruskin writes.[39] But building—and the making of artifacts—might alleviate the pain and replace it with joy. Ruskin opens *The Seven Lamps of Architecture* with the declaration: "Architecture is the art which so disposes and adorns the edifices raised by man, for whatsoever uses, that the sight of them contributes to his mental health, power, and pleasure."[40]

The future Le Corbusier adopted this approach as his gospel and took it in his own direction. There were to be no false skeletons or columns in his work; the pilotis are really the legs of the building, the concrete walls the true body. He was to paint surfaces in vibrant hues or with lively murals but never imitatively; notions like combed graining or imitation marble, however much they dominated the vocabulary of Le Corbusier's contemporaries, were anathema to him. Ruskin's candor and frankness, verbal and aesthetic, became his own.

For Ruskin, the most sacred and significant of all the arts was "architecture, [with] her continual influence over the emotions of daily life, and her realism, as opposed to the two sister arts which are by comparison the picturing of stories and of dreams."[41] Jeanneret, accepting the call, knew that his first step was to travel to places where he could be exposed, firsthand, to buildings in all their greatness.

Life at home intensified Edouard's urge to get away. His parents were being increasingly protective of Albert, who was showing signs of psychosomatic illness. They both pampered and favored their older son by continuing to fund his education while requiring Edouard to pay his own way with his architecture fees. Then, in October 1906, his parents moved to a new apartment, smaller but more modern, at 8 rue Jacob Brandt. Pauline ceased to live with them; the boys no longer had their own spaces. And father and younger son were increasingly at odds. On January 5, 1907, Georges wrote in his journal, "Edouard, all occupied with dancing and with girls, has just bought a pair of skis. He doesn't appear too healthy, this boy."[42]

Inflation was so severe that Georges could not afford to create the white enamel he needed to fulfill many orders from Longines, and he was panicked that his sons might never assume responsibility for themselves. His fear and rage grew all the more intense when, that summer, Edouard declared he was going to Italy. The elder Jeanneret's only response was: "Voilà—taken from us for one or several years. God be with him!"[43]

III

1

These are my Wanderjahre. I'm going to spend them in acquiring the education I never got at . . . school. . . . But it's not only knowledge of men and books that I want to acquire; that's only an instrument; I want to acquire something much harder to come by and more important; an unconquerable will. . . . You have to persuade men to action not by reasoning, but by rhetoric. The general idiocy of mankind is such that they can be swayed by words. . . .

I'm sure one can do anything with oneself if one tries. It's only a matter of will. I've got to train myself so that I'm indifferent to insult, neglect and ridicule. I've got to acquire a spiritual aloofness so complete that if they put me in prison I shall feel as free as a bird in air.

— W. SOMERSET MAUGHAM, *Christmas Holiday*

It is not surprising that Georges Jeanneret bristled. With his fees for the Villa Fallet in his pocket, the nineteen-year-old Edouard told his father, "I don't ask you for money, don't ask me where I am going nor what I am doing: I myself have no idea."[1]

Or so he said. Among the few things in Edouard's backpack was John Ruskin's *Mornings in Florence.*[2] He was on his way to meet up with Léon Perrin, one of his classmates in L'Eplattenier's advanced course, in the Renaissance city.

He left La Chaux-de-Fonds on September 1. When the train carried him on its spiraling tracks through the St. Gotthard Pass to the Ticino valley, the weather was so bad that he could see nothing of the canyon walls or of the Devil's Bridge, which he was longing to view, having read a comparison of its marvelous construction, a single sweeping arch, to the vault of a Gothic cathedral. Then Jeanneret saw as never before. After the fog and storms of the evening and the hours in tunnels, he spent a magnificent

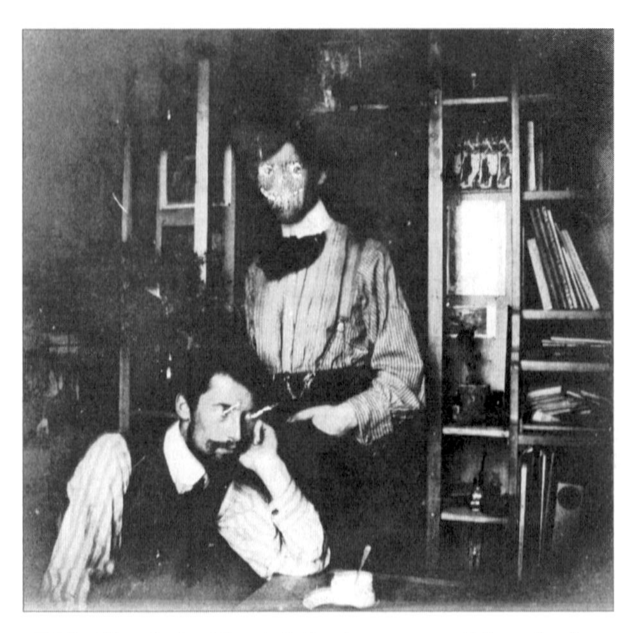

With Albert in La Chaux-de-Fonds, ca. 1905. Edouard redrew his own face on the photo.

morning in Lugano, where the mountain peaks were reflected perfectly in the clear lake. He thrilled even more in the cavernous glass-and-steel train station in Milan. Standing in the wide piazza dominated by the Milan cathedral, the young man from a mountain hamlet was overwhelmed. The feathery finials of its hovering triangular form and its endlessly variegated facade give a lightness to its mass that dazzled him. This marvel of human building was beyond anything he had ever imagined—larger and more physically impressive than he had fathomed from the illustrations in Ruskin and Owen Jones. The testimony to ingenuity in the center of a metropolis, forthright and graceful at the same time, was inestimably powerful. He sketched it feverishly.

He began to explore Milan. Only at seven the following evening did Jeanneret realize that, in his first experience of a big city, he had gone since noon the previous day without taking in a morsel of food. Jeanneret determined that Milan was enchanting in the evening, "but by day, what hell!"[3] During the hours of commerce, he had to flee the cathedral square because of his disgust at the wastefulness of humanity squandering its energy and resources. "This is the kingdom of fools throwing away money with both hands," he wrote to his frugal, hardworking parents.[4] To L'Eplattenier he described the "colossal crowd of dolts" on that great urban square where one encountered "nothing but stupidities and obtuseness."[5]

But the cathedral was his refuge. "There was such a racket that I escaped inside. *There, what grandeur!* The forest's mystery. Fabulous. Demented."[6] Within the walls of the great building, an enraptured Jeanneret felt that the relationship of the human being to the constructed space was an essential element of architecture. "The Duomo is magnificent from outside and imposing within, above all *enormous,*" he wrote his parents.[7] It took time to adjust to the grandeur: "Gradually, one gets accustomed to it, suddenly you see a tiny man beside a column; your eye begins to measure proportions, and one remains astonished."[8] That emphasis on human experience and the direct emotional impact of scale underlay his approach to architecture forever after.

2

Jeanneret studied buildings from every angle and with an intensity few tourists could imagine. When, after an overnight stop in Genoa, he arrived in Pisa, he could not stop gazing at the diaphanous surfaces of its Romanesque cathedral. He was so obsessed that he gave little note to having his pocket picked. What riveted him was not simply the building but the variations caused by the changes of light and the state of the sky. He wrote to L'Eplattenier: "Friday in the cathedral square, on the grass, with peace and the lovely blue sky for companions. First contact with the great marvel; I got myself 'pinched' (as you so nicely put it) after a few hours. I remained in this square four hours and cleared out only a few hours on Sunday and Monday for the Museo Civico. I almost came to the point of drinking *schmolli*s with the attendants in the little leaning towers 'of Carrara marble.' *(Signorino, Una, Lira, Chquante!)* This facade of the cathedral is simply marvelous, and I've never, ever seen anything like it. . . . The cathedral at six in the evening is an enchanted forest of color, the quintessence of yellows of every value, from ivory white to black patinas, and this against an ultramarine of an extraordinary quality; by dint of staring at it, it becomes black. . . . At seven in the evening the cathedral is more beautiful than ever, what hues! There's a certain brown, a certain blue, and all of a tranquility! Behind me the sky is orange and mauve; the green of the bronze doors is dead now, and the yellow marbles reveal themselves; they are matte siena. The columns, though, are the pinkish white of an eglantine petal. . . . On Saturday morning I sat on the cathedral steps: the facade is in shadow and colors of a hitherto unknown delicacy emerge and become even more delicate. Last evening occurred a magnificent song, the allegro of golden marbles with deep ultramarine. This morning the black marbles, which have been washed for eight hundred years, are as blue as if they still formed the lining of the vault, and the delicacy of this blue behind the alabaster columns makes a sort of ineffable mist. . . . The marble, once white, is now raw yellow and raw black, a curious patina accentuated by the outline."[9]

The heightened sensitivity with which the young traveler felt color and saw design details drove him to a frenzy of excitement. He began to sketch and make watercolors of frescoes, pulpits, cornices, and architraves, and he annotated some of these images with notes squeezed to the edges of the page. Architecture induced unparalleled ecstasy.

JEANNERET, who arrived in Florence on September 9, was elated when Perrin got there five days later. Now, in addition to sketching and writing about the marvels he was discovering, he could discuss them with a friend.

The physical hardships of life on a budget of sixty francs per month only added to its luster. For a month the two young men shared a room in a *pensione* on the Piazza della Signoria, where the strong wind that blew through the leaky windows made Jeanneret so cold that he had to sleep under his loden coat. The light in the room was "atrocious," and his eyes troubled him.[10] The "bourgeoise *Minestra*" that was the main substance at supper each evening had a tomato color that he associated with Giotto's frescoes and admired on the walls of Santa Croce—but not in his soup. Having instructed his father to ask no questions, Edouard now described to Georges and Marie how his hands were cramped from writing and sketching, and reported on his eye problems, his exhaustion from travel, and his inability to sleep because of the city noise.

The adversities gave him a feeling of worthiness. Jeanneret happily abandoned eating during the day so as to utilize every moment of light and of the hours when the museums were open. Euphoric, he recognized sequence as an essential ingredient of his emotional transport; Florence was more exciting because he had gone there after Siena, which had been so wonderful that it had put him into a mood of heightened sensitivity.

At the same time, Jeanneret was struggling to come to grips with his break from home. In his room in the *pensione,* he made a display of family photographs. There were pictures of his grandparents with Aunt Pauline, of his brother, and of his parents—including one of his father with L'Eplattenier. Jeanneret reflected that the pictures "afford me tremendous joy; it is really strange how the notion of a long absence can separate us so much, in thought and in memory; when I see your faces again it all seems quite abstract; I no longer live at La Chaux-de-Fonds; when, for instance, I evoke the bridge of the Hôtel de Ville or the facade of Hartmann's, they strike me as very peculiar and *oneiric.*"[11]

He was a sibling fighting for his space. Writing to his parents two days after his twentieth birthday, Edouard concluded a letter of eight dense pages with a pathetic lament: "I have a notion that you always begin your letter-writing sessions by the Epistle to Albert, and that what's left for me is only a tiny quarter of an hour between 11 and 11:15." He signed off like a little boy—"Kisses all around to Aunt P., to dear papa, and to dear mama. Edouard"—and then added the postscript, "You cannot imagine the enormous pleasure a word from those near and dear can give to someone who deals only with people of stone or metal all day long."[12]

Even if his parents did not respond adequately, they afforded him the chance to voice the new fire that was burning within him: "To think that at this very moment I have seen and frequently touched the most beautiful things ever produced by the human mind. Michelangelo, Giotto, Raphaël, Donatello, Rubens (portraits), *tapestries,* goldsmith work, enamels, ceramics, ivories, even mummies! They all fascinate me, and I can never be grateful enough *to the masters* who initiated me and gave me a thirst for the beautiful: I feel I possess a very *sure* critical sense, and I am more than pleased to find that I get worked up only in front of the loveliest things . . . oh, the Palazzo Vecchio! What a wonder; I admire it much more than the campanile, and certainly more than the cathedral. Orsanmichele, too, as well as Santa Croce. All the same, Pisa remains number one among all my beautiful moments."[13] It became one of the struggles of Le Corbusier's life to find people who understood that intoxication with visual beauty.

3

The accepted wisdom about what was good or bad in Renaissance art meant nothing to Jeanneret. He refuted the popular idea that Raphael was a poor colorist, praising the paintings at the Pitti. He deemed Giotto as a painter "the master of simple, ample, and powerful composition, of sumptuous color," but disparaged him as an architect.[14] "The best-known example of Giotto's architecture does not win me over: not the least bit 'constructive,' it would please a painter more than an architect, enchanting by proportion and color. The cathedral, misunderstood inside as out—an accumulation of materials which don't look like what they are—makes me regret Milan."[15]

Jeanneret told L'Eplattenier that "the city seems to me *anything but rich* in architecture."[16] But in this instance he took the rare step of questioning his own reaction. He asked: "Can it be true? Or are my eyes still dazzled by

Pisa? As I was saying, the Palazzo Vecchio is a great wonder but difficult to study, its power is abstract as the sculptures are superfluous (no use, it seems to me, even trying to copy Raphaël or Botticelli). But perhaps I'm taking the wrong path and should be drawing the city's palaces instead. A word from you on this matter would be a great help."

At the Uffizi, Hugo Van der Goes's powerful *Adoration,* a work that puts others off because of the coarseness of the crazed peasants, affected Jeanneret viscerally. He saw in it "that knowledge of the great masters in the balancing of masses, colors, lines, etc."[17] Titian's and Botticelli's paintings and Donatello's sculpture moved him similarly with their power to conquer viewers.

But the monument in Florence that excited him above all was Orcagna's tabernacle in the small chapel of Orsanmichele. Andrea Orcagna—an accomplished painter, sculptor, architect, and poet—had been commissioned to make this ornate niche in the church of the guilds of Florence in 1340. A complex composition with bronze girders and supports encasing angels and prophets in half relief, it surrounds a Madonna who ascends to heaven with a gloria. Every centimeter is charged with a sense of urgency and unbridled emotional intensity. The participants in the holy scene are consumed by religiosity, and there is a feverish animation to the movement of drapery and limb, the crevices and swells of the chiselwork. Jeanneret wrote to his parents, "The fabulous wealth accumulated in this marble shrine by a genius like Orcagna exceeds the imagination, you have to see it, touch it, caress these polished marbles which have become transparent by dint of delicacy, your binoculars must search out the darkest corners. I am always on tiptoe, supposing the two centimeters I gain thereby will enable me to enjoy an even intenser pleasure. And the whole thing was created, as the artist knew, to be placed in a dark church where only an artist's eyeballs can manage, by sheer force of will, to penetrate the darkness. Moreover the same thing goes for all the masterpieces here; the Giottos cannot be seen. You have to hunt them down. Luckily, all the fashionable world doesn't give a fuck (excuse the Donatellian vigor of the expression), and only those who have something in their belly can enjoy them. This is no longer the fashion-magazine of the Uffizi where you can see crowds fainting with ecstasy in front of wretched daubs. This tabernacle, six meters wide and deep, eight meters high, is built of the most beautiful yellow marble that looks like ivory. Angels and prophets, sculptures, bas-reliefs, and tondos, but the bas-reliefs above all, marvelous in their control of volume, gesture, and sobriety; and everywhere, in the tiniest corners and of course in the darkest places, inlaid enamels, intense blues and golds, vermilions, greens, all vibrating and gently flashing in a rich and robust symphony by Sinding accentuating the construction, or suddenly exploding in the darkness, just where you weren't expecting it. Just remarkable."[18]

After six hours sketching the tabernacle, Jeanneret was so energized that he violated his usual rule of fasting by day and indulged in a late lunch: "a veritable feast: 15 centimeters of fried potatoes then a little farther on, four sous worth of salami and one of bread!"[19] Orcagna, versed in four art forms, capable of making art beyond all expectation, had become his hero for life.

4

Much as Jeanneret loved Orcagna's tabernacle, he lamented to his parents about "the parade of imbeciles lasting all morning, Baedeker in hand, striding around the marvel, blinking and making their escape, fully satisfied to have seen Orsanmichele, and to be able to tell some Kreutschner, 'When we saw the tabernacle . . . oh you can't imagine!' "[20] Le Corbusier always evinced this contempt for people who look without seeing.

At age twenty, he had already developed a completely independent sense of judgment. The "red ochre, ultramarine, burnt siena, yellow ochre" of an obscure Etruscan tomb painting that he copied in the garden of the archaeological museum made it "stronger as decorative painting than all the Giottos in the world."[21] He prized legibility, declaring of the first Greek vases he ever saw, "How beautiful, what style, how easy to read!" After his initial evaluation of Masaccio's frescoes in the Brancacci Chapel—"ultimately, they cheat you"—he retracted his view, for he realized that this impression had been caused by the darkness of the small chapel, to which he conscientiously made a second visit. On that occasion, he noted *The Expulsion from the Garden of Eden* as "splendidly composed, lovely simplified figures, ample gestures."[22]

Jeanneret observed urban life in all its variety, well beyond the dictates of guidebooks. He wrote his parents that Florence was "the city of wind and cats." He depicted those cats with a novelist's flair: "big ones too, burly and complacent bourgeois, with solid muscles, eyes a little dimmed by idleness, their fur unbrushed. You see them everywhere, anything but fierce, sitting with their tails wrapped around their feet on every doorstep."[23] On one occasion, he decided to share his lunch with a cat, and in a letter home feigned offense at the way the creature strode off without a thank-you or a backward glance.

He reported almost everywhere to his parents. Comparing the husband-hungry ladies of Florence to streetwalkers, he wrote Georges and Marie that the Italian city had a "nuptial atmosphere; women not of the upper class all look more or less vicious, they pass you at the corner of the Palazzo Vecchio at high noon; usually mama accompanies the young lady, she smiles at you quite pleasantly and makes her proposition in French, if you please; it's with her, I assume, that the agreement is reached! Most of these transactions occur on the steps of a church; singular morality. I may be making too much of this—I confess to not being preoccupied by it in the slightest. I leave such commerce to those to whom Angelico has nothing to say."[24]

And how Fra Angelico astonished him! "I've also seen the most extraordinary, the most *disconcerting* thing at the Academia: a picture by Angelico painted 500 years ago and which I swear dates from . . . tomorrow."[25]

JEANNERET was crystallizing the passions that were to determine his life's course. "Ah! The monasteries! I'd like to spend my whole life inhabiting what are called their cells," he wrote L'Eplattenier.[26] He was referring both to those simple white cells at San Marco rendered sublime by Fra Angelico's graceful frescoes and to a lesser-known sight that was to exercise a lifelong grip on his conscience: the Charterhouse of the Valley of Ema.

No single architectural monument—even the Parthenon, which he visited four years later—had such an impact on the future Le Corbusier. The intelligence of the plan that gracefully combined community living and the sanctity of the individual's private existence made the monastery a perfect small city. The access to nature was ideal, and the internal arrangements of the cells reflected a logic Jeanneret found admirable. He had traveled the six kilometers from the outskirts of Florence to this fifteenth-century Carthusian monastery because of John Ruskin, who sent his readers there. After studying the monks' small houses with their private gardens and observing the church and refectory and the central courtyard that served as meeting places, he wrote L'Eplattenier, "This is the solution of the unique type of workers' habitation, or rather of the earthly paradise."[27]

In *Details Concerning the Present State of Architecture and Urbanism,* a pivotal text Le Corbusier wrote in 1930, he discussed the direct impact of this highly intelligent organization of space on his own mature work: "I've seen, in the musical landscape of Tuscany, a *modern city* crowning the hill. The noblest silhouette in the landscape, the uninterrupted crown of monks' cells, each with a view over the plain and opening onto a little walled garden down the slope. I believe I've never encountered such a joyous version of habitation. The back of each cell leads through a door and then a gate onto a circular street covered with an arcade: the cloister. All the common services function here—prayers, visits, dinners, burials. This 'modern city' dates from the 15th century. The radiant vision of it is always with me. In 1910 [*sic*], returning from Athens, I visited the monastery once again. One day in 1922, I mentioned it to my associate Pierre Jeanneret: on the back of a restaurant menu we spontaneously sketched our 'villa apartments': the idea was born."[28] In 1948, in *The Modulor,* he referred again to the impact of Ema as the exemplar of "individual freedom and collective organization."[29] In 1950, when writing about his intentions for l'Unité d'Habitation in Marseille, he again cited Ema as his model: "The harmonious organization of collective and individual phenomena is here resolved in serenity, joy, and efficiency."[30]

The day after visiting Ema, the twenty-year-old vowed to his parents that he would never forget that all human housing should provide some of the solitude and tranquility enjoyed by monks. For "at least they knew how to arrange a delicious life for themselves, and I am convinced that, all things considered, they are blessed, especially those who have Paradise in view!"[31] The goal of his architecture was never to shift.

5

After writing his parents about "the thirst for the beautiful" and proudly declaring, "I feel I possess a very *sure* critical sense, and I am more than pleased to find that I get worked up only in front of beautiful things," he proceeded in the same breath to ask his father to send him, "*by return mail,* an American razor of *first quality,*" for which Georges should use funds Edouard had left behind for such purposes.[32] He instructed his helpful parent to unwrap the razor to make it appear used, a deceit intended to avoid customs duties. Jeanneret explained that in Italy a shave cost ten sous, and "they stick their fingers in your mouth it's disgusting and the hair grows too thick."[33]

His preoccupation with money and hygiene dominated the letters home. He reported about a train on which he was so black from smoke that he had to go to the toilet twice to wash, differentiating himself from the Italian "swine."[34] With his need to impart personal details, he described dinner at the *pensione* in Florence as "an enormous plate of soup with macaroni, then meat and the problem of Italian-style vegetables, and mystery, yes, of course, good or bad, who knows what to call it: *constipative . . .* certainly!"[35] The state of his bowels was a major issue for him, of which he kept his parents apprised with frequent reports of both constipation and bouts of diarrhea.

6

He was, however, as poetic as he was mundane. From Padua, Jeanneret wrote his parents, "Before falling, the leaves become gray here, a splendid, fine gray; the fields remain intensely green, and only the plowed fields strike a vibrant note. The soil of Italy is extraordinary; salmon-red, tile-red, and with the occasional groves which turn a brilliant lemon-yellow, the plowed fields with their deep and regular furrows, the clumps of small trees, the little walled gardens, the narrow paths of a rich, gray color: it all forms what the famous frescoists have left us on their walls, a gift to the eyes and to the imagination. In Ravenna, on the other hand, the grass is a raw acidic green and the earth is violet."[36]

That instinctive feeling for color and nature governed Le Corbusier's approach to architecture. He designed his buildings in close relation to their surroundings. Le Corbusier never envisioned a project merely as a static model or as blueprints and plans made under artificial office light. Rather, he acted in accord with the realizations of this eye-opening trip to Italy: buildings live and breathe in constant connection to the specific environment in which they are set, and they change with the same frequency as weather and light conditions.

CONSIDER, FOR EXAMPLE, the sight of Le Corbusier's Atelier Lipchitz (1925) in late autumn—the same season when the future architect marveled at the subtle colors and transformation of leaves in northern Italy. Le Corbusier made this studio/residence for Jacques Lipchitz when both he and the Cubist sculptor, a friend, were enjoying their first periods of critical and financial success.

On a quiet residential street in a Parisian suburb, Lipchitz's house is dominated by a massive, silo-shaped concrete cylinder, set down with the weight of a kettledrum against the light piccolo tone of tubular-steel balustrades and playful openings along the facade. That counterpoint between the immense central volume and the jubilant smaller elements evokes the paintings of Le Corbusier's and Lipchitz's mutual friend and colleague of that time Fernand Léger. But the careful orchestration of concrete, steel, and glass is only part of what occurs.

This impeccably engineered assemblage of man-made forms exists in constant interplay with nature, for Lipchitz's house is covered in vines. Sounding the same "vibrant note" of the foliage Jeanneret observed in

Padua, these vines produce a flurry of large red-and-gold leaves, bowing forward in their last moment of life. Higher up on the building walls, the vines form a bare network of infinite complexity, woven out of more elements than a spiderweb. This tracery of lacework is remarkably like the filigree patterns that so enthralled Jeanneret in Pisa. What makes the Lipchitz house so intoxicating is the coupling of architecture with the never-ending motion of the universe that caused Padua to be "a gift to the eyes and to the imagination."[37]

7

> The rains had come, the rains had gone, and the sun was back
> on its throne like an absolute monarch kept off for a week
> by his subjects' barricades, and now reigning once again.
>
> —GIUSEPPE TOMASI DI LAMPEDUSA, *The Leopard*

On October 25, Jeanneret and Perrin arrived in Venice. The rain was merciless. The downpours continued for five miserable days, with such intensity that one night a shower woke up a flock of ducks settled in under the windows of their *pensione.* Then came two days of opaque fog. The Adriatic flooded the Piazza San Marco. Having known only a mountain climate until then, Jeanneret wrote L'Eplattenier, "One feels like scratching everywhere on one's body: are these fins breaking out . . . or simply mosquito bites?"[38]

At last, the sky shifted. The effect was to be paralleled when the clouds whipped by overhead at Le Corbusier's funeral fifty-eight years later. The change in light was a miracle for the twenty-year-old Jeanneret, who wrote: "Two or three patches of sunshine allowed us to judge Venice at its finest, and the other evening we even observed a real apotheosis, a dramatic sky entirely covered with black clouds drowned in the yellow mist, and the brilliant sun next to the lantern of Santa Maria della Salute; sea, sky, and houses making a single enormous torch seen through tears."[39] To cry at beauty, especially after darkness, was his norm.

The apotheosis continued: "The blue sky is a miracle. At such moments, everything sings. I have seen the most extraordinary colors in the canals. The theory of complementaries set to work by a superior magician."[40] And if San Marco, the Ca' d'Oro, and the Palazzo Ducale enraptured him by daylight, they were even better at night. Brightly lit by "the glow of gas lamps," they became "a marvelous and supernatural specter."[41] Now, even more than in Milan and Florence, Jeanneret dreamed of making public architecture that could stir the soul.

8

The travelers' next destination was Vienna, where they hoped to find work in an architect's office. Jeanneret became obsessed by his clothing. He wrote his parents about "my shoes, which gaped all around the soles, the toes were likely to extract sighs on the delicate porches of Ravenna; bought a pair for 17 f.25 (secondhand!) in town: splendid yellow 'melon slices' as P. would say, the envy of the entire population of Ferrara. As well as a necktie, which happened to have been embroidered one fine day by the subtlest of lace makers. Now it's my nightshirt that's giving up the ghost, I'm sorry mama saw fit to give me one in such poor condition, the Italian air doesn't suit its failing lungs. I've bought myself an elastic collar, quite practical."[42]

He was determined, as he set out to join the workforce in a sophisticated city, that his wardrobe be pleasing. He instructed his parents that he needed "another very practical zephyr shirt, size 7, collar 37 centimeters from one buttonhole to the other. In case anyone wants to buy me more, maybe in brighter colors, less drab-looking. Not any more collars, please. As for shoes, it's pointless to mention spats and dress boots. *Rubber soles, yes, and leather slippers too.*" And he hoped for "my (chic) brown *kid gloves.*"[43]

He was in a state of anxiety—both about that trunk he hoped would await him in Vienna and about his first sea voyage. He enjoined Georges and Marie to participate in his nervous anticipation: "One does not leave a place like this behind without great regret. Including tonight, including the ball! Luckily the sea doesn't look at all threatening. . . . *Au revoir* and wish me a good crossing! Kisses all around."[44] This entreaty to his parents was illogical. Surely Edouard knew that by the time they received his letter in the post, he would already have arrived at his destination. He needed, however, to imagine his mother and father cheering him on. So he would always be: a brave traveler and a child in need of comfort.

IV

1

Architecture can be seen as silent music.

—JOHANN WOLFGANG VON GOETHE,
"Conversation with Eckermann"

Vienna hardened him. There, Jeanneret developed both the cynicism and the escape routes that enabled him to survive serious depression. His high spirits began to plummet when, after four days, he and Perrin still had not found a place to stay, the trunk he was expecting from Switzerland had not arrived, and everything was closed for an unidentifiable holiday. He had also discovered that design school was expensive and had no places for new students. The paving stones were hurting his feet in his search for "unobtainable information from undiscoverable people."[1]

The man who later devoted himself to improving urban life felt crushed by this first effort to try to earn his keep in a metropolis: "Sad day; no purpose whatever; mortal boredom; one rages, one rears up, one is a tiny angry god in solitary combat against this mocking inert mass, the inexorable *indifference* of the big city." He was further appalled by the new art he saw in the large "Secession" exhibition. The rage for the stylized modernity of this popular movement convinced him that people in general were "imbeciles," inclined to be "chic" rather than tasteful or original.[2]

Jeanneret was formulating his concept of how the world functioned. He wrote L'Eplattenier that in Vienna "nothing gets done unless you have connections and recommendations." His initial impression of the modern architecture he was supposed to admire was that "the whole construction is masked and faked." Like the people, it was "weak, oh, how weak and empty, discouraging, disconcerting (judging quite objectively, with no special pessimism!)."[3] What was being done in this hotbed of modern design was "*wretched, awful,* absolutely zero as far as experiment goes, *it's stupid.* And that's speaking objectively."[4]

After three months in Vienna, the moral corruption he perceived in the new architecture combined with his inability to find work left him sinking into melancholy. His main tool for combating the gloom was to make order in his immediate details. When his trunk finally arrived, he was overjoyed by the care his mother had taken, and at least he could put on a clean white shirt. The white that restored his state of grace was the same salubrious color as the snowcapped peaks of his childhood; the elixir of purity, it had the brightness in which he was ultimately to try to house humankind.

The organization of his own belongings gave Jeanneret a sense of equilibrium he found lacking in the world around him; it compensated for the horrors of the design scene about which he had just complained. "Everything's in good shape now, I have a lot of drawers, and everything's in its proper place," he reported to his parents with glee.[5] In time, he was to provide the inhabitants of his architecture with ingenious closets whose orderly shelves and bins were paradigms of crisp, charming geometry; he saw such artful organization of private details as a means to escape inner darkness.

Simple domestic grace was salvation. If contemporary Viennese art disgusted him, a dustcloth could be inspiring. "I worked yesterday, my hands in the dirt, with a determination worthy of a nobler object."[6]

Yet after unpacking happily and thanking his mother for all she had done, Jeanneret harshly rebuked her for what she left out. "But why the devil didn't you specify the following objects in the order of their primary necessity? I'm not blaming you of course, but I really don't understand this omission," he wrote before detailing nine categories of objects missing from the trunk. His aluminum drawing pen was absent: "What the devil do you think I can do without that?" Where was his postcard collection, his photos of rustic Swiss architecture, and his new brown gloves? He couched the exegesis with a sideways apology—"I have nothing else to say to you; furthermore you have nothing to complain about, I realize I'm in the wrong; I'm doing it quite selfishly."[7] But he needed those gloves. After all, he wanted to go to concerts. He had to put on a face to the world: "My neckties are threadbare, I'm going to buy new ones. Shoes too, though my yellow ones still arouse great interest and are of excellent—striking!—quality. Bravo Ravenna! The drape of my coat, when I turn my collar up, gives me the look of a Steinlen drawing, as Perrin would say."[8]

To make his first foray into Viennese society, Jeanneret bought a felt hat—"the sponge one was just too cheap—just over six crowns!!!" The event was a concert of the Philharmonic, with Richard Strauss conducting. Jeanneret's opinions were characteristically sharp: "Some Spohr, rather cold though very skillful, some Wagner (the 'Faust Overture'), very tiresome, some Debussy, really stunning; such clarity after all that German blur."[9]

Having gone to Vienna ostensibly to study modern art and design, Jeanneret spent most of his time there listening to music. Attending concerts every Sunday afternoon at the "Grosse saal" of the Musikverein, in his eyes the most sumptuous and beautiful place in Vienna, he determined that Tchaikovsky was a genius. When Gustav Mahler was conducting the Viennese Opera, Jeanneret stood in line for four hours in the damp cold to get a standing-room ticket. The performance of *Siegfried* was torture for his legs, but "as music it's marvelous, amazingly rich, the themes imaginative, the sonorities splendid. To manage not to repeat oneself, *not to go on too long even once* in five hours, that's really something. The scenic effects are magical, the lighting too."[10]

Wagner's opera had a depth and authenticity he deemed lacking in Josef Hoffmann's silver, Gustav Klimt's paintings, Otto Wagner's architecture, and all the other exemplars of the new visual trends he deplored. "Here in Vienna, if it weren't for the music, one would commit suicide—proof: each time I went out looking for art I came back with a terrible depression," he wrote.[11]

TWENTY-YEAR-OLD JEANNERET believed that in this "painful moment" young architects had "no father in the movement to guide them."[12] With all that Vienna offered, L'Eplattenier was still the only teacher in whom he had retained confidence. Yet, he assured Georges and Marie, he still had one constant source of joy: "Music overwhelms me."[13]

2

By the start of 1908, Jeanneret was using the vocabulary of true clinical depression. He wrote to his parents about "the demon of doubt, depressing uncertainty. . . . It's precisely because I have disappointments that I feel the need to tell someone about them." He was designing a villa to be built back in La Chaux-de-Fonds and attributed his anguish to problems with the project—as well as to one of his frequent colds. "I fumble, I make risky, almost always illogical choices, and fail to keep to the straight and narrow!"[14]

He was completely candid with his parents about his burgeoning awareness of the opposite sex. His lack of self-confidence came through in an idiosyncratic narrative about an incident in the studio of the sculptor Karl Stemolak, where he had briefly studied drawing. "With Stemolak, I learn how to see, but I get a good talking-to every day: *ganz schlecht, Herr Jeanneret, ganz schlecht!* And now and then an encouragement: '*ah ah, jetz gehts besser.*' The pretty harpist having done her number, I finished the first sketch as best I could and gave her as good as I got this morning, which gained me exactly one nice smile. I'm the one who's assigned to the wardrobe and who helps her on with her jacket at noon (she's twenty, and with eyes!). . . . It's a fact that the scales have fallen from mine, and since I've come to Vienna I'm beginning to see what a woman is, it's the inevitable attraction of the Eternal Feminine making itself felt—rather late in the day in my case. I've spent my entire youth without ever having looked at a girl. Now there's a sweet music in my ears, and I frequently soften up *in-petto.* It was ever thus. Have no fear, if you please, it's all very pure and I have no nuptial intentions; proof: if I did, I'd be able to have myself a nice hump on *Sylvesternacht.*"[15]

The dour Calvinists probably recoiled from their younger son's subsequent report of the proliferation of prostitutes at midnight on the Stephanplatz, the center of city life, and his explanation that, were he less virtuous, he could have had one of them. He described women showering kisses, with one of them practically having her clothes torn off by a mob, and continued, "More than once I've found myself, pushed and pushing, first in line in front of a young lady. But, without aspiring to chivalry, I confess that hugging a woman in that kind of danger would be repugnant to me. So I resisted with all my might and thereby managed to liberate one or two young goddesses. Which has not kept me from receiving a first-rate slap from one little student who, in imminent danger, distributed such treatment all around. And that was my one and only kiss!!"[16] Jeanneret was consumed for years by this internal war of desire and inhibition and the fantasy of what he might have enjoyed had he not resisted it.

3

His sweetest moments in this difficult time period, he assured Georges and Marie, came when he looked at the many family photographs he had scattered all over his room. "I love you, and right away I begin shedding tears even as I write the words," he wrote. "The house is too sacred a thing for me ever to forget it, and the parents are a young man's whole life before he gets married."

"The realm of the affections has an enormous role to play in my life's goal," Jeanneret informed his parents in the stilted tone of an engineer discussing a machine. In the same voice, similarly poignant for the stiffness with which he expressed his emotional depth, he assured them he would let down neither them nor his teacher. "I'd be too afraid of disappointing you, of falling back into the condition of an ordinary man, whereas for twenty years you have nourished us on noble ideas. And so, my dear M. L'Eplattenier, I say this quite frankly, it's for his sake that I'm trying to make something of myself."[17]

Even more pompously, Jeanneret informed his mother and father, "My readings are not frivolous; any more than my person."[18] To drive home the point, he explained that he sometimes saved a roll from his evening meal to have for breakfast the next day. He spent his nights reading and writing letters but never let a day go by, even a Sunday, without visiting a museum or an exhibition or a corner of the city. He never permitted himself "to relax," insisting that "a young man of my age must keep his artistic fibers vibrating on all occasions."[19] Unlike other young people, he did not seek more personal pleasure. "One is devilishly alone here," he wrote home.[20]

Jeanneret was desperate for his parents to know how eager he was to improve himself. "I have a serious defect, which is always to be judging," he wrote. "I reproach myself for it and frequently realize how exasperating it is: a constant danger for an artist, whose entire life consists in *sifting* and in quite coldly excluding, in being frank with himself. He becomes noble when he can keep this to himself and manage to rein in his indignation, which frequently flares up. Thank you for warning me of the danger—you must chastise me often and harshly."[21]

While they were supposed to keep him in line, he would instruct them on how to live. Edouard told his father to hire an assistant and his mother to continue with her music. This was feasible, he explained, because he was earning enough from the fees for the architectural work he was doing at long distance that they could stop setting aside money on his behalf. But if Charles-Edouard Jeanneret believed he was going to lighten his parents' financial burden for long, he was delusional.

V

1

As a last-ditch effort to find work in Vienna, Jeanneret barged, unbidden, into the offices of the city's two leading architects, Otto Wagner and Josef Hoffmann. Twenty-five years later, Le Corbusier claimed that Hoffmann offered him a job for two hundred crowns and introduced him to Klimt and other artists, but in a letter he wrote L'Eplattenier at the time he said that Hoffmann was not even in his office and that they never met.

L'Eplattenier advised his two students to go to Dresden or another major German city; Jeanneret responded, "You're violent and treat us like ten-year-olds."[1] Jeanneret knew what he had to do: "In order to create a new art, you have to be in a position to calculate arches, large roof spans, bold cantilevers, in short everything our traditionalist 'masters' fail to do, for you can imagine that my ambition goes further than making little rental houses and villas."[2] He could not acquire this technical knowledge in the German language; besides, he needed to gain his living. He had made up his mind to move to Paris.

GEORGES AND MARIE were enraged. They were upset both by the idea of Edouard's going to the French capital and his failure to communicate with them directly. He responded that there had been no point in explaining the decision to them since they did not even know the names of important architects.

He then pinned his secrecy on his reluctance to trouble them: "That would have made a constant disturbance for you, my beloved parents, for you're so kind, you live so little for yourselves and far too much for us."[3] He explained his choice of Paris with the sort of verbiage of which he became the master: "Whereupon I returned to my bourgeois common sense and once again burned what I had adored; i.e., when one is young one speaks for the sake of speaking, and goes on doing just that, actually, more or less until one dies. (Those who say nothing are the smarties, of course; and I've noticed I always had a chattering temperament.) The received opinion is this: that I lack any solid basis, that I don't know my trade, which is exactly what I must now learn." The solution was a job in France: "My tastes are Latin tastes. . . . In Paris (nor does one have to be somewhat cracked to believe it) . . . they build just *as big* and with just as modern methods as they do in Germany."

"One thing you can be at peace about," he assured his parents, "I'm anything but a 'vain boaster,' and I need to muster all my courage in order to face up to the future as it looks to me. I'm too much of a worker, and I make myself *stupid* because of it. No question about it, I must let the *young man* in me speak, otherwise I'll shrivel away to nothing, and I spend my evenings making projects solely in order to do nothing or to kid around. . . . My trade or my vocation is uniquely or rather *must* be in art, a young man of my age must keep his artistic fibers vibrating on all occasions. One must have a daily bread in art, an atmosphere of art. Here in Vienna, if it weren't for music, one would have to do away with oneself."[4] In Paris, on the other hand, he would see Notre-Dame, the Louvre, and other great sights he knew only from photographs.

"Before me stretches the vast battlefield of Art, which devours so many men's lives but which I must embark upon, and right away. *That is why I am going to Paris.*" His parents had to understand that he had endured all he could; he begged for their support. "I need your confidence. Above all, my dear good parents, stop saying I make you bitter. Whom else can I love except you? . . . Trust me, I love you, and you know quite well that all I have is you. I embrace you both, and thank you eternally all over again."[5]

To reconcile his need for his parents' approval with his indomitable will to go his own way was his most urgent task.

2

When Charles-Edouard Jeanneret arrived in Paris, he had all the expectations of a provincial. The disappointment stung.

His train reached the French capital after nightfall. Throughout the long journey, he had been picturing his life in the city of light. When he walked out of the Gare de l'Est on that March evening in 1908, little was as he had imagined. Rain was bucketing down. As he wandered into the aftermath of the celebration of Lent Tuesday, the masks and confetti in the mud struck him as sinister.

He had in his pocket the address of a hotel where one of his classmates from art school was staying. It was on the rue Charlot, a narrow street populated mainly by wholesalers and small businesses, not far from the sprawling place de la République. Finding his way on foot, Jeanneret encountered none of the monuments, bridges, or parks that composed his image of Paris. Even at night, the rue Charlot was commercial and noisy. The hotel itself was a disgusting hovel. As it would be told in the biography he masterminded a quarter of a century later, "His first contact with Paris—the Paris of fiacres, buses, double-decker trams—far from affording him the anticipated amazement, filled him with sadness and caused him something very like anguish."[6]

In Paris, ca. 1908

Two letters awaited him at the front desk. One, from L'Eplattenier, chastised him for this rash move. His former master and guide warned him that Paris had become a hotbed of artistic decadence. The other, from his father, alerted Edouard that he would receive no support in this "modern Babylon."[7]

At least that is how Le Corbusier spun the tale via Gauthier—in whose book he arrived in Paris a month earlier than was the case. The reprimands had actually reached him when he was still in Vienna. But it makes a better story this way. The image of the solitary survivor, braving opposition with only a few sous in his pocket, was embellished by making those hostile letters part of his greeting to his new life. Similarly, Le Corbusier removed Perrin from the picture, although his old friend was with him; it's a more dramatic tale if Charles-Edouard Jeanneret was entirely alone.

3

What Le Corbusier later presented as a struggle against all odds, with a prolonged stay in the hovel, actually took an upward turn the day following his arrival. In his contemporaneous letters to L'Eplattenier, his spirits lifted as soon as he saw Notre-Dame and the Eiffel Tower. Almost immediately, he took a pleasant room in a small hotel on the rue des Ecoles, in a charming neighborhood on the Left Bank.

The architecture of this area, on one of Paris's highest hills, was on the same scale as in La Chaux-de-Fonds. But while the Swiss city was a rigid grid of rows of unvaried five-story structures, this corner of Paris consisted of ancient townhouses abutting more recent Art Nouveau facades on angled byways that together resembled a spider's web. A vitality and playfulness replaced the dour elevations of Jeanneret's hometown. Now he was surrounded by both grandeur and intimacy—from the massive Ecole Polytechnique, completed in the aftermath of the French revolution, and the imposing Pantheon, to picturesque squares and narrow streets with a proliferation of food shops and fine bakeries. From the solitary window of his attic room, he could "contemplate at the same time the gilding of the Sainte-Chapelle and the whiteness of Sacré-Coeur."[8] All of Paris, from Vincennes to the Arc de Triomphe, opened before his eye.

On one of his long daily walks, Jeanneret accidentally found himself at the Salon des Indépendants. A large canvas by Henri Matisse made him stagger backward in consternation over "enormous women with skin that looked boiled."[9] The young Swiss who in those days was painting small-scale, tame watercolors could not fathom Matisse's distortions of form and color.

When he audited a course at the Ecole des Beaux-Arts, however, he loathed the academic style it promulgated. What mesmerized young Jeanneret, rather, were the qualities of freedom and inventiveness he discovered in the glasswork of Lalique, the sculpture of Rodin, and the buildings of Art Nouveau architect Hector Guimard, for whom his companion Perrin went to work. Unlike Vienna, Paris had artistic practitioners with taste and imagination.

4

Jeanneret soon began to bang on the office doors of Paris's best-known architects. Frantz Jourdain, architect of the Samaritaine department store and founder and president of the Salon d'Automne, liked the drawings the audacious young Swiss had made in Italy. Jourdain paved the way for him to meet others in the Salon hierarchy, who asked him to work on a polychrome decorative frieze for a cornice. Jeanneret deemed the task beneath him and went instead to see Eugène Grasset, whose book on ornament had obsessed him in art school. Armed with his new Parisian *cartes de visite*, he talked his way into Grasset's office and got the master to look at the same drawings that had won over Jourdain. Grasset's response was to rail against the current Parisian architecture scene: "complete decadence, inveterate academicism, the low bourgeois utilitarianism of the rental-warren." Jeanneret asked the oracle if there was any hope whatsoever, which prompted Grasset to make a pronouncement that changed his young listener's life: "Everything can be saved by a method of construction which is beginning to be widespread: you make board boxes, you put iron rods inside and fill them up with concrete. . . . The result: pure forms of coffering. It's called reinforced concrete. So go and see the Perret brothers."[10]

Charles-Edouard Jeanneret followed the advice without a moment's hesitation.

AUGUSTE PERRET was forty-four years old, Gustave forty-one. The sons of a Belgian building contractor, they had developed a speciality in reinforced concrete and were engaged in unprecedented feats of construction. Four years prior to the arrival of Jeanneret at their door, they had completed a bold reinforced-concrete apartment building in the sixteenth arrondissement on the rue Franklin, near the Trocadéro, which served to demonstrate the technology and their quality of workmanship.

Coming up from the Seine, looking across the rue Franklin, Jeanneret faced a lithe yet massive seven-story structure visibly standing on tall, narrow concrete legs. The lively facade presented the structural skeleton unclad, as one would normally find it only in buildings still under construction. The candor was unprecedented.

Instead of flowing smoothly along the line of the street like its neighbors on either side, the front of 25 bis was a sequence of deeply cut recesses, bold iron railings, and large-paned windows. Because the narrow site did not permit an interior courtyard, an equivalent courtyard—sliced by the line of the sidewalk—was moved to the front. In this three-quarters court, the upbeat apartment house embraces the daylight.

On its slope facing the Eiffel Tower, the building was—as it still is—more energetic and animated, as well as taller and whiter, than its nineteenth-century neighbors. A panoply of decorative coverings made it the machine-cut descendant of Jeanneret's beloved cathedral facade in Siena.

Charles-Edouard Jeanneret absorbed all of this as he walked into the Perret brothers' offices on the ground floor. He was stunned even further by the absence of internal structural columns—possible because the entire building was supported on external concrete posts. The effect was liberating.

Again, the young man presented his Italian drawings as his entry ticket to the office of an important architect. Auguste Perret took one look at the sheets of Italian scenes and announced, "You will be my right hand."[11]

The four months of searching had paid off. In his new workplace, the cocky young Swiss was at home as never before. The Perrets' courage to buck the artistic tide, their intelligence and honesty, and their technical sophistication were unlike anything he had encountered in so-called modern Vienna.

Auguste and Gustave Perret believed that the design and appearance of a building should honor its function and program. It was also vital to build with accessible materials and to utilize current technology. Jeanneret thrilled to their startling insistence that building design cease inserting antiquated forms and obscure substances into our lives. They offered the voice of truth.

5

For fourteen months, Jeanneret worked five hours every afternoon for the Perret brothers, doing drafting and preparing blueprints. He earned six francs per day, which enabled him to move into nicer digs, another single room tucked under a mansard roof, but now at 3 quai Saint-Michel, overlooking the Seine. When he wasn't working, he went to museums and sketched. He focused mainly on vernacular art: Greek and Etruscan pottery, Egyptian and Persian painting, medieval tapestries and statuary, and Chinese and Hindu bronzes. In the dusty and obscure rooms of the Musée d'Ethnographie at the Trocadéro—a place to which he often repaired with great pleasure, relishing the solitude—he succumbed to the enchantment of Peruvian pottery, Aztec sculpture, and African textiles and wood carvings.

Jeanneret took it upon himself to go to the Ministry of Beaux-Arts, the administrative office for Paris's monuments. There he managed to obtain a bunch of keys that opened locked gates and doors within the great Gothic cathedral of Notre-Dame. He had often studied its exterior from his apartment window; now he explored the tops of the steeples and climbed the pinnacles and buttresses. The structure and construction thrilled him, but the decorated surfaces were an irritant. "The plans and the Gothic cross-section are magnificent, full of ingenuity, but their verification cannot be achieved by what meets the eye. An engineer's triumph, a plastic defeat."[12]

He continued to write regularly to his mentor L'Eplattenier, but the more colorful, worldly Auguste Perret was becoming his new role model.

"Auguste Perret has a nabob's tastes," he wrote. "He would like to sit enthroned while grinning in secret; he loves things *preciously* made, a Japanese *netsuke,* a piece of woven Moroccan leather, a shapely sword, delicate cookery . . . he's sublime with clients. He holds his head high . . . chooses his neckties very carefully. . . . His worktable is always impeccably arranged. . . . He'd have liked to be the shah of Persia, but he'd have decapitated his enemies with a wooden sword and offered his victims cigarettes after a session of torture. He liked to consider himself a revolutionary figure, and in fact he carried out his revolution meticulously, with deep love, respectful and assiduous in his vocation, which is *to build.* And to build meticulously with reinforced concrete, in this period of utter decadence."[13]

Meanwhile, *Don Quixote* and writings by Nietzsche, both of which he read continually, corresponded to his own experience of the world. In July, he wrote L'Eplattenier, "Life, at this particular period of my existence, is a grueling combat. If every day I see new difficulties cropping up, if I find they are more numerous than those which my colleagues working toward the same goal must overcome, it is because I feel I'm an 'outlaw.' "[14]

As if he were his own advisor and pupil at the same time, the young man laid out his goals to his old teacher: "I'm attempting to establish a rational program for myself, one which will gradually allow me to learn the tricks of the trade. Every day I do my work, and I frequently catch myself getting excited over a difficult, mysterious problem, enthusiastic when I've found the solution. For the rest, aside from the abstraction of pure mathematics, I read Viollet-le-Duc, a man so wise, so logical, so clear, and so exact in his observations. I have Viollet-le-Duc and I have Notre-Dame, which serves as my laboratory, so to speak."[15]

After conjuring for his parents the nineteenth-century French architect who had led the Gothic revival and restored Notre-Dame, Jeanneret put himself down: "I feel deeply disgusted with myself. No, honestly, I am horrified every day by discovering my inability to hold a pencil; I don't feel the form, I can't make a form revolve: it drives me to despair." The self-denigration sparked an intense drive to do better. "I try to control myself these days, to wrench myself out of this disgust: I seek geometrically the principle of the model, the decomposition of light and shadow on a sphere, an oval, a vase or some other object."[16] That rapport with light effects was to be Charles-Edouard Jeanneret's salvation and a fundament of Le Corbusier's genius.

6

At the start of July 1908, Jeanneret wrote L'Eplattenier, "What constitutes the great disaster, or perhaps the great success—disaster because synonymous with struggle, success because it is a thirst for ideals, for aspiration—is that the critical faculty grows sharper, becomes imperious, decisive, commanding. It turns you into a painter, an incompetent, a fraud; it says to me: 'You're nothing but an imbecile, and I never would have thought such a thing of you. I had illusions about you, fantasies, I saw you heading for triumph, swimming through clouds of glory.' . . . How severe the critic becomes, a fellow who doesn't mince words. . . . But God has made us in His image and He remains the great face, the great passion to make the Good and the Beautiful, and at times that power prevails over all else, which is why at this very moment I am not a clerk in an office or a grocery clerk!"[17]

Aspiring toward the "beautiful" and trying to cope with his meandering mind, he tried to pare down his life to the rigor and bare simplicity of a tent in a battlefield. Jeanneret embraced a leaner, purer, tougher existence. "I am sometimes invited into bourgeois homes, which awakens tremendous exasperations," he wrote L'Eplattenier.[18] Middle-class life was a trap, dominated by heathens who mocked Rodin and did not understand Wagner. Superfluous comforts and material well-being were deadening. Even Jeanneret's fellow students drove him to despair with their false values and lack of idealism. "Oh, how eagerly I wish that my friends, our comrades, would discard that mediocre life with its everyday satisfactions and abandon what they hold most dear, supposing as they do that such things are good—if only they realized how petty their aims are, and how little they're *thinking,*" he wrote.[19]

Alone on the quai Saint-Michel, Jeanneret relished his "fruitful hours of solitude, hours during which one undermines, when the lash bites into the flesh. —Oh, if only I had a little more time to think, to learn! Real life, paltry as it is, gobbles the hours."[20] He was to refer to the flagellating whip for the rest of his life.

In his hermetic existence, the sole encounters he valued were with Grasset and other elderly men who had devoted their lives to art: "Such men's hair has turned white; yet it is they who are keepers of the true devouring flame. Such men have the already idealized, already paradisiac faith of those initiates who have seen and know the truth. One leaves their presence scourged but with a high heart."[21]

Jeanneret counted on L'Eplattenier to understand all this. He wrote his master, "It is by thought that today or tomorrow the new art will be made. Thought withdraws and requires combat. And to encounter thought in order to give battle, one must proceed into solitude. Paris affords solitude to those who ardently seek silence, the aridity of retreat." If he acted properly, this magical metropolis was a place to be productive: "Time in Paris is fruitful for those who seek, from the passing hours, a harvest of strength. Paris the great city—of thoughts—*in which one is lost* unless one is severe and pitiless to oneself."[22] It was a religious quest, worth the requisite sacrifices because it replaced his anguish of Vienna with values and purpose.

"Vienna having given the death blow to my purely plastic conceptions of architecture (no more than the search for forms), and having arrived in Paris, I felt an enormous void and said to myself: wretch! you still know nothing at all, and alas you don't even know you know nothing." His self-prescribed program in the French capital had succeeded: "I suspected from the study of the Romanesque that architecture was not a matter of the eurythmia of forms." His instruction in "mechanics" and "statics" had added to his growth: "It's arduous, this mathematics, but beautiful—so logical, so perfect!"[23]

Now that he had recovered from Switzerland and Austria, his ascendancy was under way.

7

Paris had effected his metamorphosis. "These eight months in Paris shout: logic, truth, honesty, behind the dream of the arts of the past. Eyes open, forward! Word for word, with all the value words can have, Paris tells me: Burn what you have loved and worship what you were burning," he wrote to L'Eplattenier. This outburst was also a diatribe: "You, Grasset, Sauvage–Jourdain, Paquet, and the rest, you are liars—Grasset, that model of truth, a liar, because you don't know what architecture is—but the rest of you, architects all, liars all, yes, and cowards as well." He was enraged that none of his former mentors had led him toward the realization that "the architect must be a man with a logical brain . . . a man of knowledge as well as of heart, artist *and* scientist."[24]

Jeanneret charted his course accordingly. A new art would be born in Paris, and he would be part of the breakthrough. His excitement took him over the edge of logical thinking: "As a tree on a crag which has taken twenty years to anchor its roots and which generously concludes: 'I have struggled—my offspring will gain by it!' and lets its seeds fall on the few patches of soil mottling the crag, soil which the tree itself has formed with its dead leaves—with its pain; the crag warms in the sun, the seeds flourish, and the rootlets grow—with what vigor! what joy! to stretch the tiny leaves to the sky. . . . But the sun heats the crag; the plant in anguish feels the stupor of excessive heat; it tries to send its rootlets into the shade of its great protector. Yet the tree has taken twenty years to anchor its roots, and with what a struggle—its limbs filling the crannies of the rock. In anguish, the seedling reproaches the tree that has created it. The seedling curses the tree and dies. It dies of not having *lived*—by itself. . . . That is what I see in this country. Hence my anguish. I say: create for twenty years and dare to continue creating still: aberration, error, prodigious blindness—unheard-of pride. Trying to sing when you do not yet have lungs! In what ignorance *of your very being* must you be plunged? . . . The parable of the tree inspires me with fear . . . fear for the tree that prepares itself for suffering. For you are a being so full of love that your heart will be plunged into mourning to see the incandescent life—the life that must be gained in order to struggle against it—coming like a cyclone to burn the little plants which so proudly, so joyously aimed their leaves at the sky."[25]

He announced to L'Eplattenier, "My struggle against you, my beloved master, will be against this error." His "struggle against friends" was "the struggle against their ignorance. . . . They do not know what Art is." He, on the other hand, recognized his pathetic state: "I *know* I know nothing." As he beat the evil out of himself, Jeanneret swooned over the new truth he at last glimpsed: "Vienna gave me too strong a shock. At present I am a man without resources, incapable of creating or of executing anything. I no longer see in works of art, or in nature when I go for a walk, anything but *life,* the mad sinuous curves and spirals, the shoots opening into magical palmettos. I say 'seeing them'; it would be more correct to say that I *foresee* them. But the shock of Vienna was so powerful, the disgust so deep, that I am no longer attached to execution; only fragments of art delight me. And so I do not know one iota of my trade."[26]

8

Jeanneret read Ernest Renan's *Life of Jesus*.[27] He marked the most hypnotic passages and wrote their page numbers on the title page.[28] Language he was to use for the rest of his life came from Renan's phraseology.

Jeanneret drew excited lines next to "Jesus is not a spiritualist; for him everything has a palpable realization. But he is a fulfilled idealist, for him matter is only the sign of the idea." In the margins, the young architect scribbled: "And I herewith create everything anew! This is the feature all reformers share." He marked with a double line the statement that Jesus "had renounced politics; the example of Judas the Gaulonite had shown him the futility of popular sedition." Renan's Jesus was his model, or at least his excuse, when he later worked with any regime that would allow him to build. By declaring politics insignificant, he revealed to the world this truth: "that the nation is not everything."[29]

The other text he double marked was the single sentence "For him, freedom is truth." And he pressed his pencil so hard that he dented the margin next to Renan's conclusion: "Inevitably a moral and virtuous humanity will have its revenge, and one day the sentiment of the honest man, the poor man, will judge the world, and on that day the ideal figure of Jesus will be the confusion of the frivolous who have not believed in virtue, the selfish who have been unable to achieve it. . . . A sort of magnificent divination seems to have guided the incomparable master here, and to have sustained him in a generalized sublimity embracing many kinds of truths at once."[30] The man who would make himself another "LC" was to rail forever at those frivolous and selfish creatures who could not recognize a savior in their midst.

9

On May 12, 1908, Georges-Edouard and Marie Charlotte Amélie Jeanneret celebrated their twenty-fifth wedding anniversary. Georges wrote in his diary, "Thanks be to God this quarter of a century of life together has brought us more intimate days than pains, aside from everyday cares; we have acquired a modest comfort, at least our daily bread is secured for the morrow; our two sons have caused us no moral torments, their behavior has been excellent, their moral nature is intact: their careers are not yet certain, yet they pursue them with great and cheerful energy. My wife has been a discreet helpmate who never flinched from duty. Our health, aside from a few minor cares, has remained good. The four of us live in harmony, closely linked by affection."[31]

Georges could overlook his rage at Edouard's trip to Italy and subsequent move to Paris now that the younger son had a job. That was more than could be said for Albert, who, after earning his "diploma of virtuosity" from the music conservatory in Geneva, went off into the mountains alone. Albert declared himself utterly confused, unable to do much of anything. Although he then returned to Geneva to teach and performed publicly in La Chaux-de-Fonds, in March 1909 Albert said that he had to stop playing the violin for at least a year, as he was suffering from pains in his arms. Making matters worse, a lull in Georges's work meant that Marie's piano teaching was their main source of support.

At the end of 1908, when Edouard had finally returned home after an absence of a year and a half, he had begun to assume the role of the easier child. Georges reported in his diary in January, "Though he still dresses rather deplorably, we found him to be a good talker, of solid morals and firm opinions (despite the complete modification of his beliefs and his faith); tall, with a new reddish-blond beard; still confident in the future, energetic, and in good health!"[32]

IN MID-MAY OF 1909, Georges and Marie Jeanneret visited Edouard in Paris—the first time they had ventured so far from La Chaux-de-Fonds. Georges felt that the eight francs a night they paid for their twin-bedded room at the Hotel du Quai Voltaire, convenient to Edouard's apartment and the Louvre, was warranted. This was high living for the Jeannerets, but although the total they dispensed for the trip depleted the accumulated interest in their savings account, it did not touch the capital. The watchcase decorator and piano teacher took great pleasure in the sights Edouard had chosen for them to see, including a performance by Sarah Bernhardt. Georges made another happy diary entry: "Our son knows his town like a native and was of great assistance to us, and of great interest through his knowledge of art, his sure judgment, his amiability, his good manners, despite his unfortunate clothes."[33]

In September, however, in one of his most bizarre mis-

Dressed as a "rapin" in his garret at 9 rue des Ecoles, Paris (1908–1909). The rapin coat was the unofficial uniform for students in Beaux-Arts courses.

sives to date, Edouard suggested to his parents that good clothing was not his only lack. "To make love, *le bel amour,* takes cash, fine clothes, and the gift of yourself, and for lack of cash, fine clothes, and the capacity to give myself, such a thing is quite impossible for me, since as I've told you I belong for the time being to Mistress Escapade, and of course all substitutes find me retrograde, inferior, and, on the other hand, sometimes quite severe! . . . One lives a life *contra naturam,* that's obvious, and in spite of all that might be said, one needs *woman,* that subtle element consisting of everything we lack, but without which we are incomplete."[34]

THE JEANNERET SONS both seemed determined to jolt their parents.

Albert, who spent a few weeks in Edouard's room with him, reported deliriously about their drinking multiple liters of white wine one evening and cavorting in the countryside on a Sunday when the temperature reached forty degrees: "We terrified a young virgin (approximately 40–50 years old) who had ventured to accompany us, but who quickly changed direction at the sight of our extremely light garments. Unfortunately (and this will be imputed to us by daylight) we introduced certain germs into the hearts of other passers-by." The Jeanneret boys ended up spending the night outside, sleeping on their backs with their feet practically in the Seine; "we tasted the delights of letting ourselves live." Edouard told his mother and father, "We must find a way to walk the streets stark naked," but added, "I find I have a character likely to overload itself with work and insufficiently disposed to enjoy life." When he wrote that he was "stupidly delighted" in the garden of the Palais Royal with Albert, it was "not for the sake of a good time, but because it was a mistake to work with an exhausted mind."[35]

With Albert behind him at 3 quai Saint-Michel, 1908

THEN, ON NOVEMBER 9, 1909, Edouard terminated his connection with the Perrets. Postponing his return until his money ran out, he wrote his parents, "In my hours of freedom, I feel the rebirth of an artistic fiber, and I rejoice in this vacation during which I can surrender a little to poetry."[36] At the end of the first week of December, Jeanneret returned to La Chaux-de-Fonds. His plan was to spend three months in a rented farmhouse. Although he had initially rejected L'Eplattenier's counsel that he work in Germany, now he wrote his master that he had decided to go to Munich and then Berlin. Yet again, everything had changed except for his burning goal: to understand architecture.

Self-portrait drawing as the "Grand Condor," on a postcard to his parents, Christmas 1909

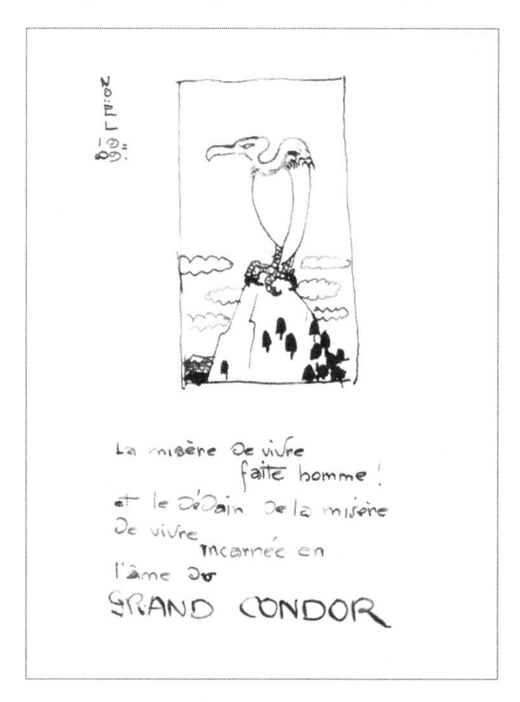

VI

1

In the books Le Corbusier wrote or authorized about himself, his three-month return to La Chaux-de-Fonds exists solely as the occasion when he diligently took the opportunity to study reinforced concrete. But his self-imposed isolation at age twenty-two in a barn during an especially severe winter was significant in many ways.

This primitive structure Jeanneret rented on Mont Cornu, three kilometers outside of La Chaux-de-Fonds, was dominated by a wooden-shingled roof shaped like an inverted, flattened V. The second-story hayloft and the covering of thick snow on that sloping roof were the main sources of insulation against the biting cold. The warmest place was the kitchen, a windowless room contained by masonry walls in the middle of the barn and heated by a fireplace serviced by the wide central chimney. More than forty years later, Le Corbusier's exuberant church at Ronchamp was to restate the form of that primitive barn.

With his parents in La Chaux-de-Fonds, 1909. Charles-Edouard's bohemian appearance, a vestige of his new life in Paris, shocked his parents.

IN APRIL, Jeanneret took off for Germany. His ostensible goal was to learn still more about the technology of reinforced concrete. But once he was in Munich and the sole architect he admired, Theodor Fischer, did not hire him, he focused on Wagner's operas, the paintings of Rubens and Rembrandt in the Alte Pinakothek, and the hearty cooking at inexpensive *bierstuben.* When he went to the Neue Pinakothek to see the latest paintings, he spent precisely seven-and-a-half minutes—he recorded the time—and then declared the visit to have been a complete waste. He preferred the force and purposefulness of Baroque architecture to the stylization and autobiographical content he disdained in more recent artistic trends.

Jeanneret also crystallized his views on Germans in general. He admired the German people for their organizational instinct and deductive reasoning, but thought that they lacked imagination and creative genius. While the Germans credited themselves with having launched a new aesthetic movement, Jeanneret was convinced that their sole achievement was the discovery of Latin genius; for him, they were subordinate to the French, who reigned supreme in the realm of art.

Shortly after arriving in Munich, Jeanneret met, on L'Eplattenier's recommendation, the man who was to affect him above all others. William Ritter, a music critic from Neuchâtel, was immersed in the work of Anton Bruckner, Leoš Janáček, Gustav Mahler, Richard Strauss, and Bruno Walter, all of whom he knew. Ritter was forty-two and undisguisedly homosexual in an era when to be so open was unusual. Since 1903, he had been sharing his life with Janko Czadra and would do so until Czadra's death in 1927. Ritter's intensity and artistic passion, and his personal courage, made him a hero to his fellow escapee from French-speaking Switzerland. For years to come, Charles-Edouard Jeanneret bared his soul to this father figure who provided him with unequaled emotional companionship.

For now, however, the traveler's letters were to his mother and father. "The first thing to regret is the exaggerated flight of time," he wrote them shortly after arriving in the Bavarian capital. "The same old song. Too much to deal with, turning every which way in order to have time to realize that it's already ten at night."[1] Georges and Marie Jeanneret, on the other hand, felt that Edouard was wasting the time he deemed so precious when, after more than a month, he still did not have a job.

Portrait of William Ritter by Charles-Edouard Jeanneret

Edouard replied to their admonitions with the rudeness and self-righteousness he never lost. "My dear parents, You're absolutely right to ask for *clearer* details, but you're not going to get them! Which is called the rebellion against proper authorities. . . . Yet I want you to know that my mystery is utterly chaste and my silence merely one virtue added to many others. This silence of mine is the sign of a modest, prudent spirit which regards things according to their causes and their consequences, having sounded the mysteries of human psychology."[2]

Even as he feigned control, Jeanneret continued with senseless allegories and a strained humor that bordered on hallucinatory. "Yet I hear the voice of the race, while liable like Icarus to break my neck tripping over a wire; I should like to raise you to the level of my conceptions, but let us postpone such elevation to my next, in order to avoid a flood of amphigoric terms. Speaking positively: did you know that everything depends on elegance here and that I am actually studying the cut of the frock coat I must wear! The bohemian-student type is discountenanced here. One must dress up. And all modern artistic Munich hoists the flag of elegance. And since I am trying at all costs to penetrate this milieu, I too must be gorgeous. At what cost? I who am a monster by nature! O Divinities of India, so plump, so opulent, yield something of your style to the poor admiring wretch who loves your bellies and your smiles. . . . And to hell with that pianist downstairs in absolute Nirvana! Divinities of India, plenitude inscribed in stone, hear my prayer, and even if you need to summon Bacchus himself, do your work!"[3]

With style and wine, he might have women.

2

Two months after Jeanneret arrived in Munich, L'Eplattenier wrote with news that turned his life around. L'Ecole d'Art of La Chaux-de-Fonds had awarded him a grant to write a report on the applied arts and architecture in Germany, so that his findings could be applied in Switzerland. It was the first time that the future Le Corbusier was asked to offer expertise on the aesthetic and technical aspects of design and its connection to human experience. He traveled to Frankfurt, Düsseldorf, Dresden, Weimar, and Hamburg, visiting the latest factories, office buildings, and design studios. A modest pamphlet—*Study of a Decorative Arts Movement in Germany*—resulted.[4]

He then wrote an essay called "The Building of Cities."[5] In it, he extolled the merits of curved streets of varying width and incline. One should, Jeanneret proposed, imagine the donkey as one's guide, ambling through urban space with unexpected twists and turns. Jeanneret fastened on to the diversity of old towns that invited circuitous wandering and provided the thrill of variety. The places he enjoyed and the urbanism he now advocated complemented the leaps and wanderings of his soul.

Jeanneret pointed out that, by contrast, in a plan based on a grid—a large square subdivided into smaller squares—the only way to walk from diagonally opposite corners is by following a ridiculous zigzag path. He mocked such orderly layouts and the unimaginative bureaucrats who imposed them on people. La Chaux-de-Fonds, of course, was built on such a stifling concept, with no relationship to the life and vitality of the larger universe and no sense of progression or hope. Fortunately, Milan and Pisa had introduced Jeanneret to the marvelous variability that occurs where every small street stemming from a piazza leads to a different adventure.

As he wrote "The Building of Cities," the zealot came alive. Eventually, he refined its ideas in his 1924 book *Urbanism* (also translated as *The City of To-morrow*).[6] For the rest of his life, he espoused these ideals, by which he hoped to give millions of people lives full of diversion as well as calm.

3

In mid-October, Jeanneret traveled to Berlin to attempt to work for the architect Peter Behrens. Nineteen years his senior, Behrens was well established as a designer for German industry. He had developed a streamlined functionalism that was a radical break from all past architectural traditions. Behrens had just finished his renowned AEG Turbine factory, a powerful exaltation of machined forms. His name topped the list of architects Jeanneret admired.

Behrens denied him an interview. The twenty-three-year-old fell into a downtrodden state that echoed his humor in Vienna three years earlier: "Berlin has not conquered me; once you leave the grand boulevards, everything is horror and filth. . . . Exploring the museums disgusts me in advance. My moods have taken a pathological turn. Yesterday I visited the Kaiser Friedrich Museum, and I can assure you the experience was anything but gay."[7]

To his new friend William Ritter, who believed that cities had their own personalities and exercised a powerful effect on their inhabitants, Jeanneret reported that the German capital induced "a feeling of the blackest desolation. Even London could not show me a great city under so monstrous an aspect."[8] But the possibility of working with Peter Behrens justified staying, and Jeanneret was so persistent that he wormed his way into his hero's office and landed a job. Ten days into it, Jeanneret described his forty-two-year-old boss to his parents: "A colossus of daunting stature. A terrible autocrat, a regime of terrorism. Brutality on parade. All in all, a type. Whom I admire, moreover. My masochism thrills at taking the bit between my teeth when the horseman has such style."[9]

Jeanneret was eager that his parents know him as he knew himself: "I must confess that my anxious soul is increasingly tormented. The goal is terrible. Why have I placed it so high? What devil has placed it so far from my myopic eyes? Everything conspires to destroy serenity: lowest details and the highest ideals. . . . Doubt is a horror. The further I advance, the higher IT rises. Doubts, Stumbles, Hesitations, painful Shocks."[10]

As a draftsman for Behrens, he was broke, depending on his commissions from the work at home to pay the twenty-eight marks per month—heat and dinner included—for the room he had rented. "The boss doesn't pay; it's all a huge exploitation. The salaries are ridiculous."[11] But at least he was directly exposed to the making of architecture that was unprecedented in its blend of brave simplicity and visual charm. He wrote L'Eplattenier, "Behrens, a severe master, demands rhythm and subtle relations and many other things previously unknown to me."[12]

Jeanneret worked from 8:20 a.m. to 1:00 p.m. and from 2:00 p.m. to 6:00 p.m.—with Saturday afternoons and Sundays free. Soon he began to receive two hundred marks per month—a pittance, but sufficient to change his housing. He was delighted to move from an overstuffed room whose comforts were anathema to his taste to an austere but blissfully isolated garret. He wrote his parents: "I am . . . abandoning my huge bedroom for an attic, my armchairs for kitchen stools, pier glasses for a tiny shaving mirror, and racket for peace. There we are. Besides, the slate roofs of Paris are inscribed in my memories, and an attic is much more poetic than too many armchairs, glistening armoires, objects of the most deadening banality which yours truly cannot endure more than a fortnight."[13] One's surroundings and one's inner state were inseparable.

4

On December 2, 1910, Jeanneret wrote his parents a poignant letter that obliquely indicated a sexual dysfunction and his general sense of impotence. He began by quoting one of his happy-go-lucky friends from La Chaux-de-Fonds: "Octave Matthey wrote me this week: 'Since you've fulfilled all the requirements for fucking off in less than no time, why don't you just fuck

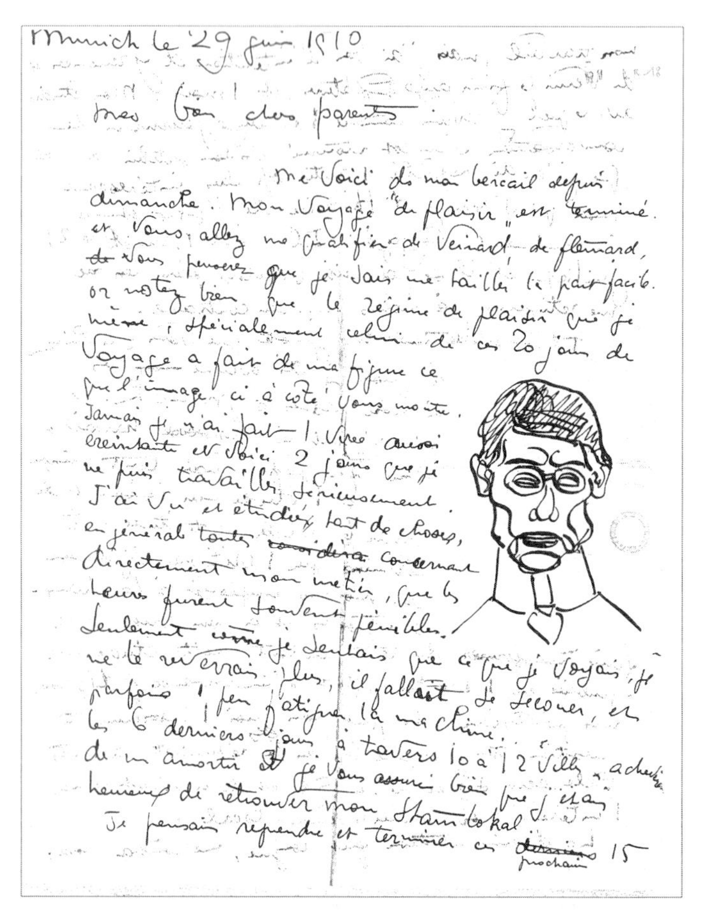

Munich le 29 juin 1910

Mes bien chers parents

Me voici dans mon bercail depuis dimanche. Mon voyage "de plaisir" est terminé et vous allez me qualifier de veinard, de flemmard, vous pensez que je suis ne faillir la part facile. Or notez bien que le régime de plaisir que je mène, spécialement celui de ces 20 jours de voyage a fait de ma figure ce que l'image ci à côté vous montre. Jamais je n'ai fait 1 vie aussi éreintante et voici 2 jours que je ne puis travailler sérieusement. J'ai vu et étudié tant de choses, en général toutes ~~considéra~~ concernant directement mon métier, que les heures furent souvent pénibles. Seulement comme je sentais que ce que je voyais je ne le reverrais plus, il fallait de secouer, parfois, 1 peu fatiguée la machine, et les 6 derniers jours à travers 10 à 12 villes, ... je vous assure bien que j'étais heureux de retrouver mon Stammlokal. Je pensais reprendre et terminer ces ~~derniers~~ prochains 15

Self-portrait in a letter to his parents, June 29, 1910

off. You know you'll never do anything else as long as you live—it would take such an effort you'd never manage it, even if you died trying. Try it and see!' Octave's irony; he knows my sickness and laughs at it. As for me, what sickens me most is not being able to get well. Each day begins by opening a big hole in front of me and dropping me into it because I thought I wasn't being an idiot, which I am, and in a way that's disgustingly and unacceptably unfair. Of course it's my own fault, but my sickness is right there, mocking me, frustrating me. You no longer understand such a creature, my dear parents, nor do I. I've given up—first victory, or already a first defeat: trying to analyse why. It's all summed up in a single word of two syllables: Boredom."[14]

Disillusioned over his new job, he also poured out his thoughts to the receptive, warmhearted Ritter, in the first of many twelve-page letters in which Jeanneret's fountain-pen scrawl reached all four corners of the sheet in a stream of associations: "The work I'm required to perform leaves me indifferent. I now judge quite severely a man who has allowed himself to be surrounded by the fatal cortege of fame; though a powerful personality, Behrens has become a victim of his successes. Eager to make money, he undertakes too many projects, losing all effective control over what we, his twenty *nègres,* often produce reluctantly, merely obedient to an authoritarian and unjust rod. I'm so fond of Behrens as a person and as a man that in order to preserve my admiration, I've decided he must be sick."[15]

Having initially felt warm toward his office mates, Jeanneret had become contemptuous: "My colleagues are, in every sense of the word, what last Sunday, when I was at home, you feared I might become: superficial architects with no artistic fiber, no passions but the extremely vulgar ones of drink, dancehalls, and an occasionally disorderly life." Struck by his employer's instability—"Behrens is a sick man and consequently intractable, unapproachable, immersed in his rebarbative ill humor"—Jeanneret was creating his concept of the ideal architect: "An architect, as I envisage him, must be above all a thinker. His art, consisting of abstract relationships which he cannot describe or depict except symbolically—his art does not require a cunning hand. Indeed, such a hand could be fatal. But this manipulator of rhythms must possess a fully developed brain of extreme flexibility."[16]

Shortly thereafter, he wrote his parents about hearing a Tchaikovsky overture remarkable for "the slow, panting, anguished release of the orgiastic orgasm of liberation painted in all the colors of experience and seen as such by the homosexual martyr Tchaikovsky."[17] In his own responses, Jeanneret himself possessed the mental suppleness he craved in others.

5

Soon his state of mind devolved into a "crisis of profound boredom" even more extreme than his depression in Vienna. In his despair, he asked Ritter, "What accounts for this terrible disenchantment? I'm searching my soul to find out."[18] But the ultimate sources of his misery eluded him; something far worse was going on during that Berlin winter than his lack of friends or Behrens's gruffness. He had lost all hope of pleasure or serenity in life.

To his new confidant, he obsessed about his anhedonic state: "Aesthetic joy is over and done with. Since I've been here, I haven't heard one note of music. So tight is our regimen that it is impossible to attend a concert with any pleasure. It would be exhausting."[19] His absorption with his own misery made him overlook the performance where he had heard the Tchaikovsky overture. "I'm ashamed that once my lucky star guided me to you, all I've had to show you was an exhausted, mentally debilitated being," he wrote. "Never, believe me, have I lived through such a lamentable period. It's a mistake to blame external phenomena. They're not all that unfavorable. Here's another aphorism that I picked up somewhere: 'All young men, after great enthusiasm, go through a period of depression.' Perhaps the aphorism itself has done the mischief? You with your profound experience of artists' lives could enlighten me; berate me mercilessly, or else tell me the cure."[20]

He loathed his own appearance, linking it with his unfulfilled craving for women. "Good God! Yet I could, if I really wanted to, eventually consider some young lady 'inexpressibly lovely'! Hear me out: in my entire life as a student, I cohabited with cats, always above the gutter and never below it. The window was usually no more than a peephole. And when, in the shadows, the mirror afforded a reflection, it would be tiny, wavering, affording my imagination 'infinite spaces.' O Prussian inhospitality! My bedroom—I moved out two weeks ago—was a huge monstrosity, two windows took up one wall, and there was even, in the corner, an enormous pier glass, maybe six feet tall and two feet wide. The light came in from the opposite side, and I saw everything in that mirror; I couldn't believe it, but I went on looking: I saw rickety legs and huge red dangling paws, swollen with disenchantment; a nose straight on which seemed to define the creature underneath, a wrinkled forehead, a crestfallen coiffure and a lot of skin and bones. An unhealthy complexion. The Sunday clothes—the same moreover as those of everyday—were ill fitting. I saw everything; I told you there were two big windows on the opposite wall which showed everything. There was no getting away from it."[21]

While he believed that no beautiful woman could possibly find him appealing, he perpetually imagined meeting one. "You'll understand that I'd be *moved* to see the inexpressively lovely young lady!" he wrote, including Ritter's partner, Czadra, in closing, "Some happy day I hope to make tangible my respectful admiration and my gratitude to you both. Yours devotedly, dear gentlemen."[22]

6

At the beginning of 1911, Jeanneret's gloom turned to fury: "With Behrens there's no such thing as pure architecture. It's all facade. Constructive heresies abound. No such thing as modern architecture. Perhaps this is a better solution—better than the anything-but-classical lucubrations of the Perret brothers. They had the advantage of experimenting with new materials. Behrens, on the other hand, opposes all this, so with him I'm learning absolutely nothing but facade in everything. The milieu is hateful, my life here is hateful, my life here is idiotic. Exhausting work all day and no reaction possible by night. The better I get to know these people, the emptier they seem. No friend possible except Zimmermann, whose artistic soul is inadequate. No contact, ever, with Behrens."[23]

Again, music saved him: "The Jacques-Dalcroze orchestra, virtually the antithesis of that of Richard Strauss, offers me an atmosphere of joy and health spangled with whims and impossible choices, a heaven of gold like those smooth skies of Duccio or the serenely inimitable vistas of Perugino—but resting on a faraway horizon, solemn and sometimes tragic."[24]

Everything was reduced to the battle between Latin and Germanic cultures. Strauss, he believed, suffered from uncontrolled hysteria. Similarly, "in Germany, painting and sculpture, virtually the sole metaphysical exteriorizations of our period, are stupid and always backward," he wrote to L'Eplattenier.[25] To Ritter, he lamented, "German painting has stubby wings—how clumsy it looks compared to the French school."[26] The entire German nation, he subsequently harped to L'Eplattenier, was blinded by its unwarranted "artistic pride."[27] Other German-speaking places were just as bad: Austria had been a desert, Switzerland a bastion of poor design.

If only he could head back to Italy and even farther—to Greece, the cradle of ancient civilization! Jeanneret began to hatch a plan.

7

He was thinking about love as much as art. To his homosexual confidant, Jeanneret revealed his amorous musings: "I stole a kiss the other evening from a young lady; today a cat I was holding in my arms disturbed me with its glowing eyes; and this evening in the woods, under the pink sky of twilight, I stood for a long time watching a blackbird singing its heart out; incontestably he was doing his best, he wanted his song to be beautiful; and since he was alone at the edge of the woods, I wondered why he was pouring out his heart so passionately!"[28]

The gloom of winter was giving way to manic enthusiasm; Jeanneret was ready to blossom. "My spring will soon be coming into its own," he wrote. "Summer will be here all too soon. After four years of absence, they're calling for me at home. Now I feel ready to open myself to everything. The period of deliberate concentration is past! Open the floodgates! Let everything rush out, let everything live within!"[29]

He had decided to embark on a long trip with Auguste Klipstein, a friend he had met in Munich. With no timetable, no fixed destinations, and no names to call upon, they would go to unknown Balkan villages, the great cities of eastern Europe, Greece, and maybe Egypt. Again, his father disapproved, and L'Eplattenier told him he was not sufficiently mature to profit from the trip and that it was a waste. But Jeanneret, excited because Klipstein was "a boy who knows how to have a life even while he's working away with great deliberation," was soaring out of his gloom. "I'm making my escape after five months of penitence; gray hours, interminable weeks, leaden months," he informed Ritter. The trees were budding, a concert of birds emanating from their branches. "Spring is approaching and with it the sun, blossoming, expanding! I feel joy again, the monotonous gray is disappearing."[30]

He was imagining naked women "in broad daylight," the joys of a blue sky and the Aegean.[31] He could picture classical architecture with its vertical columns and entablatures parallel to the line of the sea. After the trip, he would settle down to a productive life, but first Jeanneret planned to educate himself in pleasure.

VII

1

What Jeanneret saw on that journey affected his life forever after. From the start of the trip, in Vienna, previously the scene of his worst misery, he was inspired by magical sights he would never forget. Its flower market was "a stunning procession that passes between the black colonnade of tree trunks bearing an immense barrel vault that recedes as far as the eye can see. . . . The eye becomes confused, a little perturbed by this kaleidoscopic cinema where dance the most dizzying combination of colors."[1]

Could anyone have written a more apt description of the Assembly Hall that Le Corbusier later built in Chandigarh? Its entry, a sequence of tall, tapered columns with a celestial light flooding in from above, resembles a grove of trees and a Romanesque nave. After that calm glade, the assembly itself is another "kaleidoscopic cinema." The vision Jeanneret developed in 1911 made such an imprint that he recapitulated it more than four decades later.

Then, traveling down the Danube on a large white paddleboat, Jeanneret reflected, "Were I a fisherman or merchant along its banks, I would religiously sculpt out of wood, somewhat in a Chinese manner, a god who would be this river and whom I would worship. I would set him on the bow of my boat, smiling and gazing out vaguely ahead of him, just as they did in Norman times. My religion, however, would not be one of terror: it would be serene but above all full of admiration."[2] Nearly half a century later, Le Corbusier's main architectural collaborator in India, Balkrishna Doshi, observed, "I often noticed while interacting how much he believed that there was somebody, somewhere, who was creating or sending messages so that they could be implemented by him as HIS instrument. He often referred to the river which internally connected the source and the destination of the water and where the creator told him to flow, but always detached from either of the banks."[3] It was on that boat deck at age twenty-three that Jeanneret began to worship such an undefined spiritual force.

2

Approaching Belgrade on the wide river, Jeanneret wrote Ritter, "The whole mystery of this journey seems so full of promises, occurring under a sky that already declares its splendor, so that quite understandably one feels happy. There is in us—perhaps only in me—a vestige of religious masochism that almost engenders a fear of such happiness. But I am gradually discarding it, soon the devil will relieve me of it, and have to find another poor leper to torment himself."[4] Jeanneret sketched a square shape divided in the middle horizontally by a wavy double line. The top half he marked "sky," the lower one "water"; "earth" was nothing but a narrow slit between the two roughly parallel lines in the middle. Le Corbusier always viewed earthly existence as such—a fragile platform that is a minuscule part of the larger scheme—but he was learning how to enjoy being there.

BEFORE THE SHIP reached Belgrade, the captain arranged for the two young travelers to board a small raft at daybreak. Journeying via stream to one small village after another, Jeanneret thrilled to the throngs of pilgrims chanting psalms, the peasant women bearing small baskets of fruit and vegetables in crowded marketplaces, and the oxen, cows, and goats grazing peacefully. He also reveled in the straightforward building style that achieved protection and enclosure in their fundamental form: "Each house has its own courtyard, and the intimacy in them is as perfect as in the gardens of the Carthusian Monastery of Ema where, as you may recall, we had a fit of spleen. Beauty, joy, serenity gather here, and a wide, semicircular portal, closed by a door lacquered in either red or green that opens onto a spacious exterior! The trellis assembled from latticework casts a green shadow, its white arcades bring comfort."[5]

Village life in this powerful landscape sent him soaring: "The three great whitewashed walls, which are repainted each spring, make a screen as decorative as the background of Persian ceramics. The women are most beautiful; the men clean-looking. They dress themselves with art: flashing silks, . . . the thousand folds in the short dresses where the silk flowers ignite under a sun of golden fire."[6] He was finding the beauty that was to be his lifeblood.

3

When he got to Istanbul, Jeanneret learned that William Ritter had mentioned him in a newspaper article that would be read in La Chaux-de-Fonds. Jeanneret wrote Ritter, "Will my distinguished papa deign to smile if one day he sees his son's name in cold print?"[7] He allowed to Ritter that his father was convinced that his sons would never amount to anything.

L'Eplattenier had recently asked him to teach for twelve hours a week at a new school; his father, whom one might have expected to be pleased, was indifferent about the offer. "You understand that my dear papa, who has no ambition for his sons beyond a stable position, could be quite happy. Yet it's he himself who catalogs all these wonders while commenting on them with a lack of enthusiasm, of warmth, which neither surprises nor disturbs me."[8]

Suddenly, his world was falling apart again: "In any case, the watercolors are going nowhere. Besides, who knows if Constantinople is right for watercolors. Is Santa Sofia lovely? Internally speaking, of course. Perhaps Constantinople is a mirage? K and I are in a strange state of mind, and each evening we question each other: 'Perhaps I've gone mad? Tell me, Klip, do I look like a donkey? I think this damn tobacco has played a trick on me, and now I've been mummified!' Etc."[9]

The "tobacco" was probably hashish. It had him wavering between a self-nourishing negativism and an enthusiasm he voiced to Ritter in a language a young man from the provinces might have used to try to impress a duchess.[10] This shift in mood within a two-page letter reveals the precipitous emotional leaps and descents to which Jeanneret was increasingly subject: "We came by way of Rodosto in order to proceed through those waters I'd always adored; by sea so classically, so majestically, in order to take it all in. We saw Andrinople, and how we loved it! Kazanlik at the foot of the Balkans was simply exquisite. Tirnovo gives you an attack of spleen, but I've had the revelation of the Chapel of Paradise."[11]

The experiences of color and smell were intertwined with sexual cravings, about which he also wrote Ritter in a pretentious literary style: "Strange how your incisive words about Bucharest express just what I felt there: that terrible itch of the flesh, that thirst for Theodoran debauchery (I'm creating adjectives), and then that disgusting odor of the lilies the handsome gypsy women were selling. And to think that painters here produce such filth instead of *painting* filth in a gypsy *plastique* and in chromatics where lemon yellows would excite dirty greens and corrupt violets, and where the blacks, absolute blacks, would blacken everything that's rotten, cynical, bestial. And inside blooms that weird rose of sensuality which savage peoples adore because it's the true color of flesh. And it all stinks of lilies until your brain cracks, your arteries burst."[12]

The bursting arteries were in his penis; he wrote Ritter, "And it was hot here, so hot we were kept awake all night! And believe me, one hard-on after the other!!!" The freedom to enjoy himself was still a problem, however. "It takes an act of will to let oneself go here, to fill one's lungs and enjoy a real vacation of doing nothing. Yet even so, one conscientiously torments oneself every day: the devil's always had a hard time turning white."[13]

JEANNERET was determined to be liberated from his shackles: "One expires from impoverishment and Christian torture. I've been so stifled that I've had to throw off the heavy cape. Now for action." But although the local women were enticing, he considered them strictly off-limits: "The little ladies: white silk, cherry-red, black silk, too. But it's all impossible, absolutely forbidden. So then one hugs one's pillow, too bad!"[14] This was one of many undisguised references Jeanneret made over the years to embracing his pillow in the absence of a woman; he frequently described his relationship with his pillow to Yvonne.

The physical experience occurred in solitude, yet he felt compelled to tell someone else about it.

4

From Constantinople, Edouard wrote his parents that he hardly had money for postage stamps because he had been unable to resist buying a marvelous Persian miniature, brocades for his mother, ceramic pots, and some icons. Georges was outraged at the expenditure, but Edouard insisted that they were bargains and good investments and that he and Klipstein were living on three or four francs per day, including rent. Besides, he would soon be on his own financially.

The tension mounted when Georges corrected a draft of Edouard's essay on the design of cities. Georges—whose own published writings for the Adventurers' Club newsletter have a succinct, no-frills style—gave valid counsel: "Your sentences are . . . too complicated, too long; we get lost."[15] He also informed his son that L'Eplattenier had telephoned the editor in La Chaux-de-Fonds asking him to delay publication of the article until

Edouard had restructured it and made its views more acceptable to the local authorities. Georges meant to soften that blow when he wrote, "I'm giving you fatherly advice," but Edouard showed no such grace in his response.[16] In a long and relentless diatribe, he retorted, "It's dangerous to interrupt someone else's work; it's an ungrateful role as well as a sacrificial one, and it pains me you're taking it on."[17] After announcing that he would not communicate from Constantinople again, he sulked for a month, finally writing only to inform his parents that he had not died of cholera.

He did not even bother to let them know that he had escaped the great fire that destroyed some nine thousand houses in Constantinople that summer, although his account of it to L'Eplattenier afterward would have served to reassure them that he had survived. Jeanneret fastened onto every detail of the tragedy. As flames shot out from the military headquarters, barefoot firemen ran around "like raving madmen."[18] Water blackened by soot rushed down the street, while "the inquisitive crowd" clambered toward the scene of the disaster.[19] Having emptied their establishments of all merchandise, shop owners now sat smoking with their friends as the flames approached and fire burst out in three separate places at the same time. Jeanneret calculated that two million square meters were burning.

He observed with a smug satisfaction the selfishness evident when the "unperturbed and curious" crowd blocked the streets and got in the way of people desperate to rescue their possessions.[20] "Neither a gesture of compassion nor one of solidarity induces this multitude of idlers to offer assistance," he wrote of the way that, during a downpour of burning embers, street vendors sold lemonade, ice cream, syrups, and fruit. In the face of this tragic devastation, he applied his cynicism to himself as harshly as to other impassive bystanders: "Since we do not see a convulsive face, we have no sense of horror. We hear no groans, no cries, no blasphemies. . . . We are captivated by a scene of formidable beauty and haunted by its magnificence."[21]

Thirty-four years later, at the end of World War II, Le Corbusier was similarly excited by the totally destroyed city of Saint-Dié. Making a reconstruction plan, he treated the eradication of the homes of hundreds of thousands of people as a clean start, a wonderful chance to build. At age twenty-three, observing the burning Constantinople, he wrestled with that same enthusiasm. "We can only seek to appease this passion that overwhelms us by its diabolical beauty," he wrote of the "brocade of fire; . . . the colossal blazing mass as though it were a sculpture; . . . these fabulous columns of smoke, streaming with fiery embers. It is an exaltation of joy! What utter joy!"[22] Color and form, explosion and destruction, intoxicated him so completely that he willingly shut his eyes to their horrors.

VIII

1

Following Constantinople, Jeanneret and Klipstein headed to Mount Athos. Known also as "The Garden of the Virgin Mary and the Holy Mountain," this self-governing state inhabited exclusively by monks has been a religious retreat for more than ten centuries. Jeanneret had long been determined to be one of the rare laypeople to visit the sacred territory. Athos is dotted with twenty monasteries, extraordinary in both their architecture and their isolation, and he counted on expanding on the fantastic experience he had at Ema.

Entry to Athos, however, was an arduous affair. The instinct and tenacity to make this pilgrimage to the Holy Republic distinguished Jeanneret and Klipstein from virtually everyone else they knew. Few of their contemporaries raised in the stronghold of Protestantism would have dreamed of hazarding the trip to the territory of total maleness, religious devotion, and physical isolation; even drinking the thick foreign coffee that coats the teeth with bittersweet muddy powder, a staple of this journey into the Turkish empire, would have been unthinkable.

In Constantinople, Jeanneret had had to obtain a letter from the Greek patriarch, which necessitated a recommendation from an embassy. There was, however, no Swiss embassy there. He had had to turn to the French authorities, who were not inclined to help someone who wasn't one of their citizens. Armed with letters from L'Eplattenier and Perret, he asserted himself until, finally, after several weeks, entry documents in hand, he was on his way.

MOUNT ATHOS IS one of three peninsulas in Macedonia in northern Greece that stretch down into the brilliant blues of the Aegean Sea. The most easterly, it has the form of a splayed claw. Its jagged mountain peaks, treeless and rocky, are virtually inaccessible, although Lord Byron claimed to have scaled the bare summit, 2,030 meters high, and to have seen the plains of Troy from it.

On the fertile cliff-top plateaus near the sea, large monasteries were built starting in the eleventh century. The pine forests around secluded coves lined by sandy beaches were scattered with dwellings for smaller groups of monks who preferred even greater isolation, as well as with huts for monks requiring solitude.

The monastic republic is accessible only by sea. Jeanneret and Klipstein first had to travel on rugged roads for many hours from Thessaloniki southeast to the port of Ouranapolis to get their boat. To their surprise, rather than sail directly to Athos's entry port of Daphni, they first were forced to take a small dinghy to a desert island just offshore from their departure point. There they spent four miserable days quarantined in a cell that Jeanneret compared to a cage for chickens and where his and Klipstein's underwear was taken so it could be boiled. Finally, they were released and boarded a large boat for the three-day crossing.

But the moment Jeanneret stepped off the boat at Daphni on August 24, he was transported. The town was inauspicious—a cluster of a few ramshackle wooden structures for customs officers—but Jeanneret was captivated by the landscape, which struck him as sacred. The grandeur and majesty of the mountain in front of him was more impressive than any man-made construction he had ever seen. And he exulted in the myth of this bold pyramid form shooting up from the sea—said to have been the rock that Athos, the leader of the Giants, had cast at his foe Poseidon, the leader of the Olympians, but that had missed him and fallen into the ocean.

In early Christianity, a tradition developed that Athos was holy ground and had been visited by the Virgin Mary. The mountain was dedicated to the Mother of God and her glory, so other females were not permitted there. Edith Wharton had written in 1888 when she peered at the sights of Athos from a deck without being allowed to land, "The early established rule that no female human or animal, is to set foot on the promontory, is maintained as strictly as ever; and as hens fall under this ban, the eggs for the monastic tables have to be brought all the way from Lemnos."[1] The idea of this haven conscribed exclusively to the Holy Mother impressed itself on the traveler who four decades later designed his chapel at Ronchamp, dedicated to this same Marie.

2

For about two weeks, Jeanneret and Klipstein traveled by mule and stayed in various monasteries. The high-perched building complexes were unlike anything Jeanneret had ever seen. So was the endless horizon, devoid even of boats. Sleeping on cots in the spare rooms, savoring those vistas of sea and sky, dining with monks in the refectories, Jeanneret felt his life change.

He wrote of the trip to Athos, "To go there requires physical courage not to doze off in the slow narcosis of so-called prayer but to embark, rather, upon the immense vocation of a Trappist—the silence, the almost superhuman struggle with oneself, to be able to embrace death with an ancient smile!" The sea journey itself provided a new sense of what mattered in life: "Lying motionless at night, I feigned sleep, so that I could gaze, with eyes wide open, at the stars and listen, with ears fully cocked, for every trace of life to subside, savoring silence in its glory. These were the happiest hours I have ever experienced."[2]

The obsession with the horizon that Jeanneret developed on Athos was to determine the way he positioned almost all of his subsequent architecture. The smooth and continuous line where sea and sky meet had a meaning well beyond its visual beauty. "I think that the flatness of the horizon, particularly at noon when it imposes its uniformity on everything about it, provides for each one of us a measure of the most humanly possible perception of the absolute," he wrote.[3] In his future, there were to be other forms of horizon: the bumpy juxtaposition of gentle fields and sky as seen from the terraces of the Villa Savoye; the wavy border of the earth appearing like a mirage in the blazing Indian sunlight at Chandigarh. But whatever the base, the boundary between earth or sea and the infinite cosmos of the sky became the focal points of the vistas that Le Corbusier made essential components of his buildings.

The pure and honest architecture on Mount Athos conquered Jeanneret as much as the cosmic setting did. The monasteries built there nearly a millennium earlier as self-sufficient villages eventually spawned his all-inclusive apartment complexes; the stone and plaster constructions where religious contemplation was the goal were reborn in concrete and steel in his monastery of La Tourette.

Immediately recognizing the impact of those monasteries, he wrote in his journal of his "yearning for a language limited to only a few words."[4] In this anonymous architecture, built modestly and purposefully, he saw both the salient honesty and the celebration of life's wonders that were to be the goals of his own architecture.

Jeanneret found the heat oppressive, yet the sun's warmth, which served to remind him of its actual fire, also excited him. This landscape with olives and lemons and almonds growing in profusion, with the sea nearby for long swims, became his ideal setting to live in, especially when it offered a view to the infinite.

3

In *Journey to the East*, an account of this trip published many years later, Le Corbusier mused erotically about his time on Mount Athos: "The night was conducive to any emotional contemplation made languid by the warm, moist air, saturated with sea salt, honey, and fruit; it was also conducive, beneath the suspended, protective pergola, to the fulfillment of kisses, to wine-filled and amorous raptures."[5] What did he mean by these ambiguous remarks about the all-male domain? Was this a memory or a fantasy? Was he revealing a homosexual encounter on the spot where Lord Byron had trod a century earlier? Or was he insisting that abstinence, psychologically, was impossible, that the territory set aside for men to be celibate had the opposite effect and filled the mind with the longing for a woman?

Le Corbusier was deliberately obfuscatory. At that time, he lacked a clear direction and lived mainly in his head. But he observed richly and imagined mightily, especially when describing his thoughts in Karies, a village in the hills in the middle of the peninsula. Full of hazelnut trees, Karies had been established as the capital of Mount Athos in the tenth century. Jeanneret wrote: "With the overwhelming heat of the evening and our sudden transplantation into the sensuous night of such a place, a more than Pompeii-like feeling resonates with a heavy languor, and the loneliness of my heart conjures, in this glowing warmth, the black outfit and dismal figure of a marquis standing away from the group, far from the tables beneath the lattices and vine leaves, and leaning against the railing, back turned, lost in the contemplation of the sea. No, for more than a thousand years, this very simple and unique inn in Karies had lodged neither a marquise nor a courtesan, not even a simple woman traveler. For this land with the most Dionysian of suns and the most elegiac of nights is dedicated only to the dejected, the poor, or the distressed, only to the noble souls of Trappists, only to criminals fleeing the laws of men or sluggards fleeing work, only to dreamers and seekers of ecstasy and solitude."[6] That his reverie was simultaneously so vivid and so ambiguous was both a gift and a burden to the young man trying to forge his identity.

4

Jeanneret and Klipstein decided to approach some hermits living in *sketes*—the dry stone huts that provided maximum isolation. The recluses responded to their greetings by offering large bunches of grapes, which the visitor from Switzerland considered symbolic of both human generosity and the earth's bounty.

Of the monasteries, Lavras, which had been founded in 963, impressed Jeanneret especially. Its design has an abiding simplicity and derives from the purpose of providing proximity to nature in a tranquil setting. As one approaches the rambling structure from the sea, its rows of bedrooms look like white linen hanging on a laundry line in the wind. The top stories are perched on skeletal structures that project them in the direction of the horizon. Inside, the plain white walls are clean and silent. All of these elements reappear in Le Corbusier's luxurious villas and large apartment buildings, while other details—the large bell next to the chapel, the minimal Christian crosses, and the outdoor places of worship—all show up at Ronchamp.

The monastery's refectory was to have an equal influence on Jeanneret's work. It is an extraordinary salubrious space for human congregation; the overall impression is of rough plaster—painted with a marvelous bright whitewash—and then of the subtly colored frescoes that cover many of the walls and convey a biblical narrative cogently and gracefully. The tables in the refectory are semicircular, thick, coarse slabs of marble, quarried on islands in the Marmara Sea and, like Carrara marble, dominantly white with grayish-blue veins.

These slabs and the benches that accompany them ennoble the act of eating and sitting. The wooden seats are long planks set into whitewashed plaster bases that echo the curves of the tables. Le Corbusier made similar custom-fitted furniture in the lakeside villa for his mother, in his own *cabanon* in Roquebrune-Cap-Martin, and in other residences. Like the anonymous architects of Lavras, he, too, unified functional, dignified furniture with luminous architecture and colorful art so that all the elements work in tandem.

Jeanneret reveled in the ambient honesty and strength of these surroundings and the monks who inhabited them: "We sit down on the white wooden benches. The monks' hands are rough and calloused, swollen from working the fields, and their robustness is at one with the plates and enameled earthenware common to the country and implying the soil. Beyond each guest are three earthen bowls containing raw tomatoes, boiled beans, and fish, nothing else. And in front of him is a wine pitcher and a tin goblet, together with round, heavy black rye bread, the daily treasure, the meritorious symbol. In front of the apse, the superiors break the bread, eat their food and drink their wine from the earthen dishes and the green jugs on the unvarnished wood boards, and nothing more. A joyous atmosphere."[7] This became his ideal: earthy materials, lack of pretension, the interplay of work and simple pleasure—all nourished by the southern sun.

5

On Athos, Jeanneret was also awakened to the relationship of a garden to the life it supports. The terrain cultivated for melons and peppers and other fruits and vegetables at the monasteries in time led to the well-planned courtyards and terraces in Le Corbusier's villas and to the parks he designated for the outskirts of large cities. The necessity of a growing space in communion with a living space seized his consciousness forever.

But while he retained the memory of the pink Judas-tree blossoms and the profusion of delicious sun-gorged vegetables of the Holy Republic, the reality of his time there was less than perfect. In a letter to Ritter, he blamed the monks of Iviron for the food poisoning from which he suffered shortly after arriving there: "Endless diarrhea due to those dear monks whose culinary preparations had wandered into forgotten cupboards."[8] Suffering from at least two intestinal attacks on Mount Athos, he was extremely sick for ten of his days there.

Jeanneret treated the illness with retsina, of which he drank great quantities at night. He marveled at the curative effects and credited the rough wine with his ability to spend the days on muleback ascending and descending the island's steep hills. This was how Jeanneret found a rather ordinary building that staggered him with the clarity and grace of its architecture. It was a simple, small Byzantine church in the monastery of Rossikon: "Two things: the straightness of the nave, like an immense forum, and then the hollow onion bulb of the dome proclaim the miracle—the masterpiece—of man." This modest structure had none of the scale of Hagia Sophia or other famous buildings, but it was a kernel of truth. "This architecture, however diminished in volume, commands my admiration," he wrote, "and I spend hours deciphering its firm and dogmatic language."[9]

Undeterred by his ill health, Jeanneret "felt quite strongly that the singular and noble task of the architect is to open the soul to poetic realms, by using materials with integrity so as to make them useful."[10] This church at Rossikon enabled him to recognize the inestimable value of building with a clear conception and a worthy purpose. Jeanneret's travels convinced him that the standards and integrity essential to such a creation were practically extinct; he would revitalize them: "The hours spent in those silent sanctuaries inspired in me a youthful courage and the true desire to become an honourable builder."[11] He was, for the rest of his life, to strive for this same marvelous combination—logic and directness in tandem with the inexplicable—that he discovered on Mount Athos.

6

Leaving Mount Athos, Jeanneret remained "haunted by a dream, a yearning, a madness."[12] His goal was to see the Acropolis.

On the voyage, for the first time ever, he immersed himself nude in the ocean. He could not yet swim. But, surrounded by water, entirely alone, he felt himself gloriously connected to the larger world. He wrote Ritter, "I look up and it's splendid. I was plunging naked just now in these classical waters. I have a notion that there was fighting here once. Eleusis is across the away—a few thousand yards. And now, cobalt has filled the folds of the mountains and the beach rising out of the sea. Eleusis? The site of mysteries so long ago! I've seen Olympus, first the Asian one, and then two days ago the real one where Jupiter and company were enthroned. A fine mountain with a lovely profile I neglected to mention. Lord! I've seen Lemnos and Pharos days on end without flinching, all very beautiful."[13]

The man who was so intoxicated by the ancient world and had just bathed naked was thinking more and more about sex. He revealed to Ritter that he was acquiring a very specific taste for large, full-bodied females with enormous breasts—the same creatures who were to dominate his paintings toward the end of his life. He saw the prototypes of these voluptuous earth goddesses on the island of St. Giorgio, near the port of Antiparos, when his boat stopped there on the way from Mount Athos to Athens. The twenty-three-year-old wrote his mentor in Munich, "Back to my old crones, or rather forward to two enormous Greek women who came down to the beach one evening, surrounded by a thick cloud of patchouli, which I greedily inhaled. Lord what women! Splendid animals. I told everyone the identical creatures were to be seen in the two caryatids at the treasury of Delphi. They

Sketch showing a view of the Acropolis, September 1911

sat down at a table and proceeded to stuff themselves like the peasants they were, working their jaws to great effect. What arms, what heavy round chins, and what adorable breasts!"[14]

In the bazaar, he purchased, for one hundred sous, an archaic earthenware figure with a full-bodied form that he likened to Aristide Maillol's work. On top of the Persian miniatures and the bronzes he had already bought and shipped home, the purchase left him penniless but overjoyed. Clutching it, he wrapped himself in a brightly colored Romanian rug he had acquired on the trip and slept on the deck as the ship made its way toward the Greek mainland. He ate octopus from Mycenae and drank Sicilian wine, which was stored in a cask. In a language he scarcely spoke, he raved about both to the cook.

Then, from the sea, Charles-Edouard Jeanneret had his first glimpse of the Acropolis. As light conditions changed before his eyes, he marveled at the overall order evident in the assemblage of temples: "For all the majesty of the natural surroundings, the focal point was an amalgam of buildings perfectly placed on their sites by human beings."

Toward the end of his life, Le Corbusier acknowledged the indelible effect of both the ocean and the ancient temple ruins at that moment: "Over the years I have become a man of the world, crossing continents as if they were fields. I have only one deep attachment: the Mediterranean. I am Mediterranean Man, in the strongest sense of the term. O Inland Sea! queen of forms and of light. Light and space. The essential moment came for me at Athens in 1910 [*sic*]. Decisive light. Decisive volume: the Acropolis. My first picture, painted in 1918, was of the Acropolis. My Unité d'Habitation in Marseille? Merely the extension. In all things I feel myself to be Mediterranean: My sources, my diversions, they too must be found in the sea I have never ceased loving. Mountains I was doubtless repelled by in my youth—

Resting on a column of the Parthenon, September 1911

my father was too fond of them. They were always present. Heavy, stifling. And how monotonous! The sea is movement, endless horizon."[15]

ONCE HE AND KLIPSTEIN got to Athens, Jeanneret postponed the experience of actually walking up to the Acropolis. Even after he resolved to do so, he put it off again to forestall what he knew would be overwhelming. He told Klipstein that he must make this journey alone; he was in too excited a state to be accompanied or let anyone else determine his pace.[16]

On the designated day, after being on edge all morning, he decided at midday to wait until the sun had gone down. He wanted the effects of moonlight and the solitude of night to be present before going closer to the ancient temple. He calculated that afterward, once he had walked back down to the city, he would have only to go to sleep.

Jeanneret felt overcome by "the deliberate skepticism of someone who inevitably expects the most bitter disillusion."[17] But when he finally reached the Parthenon, the building's scale stupefied him, and he was exhilarated beyond all expectations. After climbing the steps he considered too large, he walked into the temple on its axis. He looked back between the fluted columns to see the vast sea and the mountains of the Peloponnesus spread before him in the changing light of dusk. Conscious of standing in a place once reserved for gods or priests, feeling himself thrust into an era two thousand years previous, Jeanneret was "stunned and shaken" by the "harsh poetry."[18] In that delirious state, he began to walk around.

ANYONE WHO HAS looked over one of the perfectly scaled parapets on the terraces at the Villa Savoye, who has stood on the roof of l'Unité d'Habitation in Marseille and taken in the mountains to the north and the sea to the south, who has felt the merging of garden and house at the Villa Sarabhai in Ahmedabad, will recognize that these ever-changing compositions are rich echoes of the marriage of nature and building that Jeanneret perceived when he first took in all that was contained and exposed on the hill overlooking Athens. What affected him above all at the Acropolis was the integration of the temples into their site. The relation of buildings to their natural setting; the universal vistas; the equal importance of air, water, and light to stones and mortar—what was evident in the Greek monuments was to be palpable in all that Le Corbusier built.

So were the roles of color and light. "Never in my life have I experienced the subtleties of such monochromy. The body, the mind, the heart gasp, suddenly overpowered."[19] Now more than ever, he wished to create such thrills for others.

7

Jeanneret both worshipped and detested the godlike power of the Parthenon. He summed up the experience as "admiration, adoration, and then annihilation." After twelve days of daily visits, he suddenly disliked going up there: "When I see it from afar it is like a corpse. The feeling of compassion is over." Jeanneret began to sense the presence of death everywhere around him. The nights seemed "green," with "bitter vapors" under the black sky. In the streets of Athens he saw—or thought he saw—corpses being carried by black-robed Orthodox priests; the skin of the exposed faces of the dead bodies was also green, with black flies swarming around them. "The torpor of the land" merged in his mind with the weighed-down clouds.[20] Yet for nine more days, he kept going back to the Acropolis. He was in love, then out of love; ravenous, then satiated; ecstatic, and then despondent.

Finally, Jeanneret had had enough. He later wrote L'Eplattenier, "I've seen Eleusis and Delphi. All well and good. But for three weeks I've seen the Acropolis. God Almighty! I had too much of it by the end—it crushes you until you're ground to dust."[21]

At the Acropolis, September 1911

8

In Athens, Jeanneret received a letter from Charles L'Eplattenier, asking him to come back to art school and form a new division there.

Having taken this long voyage to cure himself of his previous misery and, he wrote Ritter, having succeeded in enlarging his vision of life and acquiring a new serenity, he was tormented by the offer. The need to reconsider his future was a "catastrophe." He feared that if he decided to go back, he would become like L'Eplattenier, a prospect he equated with spiritual death. But he had to contend with reality and the obligation he felt to return to his hometown.

Jeanneret told Ritter that he blamed himself for his suffering; his own tyrant, he tortured himself. Since the age of fourteen, he had pushed himself mercilessly, so that now he was more anxious by the day and made women afraid. His brother, Albert, by contrast, was generous, full of sunshine and love.

Miserably, he was resigned to accept L'Eplattenier's proposal but still would not give his parents the satisfaction of knowing he was coming home. He told them only that he was leaving Athens and going to Calabria rather than Cyprus because of his digestive issues: "I'm dragging my guts around Athens . . . it's the cooking here that's doing me in." He believed he would stop his diarrhea with Italian macaroni. "I think that'll put the cork in it."[22]

In Pompeii, the cure worked. But in Rome he became upset about a misunderstanding. He learned that a postcard he sent home from Constantinople showing himself and Klipstein disguised as women had flopped. His parents "failed to recognize their own son with towels for breasts and purebred elbows" and were not amused by the "bazaar finery."[23] Then, on October 4, Jeanneret learned that his father's workplace and his aunt's apartment had been destroyed by fire.

He responded by writing that, although the fire was a serious matter, it neither troubled nor saddened him. While he offered to rush home if his help was needed, the event was an opportunity for a fresh start: "Now comes a resplendent purity," he assured his parents.[24] Jeanneret told his mother and father that he had, however, cried because of the probable loss of two books that he wanted to use for his own research: the *Encyclopedia* and *La Patrie Suisse.* He also grieved the loss of "Papa's suspenders, his smoking-jacket, his slippers, his checked celluloid cuffs."[25] But the idea of giving everything up and starting all over again was consolation.

He longed to be in the same situation. From Rome, Jeanneret sent L'Eplattenier a postcard declaring, "I hear the death-knell of my youth. Within a month or less it will be over. Ended. Another man, another life,

Auguste Klipstein and Charles-Edouard Jeanneret performing the dance of Salomé in Pera (Istanbul), July 1911

clear horizons, and a road between walls. . . . Of course I'm often sad about it: gray fits of melancholy mingle with the joys of my return. I leap from dark to light and back again, and there's no doubt something harsh and tragic remains."[26]

But Charles-Edouard Jeanneret had now made a resolution. If he had to be back in Switzerland, at least he could use it as a stepping-stone toward becoming an architect. His lack of the requisite diploma was no obstacle.

IX

One can never forgive the city where one has learned to know one's fellow men.

—STENDHAL, AS QUOTED BY LE CORBUSIER

1

The return to his hometown felt like a form of death. The train from Milan took the traveler back through the mountain passes through which he had first fled La Chaux-de-Fonds four years earlier. He wrote Ritter that he was heading toward "an ugliness sadder for being pretentious . . . that's what my future will be: hard, hurried, arid, dangerous." As he left "the tragic tunnel" on the train that was to deposit him in his birthplace later that afternoon, it was "the last day of a condemned man."[1]

AT AGE TWENTY-FOUR, Charles-Edouard Jeanneret teetered in borderline territory between genius and insanity. His consuming love of female beauty and craving for sex, his determination to make a new architectural dogma with universal application, and his passion for the visual overwhelmed him. For he had no idea how to realize his goals.

He revealed the rich confusion of his unusual mind in a letter he wrote Ritter on November 1, the day of his return home:

> I've had my fill of death. In Italy everything has crumbled or collapsed. For me Italy is a cemetery where the dogmas that were once my religion are rotting where they stand. Who could believe such a hecatomb? In four years, I've suffered and survived a terrible evolution. I've gobbled up an East of unity and power. My gaze is horizontal and cannot see the insects at my feet. I feel my own brutality. Italy has made me a blasphemer. I sneer at everything, and my feet are ready to kick things out of the way. I was obeying my destiny when I left

everything behind in order to travel at any cost. All that bric-a-brac I treasured disgusts me now. I stumble through elementary geometry in my hunger for knowledge and eventual power. In this mad dash, red, blue, and yellow have become white. I'm besotted with white, with the cube, the sphere, and the cylinder, with the pyramid of great empty spaces. The prisms rise, balance, and advance according to various rhythms, having a huge black dragon writhing on the horizon in order to hold them together down below. Above them is nothing but a white sky: they stand on the marble paving where they compose monoliths unpolluted by color. But at noon the light spreads the cubes in one immense surface; by evening a rainbow rises out of the forms. In the morning they are real again, with lights and shadows, bright as a diagram. One senses their tops, their bottoms, their sides. More than ever, the night is black and white, the white whiter than ever, the black blacker. There are scarlet rooms with luxuriant bacchic evocations, stifling rooms filled with shadows, a sort of paradise aglow with local golden Buddhas. These would be refuges for hours of great anguish and madness. But we would be living between huge walls as smooth as they were white. It would be so ennobling that our progress would be regular, our gestures graceful, and everything would assume color. The world would take on grand and lovely proportions. Painters and sculptors would gradually become masons. Listen to the music of it! Can you see the developing architecture of a tragedy? Can you see the joyous inferno of a *commedia dell'arte:* Captain Fracasse, Pulcinella, Pierrot, Harlequin, and a black-swathed Don Salluste passing by.

Narrow streets with a checkerboard of windows in the facades. No ornamentation. The whole city one color, one substance. Cars surge past, planes pass overhead with no one paying much attention. There would be avenues across the rooftops amid flowers and trees; huge staircases to climb and long bridges to cross and then the descent down a superb staircase, which confers the gait of an emperor and fills one's heart with generosity.

Here and there a temple: a cylinder, a half sphere, a cube, a polyhedron. And empty spaces, for breathing.

Up on such rooftops, what else would we be but gentle madmen, leaving the crowd, with all its bright rags and celluloid collars, on the *piano nobile* below?

What is to be done with women? Steal your best friend's wife for a night, abandon your own for another, make love when the impulse seizes you, a debauch at essential hours. A splendid resurrection of hetaerae murmuring endearments and performing acceptable coitus. From great white halls you would pass into red ones. And then proceed on your way forgetting the episode, recovering your habitual companion. I desire such things, perfect fool that I am, for what exists today is intolerable. I have lost all religion, and upon seeing two young newlyweds crossing the square in front of the cathedral tonight, entwined just closely enough for the sake of hygiene, I wondered what the devil we were doing here on earth. Surely the stupidest question to ask, for the answer is: do your work, burn your candle, the one you manufacture and sell for the sake of light, and above all, do not concern yourself with whoever furnishes the tallow and with what those you illuminate are doing.

Since the blade has already fallen, I shall not die tomorrow. I am in the next world already. My muscles are prepared, capable of hard work. I shall perform at the top of my powers for several years. And I shall see the two young newlyweds entwined for the sake of hygiene—perhaps she will be the one, the unknown woman who awaits me, and I—I shall be cast into the void wondering *Warum*?

Starting tomorrow L'Eplattenier will hire a good mason and we shall make Art! A ridiculous notion! Never again must we make Art but only enter tangentially into the body of our epoch and dissolve there in order to become invisible. And when all of us have disappeared in this way, the stone will have become one great block. What will survive us then will be Coliseums, Thermae, an Acropolis and certain mosques, and the Jura, our mountains, will provide a frame as fine as any sea. Long afterward young people will pass by, their passions aroused.

Let me propound my new dogmas: we are remarkable men—great and worthy of past epochs. We shall do better—that is my credo. The primitives are in fashion. Their day is past. They were savages, and we are civilized men. I must raise two altars—to Michelangelo and to Rembrandt. All the others in the history of Art are so much dung. Piero della Francesca is a poet. Cimabue is a painter. And Giotto a decadent. I shall betake myself to Egypt. Asia is our crucial resource. All art critics must be destroyed, excepting only those who reveal contemporary art. Those must sit in judgment. The world must be made white. The fruits of the earth must be eaten and drunk. To make love with the body and thereafter to be stoned to death, having put up a splendid resistance—what a beautiful fate!

Must, must. . . . There is no escaping it. Must: the dogma of the new. A hard look and a whip for those who refuse. That sounds like me. Who else?

Yes, I long for imperatives. Such is my destiny, as you well know. Yet wrought up as I am, I aspire to being so for its own sake.

This was just a small part of the fifteen-page missive he wrote as he anticipated losing the gains of his time away. "I shall turn back, mow down my friends, be called a crazy fool, and once there is a void around me, I shall remember that you shouted: 'Sir, sir, whoa there, breakneck!' but there is nothing for it. Go your ways."

This was the occasion when Jeanneret put, on the back side of the envelope, as the return address, "La Chaux-de-Fonds de m . . ."—La Chaux-de-Fonds of shit.[2]

2

Georges and Marie Jeanneret did not have room for Charles-Edouard in their apartment. For four weeks, he stayed with L'Eplattenier. Then he visited Octave Matthey. The friend who had advised him on sex was living in an ancient granary, similar to the primitive barn he had rented on Mount Cornu two winters earlier. The moment he saw this rough structure, constructed in 1670 in open countryside, he decided to move in. If he had to be back at La Chaux-de-Fonds, he would do so in wilderness rather than bourgeois oppressiveness.

It was, Jeanneret wrote Ritter, "exactly two minutes from the top of the town, an outbuilding of the old convent which has lately been inhabited by tramps. I was jealous of the place; I had them cut out a huge room from the

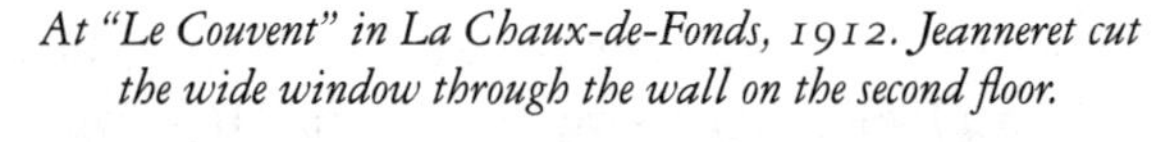
At "Le Couvent" in La Chaux-de-Fonds, 1912. Jeanneret cut the wide window through the wall on the second floor.

barn, forty or fifty feet on a side, low ceilings, but with enormous and very beautiful brown rafters and very white walls, I insisted on that. I tell you, my big barn is adorable. You get in up a steep, narrow staircase, and out the window I see a mountain ash, and beyond it the melancholy Mont Sagne bristling with stubby firs. O these horizons under your nose! My friend Octave lives in the apartment underneath, a friend from Coulon days. We share an enormous kitchen, with a fireplace between the arches worthy of a Hindu cult. It is pitch-black, dark as a cave inside, really too dark. . . . And to get my barn in working order took these cheating workmen a whole month."[3]

Matthey had an "Egyptian"'s triangular torso and square shoulders, yellow skin, hair that was practically blue, and Dante-like nose. One day, when a former girlfriend of Matthey's was in his room, Matthey knocked on Jeanneret's door. The woman, who lived in Zurich, was visiting for two days. Matthey remarked that since Jeanneret had shown him his Maillol—as they called the little terra-cotta from the island of St. Giorgio—Jeanneret might now want to come see *his* "statue."[4] Matthey added that Jeanneret could stay as long as he wanted, but he should come on tiptoe, since she appeared to be sleeping.

To Ritter, Jeanneret described the encounter with his unique mix of specificity and incoherence: "One shawl spread across the six-paned window, another at right angles hung from the ceiling, both forming—with the partition opposite the second shawl, the ceiling, and the floor—a tiny hollow cube in which the triangle of the two splendid armchairs and the wicker chair produce a design of their own; a pedestal-table covered with what appears to be a service of black and white china, on the far sideboard an enormous pot of dried chrysanthemums, the various stems protruding under their weeping tresses. *She* was stretched out in one of the big armchairs covered with a big scarlet rug, naked and asleep, her feet thrust toward us, her head in a cloud of red curls hiding the face tilted toward her armpit; the almost complete darkness made her body look colossal."[5]

After creeping in, Jeanneret sat down in the second armchair. Matthey offered him a cup of tea, but Jeanneret was too mesmerized to do anything as ordinary as sip a beverage.

His mind went through complex gyrations as he faced the sleeping, naked woman. He wrote his mentor, "We were talking softly about the Beauty Sanctuary constituted then by the huge spherical lantern of orange and white paper with a big blue eye in the center which Octave lit and hung above us. We decided it had to be painted. Octave took his brushes; the shawl spread in front of the six little panes of the window made a green fluid immobilized above the dishes which looked, in the warm light of this sanctuary—pink flesh in a vermilion matrix—as if they were made of some black and white substance. That was when I left. And here on my desk upstairs there was the blue cover of a book of Mallarmé's poems—I read the 'Soupir' and his translation of 'Ulalume.' "[6]

Matthey's girlfriend returned to her family. Two days later, Jeanneret did a watercolor of the sleeping woman from memory. It released a new energy in him, and he began to paint with zeal. Drawing on recent memories for his subject matter, he believed that by making art he could create the vibrancy absent in his everyday experience. He painted the Parthenon in emerald green and vermilion, and the temple of Jupiter in green and "*rose-caleçon*"—a pink Jeanneret inexplicably identified with boxer shorts.[7]

Yet nothing was good enough for Jeanneret. On a postcard he had bought in Florence in happier times, he wrote Ritter, "I don't know what I'm doing. What appears disgusts me; I spoil everything in ten minutes and yet I don't give up. I'm telling you I no longer have any control over the thing. I look into myself with a deep expression of exasperation. But isn't it true to make a sky exploding with light you have to leave the paper blank from top to bottom, not daubing it at all? Yet this strange persistence of black and of dirty grays produce a kind of tragic harshness. You can imagine how sick I am of the whole, can't you? I walk like a drunkard with huge gaps, light and darkness."[8]

Then, for six weeks, he stopped writing even to Ritter. When, at the start of February, he broke the silence with a postcard, he again utilized the term "depression." He felt outside of himself; it was as if his mind as well as his body were freezing in the barn. Matthey had left their shared home without warning—giving the incident of the sleeping woman in the armchair as the reason but specifying nothing more. Without a roommate, Jeanneret's financial affairs were in chaos, and the city government had failed to give him an office.

SUDDENLY, HE BEGAN to soar again. A sentence Jeanneret had read in Ritter's "Musical Life" was so beautiful "that it may help me to disperse the mists which imprison me."[9] He was designing two villas, one of which was to be a new house for his parents; in his new role as a teacher, he was gaining a wider audience. Elation replaced gloom.

Le Corbusier later compared L'Eplattenier's new division of l'Ecole d'Art to the Weimar Bauhaus. It taught everything that pertained to the art of building. Teaching twelve classroom hours per week, Jeanneret enlarged students' understanding of basic geometric elements and enabled them to apply that knowledge to architecture, furniture design, and interior decoration, with the emphasis on abstraction more than structure.

He began to relish his role of embattled martyr: "People hate us a priori because we were trying to do something fine. The minnows and the piglets have protested—they hate us because we were trying to clear the muck out of their stable. In the same way that the socialists hate L'Eplattenier because the monument has made him radical, the bourgeoisie hate us, the young ones because we don't have anything to do with them since most of my friends are boors, wild men with red beards and clumsy gestures whose elocution offends them more than spelling mistakes."[10]

If only he could reconcile the world of watchmakers and the love burning inside him. "What I'd like is to be able to do whatever I do with a great deal of passion," he wrote. "Anything deserves to be well done. It's true—to adapt yourself to the milieu, to love and express it: the roots of the trunk of the tree of art. So that we no longer rebel against the Convent. That would be too easy. We smile at the Gray City which does not smile back. The Gray City would like to spit on us, a business of carefully ejaculating a gob of saliva; pleasures of smokers and drunks." Even his mother was against him: "Bare-faced lying, if there's any hope for success. They've just covered my head with ashes and called me a chimney sweep; that's my mother for you: chimney sweep because it's not yet practical."[11]

But this time, rather than sink into incapacitating depression, Jeanneret resolved to work fiendishly hard. "All action is an act of optimism. In all inaction is a fall into the gray void." Yet he was completely confused about what direction to take: "To make 'beauty' for others—is this a necessity or an impertinence? It is either civility or altruism. It is? Damned if I know. I'd like to be a milestone of positive contribution, not of combat. And to make a contribution is to be a tiny thing in a great mass. To be avant-garde is to set yourself up alone on a pedestal, very high in spite of yourself, with principles of movements. To be a poet and describe a flower! It seems to me that it's permissible and necessary even for certain individuals to be the pope. Sometimes the poet and his flower seem selfish to me, and sometimes so wise. Every problem is a question for me, and I am not sufficiently indifferent to life not to ask it."[12]

3

Charles-Edouard Jeanneret managed to harness his energy and to set his course in spite of that burning tendency to turn belief into doubts. By the middle of the year, he had determined that making beauty for others was all that mattered in his life. It was insignificant that he was not certified in his profession; in fact, he never attained the official qualifications to practice architecture. Having decided who he was, he opened an office at 54 rue Numa Droz in La Chaux-de-Fonds, with the mathematically satisfying telephone number 939. The letterhead declared, "CH.-E. JEANNERET * ARCHITECTE." The description beneath the name was "Architecte des Ateliers d'Art Réunis." A list of services followed: "CONSTRUCTION OF VILLAS, COUNTRY HOUSES, APARTMENT BUILDINGS—INDUSTRIAL CONSTRUCTION—SPECIALIZING IN REINFORCED CONCRETE—REMODELING AND REPAIRS—INSTALLATIONS OF SHOPS—INTERIOR ARCHITECTURE—GARDEN ARCHITECTURE."

WITH VILLAS UNDER CONSTRUCTION and spring sunshine, he wrote Ritter, "The irises and the lilies of the heart bloom and open and spread their perfumes of the heart out the furthest fiber of the corollas, the same generous gift has risen and has traced, violet and blood-red on a field of mourning, a line of life. The rose of Hope is reborn each spring, which must afford us great comfort."[13]

Hope brought dreams: "Of Venice and of Ravenna, of huge, opulent women, smiling giantesses of Ferrara. Sickly Paris, Paris of the Folies Bergère, military service. Colombia: oaths, ecstasies, enthusiasms—youthful impulses. Enormous desire. Kindness in virtually everyone. . . . Paris glistening like a paradise and our thoughts transport us to the land of dreams, sometimes."[14] It was, however, time for a clean break: "It's all over between L'Eplattenier and me . . . There is nothing left between us but masks. Masks that must be torn away."[15]

It was to be a pattern of Le Corbusier's life: worshipful attachment followed by total rupture. The end with L'Eplattenier left him "a soul still sad at the agonizing spectacle," but severance was the only possibility: "I've had to put down others. Oh, yes, eliminate and destroy many things, hopes, people I loved and who I believed loved me, who themselves believed they loved me."[16]

Like the fire in his father's workroom, catastrophes opened doors: "It's a great deliverance. The grim, huge, melancholy, the swamp of stagnation, gives way to the rush of light. Yes! This is a cruel landmark."[17] Throughout Le Corbusier's life, conflict was a sublime stimulus; there was nothing like annihilation to clear the air.

IT NOW WAS, Jeanneret decided one August morning at his parents' kitchen table, "the modern moment!" "To raise a tower, first you must dig," he declared. He blasted himself for the work he had done locally. "As for the houses I built this year, I have committed certain anachronisms in their regard. I have been old, old-fashioned. With a fool's ear, I listened to dubious gossip, citations, unlikely aphorisms. I have been scandalously unsuitable. The absence of suitability, which has flung me this year into an abyss, has shown me the darkness of this condition. And now I see white!"[18]

He was in a manic upswing. "The hour of battle sounds in music. . . . Music is the great promoter of joy. I listen, and I hear so much! Music, by its rhythms, is of all forces the one which is combat," Jeanneret wrote Ritter. He was determined to understand and harness his euphoria. "What are they physically, then psychically, these explosions, these discharges, these outbursts, these ecstasies experienced, suffered?—once at the age of twelve in the presence of flowers, another time in front of that Alp, then inside that charterhouse near Florence (ineffable, agonizing vibrations), here in Palestrina's mass, there in Paris, along the Seine." The list of stimuli went on: the minarets he had seen in the east, the Parthenon viewed in conjunction with the sea and the sky: "Each thing offers itself to the eye."[19]

Now determined to celebrate rather than deny pleasure, he compared his responses to art and music to his sexual emissions when he was sleeping. His aesthetic reactions resembled "the effervescence of carnal dreams." Ritter was the one person who would understand. "I ask you—you who have inhaled life with such generous lungs—what becomes of and what use are the fugitive hours when we no longer belong to ourselves and where tears, cries, prayers, and blasphemies emerge pell-mell in our seething nonconsciousness? I'd like an answer from a man who has inhaled life with generous lungs."[20]

That zest for existence in all its magnitude brought with it a keen awareness of death: "Can it be possible that Life withdraws from those who love it? I am agonized by this question. Is all we have experienced . . . lost? Does it vanish, devoured by the grim indifference of external things? How to emerge from this abyss? Do you believe that with a sincere effort and a love of reality (and I know how readily the REAL can be masked!)—do you think that such things may keep us from dying?"[21] The questions were not rhetorical; they burned inside him.

DEATH BECAME MORE than theoretical when the thirty-seven-year-old journalist Auguste Bippert died demonstrating a small plane with a professional aviator on October 15, just after Jeanneret's twenty-fifth birthday. Bippert was "one of the only men hereabouts (perhaps the only one) who was interested in art, who understood something about it, who was really alive." At least to perish in an airplane was better than to be one of the living dead around him: "How much enthusiasm it takes, how much faith, and how many inner demons!"[22]

He focused more on Bippert's risk taking than his death: "The law of equilibrium demands that some exaggerate and caper since the rest are clams and rotting lobsters." Jeanneret disparaged the cliché that the accident was predestined: "The believers have already cited the Finger of God, turning Him into a kind of boulevard swindler."[23] It was the contrary; Bippert, rather than fall victim to death, had commited a heroic act. The end of life must be the way Orcagna represented it, as a triumphant moment. At age twenty-five, Jeanneret resolved that, whenever the time came for him to die, it would be according to his own will and in a blaze of glory.

4

Albert had taken to performing silent pantomimes of someone playing the piano. When he was in these disturbing trances, no one could get through to him. In the same period, Edouard began to have upsetting, complex dreams, which he described vividly to Ritter: "I dreamed once of a Biberstein autumn, deep puddles of blood as far as the eye could see from your windows. Then the snow fell, rising above your roof. We were guarding your books, which the snow was gradually burying. Wolves had passed; then two exhausted Moujiks appeared, whom you greeted. The potters' workshops had vanished under the snow. The Romanian blouses were covered. There were no longer any windowpanes and I stepped inside through the open windows. Yet even tilting, the Plain of Biberstein was one great puddle of blood. Yes, but there was the sky, the sun setting over that anguish."[24]

A perpetual lack of sunlight and the premature turning of the leaves added to his gloom. He wrote Klipstein, "It rains incessantly, tearfully. Enough to drive you to suicide."[25] When five hundred copies of his *Study of a Decorative Arts Movement in Germany* were published at the end of 1912 and there was "no reaction, no response," his depression worsened.[26] Jeanneret was exaggerating—he had heard from readers in Paris, Berlin, and Brussels—but he had not started to change the world as he hoped.

After the highs of early summer, he had now crashed completely: "No music for months and months, no shocks, no jolts, no excitement, no joy. Your footsteps track the rainy days over the squelching earth . . . and my soul is so profoundly unwell that whenever I attend a concert I realize I no longer hear the music. Overcome by the day's fatigue and paralyzed by the circumstances, my ears listen, but my heart remains cold. Unbalanced, I intensify my illness by a constant nonsatisfaction. The past abides like a book I've already read. It has not yet assumed the position of a witness, and uncertainty prevents me from making any resolution for the future."[27]

Even a kitten disappointed him! "I'm infatuated with cats: this morning someone brought us a kitten, the future guardian of our residence: ugly and oddly marked, the creature fails to attract me. How many women, too, generous though they may be, wake no response because they are not lovely?"[28]

The man who half a year earlier had been exulting "the rose of hope" and "ecstasies, enthusiasm . . . enormous desires" now lamented, "Alas, most of one's dreams will never come true."[29] There remained, however, one sole, splendid prospect: the great white villa he was in the process of building on the slope over La Chaux-de-Fonds for his parents, brother, and himself.

5

Charles-Edouard Jeanneret first conceived of a new house for his mother and father and Albert at the start of 1911. His parents owned a large lot on the hillside overlooking La Chaux-de-Fonds. Edouard designed a sprawling structure that was fit for gracious entertaining they never did and was luxurious beyond their wishes. It is astounding that Georges and Marie agreed to it, but by the end of April 1912 the foundations were laid, and by the start of 1913 his mother and father were in their sumptuous all-white bedroom, with an "ennobling" blue floor, and he and Albert were in their capacious semicircular aeries on the floor above. The place he created as if his family would spend many more years intact—the sons unmarried, the four of them under the same roof—was imbued with boldness and grace. There were vast living and dining rooms and a terrace overlooking the landscape of woods and Mont Racine.

The proud son was bursting with excitement: "One feels one is very high up, dominating a landscape somewhat reminiscent of Mount Athos—minus the sea!"[30] He wrote Ritter, "My dear Sir, within my white walls my mother has become a slender girl again, and sings Schubert at her piano as she did at thirty. Is peace created here at home? In any case, I have experienced great joy on account of my mother's happiness and my father's contentment."[31] With the Villa Jeanneret-Perret, also called the Maison Blanche, he was, for the first time, the author of human joy.

Then, even before the great family house on the hill was totally finished, reality hit. Charles-Edouard Jeanneret had destroyed his parents financially. "Where is duty?" he asked Ritter rhetorically. He answered for himself. "Duty: I have a papa and a mama."[32] He was shattered by what he had done.

It is unclear if anyone had ever discussed a budget for the Jeannerets' mansion. But what is certain is that the final cost was about fifty thousand Swiss francs. The sum would have been substantial no matter what the clients' circumstances; it was exorbitant for people of the modest means of an enameler of watchcases and a part-time piano teacher. The entire savings that Georges and Marie had acquired through years of hard work had been depleted by the construction of their new home.

Jeanneret heaped blame on the people he had hurt. If they had led their lives differently, his parents would not have been in this predicament. Edouard considered his father's work "a stomach-turning and degrading *métier.*" Nearly forty years of doing the same thing had turned Georges into a passive person who had few personal pleasures beyond some limited time for reading and hiking. He admired his father's intelligence but deplored his isolation: "My father has nothing to do with anyone, neither relatives nor friends." His mother, at least, was, at the age of nearly fifty, still "ardent and youthful" and adored by her piano students.[33] But in his frenzy, he resented everyone. Even if one of the main reasons he was back home was because of L'Eplattenier's asking him to form the art school he would later equate with the Bauhaus, he acted as if he had been obliged to return from Greece to assume an immense burden of responsibility for both of his par-

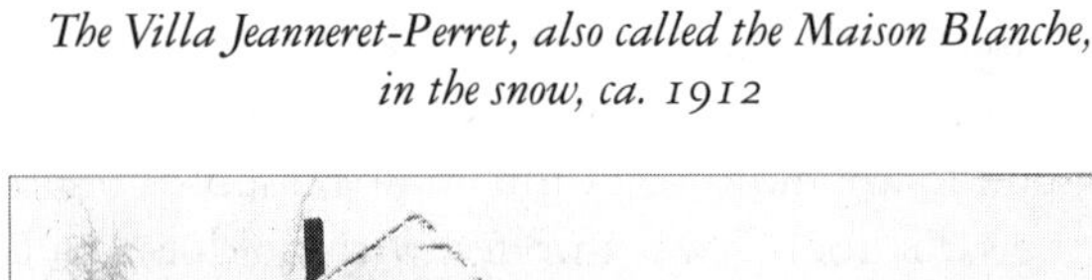

The Villa Jeanneret-Perret, also called the Maison Blanche, in the snow, ca. 1912

ents because Albert was away. Now, in his devotion, he had gotten them all into deeper water with the new house, an enormous blunder. Not only had he encumbered his parents financially, but he had foolishly established them away from the city and their neighbors.

The irony is that when the house that broke the bank was completed, in June 1913, it was the first architectural achievement in which the future Le Corbusier assumed his own voice. Unwieldy to run and made of materials too fine, it was, nonetheless, a superb and original design. Its gentle, sweeping forms and lively details lent harmony and charm to everyday life. This house had infused Jeanneret with an energy and originality that enabled him to go beyond the static formality or overly local style of his previous work.

The rear facade was bold and playful. For the first time, he made a wall by building a straightforward slab and perforating it so that the long, continuous form was a syncopation of thick and thin, glass and stone, mass and opening. Delicate steel mullions balance thick stucco; feathery lightness jibes with dense weight. The dominating whiteness is punctuated by a band of vibrant blue. The octagonal rectangles of the white shingles that cover the house—a pioneering concoction of compressed concrete with visible fibers, each small panel nailed to the support beneath—further the impression of energy and candor.

When he had been designing the Maison Blanche, Jeanneret had had Klipstein send him photographs of religious buildings that had impressed him in the Balkans.[34] The boldness and simple massing of these anonymous Romanian buildings, and the confidence with which those majestic struc-

With his father in the garden of the Villa Jeanneret-Perret, ca. 1916

With his parents and brother in the garden of the Villa Jeanneret-Perret, ca. 1916

tures were planted on the ground, have their echoes in the villa. The influence of the Parthenon is also apparent in the way Jeanneret's cubic structure is enlivened by the sequence of evenly spaced vertical elements.

Previously, Georges and Marie Jeanneret had surrounded themselves with comfortable clutter in small rooms with flowered wallpaper. Their younger child moved them into a small palace, aesthetically more austere than anything they had ever before known but also far more luxurious. Now the closet for their clothing was the size of their former living room, and their lives were graced by noble forms and a plethora of inventive details. Edouard had realized his goal of making his parents different from the other townspeople; these modest-living, hardworking people had not been able to turn him down when he had proposed it. The problem is that, from the moment they started to live there, they knew they could not afford to stay for long.

X

1

When war broke out in August 1914, Charles-Edouard Jeanneret was exempted from military duty in the Swiss army because of his bad eyesight. He had worn thick glasses and suffered from vision difficulties at least since 1904, when the local oculist had requested that l'Ecole d'Art excuse him from engraving. Within a few years, he almost completely lost sight in one eye. He credited that problem alternately to a gradual deterioration accelerated by an intense period of painting at night in 1917 and 1918 or to an accident with a sharp pencil point. All that is certain is that Le Corbusier had monocular vision and was known to argue with optometrists that his eyeglasses, frame included, should be half price.

Albert, too, was exempted from the army. In his case the reason was a slight heart condition, genuine enough but exacerbated by hypochondria.

Years later, Le Corbusier claimed publicly that he had done his military service by directing the construction of roads. Considering French soldiers "a marvel, nothing could be finer, more robust," he implied that he had been among their ranks, but it was a fantasy.[1]

THE CRUEL REALITY of war did, however, lead him to develop a brilliant concept of housing for the victims of bombs.

In September 1914, Jeanneret received news of the partial destruction of the cathedral at Reims. He wrote Ritter, "I'm profoundly disturbed by the spectacle of these fallen stones. Reims destroyed. All I had to do was to consult images of this unique, ineffable vessel of glory in the fantastic structure of its stones in order to feel a decisive hatred, somewhat equivalent to the sadness you must be feeling. Oh, I promise you my architect's soul is suffering." That catastrophic damage to a masterpiece horrified him: "these stones arched over a tabernacle and the eloquent relics within—now hurled to the ground by a pig named Wilhelm or Kronprinz." He called it "a cruel nightmare. Everything crumbles before these criminals, and so many men will die who were beacons in the darkness."[2]

The bombing of Reims made Jeanneret wish he could "take a pickaxe, and if possible prowl around the cathedral, piously gathering up the ruins," as he said to Ritter. He was plagued by his own inability to take action: "This is a terrible screed I'm sending you, harsh and fidgety, without the slightest note of calm. Unfortunately, there's no chance of that. Despite all my efforts, I'm unable to control myself; I feel a constant, morbid compulsion to talk instead of shutting up. And at the same time, an imperative sense that I owe it to myself to do so."[3]

As was often the case, when his world was falling apart, Jeanneret came to life. The citizenry of La Chaux-de-Fonds, against L'Eplattenier's new section for having violated the traditional approach to art education, forced its dissolution. Plans for a building by Jeanneret to house that innovative institution would never see the light of day. His parents were becoming upset over problems with their house. And now Flanders had erupted in a military conflagration that threatened the fiber of everyday life. This was when the future Le Corbusier's first major innovation, the Dom-ino system, rose from the ashes.

2

Dom-ino was a form of housing conceived for the victims of war. Based on standard elements that could be combined quickly at low cost, it could exist anywhere.

The plight of people ravaged by the forces of destruction and suddenly left homeless offered Jeanneret the fresh start he craved, and he came up with a snappy, elegant idea that was totally original. The Dom-ino system is a structure of three parallel slabs, stacked at intervals like toasts in a club sandwich. The uppermost two slabs are supported by lithe columns of reinforced concrete; inside, the levels are joined by concrete stairs. These straightforward units have an airy, ethereal appearance. With their tensile lightness, they use the latest technology in materials and engineering. Their aesthetics are fresh and contemporary; every form is simplified and pure, virtually a Platonic ideal of its type.

The flat-roofed structures could theoretically be joined in infinite combinations; the columns were within the space and not in the walls.[4] Jeanneret planned entire Dom-ino complexes to replace areas that had been destroyed by the war. This early idea of mass production—dedicated to the well-being of all inhabitants, respectful of human scale—was to have echoes in the city planning with which he altered the face of civilization.

JEANNERET'S FRIEND Max du Bois worked with him on Dom-ino. Du Bois, from Le Locle, near La Chaux-de-Fonds, had known him since he was a toddler and was a key figure in the younger man's rise to success. An engineer in Paris, Du Bois attended to the technical details and development of Dom-ino, while Jeanneret masterminded its design; Du Bois also applied for its patent. Then Jeanneret developed grandiose ideas that the Dom-ino patent might be worth a lot of money and became suspicious that Du Bois would put everything in his own name. In fact, Du Bois, who had done the work mainly out of friendship, did not even have his name on the patent when it was received, but Jeanneret had by then damaged the friendship by accusing his helpful, more established colleague of selfish motives and insisting that no part of the authorship of Dom-ino be attributed to him. Dom-ino is one of many designs today associated with the name of Le Corbusier where credit should be shared; Du Bois was only the first of many people to feel that Le Corbusier erased his significance from history.

3

Jeanneret loathed what he considered the Swiss obsession with money: "Liveliness, originality, even wit are not Helvetian qualities to anything like the same degree as seriousness, conscientiousness, strength, clarity, and initiative—the sense of practice and of exploitation—altogether remarkable."[5] He considered himself as culpable as his fellow countrymen in having viewed war for its potential financial gain by joining the speculators who, as early as 1914, were imagining how they would heap profits during the inevitable period of reconstruction. He railed against this "civic consciousness built on the ruin of others. I yield to such consciousness. We spend hours in the speculators' offices, and we talk figures and realities."[6]

Following the demise of the new division, the local officials who, exceptionally, admired his work, tried to commission different projects, but he was too angry toward his former foes as well as toward himself to accept the offers. On November 28, 1914, he wrote Ritter, "My history of being-in-opposition has turned against me and disgusts me now. I have had valiant defenders and, the conspiracy having failed, I triumph, but with such a feeling of bitterness that I'll probably decide to send in my resignation."[7]

In Jeanneret's mind, everything became associated with the relationship to one's parents and home territory. He wrote: "A touching story: our little cat, the son of the one you saw, was given a month ago to some poor people on the west side of town who had asked for him; and after dinner today he turned up here, apparently guided by instinct, amazingly enough. He's taken up residence in his mother's bedroom, napping beside her. The minute his mother shows any sign of attention is followed by a session of tentative licking: the prodigal wants to nurse, and so the old woman's bourgeois peace is troubled; whereupon quarrels, unpleasantness, abandonment. Appearing so miraculously from so far away, the sad little cat recognizes the premises, jumps into his old basket (in which he was born), feels reassured, starts to play. He is terribly skinny, his fur matted; the tiny creature is quite melancholy, though at the age of wild frolics. . . . The old woman was annoyed and upset, and the little cat is gone again. Fascinating story! It moves me nonetheless, this cat business!"[8]

Not only did Le Corbusier always respond deeply to cats, dogs, birds, and donkeys—to their honesty and chicanery as much as their innocence—but he identified with these creatures of instinct, often wounded, always pure of heart. The affectionate, needy kitten, morose just at the stage of life when he should have been playing carefree, spurned by his own mother but desperate for her love, was Charles-Edouard Jeanneret's image of himself.

4

In June, Jeanneret handwrote and sent Ritter a three-page text called "First Step in a Residence." For this evocation of a salubrious dwelling, he delved into memories from Ema to Balkan villages to Athos. The goal—which was to permeate all of Le Corbusier's domestic architecture—was to sanctify the myriad acts of everyday existence. His idea derived from "the nostalgic architecture of the red rocks of Dalmatia; a distorted antiquity whose every theme is atrophied, accumulating symbolic motifs to excess. And this becomes an evocation, chalk-white and terra-cotta. Roman, Etruscan, Byzantine. Everything strong, rich in values suggested by great heights, and the violence of the volumes. A vestibule whose door opens onto a courtyard. Further suggestions of enormous volumes. The peristyle was of square columns, bristling out of the earth." There would be relief sculptures "suggesting good meals and high life. A tiled structure drowned in a big cement pool. . . . The ceiling simulates low, white beams separated by black intervals, and over each of the narrow doorways, an exaggeratedly prominent pediment, white with a black tympanum—which will be the *leitmotif* in the courtyard, though made of red terra-cotta in a whitewashed wall. This is what gives strength, freshness, height, and generous lodgings for people who love action and dreams."[9]

In this ideal residence, water would be everywhere. There would be a pool made of smooth marble and a tiled basin receiving the flow would emerge through six tiled channels in a niche on one side of the courtyard. "In the vestibule, almost all the reliefs are engraved in the mold, in the fashion of old Greek, Byzantine, Sassanian, and Etruscan coins."[10] This exotic vision of home conjured in 1915 has a luxuriance that, however concealed, underlay Le Corbusier's most machined buildings.

EARLY IN JUNE, Jeanneret went to the south of France to meet Auguste Perret. The first leg of the journey was a train from La Chaux-de-Fonds to Lausanne. Before boarding, a stranger approached and asked Jeanneret to take charge of a teenage girl taking the same trip. "I was introduced to her and then I was requested to be sure nothing happened to her," he later wrote.

He was bowled over by the adolescent's beauty: "I saw her for the first time, and perhaps for the first time as well I the solitary and hitherto unlikely connoisseur of women, found a depth, a tranquility, deep and distinctly apparent, a wealth of impressions leaping from the heart as well as from the lovely lips, charms as in a pretty round face, smooth and well-proportioned, and in gray eyes rimmed with ochre, clear and straightforward, all of the qualities which are not those of a doll but of a woman of ravishing sensibilities."[11]

Changing trains with his temporary ward in Lausanne, he witnessed a heartbreaking scene on the platform that both saddened him and awakened his voyeurism. A woman had accompanied her fiancé, a soldier, from Geneva to Lausanne, where he was being mobilized to Italy: "They were pressed close together against each other on the step of the railroad car, their faces constantly united, seizing, sucking, drinking each other, drenched with the young girl's slow tears. And long, sudden hugs, like bedroom recollections. Broken apart, having continued, having certainly given the totality of gifts in this last afternoon of the first stifling summer day, having pressed against each other with all their skin, with all their strength, in alternating anguish and delight, and the hideous suggestions of possible outcomes. The mother of the mobilized soldier was eagerly watching this supreme expression of her son's heart, whose last moments she reserved for herself. The train left. The girl beside me was weeping gently. I dared not look at her; I registered the faint sound of her tears. Bellegarde. Culloz. So many other tiny stations where the train kept stopping. Staring at people and weighing the silences, the smiles, and that friendliness of men over forty which one sees so much of everywhere, and then at each stop, seeing getting into the train not even accompanied, without embraces, without anything, one, two, five soldiers with red trousers. I was quite overcome. At each station, my nerves were at the edge of my eyelids. One of those famous artillerymen, a *chasseur alpin!* Very masculine, short, but tough and nervous. And all with such gentle expressions. Ambérieux. 'For the wounded': this young woman is selling short-stemmed roses, I walk off with mine, hide myself in my compartment, remembering those fragments of sentences I feel it necessary to write, for this is a unique year, and each episode of this country's history is like a temple corridor or gallery to me. The day before yesterday, I was telling the young Jewess about my desire for action and the cravings, which sometimes grew so intense to fight as well as the others. I am timid here, feeling so useless I only dare glance at them out of the corner of my eye, these *poilus* who are going back to the front—these *poilus,* fresh, clean shaven, well brushed, quite short: not husbands, not fathers, but mama's boys. That rose for the wounded I had bought is quite pale and not the royal flower of the lips. Its perfume is scarcely apparent, something like a big eglantine. The train pulls out."[12]

The "young Jewess" to whom he was referring was the girlfriend of his friend Charles Auguste Humbert. She was another of his friends' girlfriends who obsessed him while he still did not have one of his own: "with black hair, blue eyes, heavy eyelids, matte-white skin, she would make a wonderful seraglio odalisque, and were it not for La Chaux, I would declare myself the Sultan!"[13]

Continuing on his journey, Charles-Edouard Jeanneret became increasingly devastated by the wounded soldiers, young wives in mourning, and military men armed for battle. With his penchant for good machinery, he admired the weaponry—"The first bayonet. A terrible device at the end of a rifle. Long, black, splendidly sleeved"—but even if he respected the mechanism, he was shattered by its significance. "The afternoon Lyon–Marseille express, dear friend, is the train of women in mourning. Black crepe in almost every compartment. In the streets of Lyon, life was so normal that I returned to the station, curious about what had come over me this morning and annoyed with myself for still being a man of pathos, of immediate sensations, of indiscreet emotions. The train full of these women in mourning brought it all back."[14]

FACED WITH the human suffering wrought by the war, Jeanneret was anguished by Swiss neutrality and his own distance from the action he was witnessing in France but had essentially ignored at home. He lamented "a lack of awareness for which I cannot forgive myself. For after all, this country is at war, and it's been nine months now that I've imagined these horrors. . . . No one talks about it. Up till now, there's been no sign of a black soldier, a Gurka, nor a cannon. Now the train is full of soldiers. We share a car with officers. All quite clean and calm, very calm. They're about to do their fortnight in barracks! Is that what war is?"[15]

As the train wound its way south, and he scribbled away at this twenty-eight-page letter to William Ritter, Jeanneret's flickering mind jumped from the human drama to the changing landscape outside the train window:

> Here we have it! Classical lands! It begins before Orange, with ruins clinging to an ochre pinnacle; there was a stone church with a tiny germinated window; there were whole mountains covered with glistening gorse, the first olive trees, the cypresses, and since the sky is full of melting clouds, it is van Gogh before Cézanne. Then, to the left, the last Alps, strangely silhouetted like cumulus clouds in a stormy sky on a stage set of the Vieux Colombier. Then: the gray walls, the pink earth, the gray olive trees, and all of a sudden, as a kind of hors-d'oeuvre, a huge bed of the most radiant pink and blue foxgloves. . . .
>
> But back to van Gogh. Under the steely sky, the writhing cypresses; the gamut of the intensest emerald: green-green-green, no black, no red; yes, one red roof. . . . Then van Gogh, the drawings . . . : wheat fields, oats, vineyards, olive trees, fruit trees, vegetables in geometric patches. . . .
>
> Cézanne will not be at the party today. The "motif" is not here. It's true, Monsieur Cézanne does not do "skies with pale gray mixed into the blue," so today there will be no painting the earth of Provence, whose soul belongs to a man of the north, his pathetic passion so imperiously interposed between us.[16]

Even as he failed to make sense, the power of color on his brain and his fascination with the vision of great and radical artists was clear. He then noted the saline and eucalyptus smells in the air. Recalling a large bouquet of anemones he had arranged the day before, he launched into a diatribe against geraniums and a commentary on the sweet smell of roses in the warm air, which led him to memories of Mount Athos. "The flora, the sensation, the smell, the evocation of the mornings on Mount Athos where the sea, as here, was always present, but larger because we were seeing it from higher up, but paler and more intoxicating because the season was August instead of June. And because we had the recollection of having seen the islands as red, while they are green, and because we were after all in Greece itself, while here it is only Magna Graecia."[17]

Then, at long last, the train brought Jeanneret—and, we presume, the teenage girl of whom he had taken charge—to the Mediterranean port that ultimately was one of the most important places in his life: "A stir and a rising of the waves in sparkling sheaves, a spreading apostrophe. Marseille! Marseille!"[18]

5

Jeanneret's reunion with Auguste Perret in the salubrious setting of Provence made him burst with joy. They talked animatedly about Paris and the new ways of seeing that were being promulgated there. The reborn Jeanneret reversed himself about Cubism. Previously he had disparaged the artistic movement recently launched by Braque and Picasso; now he was at home with its multiple ways of seeing at once: "Let's hear it for cubists: let's understand everything the world offers by way of 'fantasy,' 'evocation,' 'spirit,' and everything the world has to offer aside from photography and banality and ready-made vision."[19]

Jeanneret wrote Ritter that he greatly admired Perret's Théâtre des Champs-Elysées and regretted not having been able to accept his former boss's invitation to return to Paris and work on it: "As far as I'm concerned, it's the best piece of architecture in a long time. Auguste Perret has no diploma, he tells me. His thoughts are permanently molded, like reinforced concrete."[20] Here was a role model to replace L'Eplattenier. Modern technique, steadfast resolve, no official credentials: these were the ingredients of genius.

The halcyon setting lent magic to their reunion: "But Marseille, gateway to the east! . . . A city of life, swarming life. . . . A city of fortresses and a city of peoples. The empire reigns at the gates of the port, and the empire is all of Europe. The Hotel de Ville is at the very least the Great Khan, China, and the Indies. It is the port of masks, the sea glimpsed beyond the forts, a second Attica, Magna Graecia. . . . A port, but what a port! Negroes, ships, waves, fish with fantastic scales, shellfish, masked crowds, Chinamen, Gurkas, and Kamerat!"[21] The love affair with that exotic seaside city was, after yet another world war, to culminate in one of Le Corbusier's masterpieces.

6

Back in La Chaux-de-Fonds, the twenty-seven-year-old worked on a series of interiors where the lacquered inlay and other bows to tradition came to represent "corruption of the most banal sort and the most vulgar."[22] Then, in August, he returned to Paris.

As usual, his mind was full of contradictions. He wrote Ritter, "What a paradox this war is, this mass uprising. Yet only man is so rich a marvel that he includes all consolations. Paris, a harmonious city. This war has destroyed the old sense of greatness. It is very harmonious here. But the city, all cities prove to me that we are living on conventions: the convention of an old and absurdly idiotic abode."[23]

Humankind appalled him: "But the contortions, the grimaces of Paris! If you saw the faces here, the whole greedy and insane swarm, the cruel egoism: life as a funnel down which one slides to the depths."[24] Yet the French, compared to the Germans, gave him cause for hope: "there are many flagrant proofs of this people's charming and serious ingenuity—much more profound than across the Rhine—which frequently exalts me and gives me the courage to follow my star."[25] Even in his rage and confusion, Jeanneret's exaltation and inner strength were returning as he zeroed in on the idea that that star was to make cities that were "explicitly modern."[26]

XI

1

> He did not wish to lose any time in putting his plan into effect, for he could not but blame himself for what the world was losing by his delay, so many were the wrongs that were to be righted, the grievances to be redressed, the abuses to be done away with, and the duties to be performed.
>
> — CERVANTES, *Don Quixote*

In Paris, Jeanneret stayed with Max Du Bois. In the course of the visit, he met Aristide Maillol, considered the greatest sculptor alive. In that first encounter, Maillol was making a stone wall. If Jeanneret's account can be trusted, the sculptor praised Jeanneret's architecture, although he could have known it only from hearsay or drawings or a few photos, since nothing had as yet been published. Jeanneret began to dream of making a building for Maillol's work.

Aristide Joseph Bonaventure Maillol was Jeanneret's senior by twenty-six years. He was the colorful sort of character who would, life long, appeal to Le Corbusier. Born on a farm near the small port of Banyuls-sur-Mer, Maillol had grown up admiring a smuggler grandfather, had been expelled from boarding school, and—after showing his work to Jean-Léon Gérôme, a Beaux-Arts academician, and being told he knew nothing whatsoever—had jumped at the chance to make art in his own way.

After war broke out in 1914, Maillol had buried his statues to protect them against enemy bombs. That act led to Maillol's being accused of spying for the enemy. A public prosecutor issued a search warrant to try to find grounds for arresting Maillol for treason, and, although the investigating judges dismissed the charges, a mob burned Maillol's workshop.

When Jeanneret met Maillol, he felt immediate sympathy for someone he considered, like himself, society's victim. And he admired Maillol's robust, overtly sensual sculptures, which were like spirited fertility symbols.

On the second and third of August, Jeanneret stayed at Maillol's house in

Marly-le-Roy, not far from Versailles. It was the setting of a great sexual awakening. The sculptor himself was not, however, present. Jeanneret wrote up what occurred in an account full of literary flourishes that he sent to William Ritter. Titled "*Grandeur et Servitude . . . ,*" it began, "There stands the house that Maillol built the year before the war. He did everything himself: plans, financing, supervision, employees: 15,000 Swiss francs is a lot for such mean walls, and the house is little more than a shed but so agreeably arranged. Untrained architects always have a verve of their own, and it's good Maillol didn't seek professional help."[1]

The visitor from La Chaux-de-Fonds admired the carefully chosen mixture of the ancient and modern objects: "In the large room downstairs was an old, Flemish (?) tapestry on the wall: a wonderful effect, something like Bonnard, something like Gauguin." Jeanneret responded viscerally to the sculpture—"one of those powerful figures by Phidias at the Parthenon"—and Maillol's plaster for " 'Pomona' . . . with her apples in her hands, the tits even more beautiful as fruits go, her huge thighs." This voluptuous piece and the woman who had modeled for it were his ideal type: "A Spanish woman from Banyuls, actually more powerful than that, with a chest out to here! Well, really something. The Pomona, still in plaster, was lying on the ground, maybe two-thirds life size: amazing." There was also an "admirable Gauguin, perfectly hung near the big glassed-in area (the former studio) where the fig tree outside presses its leaves against the panes, creating a green undersea atmosphere where the green Gauguin seascape of waves filling the whole frame sings as it rises up the long pink snake of beach."[2]

Unbridled colors, the moving evocation of the sea, the glories of nature: again Charles-Edouard Jeanneret's eyes were opened.

HAVING SET the scene, Jeanneret introduces one of its key players. He is Gaston Béguin, from Locle, one town away from La Chaux-de-Fonds, to whom Jeanneret gives a Latin-style Rabelaisian name: "*Gastonibus Béguinus,* a Calvinist Swiss, from Locle, models a bust of Jeanne, Maillol's niece. Soon she looks like a frog, so strongly are the planes, spheres, prisms, etc. brought out; a tin frog made by a roofer. Was this the influence of cubism? Indeed, Maillol might have reason to complain when he comes back from Banyuls."[3]

Jeanneret then interrupts his account of Béguin at work to extol the charms of Maillol's own oversized, well-endowed nudes. These sculptures, with their capacious bosoms and ample hips, exemplified a Mediterranean sense of pleasure he found irresistible. "This is certainly the Olympus of monumental, earth-mother buttocks, the breasts that fill your hand." The *Pomona* was particularly inspiring: "I'll take this torso and put it in my bedroom. That would give me a splendid Maillol of esthetic value equal to the financial."[4]

The Swiss Calvinist Béguin is ill at ease in the luxuriant scenario of Maillol's studio: "No, everything cracks and crumbles under the shed roof; this autumn, apples from the apple trees between the breasts of the huge, broken torso, fill the valley of her thighs, a new Pomona that rots, bringing to an end this splendid health concretized so magnanimously. It inspires serious thoughts of theft and a new concept of others' possessions. Gaston Béguin's role is not an easy one, having to observe these slow deaths."[5]

Again Jeanneret jumps from describing the awkward Béguin, now to amplify the merits of an artist who lived simply while cultivating monumental work: "The trees here are quite small and cover the ground. In fact, everything is small, the fruit, the cottages; the suburbs of Paris know nothing of the *Kolossal* and Aristide Maillol; 'the world's greatest sculptor,' according to him, lives in a little house whose modesty reassures, comforts, and inspires thoughts of the futile and disappointing pomps of this world. The huge thighs of the torso of Phidias afford an adequate sensation of grandeur. And such grandeur is superior in terms of reverie. This odd combination of a Parthenonic Hellas corresponding to Hymettus and the Pentelic heights, of the Gulf of Salamis and the Peloponnesian rumps, ever so gently caressing the reveries of a man lost in the outskirts of the huge capital, in a minor jungle of sweet fruits in endless profusion."[6]

Jeanneret turns his sights to Jeanne, the wife of Gaspard Maillol, the sculptor's nephew, who worked for him. Maillol was sculpting her. She is a "lovely young woman of magisterial bearing, shoulders as broad as her smile, and God knows voluptuous, to cut short the definition; in any case her lips are distinctly sinuous and the high cheekbones make her eyes squint in a countenance quite used to receiving *à la française* its constant coating of powder."[7]

Then, in his most competitive voice, Jeanneret deprecates a portrait Gaspard had painted of this beautiful woman to whom he had the good fortune to be married: "The gentleman who painted this must be as coarse as that famous brown and yellow oilcloth that covers the walls of the poor of Paris, as I discovered as a student in the hallways and W.C.s of cheap furnished rooms and on the partition walls of the blocks of slums still being torn down today. Poor powerful Jeanne whose behind or whose pink cretonne gowns serve as a pretext for this fake Douanier Rousseau."[8]

The sublime Jeanne is not only sexy but unpretentious and easy to talk to, as opposed to "Gastonibus Béguinus who does his little-king number. I cast him as the perfect concierge of Aristide Maillol and company—you can't imagine the royal airs he puts on, clattering heels and high-pitched voice. . . . Certainly Gaston, in this household abandoned by the husband 'who's always in his warehouse' (a malingerer, a southern no-good, etc., etc.)—certainly Gaston gropes the girls, greedily steals the jam off Jeanne's lips, etc. . . . etc. . . . Oh well." Jeanneret describes Jeanne grotesquely but according to his own taste: "She's changed her dress and has greased her lips with the most generous helping of gooseberry jam."[9]

THE ACTION of the lubricious account really begins when Jeanneret goes to bed. There is the sound of a high wind in the surrounding orchard, of apples falling everywhere. Maillol's bedroom is below. With palpable excitement, Jeanneret reports to Ritter,

> The big bed of the world's greatest sculptor is in the room below mine. Banyuls is far from here, at the edge of the Golfe de Lion, and Maillol sleeps there tonight, having ended his day with "a flask of old wine," apparently quite conjugally. Which doesn't stop the whispering from keeping me awake, up here: Gaston has let me have his bed, and uses his master's. . . .
>
> This silence. Then, in the wind which gets in down below, a series of *ha ha ha's* . . . modest at first, then faster, then panting. Go for it, Gaston! Then it stops short, and Gaston is heard no more. Now his voice sounds in a lower register, *ha ha ha, Oh ho!* And then, if you know our Gaston as the little bull of Locle, comes that decisive, definitive, closing *Rrrrhan!* an exploding shell. No resistance. It's all there. Gaston has uttered his *Rrrrhan!* He's content. . . .
>
> The center of the house, the sanctuary of the life of the house: here, tonight, the sacrifice is consummated. . . . So be it, the heart has its reasons. Gaspard, poor devil, in his office![10]

Gaston Béguin—a rake from eastern Switzerland at the start of an adventure—is Jeanneret's invented name for himself. It's an obtuse tale, but what is clear is that the lovely Jeanne was in the house while her husband was still at work and that Charles-Edouard Jeanneret delighted in writing about his own orgasm.

2

In the fall and winter of 1915–1916, Jeanneret continued to work on private villas and apartments in Switzerland. Yet he felt as if he was stagnating at best. He was chronically exhausted and began to lose so much weight that his parents considered him ill. He saw himself as a victim, scorned and mocked by everyone: "There are a number of us these days who believe in the evils of the world, and worse still, in the insuperable obstacles that do you in, when everything gives you the lie and points the finger of scorn."[11] In March 1916, he wrote Ritter, "I've been feeling so depressed, so impotent, so lacking in all the resources of my craft, that everything seemed quite futile."[12] His mother often told him, "You are not kind," to which he responded that she knew him well.[13]

Then, one late April night, everything began to change with a dream. He entitled his account to Ritter, "Young Charles-Edouard Jeanneret takes the cherry of the virgin Marguerite de Nemours."[14] Even if it occurred only in his sleep, it was a momentous event.

The setting in which twenty-eight-year-old Jeanneret pictured himself taking Marguerite de Nemours for his sexual pleasure fueled his later urbanism. It was a city where the arrangement of living and working spaces facilitated the sort of encounters that only an ideal urban environment made possible. The dream began there on a Saturday evening at the hour when everyone was leaving work in factories: "The proletarian hosts have already dispersed. One crosses the town. At the South Gate, one takes the boulevard to the right. On the left side, apartment buildings five to eight stories high form a square. Good God, I've got to stop!"[15]

What makes him halt is a sight that recalls certain lewd paintings of Goya. A profusion of bare women are standing on the balconies of every floor: "Naked women busy with their toilette: bowls of water, combs, brushes; the one on the nearest balcony scrapes the scabs off her filthy thighs—Francion version—I glance out of the corner of my eye, as one does when two dogs are going at it."[16] The term "Francion" referred to the libertine hero of an early-seventeenth-century French comic novel; in search of love, Francion was a character beloved to Jeanneret.

He then saw something "staggering . . . zany. At the top of the pediment of the tallest house, in the middle of the facades, Marguerite Frochaux representing the figure of Justice holding a mirror. Exactly like the Cabanel version—the one with a famous, prominent, and glistening hip, and on the side of her raised arm that wonderful straight line from her big toe up under the armpit all the way to the mirror. Next to her, Marie Frochaux represents 'The Wave.' Not a shred of body hair on either one. All the balconies are swarming with figures. It's mythology come alive."[17]

Marguerite and her fiancé are seated at a piano, performing their own composition—"the mystery of St. Sebastien"—which Jeanneret hears in his dream. During the "poem symphonique," Jeanneret becomes so captivated by Marguerite's alabaster body that he is sexually aroused in his sleep. "Marguerite, ashamed, lowers her lovely arms over her sex, which she fails to see is not in the part she plays. Historical exactitude! Well, what can I do? Marguerite, your body's pallor is suitable for martyrdom. I'm actually beginning to get a hard-on. Maurice Barrès, that Sodoma!"[18]

Following this swipe at the monarchist Barrès, a hero to the rightist movement Action Française, the vision evolves into a sadomasochistic drama with Jeanneret in the role of harem master: "I unroll all seven yards of my Turkish girdle and command: 'Raise your martyr's arms; I, the executioner, shall conceal your sex. I shall bind your hips with Orient wool.' I am of the opinion that at this moment a screen would descend, shielding the public's eyes widened by expectation from the scene of the binding. The bridegroom acquiesces, the screen appears, separating the inspired musician from the body of his beautiful beloved."[19]

The naked Marguerite succumbs to his will: "I have begun binding one thigh, then the other. I return to the first, then to the latter. Her hips widen. The girdle describes a figure-eight, which it repeats. I have not passed my woolen strip over the belly nor over both thighs together: one after the other. Marguerite seems moved by my presence, as am I by the odor of her body. 'Raise your arms, St. Sebastian, against the trunk of the tree!' I attach her hands to the lowest branches."[20]

Different music now accompanies the fantasy: " 'Put your ankles together; your martyred body weighs heavily on these columns to which I have also tied two heavy astral lamps.' I bind your martyred ankles. Shriek of oboes, glissando of flutes, the harp lacerated."[21]

Jeanneret becomes even more excited and irrational in describing the subsequent events with a panoply of literary flourishes: "The sky is entirely pink, reddening with the final reverberation of this splendid early-spring twilight above the factory gates at Landeron this Saturday evening. Marguerite bound, Marguerite at my mercy. My bow is drawn, intoxicated archer. Your torso struggles, St. Sebastian. I embrace it, adolescent; I force open the propylaeum. The girdle was a lure. The figure-eight had a defect in its armor."[22]

Jeanneret then hears the plaintive cries of Marguerite's fiancé, who is seated, out of breath, at the piano. The atmosphere becomes a mixture of guilt and high drama. The poor fellow inquires desperately.

"Oh, Marguerite, what ails you? My music, your nerves?"

"No, my bridegroom, the gentile's javelin has pierced me through!" she replies.

The scenario is again accompanied by a shift in the music, which has the overstated melodrama of a silent-movie score: "The piano resumes, panting, suffering, dying away. . . . Go to it, Léon!"[23]

At this point, Jeanneret awakes, having had a wet dream: "I awakened bathed in the blood of my blood." This last sentence was accompanied by a drawing of a maze of curlicues from which a small bird emerges in flight. The image suggests pubic hair with a sperm in flight from it: ejaculate as annunciation. Under the drawing, he has written, "Behold, dear Monsieur, this vile pornography."[24] Again, he was determined to put his pleasure on display.

AFTER DESIGNING a movie theatre but losing money on it, and then feuding with a collaborator who worked on two houses with him, Jeanneret, again desperate to leave La Chaux-de-Fonds, resorted more and more to fantasy. "Ever since I learned that Europa was raped on the Bosporus," he wrote, "the myth has struck me as full of life. . . . A dream which finds its victim, and away we go! O how I'd like to leave for an unknown shore: the flood, the naked bodies, that woman on the bull's shiny rump; a swoon, a regret, but so many hopes, and then the notion that after all one might take the risk."[25]

The time had come to head for that unknown shore and become one of the naked bodies. He proposed a solution to his own anguish: "Get some water on your body and get out."[26] The sense of duty to his parents and his hometown was to imprison him no longer. Charles-Edouard Jeanneret was ready to leap and become Le Corbusier.

XII

1

The milestone of Jeanneret's thirtieth birthday was looming (see color plate 1). When he was invited to Frankfurt to work on some municipal building projects, he accepted. But at the passport office in Neuchâtel, as he stood at the wooden counter awaiting the visa stamp, he changed his mind.

Having walked into that office to gain the right to move to Germany, he requested a passport for an unlimited time period in France. The change of heart took him by surprise, but knowing that he could count on Max Du Bois to help set him up in Paris, he had no doubt. Du Bois had forgiven Jeanneret for his treatment of him on the Dom-ino project, and repeatedly insisted that he was destined to perish if he did not leave their stultifying natal city and move to Paris permanently. Du Bois had founded the Société d'Application du Béton Armé (SABA) to promote the use of reinforced concrete, and he wanted Jeanneret to join him in making this durable and efficient new material available through mass production.

All that was left for Jeanneret to do was raise some funds and pack up. After returning to La Chaux-de-Fonds, he arranged a bank loan, which was granted because of fees he was still owed for the movie theatre. He also found three local businessmen who gave him a small amount of capital to invest on their behalf in new enterprises associated with the construction business. With twenty thousand francs—roughly the equivalent of thirty thousand dollars today—and a couple of suitcases, he again took the train to Paris. For the rest of his life, the French capital served as his home and the campaign headquarters for his battle to change all human habitation.

2

The Paris Jeanneret encountered when he arrived on February 9, 1917, had been torn asunder by aerial bombardment. Many people were at the brink of starvation, and everyone felt constant danger. But to the young man from the Alps, the French metropolis was "the crucible, the diapason, and the torch."[1] He knew it had been the source for Géricault, Degas, Ingres, Manet, Courbet, Monet, Seurat, and Matisse. He was determined to join their ranks.

Jeanneret stayed in Max Du Bois's fifth-floor walk-up apartment. In his later reconstruction of his personal history, Le Corbusier presented himself as the intrepid country boy who went to the big city to make his way aided by nobody and who launched himself in solitude. He would have people think that, entirely on his own, he found a place to live, began an architecture practice, became a businessman, and located clients. He obfuscated the central role of Du Bois—who not only put a roof over his head and gave him a job with SABA but also introduced him to wealthy Swiss and members of the French business community.

While in Du Bois's flat, Jeanneret set up a small office in a former kitchen and maid's room on the seventh floor of a charmless apartment building on the rue de Belzunce, near the Gare du Nord. It was a "dirty hole," but the rent was cheap, and within five days he stripped the rough hovel into a fresh, clean space.[2] "I have 'boned' my workplace with complete success," he wrote his parents, jubilant at having cleansed it of its layers of excess and cut through to the structure. In these rudimentary headquarters, he began work as a consultant for SABA.

Next, Jeanneret found his own place to live. This apartment, which he was to inhabit for seventeen years, was, like his office, high up in former servants' quarters. But the building—at 20 rue Jacob—had far more charm. The narrow and quiet rue Jacob was one of the most lovely streets of St. Germain-des-Prés, near the Seine, in a neighborhood populated by artists and writers and full of small bistros and inviting cafés. Number twenty, a distinguished seventeenth-century residence built around a cobblestone courtyard with fragrant linden trees, was the former town house of Adrienne Lecouvreur (whose name may have subtly been one of the many factors contributing to the one Jeanneret soon chose for himself). To reach his small space there, he ascended an oval spiral staircase constructed in dark wood. Under the mansard roof, surrounded by plaster that dated back to the reign of Louis XIV, he in time dreamed up his streamlined modernism.

He was enthralled to be in a space that had been inhabited by the colorful Lecouvreur, an immensely popular actress early in the eighteenth century. Her romance with Maurice de Saxe, a distinguished nobleman in the court of Louis XIV, was the subject of a poem by her friend Voltaire, as well as of an opera and a play. It ended tragically—Lecouvreur was apparently poisoned, at age thirty-seven, by her rival in de Saxe's life, the duchess of Bouillon, and the Catholic Church denied her a Christian burial—but

At 20 rue Jacob, late 1920s. Photo by Brassaï

Jeanneret often referred to the golden time when de Saxe constructed a small temple that still stood in the garden. Jeanneret sketched it for Ritter and wrote him, "I'm thrilled to be able to paint the roof tiles of Maurice de Saxe. Shall I manage to live worthily in this residence?"[3]

The reality of Jeanneret's own life was less ideal. The rooms at 20 rue Jacob were sometimes bitterly cold, and no heating fuel was available. He had scarcely enough food. But, through the tricks of art, he transformed the garret. To warm up the flat, he painted on one wall a landscape of a tropical scene with palm trees bathed by sunlight.[4] Visual illusion provided salvation and joy.

3

Jeanneret became absorbed by the prostitutes he studied and coveted in the Métro. He was a connoisseur of them, even though he considered the women mostly unobtainable. For Ritter and Czadra, Jeanneret sketched the profile of one who had bold features like a Greek warrior's, her hat and coiffure an exotic blend of pouf and ornament that he rendered in elaborate detail. He wrote, "Yesterday in the tram at La Roquette I saw two whores from the brothels out there, one of whom was a marvel; I'm eliminating the first page of this letter, or rather I'm completing it by this notation: the Lord has created a lovely animal."[5]

But sex was often a struggle for him: "The act of love is rather complicated to perform; it requires special circumstances. I no longer manage to have my old magnificent erections, and I fall back—in a fatally Oriental impulse—on visions of Spanish fly."[6] Jeanneret said "fatally" because he knew that, while a small amount of the famous aphrodisiac could help stimulate the blood flow as well as the kidneys, too much of the insect's venom could kill someone.

A few weeks later, however, he saw, on the Métro, a prostitute with whom he had had sex. In one of his most obtuse soliloquies yet, he told Ritter that the encounter made him realize that he preferred the simpler women in cheap bordellos to the higher class of streetwalker whom he had drawn: "How I hate these cows! This is the second in months. I'm quite indifferent to all of them. What I lack is a sense of the 'minaret.' You know: the minaret rises solitary above the mosque, and pierces nothing but the sky. You tell me I need a Grand Passion. Thanks a lot. Except for the selfish pleasures of the heart, a woman is nothing but a *bête d'apéritif.* In which case I prefer the brothel, simply the animal and the water closet. I have close friends. O Adrienne [Lecouvreur], unless you manage to reincarnate yourself, your Maurice [de Saxe] will not be wearing out too many bedsprings under your alcove roof, well tiled though it be. In the calm of this garden and the solitude of this empty house, there's room for the eloquent explanation of two storms; I don't dissociate love from the tempest and from danger. Beyond a sinuous mouth and a pair of eyes, I require a chin and a forehead."[7]

Jeanneret began writing a diary, which he sent in periodic installments to Ritter. In one entry, he confessed the problems of making love to these women: "But a man can't give his body to these easy girls, for he feels something like fear. There's no lust, only pity and affection, and instead of casting your seed into this public sewer, you'd like to caress these creatures, caress them gently. A lot they'd care for that!"[8]

At the end of January, Jeanneret went with Max Du Bois and his friend Marcel Rey to the Casino de Paris to see "Les dancing Girls" in *The Flags of the Entente.* An all-Negro orchestra played. Jeanneret was enraptured by their beauty and raw force. The women cavorting onstage impressed him much as the Pisa altarpiece and Balkan pottery had: "There was Gaby Deslys, whom I remember three days later as a pink vision of magnificent flesh, an image of primeval life. Idiot movements, whorehouse *plastique,* or more often just bourgeois asshole tricks. But flesh . . . but sap . . . Panting marble . . . Who cares how stupid she is, Gaby Deslys represents seduction for a sad and solitary heart like mine."[9]

Yet for all his ardor, he remained more the observer than a participant. He wrote to Ritter, "There's a lot of Woman around, as ever. How stupid all these men seem, who just because they're sitting around a piece of meat think they're becoming kindred spirits! But of course it's for the sake of the nozzle this crowd gathers, each man wild to satisfy his brute need, his vital egoism. How stupid a man is in the last analysis! Yet what a piece of work is man."[10]

In a diary entry a few weeks later, he linked a town center he loved with its beautiful women. "Pisa is surely one of the towns I love most. Life there seemed to flow slowly enough to let me enjoy the centuries as they pass. And Orcagna drew unforgettable women there."[11] From there he jumped to comments on Paul Poiret's coiffures for music halls. Almost as much as he liked the Pisa cathedral, Jeanneret was fascinated by the ostrich feathers arranged like a peacock tail on Gaby Deslys's head, which nearly doubled the height of her body. For months, he painted these women. But that was the extent of it: "What I need is to caress someone: my life is murderous," Jeanneret reported in the diary he eventually sent to Ritter.[12]

Jeanneret was vaguer to his parents about the simultaneous attraction and repulsion he felt to prostitutes, but he wrote them as well about his struggles: "Yet this expression which I understand but which I fail to estimate properly, alas, for lack of having enjoyed that bittersweet fruit: the wild distress when there is passion in carnality, the thirst of one's entire being, the indispensable presence, copenetration, reabsorption of every molecule."[13] The allure of "that bittersweet fruit" haunted him.

THE ACT OF LOVE and the making of buildings were inextricably linked in Charles-Edouard Jeanneret's mind. Going to brothels and realizing architecture required similar determination; the challenge was to get from the fantasy stage to efficacy. In his diary to Ritter, Jeanneret wrote, "I'm an architect, a builder. I like my drawing tables on their trestles, my telephone, my typewriter. I like the hiss of automobile tires and the clamor of the street. I'm not a castrato. I'll pay my visits to that seething Montmartre sloping up toward Saint-Augustin. I won't withdraw from life, I'll do what everyone else does. And I'll rent a big room, a workroom in which my furniture will shrink to nothing, and then the big walls will impose a grand design on me, in which my chaos will espouse the kinds of violence oriented toward a geometry as deliberately inscribed as the wheels and pulleys of a machine, and with the same lucidity, the same fantasy, the same concision."[14]

Determined as he was to show his virility—to go to "that seething Montmartre" meant frequenting brothels—he couldn't bring it off: "I complain: this is ridiculous. I had gone to the restaurant to pick up a girl. There are no girls left. My celibacy weighs on me." On the Easter Monday when he recorded this, he was drinking cheap Chianti: "My life flows past, stupid, monotonous, tense, alone, unfortunately. . . . Now I'm at home drinking some kind of nasty alcoholic brew; I've turned on all my lamps. It's cheerful here, this nest of mine—the former residence of a maid of Adrienne Lecouvreur. I'm alone, except for the mice doing their minuet on my ceiling."

He envied an acquaintance who had "a mistress who is a real woman; he's beyond me, I'm isolated, wounded, I suffer. I see the irony, the grotesquerie of life; I'd like to experience its beauty, its energy, along with this springtime, this joy, this *living* in spite of everything, this song of the sparrows, these skies of hope. My mind abandons itself to melancholy and assigned projects. How I long for the release of a natural, beneficent flowering."

Jeanneret prized sexual potency as a mark of greatness. "To have or not to have . . . an erection. He who gets hard and stays with it is a man capable of strength, still a beast deserving to live in the sun." Swiss men, he claimed, were eunuchs, but now he had left their neutered land behind: "I'm telling you this because it's true. Since I get my erections normally, I believe in life, desire it, and this spring I even have the impression that the desired act is fulfilled and that I'm entering the CITY. I'm through with what's back there. . . . I was a child of La Chaux-de-Fonds, brought up far from life and in fear (in the fear of God, they have effrontery to say). . . . I'm entering the age of realization. . . . Now I'm a man nearly six feet tall named Jeanneret who's an architect, who has no diploma, who's capable of solving a problem and achieving his goal."[15]

It was not to be as easy as he hoped.

4

At the end of April 1917, Jeanneret sent a postcard to Ritter from Chartres. It was of a single thirteenth-century figure from the North Portal, a solemn woman, looking downward, carved with great dignity, who represented "la Vie Contemplative."[16]

On this card showing another tormented observer frozen into inaction, Jeanneret wrote, "Yes. Alas, one must look ahead and fulfill one's destiny. This cathedral is as much the house of the Devil as of God. The tragic heroism of these stones deserves a portico of hell; here, in a titanic effort, man expresses his own damnation. No one could imagine Chartres from looking at other cathedrals: the foundations are like the successive movements of a symphony and of fatally incomplete thunders: there is moonlight in these stones, and an unheard uproar."[17]

World events were making his incertitude worse. In February, the Bolsheviks had overthrown the monarchy in Russia. On April 6, the United States had entered the war in Europe. No place seemed stable, even if the epidemic of mutiny in France had been ended when Henri Pétain, the new commander in chief and future Maréchal, and Georges Clemenceau, the new premier, restored order.

Yet three days after sending that postcard from Chartres, Jeanneret was so enthusiastic about the richness of human history and the bounty of nature that he was displaying symptoms of what today is called "rapid cycling." He wrote Ritter and Czadra a single, rambling, manic sentence:

> Dear friends. It's the fault of too many buds bursting into bloom outside the open windows, of too many branches shaken by a warm wind—old branches, as old as Maurice de Saxe, above the flowerbeds entirely covered with ivy; of too many irresistible appeals from the old bridges of Androuet du Cerceau, with their cornices of flags and banners, their opulence of royal pomp; of too many quais between which flows a river as joyous as silk—quais where once again the great trees spread their limbs wide in a touching blue sky; of that overpowering murmur I hear from my desk, coming from far away—I hear it coming from the other side of my wall, coming from distant walls to strange crenellations against a sky that is pink at this time of day—that murmur in which I can make out an occasional raucous call of the bargemen on the river, under the bridges; of too many sweet, sad impressions which drown me quite "dolorously" because it is really too beautiful and because a man cannot be happy with a tangible and present happiness, and because there pass through the air shudders of unknown and troubling future things, inevitably sad since I feel I cannot measure my happiness, that I lack an inner vitality strong enough to silence those far-off enthusiastic branches: all too often the calm of my walls yields to the raucous call of the passing Unknown, and as I follow the flood of a destiny to which I attribute so many surprises, I proceed beyond my crenellations one after the next, toward the boundaries of nations, and toward places where there are people I think of and whom I can beguile with such spleens as these. That is why I have waited so long to write.
>
> Man is very much alone.[18]

The frenzy of enthusiasm required an outlet if he was to overcome that solitude. He continued: "I feel that I cannot discern my happiness, that I lack a soul generous enough to deck my heart with flags." Sooner than he imagined, however, he was to channel his ecstasy into architecture.

5

On the evening of May 17, 1917, Jeanneret went to a performance of the Ballets Russes at the Théâtre du Châtelet that, in retrospect, stood out as a milestone of modern cultural history. When the dancers from Moscow, impeccably trained in the imperial tradition, soared above the Parisian stage to the strains of music as advanced as the latest progress in air travel, the possibilities of human motion took a new dimension.

That night, an art form that had been the precinct of the elite embraced mass culture. This revolution, a triumph of modernism, thrilled the onlooker from La Chaux-de-Fonds. That it was loudly booed and brought on the rage and opprobrium of the sleepy, reactionary bourgeoisie enhanced rather than diminished his pleasure.

The ballet, called *Parade,* reflected a radical preference for settings like fairgrounds and the circus tent. It moved as far afield from the refinement of the Bolshoi and its ballerinas enacting fairy tales in tutus as Jeanneret had when he shifted his sights from the splendors of Versailles to humble dwellings in Balkan villages. The new ballet had been the idea of Jean Cocteau. In 1915, Cocteau and the composer Erik Satie created *Parade* for the dynamic Russian choreographer Sergey Diaghilev. Pablo Picasso designed the sets and costumes.

Parade threw off the shackles of elegance and embraced the tawdry atmosphere of the music hall. Three characters, ten feet tall, became moving skyscrapers; one turned into a tree alongside a boulevard while another was a horse. Two acrobats flew into the air, and a Chinese conjuror removed an egg from his pigtail, ate it, and then discovered it on the toe of his shoe. An American girl rode a bicycle, danced a ragtime, imitated Charlie Chaplin, snapped photos, boxed, and went after an imaginary thief with a revolver.

Charles-Edouard Jeanneret was fired up. But most of the audience was incensed. When the performance ended, several threatened the producer physically. Many shouted "Filthy *Boches*"—a swipe at Germans uttered often during the war. As tempers flared, the poet Guillaume Apollinaire took the stage. Recently wounded in battle, he had a bandage wrapped around his forehead. He was dressed in his military uniform and wore his

Croix de Guerre. The irate crowd had no choice but to accord him the respect warranted by a hero and calmed down. Apollinaire urged them to be more tolerant.

For the program that evening, this proponent of modernism had written an essay entitled "*Parade ou l'esprit nouveau.*" Apollinaire animatedly defined that "esprit nouveau" as the means by which art was successfully combined with the most recent progress made by science and industry. In its brazen simplicity, "l'esprit nouveau" became Jeanneret's gospel. He enthusiastically scribbled notes in the program and sketched some of the sets. The élan of *Parade* and the boldness of Apollinaire's text signified the future.

6

At the beginning of July, Jeanneret told Ritter, in scintillating detail, "the epilogue to 'the night at Aristide Maillol's': Today Aristide Maillol told me: 'I kicked Gastonibus out, because the worst of it, after living four years in my house, was that Gastonibus, instead of vanishing somewhere into the crowds of Paris, came to rest in my own niece's house, a house that belongs to me." Jeanneret reiterated the horror of the lovers using Maillol's own bed, instructing, "Reread for memory's sake in what bed this all took place that night, already two years ago! Keep the gossip between ourselves, Gastonibus being the present and future glory of the chamberpot city under the mountains."[19]

The place like a toilet was La Chaux-de-Fonds, and Gastonibus Beguinus was merely the first new persona Charles-Edouard Jeanneret would assume in order to have the virility he craved.

7

In May, Jeanneret founded the Société d'Entreprises Industrielles et d'Etudes, leasing a new office at 29 bis rue d'Astorg—a location near the Madeleine that put him at the center of bustling, commercial Paris. In his free time, he dedicated himself to watercolors (see color plate 2).

Beyond that, on October 16, ten days after his thirtieth birthday, he opened an enterprise to manufacture reinforced-concrete bricks. Max Du Bois had provided the financial backing for him to rent space in the St.

Lumière power station in Alfortville, on the Seine on the outskirts of Paris. The blocks were made of by-products from the station and could easily be shipped from the location on the river. Jeanneret designed himself a coat of arms bearing the statement "The world is without pity," but he was ebullient as he launched the commercial venture with which he planned to earn his fortune while also practicing architecture and painting.

Jeanneret entered one of his periods of ecstasy. Moneymaking and the betterment of the world could go hand in hand. With his start as a businessman, he resumed the diary he sent to Ritter: "Alfortville is begun! We're going to make bricks. The factory, the site actually, is attractive, the machines powerful, the situation magnificent. Enormous gasometers, the four overwhelming Est-Lumière chimneys right next to our property." The fast pulse of industry was pure poetry: "Coming home at nightfall, I saw the water shimmering and the great factories smoking, their luminous bays reflected in the river."[20]

Still, Jeanneret deprecated the old-fashioned style and suburban ambience of the Napoleon the First building where his business was housed. And he disdained himself for his new alliance with the lowest of all human forms: the bourgeoisie: "I breathed deeply over my property: the bureaucrat, the *trustee,* the businessman, the eunuch architect will vanish someday—eventually! I'll make fine engravings of my factory, and I'll be able to speak of 'my stocks' and of 'my sales' like any wine merchant."[21]

His mental swings were rapid and extreme. Suddenly, the self-loathing entrepreneur, after thinking of great architecture rather than business, was riding high again: "Tonight I leafed through my files from the Bibliothèque Nationale (more than five hundred sketches of cities). The whole world in extracts from old engravings. What flavor! Amplitude and imagination above all; overflowing. I am jubilant. And delicious inscriptions, 'sweet smelling roses' of Jacques Callot. And the big cartouches of the Roman engravers. Those letters! If William Ritter were here, he'd rejoice for days. And I'd be hearing him. Rome inundates me, hypnotizes me. Good lord, what laughter! The scale and the poetry. And their consuls, and their old men. L'Eplattenier dared tell us they were corrupt; the wretch!"[22]

Then, as if a narcotic had worn off, he plummeted again. Only hours after committing his jubilance to paper, he lost confidence: "Sick all day. Solitude, entirely impregnated with Michelangelo. Still Rome! Tragic life, forced labor, implacable destiny. Tenderness, affection, the heart of that good, dolorous man. Fog outside. Silence here. My painting is still ten times less than what I wanted. I still don't know how to set down a flat tone, nor how to shade a cube without 10 reflections, which do away with strength."[23]

8

This time, Jeanneret remained glum until he immersed himself in architecture with such fervor that nothing could burst the bubble. When All Saints' Day came six days later, he made his way through the rain to attend a morose mass at Notre-Dame and then chose to copy Rogier van der Weyden's *Déposition.* It was a perfect recipe for gloom.

The copy was his fifth oil painting. Trying to master the medium, he transformed the Flemish master's gripping scene of death and mourning, its dramatic gestures and anguished faces, into a freer rendition with his own modern coloring. The painting then fed a fantasy of his own death.

Jeanneret's cold had evolved into a dreadful grippe—the sort of flu and sinus symptoms that would plague him regularly throughout his life. In the middle of the night after All Saints' Day, he was hardly able to breathe. The problem intensified; suffering from the barklike gasping of croup, he had the agonizing sensation that he was suffocating.

Semiconscious, he thought he was having a nightmare but then realized that the torture was real. At 3:00 a.m., he became completely miserable in "absolute silence. Abandonment, oblivion of mankind." For the third time in as many days—first when the illness initially hit him, and again the following day—he thought his life was over: "I had the feeling I was giving up the ghost, and I resigned myself to it with complete simplicity."[24]

Then, he did one of his typical about-faces. "But the hell with dying; since this is hardly the time for it, let's try something better."[25] Again he was resolved to reconfigure the settings of everyday human existence.

XIII

The big break occurred when Charles-Edouard Jeanneret was asked, at last, to submit a design for an architectural project of substantial scale. It was to be in Challuy—near Nevers, in the center of France. "Right now I'm studying a big slaughterhouse," he wrote. "I could never have guessed how magnificent this problem is—and leads to true architecture. An architecture from America and Chicago, and its canned goods are letting me create a château on the Loire."[1] Not only would he bring the boldness and candor of American industrial architecture to the French countryside and build a monument to rival Blois and Chambord, but his factory for killing animals would be an unprecedented declaration of truth.

After the initial charge, he descended into worrying: "Dubious and less than likely attribution, this work leaves me reticent and melancholy. Ah, life is hard, and a torment for those who are young and believe in ideals!"[2] Nonetheless, in November and December, he plunged in. First, he ruminated about the project's requirements. Then—and this is how inspirations always hit Le Corbusier—the design idea came to him in a flash. On the train to Nevers to study the site, he hastily sketched his concept while sitting in the restaurant car.

It adhered to the tenets of Taylorism, the theory of assembly-line efficiency that called for increased productivity through standardized tools, more attention to workers' abilities and training, and improved working conditions. These ideas had been put forth in the American Frederick Winslow Taylor's *Principles of Scientific Management,* recently translated into French. Taylorism was then sweeping the industrialized world: it put in place conveyor belts to facilitate man-made production and organize factories for maximum efficiency. Jeanneret envisioned three separate buildings—housing animal stalls, refrigeration units, and the actual slaughterhouse—linked by bridges and Taylor's mechanical bands.

There seemed a real chance that the commission might be completed and paid for. He was ebullient. The little apartment on the rue Jacob began to feel like paradise. The man who was soon to streamline interiors to bare white walls and stovepipe railings had covered his bedroom with a black wallpaper decorated with bowls of fruit that went well with the Louis XV wood carving in the alcove, where an enormous divan nearly filled the entire space. Rugs of black, white, and red stripes were underfoot; no bare floor whatsoever was visible. An abundance of cushions and pillows offered many possibilities for comfortable seating. Once wartime restrictions on fuel were lifted and Jeanneret was able to maintain the gas heat at his ideal temperature of eighteen degrees Celsius, this overstuffed, small apartment was everything he wanted: "It's a perfectly appointed living room, suggestive of the most complete intimacy. Surrounded by the absolute calm of this residence, all I need do is wait for Sleeping Beauty to awake." As of yet, the mythic female was only a fantasy.

As 1917 drew to a close, he learned that the slaughterhouse proposal was going ahead. Just before New Year's, Jeanneret experienced his first charrette, the nonstop, round-the-clock campaign in which architects complete building plans. He was ecstatic.

The making of the slaughterhouse was a "new baptism": a purifying rebirth that was his own renewal. "The further the project advances, everything grows clearer, more orderly, better organized. Backup draftsmen arrive, my drawing workroom, so lamentably empty, is filling up: until midnight Saturday, Sunday, and Monday, just before Christmas, 44 hours without stopping, eating on a drawing board, the excitement, total reliance on nervous energy." When he observed "we advance, but we shall not arrive," it was not a lament; the quest was what thrilled him.[3] Throughout his life, the urgent sense of necessity infused Le Corbusier with a happiness rarely matched by the end results.

He was much too excited to react to the gore of the project with anything but amusement: "From 'Industrial Cold' this Christmas morning came the nicest secretary, diminutively blond and neat, out of a nice warm bed. And to *M'selle* Yvonne I dictate memoranda on dung heaps, liquid manure, slaughtering, emptying cow bellies, guts, etc. A thousand pardons!"[4]

"Working myself to death," he wrote without irony. The more the martyr suffered, the more he knew who he was. At three in the morning, when the draftsmen had all left the office, he remained. This was the moment to take the project to a new stage and to draw the ensemble of factories as a vision without precedent. At last he was an inventor, not just someone who rehashed old ideas of what buildings should be. In his hands, radically new forms were conceived: "Energy and flexibility are needed. I'm stiff with physical exhaustion."[5]

When Jeanneret finally put down his pencils that December evening and left his office at 29 bis rue d'Astorg, he found himself in a swirling snowstorm. Walking along the wide boulevards of the Right Bank, he lost his way. Then he circled the Madeleine, the enormous nineteenth-century structure built in antique style as a temple to the glory of Napoleon's army, and the next thing he knew, as if he had no control over his own footsteps, he was back in his office. Aided by the eight people who had just arrived to start a new day, he finished the project. He was nearly as thrilled by his exhaustion as by his achievement: "The big plans, impeccably drawn in ink, describe the really good arrangement of this project, its boldness, its grandeur, its harmonious modernism. It fills me with joy. But how weak my legs are!" The feeling of having given his all was his intoxicant. When those neat drawings were, at last, ready to go, Jeanneret declared, "One is stupefied, like a woman who has just given birth."[6]

He believed that if the slaughterhouse project succeeded, it would be the beginning of his changing the world: "I'm getting excited just writing this. I see the happy days shining anew, and I wrest myself from the spleen of those days of terrible cold. The flowers freeze with the water in my vases. The river at Alfortville is magnificent, lashed by snow, a mordant green, cruel to the citizens, cruel to my plans. Everything has a color exceeding the beauty of what has ever been seen on this river, but to stop now would be death."[7]

XIV

1

> The difficult task of knowing another soul is not for young gentlemen whose consciousness is chiefly made up of their own wishes.
>
> —GEORGE ELIOT, *Middlemarch*

Auguste Perret liked to introduce to one another members of the next generation who were on the right path. He had as a neighbor a promising young artist named Amédée Ozenfant, whose father owned a construction company that sought out the latest technological advances in building and had consulted Perret about reinforced concrete. He was determined that Ozenfant meet the creatively possessed if notably eccentric Charles-Edouard Jeanneret. "He's an odd duck," the elder statesman warned Ozenfant about the recent arrival from La Chaux-de-Fonds, "but he'll interest you."[1]

Portrait of Amédée Ozenfant by Charles-Edouard Jeanneret, ca. 1920

Amédée Ozenfant was born the year before Jeanneret. At age twenty-six, he had conceived and built an aluminum car on the chassis of a Hispano-Suiza, with large whitewall tires and a streamlined, elegant body. He also painted and was devoted to ancient art—like Jeanneret, he had formed his artistic sensibility in Italy and at the Louvre—and, having traveled to Russia, was so attracted to Slavic culture that he had married a feisty Russian, Zina Klingberg.

Exempted from the military because of persistent bronchitis and pneumonia, at the start of the war, Ozenfant founded an avant-garde review called *L'Elan,* which featured André Derain and Pablo Picasso among the painters and Max Jacob and Guillaume Apollinaire among the poets.[2] The goal of the publication was to support the French war effort by serving as a propaganda tool for manifestations of the French spirit: the lightness, energy, and charm encapsulated in its title.

Ozenfant's father died suddenly in 1917, forcing Amédée to become the supervisor of a large building project for a munitions factory in Toulouse. He camped out in a small hut directly on the building site. In the evenings, burrowed inside this shelter intended for explosives, he wrote about "Purism"—a term he had developed to describe a new artistic approach. The workmen were stunned that this odd young man spent more time than was necessary in the midst of dangerous materials, but just as Charles-Edouard Jeanneret could gaze at flames and see art more than peril, Amédée Ozenfant was focused only on change and progress.[3]

2

In 1916, Auguste Perret had founded and became president of Art et Liberté, a group of pioneering practitioners of all the arts who opposed historicism.[4] Ozenfant was a charter member. Perret brought Jeanneret to one of their luncheons so they could meet.[5]

They took to each other instantly, and with their friendship Charles-Edouard Jeanneret was exposed to a whole new milieu. In addition to his work at the family business, his publishing, and his painting, Ozenfant was running the Jove couture salon, one of the most prominent dress shops in Paris. Frequented by wealthy courtesans and other stylish women, Jove was owned by the fashion designer Germaine Bongard, sister of the couturier Paul Poiret and said to be Ozenfant's lover. Ozenfant occasionally organized art exhibitions in the salon; the first show included two paintings by Henri Matisse, for whose daughter Bongard had designed spectacular outfits in which she posed for her father.

His new friend opened Jeanneret's eyes as never before to the visual as a source of amusement in life. Ozenfant's mother wore the sort of fine clothing he helped sell; Marie Jeanneret and Aunt Pauline, on the other hand, would never have imagined donning anything more extravagant than the plain offerings of the ladies' establishments in La Chaux-de-Fonds, where sensible women paid reasonable prices for what went well with solid shoes. Nor did they approve of anyone who presented herself in an entertaining style: Jeanneret was furthering his education in the art of pleasure.

More than two decades later, Le Corbusier would ask, " 'Was Jeanneret more valuable to Ozenfant than Ozenfant to Jeanneret?' It would be extremely difficult to decide the question."[6] And Ozenfant eventually made it one of his major pursuits to assume credit for having originated and invented almost everything they ever did together. But for a few seminal years, the two young modernists were devoted partners, each bolstered by having a colleague.

INITIALLY, OZENFANT SERVED the vital function of being Jeanneret's latest vehicle for self-improvement. He wrote his new companion, "In my confusion . . . it seems that an abyss separates us as to age. I feel on the threshold of my studies, while you are carrying out your plans, . . . I am a bricklayer, working without any plans, in the trench. . . . You are nevertheless, of those I know, he who seems to me most clearly to be carrying out what is stirring within me."[7]

Ozenfant's idea of Purism became his and Jeanneret's mutual rallying cry. It emphasized visual reduction, clear lines, and concentrated forms. Jeanneret had already been attracted to these values inside barns on the outskirts of La Chaux-de-Fonds. Most designers, however, still decorated every possible surface; the Beaux-Arts architectural style blanketed building fronts and room paneling with echoes of the Renaissance and the Baroque. Even Jeanneret's own early architecture was laden with ornament; Purism presented an alternative.

Ozenfant proposed "cleansing the plastic language of certain parasitical terms, as Mallarmé had done with the verbal language."[8] He wanted to continue the quest to understand and abet the process of perception that had been launched by Ingres, Seurat, and Cézanne. For Jeanneret and Ozenfant, the connection to the ancient past was also an essential component of their modernism. They intended to achieve freedom by emulating the balance and clarity of Classicism.

3

Jeanneret challenged all the usual ways of thinking.

At the end of January 1918, he was on the Pont des Arts, a lovely bridge spanning the Seine between the Left Bank and the Louvre, when a bomb exploded. An air alert a few minutes earlier had sent most people to the Métro or to cellars, where they huddled together and enjoyed the protection of being underground. Jeanneret had opted to be among a smaller group out in the open air, facing the spectacle directly. Standing there brazenly, looking up and down the Seine, the young Swiss took in the bombing as a concert of sounds and a visual panoply. Transfixed by the explosions, he felt no fear and experienced no horror.

The next day, he wrote Ritter, "Yesterday I watched the bombing from the Pont des Arts. I couldn't make anything out of it. There were a good fifty of us on the bridge listening to the roar of the cannons, the enormous explosions close by, watching the glow of fires. Bombs were exploding a hundred meters from us; we didn't realize they were bombs."[9] He was as interested in this lack of cognition as in the horrific event itself.

It was the beginning of the heaviest action of the war in Paris. Yet, two weeks later, Jeanneret tried to be as circumspect as possible to his parents: "The spectacle was fascinating, the sound of it overwhelming. . . . But in the roar of the cannons and the violent explosion of the bombs, I couldn't tell what was happening, and it was only next day that I realized that this time the Goths had reached Paris and were actually spitting their bullets. Now the moon is back; the *Boches* will return with it. Right this moment, during this freezing night, you can hear the hum of pursuit planes: the moral security offered to the Parisians."[10] The only thing that terrified Charles-Edouard Jeanneret was the prospect of missing the excitement.

HAVING BEEN CALM during the bombing, within a month of that violent disruption Jeanneret believed, just as he had a few months previously when he had his grippe, that he was dying. He wrote Ritter, "And tonight, all of a sudden, alone in my office, I had the strangest feeling: an insuperable pang. I was distinctly convinced that I would die tonight. Now my mind is utterly calm. I want to write that if I were to die tonight, I protest against the life that tempts me so and that is so low and cynical."[11] Again, the verb he used for the process of dying was "*claquer*"—abrupt engineer's lingo, with the sound of a machine.

Contemplating his own death, he mapped out a plan: "You must forge your own weapons for the life you want to have. You must make yourself a superior being, to see only what is high. And detach yourself, turn away from everything not involved in the realization of something superior. It is, after all, only the abstract which will survive and which is worth the effort."[12]

4

Jeanneret had made the short list of eight finalists for the slaughterhouse project, and he remained after the group was whittled to two. At the end of January, a commission presided over by a government minister did the final review: "The Fixari project is the board's favorite—unrealizable! It costs twice as much as ours. Mine is a personal creation; it is alive—an organism."[13] The injustice stung, and the certainty and excitement he had felt at Christmastime collapsed.

With German aircraft continually buzzing Paris, by mid-February he was confined to the very center of the city and could no longer wander even as far afield as Montmartre or Montparnasse. The bombing intensified; by mid-March, he did not dare to go to sleep at night in his apartment. While Woodrow Wilson was formulating fourteen points for a peace settlement that might end the war, there were so many Luftwaffe attacks that Jeanneret often stayed in the freezing cold cellars. "Paris is unrecognizable: impenetrable darkness: no way of knowing where you are, of finding your way. And during the bombing, it's *absolute* night without a single light anywhere," he wrote.[14]

Then an art collector he knew, Barthélémy Rey, was killed by the Germans directly in front of the Ministry of War, at the moment of presenting himself to enlist. The event was a turning point in Jeanneret's life. He realized he had to summon incredible toughness and self-mastery just to endure. He wrote his parents, "So now we have bombs all the time, which means that the women are hysterical. How they go on! Myself, I pay no mind. Though I've decided to zigzag nightly to where the cellars are, after the events of these last days, which were more demonstrative than others. I repeat: I'm quite unconscious of the danger in every respect—in business as well; I'd make a good campaigner."[15]

Max Du Bois, on the other hand, was crumbling. Jeanneret could not stand it. "Du Bois's nerves are very bad. It's impossible to be around him; he's setting up a kind of satrapy, a despotism, a czarism. I feel a complete indifference for so much fuss, given the facts. A bomb will have to come and find me, I'm not looking for it. At times like this, when I'm calmly puffing on a dreadful cigarette butt as I calligraph this epistle (for I do calligraph), I know several little women who are completely overwhelmed, crouching on a corner of the couch, a candle nearby, blankets, shawls, provisions, letters from their lovers, everything ready for the descent into the realm of the rats. . . . Now in my neighborhood, my slimy rue Jacob, as Colette Willy [later known as the writer Colette] calls it, the bathrobes of the young heiresses are more ordinary than ermine, so that when you have to spend an eternal 4 hours in some cellar corridor waiting—what else is there to do but flirt, since you can't smoke or drink?"[16]

Barthélémy Rey's death, unlike Du Bois's weakness, was noble: a heroic act like his friend Bippert's fatal flight. Even though Rey was a rich dilettante with impulsive taste, morally he was a superior being, for he had given up his life of ease, closed the doors of his bank, and torn himself from his wife to present himself at the ministry that fatal day. "But this time, our friend Barthélémy Rey, the father of our friend Marcel, was killed, his chest ripped open by an explosion. That chest which a minister has come to close by pinning on it the Cross of the Legion of Honor." Charles-Edouard Jeanneret focused on Rey's courageous control of his own destiny. "He had real panache. His life had no purpose. He died splendidly, illustriously. That's something in a man's life."[17]

Again he addressed the issue of his own mortality: "Death doesn't scare me, mine or other people's. It's so natural . . . I believe I won't experience any of those distresses which are so many weaknesses: a tree against its stake, a stake against its tree. . . . Separate them; is there suffering? No, there's a nuisance. Look: we're separated. And our thoughts? No. Even when space stretches to infinity, thought remains."[18]

Fear or weakness was worse than the end of life: "There's only one painful and dangerous sentiment, dangerous because it's exclusive of will: panic! The collective effect is huge. Yet up till now, I've escaped it, and this is why: my spirit of contradiction."[19] By always challenging the status quo, he avoided the nightmarish impotence that destroyed the lives of people who complied. His brave contentiousness defined him.

5

Jeanneret loved telling his parents about his wonderful new friendship: "Ozenfant is a boy endowed with a wealth of remarkable gifts without at all belonging to that genial hermaphrodite race that is to be encountered among musicians and that is utterly exasperating. Ozenfant is a heroic worker. And he navigates the business labyrinth even as he accomplishes his own work. He writes well; he paints very well. And he's all for freedom of the seas! We often take dinner together in a little dive down the street and spend the rest of the evening in my office."[20]

The routine was convenient, since Ozenfant's flat was near Jeanneret's office. On one Sunday evening in mid-March, however, Jeanneret served the friend whom he described as having a "sharp Mohican's face" a dinner on the other side of the Seine, in his own apartment on the rue Jacob.[21] For someone brought up on the heavy fare of landlocked La Chaux-de-Fonds and never taught to cook, the repast was remarkable—especially during wartime. He started with Portuguese oysters accompanied by a white Graves. Then came hearty dried sausage. The main course was pork chops with poached eggs on top and buttered baby sweet peas on the side. By then, the two comrades were drinking a St. Emilion, although Jeanneret had planned a red Burgundy. The cheese course was brie with an apple marmalade. Then came

Letter to his parents, with the menu of his banquet for Ozenfant prepared during World War I

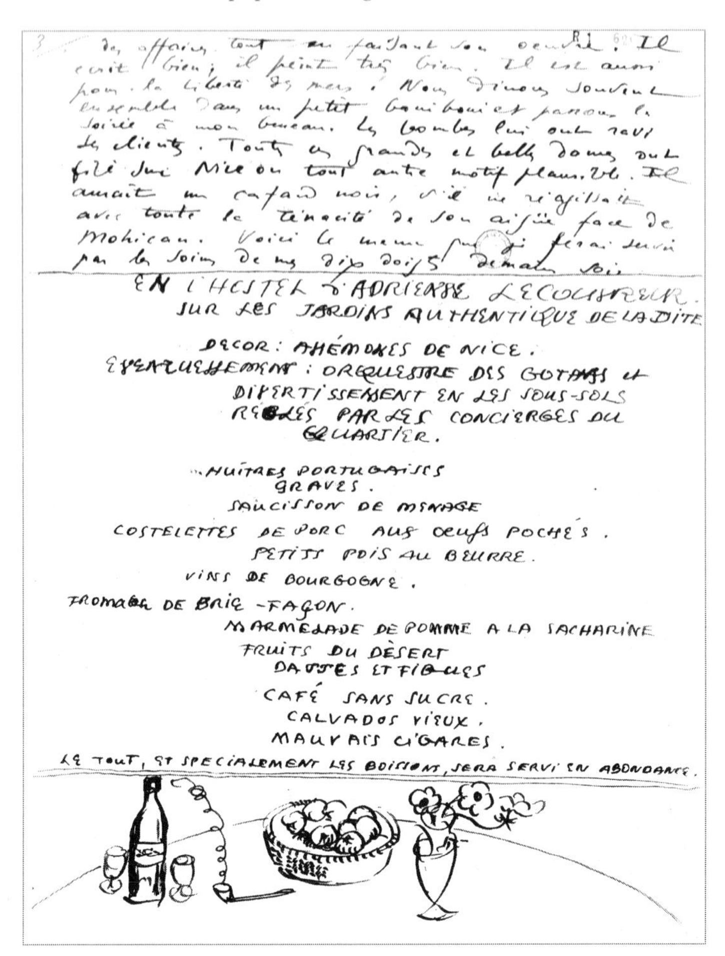

des affaires tout en faisant son oeuvre. Il écrit bien; il peint très bien. Il est aussi pour la liberté des mers! Nous dînons souvent ensemble dans un petit boui-boui et parfois le soir à mon bureau. Les bombes lui ont ravi des clients. Toutes les grandes et belles dames ont filé sur Nice ou tout autre motif plausible. Il aurait un cafard noir, s'il ne régissait avec toute la ténacité de son aigüe face de Mohican. Voici le menu que je ferai servir par les soins de mes dix doigts demain soir.

EN L'HOSTEL D'ADRIENNE LECOUVREUR.
SUR LES JARDINS AUTHENTIQUE DE LADITE

DECOR: ANÉMONES DE NICE.
EVENTUELLEMENT: ORCHESTRE DES GOTHAS et DIVERTISSEMENT EN LES SOUS-SOLS RÉGLÉS PAR LES CONCIERGES DU QUARTIER.

HUITRES PORTUGAISES
GRAVES.
SAUCISSON DE MENAGE
COSTELETTES DE PORC AUX OEUFS POCHÉS.
PETITS POIS AU BEURRE.
VINS DE BOURGOGNE.
FROMAGE DE BRIE -FAÇON.
MARMELADE DE POMME A LA SACHARINE
FRUITS DU DÉSERT
DATTES ET FIGUES
CAFÉ SANS SUCRE.
CALVADOS VIEUX.
MAUVAIS CIGARES.
LE TOUT, ET SPECIALEMENT LES BOISSONS, SERA SERVI EN ABONDANCE.

dates and figs. "Coffee without sugar," "old Calvados," and "Bad Cigars" followed. He illustrated a menu in the style of Raoul Dufy and said that everything, especially the beverages, was to be served "in abundance."

Jeanneret was determined that his parents get the point that living with panache had the power to ward off sadness and obliterate evil: "The lecture for today: *Harmony Above All.* Some Greek terra-cottas on the table, and then the bottles, the fruit in wicker baskets, the sugar in Daum cups. The wine was good, the anemones superabundant, as were the pinks. A suitable lighting from candles in the polished bronze of a Dutch candlestick. The table offered a rich still life, attractive and unstudied. Everyone talked at once, a thousand questions were broached without sterile controversies but in a restful unison. The cigars were splendid, the weather fine. It makes you feel good. You forget the war and the bourgeois (which is the same thing). *Proportion.* That's it, the Whole of life, the goal, the truth."[22]

IT WAS TO BE a long time before Jeanneret had as romantic an evening with a woman; after the Sunday-night dinner with Ozenfant, he was as high as someone in love. For a brief but shining moment, Charles-Edouard Jeanneret was less alone than he had ever been.

6

In little time, as Le Corbusier, he would flaunt self-assuredness and appear confident to the core. But less than a week after his feast with Ozenfant, his faith was sullied by doubts. He wrote Ritter, "I'm living in a torment, a little tempest in my teapot: the heaviest cares, yet fine reasons to be confident, the crest of a wave, the gulf between two waves, enough to disjoint a man. . . . I'm a man flung into the whirlwind of affairs carrying in outstretched arms over his head, above the filth, his dream."[23]

The wailing air-raid sirens and his self-disgust at not being part of the war effort plagued him. "The moon is sparkling over Paris, and the sky is full of buzzing planes. The *Boches* have come with their Gothas. We've gone down into the cellars," he wrote. There he noticed "a pretty girl of about twenty with a touching expression (many girls touch me, but I don't *touch* them). . . . Myself, I'm all for the conquest of money and fucking off afterward. I find money tragic, not just stupid. Luckily my instincts are the non-sensation of the value of money. . . . Some people have confidence. Not me—I've spent everything; will I come out on top? I think so, for I'm following my lucky star."[24]

The lucky star was art; at least he was now doing what he loved: "And art, ideas, but ten times more than at La Chaux. How I love them, as I practice them. I draw, I paint between eleven and midnight." Yet he was troubled by his own emotional isolation: "I have moments of sunshine when I see the hour of my rehabilitation shining before me. The bastards will hear my fanfare! Yes, I've known that great bitterness. . . . But how sad I am that my heart's rind still remains hard and intact. . . . Am I doomed to a melancholy solitude?"[25]

7

The tortured Calvinist dreamed of going to a whorehouse, "to bury myself effusively in the damp warmth of an armpit." He went, but found the prostitute "Alas, indifferent!" The bought sex, he told Ritter, was "a nostalgic abandon of one's energies, having struggled all day long and all week long, between the hands and the arms encircling you, which will close your eyes in order to make appear certain joys, alas quite false, alas contested in advance, alas inaccessible or sad, sad then." He imagined something nobler. "I dream of Max Elskamp, with his nostalgic '*Maisons de Mauvaise Vie*' where he never set foot. . . . How indifferent I am to all this. I'd like to be cut down on a splendid page of life, in full ardor, at the top of my bent."[26]

It was heroic to do battle and cowardly not to. He was in hot dispute with his father, who favored Swiss neutrality and declared that in war men become beasts. The younger Jeanneret insisted to his parents that "the man in the trenches is not an animal, he is of the most sublime nobility; and there are millions of them just like him in every country. The war, quite the contrary, has *raised up* humanity . . . the question is to know why and for whom one is fighting, by virtue of what ignoble false idol, false belief, criminal false-ideal." The son lashed out: "I've already told you a hundred times: in your hateful business you had the best remedy: there is still time. You should write the Journal of a Bourgeois during the War."[27]

When, in the middle of the night, Jeanneret heard air-alert sirens and got dressed and escaped, like so many Parisians, into the nearest Métro station, he felt revulsion when it turned out to be a false alarm that had everyone running through the streets. He declared himself a useless observer of the world: watching from a distance, judging, masturbating. He should take action, and so should his father: "Now then, I'd like to know I have a papa who *reacts* with all his might against the invading depression."[28] His mother, too, was guilty of lapses—mainly by playing away at the piano without taking pen to paper to write to him.

Edouard also lectured his parents about Ritter and Czadra. He told Georges and Marie that while they had everything, they must not forget these kings in exile, so misfortunate and in need of affection. He verbally wagged his finger at his father and mother by writing, "I really don't want to believe your silence is indifference."[29]

Unlike the rest of them, the youngest member of the family knew how to conduct his life. "There are two ways of regarding life: FORWARD and BACKWARD. There's the wisdom that ends in indifference. But there's the strength that produces passion. And there's the conscience which produces hate. All three are necessary." Jeanneret was grandiose and humble in the same breath—and desperate to conquer his own demons sufficiently and become steady. "So then there's the conflict within oneself from morning to night—but what a turmoil! The years fly past in pursuit of realization. In this torrent it's good to come up against others, it *tempers* you. All of which may be empty words; Ritter, that observer buried in his den, would demolish my system in three strokes of a pen; never mind. The turmoil is the fact of an imbalance. The important thing is not to fall."[30]

AT THE END of March, he wrote his brother that the cellars of his building had become a shelter, but he now considered that scurrying down to the basement was like the mindless pursuit of money: something most people did like a swarm of insects. He would never again bow to fear.

8

On May 6, Jeanneret got his first substantial order for the brick factory. His spirits soared; his business was sure to succeed.

Music again moved him to rapture; he attended the first Debussy concert following the composer's death, making Debussy's vast accomplishment seem of a piece, with *Le Clair de Lune* leaving him elated.

He was also euphoric that the days were getting longer: "How lovable this country is, how loving, how the sob of life gently follows the obtaining of frivolous loves. How this country accounts for itself, how it soothes my mountain man's heart. How gladly I surrender to the sweet light. . . . This city is lovely, and life here promises well."[31]

Then, just as he was flying high, a contrary force took hold of him. Determined never to let love weaken his control of his destiny, he would not waste the time and energy required to maintain a serious relationship, yet his solitude was unbearable. Mostly celibate, and still skeptical about his sexual performance, he was crazed by vivid erotic fantasies and his craving for voluptuous women.

He tried to create and possess his ideal female in his watercolors: "My artistic thoughts rise toward plasticity, a form and a line ever more esoteric. My attempts are shapeless, disappointing . . . and I paint trash. My women are of a bestial, gross lasciviousness. And I hesitate to touch a naked woman, for her back, her breasts, her mouth are of an adorable substance, are a kind of dream my crude fingers would spoil. My sensual excesses remain almost entirely outside the bed, and I have a more intimate and painful joy in thrusting my tongue into a big, fresh rose."[32]

Art counted more than flesh: "If I yield to the lure of the boulevards where the women are, it's to find an expression of the ideal mathematics for that dream my brushes are busily seeking to create." Attracted as he was to those prostitutes, it was his job as a martyr to resist the lure of sex in deference to his higher calling. He focused on the dream women of Italian art, not the streetwalkers of Paris: "Sudden encounters: yesterday a word of a conversation about the Medici tombs, and it's that entire Sunday when Michelangelo and Leonardo obsess me. The women of Titian and Giorgione. Italy forever!"[33]

His increased alienation from his parents was exacerbating his feeling of isolation. His mother's concern with the effects of the power structure in La Chaux-de-Fonds, which he was determined to put behind him, made him write Ritter, "All alone a man is in the world. I've just received from Maman a long letter entirely beside the point. First of all, those cannons, those Goths, which no longer exist and which have never bothered me more than a bramble that pricks you as you're walking through the fields. Then an inconceivable excursus on my pathetic present and my agonizing future!" What upset him the most was his mother's and father's failure to grasp the progress he had made: "Enterprising as I am, I'm happy. My whole being is happy. I may suffer in my private heart, sufferings of the bird peeping in the spring in a flowering tree. Ah, poor parents, once again how little you understand your children, how you persist in not seeing what they really are!"[34]

9

Then Paris was bombed some more—and Jeanneret was revived from what he called his "pathetic languor." The cacophony of sounds and the fluid violent forms mattered far more to him than the destruction they accompanied: "Inevitably, here are these she-camels of sirens. A magic and opulent sound over the city. A new note of the coming symphonies. A roaring which catches like fire over all Paris. Cannons. Trumpets. Nightfall. An admirable clamor that, through so much moonlight, and over such handsome blossoming chestnut trees, is no longer of distress but only music. It fades in the distance. The sound of our Notre-Dame first of all, then that of Saint-Sulpice. Those over all the churches and the town halls, all the sirens of the earth. The other sirens have come down the rue Jacob to mark the crescendo. There is silence, and there will be cannonading in the distance, and then roaring over the city, and then the great thumps of the autocannons in the streets, and here and there violent explosions. The *Boche* is approaching and in five minutes will be here with his filthy idiotic bombs."[35]

He was similarly intoxicated by the brute power of industry at Alfortville: "The two daunting chimneys of the Thompson-Houston spitting blackness. The four daunting chimneys of Est-Lumière. . . . The barges swollen with coal, the cranes sweating with black efforts, the tugs valiantly struggling." Then a bomb fell directly opposite 20 rue Jacob: "Six-thirty a.m. of May 27th, the cannons have spoken! One Monday morning when the factories are opening, the signal, the *Boche* has the coquetry of order. . . . It was a blast of all the devils at once: it *collapsed,* O Zbinden Fritz, three floors of the house across the street."[36] As he addressed imaginary Germans, Charles-Edouard Jeanneret was still determined to appear excited rather than panicked.

10

In the spring of 1918, Georges and Marie Jeanneret realized they absolutely had to sell the Maison Blanche. The fantasy was over; there was no longer a chance that they could afford it. With the war, the watch industry had bottomed out, and Georges went from earning a mere five francs per week to having no work whatsoever. He had developed such severe arthritis that he could not imagine starting up again, and the construction and upkeep of the new house had completely depleted his pension fund. Marie's meager income from piano lessons, also reduced during wartime, was insufficient to keep them afloat. The only option was to divest themselves of their son's folly.

The consequences lasted for the rest of the lives of all the major players. Edouard had charged his parents a 6 percent architect's fee; this was less than his usual 10 percent, but it was still the type of arrangement that destroys family relations. Worse yet, when Georges and Marie finally sold the house in 1919 for sixty thousand francs—which, given the high rate of inflation during the war years, represented a horrendous loss—the pur-

Letter to his brother, with a sketch for a small house in Hyères for their parents, June 1918

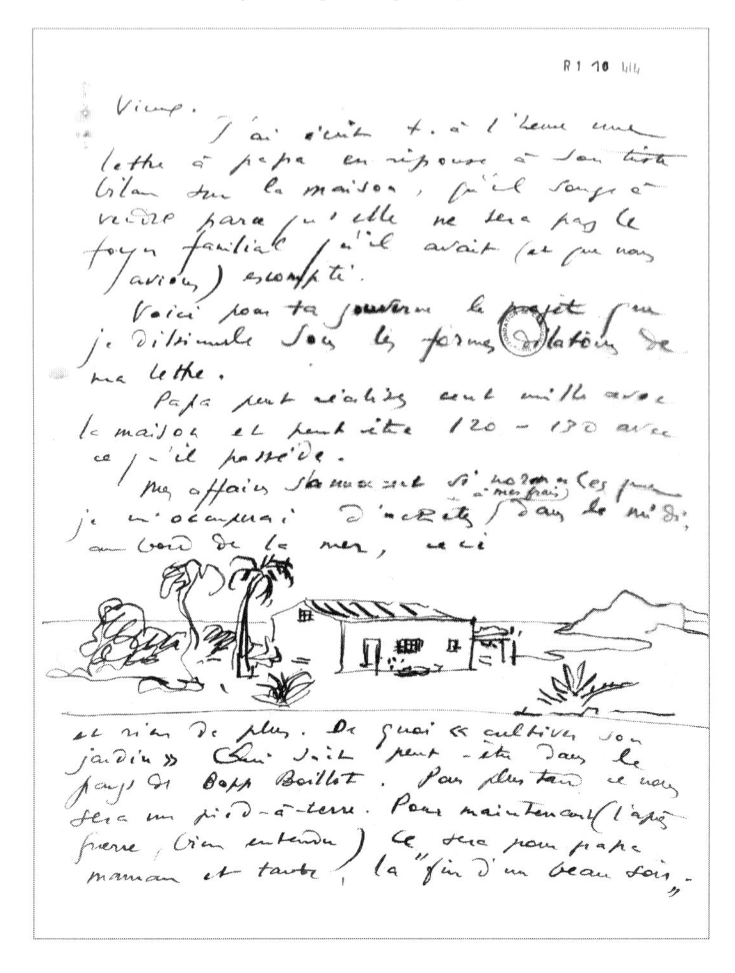

R 1 10 44

Vienne.
J'ai écrit tout à l'heure une lettre à papa en réponse à son triste bilan sur la maison, qu'il songe à vendre parce qu'elle ne sera pas le foyer familial qu'il avait (et que nous avions) escompté.
Voici pour ta gouverne le projet que je dissimule sous les formules de ma lettre.
Papa peut réaliser cent mille avec la maison et peut-être 120 – 130 avec ce qu'il possède.
Mes affaires s'annonçant si normales que (à mes frais) je m'occuperai d'acheter, dans le midi, au bord de la mer, ceci

et rien de plus. De quoi « cultiver son jardin » [illegible] peut-être dans le pays de Bopp Baillot. Plus tard ce nous sera un pied-à-terre. Pour maintenant (l'après guerre, bien entendu) ce sera pour papa maman et tante, la "fin d'un beau soir".

chaser then defaulted on his payments. The house was repossessed, and the Jeannerets lost an additional twenty-five thousand francs. Any hope they had of preserving even part of their lives' savings was obliterated.[37]

When Le Corbusier's mother was in her nineties, in letter after letter he offered her financial support and begged her to allow herself more luxuries, like having a maid do the occasional load of wash. As the most prominent architect in the world, he made bank drafts and transferred funds simply to cover the cost of a small Christmas turkey. The financial past was never discussed with any of these gestures, but neither in his eyes nor hers did he ever make up for the havoc caused by the extravagance of the Maison Blanche.

Edouard insisted at the time that the reason for putting the Maison Blanche on the market was that it was too big for two people, that his parents would stagnate in old age if forced to ramble around such a place. He announced optimistically they could get as much as 130,000 francs for it. That estimate was as unrealistic as the grandiose villa itself had been.

To compensate for his mistake, he developed a new dream house for his parents, which he sketched in a letter. He had found the precise spot for it—on the Mediterranean coast of France, facing the islands off of Hyères. He told Georges and Marie they must leave La Chaux-de-Fonds completely, spend a few weeks in Paris and the rest in this idyllic, simple retreat. After their years of toil, they deserved no less "for the final days of a fine life," he explained to Albert.[38] All that was needed, urgently, was a down payment of thirty-five thousand francs for the land.

He sought his brother's complicity: "So, instead of the parents seeing before them a sinister dead end, we can open the door to the happiest old age they could ever have. I have no reason not to achieve this, and there will be no more winter for them."[39]

This time, however, there was no cash to throw into Edouard's fantasy. Nothing came of the son's idea that his taciturn parents should move to the south of France.

11

In mid-June 1918, Charles-Edouard Jeanneret decided that all of his problems were over. He wrote his father, "I have, it is true, ten painful years behind me, and my joy which I do not disguise marks the definitive recovery of my optimism, curbed hitherto by so many struggles and pains."[40] He begged that the Maison Blanche be seen as a cup half full. After all, the family had had six good years there, and they all loved one another.

Edouard rationalized the financial catastrophe. The new house had served well as a workplace for Georges and Marie alike, but now they had worked enough, and it was a good thing that they would be forced to move from "a hard, dry, brutal country none of us has ever loved."[41] Moreover, it was the war that had put in motion the inflation that was the cause of their problems.

The youngest member of the family acted as if he were the one in charge: "I confess to having had, in 1914, a certain doubt about the entire destiny of our family. Today I find myself happy, and I believe I have the solution. Everything is oriented for each of us toward its just solution. And I believe that the labor and honesty which have been *all* our actions will bear their useful fruits." Now Edouard preached unembarrassedly: "Love your last watch dials. You owe them that much. And cultivate your garden, your flowers, and your potatoes. Whistle as you listen to the birds. And forget about the price of coal." Chagrin had given way to pomp. But he also had a heartfelt wish. His goal for his father and mother was that "the last rays of your life might be from a beautiful, limpid, favoring sun."[42]

12

On a Sunday in that June of his rebirth, Jeanneret made a diary entry on the subject of flowers. His sensual response to the miracle of nature discombobulated him.

> The bouquets in my vases are select flowers from hothouses and flowerbeds and the fields of the south. My bouquets have a simple arrangement. One, two or three flowers, and the blossom alone triumphs. Corolla, perfume, weight, scallops, calyx, with the altar raised in the center and the pollen hanging for mute communions. The calyx have a vase, offers the oriole of its blossom. And the vases are arranged so that they help the rhythm of the bedroom as the nipple of a breast glows in the warmth of flesh and establishes the peaks. My ostensible witnesses, my living friends, my companions of voluptuous hopes, my stimuli of wicked thoughts: the roses! Always the flower that I kiss; the tulips, which I question and insult, the red tulips with regular and heraldic yellow streaks like the old playing cards, which speak to me of gambling houses, *lupanars,* protruding breasts, and kohl around the eyes, on the hard lips, on the cheeks of shrill vermilion below the bistre of the eyelashes. That blue, cold leaf of serpentine bronze encir-

> cles with a twin embrace the flower without calyx possessed of a geometric brutality, its empty odor, its pistils offered like bloodless lips in the depths of a womb. For me it remains the ideal rose. Mama used to make admirable bouquets. . . . They were all candor, ingenuousness, ingenuity, caprice, freedom, impromptu, talent. Mama's bouquets used to delight me, their renewal amazed me. All her artist's soul was in them, more than anywhere else, no repetitions, nothing learned or copied. It was all inspiration.[43]

The mature Le Corbusier craved order and efficiency because it provided a framework for this sort of feeling of abundance. Overcome by his own mind, with its cascade of associations from flowers to sexuality to prostitutes to his mother, he needed mechanisms for stability. Moreover, the machines he loved paralleled nature. Rather than being merely dry or mechanical, they resembled flowers in the harmonious workings of their parts.

The natural world and effective machinery were sublime, while the world of business was fit only for con artists. The person about whom he was now most cynical was himself, in the management of the factory at Alfortville: "At 6 in the morning at my factory, what color, what design! The ferryman, the chimneys, and those men of mine who by shrewd accountability and a soon-to-come redistribution, sweat and strain twelve hours and earn my living for me." Jeanneret relished "that force of the master who comes to command all those who produce." Machinery responded similarly to proper controls. He noted "the powerful machines, which ask nothing better than to produce, which ask only to serve, which bestow abundance upon the man who knows how to love them properly."[44]

Jeanneret himself was at last in the position he wanted: "Like a little centaur, I return along the riverbanks, drawn by its fine piers worthy of Seurat, that river worthy of all the love and caresses it receives, by so much gay sunshine on the world and in my heart. In my heart that decision of beneficent calm, that will to pleasure, for it had been too long I had tried to force life instead of simply giving myself up to it."[45]

Giving himself up meant that he would spend more time painting. He was convinced that the brick factory had achieved its objectives and was functioning on its own, with no risk of a downturn, so he now had his afternoons free to concentrate on art. He was delusional in believing that he and Max Du Bois and a third man, Edgard Louis Bornand, had been offered full control of SABA, and that since it was already doing 1.5 million francs' worth of business a year, it would do 2.5 million the next—enabling him to work only a few hours a day while earning a fortune for the rest of his life. But the fantasy gave him the assurance to believe he might throw himself into his painting as never before.

XV

1

On July 4, Jeanneret joined the spectators watching the American soldiers march through the streets of Paris. No one else could have seen or heard that event in the same way, or calibrated human behavior as he did. He wrote in his diary, "July 4: Independence Day. American troops by the thousand paraded stiffly across the place de la Concorde in an oppressive silence, faces impassive above their helmet straps, though a few flowers were tossed. A strange stream of massive steel followed, rumbling tanks maneuvering slowly down the boulevards. Soldiers of the Second Crusade, with the sentiment that, having come here from so far away in order to die, it was for God or his equivalent; the innumerable crowd manifested in stupefaction the fruits of their victory over the demoniac madman. There followed the YWCA, homely and clumsy women in Salvation Army outfits, here to save the world. And the soft skies of Paris witnessed such things with astonishment, and the grace of the huge palaces and the charm of the parks seemed disconcerted. Then came the *poilus,* their short, sharp bayonets unsheathed, as if for harvesting wheat. The blue horizon of this womb of the Ile-de-France enskied the crowd's *grisaille,* and all the soldiers were covered with pale pink chrysanthemums, their bayonets garlanded with daisies and cornflowers. The mob of women, relieved that the massive khaki vision had passed like some kind of strange carapace, cried out: '*Les poilus, our poilus!*' and the men laughed and wagged their heads. Bugles blew, and an armored plane looped the loop around the Obelisk of Luxor. There was great enthusiasm all over the country, a huge rush of confidence. America had surpassed all expectations, it had confounded all expectations. Mammon? no; a Protestant preacher in a black frock coat, yes. Wilson—Peter the Hermit. These cowboys in the Paris of eternal *grisettes,* in the festivities celebrated among the trees and in the clouds, were, for all their athletes' build, communicants of a sort on church steps: the fields of Champagne, the hills of the Vosges. These troops of bodies efficient as machines would serve to give Hindenburg the poignant terrors of nightmare."[1]

It wasn't the only time that American soldiers impressed him with their strapping bodies and innocent strength. Male power—which L'Eplattenier, Perret, and Ozenfant possessed in their artistic achievement as surely as these young military men did in their physiques—intoxicated him. Only when he felt endowed by it himself would he fully escape La Chaux-de-Fonds and the weak air of compromise he associated with his father.

2

Weeks after Jeanneret had determined that his business was flourishing and his finances solid, production at the brick factory dropped precipitously. He could no longer afford to imagine more time painting; he had to throw himself into the work at Alfortville: "My business has taken its revenge. I must get back into harness, and how!" In July, he borrowed thirty-five thousand francs that would be due on August 15; it was his only hope. A heat spell and drought made everything worse; suddenly, city life was losing all its appeal, and he began to contemplate escape from his paradise of a few weeks earlier. Nietzsche offered the latest solution: "Opened *Zarathustra* at random, and at random found: 'Do not stir the swamps. Live on the mountains.' We shall see."[2]

HE WENT ON another rampage about prostitutes, whose lives increasingly obsessed him. Other men had the hypocrisy to call commercial sex "lovemaking"; he knew better. The term was a travesty; these victims who sold sex took no pleasure in it. The one great thing—for him as well as for them—was women having sex with one another: "And that eternal comedy, tonight more cynical than ever. And they call lovemaking LOVE!!! 2 a.m. In the stupefying silence of the city, the rumble of cannons at the front. And the only real pleasure was that I 'did her portrait.' And she carried it off to end up in some joke with another man's condoms. These women have no use for men. And they let themselves be had! Women loving women—that's what appeals to me, the only decent, the only passionate love."[3]

Jeanneret painted lesbian sex in a series of watercolors (see color plate 9). He celebrated the subject with pen-and-ink strokes and splashes of color as robust as the women who were his subject. One work depicts, from above, a heavyset woman, the curves of her buttocks center stage, performing oral sex on another amply proportioned woman, who leans backward, savoring her pleasure as she looks at us in brazen delight. Another image shows three women wrapped around one another. They loll on a sofa in a display of unabashed hedonism, with a bottle and glasses of red wine completing the scenario. One woman is entirely naked except for green stockings that stop just above her knees; another is scantily clad in a blue dress that leaves her breasts exposed.

Jeanneret wrote Ritter about a taxi he had jumped into just after a woman got out in front of his office building: "And all the same I held on to that sensation of the odor of calm voluptuousness . . . in a taxi which I took the moment a woman of tremendous elegance left it outside 'Alex,' her dressmaker in the apartment building of 29 bis. The taxi was full of that perfume, and I got my hopes up all over again, the slave yet again of 'wealth.' "[4] The more he had to study sheets of numbers through his thick eyeglasses, the more he longed for the sensual experiences that beckoned at every turn.

3

If only he could reconcile his desires with his actions.

Jeanneret continued to report ebulliently to Ritter about his solitary erections. The complete sexual act—which for him meant being with a prostitute—brought greater guilt and conflict: "I thought I recognized a woman I had slept with and whom I remembered as charming. In a corner bistro, her hair done up and her face plastered with makeup, she was fraternizing with four or five professional tarts, women in wigs and so insolently crude and bestial I never even look at them. Of course any painter would fall to his knees. Coulon [a colleague in the Briquetterie d'Alfortville] calls me a pig."[5]

Even with the whores who were more to his taste, he was aware of his essential solitude. "Women so pretty, so well dressed and fresh and cheerful, Paris still so much a bouquet of pink flesh. The heart remains alone when the body does its thing. There's no time for love, and that's the problem. Amusement. One would easily understand, lacking the sob of the *sveltes jets-d'eau parmi les marbres,* the spasm of resignation of the eternal solitary, ever more confirmed in this noisy void."[6]

By the end of July, Jeanneret was experiencing "black days . . . the great wave of pessimism is about to break over so much previous optimism." His foreman at the brick factory gave notice. The enterprise was a complete failure; Jeanneret sadly reported that "Alfortville will be empty and silent after all the uproar of the machines."[7] He was completely discouraged about his architectural work as well.

But then, at the last minute, he managed to get a loan of thirty-five thousand francs from members of the Swiss community in Paris, which enabled him to repay the bank for the cash advance that was about to be due and was plaguing him. "Acquaintances in the Swiss colony, friends of friends. And tonight it happened: the 35,000 francs are here," he wrote on July 26. It was a vital life lesson: "In my success I had many enemies. I discovered many friends in difficulty."[8]

He wavered between hope and despair. At the end of July, Jeanneret had a dream that, as bombs were falling, he was embracing the dancer Mistinguett—famous throughout France for her good legs. He treated the dream as if it were reality: "This morning I was in Mistinguett's arms. We were lovers. We were dancing pressed close together. I kissed her deeply. She had chosen me because I had a funny priest's face. We were waltzing slowly, all our senses aroused; there were planes dropping bombs. I asked her if she had loved my compatriot Maurice Barraud. At this she turned to ice and let me go and I woke up. I'm bored with women and yet I'm exhausted *for them.*"[9]

HE STILL HAD his parents' housing to resolve. Georges and Marie Jeanneret had agreed to move near Montreux, on Lake Geneva. Edouard began to design their new dwelling and work out all the details of size and cost. In the meantime, he found a place for them to rent that had room for Pauline as well. Their acceptance of his authority put him back on course.

Every evening from nine to twelve and throughout the day on Sundays, Jeanneret was drawing and painting. In his diary of August 2, he wrote, "I'm drawing *médoc* bottles, coffeepots, and pipes with a pencil sharpened like a needle, determined to create form in terms of volume. My palette has been reduced to four colors, red and yellow ochre, ultramarine, and black. And I'm approaching the paradise of power; I feel I'm on the way. Soon I'll be using oils and in 3 or 4 years, I'll have something to show."[10] Painting even more than architecture, he now believed, was to be his means toward clarity and stability.

4

In July 1918, Ozenfant divorced his wife, Zina. He told people this was in part because of his new closeness to Jeanneret. The two men had become "we." At the start of September, Ozenfant invited Jeanneret to go to Andernos, near Bordeaux on the southwest coast, on the Bay of Arcachon, for ten days; it was a holiday from their regular jobs but also the chance to develop a mutual manifesto about art.

Ozenfant read out loud to Jeanneret about Purism and proposed that they collaborate on a book presenting their ideas on it. In a rare moment of self-effacement, Jeanneret accepted with the insistence that Ozenfant's name go first, contrary to alphabetical order. They painted simultaneously, and their canvases of bold, abstract forms were similar, even though each signed his own pictures and had his particular characteristics. Their shared vision mattered more than their individual selves; the two stalwarts wanted the world to consider them a perfect unit.

JEANNERET worshipped Ozenfant's precise thinking, his strength and calm, and his clear sense of what art was. His new savior was also the master of the technical know-how Jeanneret considered imperative. He wrote Ritter, "Above all he's understood the *métier;* he paints as well as the painters of automobile bodies. He's the master I have been searching for all this time, he achieves what I was crying for so loudly in the course of my disappointing ejaculations of this last year."[11]

Ozenfant also demonstrated the courage to start at zero, which was another of Jeanneret's imperatives for a purposeful existence. He had recently divested himself of an accumulation of luxurious possessions and had reduced his holdings to a sofa bed, six bentwood Thonet chairs from 1840, a plain round mahogany table that belonged to his grandmother, an easel, a few plates and casserole dishes, and the books on his bedside table. He had even destroyed many of his own early sketches and paintings that he disliked. Living austerely in an apartment, which had the cachet of having been Stendhal's one hundred years earlier, Ozenfant was an even better god than L'Eplattenier and Matthey combined.

5

Jeanneret wrote Ritter and Czadra: "Everything is at the zenith, after so much misfortune."[12] He had been named administrator-delegate of a company that made large blocks, conglomerates of asbestos and cement used to cover apartment buildings; beyond that, he had overcome his loneliness. Jeanneret and Ozenfant were preparing for a joint exhibition of their paintings while writing their book. "Our collaboration is an intimate one. Ozenfant is noble and broad-minded. Intimacy. We giggle like boys. There is grippe all around us; we drink camomile tea, cognac, we smoke—how we smoke!"[13]

Because he did not want it known that he was not devoting all of his time to his business ventures, he kept his painting private from everyone other than Ritter and Ozenfant, but it was his refuge. "When I'm drawing I seem to be elsewhere. I maintain absolute secrecy; it would be a scandal if anyone knew I was daily tickling the muses." How grateful he was to the friend of Picasso and Apollinaire who had given him this impetus: "All this is due to Ozenfant, and to my star."[14]

6

Ozenfant and Jeanneret decided to call their book *After Cubism.* Having scrapped their decision about the order of their names, they now planned to publish it anonymously, to give their words the ring of a religious doctrine.[15]

Whenever Jeanneret embarked on a new venture, it was both an exaltation of the good and a fight against the bad. On October 1, he wrote Ritter, "We're all too sensitive to the subtle and facile and lazy talent of Apollinaire and his friends, so that having settled down to work, having realized the great seriousness of life, we react against the facile buffoonery of these older comrades."[16] Painting and writing with Ozenfant, Jeanneret felt he was now working "with courage and simplicity, and in harmony with what we love around us. As an artist, how far I feel from artists. Things are clearer to me now; I see my way, having spent many years in confusion."[17]

Then, in late December, an hour after he put the text for *After Cubism* into the mail, Jeanneret learned that Apollinaire had died. "I regret Apollinaire's death, the loss of a powerful adversary. There are so few strong men and so many inert followers!" he wrote Ritter.[18] As the inventor of the term "l'esprit nouveau," Apollinaire had been an ally, but Jeanneret considered his defense of Cubism the mark of decadence. Nonetheless, the people who counted were the ones who took a stance; a fighter and believer was better than a eunuch.

Jeanneret himself was now working eighteen hours a day, including Sundays. Happily he gave up dinner with friends; mere socializing was a waste of time. He had even forgotten both his parents' birthdays. The lapse brought on manic excitement rather than regret; he wrote them, "Forgive me. You know my credo in life. You must see the bright and the dark and keep only the bright."[19] Now that he was making and writing about art, he was convinced the gleam could last.

XVI

1

> The war has left throughout Europe a mood of disillusionment and despair which calls aloud for a new religion, as the only force capable of giving men the energy to live vigorously.
>
> —BERTRAND RUSSELL

When *After Cubism* appeared following the armistice, Jeanneret and Ozenfant were convinced that their cry for artistic revolution at this transitional moment of history was the most important doctrine of the new era. Their manifesto begins with a flourish: "The war over, everything is reorganizing, clarifying, and focusing; factories are being built; already nothing is what it was before the war: the great rivalry has tested everything, has discarded senile methods and replaced them with those which the struggle has proved to be superior. . . . Never since Pericles had thought been so lucid."[1]

Ozenfant and Jeanneret's premise was that Cubism, embraced by a decadent bourgeoisie, was inadequate for the changed civilization. What was needed instead was a new, orderly world, in which science and art would function in tandem. Machinery, industrialization, and technology were the modern gods; painting and architecture should reflect their capabilities and truthfulness.

Jeanneret and Ozenfant advocated the "tendency toward rigor, toward precision, toward the best utilization of forces and materials, with the least waste, in sum a tendency toward purity"—as it was found in ocean liners and other streamlined and efficient objects.[2] Their goal was to create a pure and serious art based on invariable laws, mathematics, and order as it exists in nature. They extolled the human body as an excellent mechanism, symmetrical and harmonious, organized for maximum efficiency, and they pointed out that "nature resembles not a fairyland without plan but a machine." The writers belittled all that was "garish" or "noisy" or "incoherent" in contrast to this seamless union of science and art. As opposed to artistic movements like Dadaism and Expressionism, with their emphasis on the haphazard and the emotional, their Purism depended on simple, universal subject matter like a bottle of ubiquitous form, "banal for the indifferent observer," or an ordinary tree. General, invariable characteristics counted more than personal expression. "Chance is what art casts out; it is the opposite of art," Jeanneret and Ozenfant declared. "The true purist work should conquer chance and channel emotion; it should be the rigorous image of a rigorous conception. . . . Purism expresses not variations, but what is *invariable*."[3]

The idea was noble, but the art in which Jeanneret realized the strict intentions of Purism has a stifled quality. Working out the need to take rigid control of his emotions, he suffocated his pictures. Fortunately, in his subsequent architecture he moved beyond the tight guidelines he imposed so stridently on his vision in 1918, and permitted the quirks that breathe in the force of life requisite for masterpieces.

2

On November 12, the day the armistice became official, the Americans jumping and dancing in the streets of Paris again struck Jeanneret as different from other people.

Riveted by these revelers from across the Atlantic, he decided that they had the boldness and directness of their silos and factories. Black and white, they kissed one another and threw dollars in the air. "The women want to spend their dollars and they want that sensation in that little vice of theirs—the transoceanic sensation," Jeanneret raved to Ritter.[4]

The armistice itself, however, was a nuisance. He and Ozenfant were supposed to have their exhibition open at THOMAS Tableaux at just the time when people were too busy celebrating, and Jeanneret resented the intrusion on his career. On November 20, he complained, "The show had to be postponed on account of the armistice. The armistice has disorganized a lot of things. People have been celebrating for the last eight days. Not me, of course."[5]

The only comfort was that the postponement gave him additional time to tear into his work and perfect his paintings. He continued as he had for three months, sleeping little and painting in every minute left over from his other work. On December 19, two days before the new opening date at THOMAS, he wrote Ritter, "I see more clearly these days. My place is set

In his apartment at 20 rue Jacob, just prior to his show at THOMAS Tableaux, December 1918

for me in Paris, more or less at the high table. I have been made the administrator of two huge deals. I feel I am an essential cog in the machine, and there is a decisive clarity in my ideas for which I am esteemed. I count. This is the beginning for our generation: it is our turn to take action. I have put my ideas of art in order, and some order in my life. I still flounder in my affairs because they are not yet sorted out, but 1919 will do the trick. Then I will be complete as a man and more extensive in my work. On the whole, I am making progress, not without difficulties, not without effort. I have the distinct sense of having become my own judge, a rather clearheaded and demanding judge at that. Other people's opinions are a matter of indifference to me."[6]

On Saturday, December 21, at 4:00 p.m., the exact moment when the vernissage was beginning, he proudly finished his last painting for the exhibition.

3

THOMAS Tableaux—at 5 rue de Penthièvre, near the rue La Boétie, the fashionable street of galleries that was then the center of the art world—was normally Jove, the dressmaking shop where Ozenfant worked. It had been renamed for occasional exhibitions two years earlier by its owner. The gallery was open only from 2:30 to 6:00 p.m. on weekdays, but its connection with Matisse and other well-known painters made it a worthy showcase for a first exhibition, sure to attract the press.

There were twenty works by Ozenfant and ten by Jeanneret. Jeanneret's friends, who thought he only built slaughterhouses and made bricks, were amazed. The critics, however, disapproved. Louis Vauxcelles, the predominant art pundit of the day, wrote that Ozenfant and Jeanneret were "like clergymen putting on blinders when they walk down the grand boulevards, in order to keep from being tempted by the pretty girls."[7]

Vauxcelles had a point. Jeanneret's carefully preconceived canvases revealed meticulous execution, but the freshness and spontaneity of his travel sketches were absent. Jeanneret told Ritter these were "painted according to the strictest rules, the paint as smooth and uniform as Ingres (if not so good). . . . No longer a matter of vibration, of excitement, of noise."[8] He was using painting as a sedative.

Jeanneret's early forays into painting were also limited by a lack of originality. Ozenfant was not out of line to claim "our two drawings were as alike as twins, especially because at the time Jeanneret saw through my eyes and, in painting, I did his thinking for him."[9] It would take architecture for Jeanneret to realize his own brilliance.

4

For a while, though, Jeanneret remained unsure about where the ultimate focus of his life's work should be. And the two years in Paris had made him no more certain about the issues of women and sex than he had been when he arrived.

The first of January 1919 inspired one of his grand statements about carnal and artistic passions. Jeanneret again described to his two homosexual friends his ambivalence about prostitutes. His natural impulses were coun-

1. Self-portrait, watercolor, summer 1917, Paris

2. Paris, watercolor, 1917

3. LC4 Lounge Chair, covered in panther skin

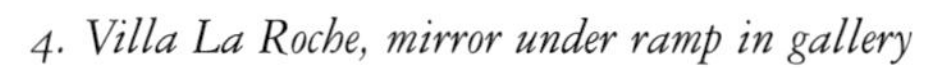

4. Villa La Roche, mirror under ramp in gallery

5. Villa Savoye, exterior room and ramp to top level

6. Villa Savoye at Poissy

7. Villa Savoye, built-in bath

8. *South America (self-portrait with Josephine Baker), pencil sketch,* 1929

9. Two Naked Women Lying Down, *watercolor*

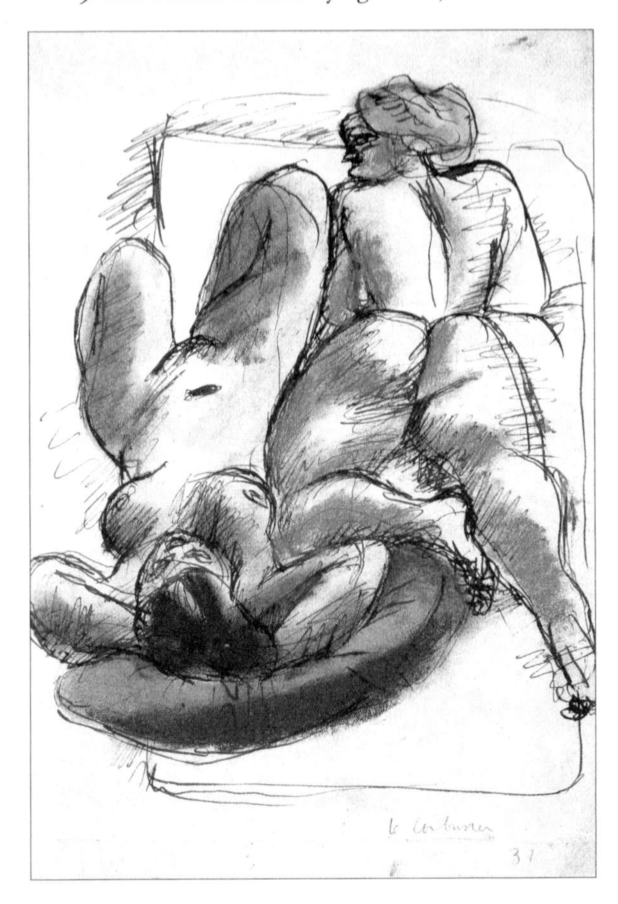

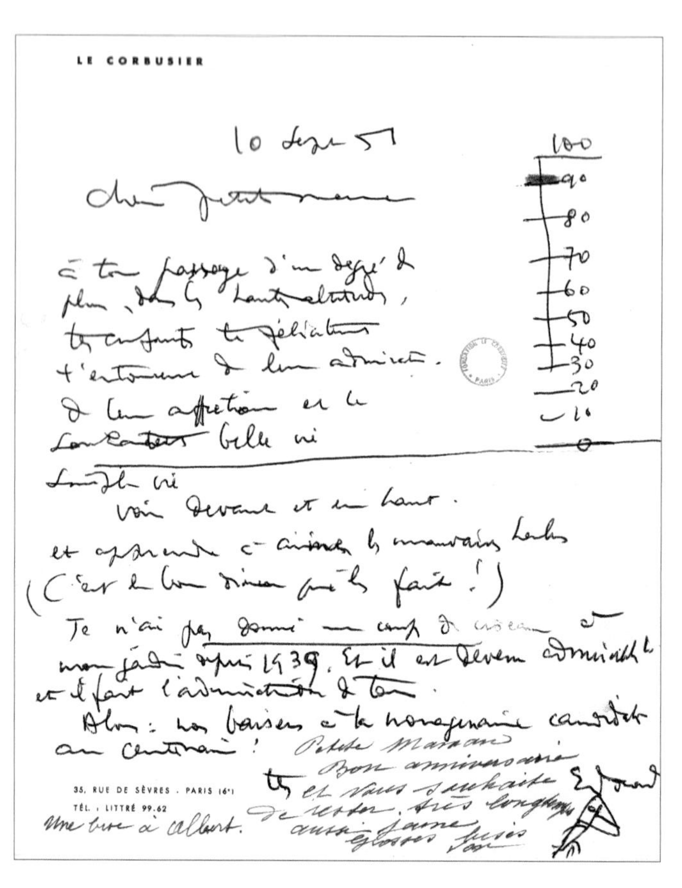

LE CORBUSIER

10 sept 51

Chère petite maman

à ton passage d'un degré de plus, dans les hautes altitudes, tes enfants te félicitent t'entourent de leur admiration de leur affection et te souhaitent belle vie longue vie.

Vois devant et en haut.

et apprends à aimer les mauvaises herbes (C'est le bon Dieu qui les fait !)

Je n'ai pas donné un coup de ciseau à mon jardin depuis 1939. Et il est devenu admirable et il fait l'admiration de tous.

Alors : nos baisers à la nonagénaire candidate au centenaire !

Petite Maman Bon anniversaire et vous souhaite de rester très longtemps aussi jeune. Grosses bises Yvonne

Une bise à Albert.

Edouard

100 / 90 / 80 / 70 / 60 / 50 / 40 / 30 / 20 / 10 / 0

35, RUE DE SÈVRES · PARIS (6e)
TÉL. : LITTRÉ 99.62

10. Sketch in letter to his mother, September 10, 1951

11. Unité d'Habitation, Marseille

12. *Maisons Jaoul*

13. Cabanon, *interior*

14. Le Corbusier and Yvonne's bedroom at 24 rue Nungesser-et-Coli

tered by his self-judgment. The inner combustion he revealed to Ritter and Czadra linked his approach to sex with his attitude toward everything else in life: "The women are leaving here, including Raymonde, opulent and magnificent; can I love them? Can I love Raymonde? So much heft and health, so much good nature; so *nice.* I still think so. I'm still a kid, and such women are for going to bed with, no other functions. So much confusion in my life, so much paradox, so much rationality to apply. Not to let all streams flow. Take responsibility in business, in art, and in the realm of the senses, where the love of plasticity impels toward the embrace, toward natural effusion. I tend to strike out in all directions, I want to embrace everything, I am wildly dilated. Everything enthralls me and pulls me up short. An artist without calculation: this year opens like a fan. I am ready to believe everything and to do anything. Reckless and what of it: the heights and depths of society, ecstasies and depressions, wild ambitions—it's all wonderful. Yet responsibilities accumulate everywhere, and everywhere a maximum effort is required. Everywhere ardor. Love it all. . . . Why not? What a child I am! Tonight I'm completely overwhelmed! And yet I long to act—in every realm. Everywhere I sense tension, expectation, desire. What a symphony! From time to time my heart sings. But how to sacrifice and select? In art I see clearly. Elsewhere I lose my breath and believe in everything. I am terribly tired. 1919? Anything goes until a choice is made, the choice that will come later. Life is too beautiful now."[10]

The office at 29 bis rue d'Astorg was busy. He was undertaking a number of architectural projects for new industrial clients, and he had begun work on *Toward a New Architecture*—a text that in time became one of the most important treatises in twentieth-century design. But then, as in his soliloquy, came the "pulling up short." Having thought the sale of his parents' house in La Chaux-de-Fonds might realize 130,000 francs, he now saw it go for 60,000. Edouard was probably intensely guilty over the financial loss he had imposed on his father and mother, but his way of dealing with it was to insist that they know how important he had become in Paris.

Like a rooster strutting across a stage, he wrote them about attending a breakfast where he was seated between Le Marquis Boniface de Castellane and Le Duc de Clermont-Tonnerre, at de Castellane's house. He had been sent as a delegate from the Technical Commission for the Renaissance des Cités. "I was royally entertained in '*cet hostel*' where I proclaimed the beauties of modern life," he wrote. He also proudly described his Christmas Eve: "an extremely select '*soirée*' at the house of Poiret's sister, a setting of the last refinement and exquisite art, with Ozenfant, Auguste Perret, et cetera."[11]

It was essential that Georges and Marie recognize that the child who had cost them their lives' savings had now worked things out: "I'm going to buy a first-rate gramophone so I can hear the fine Italian masses, the Beethoven quartets, Rameau, Ravel, Granados, Moussorgsky, etc. with a perfection which is a real revelation to me. I never go to concerts now, they bore me. To have perfect execution by Capel, by Risler, by Chaliapin, and by don Perosi, at my worktable and in the most flagrant intimacy is a windfall I owe to the wonders of science." With this ability to listen to the great musicians of the day, his place on the rue Jacob was "a marvel of tranquility and of exquisite proportion," but he was looking for something else as well, nearer to work, that would allow room for the entire family; and he intended to buy a car, a further sign of success.[12] "There are two architects in Paris: Perret and Jeanneret," he boasted. He had been asked to advise on the restoration of the cathedral at Reims. And again he let his mother and father learn about all the important people he knew, while assuring them that he was above it all: "Senator Risles, next to whom I was seated, showed great friendliness toward me. I accept it all without batting an eye."[13]

Yet something was deeply wrong. "Your letters continue to be very incoherent," he snapped at his parents, after first chiding them for not having written enough.[14] The boastfulness and anger were a transparent mask for his remorse and embarrassment over the crisis of the Maison Blanche.

5

One afternoon, Jeanneret ran into an old friend, Alfred Vallette, the director of the Mercure de France, where Jeanneret hoped to publish a new version of *After Cubism.* They met on the rue Condé. Standing on that narrow street of old buildings with high-pitched roofs and ornate facades, Vallette accosted him with the remark, "Oh, it's you, the flat-roof-man." The publisher was referring to Jeanneret's latest architectural proposals for flat-roofed, cast-concrete structures in Picardie, the Somme, and Champagne, which were the subject of an article he was writing and which he predicted would be frightful.

"Not in the least," Jeanneret replied. "This village will be as lovely as a machine." The young architect described the incident and dialogue in graphic detail to Ritter: "He gave a start. 'You don't mean it!' 'Of course I mean it, it's not a slip of the tongue: a village as lovely as a machine.' He backed off, groaned, acknowledged that 'I had a point,' but that it was frightful. 'I won't forget your remark, a village lovely as a machine, a village lovely as . . . !' I authorized him to make a grenade out of it. 'You could put it as an epigraph to your article.' We left on very good terms. He's always quite cheerful, chubby, and in slippers. He regards the enterprise of modern life with terror; he understands my optimism but rejoices at the imminence of his death. Life extinguishes them, these good librarians, these extractors of quintessence."[15]

Thus was born the much misunderstood rubric for Le Corbusier's work: his intention that a house be "a machine to live in." This line that gets quoted more than any other of his—often to suggest the sterility of mechanization—has come to have a significance that distorts its true meaning. The architect did use that expression and did want efficiency, but its purpose was to facilitate, not stifle, rich and complex living. His idea was a beautiful and well-run vessel for the diversity of nature and human existence. And the language he had chosen had been a deliberate sally in the sort of verbal fencing match he loved.

YEARS LATER, when a world still unable to fathom Le Corbusier's industrial windows and stovepipe railings continued to hammer "machine for living" to death, he defended it via his biographer Gauthier.

> *Machine for living!* This is one of the expressions for which Le Corbusier has been most frequently and most violently reproached. But what is a machine? *An instrument for communicating a certain freedom of movement,* according to Littré; in other words *a motor,* but also a house, according to Diderot's *Recherches philosophiques sur le Beau:* Every machine involves combination, arrangement of parts tending to the same end. And is not the goal of a house to make life easy and agreeable? And is it not consequently important that the arrangement of all its parts tends to this same end?
>
> What! You're saying that our family roof, the sacred shelter of our household gods, the hereditary asylum and love-nest, the villa of our relaxation and the castle of our dreams—all just machines?
>
> Le Corbusier says *machine* for *house* the way Mme. de Sévigné, writing to her son-in-law, says *machine* to indicate her daughter Madame de Grignan: *If out of tenderness and pity, you fail to give a rest to this lovely machine, you will inevitably destroy it. . . .* Le Corbusier says *machine* for *house,* but Voltaire: *Man is so much a machine. . . .* Le Corbusier says *machine* for *house,* but La Fontaine: *Is there a poorer man in the whole round machine?* But Boileau: *But to think that God turns the world / and regulates the springs of the round machine.* But Béranger: *Observing the machine of the universe. . . .*
>
> And then we have the expression: *the machine of State;* Chateaubriand went so far as to invoke *the grand machines of Christianity;* The Dictionary of the Académie-Française allows us to exclaim that Veronese's

> "Last Supper" or St. Peter's in Rome are *Grand machines;* and Victor Hugo has observed that: *The marvelous is the epic's essential machine. . . .*
>
> A machine for living, Corbusier says, and he is right. For by expressing himself in this fashion he puts the problem where it belongs. He incites us to a *healthy conception of the residence;* not to forget, for instance, that a house must be above all a shelter sealed against the elements, thieves and prowlers, and at the same time a receptacle as open as possible to pure air, to light, to sunshine; to consider that order, in the rooms we live in, is one of the chief conditions of our peace of mind and that, consequently, we must achieve it conveniently and comfortably. In short, we ask architects, who are or should be artists, to prove themselves to be at least as endowed as the industrialists, creators of airplanes, automobiles, steamships, typewriters, office furniture, trunks, a thousand manufactured objects, in order to perform precisely the services we are entitled to expect of them.
>
> Such objects, such furniture, such maximally productive machines, all of which are obtained by a minimum of means and matter, Le Corbusier designates standards. Hence a *standard* is a necessary product because it corresponds exactly to one or more needs of our life; it is also, from the technological point of view, a model composed of simple elements, easily assembled. The *standard* is not perfection. It is merely the path, the basis, the springboard, the preparatory phase. . . . Before ultimately creating the Parthenon, which is architecture, a work of the highest spirituality, the Greeks made countless temples, always of similar construction but each time further refined. The *standard* expresses ineluctable realities, belonging to the economic and social realm. The architect, on the solid basis of the standard, has the possibility of attaining perfect beauty, but only the possibility.[16]

This was the battle he had begun as Charles-Edouard Jeanneret, trying to explain his goals to one of the many skeptics who did not understand the humility with which he tried to enrich other people's lives.

6

While Jeanneret was reformulating his own life in Paris, he was also trying to take control of his parents' future at a time when his mother was both wage earner and housekeeper. He wrote Georges and Marie: "I understand your silence and have been stirred by the awareness of the enormous difficulties you have faced, all the more unendurable since they were continuous and tormenting. And the cold, *as I know by my own experience,* can be depressing, especially for you who no longer have the resources of youth. But now better times have come, and I hope that your morale is better too. For you know, don't you, how to give things their real importance. You must envisage a future solution; there is where the search must be made, and I hope to search with you. I realize the crushing task Maman has *imposed* on herself; I can hardly congratulate her for having done so, but I know her courage and her strong will, and Albert must surely understand the reasons for my reticence. For you see, one must know how to choose happiness. And I can just hear dear Papa disparaging morale for irrefutable reasons, going at it in good conscience. But we must allow ourselves to be upset only in proportion to things as they are."[17]

The issue, as always, was how to wrestle happiness out of life, given the obstacles within one's own mind and the impositions of a flawed world. "I am often, believe me, forced to confront very melancholy realities," he wrote. "So long as they concern only myself, my feelings, my suffering, my harsh and violent struggles, I pay no mind. I have a remarkable power of endurance, I resist to the end, and always manage to survive. But there are so many kinds of suffering which other people do not survive, which are dreadful fatalities, and which actually make me realize to what degree I am a happy man." He recognized the effects of his own personality: "I'm an odd duck, and I know I disconcert those who don't know me well; those who do, make no secret of their esteem. It is all or nothing."[18]

Jeanneret intended to use this period of life to make money so that within two years he could have the financial independence to paint and do nothing else. He also declared to Georges and Marie that he intended to support them and Albert in perpetuity. All was perfect; he would be a whiz at business, a creative genius, and the bastion of the family.

7

"The ideal is one of purity, as old as the Greeks. And to achieve this ideal, it is the machine which affords us the means to exceed the greatness of Rome," he wrote Ritter and Czadra in April. Emboldened by his sense of purpose in fostering that credo, Jeanneret himself was "a motor which has been switched on."[19]

The lover of impeccable functioning was bowled over by Ozenfant's new car. The two friends spent a May afternoon in Versailles, zooming around in the spiffy model made of two "airplane bucket-seats" on a single chassis. Weighing only three hundred kilograms, endowed with an exceptionally strong motor, it could readily pass everything else on the road. Jeanneret wanted the speed of his life to echo the velocity of that automobile. "One is moved by this accelerated rhythm, and I take no pleasure strolling on foot through the woods," he wrote his parents.[20]

He had expanded his office at 29 bis rue d'Astorg to occupy four floors, and at home he had begun what became his habit of doing gymnastics every morning. Despite occasional migraines, he painted every night and on Sundays, side by side with Ozenfant. Earning twenty-eight thousand francs per year with his business enterprises, he was convinced that his plan to devote himself full-time to studio art was about to become reality.

XVII

1

Not everything was as clear as Charles-Edouard Jeanneret had thought. "All is confusion within me since I've gone back to drawing," he wrote Ozenfant that June 9. "Sudden rushes of blood force my fingers into the realm of the arbitrary, my mind no longer guiding me. . . . Yet I feel such *joie de vivre*! . . . In my business affairs, I have discipline enough, I lack it in my heart, in my ideas. I have given too free rein to the habit of impulse."[1]

He confessed to his role model, "In my confusion I evoke your tranquil, clear will. It seems to me there is an abyss of age between us. I feel that I am on the threshold of study, you are already at the stage of realizations. Behind me I sensed the fluttering of a thousand intentions, violent, successive sensations, and I kept telling myself: 'The day will come when I will build.' The days have come, and I am a wretched mason at the bottom of the foundation pit, without plan! . . . And the things I paint have no weight, no massiveness, no indispensable existence."[2]

IN MID-OCTOBER, he sold one million bricks in a single day, and felt his optimism and energy renewed, but a month later all was gloom again. He wrote his father, a sure comrade in depression, "Here winter is raging, the price of life has become exorbitant, the labor question insoluble. I have just spent fifteen terrible days, and nothing has changed." They were joined in their suffering: "I suspect that on your side, too, things have not been very cheerful. . . . We think of you often, but we lead on the whole a tyrannical existence, and what is most disturbing is that the circle of difficulties widens every day."[3]

He claimed to his parents that he had slept for forty-eight consecutive hours. As 1919 came to an end, Jeanneret's energy was so depleted that he felt he could do nothing whatsoever.

2

At the end of January 1920, Jeanneret had another encounter that changed his life. Edouard's second cousin Pierre Jeanneret, whom he had met a few years earlier, arrived in Paris to study architecture at l'Ecole des Beaux-Arts. Pierre—who was born in 1896 in Geneva and whose father was Georges Jeanneret's first cousin—had studied at l'Ecole des Beaux-Arts de Genève. There, he won first prizes in painting, carving, and architecture. He had recently done his military service in the cyclist corps.

Edouard's initial reaction was a mix of moral superiority and sheer contempt. He wrote his parents, "I am actually stupefied by the apathy of this boy of twenty-three; his nature is thoughtful enough but so rarely individual. At twenty-three, I had seen the Acropolis and built the Villa Georges Favre, and I was already a tough customer. He is just beginning his studies and hasn't a clue what direction to give them."[4] Yet, in spite of his reservations, Edouard sensed a potential alliance of great significance.

He was also encouraged by the aftermath of his show at THOMAS. Now an exhibition of Jeanneret's paintings was scheduled to open at Druet, one of the most prominent galleries in Paris, in January 1921. Needing to complete fifteen canvases in less than a year, he was painting at every moment that his other work allowed.

Relations between Jeanneret and his parents were on the mend. Georges and Marie were happier now that they were in a rental in the village of Blonay, and the sale of the house was behind them. Edouard was jubilant over a cheerful letter from his father, writing back, "Everything goes well here and now it's spring. . . . You're happy! What a difference it makes for me to hear that you're in that state of mind, whereas in 1918 it was the blackest depression." His own work was soaring: "I receive the greatest encouragements, and I have complete confidence in the future."[5]

Again his goals were in sight. On June 19, 1920, Jeanneret wrote Ritter and Czadra, "Paris is the line of fire. A different song. And my ambition has impelled me to the same excesses of work, but differently conceived. I believe this will produce results. It appears that I have something in me, for I'm constantly grappling with all the big guns here—in business as in art. In art above all. My life is programmed, but the days have only twenty-four hours, and I must sleep seven of them. So everything must be done outside of the ten business hours: thinking, acting, writing, painting, even caring for this little heart ever continually crushed and baffled by other pains.

When the program is major and organized as ours is, a hierarchy of access to time is set up. This would be untenable, physically and morally lethal, if it were to last all one's life. I have arranged a very brief interlude at the expiration of which there will be painting."[6]

It was a productive summer. By July, he had finished ten paintings. Although he had initially set out to complete a total of fifteen, he now decided to reach twenty before the exhibition. Nothing stood in his way, not even the excessive heat. He felt guarded about his progress yet essentially victorious, writing Ritter, "What is wrong with oneself is nothing compared to the weakness of others whom fate has not armed with fangs. There is not only high life in Paris. And I am sometimes anxious about always feeling so strong, so implacable. Considering other people, one realizes one's own happiness and the joy of one's destiny. Paris, with its host of sufferings, has allowed me to be happy with mine."[7]

Charles-Edouard Jeanneret was preparing to create another self, with another name. This alter ego, relentlessly fired by purpose, was meant to be devoid of the vulnerability that had been the burden of his youth. He was already on his way to that loftier place, for he and Ozenfant were about to start a magazine that embraced a new way to live.

3

> We founded *L'Esprit Nouveau* in order to open paths toward that laughing, clear and beautiful sky.
>
> —LE CORBUSIER

The intention of the magazine *L'Esprit Nouveau,* first published in October 1920 by Ozenfant and Jeanneret with the avant-garde poet Paul Dermée, was to promote artistic balance and mathematical order as a means toward the contentment that was now possible with peacetime. "The goal of art is to put the spectator in a state of mathematical quality, that is, a state of an elevated order. . . . The highest declaration of the human mind is the perception of order, and the greatest human satisfaction in the feeling of collaboration or participation in this order," they wrote.[8]

With the inception of the new publication, Charles-Edouard Jeanneret underwent the transformation of his name. He signed several essays "Le Corbusier." The pseudonym had the right ring. In one essay Jeanneret and

With Ozenfant and Albert Jeanneret in his studio in the Maison Blanche in August 1919, shortly before it was sold. The Serbian pot on his head was an acquisition from the journey to the east of 1911.

Ozenfant defined a work of art as "an artificial physical object destined to produce subjective reactions"; the name "Le Corbusier" suggested such an object designed to accommodate the "need for order . . . the most elevated of human needs."[9]

Charles-Edouard Jeanneret had long sought a means to counter the perpetual vagaries of his own mind. With his new name, he invented a person who had a protective shell.

Ozenfant adopted, for some of his writing, the name Saugnier, which had been his mother's maiden name. Jeanneret said he hadn't picked his mother's maiden name because it would only create confusion, being the same as that of the architects Perret. The explanation for the new name, promulgated by Le Corbusier himself, was that it derived from the name of his ancestor Lecorbesier. But there were a range of other reasons that led him to invent this sobriquet that had a more authoritative sound than "Perret" and endowed its bearer with the ability to have others "*courber,*" or bend to his will. Above all, "Le Corbusier" gave Charles-Edouard Jeanneret the toughness and resiliency he felt he needed.

4

When the first issue of *L'Esprit Nouveau* appeared on October 15, 1920, an article signed by Le Corbusier and Saugnier, entitled "Three Reminders to Architects," declared the universality, timelessness, and supreme beauty of "cubes, cones, spheres, cylinders, and pyramids." It cited the fundamentality of these forms to ancient architecture—from the Egyptian pyramids to the Greek temples—and to American silos and factories. Engineering had infinite value, whereas design for its own sake was decadence; mechanical calculations were superior to architectural folly.

On paper, everything was clear and certain; in reality, it was not. By November 1920, Jeanneret was again having serious problems at Alfortville, where the factory had a surplus of bricks. Making five hundred thousand per week, it now had a stockpile of 1,300,000 that no one wanted to buy.

Having only recently encouraged his parents to come to Paris and participate in its pleasures, he now wrote them, as if it were the only truth, "Life has been hard for me. It becomes harder and harder. Don't think I'm becoming insensitive. I am forced to choose, for the years pass tragically fast, and my work must not escape me. You cannot imagine what the struggle is like here in Paris. You have to have put yourself forward in order to realize it. This in the realm of ideas. There are distances created which are those of the mind and of comprehension. These distances have, for instance, alienated many of my old friends. But false good manners fall away and what remains is esteem and affection, which I feel very strongly here, where I am full of courage and certainty."[10]

Having deliberately shed the family name and set his sights on spreading his gospel everywhere, at age thirty-three he still cared desperately about open and truthful communication with these two people who had raised him. "In any case, you are resting now, and it is your lack of calm and ease which so strongly affected me. It was this way of referring everything to your own level of comprehension and thereby creating for yourself, through us, through me especially, cares and disappointments you had no need to experience. Next time, do not struggle so; let us gently make contact with the happiness of being with the two of you rested, serene, happy."[11]

That tight and complicated connection with his aging parents in the Swiss mountains, the interdependence of their happiness and his own, was a secret Le Corbusier carefully guarded from all who knew him in his new life. It both tortured and fortified him.

XVIII

1

The Galerie Druet normally exhibited artists of the School of Paris, among them Matisse and Bonnard. Art as didactic and programmatic as the recent work by Jeanneret and Ozenfant, both of whom kept their old names as painters to make the distinction from their *L'Esprit Nouveau* selves, was a departure. Madame Druet, the widow of the gallery's founder, had been persuaded by her director, Athis, to exhibit the two stalwarts of Purism, but it was not her personal taste.[1] Once the show was installed for its opening on January 22, 1921, Druet glanced at it and promptly walked back into her office—never to be seen in the gallery during the two weeks the work was up.

The twenty-five paintings by Ozenfant and twenty by Jeanneret were all the same format: one hundred by eighty-one centimeters. Those dimensions had an underlying mathematical purity; one hundred was ten squared, and eighty-one was nine squared. The formula facilitated the use of regulating lines—a passion of the painters, who had written about such proportional systems for the organization of building facades.

Jeanneret's canvases at Druet evinced considerable progress since his show at THOMAS. However formulaic and technically serial, they are lively and animated, more bold and audacious than his previous work or than Ozenfant's paintings. The deliberately compressed surfaces of these elaborately structured canvases present highly charged forms with multiple meanings. A shallow plate reads as the sound hole of a guitar and the top of a smokestack at the same time, so that the musical instrument and the massive pipe have the same monumentality. The compositions are charged with a lively interplay between distinct flatness and three-dimensional dynamism. Jeanneret emphasized the recesses and curves, the masses and voids, with the eye of an architect.

Music was often one of Jeanneret's main motifs, with violins and guitars the dominant subject matter. As in musical compositions, each work has a powerful sense of progression; a major statement is followed by a sequence of reactions, with the elements different from one another yet carefully related. The earthy colors respond to one another as carefully and successfully as the four different instruments in a well-composed string quartet. The underlying plan is essential; true to his earliest training as a draftsman for the watchmaking industry, Jeanneret drew and painted on a modified grid.

The paintings were signed "Jeanneret," the drawings "L-C." In pencil, L-C was neat and precise yet bold. He made a very physical rhythm, endowing forms with a sculptural mass, so that the viewer feels the tough and sturdy cylindricality of stovepipes; you have the sensation that you can grab the doorknobs and pour from the pitchers. L-C imbued simple objects with majesty; to render everyday life bountiful was his goal in all media and under all his names.

2

For eighteen months, Jeanneret had been so devoured by the need to paint that he had "withdrawn from everybody in order to execute a difficult task. I have not had enough of all the hours of the year, in an agitated life and a crushing load of work, to be able to give time even to my closest friends." Obsession was Jeanneret's mainstay; without it, he was worthless. He needed the urgency of work and his relentless pace to feel alive. "There was not a *single* hour of relaxation in the whole year," he wrote Ritter and Czadra about his and Ozenfant's preparations for the show.[2] The intensity suited him. To halt or even falter for a moment would be like becoming a broken watch, with its hands frozen in place.

Once the show opened, the audience response stung. It confirmed his horror of bourgeois taste—which did not ameliorate for the rest of his life: "The public reacts: praise or scorn and indignation. We thought we were so docile and we are treated like madmen." Louis Vauxcelles accused the work of lacking humanity. Writing Ritter, Jeanneret responded as only he could: "Vauxcelles finds all this glacial and advises me to go sleep with a trollop in the Meudon woods. Vauxcelles is also called the Knight of the Doleful Countenance, for he is sad, very sad, and it takes paprika to enliven him; paprika and ringing gold coins."[3]

He continued, "Our paintings are taxed with being mechanical; myself I am certain that they imply a dream, a dignified and austere dream, but of an order above the gonads and the 'heart.' "[4] Jeanneret had hoped for a better response in part because he desperately needed to sell these paintings to survive. After his brief flash of success in his business ventures, following three years of trying to secure his fortune, he had been wiped out.

He now definitively abandoned his efforts to work with industry, blaming the overall international financial crisis for this debacle. But Jeanneret did manage to find the funding, from a range of sources, to continue *L'Esprit Nouveau.* Its message was so imperative that it had to be saved at all cost.

In an article for issue 10, Le Corbusier and Saugnier showed Greek temples and automobiles side by side. This was the essence of their gospel, for the comparison made the achievements of ancient Greece applicable to the modern world. "Geometry is our greatest creation and we are enthralled by it," the authors wrote.[5] Promulgating those values, Le Corbusier was on the upswing; it was a "period of healthy courage and clarity, the twilight of impressionism, of symbolism, of what was beside the facts."[6]

Le Corbusier had a new realism about finances that Jeanneret had lacked in the days of the Maison Blanche. He recognized the necessity of funding to realize his artistic ideals, and beyond what he had found for the magazine, he succeeded in raising one hundred thousand francs for his other ventures. Cynically, he attracted the investors because he pandered to their wish for "profits, to be realized at a friendly businessmen's lunch—convinced, between the fruit and the cheese, of the necessity of ennobling the financier's profession by some vague investment on the dreamers' behalf."[7]

For all the setbacks, his life plan was now working. To Ritter, he extolled his emergence on the world stage only three years after he had made his pivotal move from La Chaux-de-Fonds: "It so happens that today I exist, much more rapidly and more powerfully than I would ever have thought. This in a country of astonishing health. The German *morbidezza* is alarming, and the many books and periodicals we receive appall me, outrage me, stupefy me. Yet I could not have come to anything without this desert of ordeals, which is Paris, this city where choice functions with a terrible brutality, because I have created my identity on my own foundations, on my own terms."[8] Having mentally planned his new self, he was now succeeding in constructing it.

XIX

1

Following the war, geniuses in many domains voraciously explored new means of living well. Jeanneret had believed he would change the world as a painter. Now, as Le Corbusier, his mission was to transform the human condition through architecture. Convinced that the right visual environment had the power to elevate the souls of its inhabitants, he was determined to create settings for "healthy activity and industrious optimism."[1]

That happy state was the goal of the Citrohan housing type, which Le Corbusier developed between 1920 and 1922. In a 1921 *L'Esprit Nouveau* article called "Mass-produced Houses," he and Saugnier explained that they had deliberately used a name based on the Citroën motorcar because they intended a "house like a car. . . . One needs to consider the house like a machine to live in or like a tool . . . what one can be proud of is to have a practical house like a typewriter."[2] The further use of the phrase "a machine to live in" would be overinterpreted, but the building concept was clear. The house had a shoe-box shape. A forthright and bold rectangular block, its main element was a two-story-high living room flooded with light from a wall almost entirely of glass.

Le Corbusier had been struck by the idea when he was eating at a bistro on the rue Godot de Mauroy across from Ozenfant's apartment, where the two artists ate together almost every day. The space was very high and four times as long as it was wide. A two-story dining area opened to the street in front; the kitchen was in the back, in the lower part of a space sliced horizontally into two, with a small dining balcony on the top.

One day, Le Corbusier realized that this was the perfect solution for a human dwelling. The kitchen and a maid's room and a dining area could be in a space one story high in the back of the house, with a bedroom and bathroom and boudoir above them. A spiral staircase could link the two stories tidily. These nested rooms could open onto a two-story living room. The flat-topped roof could serve as a solarium in front and, toward the back, as the base for two guest rooms reached by outside stairs. All of the light would come in through industrial-style windows on the two short ends, making the structure simple to build and easy to monitor against crime.

Le Corbusier was convinced the concept had endless applications as an ideal habitation. Simple to clean and hygienic, it could be built of whatever materials were most readily at hand. "With this house, we turned our back on the architectural conceptions of the academically oriented schools as on the 'modern' ones," he joyfully explained.[3] This "house like a car" had a zip and aura of victory that would be felt by all who entered it.

The dream of the man who had just changed his name into that of a powerful tool, who would soon refer to himself in the third person, was stability and clarity. Having organized form in his paintings to counteract emotional turmoil, he now had developed architecture that provided systematization and effectiveness as anchors in shaky territory.

The Citrohan design was a precise shell in which the rich tapestry of human life might flourish. Its geometrically organized and rationally programmed environment would allow the vagaries of existence, the unfathomable struggles and the sublime pleasures, to be realized in harmony. The inhabitants could feel serene and secure in logical dwellings that worked well and gave pleasure through their agreeable lines and forms.

In one way or another, all of the architecture to be made over the next half century by this man who could be so warm and so cold, generous and arrogant, insightful and shallow, was marked by that same combination of the Romantic, the Classical, and the Modern.

2

Le Corbusier's enterprise of his new self had taken off beyond expectations. In midsummer, he wrote Ritter and Czadra, "The Le Corbusier campaign is bearing fruits I had not hoped for so soon. I am being asked for houses, which is too bad since I wanted a year's rest." The notion of stopping was, of course, specious. Besides designing houses, he was painting and editing his magazine: "The Paris of internal struggles would be stifling for anyone who failed to engage in the fight. It's a tough battle, but for what stakes! Ambition? Of course, or let's say determination. For this one is determined."[4]

He was, he told his confessor figures, "full of good humor, with a bad character." Their faith in him was a major factor in his life. "I know that you still have all your confidence in me; how gratefully I preserve my precious memories of you. I often write you imaginary letters, thinking you would be in agreement with me. But imaginary or not, you would be, deep down."[5]

They were no longer the only ones to relieve his solitude. Le Corbusier was finding a group of admirers in Paris. The painter Fernand Léger described their first encounter: "I met Le Corbusier in 1921 or 1922, in a rather odd way. I was living in Montparnasse and from time to time I would sit on the terrace of La Rotonde with friends and models from the neighborhood. One day one of them said, 'look, there's a funny specimen. He's riding a bicycle in a bowler. . . .' A few minutes later, I saw coming toward me, quite stiffly, an extraordinary moving object, a kind of Chinese shadow topped by a bowler hat, with spectacles and a clergyman's overcoat. This object advanced slowly on its bicycle, scrupulously obeying the laws of perspective. This picturesque personage, indifferent to the curiosity he awakened, was the architect Le Corbusier. Shortly afterward I made his acquaintance. I must say that our tastes had many points in common. He, too, painted."[6]

These two robust enthusiasts of modern life, who regarded smokestacks and scaffolding with a rare delicacy of perception, whiled away long evenings at La Rotonde and began bicycling together. Unlike many of Le Corbusier's relationships, this was a friendship that was to last. With the rare individuals who, like him, combined a passion for modernism and human simplicity, he was truly at home.

3

Le Corbusier was ready to redesign the world. Having planned what he considered the perfect individual dwelling, he leapt to the idea of varying and multiplying it on a vast scale. In 1922, at the Salon d'Automne, where he exhibited the Maison Citrohan for the first time, he also presented drawings, plans, and models for a city of three million inhabitants.

This imaginary metropolis was impeccably organized. At the center there was a seven-story-high structure that was a terminal for trains, subways, and automobiles, with an airport on top. Twenty-four cruciform, glass office buildings, each sixty stories high, surrounded it. Beyond the skyscrapers there were apartment houses, one type containing standardized dwellings around a communal garden, the other with luxurious two-story units similar inside to the Citrohan house, with two-story-high living rooms. Each of these cushier residences had a private roof garden, so that the privileged few could connect with nature there as well as in the public spaces. Four hundred thousand people would inhabit the business district, six hundred thousand the area of urban housing surrounding it, and the remaining two million a garden city on the outskirts.

Like Freud, Le Corbusier had sought to discern universal laws and truths: "standards of the mind, standards of the heart, the physiology of sensations (of our human sensations); then standards of history and statistics. I touched human bases, I possessed the realm where our actions occur."[7] Charles-Edouard Jeanneret's belief that he knew best about how others should live had reached a new scale.

THE BASIC BUILDING MATERIALS were concrete, steel, and glass. They facilitated the height of those living rooms and the large windows that let in the abundance of nature and made the sky present. Le Corbusier was using modern technology to re-create the combination of community living with a direct connection to the universe he had discovered at Ema and to make a haven like the monasteries on Mount Athos: "You are under the shade of trees, vast lawns spread all around you. The air is clear and pure; there is hardly any noise," he wrote about the life he would give three million people.[8] "The materials of city planning are sky, space, trees, steel and cement, in this order and in this hierarchy."[9] He envisioned an "immensity of space . . . the sky everywhere, as far as the eye can see":[10] that uplifting vista he had first known on Athos.

Le Corbusier deplored the helter-skelter aspects of urban living, the elements that were random or inchoate. But a well-run city could be the perfect engine of human life. His new metropolis was the solution: "As the seat of power (in the widest meaning of the words; for in it there come together princes of affairs, captains of industry and finance, political leaders, great scientists, teachers, thinkers, the spokesmen of the human soul, painters, poets and musicians), the city draws every ambition to itself; it is clothed in a dazzling mirage of unimaginable beauty; the people swarm into it. Great men and our leaders install themselves in the city's centre."[11]

Having located himself within walking distance of the Assemblée Nationale and the Elysée Palace, Le Corbusier had put himself in the cockpit he described. From here he intended to launch a new city and build its clones all over the world.

4

The architecture historian Vincent Scully has said that the drawings for the City for Three Million reflect "a monocular vision."[12] Being unable to see with one eye causes distorted depth perception, which is why, in Le Corbusier's perspective drawings of the superhighway running through the new city, the vanishing point is much nearer than it would be in actuality, with the extreme foreshortening creating an artificial impression of energy and speed. Moreover, Le Corbusier had become partially blind to most other people's experience. What he showed at the Salon d'Automne was exciting, imaginative, and bold; had it been built, it would probably have made many people miserable.

To Ritter and Czadra, he acknowledged his partial blindness: "I am a Cyclops in spite of myself, a nasty joke. And for this very reason things are quite complicated for me. You get used to it: it's been going on for two years. The cause: overwork."[13] In spite of the ocular problems he had had since his youth, he was convinced that the loss of sight in his left eye was a direct result of his detaching his retina when working at nights with very hard graphite—an explanation that supported his sense of martyrdom even if it made no sense medically.

As a Cyclops, he was in his self-image a giant with a foul disposition, but also the primordial son of Earth and Sky.

5

Le Corbusier observed his own ascent with pleasure. In April 1922, he wrote Ritter, "A new incarnation seems to dawn for Le Corbusier; glowing prospects, art as free as possible. On every side, in every realm, the battle lines are moved forward. One is observed, appreciated. One must do well. It might be said that I have reached this point: of being at grips with the powerful figures, the ones who count. In architecture, complete success: I am alone in my category."[14]

For all the gloating, though, he remained daunted by the challenges: "*Succès d'esteem* in the press and elsewhere, in Paris and abroad. All of which is of no importance. Every day I face the work to be completed, occasionally sick to my stomach, then leaping forward, etc. A thrilling life, but not on days when I am sick. At thirty-five, you are old enough to be given credit, but it is an age when you must produce. I am not complaining, I am content. Content especially with being, at this moment, of my generation, for the period requires an adaptation of full consent in order to grant you understanding and a reason for working. Art is eternal, of course. Only what has *contributed* lasts."[15]

He had severed his old life: "Switzerland alienates me. I feel I belong to the Mediterranean coast, and not Norway." He told his friends that he had destroyed his old possessions, burned his archives, and saved nothing. Even if this was only partially true, he was now living in empty white rooms, with no furniture and nothing on the walls. The apartment had the purity and simplicity of Athos: " 'Everything's been said, everything's been done, there's not even a new sin,' you wrote me that last year. Yes and no. About sins you're right, but not about painting: observe this figure." Here the man with a new name and a new profession drew a line like an uncoiled spring, looping its way along, with an A on top toward the end. "We still are entitled to try to be at A. That's what matters."[16]

6

That summer, Le Corbusier shortened the issues of *L'Esprit Nouveau* from one hundred pages to fifty in order to save money. His financial mistakes were over. "In an enterprise of ideas like this, money talks, and talks tough," he wrote to Ritter. What was required was a "magazine that will be more direct, swifter, and more readable. . . . The speed factor intervenes."[17]

Le Corbusier was approaching his own life with that same enterprise. He sought efficiency and structure. Set on his course of changing the world through architecture, he would do what it took to navigate effectively toward that goal.

Yet even as he forged ahead, Le Corbusier was still subject to Jeanneret's bouts of doubt and sadness. That September, he went to Venice. On a postcard of the Piazza San Marco, he wrote Ritter and Czadra, "Dear friends, I have made my escape and I'm doing water-colors, happy as a clam. This is a city for water-colors, a technique for such beauty. Taking the train I indulged in bitter reflections on the ravages of time; I am no longer young in body and mind. Life has become hard with ever-higher ambitions. Harsh labor, endless struggles. I was telling myself (leaving the hospital) that the heroic age was probably past, an age unfamiliar with weariness. So I'm doing water-colors and enjoying this theatrical city. Best regards and forgive me for such a long silence."[18]

The reason for the hospital stay was a hemorrhoid operation, which left him physically uncomfortable, aware of age, and vulnerable. But the Veneto restored him. Le Corbusier fired off another postcard to Ritter and Czadra, pressing words so tightly into the margins around his message in every direction that it had to be turned 360 degrees, and required the use of a magnifying glass, in order to be read. The picture side of the card showed a Tiepolo from the Villa Zileri in Vicenza that, appropriately, depicted *Time*

Revealing Truth. In the dramatic allegory, winged creatures with ardent expressions on their faces flaunt banners emblazoned with their noble crests. Jeanneret wrote to the two men, "I think of you united with me in my enthusiasm for Vicenza, Palladio, and Tiepolo. . . . It would be nice if you would write me a letter of twenty lines about your Tiepolesque delights."[19]

Le Corbusier himself was ready for his own version of those delights.

XX

1

From 1922 on, Le Corbusier made houses and villas of tensile lightness and refined proportions that took domestic design into virgin territory. In steel and glass, and in concrete as light and taut as a sail perfectly rigged in a high wind, Le Corbusier's neat, rhythmic structures used modern technology to create a new form of aesthetic luxury: habitations of unprecedented simplicity and airiness.

He built a tapered, five-story studio/house for Amédée Ozenfant—who had recently inherited the wherewithal from his father—that has a triumphant grace and neatness. Here, Le Corbusier realized his desire to make urban life easy and pleasant and to give it many of the charms of the countryside, in a radically modern shell. The Ozenfant dwelling stands opposite the large Montsouris Reservoir, which, as the source of much of Paris's water, resembles a lake at the edge of the city. The crisp and straightforward factory-style windows open to these bucolic charms. The roof is a progression of angled skylights that bring the sun and sky in. The house embraces the treetops and the reservoir as totally as it reflects mass production and industrialization. And when one views it from across the street and looks through the sequence of large sheets of plate glass set at right angles in the studio, it is like a weightless container for air and light.

The architect who was in the process of developing for himself a skin against the outside world designed an attractive, plain white concrete covering to sheath the rooms. These walls are nuanced with little indentations and slight protrusions, useful in their function of letting in light and warding off rainwater as well as artful in their rhythm and shapes. Ozenfant's villa is as refined and subtle as a late abstract composition by Mondrian, thanks to Le Corbusier's judgment and precision about where to hold a border back and where to let a plane protrude.

One touch above all brings the structure to life. This is the curving exterior staircase with its ribbonlike banister. The pirouette of the stairs leads to a right-angled composition made by a ledge—to shield an entrance door from the rain—and a vertical slice of glass above it. Nearby, a cantilevered

Exterior of Ozenfant's studio and residence in Paris, 1924

square projecting at a right angle to the wall under a window grid is action and void; in counterpoint to it, another cantilever over the exposed corner of the house serves the practical purpose of shelter while providing a spiritual lift through its sheer élan. Visual diversion and effective architecture are synonymous. Life inside Ozenfant's residence and workplace is marked by both plenitude and clarity.

Another of Le Corbusier's inventions was the study that is like a monk's cell within the studio. To reach it, one has to climb difficult stairs, with risers of double height. Accustomed as he was to hiking up seven such flights of steps whenever he arrived at his own home, Le Corbusier valued the journey he now gave to his friend. The reward for the energizing ascent was one of the first of the architect's small spaces meant to provide quiet and solitude. It mimics a boat cabin or a sleeping compartment on a train, with everything necessary for thinking and working in a tidy, aesthetically satisfying, and comfortable enclosure as carefully conceived as it is small.

There was also a garage—unusual in 1922, but a prescient acknowledgment of the need for a car. And the housekeeper was given a real bathroom nearly the size of the one for the master bedroom—a rare statement of social equality, initiated by the architect.

For all that had been done in Berlin and Vienna, nowhere else were the angles quite so rhythmic and pleasing, the lines so playful, as in this house

Interior of Ozenfant's studio

on a corner with its bold, boxlike form and double-peaked roof. The juxtaposition of textures—buffed glass, shimmering and translucent against the black steel mullions supporting it; white concrete, solid against the openness of the window wall and banding—is infinitely satisfying. The black-white rhythms have the quality of cinema. The purity and refinement and understatement were unprecedented in domestic architecture.

2

In 1922, Le Corbusier elevated the second cousin he had initially disparaged to the position of partner. The principals of the office were, officially, "Le Corbusier–Pierre Jeanneret." But it was called l'Atelier Le Corbusier; there was no question as to which one had more authority. There was room for only a single genius in the partnership, and while Le Corbusier did most of the designing, the competent but less imaginative Pierre was better suited to be the loyal, skillful manager with his feet on the ground. Few people even knew that the two men in truth had the same last name.

Toward the end of his life, Le Corbusier wrote, "Our work as a team permitted an important architectural and urbanist production. Supporting each other, we were able to produce significant mutual work. Between the two of us, there was always total confidence, despite the difficulties of a working life. . . . Our personal characters in all this advanced side by side, Pierre and I confronting all obstacles together."[1] In fact, there was to be one long-lasting feud over the issue of Vichy, but Pierre's presence in Le Corbusier's life made a great deal possible.

THAT SAME YEAR, Le Corbusier began to live with Yvonne Gallis. They met because Yvonne was a salesgirl and model at the couture house of Jove when Charles-Edouard Jeanneret showed his paintings there in 1919.

She had been born Jeanne Victorine Gallis in Monaco on January 4, 1892. Her father was a gardener, and her mother owned a small flower shop. Full figured, with large dark eyes, a delicate chiseled nose, and cupid-shaped lips, Yvonne was unabashedly sexy and coquettish. When Le Corbusier first met her, she parted her black hair in the middle, pulling it back straight and then letting it cascade in neat waves that draped around gold hoop earrings, so that she resembled an exotic gypsy. She laid on her mascara, eyebrow pencil, and rouge as if with a shovel, and she applied her dark crimson lipstick as boldly as he painted bottles of red wine in his Purist still lifes.

To him, she was "Vonvon"; to her, he was "Doudou." From the start, she made him laugh and gave him a sense of well-being. She had none of his intellect and drive, but she believed in him totally, at least initially. The zealot who was slaving away for long days at the office revolutionizing world architecture and designing everything from private houses to entire cities, and who sanctimoniously told his parents that he had completely sacrificed the pleasures of friendship and private life, let down his guard with this girlfriend who embodied the Mediterranean spirit he craved. With her, he had fun and felt robust.

Although they were to be together thirty-seven years, the first ten unmarried, Yvonne remained almost completely out of the public eye, even as Le Corbusier became world famous. She rarely attended official events and scarcely appears in the material published about him. The architect's close friends and office staff knew her, but otherwise he kept her like a well-guarded, secret treasure.

The one statement Le Corbusier put in print about this eccentric beauty makes clear the role she played in his mental construction of his life: "Yvonne is the best girl in the world. But she has her own ideas, her habits. She's a willful little creature, and it's no use trying to alter her nature. What would be the point? To make her a commonplace *bourgeoise*? Wasted effort!

You would get nowhere. The game isn't worth the candle. What I can say is that her tastes and mine fit together, harmonized by being different. . . . Yvonne, the empress's daughter, used to giving despotic commands, a great sport of a girl, so kind, so pretty, so charming, so affectionate."[2]

Yvonne was famous for her practical jokes as well as for her sharp remarks. When the distinguished architectural patron Père Couturier, a Dominican father known for his support of modern art, came to call on Le Corbusier and his wife in the early 1950s, Yvonne, sounding like a well-brought-up Catholic schoolgirl, reverently told the prelate to have a seat on the living-room sofa. He lowered himself gently in his immaculate white robes, only to bring about the sounds of booming flatulence from a whoopee cushion. Yvonne began to giggle like a ten-year-old, as did the admiring Le Corbusier, who retailed the story. She was salty, generous, and famously difficult.

THE FIRST EVIDENCE of Yvonne's residence in the garret apartment on the rue Jacob is a letter dated September 27, 1922, which Le Corbusier sent to "Mademoiselle Yvonne Gallis, chez M. Ed. Jeanneret, 20 rue Jacob."[3] On his way back to Paris, he visited his parents and brother in Switzerland, where there was no possibility of his being joined by a girlfriend, let alone of revealing their cohabitation, but where he hastened to write her in secret.

Le Corbusier described cutting wood with great strokes of an ax; now his hands were full of blisters. He wrote Yvonne in baby talk, instructing her to rest up and to sing, to be at her best when he got back: "And it would be nice if you made me some little drawings. You'd have fun doing it, the time would pass more quickly, and your Doudou would be so proud."[4]

He counted on her to understand him, continuing, "My parents are as nice as could be. But they're terrified of their sons and their damn ideas. Fortunately I never talk about painting—that would stir up a storm."[5] To post this letter secretly, Le Corbusier needed to walk through the countryside for nearly an hour in the wind and rain. Sneaking out of the house for love, he felt a sense of true companionship and could fancy himself a Mediterranean at last.

3

The architect was having his bachelor digs remade to suit his girlfriend's tastes, and wrote her from Vincenza about the details. Pierre had wallpaper installed. While Le Corbusier was traveling in northern Italy, Yvonne was hanging curtains and applying yet another coat of polish to the parquet. He wrote her that his consolation each evening when he returned to his hotel room was to look at her photo and think of her in their new domesticity. After a six-week separation, he was counting the days until he would be back "in my little nest in the rue Jacob with you my happy little song-sparrow." Anticipating the hard work he faced in Paris, he wrote, "You'll be there to soothe me with your caresses. . . . I know I've got a bad character, but I wouldn't do any harm to a nice little friend like you."[6]

He instructed her not to come to the station when he got back. His train was to arrive early in the morning and might not be on time; this would fatigue her. He would head straight home; she should await him in bed.

Le Corbusier now considered himself a connoisseur of women and wanted Yvonne to know of her high standing: "Venetian women are lovely—dark and distinguished, built rather like you; so I kept thinking of you, and I was quite pleased with you in comparison."[7] His way of being faithful to her, he explained to his mistress, was by embracing his pillow. He urged her to ask him, once he got back to Paris, what his ideas had been when he was doing so.

4

Within months of their beginning to live together, the relationship between Le Corbusier and Yvonne had advanced to a point of complete dependence for both. But even a year into the affair, he remained nervous about the need to keep her existence secret from his parents. In August 1923, when he went to Blonay, he instructed Yvonne that if she wrote him at his parents' rented chalet, she had to be sure to address the envelope with a typewriter, to prevent his mother from having any ideas about the sender.

Pierre, on the other hand, was in the inner circle. During that holiday, the quieter cousin was in charge of Yvonne's entertainment and well-being in Paris. Following Pierre's report that Yvonne was grimacing when she took her cough syrup, Le Corbusier, like a tough parent who had put a caretaker in charge, wrote that if she was still coughing when he got home, he would give her a "good thrashing."[8]

At first, she was nothing but worshipful and sweet to her lover. But by their second year together, she periodically burst out angrily. Le Corbusier appeared to handle her anger rather than rise to it. With his mother and colleagues, he feuded; he dealt with Yvonne as one might cope with an enchanting pet cat, accepting and enjoying the limitations of control.

But how he admired his inamorata. He credited Yvonne with "a quality which makes for peace in the house," while complaining to her about his mother's chronic restlessness and twitching, her need always to be doing something, and her inability to sleep.[9] The contrast between these two totally different women, which Le Corbusier often pointed out to both, obsessed him.

When Le Corbusier returned to be with his mother and father in Switzerland for Christmas that year, Yvonne again remained in Paris. Back in his parents' world, the thirty-six-year-old architect simply did whatever was expected of him. He again cut wood for the winter and helped slaughter pigs for the holiday meal. He slept on a board in a freezing room under the roof, and when his father took off on mountain outings in brutal weather, he joined in cheerfully. But in the letters no one saw him mail, Le Corbusier emphasized to Yvonne how much he missed her. He complained of his loneliness and the sexlessness of life there, conjuring up a picture of the bare planks on which he slept solo, in contrast to their warm bed at home with her in it.

Realizing that she would be alone for Christmas, Le Corbusier wrote on December 24, seemingly unaware that, even if in his mind he thought he was comforting her on Christmas Eve, she could not possibly receive the letter until a day or two after the actual holiday: "Yet your Doudou will be thinking of you and sending you a nice kiss during the night. In my chilly room under the eaves, I'll be thinking of my brave little girl far away in her soft beddy-bye while I'm sleeping on a plank. I'm scouring the countryside, which is covered with snow, and it's cold and wet and dreary, and I'm out looking for sites. No fun, but my parents are so happy about the future house that I'm glad to take on this task."[10]

The separation and hardship and foul weather were all worth enduring for that chance yet again to create a place where his parents would live. He had a new idea in his mind, and this time, with a different name, advanced skills, and a sense of reality, he would not let them down.

XXI

1

Raoul La Roche, a Basel-born director of the Crédit Commercial de France to whom Max Du Bois had introduced Le Corbusier, had become keen about the architect's work. La Roche, who spoke with a thick singsong accent like Le Corbusier's, was a man of strong opinions. La Roche had been supporting *L'Esprit Nouveau* ever since 1920, and he valued Le Corbusier, four years his junior, as an aesthetic guide.

In November 1921, Ozenfant and Le Corbusier bought for La Roche six Picassos—"the most beautiful," said Le Corbusier—and a major Braque at a foreclosure auction of work coming from the collection of the dealer Kahnweiler.[1] They acquired for themselves two Picassos that Le Corbusier kept at the rue Jacob and a Braque that Ozenfant had in his studio. The prices, Le Corbusier proudly noted, were a fifth of what they would have been in galleries. Le Corbusier and Ozenfant continued to coach La Roche on his collection, which, while deliberately excluding Matisse, whose pictures they considered lacking in gravity, also had work by Léger and Lipchitz. La Roche was so grateful to Le Corbusier for steering him toward foreclosure sales where art could be bought at low prices that he eventually gave the architect the Braque.

The prosperous banker also bought up work by Ozenfant and Jeanneret—as he continued to be known as a painter. In 1923 alone, Jeanneret sold him six major paintings. That same year, his devotee commissioned what was to be Le Corbusier's most significant building to date. This was a house in Autheuil, on the outskirts of the sixteenth arrondissement, intended primarily as a showcase for La Roche's collection and as a place for the banker to give parties.

The project became doubly important because, while Le Corbusier was enjoying new prosperity thanks to La Roche, Albert Jeanneret had befriended Lotti Walden-Raaf, a widow who had come to Paris as a member of the Swedish Ballet Company when it was performing at the Théâtre des Champs-Elysées. Albert and Walden-Raaf were wed in June 1923. Walden-

Pastor Huguenin, Lotti and Albert Jeanneret, Pierre Jeanneret, and Le Corbusier at Lotti and Albert's wedding ceremony, June 26, 1923. Charles-Edouard Jeanneret's painting in the background, now owned by the Museum of Modern Art in Stockholm, was his wedding present to them.

Raaf, who had a private income, commissioned a house adjacent to La Roche's, where she and Albert and her two young daughters could live.

The adjoining villas changed forever the way that human beings might choose to feel at home. Notions of what required concealment and what was permissible to see were radically altered; concepts of separation and openness, physical and emotional, were never again the same. The inventive forms and pioneering materials inaugurated a revolution in domestic design that echoed almost everywhere in the world where people construct houses.

THE VILLA LA ROCHE is a marvel of playful rhythms and luminescence. The interior details—the sloping, shiplike interior ramp connecting the second and third floors through the capacious gallery (possibly a prototype for Frank Lloyd Wright's ramps at the 1959 Guggenheim Museum); the gallery table that is a bold plane supported by an upended triangle at one end and a slab at the other; the recessed shelves here and there; the soaring interior atrium/hall with its lively balconies and ramp ways—have the weightlessness and the upbeat spirit Le Corbusier felt in the music he loved (see color plate 4). The original container was equally daring. As absolute in

Facade of the Villa La Roche, ca. 1925

form as Jeanneret's most pared-down paintings and more massive than the studio for Ozenfant, it was like an enlarged version of the shoe-box Citrohan houses.

With this showcase for an art collector, Le Corbusier opened new possibilities for the concept of luxury. Flat surfaces, machined materials, right angles, sharp edges—all were taken from the realm of industrial fabrication and made the essence of domestic graciousness. A solid block might be as suitable for a rich person as rococo panels; concrete could serve where once there would have been gilding.

THE PROCESS, however, had none of the grace of the results. La Roche had put his total budget at 250,000 francs. By the time construction began, the estimate for building was 200,000, on top of 207,000 for the land and various fees and an additional 80,000 for furnishings and other expenses. Construction began in July 1923, yet the interior elevation drawings were still not complete more than a year later. The interior walls, constructed of brick covered in plaster, were not strong enough to support the doors Le Corbusier specified, which were made of "Ronéo," an exceptionally heavy metal; some walls had to be rebuilt out of concrete, and the doors' size had to be altered. The windows had flaws, and the technical systems were a disaster.

Raoul La Roche with his collection, ca. 1925

The strip lighting Le Corbusier and Pierre Jeanneret designated for the library and gallery gave insufficient light for reading. In October 1925, La Roche wrote Le Corbusier that the dining room ceiling was still "full of holes. . . . It's six months since I moved in and I am still obliged to use illumination which . . . relies on ad hoc arrangements. What must the many visitors think, and what do you want me to tell them? I come back to the point that a perfectly banal system would be the best solution."[2] It was only in further revisions, undertaken in January 1926 and then in 1928, that the lighting was satisfactorily resolved.

Such disagreements—and on many occasions a schism between architect and client—became the norm for a commission by Le Corbusier. Yet the airy court of the Villa La Roche, with its ramps and parapets and sequence of visual vignettes, remains a triumph.

2

The Villa La Roche led to a dispute that sundered Le Corbusier and Ozenfant. Le Corbusier credited himself and Pierre with installing La Roche's paintings according to the collector's "precise instruction."[3] Initially, the cousins had hung the Picassos in the gallery, but when the collector insisted that it be used solely for Purist works, they reinstalled La Roche's collection. When Le Corbusier subsequently arrived at the villa to discuss an unrelated issue, he found that Ozenfant had made major changes in that hanging.

Le Corbusier's subsequent letter to Ozenfant about the problem exemplifies the insidious form of diplomacy that became his speciality. The architect presents himself as the paradigm of balance and even temper. Touting his own virtue but seeming amenable to compromise, he is initially solicitous; then, subtly, he begins the attack. He writes, "Nothing could please me more than that you should carry out the hanging, but I would like it done by agreement with me—not with the aim of protecting my own interests (since you will have seen that I kept a good place for you)—but simply with the intention of insuring that the La Roche house should not take on the look of a house of a (postage-stamp) collector." Following that deceptively gentle language, he shows his will of iron: "I insist absolutely that certain parts of the architecture should be entirely free of paintings. . . . Since this intention appears to have been modified by the new arrangements which you have made, I appeal to you as a good friend, first to take note of it and secondly to come to an agreement with me over it."[4]

Then, in 1926, Le Corbusier wrote an article in *Cahiers d'Art* criticizing La Roche for undermining the impact of his architecture through the dense installation of the pictures. This prompted La Roche to write the architect a charming riposte: "Do you recall the origin of my undertaking? 'La Roche, when you have a fine collection like yours, you should have a house built worthy of it.' And my response: 'Fine, Jeanneret, make this house for me.' Now, what happened? The house, once built, was so beautiful that on seeing it I cried: 'It's almost a crime to put paintings in it.' Nevertheless I did so. How could I have done otherwise? Do I not have certain obligations with regard to my painters, of whom you yourself are one? I commissioned from you a 'frame for my collection.' You provided me with a 'poem of walls.' Which of us two is most to blame?"[5] Not all of Le Corbusier's disputes with his clients were handled in such gracious tones.

But Raoul La Roche was a man of exceptional humor. Violaine de Montmollin, the seven-year-old daughter of another of Le Corbusier's Swiss banker friends, Jean-Pierre de Montmollin, was invited, with her brother, to the formal inauguration of the villa in 1927. The little girl found Le Corbusier, with his strong mountain accent, amusing and extremely charming to her in particular. While others drank champagne, the two de Montmollin children continually slid down the gallery ramp on their backsides; Raoul La Roche and Le Corbusier were the only people present who approved.[6]

3

Le Corbusier chose the furniture and interior fittings for the Villa La Roche: white curtains, a blend of flannel and cambric, from the department store Printemps; graceful bentwood Thonet side chairs throughout; classic French garden chairs for the roof garden; leather armchairs from the designer Maples. The client mostly acquiesced, but not always. Sometimes, he initially tolerated something he did not like but then changed his stance. In December 1927, when pipes in two of the gallery radiators burst in a cold snap, the complicated repair required rebuilding the wall that supported the gallery ramp, and La Roche used the occasion to change the floor covering.

It was in this period that the remarkable marble-topped table, nesting on a V-shaped tubular-steel support and a tiled miniature wall, appeared in the gallery. In a splendid embrace of modern technology for domestic design, the parquet floors were replaced with pink rubber made by a company called Electro-Cable. Lighting fixtures that looked like gigantic arms were installed. By this time, Le Corbusier and others in his office had become more active in creating furniture and lighting, and the Villa La Roche was a showcase for their snappy new designs. La Roche was the epitome of forbearance, graciously dispensing substantial sums of money to improve his house. In February 1928, the client received a cost estimate of nearly thirty-three thousand francs for revisions; by the end of the year, he had spent almost fifty-one thousand.

Within the next decade, the banker from Basel shelled out even more substantial funds to repair or replace items that should have functioned correctly initially. When the handsome, modern windows failed to shut properly, he paid for replacements. The roof leaked, threatening his precious collection; he had it fixed. The coal-burning boiler Le Corbusier had designated was never sufficient to heat the large spaces of the house; La Roche replaced it with an oil-burning one that, alas, was noisy, smelly, and also inadequate.

Then Raoul La Roche had his patience tested even more severely. He felt cold dampness on the sleek white walls of his gallery; the smooth continuous surfaces the architect had given him had become a breeding ground for mold. Knowing that a creeping incursion of blue fur would have followed, the collector insulated the gallery walls with panels of *isorel*—a trademark hardboard. It was less aesthetically pure but sufficient to stop the slime.

There was no rage or talk of legal action that today would occur between

Master bedroom of the Villa La Roche, known as the "Purist Bedroom"

a wealthy client and his impractical architect. Because of the problem with condensation, La Roche simply relined the space he had already rebuilt once following the radiator disaster, and he rehung his art on walls that now had seams. The pristine had to yield to the practical, and that was that.

IN *THE COMPLETE WORK,* Le Corbusier described the Villa La Roche as "an *architectural promenade.* You enter: the architectural spectacle immediately presents itself; you follow an itinerary, a great variety of prospects open; you enjoy the afflux of light illuminating the walls or creating shadows . . . architectural unity. . . . The assertion of certain volumes, or, on the contrary, their effacement. . . . Here, living again before our modern eyes, the architectural events of history: pilings, vertical windows, roof gardens, glass facades. *Still, you must know how to appreciate, when the time comes,* what is presented and you must also renounce things you have learned, in order to pursue truths which inevitably develop around new techniques instigated by a new spirit born of the profound revolution of the machine age."[7]

The villa in Autheuil, sleek and modern on the outside, also has, in its interior, a religious dimension. The large open space is a paraphrase of a cathedral interior. The small balconies that jut into it resemble pulpits. Light floods in from above. With the whiteness, boldness, and simplicity, the building offers a spiritual awakening.

Le Corbusier's roof garden for Raoul La Roche is also a setting for reverence. The large terrace on top of the villa, with its cantilevered overhangs and smokestack-like chimneys and immaculate tiles, is the stage for a rich array of plantings that present the luxuriance of nature. Le Corbusier had organized the "arbor vitae, cypresses, okubas, euonymus, Chinese laurels, privet, and tamarinds" with even greater care than the paintings downstairs.[8] One of the architect's proudest moments was when his client invited him to see his lilacs and exclaimed, "There are more than a hundred clusters of bloom!"

This more than anything was Le Corbusier's goal: to bring sunlight, and the natural growth it facilitated, into urban life.

NEVERTHELESS, the architect was not totally satisfied. In his own words, "The plan seems tormented, because certain brutal constraints have required and strictly limited the use of the site: the constraint of *non-edificandi,* age-old trees to be respected, constraints of height. Further, the sun is behind the house, the site being north-oriented, so that it was necessary, by certain stratagems, to look for the sun on the other side. And despite this torment imposed on the plan by antagonistic conditions, one idea obsesses: *this house could be a palace.*"[9] He was heading toward that dream; orienting himself toward the sun, Le Corbusier was soon to build its palace.

4

Passion can create drama out of inert stone.

—LE CORBUSIER, *Toward a New Architecture*

When the first edition of *Toward a New Architecture* came out in 1923, on its cover and title page the name given for the author was "Le Corbusier–Saugnier." With their new names combined, Charles-Edouard Jeanneret and Amédée Ozenfant left behind their individual personalities as readily as they discarded ornament and brownstone. That attitude changed with the appearance of the second edition, a year later, which cited as its author Le Corbusier. It was, however, now dedicated to "Amédée Ozenfant." In the next edition, that dedication was removed.

Beyond the disagreements over the Villa La Roche, there had been further discord between Ozenfant and Le Corbusier because of Ozenfant's infatuation with Surrealism, which Le Corbusier mostly disdained as poorly executed and self-indulgent. Then Ozenfant designed his own dress boutique, for which he used the name Amédée. Le Corbusier considered this emporium a frivolous endeavor.

Le Corbusier told Ozenfant that the lack of dedication in the third edition of the book had been a mistake on the part of the printer. Ozenfant responded that La Roche and Lipchitz had told him that Le Corbusier had deliberately thrown it out. Then Le Corbusier wrote one of his vituperative letters. After voicing concern for the health and well-being of "*mon cher ami,*" he lambasted Ozenfant for his connection to the world of fashion, accused his former hero of vanity and selfishness, and labeled him a dilettante jealous of Le Corbusier's greater abilities. Now that he had a live-in girlfriend and a burgeoning architectural career, the symbiotic relationship that Jeanneret had so cherished when he was serving oysters to his soul mate was over.

LE CORBUSIER achieved his objective concerning the authorship of *Toward a New Architecture.* Today, the book is considered his alone, although both men wrote the *Esprit Nouveau* articles that comprise it.

An attack on almost all current architecture, this entreaty for a fresh approach proposes a revolution based on "the Engineer's aesthetic": "The Engineer, inspired by the law of Economy and governed by mathematical calculation, puts us in accord with universal law. He achieves harmony."[10] With that equilibrium derived from necessity, architecture can give a sense of order, move our hearts, increase understanding, and induce "plastic emotions."

These wonderful occurrences depend on the use of simple forms arranged systematically, according to a well-conceived plan. It is requisite for the architect to listen to materials and suppress his own ego to achieve balance and rhythmic harmony, qualities elusive in everyday life. Airplanes and automobiles and boats succeed brilliantly because of their designers' knowledge of the impact of materials and their awareness that the exterior must be determined by the requirements of an interior designed on human scale. All machines for living should be built for the creatures whose living they are meant to improve.

In the era when Bolshevism, Fascism, and Nazism were all on the rise, the book accords architecture the power of a political movement that can provide the solution to all of society's problems: "It is a question of building which is at the root of the social unrest of to-day: architecture or revolution."[11] Photos of Le Corbusier's own work are used throughout the book to illustrate that he and his buildings were the salvation of humanity.

XXII

1

Le Corbusier was becoming everything Charles-Edouard Jeanneret intended. By the end of 1923, not only had he published *Toward a New Architecture* and begun the villas La Roche and Jeanneret, but his latest paintings were on view at the Salon des Indépendants and in the gallery of the renowned art dealer Léonce Rosenberg on the rue de la Baume.

Then he made a decision as calculated as the adoption of his new name. He decided to conceal his "painter" side. For the next fifteen years, he painted for four to five hours per day, but he was resolved to show the work to virtually no one, claiming that it would detract from the way he was regarded as a designer and urbanist.

At 20 rue Jacob, mid-1920s

As an architect, his international importance was soaring. Swamped with work, in the spring of 1924 he complained to Ritter about the hectic pace, but, in his usual disjointed language, exulted in the overload: "Existence continues to be exhausting but quite interesting, complex, impossible even to dream of such a thing as rest: one is squeezed into rigid postures. Life augments, and difficulties as well; luckily, one is not too fond of money and there are other satisfactions."[1]

Even if money was tight, there was now enough work for Le Corbusier and Pierre Jeanneret to open a larger office. They did so in the hallway of a Jesuit convent at 35 rue de Sèvres, just a minute's walk from a major Métro stop and in the middle of one of the liveliest neighborhoods in Paris. They were diagonally across from the great department store Le Bon Marché and half a block from Le Lutétia, the largest hotel on the Left Bank, with the perennial whistles of its doormen summoning taxis for visitors from all over the world. The artists' neighborhood of St. Germain, and Le Corbusier and Yvonne's own apartment, were nearby. The setting where Le Corbusier was to create the buildings that have come to define modern architecture lay behind a quiet, classical facade. It was as seemingly traditional as its boss's appearance. Yet once one had passed through the convent and a courtyard, under the surveillance of a concierge, and passed through "a huge, white gallery-corridor some thirty yards long, five yards wide," another world awaited.[2] Up a dark flight of stairs, one was in a secret hub of power.

This was the "old, dirty, smelly, and brokendown" atelier.[3] It had the same form as the corridor below. On one side, windows faced the courtyard; on the other, a long wall backed up on the Church of Saint Ignatius, from which Gregorian chants or Bach fugues could be heard. There was a hodgepodge of drafting tables, easels, and architectural models, with drawings hanging everywhere. In the beginning, the average number of people working in the office was about twelve; in time, it would swell to thirty.

Once he was in the new office, Le Corbusier established a routine he pretty much maintained for the rest of his professional life, except when he was traveling or stymied by a world war. He started his day at 6:00 a.m. with forty-five minutes of calisthenics; then he served Yvonne her morning coffee. They breakfasted at 8:00. For the rest of the morning, he painted, made architectural sketches, or wrote. By the time he arrived at the office at 2:00 p.m., he was charged with new ideas and put his employees to work making alterations to what they had done at home in the morning. If the afternoon went poorly, it wasn't long before "he would fumble with his wristwatch—a small oddly feminine contraption, far too small for his big paw—and finally say, grudgingly, 'It's a hard thing, architecture,' toss the pencil or charcoal stub on the drawing, and slink out."[4] But generally, by the time he headed back to the apartment for his evening pastis with Yvonne—she liked him there by 5:30—he felt triumphant.

He rarely socialized. Occasionally he and Yvonne ate with friends at the St. Benoit, their neighborhood bistro, or Le Corbusier recieved visitors like Gropius—the director of the Bauhaus, where Le Corbusier was greatly respected, who called on him for the first time on his honeymoon in 1926—but for the most part he devoted his time to designing, painting, or being quietly at home.

2

Le Corbusier did, however, delight in proselytizing his new faith to a widening audience. He lectured on architecture and on "L'Esprit Nouveau" at the Sorbonne early in 1924 and later in the year in Prague and Geneva. His lecture technique became legend. Dressed in his wide-lapeled, double-breasted suit, and hand-tied bow tie, with his signature round glasses and hair brushed back hard off his forehead, Le Corbusier spoke and simultaneously drew with feverish intensity. In charcoal, colored pencil, pastel, and chalk, he made his visions of urbanism more concrete by sketching away freehand on long bands of paper, about a yard wide, that he had unrolled and tacked to the walls. It might be tracing paper, cheap brown wrapping paper, or fine cream-colored stock, but the method was always the same.

The architect never used notes. Rather, he gave the impression that his ideas were still being developed. His audience felt the excitement of his thinking process. Sometimes he left meters of paper on the walls afterward; to this day, there are architects who proudly hold on to these souvenirs of having witnessed Le Corbusier in the act of creation.

LE CORBUSIER treated himself like an enterprise that needed to produce annual reports. Starting in 1924, he began to work on the publication of *The Complete Work of Le Corbusier and Pierre Jeanneret.* By 1938, there were four volumes. Once that publication ceased, it was replaced by *Le Corbusier: The Complete Work*—a series in which, for the rest of his life, he wrote texts to track his achievement for others.

The people whom he wanted to impress above all with his autobiographical report card on his diverse achievements were his mother and father. He made clear to them, however, that the modest house he was designing for them, to be on Lac Leman, was the building that counted most of all.

3

In June 1924, Edouard, as he still was to his parents, sent them a postcard saying he was finishing plans for their new home and was about to send them all the details to hand over to the builder: "This house will be exquisite, and I am quite happy with the solution arrived at. Count on us, we know what must be done so that there will be no delays."[5] The "we" was he and Pierre, in whom they could have confidence as a fellow member of the Jeanneret clan.

While Edouard never referred to the disaster of the Maison Blanche, he now gave them a house that was completed on schedule and within budget. After their five years of exile in rented chalets, the retired watchcase enameler and piano teacher would finally have a little paradise.

For more than a year, Edouard had been negotiating, in a fairly nefarious manner, to buy a parcel of land from some farmers in Vevey. When he was there with his parents for the Christmas holidays in 1923, he had written Yvonne, "One must use a certain amount of cunning with these peasants, and one spends one's time in grim dives where the talk goes on forever. I am exhausted and invoke the aid of all the devils in creation to reach a conclusion."[6] Nine months later, it had all paid off; in September 1924, he wrote his girlfriend back in Paris, "The little house will be like an ancient temple at the water's edge."[7] By the time he arrived there on December 23, Le Corbusier had seen to every detail—the linoleum for the floors, the medical-style sink, the plain-white open-weave window curtains that were such a contrast to the patterned brocades of rue Léopold-Robert. This house for two people, without servants, looking south over the lake, was without an iota of waste, as impeccably organized and efficient as it was celestial and poetic. All that was left to do before Christmas was arrange the furniture, which Le Corbusier quickly did. Once he had put the last object in place, the thirty-seven-year-old son had achieved his dream.

LA PETITE MAISON is a cosmic house. Inside, one feels perfectly aligned within the solar system. Daylight pours in through a high window facing east. To the south, a window eleven meters in length opens the interior to the water. The oceanic Lac Leman is separated from the house by only a couple of meters of land; to be in the living room is like being on board a ship, with only the deck between you and the sea. The reflections and smooth light from the lake flood the rooms.

The Maison Blanche had been excessive; La Petite Maison is reduced and taut. In this structure measuring four meters by sixteen meters—a sequence of four squares—the harmony of the plan pervades. Another architect might have made such tight organization seem stingy. Le Corbusier renders it, for all the smallness of scale, grand and sublime. The little house is neatly subdivided into rooms that provided everything Georges and Marie needed. There is a salon with a simple dining table cantilevered under the window ledge, their bedroom, and a compact galley kitchen. On the east end, there is a guest room that doubles as a second sitting room or, alternatively, can open up completely—thanks to a wall panel on hinges—to become part of the salon. To accommodate overnight visitors, Le Corbusier included a hidden closet, an extra mattress stored in the basement, and a sink concealed within a wall.

The writing/dining table is the first example of the variation that reappeared in Le Corbusier's own cabin at Roquebrune-Cap-Martin. It is a straightforward rectangular wooden slab supported by iron stovepipe legs. But while this table was as modern as the house for which it was custom fitted, Georges and Marie used old country chairs that recalled the couple's earlier years. Similarly, the elegant and old-fashioned desk Edouard had designed for Marie for the Maison Blanche, with its space for knitting needles, is in the bedroom. For all the simplicity of the architectural program, the house is not cold; it invites the charms of one's life experience to be present.

The tiny enclosure of the sole toilet in the house does not have an inch to spare. At the same time, because of a window high up in this vertical cubicle, it has the light of a chapel, ennobling the act of sitting on the toilet. In the separate bathroom, Le Corbusier put small vertical windows and skylights over the tub and sink, as he did in the closet: light, intangible and born to the sun, changes everything.

IN 1930, Le Corbusier added a "*fruitier*" to La Petite Maison. This eagle's nest for his own use allowed a view akin to what he had first experienced in the monasteries on Mount Athos. From this austere box on top of the villa, he could set his sights on the horizon.

The desk and chair in the *fruitier* are on a platform. This desk is even simpler than the table in his parents' living space; one end of its concrete top rests on a ledge, while the other is supported by a single stovepipe as delicate as a bird's leg. Le Corbusier had an ability to take strong industrial materials and imbue them with feathery lightness. The stairs to reach this aerie have a banister of tubular steel, with a graceful turn below and a handsome mirror image of that turn at the top to provide a sense of balletic grace; its concrete steps are scaled to invite easy footwork. What is weighty becomes weightless.

THE LARGE PLATE-GLASS sliding window overlooking the lake in the main space of La Petite Maison encourages the act of seeing. And what a feast that is, thanks to the play of colors within the interior. The north wall of the living/dining room is painted a light aquamarine; the east is cobalt. There is also a range of grays. The bedroom is salmon. Brown trim serves like a colored tinted mat surrounding a picture. Playful cutouts of geometric shapes, high and low, provide the satisfaction of abstract art.

All of this occurs under a flat roof that is covered with grass—a superb play of the man-made and the natural. This dwelling is the perfect shelter in which to contemplate the universal. The views, and that deliberate melding of earthly growth with the calibration of human needs, inspire thoughtfulness and reverence.

In this small, private house—his gift to the people he cared about the most—the architect who publicly swaggered across the worldwide stage, who issued pronouncements for humanity and tried to replan our cities, was charming, poetic, and divinely quiet. He sanctified everyday living while making it easy and practical. To the father who had shown him the sky and the earth, and to the mother who opened his soul to the rhythms and harmonies of music, he returned these qualities in a new form.

SHORTLY AFTER La Petite Maison was completed, the community council of a nearby town got together to forbid the building of any modern structures within the territory it governed. It did so in the name of preservation of the scenery. That slap confirmed Le Corbusier's views of Switzerland. In little time, the hostility of his native land became even more apparent; the struggle for beauty would not be easily won there. But his house for his parents was, however slight, a victory.

4

The end of February was almost invariably a time of winter lows for Jeanneret/Le Corbusier. Nineteen hundred and twenty-five was completely different.

He had garnered the respect of the other pioneers of modern architecture. This was evident when Mies van der Rohe, vice president of the Deutscher Werkbund, became project director of a major exhibition in the Weissenhof section of Stuttgart to show the latest approaches to the modern home and gave Le Corbusier the single best location, overlooking the city. Le Corbusier did two houses that expanded on the Citrohan ideas, essentially boxes on pilotis with simplified, versatile plans. Their architecture was praised for its connection to the natural surroundings while criticized for its cost; these houses were more expensive per square foot than anything else at the exhibition.

Ca. 1920

The Weissenhof houses are examples of Le Corbusier's work that must be considered in the context of their site rather than in photographic reproductions that render them as isolated objects. In that neighborhood of Stuttgart, one is on a hillside, near a bustling city center but facing a vast panorama of fertile mountains and vineyards. Especially in springtime, the shimmering white plaster of Le Corbusier's shoe boxes of modernism is a perfect foil to the fields of buttercups and bluebells catching the sunlight all around them. The utterly simple, bold pavilions, one sprawling and the other compact, one facing south and the other east, are resting points on the earth that gracefully assume second place to their setting.

Remarkably, the rolling countryside of southern Germany here resembles the surrounds of Delphi; this is more a fertile corner of the world than a particular place, with its timelessness and universality accentuated thanks to the way Le Corbusier's architecture recedes and deliberately presents a view of the distant panorama rather than the modern city. He succeeded in making Germany, the country he disliked, distinctly un-German.

The buildings serve the setting, yet they are anything but timid. These elegant rectangular blocks are both brave masses, standing strong and clear. Lighter than the villa he was simultaneously designing in the Paris suburb of Garches, they are more confident than the studio-house for Ozenfant, their bold forms exquisitely elegant without being in any way fussy.

The smaller house has a balcony that floats off of it. Its pilotis are thin and graceful, bringing to the forefront Le Corbusier's idea of the resemblance of architecture to music, with the massing of the house the kettle-drum and the balcony and these supporting elements the flutes. One goes from seeing and hearing the full orchestra to a meandering solo.

The larger house combines inside and out as a totality. Nature penetrates its balcony; the sky and the surroundings are present throughout. Le Corbusier was an architect of air; space, more than bricks and mortar, was his medium. He used the sturdiest, most durable of new materials, as befit this exhibition of current construction practices, yet rendered them weightless. A refinement and touch are apparent in every lean staircase, the tautness of the window trim, the grace with which each space opens to the next. How delicate was this bold vision that allows one to join the birds!

5

On February 24, Le Corbusier wrote Ritter his latest assessment of his life: "I realized that after ten years of really tumultuous, painful (oh very!), and exhausting life that I had rounded the cape of storms and was in fact a very happy fellow, leading an ideal life." With no time wasted socializing, he was doing what he loved: practicing architecture, painting, and writing. It made him "gay as a sparrow, more optimistic than ever, stubborn as a mule, and always focused on the same goal."[8] Now realizing more than ever what a quagmire his hometown had been, he credited Ritter, the only person he felt had had confidence in him, for his escape.

"For me architecture is a game," he wrote confidently. His struggle was with painting, "which torments me endlessly, plunging me into tremendous anxieties." But now, at least, everything was coming into perspective. His romance with business and the goal of making his fortune were behind him: "I want you to understand that for me money has lost any luster it may have had. Having earned it, but having always invested it in risky ventures, I have never had it in my hands for long; having lost it, I felt nothing. But the only good result is being able to reach that focus where, in the work itself, you feel yourself on *your way.*"[9]

Le Corbusier was determined to live simply and avoid distraction from his work: "A harsh, precipitous life furiously filled to the brim; and the modest situation of a monk (whose little heart has his little friend), in a white room, overlooking a garden. Le Corbusier is not Peter Behrens, who had a lackey to watch him eat."[10] His "little friend"—presumably Ritter knew who she was—was all he needed.

THE CLIENTS were at the door; he was preparing for exhibitions; new texts were going into print. At the same time, Le Corbusier was devising the urban scheme that, for many people, was to cast him permanently as the devil. This bombshell that the architect was about to let drop became the reason that, on first hearing Le Corbusier's name, many people still speak of him as the man who wanted to destroy Paris and as the demon who damaged cities all over the world.

This was also a time of major personal change for Charles-Edouard Jeanneret. It was the beginning of the end for his father. Freud has said that a man's father's death is the beginning of his maturity. As Le Corbusier began to assume his new role in the oldest surviving generation of men in the family, he gained a confidence of terrifying proportion.

6

With the City for Three Million, Le Corbusier had come up with an abstract urban scheme that could go anywhere. Anticipating the International Exposition of Modern Decorative and Industrial Arts that was to open in April 1925, he devised a new plan for Paris itself—or, rather, for a city that would be dropped down into the middle of an erased Paris. He had reconstructed his parents' lives by excising them from one existence and transplanting them into another; now he imagined doing so for most of the population of the French capital. He also conceived the ideal single-family dwelling that could be produced, as if with a cookie cutter, on an infinite scale and that would be the cell of this new metropolis. That his urban proposal meant bulldozing almost all that was already there did not trouble him.

The central notion behind his scheme was his belief that the automobile had changed everything. Having observed Paris empty out during the summer months, Le Corbusier had been anguished by what happened when people returned from their August holidays: "Then there came the autumn season. In the early evening twilight on the Champs-Elysées it was as though the world had suddenly gone mad. After the emptiness of the summer, the traffic was more furious than ever. Day by day the fury of traffic grew. To leave your house meant that once you had crossed the threshold you were a possible sacrifice to death in the shape of innumerable motors. I think back twenty years, when I was a student; the road belonged to us then; we sang in it and argued in it, while the horse-bus swept calmly along."[11]

In Le Corbusier's mind, the presence of all these cars became hallucinatory: "On that 1st day of October, on the Champs-Elysées, I was assisting at the titanic reawakening of a completely new phenomenon, which three months of summer had calmed down a little—traffic. Motors in all directions, going at all speeds. I was overwhelmed, an enthusiastic rapture filled me. Not the rapture of the shining coachwork under the gleaming lights, but the rapture of power."[12]

He assumed for himself a force equal to that intoxicating energy of the automobile.

> The simple and ingenuous pleasure of being in the centre of so much power, so much speed. We are a part of it. We are part of that race whose dawn is just awakening. . . .
>
> Its power is like a torrent swollen by storms; a destructive fury. The city is crumbling, it cannot last much longer; its time is past. It is too old. The torrent can no longer keep to its bed. It is a kind of cataclysm. It is something utterly abnormal, and the disequilibrium grows day by day. . . .
>
> Surgery must be applied at the city's centre.
>
> Physic must be used elsewhere. . . . We must use the knife.[13]

7

The International Exposition of Modern Decorative and Industrial Arts had been in the planning stages since 1909. This show, which subsequently gave birth to the term "Art Deco," was to reveal "modern tendencies," reflecting the era of automobiles and airplanes, in temporary structures especially erected between Les Invalides and the Grand Palais, on both sides of the Seine. Le Corbusier liked the idea but not the organizers. In March 1925, he wrote, "Countless pavilions, all decorated and decorative, are being built, truly a spectacle which astonishes me and produces the impression of pure madness. I didn't dream the level was so low."[14] The architect was particularly outraged by Emile-Jacques Ruhlmann's salon, which he said was just an updated version of an elegant sitting room of an earlier era that violated the concepts of the exhibition.

Le Corbusier, however, honored those guidelines. His intended Pavilion de L'Esprit Nouveau was to demonstrate how standardization could be applied to domestic building in a housing type made entirely through industrial means. But the organizers quibbled with this notion. "When I submitted my scheme in January 1924 to the architects-in-chief of the

Exhibition," he later wrote, "it was categorically rejected. They wished me to illustrate the theme 'An Architect's House.' I answered, 'No, I will do a house for everybody, or, if you prefer it, the apartment of any gentleman who would like to be comfortable in beautiful surroundings.' "[15]

The initial dismissal of his proposal delighted rather than discouraged the man who was convinced that he was the savior of humanity—and who expected the concomitant opposition. The dream that he could give visual beauty to the masses was too great to go unchecked. Naturally, the notion of building housing as practical and efficient as modes of transportation was too revolutionary for the mediocre minds in charge.

The official disapproval continued. In April, when Le Corbusier presented a new design for a structure at the exposition, he got no response. When a site for it was finally granted in September, the location was remote and contained trees that could not be moved.

Le Corbusier let it be known that he was injured and disgusted. But his enthusiasm did not wane. He now sought financial backing for this pavilion by approaching various automobile companies. The car, having destroyed the city in one form, could be the source of its salvation in another.

Le Corbusier offered Jean-Pierre Peugeot and André Citroën what we would today call a "naming opportunity" in exchange for funding. Peugeot was honored but refused; Citroën didn't understand. André Michelin was in Morocco. But Monservon, who worked for Gabriel Voisin, went to the office on the rue de Sèvres. Voisin, a manufacturer of aircraft with an automobile division, agreed to be the patron and gave twenty-five thousand francs. Henri Frugès, heir to a sugar cube factory in Bordeaux and a Le Corbusier supporter, matched the amount, and the three-hundred-square-meter reinforced-concrete structure was erected. The new plan for Paris, which Le Corbusier named for Voisin, was revealed inside it.

THE CONCEPT was megalomaniacal. Declaring large sections of Paris "antiquated . . . unhealthy . . . [and] overcrowded," Le Corbusier called for destroying hundreds of acres of the Right Bank, including much of the charming ancient quarter called the Marais. To ease the excessive traffic on the Champs-Elysées, he proposed building a highway that would cut through the partially leveled city. Le Corbusier retained some remnants of the past—"certain historical monuments, arcades, doorways, carefully preserved because they are pages out of history or works of art"—but the rest would go.[16]

One of the most consistent misunderstandings of the Le Corbusier legacy, however, is the notion that he intended everything to be destroyed as if by a bomb. The error is often reiterated that he wanted to obliterate the place des

In front of the diagram of the Plan Voisin, 1925

Driving a Fiat on the roof track of the Lingotto factory in Turin, mid-1920s

Vosges—that, if he had had his way, virtually every trace of Paris's architectural history would have disappeared. The Plan Voisin was radical—in most people's judgment outrageous—but, although it called for a total rebuilding of much of the area between the Seine and Montmartre, the intention was always for the place des Vosges, the Louvre, the Arc de Triomphe, the Palais Royal, and various other buildings to remain. Le Corbusier aimed to make them all the more visible. The goal was not the eradication of the past but a selective pruning that would leave the best behind to be savored in a new way. The great open spaces, such as the Tuileries and the Invalides, that had been essential to the urban idea of Louis XIV, Louis XV, and Napoleon would be returned to their former glory.

But Paris would now consist mostly of variations of the building type seen in the City for Three Million. Le Corbusier envisioned carefully spaced, cruciform skyscrapers, 245 meters high. He explained that these would attract investment from America, England, Japan, and Germany. There would, in addition, be blocks of new residential units.

THE LITTLE-KNOWN TRUTH is that although Le Corbusier invented and presented the Plan Voisin, he did not intend for it to be followed. He neither imagined it really would be done nor thought it should be. "The 'Voisin' scheme does not claim to have found a final solution to the problem of the center of Paris; but it may serve to raise the discussion to a level in keeping with the spirit of our new age," he wrote at the time.[17] No utterance of Le Corbusier's is more important to a correct understanding of his legacy. He had not wanted to ravage a world he loved. He had been deliberately provocative; he had done his utmost to stimulate new thinking; but what he put forward as a hypothetical proposal was just that.

8

The Plan Voisin and the City for Three Million were displayed in two large dioramas, each about one hundred square meters, in a rotunda within the Pavilion de L'Esprit Nouveau. Detailed plans for the cruciform skyscrapers and for entire colonies of these new dwellings hung on the walls inside this imposing silo.

The pavilion itself was the model for the standard residential unit that would have been reproduced ad infinitum in neat blocks at the outskirts of the new ideal city. If, to current eyes, the residential unit fits into a known canon of modernism, to its viewers in 1925 it offered as powerful a jolt as the urban plan. It was essentially an unadorned, unmodulated white concrete box with a facade sheathed in a taut, industrial-style window wall. The inside was punctuated by an enclosed garden with a tree popping through a circular hole in its roof. This last detail, a response to the exigencies of the wretched site, now became part of the general concept.

Walking near their office, Le Corbusier and Pierre Jeanneret had conceived of the scale after studying scaffolding in front of the three-story-high Le Bon Marché. They became convinced that human beings would profit if they followed that commercial model in residential architecture. Ceiling heights should be nearly doubled from the existing norm of nine to twelve feet to eighteen to twenty-two feet. Housing should be set back farther from the street and built higher than it had been.

Inside, the pavilion depended on commercial lighting fixtures made for shop windows. Some of the chairs and tables came from a catalog for hospital furniture; most of the cabinets and closets were built-in. The glassware to be used domestically had been made for laboratory experiments. Le Corbusier explained that the Pavilion de L'Esprit Nouveau and its contents were "the fruit of a mind preoccupied with the problems of the future."[18]

Less advanced minds did not see it this way. Controversy broke out. The jury of the exhibition, according at least to Le Corbusier's subsequent account, wanted to give the Pavilion de L'Esprit Nouveau and the Plan

Exterior of the Pavilion de L'Esprit Nouveau, Paris, 1925

Voisin its highest design award. But its vice president, none other than Le Corbusier's former employer Auguste Perret, declared, "It's ridiculous. It doesn't hold together, it lacks any logic. There's no architecture here."[19]

The Building Committee for the exhibition erected an eighteen-foot-high wall in front of the new pavilion to keep the public from seeing it. Whether this was a construction wall, simply meant to keep the project under wraps while it was in process, or deliberate censorship, as Le Corbusier makes it sound in his accounts, is unclear. But Le Corbusier always presented that wall as a symbol of the wishes of the forces against him to conceal his work, even implying that it was re-erected after the inauguration of the pavilion. He falsified and dramatized the maneuvers of the opposition; the pavilion remained plainly visible after its delayed opening. Nonetheless, the disapproval was real.

9

The printed invitation that served as an admissions card for the inauguration ceremony invited its recipients to enter the Grand Palais on Friday, July 10, at four o'clock in the afternoon. In blocky, sans-serif type, as lean and right-angled as the pavilion itself, it declared, "This pavilion is better hidden than any other in the exposition."[20] Le Corbusier wanted no one to overlook the unforgivably obscure location. But once people made their way to this structure tucked into the garden between the two wings of the Grand Palais, they were in a new world.

The pavilion was elegant: light, graceful, imparting a feeling of cheer and optimism. Inside as well as out, it was clean, fit, and energetic. Those laboratory jars and hospital furniture now used for domestic purposes were so charming and effective that they were to infiltrate the culture, so that today there are carafes resembling chemists' flasks for sale in housewares stores all over the world.

There were ingenious wardrobes and clothes cupboards built into walls or neatly suspended from them, as well as imaginative bookshelves and storage units, made out of metal by a manufacturer of office equipment, that allowed maximum space in the rooms. The new aesthetic was a revolutionary invitation to be practical, to live in a house that is easy to clean and maintain. At the same time, the clear and engaging forms were arranged at lively angles meant to lift human spirits. And bouquets of flowers burst joyously in the tidy assemblage. As always, Le Corbusier's vision was a stage on which the splendor of nature could perform in plain view.

THE PAVILION was hung with work by the same pantheon of modernists as the Villa La Roche, among them Braque, Gris, Léger, Lipchitz, Ozenfant, and Picasso. Jeanneret/Le Corbusier's own paintings were also displayed, in contradiction of his vow to keep that side of his creativity under wraps. Certain qualities of Jeanneret's Purist canvases—the " 'marriage of objects in sharing an outline' and his use of so-called regulating lines"—were echoed in the architectural organization. Similarly, Le Corbusier's deployment "of color in his architectural interiors is closely related to the palette of his canvases."[21] For all the restraint and austerity of the ornament-free shell, the overall symphony was immensely rich.

ROBERT BRASILLACH—a journalist who, twenty years later, was executed as a collaborator with the Vichy regime—wrote that the furniture, and the ideas on furnishing, would last for a very long time. But the manufacturers who the architects hoped would take up his ideas showed no interest. Having imagined the pavilion and its fittings being repeated all over the world, Le Corbusier felt mocked and lambasted.

In his new book, *The City of To-morrow and Its Planning,* he defended himself. "This is a sentiment born of the most arduous labor, the most rational investigation; it is 'a spirit of constructions and of synthesis guided by a clear conception,' " Le Corbusier writes of the Pavilion and the Plan Voisin, without attributing the quotation.[22]

His 1925 *The Decorative Art of Today* intensified the propaganda campaign. It shocked the public in part because it virulently attacks Art Deco, which had become immensely popular. The book criticizes majority taste past and present. Blasting museums for "their tendentious incoherence," it decries concepts of decoration and style in general, and laments, in particular, the contemporary plagiarism of folk art—which Le Corbusier wanted only in its genuine form.[23]

Le Corbusier cites, as objects worthy of display in a museum, "a plain jacket, a bowler hat, a well-made shoe, an electric light bulb with bayonet fixing, . . . and bottles of various shapes (Champagne, Bordeaux) in which we keep our Mercurey, our Graves, or simply our *ordinaire* . . . a bathroom with its enameled bath, its china bidet, its wash basin, and its glittering taps of copper or nickel . . . a Ronéo filing cabinet with its printed index cards, tabulated, numbered, perforated, and indented."[24] What many of us today consider the courage and imagination of that declaration of beauty struck contemporary readers as heresy.

Le Corbusier reproduces photographs of various types of fuselages and extols their merits, case by case. In this highly personal version of the history of ornament and design, he denigrates any number of classics with one of his dicta of the type that set the public on its ear: "I notice that a whole mass of objects which once bore the sense of truth have lost their content and are now no more than carcasses: I throw them out."[25]

Those who were not stunned or enraged by the narrative admired its bravery. The poet Paul Valéry wrote Le Corbusier, "Monsieur, I have only one word to tell you about your book (The Decorative Art of Today), and that is a word I use rarely: admirable. I am embarrassed, moreover, to write it to you. I think alike with you on most of the subjects you deal with. It is all too easy for me to approve of my own sentiments. . . . Please be assured, Monsieur, that I hold your work in singular esteem, that I shall make it known to others to the best of my ability, and accept the expression of my gratitude and of all my sympathy."[26]

But no praise was sufficient for Le Corbusier to abandon his role as a long-suffering martyr. He made himself the victim of "the generation of our fathers who protest, resist, refuse, mock, laugh, insult, deny. We are poor and we run round the race-track, exhausted and emotional. Our fathers sit in the stands. . . . Our fathers are smoking fat cigars and wearing top hats. They are fine, our fathers, and we are what we are—thin as street cats."[27] For the dapper and urbane son who sported fine Paris hats to portray the older generation in that way was more than ironic. His own father was lean and worn out by a lifetime of hard work. He was also on some level the man whose approval Le Corbusier still most craved.

XXIII

1

On November 8, 1925, Marie Charlotte Emilie Jeanneret-Perret wrote both her sons. "Our dear papa is lost," she informed them.

Georges had stomach cancer that had spread and formed a tumor in his liver. He had no idea how sick he was; nor could she let him find out. The doctor, who had told her this in private, said that one should hope only that Georges's suffering would not be prolonged. If he had a hemorrhage, he would be spared extended pain. Marie was now following the doctor's counsel and preparing the house so that he could be cared for there. Nurses would be required, she informed Albert and Edouard. But in fact their rugged mother was constitutionally incapable of hiring outside help and intended to do everything herself.

On November 29, anticipating Georges's birthday two days later, Edouard sent his father a letter that focused on the heating system—he hoped it was working well—and on the beauty of the winter landscape. From Paris, he conjured the eternal setting of Vevey: "In winter this site is quite stately, vaster than in summer and of an impressive, polar sweetness. One no longer sees the mountains in the background, and the lake seems a sea."[1]

Having latched onto other father figures as intellectual and professional mentors—L'Eplattenier, Ritter, and Auguste Perret among them—Le Corbusier had come to cherish his actual father as the model of beatific kindness. He wrote the dying man: "You have had many evidences of affection during your sickness. You see that you are surrounded by esteem and respect. By living without the fierce egoism which makes everything ugly, one creates around oneself a beneficent atmosphere. One would not realize this if, with the sudden arrival of the anguish of disease, those who breathe that atmosphere did not feel that their lungs would now lack it. It's quite human, such testimonies come only at acute times, moments of crisis. You will have had not pride, for that is no longer suited to your age, but a certain emotion at feeling the sincere sentiment that surrounded you." The younger son was overcome with admiration for his father's "spirit . . . so calm, so detached from all pettiness."[2] He also told his ailing parent that he and Albert feared that their mother was not up to the task of taking care of an invalid. They had begged their Aunt Marguerite to hire someone at least to run errands for her.

At the end of November, Edouard provided his father with a thorough update on his work. He was upset that the Pavilion de L'Esprit Nouveau was to be "cut into pieces by pneumatic concrete drills and transported by trucks to the suburban banks of the Seine," but the first two houses of a new project at Pessac, near Bordeaux, were complete. "So much for my little gazette of accomplishments," he summarized, going on to cheer up the invalid with the news that Albert was becoming more stable thanks to Lotti's "great serenity of spirit."[3]

As for his own female companion, Edouard made no mention of her to the dying Calvinist. But when Georges's condition worsened a couple of weeks later and Edouard rushed to Switzerland, it was Yvonne to whom he poured out his woes. He had gone to see his father in the hospital. They had opened Georges's chest and determined that the end was near. "If you knew how sad it is, how distressing, really lamentable to see my poor papa," he wrote. "His body is awful to look at: a skeleton, and he has no blood left in him; he's no more than a transparent man, and his voice is already quite remote. He thinks only of others and never complains, although he is in pain."[4]

His mother, he told Yvonne, was "heroic." She smiled in front of her dying husband, comforting him and making him believe that all was going well. Then she would go into the small kitchen of La Petite Maison and cry. That self-control in tandem with her tenderness was Le Corbusier's ideal.

It was Christmas Eve. As Charles-Edouard Jeanneret sat in the small and exquisite villa he had built for his parents to savor the rewards of life as they looked out at the vastness of Lac Leman, he knew this was to be the last Christmas with all four of them alive.

2

Le Corbusier returned to Paris to be with Yvonne at New Year's, although he told his parents it was for work. On December 31, he wrote his parents about the extent to which he felt

> family ties. I am aware of the great friendship which unites us. And the gratitude I feel toward you who raised me allows me to tell you that you can count on me.

My dear good emaciated Papa, happy new year, good luck, *bon courage,* and take care of our Maman who is not so good at taking care of herself.

My dear good Maman, *bon courage,* and count on the support of your sons.

Swift recovery for dear Papa.
Affections from your ED.[5]

EDOUARD was plagued that he had left in the middle of their last holiday time as a family—in part because Albert had remained on the scene. But if he could not win in the role of more devoted son, he could certainly out-achieve his brother. At the start of January, he informed their parents that the magazine *Architecture vivante* was about to publish an article on La Petite Maison. Even as he mocked himself by adding, "I am incorrigible," how proud he was to tell his dying father that the house was being honored in the most beautiful review in France.[6]

3

Within a few days, Edouard was called back to Vevey. He arrived on the morning of Sunday, January 10. Georges was to remain conscious for only twelve more hours. In those last moments with his mind still functioning, the elder Jeanneret discussed only what his son termed "the essentials" of life. He did not waste his breath on anything else.

At seven in the evening, the former mountain climber summoned his wife and sons. He wanted all three together at his bedside at the same time. "It's over. I'm about to die. Love each other, help each other, be faithful to each other"—these were Georges Edouard Jeanneret's departing words.[7] Age sixty-nine, he then fell asleep, never to waken.

Once his father was unconscious, Edouard lay down next to him. At four in the morning, he was aware that the older man was no longer breathing. He turned on the light. His father was dead, with one hand lying across his chest, the other positioned underneath his right ear. In Edouard's eyes, his father was "tranquil, mild, without agony." The son immediately picked up pencil and paper and drew the portrait of his dead parent. A week later, reflecting on his time with the corpse, Le Corbusier wrote Ritter, "If you knew what gentle joy I felt at being close to him this way."[8]

SHORTLY AFTER Georges Jeanneret died, Le Corbusier wrote to Yvonne. He was aware now more than ever that the human values he prized most of all were exemplified by the man who had taken his last breaths at his side. "My Papa died beside me tonight, tranquilly, without a word," he wrote. "All day Sunday he was with us, saying the essential things. I have a feeling of tremendous loss. My father is beautiful. He was the kind of man you recognized by his handwriting: limpid, pure, lofty, disinterested."[9]

4

Le Corbusier was just then working on an unprecedented number of private houses. A week after Georges died, he revealed to Ritter and Czadra the drift of his mind at this peak of professional success. The architect skimmed his fountain pen at rapid speed across the surface of three large pieces of paper, in perfect lines that appeared to rest on invisible scoring and could only have been written by a skillful draftsman: "Yes, my father is dead. You knew how tenderly all four of us were united; the two sons and their parents loved and esteemed each other; there was never any shadow."[10]

Le Corbusier pushed aside any trace of the tempests caused by the Maison Blanche and acted as if the disputes and differences concerning his early travels and career had never occurred. Rather, he celebrated the way that La Petite Maison, sitting only four meters from the lake, with its simple traincar form and magnificent vistas, had become "a place of well-being and a therapeutic of the heart."[11]

Le Corbusier assured Ritter and Czadra that the house had provided his father with a marvelous tranquility in his final days: "So, my dear father has died in perfect peace. During the last two months that his end was certain, he had established himself in the little house on the lake like a solemn music between the noble landscape and the drama that was irrevocably fulfilling itself. At this season the site unfolds its vicissitudes, and a polar majesty impregnates the soul with mildness and repose."[12]

Forty years later, near his own small house with its view of the water and horizon, Le Corbusier was, after an entirely different sort of lifetime, to try to replicate some of those same feelings.

THE EMOTIONS that consumed Le Corbusier in January 1926 belong to the sort of son who, having deliberately and ferociously gone miles beyond his own father, then idealizes the man he had been determined to outdo.

"Did you know my father well enough to know how much, day after day, he identified himself with the serenity of this site?" he wrote. "On his mortal remains, one phrase: this was a man of peace. From his silence, from his meditation always concealed in his depths, emanated nonetheless a radiant force that acted upon everyone (and powerfully upon the humble). Dead, his hands crossed on his chest, in his white shroud, he was no longer Mr. Jeanneret; he was a reformer, a man of those great centuries of bold thought. My timid father was an audacious man. Before his gently but firmly formulated judgment everyone, his countless friends, were brought up short: this was the truth; there was no thought of interest underneath it; my father was clear, felt clearly, thought clearly. He always dreamed of palm trees and sunshine and smooth, simple houses; when his features became so distinct, the silhouette of his face revealed a sharp profile; one might have said: an Arab; at least, that shape of the skull and that nose where everything is outline and pure script."[13]

Georges had dropped out of school at the age of twelve but never stopped learning. Having immersed himself in history books and atlases, he was a man of few words but great knowledge. To Ritter and Czadra, Le Corbusier now recalled his father as his greatest soul mate and champion. Behind his taciturn facade, Georges had a passion for all that his son had undertaken, and he demonized anyone who stood in the way of his success; Le Corbusier appeared to have forgotten all their differences.

The architect in particular admired the grace with which both of his parents had faced the certainty of death: "My mother has been admirable, violent and passionate as she is. This death has made her gentle and smiling, with a childlike soul, timidly beginning a new life." He, too, had passed to another level of his existence. "One no longer has the right to remain a boy," he wrote.[14]

For years he had chided his parents for their rigidity and insularity. Now he focused only on how much they had given him: "What happiness to have had a father and a mother whom you can somehow idealize; from whose example you can summarize qualities and constitute rules for your own life. About whom you feel that since the day of your first responsibilities they have guided you on your path. You pursue a tradition they have established. A line of conduct. Your life has a direction."[15]

Having fought everything he found deadening in his hometown and in the profession of his father and ancestors, Le Corbusier now considered Georges Jeanneret his human equivalent of the Parthenon. "He knew so many things, divined and perceived by judgment, appreciation. An autodidact all the way. Where you had best take him was at the end, when he gave his opinion. One realized then that he knew. Bold, libertarian, whatever, but always so polite, so fond of politeness, and having the sense of the value of traditions. Did you know that by closing your eyes in order not to see, letting yourself go in imagination, you become proud to be from the Neuchâtel mountains. But when the distance is great enough, and your forgetting complete enough, then you construct a 'type.' I have that weakness of wanting to attach myself to something, for I should prefer that my ideas had a consequence rather than being my exclusive and personal property."[16]

Now, rather than destroy the past, Le Corbusier was determined to harness the best aspects of his heritage, to go farther yet in giving his ideas worldwide consequence.

5

Fourteen days after the evening when he witnessed his father die, he wrote his mother, "So, to keep up with everyone, I spent the last 15 days on my feet from 9 in the morning till 2 hours past midnight without once sitting down, moving from one desk to the next."[17] His mother, who knew he had been back in Paris for only half that time, was used to the exaggeration. The important thing was that there was a flurry of activity at 35 rue de Sèvres and a wonderful team to produce all the square meters of plans; things were so good that Edouard let her know he would be able to buy her a new gas oven in Vevey. For Le Corbusier, the supreme antidote to bereavement was work, and he was convinced that with his success he could offer his mother the greatest possible comfort.

6

Henri Frugès asked the architect to build a new city on the outskirts of Bordeaux. Le Corbusier worshipped the industrialist's intentions of showing his countrymen the best way to live. Frugès's goal was for Pessac to have a standardized form of housing that would be life enhancing for the inhabitants and completely contemporary. It was to be well built and efficient, utilizing streamlined forms constructed of modern materials engineered according to the latest methods. "The purity of the proportions will be the true eloquence," Frugès advised Le Corbusier.[18]

Le Corbusier had envisioned such a seer and patron in *The City of To-morrow.* Now he had found the real thing. Frugès was his idea of a hero out of Balzac: rich and idealistic, and not only a businessman but a painter, sculptor, writer, architect, pianist, and composer. At the same time, he understood the limitations of his own artistic talents and ceded to Le Corbusier the task of designing the workers' housing they both hoped would become a prototype all over the world.

For Pessac, Le Corbusier devised a standardized home easily constructed out of reinforced concrete. Similar to the Citrohan and L'Esprit Nouveau structures, it had a bold, blocky exterior and an interior with a two-story living room and a neat warren of carefully prescribed spaces, as well as generous roof gardens. There was an ambient whiteness new to domestic architecture but also a radical use of color. Pale-green and dark-brown walls and an occasional light blue were deployed as vibrant accents in the whiteness. Le Corbusier believed that these aesthetic choices would lead the masses toward greater health and happiness and lend order to their lives.

Although some of Le Corbusier's designs at Pessac were executed, the scheme was never completed. Early in the construction process, local builders became defiant because of the unusual ways of doing things and had to be replaced by a crew from Paris. The new team finished the first phase of the project in less than a year, but until 1929 the city remained uninhabited. Le Corbusier blamed the authorities, whom he considered to be the typical bourgeois bureaucrats who always impede progress.

Others faulted the architect and his patron for having cut corners: "The houses were created before a complete dossier was submitted to the Mayor's office and a construction permit obtained," according to Brian Bruce Taylor's excellent history of Pessac. Additionally, Frugès and Le Corbusier had ignored French laws requiring "appropriate installations for providing and filtering water to be made at the promoter's expense." The project had been completed too quickly, in blatant disregard of those regulations, and the houses could not be sold until Frugès established "streets, water mains and drainage at his own expense."[19] By the time this was done in November 1928, momentum was lost for finishing the new city.

DETRACTORS COMPARED the architecture of the partially completed Pessac to Frugès's sugar cubes. They maintained that the new housing had everything to do with the efficiency in manufacture and packaging that had made a fortune for the industrialist—and nothing with the charms of life. But even if it appalled its adversaries, it was spectacularly inventive and beautifully intentioned.

Visiting Pessac today, one sees both how Le Corbusier succeeded and how he failed. On the three streets he completed, the houses, in various states of repair, are jewels: superbly optimistic, clean, crisp, and bright. External

At Pessac, ca. 1926

staircases and balconies make lively rhythms against the smart, compact forms; the right angles and grids and parallel lines are like the drumbeat in a jazz orchestra.

Yet these structures are mostly faded and ravaged by time, or else repainted and changed so that their purity is gone. This is not happenstance; it occurred because the architect's ideal was not what people wanted. And however charming the little community, it is nearly drowned by the mediocre architecture all around it. One must penetrate acres of desultory building to get to Le Corbusier's and Frugès's marvel. When one reaches it, it suggests the future—a future that, although constructed eighty years ago, seems bright but that was not realized as dreamed. Le Corbusier made a rarity; he did not affect the quotidian as he hoped. He created something enchanting and full of hope, but he did not come close to his intention of transforming the appearance of the larger world.

THE WRITER BLAISE CENDRARS, born about a month before Charles-Edouard Jeanneret in La Chaux-de-Fonds, was another local to take a new name, replacing "Frédéric Sauser" with an appellation that suggested fire rising from the ashes. On November 15, 1926, after a visit to Pessac, he wrote Le Corbusier. "The ensemble is gay and not drearily monotonous as I thought it would be. I also thought that given your conception of a house, you were addressing yourself to a certain French elite rather than to the working classes. That is why your 'villa' type will succeed more readily than the '*cité*.' "[20] It may not have been the total adulation Le Corbusier wanted—people from the Swiss Jura were not known to mince words—but the trenchant analysis from a fellow sufferer and escapee of La Chaux-de-Fonds moved Le Corbusier greatly.

7

At the same time that he was making houses for factory workers, Le Corbusier completed one of his most impressive private villas to date—the Maison Cook in Boulogne-sur-Seine, a suburb just at the edge of Paris. With this bold and handsome house, the architect took the flat face of a basic La Chaux-de-Fonds apartment dwelling—honoring the line of the street it parallels, providing shelter within a dense urban setting—and gave it tensile elegance, lightness, and esprit.

Working as a team, Le Corbusier and Pierre Jeanneret realized the five salient points that were the goals of their new architecture. Foremost, the Maison Cook was built on pilotis: simple, untapered columns that elevate most of the structure above the ground, so that the level one floor up is where the house begins. In romantic voice, Le Corbusier and Pierre Jeanneret wrote, in a jointly signed text, "The house on posts! Reinforced cement gives us the posts. Now the house is up in the air, off the ground; the garden passes under the house, the garden is also above the house, on the roof."[21] The goal was increased awareness of the earth itself, as well as of the sky and sun; these pilotis invited a closer rapport to what is natural, universal, and timeless.

That roof garden addressed the second of the five objectives. Again, the architect cousins were focused on the use of new technology to celebrate the glories of eternal nature: "Sand covered with heavy cement tiles, with wide joints seeded with grass, rainwater filtered through terrace gardens that were opulent: flowers, bushes and trees, lawn."[22]

Inside the house, there was a third innovation: the free plan. Reinforced concrete eliminated the need for each story to be divided in accord with what was below, allowing the architects "rigorous use of each centimeter. Great economy of money."[23]

The fourth great leap was evident in the long window band, of the type already seen in Ozenfant's studio and La Petite Maison, realized here in two handsome stripes, one on top of the other. Point five was "the free facade," which was feasible now that "the facades are no more than light membranes of dividing walls or of windows."[24]

William Cook, an American journalist of independent wealth, was a friend of the Steins—Gertrude, Michael, and other members of that family of adventurous arts patrons who had come from San Francisco and settled in Paris. Cook was interested in the avant-garde and gave the architects unprecedented freedom. "We are no longer paralyzed," rhapsodized Le Corbusier. Of the Maison Cook, he declared, "The classical plan is reversed; the area underneath the house is free. The reception area is at the top of the house. One exits directly onto the roof-garden, which overlooks the vast groves of the Bois de Boulogne; one is no longer in Paris, one seems to be in the country."[25]

In his own life, Le Corbusier was content to walk the narrow streets and lively boulevards of the sixth and seventh arrondissements between office and home and climb the seven flights of the oval spiral staircase to the nest where, through the mansard windows, he and Yvonne could look at treetops and historic gardens. But in his work for a wealthy and adventurous client, he made architecture without historical precedent in its unadorned geometric pleasures, the sheer élan of thin pilotis supporting a noble mass, and the tactile delights of glass and steel and white concrete arranged to facilitate transparency and opacity so as to reveal, in an urban setting, some of those marvels to which his late father had led him on mountaintops.

8

On March 31, even though they were living in the same couple of rooms, Le Corbusier wrote his mistress a highly official letter with instructions to guard it carefully. For this document, he used her full name, "Mademoiselle Yvonne (Jeanne Victorine) Gallis." As if addressing a docile schoolgirl, he told her that as her Easter present he had opened a bank account on her behalf.

Le Corbusier spelled out to Yvonne the terms of the account. The money he was to deposit would belong to her, but the account was to be managed by Jean-Pierre de Montmollin, and she could touch the funds only with his agreement. To prevent her from spending this money, Le Corbusier had instructed de Montmollin to keep the funds in "deeds" rather than cash; the reason for the account was that he wanted her taken care of in case something ever happened to him. One never knows what will occur in life, Le Corbusier cautioned.

With his usual meticulousness, the architect instructed his mistress which entrance to use for the branch of the Crédit Commercial de France on the Champs-Elysées. He also gave her the phone number of the bank. She was to meet with de Montmollin there. But "you are hereby informed that the shares of this account cannot serve to buy trifles, but to be useful to you, truly useful when the time comes."[26] He was starting it with a deposit of 2,500 francs—which had a buying power of roughly $2,245 today—to which he planned to continue to make additions, gradually but well into the future.

With Yvonne at a masked ball, late 1920s

HE WAS his mother's caretaker as well, though Marie Jeanneret was doing her best to cope with her solitude in the lakeside villa. Le Corbusier counseled her to be strong, not to cry too much, and to see friends. Addressing "*Ma chère petite Maman*" two months after Georges's death, he wrote, "I think so often of dear, gentle Papa and his last childlike voice, so faint, so charming. Our good Papa."[27]

He and Albert and de Montmollin visited Marie at the start of April. Afterward, he advised by postcard, "Happy to keep with me the young, ardent, intelligent memory of you. Sustain your mission among us, the disinterested love of beautiful things."[28] For the rest of her life, which was nearly the rest of his, Le Corbusier obsessed over his mother's youthfulness. He followed the postcard with a letter: "*Ma petite maman,* you must not say you feel like an old woman. You never wanted to be such a thing and you have been able to keep yourself young. So, no moral capitulations now. You are strikingly youthful. You delight me each time I see you, so apt to respond with generosity and enthusiasm. It is the proof you have never closed your heart or your mind. It is a joy for us to find you thus."[29] To remain fit and healthy, she had to stay active, accept social invitations, and, he instructed, resume her teaching, even if it meant giving piano lessons free of charge.

Edouard had assigned himself the position of family sage. He reported on a recent evening at Albert and Lotti's villa in Autheuil: "Madame is very well, and very affectionate with Albert, to whom she gives evident signs of esteem. It is true that Albert is kind, lovable, and affectionate. He seems to have inherited the best of his father and his mother."[30]

By that spring, Marie had met Yvonne. Soon after his father's death, Edouard had begun to mention his living companion, describing her as a good but fragile soul, pure of heart but also at the edge of being out of control. The first encounter went well enough, but it would be an uphill battle for his mother to accept his unlikely choice. Le Corbusier did his utmost, writing, "Little Yvonne tends on the mantelpiece, under Papa's photographs, a little altar covered with fresh flowers. Today they are wallflowers and lilies-of-the-valley. This mantelpiece covered with all of Yvonne's souvenirs and knickknacks is a touching index of her taste and sensibility; she keeps an affectionate and respectful memory of you."[31]

SENDING HIS MOTHER a long letter every four or five days, he began to act as if they were one big family: "Try, *Petite Maman,* to live this solitary life of yours stoically and serenely. We don't forget you for a moment."[32] Then he told her about a dream that he said had lasted the entire night and was haunting him. In it, she was anxious and too thin. As if to relieve that worried state in which he saw her when he slept, he informed her that he was trying to help people he knew buy property adjacent to hers, so as to protect the neighborhood.

The architect implored his mother to write down, on a daily basis, all that was happening in her mind and heart, and to send it to him at the end of each week. "I think of you often," he wrote, "realizing with true anguish how alone you are. . . . Your letters are so alive. We preserve an image of you as someone young and lively, strong in your faith. The sweet memory of papa prevails, a true poem in our emotional life, and there you are, so eager beside him, inseparable from him, purified by him; how eager you are to live, to know, to act, to love. I want you to realize that there is no barrier separating us, we are on the same footing, and there is no difference in nature or quality between us, save to your advantage. And so you are with us, the friend, the good comrade, in complete and mutual trust."[33]

9

In May 1926, in Neuilly, Le Corbusier found a dog for his mother. "The puppy mutt, a thoroughbred police dog, is very likely to become another

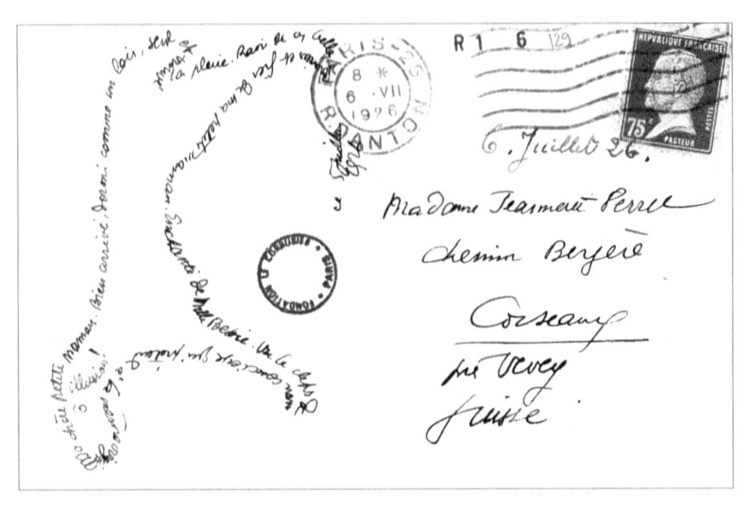

Dog formed by words in a letter to his mother, July 5, 1926

Jeanneret," he wrote.[34] His spirits were high. Important clients—American, English, and French—were pursuing him; he felt a sense of wind in his sails and of doors opening. (The clichés are his.) The novelist Colette told him she wanted to live in a "Corbusiere"—a term of her invention. They had dined together; Colette was, he told his mother, "an extremely captivating woman with magnificent eyes, painted from head to foot, and very *garçon;* she knows admirably—just like a cat—how to furnish a house which is a box of goodies."[35]

Le Corbusier lectured in Brussels about the Plan Voisin, reporting to his mother, "I was swimming like a fish in water, very much at my ease, even brilliant(!)." He let her know that, at a subsequent dinner for forty people in his honor, six speakers sang his praises. But what counted most was that when he was projecting images of La Petite Maison to his audience, he was overcome by visions of "dear Papa. Poor Papa!" And now, back in Paris, where he was writing the report from his bed, the thirty-eight-year-old Le Corbusier told his mother, "my first thought was for you."[36]

10

When he was not boasting, Le Corbusier approached his success with a sense of measure. The princess of Polignac and the Michael Steins had come to the office about major projects, his *Almanac of Modern Architecture* was about to be in the bookstores, and he was making a film on urbanism, but "at the heart of this tumultuous existence, I persist in my pictures with stubbornness and fatalism. A lot of clients come to us now from high society as well as from the aristocracy of industry. It's like a sudden launching. Of course, after such hopes there is always the counterattack of adversity; the franc is collapsing and the rising cost of houses makes chaos of our budgetary forecasts."[37]

To demonstrate his rise to fame, the architect enclosed news clippings for his mother, but he singled out one that had appeared in the obscure *Revue des Jeunes,* claiming to Marie that it was the very first time he had been moved by something written about him. For the text in this magazine intended for young people acknowledged Le Corbusier's work as "*une affaire de Coeur.* As always, everyone finds me the pitiless rationalist, the sectarian: here I am considered, above all, a man, and I am happy for that."[38]

He was also still a vulnerable little boy. Le Corbusier closed this letter, "There, Ma Petite Maman. My eyes are burning, the light hurts me and the white paper is blinding. So, beddy-bye. Beddy-bye and kisses from your son, Edouard."[39]

11

At the end of May, Le Corbusier wrote his mother about the sixty houses that were nearly finished at Pessac: "As I told you, setting modesty aside, I am astonished myself. Astonished to witness an absolutely new, unheralded architectural phenomenon, not bizarre yet telling us that things have changed, that there is a new spirit—here is a manifestation of that new spirit."[40] He was anticipating the official opening with feverish excitement. Le Corbusier, Pierre, and Anatole de Monzie, the French minister of beaux arts, were to go from Paris in de Monzie's personal train car. Henri Frugès was ecstatic that the minister would be visiting his home territory.

Albert would be there as well—all that was needed was for his mother to make the trip, too. Le Corbusier urged her, "You don't know the really beautiful countries. Switzerland is not a beautiful country."[41] Travel, he explained, was no longer a big deal; his one regret was that his father, who had studied geography so avidly and would have loved to see more places, had been denied the chance. Le Corbusier was determined to provide that opportunity to La Petite Maman.

Marie Jeanneret did not make the trip, but he described to her the event on June 13: "The mood was gay, free, unembarrassed, and one might say that the heart was in everything. The minister, Frugès, we ourselves, all of us were disinterested, pursuing only a dream of life's improvement."[42] The opening was packed with journalists and filmed for the news reports shown in the cinema. After the official speeches, Le Corbusier gave interviews.

What he had created on the outskirts of Bordeaux had the joy of the event. "The color of the walls, a procedure never yet employed, was a kind of universal festivity, and the brilliant white set off the pinks—the greens, the browns, the blues; a unity of detail in everything, a tireless variety everywhere. The big cars are in the new streets. Leaning over the banisters, climbing up and down stairs, silhouetted against the sky, a crowd occupies the roof terraces over which spill geraniums, fuchsias, bushes and clumps of reeds."[43]

The crowd on the vegetation-covered terrace was 150 people standing on the deck of the model house of Pessac, where the pine and chestnut trees surrounding the structure made the perfect backdrop to the new architecture. Everything was in place: artistic and natural beauty, the poetry of life, human generosity. Henri Frugès gave "a splendid speech, eloquent, actually ardent, setting forth his program of altruism. . . . I explain how we set about working, a technical speech, actually . . . and finish up by claiming the right to a certain lyricism, instancing the poetry of our creation."[44]

The sun was shining brightly when the minister then told the audience that he had read *Toward a New Architecture.* Le Corbusier could not hide his pride from his mother. At dinner afterward, in Frugès's house, Le Corbusier was seated next to de Monzie, and they spoke like close friends. He and Pierre went back to Paris with the minister in his "wagon salon" and slept like babies.

It was all a dream, wonderful to experience and even more marvelous to recount to the person who had given him life and raised him: "It's so you can have your own little celebration, Petite Maman; after all, you have the true soul of an architect, and weren't you the first to know how to live in a Corbusier house?"[45]

That the buildings had not received the necessary permits and that nothing could actually be inhabited was beside the point.

12

In early July, on one of the many trips he took to Vevey in the months following his father's death, Le Corbusier wrote Yvonne during a free moment while walking the puppy, now named Bessie. "DD" told his "Petit Von-

With his mother in the Villa Le Lac, late 1920s

von," in a voice of unblemished contentment, "I'm walking this little mutt and waiting for her to do her pipi. She's a handsome brute with a very becoming sky-blue leash. A boatman's dog."[46]

The dog was easier than his human intimates. His mother was insistent that he stay on with her longer than he intended, while Yvonne was impatient for him to get back to Paris. He was also having problems with Albert, who had asked their mother for money. Edouard assured Marie that he had become directly involved in his brother's latest professional endeavors, so she need not worry about his request. "I won't forget about Albert, but I'll deal with him discreetly—though actively," he wrote pompously once he had returned to France. Then, to assure her of his own financial well-being, he boasted, "As for me, we have the king's court around here. It's becoming a client a day, all over the place."[47] If he could not hope to rival his brother as their mother's preferred son and fellow musician, at least he could take the upper hand as a breadwinner.

ALBERT WAS NEEDIER, but, unlike Edouard, did not instruct or challenge his mother. Le Corbusier might conquer the world of architecture, but he never achieved his goal of upstaging his brother as Marie's favorite. The architect perpetually barraged her with news clippings about the giant he had become and emphasized his role as her protector, but the widow now had an issue she considered more pressing. The villa in Vevey had water leaking into the living room; if he was such a great architect, surely he could solve the problem.

MARIE JEANNERET was, in addition, tormented by fears about her household expenses. She could not fathom the costs she was incurring for water and gas at La Petite Maison. Le Corbusier angrily reminded his mother that she had the same income as when his father had been alive and that she used to mock Georges for his worries about money. He blamed her for torturing herself. He felt punished—as if she still held him accountable for the disaster of the Maison Blanche.

Again he informed Marie that he was working like someone possessed, pushing himself until midnight every day, including Sundays. And for all that he was doing in the world, he was occupying himself with her issues and taking care of Albert. He lectured his mother:

> Petite Maman, be careful, keep your wits about you. Don't make mountains out of molehills. Try to find a purpose in your day, recognize what's important and what's secondary. And always remember that forty percent of what the mind undertakes or what one actually does must fall through. So don't cry "wolf." . . .
>
> You're making me write this morning so that my letter will reach you without delay. But you're not getting the best of it, for I'm tense and nervous—I know I have other things to do. But of course since you're *ma petite Maman* I have written and I'm glad to do so; but it's not much of a letter—more of a porcupine. Your Sonny gives you a big hug, Ed.[48]

To please Marie Charlotte Amélie Jeanneret-Perret remained his greatest challenge.

13

In August 1926, Le Corbusier learned to swim. He had allowed himself and Yvonne the luxury of a vacation in the holiday town of Le Piquey, near the large Bay of Arcachon. In this first summer after his father's death, the warm weather and sunshine at the edge of the sea were a great comfort. He wrote his mother, "It takes an hour and a half to cross the pine forest to reach the

With Pierre Jeanneret at Le Piquey, late 1920s

ocean. Site of a simple majesty, a tremendous beach stretching in a straight line over a good deal of the coast from the Gulf of Gascony. The ocean is protected by a wide ribbon of dunes at the edge of the fields, the sand entirely sown with yellow immortelles, shifting like the sands of the desert. Then the pine groves begin, sometimes tall trunks, sometimes low bushes; a warm and intense smell of resin, of turpentine, and above it all, relentlessly, a burning sun, making the sand hot and the shade cool. A constant breeze keeps the temperature mild all day long. O deadly Paris! Here the pure sand everywhere, clean hands, clean feet, clean clothes. O filthy Paris!"[49]

He had read a newspaper article that represented Switzerland as the equivalent of Siberia. Driving home the contrast from his seaside Eden, he continued, "Here we've had nothing but an implacable sun, but all very magnificent and welcome. I find a certain humor in thinking of you fussing in your twelve square yards of garden and knowing you're quite happy doing so while we have these vast spaces of pine forests and the ocean."[50] He could have chosen to point out the oceanic nature of Lac Leman—that small garden faced what looked like a sea—but something in Le Corbusier was tortured.

One of the issues was Pessac, where he attributed the failure to hook up water to be a result of politics: "All this time the ministers administered, doing so in their very bourgeois way in order to keep up the spirits of the money-lenders who quite patriotically had invested, most of it abroad. Poincaré [Raymond Poincaré, the French prime minister at the time] is not my hero, far from it; a man of the conservatives, of the bourgeois, against whom we struggle every day. But of course, the money is with the bourgeois, therefore the bourgeois must be saved."[51]

Le Corbusier was determined to release himself from anything he considered bourgeois, too focused on money, or Swiss. He wrote his Calvinist parent, "In the last ten days . . . nobody has done anything at all. I haven't read a line nor done a stitch of work. But I've learned to swim very well, and yesterday across the dunes and the woods I made an excursion quite flattering for my age: I went to the ocean with Pierre, *running all the way without stopping once:* 24 minutes going, 28 coming back, a distance considerably greater than from La Chaux-de-F. to Le Locle (roundtrip) (9km)."[52]

One detail of the holiday he left out was the presence of Yvonne. Marie certainly knew she was there, but Edouard still wanted his widowed mother picturing him alone.

14

Le Corbusier wrote his mother about a book he had been reading by René Allendy, a pioneer of psychoanalysis in France. Born in Paris in 1889, Allendy specialized in dream interpretation and issues of sexuality. Le Corbusier reflected, "Everywhere a generalized movement appears in favor of the mind and exclusive of a narrow materialism. The former does not operate without the latter. I often experience this and often I am accused by some of a terrible rationalism, by others of being a dreamer and an aesthete. Yet architecture lives on *relations* which are a quivering lyre exclusive of practical conditions and techniques of the problem: 'touch me, touch me not,' everything is there. That's all there is to it, art is here or is not. I am moved, I am not moved. And to concern oneself with things that provoke emotion is one of the rare felicities of living, and it's because we concern ourselves with such things as these that we are happier than the rest, exclusive of material conditions."

In this confused exegesis on the balance between the emotional and the practical, Le Corbusier went on to say that his father was "permanently and constantly present: he is here, you know he is." He allowed, "My regrets, my sadnesses are constantly happy. I think: if Papa were here." He contemplated the joy Georges, "a man who passionately imagined the earthly paradises he divined elsewhere than in that severe and wretched Jurassic trench," would have known if only he had seen the places where his younger son now traveled and worked.[53]

The seacoast and the precinct of art both belonged to the sacred realm of feeling that his father had recognized as one of life's goals, however elusive and difficult it might be to achieve.

15

Returning from his halcyon holiday, Le Corbusier remained overwhelmed by thoughts of the man who had died eight months earlier. The architect wrote his mother, "Yesterday morning between Nevers and Paris his last image haunted me continuously. Moreover I kept looking at my hands shrunken by the physical activity of this vacation, and they were a little like Papa's hands. Of Papa I keep the throbbing image of those last days, of the day when I realized, precisely a year ago, that he would be leaving us. . . . That magnificent image at his death which is engraved all the deeper because I could see it so clearly in my drawing of him and then keep it in mind. That image which gives me courage for the future because I have felt the nature of the blood that flows through me so that in this dray-horse life we lead—and this jackals' life, this life of hyenas and wolves, I realize very clearly that I belong to one side and not the other, and referring myself to the testimony of our origins—our father, our mother—I move ahead, tranquil and calm, seeking one thing and not the other. You write so nicely, your letters are so true, you are so young, so frank, that I am entirely happy reading you, feeling how strong you are, how healthy in mind and body. When you write you are yourself. Your identity is complete, externals vanish. Then it is extremely comforting for a son to feel his Maman leaning over his desk in your little family dream and to know that his Papa is lying in peace, hands crossed over his chest, under the cypresses of the hill at Saint Martin. My dearest Maman, an affectionate kiss from your Ed. And to Bessie—show her my photograph so she can absorb it, you know how much I love the little creature."[54]

Now more than ever, he yearned for his mother to be happy and was desperate that she not feel constrained by the architecture of La Petite Maison or by her own mania for neatness: "It's you who makes that house alive. Knowing how to arrange each thing so that it becomes animated by a certain grace."[55] He had designed La Petite Maison to give her joy, not to impose a way of life, and to make household maintenance and daily chores as easy as possible. Le Corbusier's goals for his mother became his dream for all domestic design.

It therefore stung hard when Marie Jeanneret and Albert forgot Le Corbusier's thirty-ninth birthday. Three days after the fact, once he was sure there was no greeting that had been delayed by the post, he wrote his mother, "It hasn't happened to me since I was 16, when Papa told me: 'Now you're too big a boy.' Tender kisses from your Ed."[56] Without specifically mentioning Marie's oversight, he let her know that his Aunt Marguerite, a distant relative, had sent a card, and he had received flowers and a new pipe from unnamed sources.

This was the first October 6 since his father's death, and now his mother was happily ensconced in the small family house with her preferred child. It was more than Le Corbusier could bear.

MARIE'S DISTRACTION was understandable; Albert was having a form of psychological breakdown. In treatment with the same Dr. Allendy whose theories Le Corbusier had been reading, he had left his wife and her children in Paris and retreated to the family house, where he was mainly making music by clanking rods against bizarre arrangements of drinking glasses he had suspended upside down from strings.

Le Corbusier was forced to assume responsibility for the music school Albert had started in Paris. As he made clear to his mother several weeks after the birthday episode, he was now busier than ever before as an architect and painter of international importance. He framed his recitations of his own successes as if they were intended primarily to reassure her that at least one of her children was functioning well, but he relished his exalted position while Albert was floundering.

In spite of the birthday slight, Edouard now also sent his mother two samples of cloth and a fur collar for a coat—and he constantly inquired about the dog he had given her. Surely she must see that he had become the good child.

16

At the end of October, a new German edition of *Toward a New Architecture* sold out instantly. The success made Le Corbusier even more manic. As the hours of daylight decreased with the onset of autumn, he wrote his mother, "The day is wretchedly short of hours. And the hours themselves are even shorter. Ideas attack from all sides. I must achieve, I must act; so it's a kind of frenzy of work and an avaricious use of each minute. Now that the galley seems launched, everything begins to open up and multiply." He was, he told her, engaged in "a crushing labor."[57]

Nonetheless, he would bring the design for his father's tomb when he visited in a few weeks. He wrote, "I think of you in your tiny house, busily doing everything for everyone and often think of our Papa on this anniversary of his last sickness when it finished him off. What anguish we had last year at this time. And how a capital event intervenes in life, suddenly changing everything! And how, too, a man can straighten up and pursue his destiny all the same, a destiny quite unknown and ineffable. Tomorrow? What will happen tomorrow? There is the tomorrow we prepare for quite logically. And the other one, unknown, otherwise determined, which may suddenly intervene."[58]

Le Corbusier was desperate for his mother to attend a lecture he was giving in Zurich. He spelled out the details: "Take a ticket for Zurich, straight to Vevey. My lectures are at Zurich on the 24th and 25th, so get one combined ticket for La Chaux–Zurich–Vevey. I'll pay the difference for La Chaux–return. So it's all arranged."[59]

For once, she managed a trip. Afterward, he wrote, "You may not imagine how happy I was to be with you in Zurich and of course I was so happy that my second lecture went off well and you had nothing to blush for. I was very touched by the testimonials of respect and sympathy which you provoked. Your attitude and your lovely expression of Corbusier's old mother made respect flourish all around you."[60]

Recognition was coming at last. By the end of the year, Le Corbusier was informed by Josef Hoffmann, the man who had once been too busy to see him, that he had been named a "*membre correspondant*" of the Bund Österreichischer Architekten.[61] It was a major honor from an organization that included among its founders Klimt, Otto Wagner, and Karl Moser—even if these were the same Viennese masters whose work he had always loathed.

The future was assured: "For us, the painful hours have passed, there remains no more than what is agreeable: to make sure that it is beautiful."[62] There was no question who the "us" was: Le Corbusier and his widowed mother.

XXIV

Learn, he told himself, before you die, to live beyond the jurisdiction of their enraging, loathsome, stupid blame.

What do crows think when they hear the other birds singing? They think it's stupid. It is. Cawing. That's the only thing. It doesn't look good for a bird that struts to sing a sweet little song. No, caw your head off.

—PHILIP ROTH, *The Human Stain*

1

On January 10, 1927, in the hectic surroundings of his office, with everyone around him working away frantically, Le Corbusier suddenly wrote his mother a short letter. Eight draftspeople were in sight; these were hardly the circumstances under which he normally took the time to write.

Time was scarce in "this violent whirlwind in which I find myself," but he felt compelled by "the violent ups and downs of the idea."[1] What prompted that repetition of "violent" and was more important even than his frenzied pursuit of architecture connected to his thoughts of the previous day, a Sunday. It had been the first anniversary of his father's death. Although he was off by two days—Georges had actually died on January 11 of the previous year, not January 9—all day long Edouard had been reliving the events of a year before. This was when he recalled the vital details of his father's death and the little needle "which allowed him to leave this earth without further consideration."[2] While Edouard and Albert and their mother and the cooperative doctor were all party to the determination to help the calm and rational Georges Jeanneret end his life with euthanasia, there is no way of knowing if Georges himself participated in this decision. But this letter makes the event itself clear. The older Jeanneret had been suffering excruciating pain and had reached a terminal state. When Edouard had lain down next to his unconscious father, he had known that a well-organized death, based on carefully measured quantities of the proper mix of chemicals and proceeding at a clockwork pace, was to occur.

To find the most effective means and use them correctly was the mark of a rational, intelligent life. They had given that injection as matter-of-factly as Le Corbusier deployed water pipes, revealing rather than concealing the truths of existence. The honesty and boldness with which his natal family had determined his father's means of dying was consistent with the new aesthetic with which Le Corbusier was now triumphant. Mechanical efficiency did not displace human feeling but, rather, honored it. His father's trembling voice and wise words of departure had made clear that the time was right.

2

Founded just after the end of World War I, the League of Nations stood to benefit all of humankind by maintaining world peace and promoting international cooperation. Here, countries of every stripe and size came together as members of a global community.

When Le Corbusier was invited in 1926 to participate in the competition for the organization's headquarters on the shores of Lake Geneva, he and Pierre Jeanneret laid out a utopian dream. The complex of neat building slabs all raised on pilotis represented a fresh approach to the true meaning of community and cooperation. The wing housing the Secretariat was to be a sleek band that appeared to float in space, its form graceful and harmonious. The crowning jewel among the various structures supported by elegant and lithe legs would be a massive assembly hall built for meetings of up to 2,060 delegates. A bold, abstract composition looking triumphantly over the rest, it was sure to instill confidence in the processes it facilitated. The assembly hall was to be made of reinforced concrete and covered in polished granite, with a concave facade silhouetted against the lake. Its large windows would shimmer between trim steel mullions. Those materials encased a myriad of elements, giving unity to five hundred offices, a balcony for journalists over the enormous auditorium, a roof garden, ample toilets, changing rooms, and a restaurant.

The overall complex was designed to be welcoming and pleasant, with a covered entranceway assuring a comfortable arrival even in bad weather. Pleasantness and efficiency were central goals in every aspect of the scheme. The heating and ventilating systems, the access for automobiles and arrangements for parking, the streamlined offices geared to accommodate the latest technology, and the flawless acoustics of the Assembly Hall were all impeccable.

The structure was to be situated between the lakeshore and the mountains in a way meant to ennoble the activities that would occur within. Like an urbanized version of Mount Athos, the arrangement would enhance the serenity essential for the negotiations that were the league's mission, while providing a vista that embodied peace.

AFTER SENDING IN the plans and drawings at the end of January 1927, Le Corbusier experienced the letdown that often occurred at the conclusion of one of his creative bursts. On February 3, he wrote his mother, "Since our League of Nations plans went off to Geneva, a great sensation of emptiness reigns here. I am somewhat the worse for wear, deflated as always after a big effort."[3] He was also suffering from having given up his habitual pipe smoking earlier.

Soon enough, Le Corbusier returned to tobacco; although he occasionally halted, he was a cigarette smoker for the rest of his life. Events in Geneva were one of the reasons. At first, success seemed assured. After architects from all over the world submitted plans, Victor Horta, the president of the jury, wrote the secretary-general to say that the proposal from 35 rue de Sèvres was the only one that would not exceed the budget of thirteen million Swiss francs. Horta recommended that the Le Corbusier/Jeanneret scheme, the jury's choice, should be awarded the commission. Then the juror from France, the architect Charles Lemaresquier, director of l'Ecole des Beaux-Arts in Paris, pointed out that Le Corbusier and Jeanneret's plans had not been submitted in the requisite China ink.

Le Corbusier and Jeanneret's design had initially been made in China ink on "tracing paper," according to regulations. But what they actually submitted was in printer's ink, according to the process known as "Dorel." This was a conscious decision on the part of the architects. They thought the Dorel impressions, which corresponded to the most current practices of architectural studios, made greater sense, since it guaranteed that the plans would be completely dry, which was not the case with China ink. While Dorel in its final stage used printer's ink, it required by definition that the drawings originally be made in China ink, so Le Corbusier and Jeanneret believed that their submission fulfilled the requirements of the competition. They made it clear that they completely understood and supported those requirements—since China ink was more precise and exact than pencil, charcoal, or watercolor.

While the issue of the ink did not immediately put Le Corbusier out of the running, it caused what had seemed certain now to be in jeopardy.

Rather than award the commission to him and Pierre as originally decided, the jury now made their scheme one of nine on the short list. Then the General Assembly voted that there was more money to spend on the building complex than originally stipulated.

A battle ensued over which design to use. Sigfried Giedion, an esteemed authority on architecture, defended Le Corbusier and Pierre's proposal in widely read newspaper articles, and Karl Moser, the juror from Switzerland, championed it as well. On May 8, 1927, an optimistic Le Corbusier wrote his mother,

> Our situation is brilliant beyond our wildest dreams, and the future may belong to us.
>
> The French press has made this competition into a success, and we are among the four who have assured France its triumph. We are in fact the only moderns, the others being notorious academics. So that the field is clearer than ever: *modernism or academicism?* We have weapons. . . . On all sides the Le Corbusier victory is regarded as the victory of the modern and the other leading moderns have no standing in public opinion.
>
> Here in Paris this is a capital event in the world of architecture. It used to be denied that I knew how to make anything but "machines for living." Here is proof of the contrary.[4]

Recalling a foe who had said that "what we did was not architecture!," Le Corbusier told his mother, "We'll talk about all this when I see you next. The other evening Albert was utterly amazed. I myself maintained the most disconcerting calm, judging even at the first news that this was a manifestation of the jury's impotence. Actually, I knew we had to come out on top, for we had a well-made plan—extremely well-made—and I'm more or less convinced that no competitor had made a study anywhere near so serious. I can't separate these events from the thought of dear Papa. What deep personal joy he would have had! All the same he would have said: 'Yes, *but. But.*' . . . Those 'buts' which testified to the fact that he feared reprisals and upsets. But there are no 'buts' here, and Papa would have been deeply happy."[5]

Le Corbusier's excitement was, as usual, tinged by pain. He believed he had won the commission of his dreams, yet he was suffering from nightmares. They were about his mother. He wrote her that they were too painful to describe, but that when he received a letter from her, he could hardly believe his own relief that she was still alive to write it.

THEN, IN JUNE, Le Corbusier's confidence in a League of Nations victory began to wane. He entered the fracas directly in hopes of influencing the jurors, prompting his mother to caution him about the merits of his campaign.

On June 16, 1927, Marie wrote Le Corbusier,

> I know your experiences will soon be more firmly based; your portrait (and what a portrait, in reinforced concrete!) has been published here as well as the plans for the League of Nations. Albert tells me you are working hard for victory, and your mother must hope it is with loyal arms that you are pursuing your goal, never forgetting everything honorable and upright that our dear Papa had instilled in you. . . .
>
> I know that here on earth the struggle is a harsh one which requires tenacity and energy, and it is because I know these qualities are innate in you that I can say so.[6]

His mother enumerated those qualities: "your simplicity, your true modesty, qualities great men have always possessed, even at the height of their success."[7] Her son's conceit and boastfulness were, after all, no secret to her.

3

Marie Jeanneret harbored no illusions. She acknowledged that even the new dog was having a tough time. "Bessie is making a terrible racket; the postman is the cause, encouraging her hysteria by swiping at her with his hat. Apropos of Bessie, she is back to living her solitary little life, though doubtless regretting her races with the children at Blonay," she wrote. The loneliness and exhaustion of the dog was comparable to Marie's own: "I simply cannot do the work all by myself: curtains to wash, beds to air, closets to clean, actually a general cleanup of a ransacked house. Our friends have left, Mme. Matthey to her son's house in Herisau, our relatives for the ends of the earth! Alone! Sometimes it's hard. And I know no one."[8]

The one comfort to the sixty-six-year-old was her sons. She told Le Corbusier, "A little article by Pettarel has appeared in *La Feuille de Dimanche* about the Jeanneret family, starting of course with Le Corbusier."[9] And then there was "the fine boy," Albert. He was going to Sweden; this pleased her, but only "in part." For Marie wanted her sons for herself.

She got her wish. After Albert returned from his travels in midsummer, she wrote Edouard,

> I've just washed my hair, taking advantage of the sunshine to dry it, while my dear son has gone off to Walther's for a swim. You can imagine how happy I am to repossess my boy for me alone, a happiness soon to be doubled by your presence.
>
> And soon you'll be here, dear boy—how long you've been expected! The garden is delicious, the peaches melt in your mouth, the big plums are waiting for the birds to peck at them, and the three (count them) pears are growing larger on their tree as you look at them. Isn't it all so tempting? I add the famous swim, the frogs in the sun-warmed shallows, and the cool shade of the paulownia. . . . If after all that you don't rush to pack your bags for your native land it's because your heart no longer beats at the prospect of really good things.[10]

The dynamics never changed: Marie Jeanneret perpetually trying to manipulate her younger son's emotions, and Le Corbusier always fighting the unwinnable battle for her to renounce Switzerland and see the supremacy of his decisions and achievements. Albert—the peripatetic musician/composer, the helpless innocent of the three, unable to sustain a marriage and dependent on two powerful family members—was the only one at ease.

WHILE IMPORTANT SWISS NEWSPAPERS such as the *Journal de Genève* were in favor of Le Corbusier and Jeanneret's League of Nations scheme, others, such as the *Gazette de Lausanne,* were vehemently against its strident modernism. The mounting opposition, which Pierre, seeing the issues as having to do more with the canton of the family's origins than with aesthetics, credited to anti-Vaudois sentiment, was effective.[11] By July, Le Corbusier again began to smell defeat.

He retreated to his preferred source of sanity. In the summer of 1927, Le Corbusier concentrated with renewed energy on his paintings. He now believed that he had mastered color by understanding the need for its simplicity, which enabled him to clarify his composition. When Fernand Léger praised the new work accordingly, Le Corbusier was ecstatic.

His delight with his painting and the progress of the villa at Garches fed an overall optimism in which he became convinced, falsely, that the League of Nations project would be theirs. On July 29, 1927, in one of his phases when he believed himself triumphant on every front, he wrote his "*bonne* Petite Maman" a rambling epiphany: "Thanks for being ever brave and enthusiastic. Life is a tangled skein, and now and then one achieves a clear patch, something emerges. To know what is right, what is good, is difficult and the result not of sudden and brutal decisions but of a careful procedure during which each day brings its own contribution. . . . Life has no goal. Life is only a transition—to vain minds one lives one's life according to a beginning and an end. I myself believe one lives one's life in order to make it a mounting progress. Yet one day or another such progress slows down; age erodes the creative forces. One sees nothing but limitless ascents . . . apparently. And suddenly, the measure of a man is ossification, immobilization, a downward path. A sad certainty. One might hope to die at the right moment. But that, too, is a vanity. . . . I regard myself as an eternal student, always on the threshold of a new problem. I do not conceive of such a thing as maturity. I neither hope for it, nor do I want it. The deeper one enters into a conception (however shallow, however cloudy) of life, the more one is confused and the less one is certain of one's goal. And the more clearly one discovers that there is a means of accounting for our presence here: it is to be useful, to be generous, to be open. There are holes on all sides: they must be filled—and it is good to do so—with whatever comes to hand. A selfish life is a life without hope. The opposite kind is full of possibilities."[12]

He addressed the issue of Albert's "*neurasthénie,*" which translates roughly as "clinical depression." Le Corbusier warned their mother that she did not adequately understand this illness, but he offered her the comfort that Albert was making considerable progress with Dr. Allendy.

Where Marie could be most effective was with Bessie, "your idealized comrade."[13] Le Corbusier instructed his mother to attach a three- or four-meter chain to the catalpa tree next to the villa, "No absurd sentimentality here: what she needs is a purge for two weeks. You must not mask affection by attentions to which this creature is indifferent. And if she is tied up for fifteen days (excellent for guard dogs) she will appreciate her recovered freedom all the more. Not a wire, with all the dreaded consequences; common sense: a *chain* [underlined four times], promise me this."[14]

Try as he did to lay down the law, he knew that he was up against a force as intractable as any in his life.

4

Le Corbusier and Yvonne took another summer holiday at Le Piquey. The sculptor Jacques Lipchitz and his wife, for whom Le Corbusier had recently built the studio/residence in Boulogne, were living in a fisherman's house, where Le Corbusier was mesmerized by the tide table and perpetually mon-

With Yvonne on holiday in Le Piquey, ca. 1930

itored the sea coming in and receding, as if to measure the passing of time. He developed the idea of buying three pine trees and four square meters of sand. He would, he said, build a hut on this spot of coastline. For others, he would make grandiose villas; for himself, a modest shack facing the horizon. The idea was seeded for his ultimate refuge.

While he was holidaying, Le Corbusier learned that the forces against him on the League of Nations project were gaining strength. He wrote his mother, "The struggle is exactly what I had foreseen: *us* against *academi-*

With his mother and her dog Nora in Vevey, ca. 1930

cism."[15] He determined that at the start of September he would spend a week with her in Vevey, from where he would go to Geneva to begin to wage the battle himself, on-site.

Another fight troubled him more. The architect was furious at the builder of La Petite Maison, Colombo. He put the blame entirely on the builder for the dampness problem and leaking roof that had his mother increasingly upset. He insisted that Colombo, negligent as well as miserly, had played a dirty trick and not made an adequate foundation. He had never before had an equivalent problem in anything he had built: "Only that damn foundation is betraying us. Besides I had ordered hollow *cinder blocks* with a *hole;* Colombo made them of *cement* with *three holes.* Such walls have no consistency and no insulation. He neglected this when I was not around. I had ordered *Pitcholine* for the roof; he used *Toitex* and he made neither gutters nor connecting outlets against the parapet. It is all very clear, unfortunately. I have written Colombo to put his nose in his own doo-doo and to keep him from blaming our construction methods."[16]

To have built a second disaster for his mother was more than he could bear. He assured Marie that, busy as his schedule was with the office reopening after the August holiday, he would stay with her until he got the situation completely rectified. Le Corbusier reminded Marie that the fifty-six houses at Pessac had survived torrid temperatures and the heaviest winter storms and that there was not a single ceiling stain—even in empty, unheated houses. His Stuttgart project was being praised to the hilt. He would solve the problems at Vevey!

5

Once the house in Vevey sprang its leak, everything began to spiral downward. By the end of September 1927, Le Corbusier was convinced that his League of Nations foes would defeat him.

His cousin Pierre became his latest scapegoat. Le Corbusier could not stand being at Pierre's mercy whenever he went to Vevey to be with his mother. "That damn Pierre hasn't written to tell me what he's doing." Le Corbusier complained to Yvonne on one occasion, "If Pierre deigned to specify his intentions I'd feel better about it. . . . It annoys me, since it's the same story every year. He doesn't even realize what a lack of consideration it is. He mustn't get it into his head that I'm enjoying myself."[17]

Swimming remained Le Corbusier's emotional salvation. Trying to resolve the problems of his mother's house, which he now called the Villa Le

Lac, he could raise his spirits by taking off in the freshwater just a few steps from its doors. "If I didn't have the opportunity to swim (and I swim remarkably well) I'd be completely disgusted," he wrote Yvonne.[18] Gliding through water, he encountered no obstacles and could control his own path. For the rest of his life, up to his last breath, this was how he could feel that he controlled his own destiny.

On the milestone of his fortieth birthday, Le Corbusier wrote his mother from Paris. She was, he reminded her, "the creator of my life on earth." Le Corbusier vividly reconstructed his own birth.

> Forty years ago this must have been a very painful day: that is what is called a deliverance. Maman was delivered, and a big baby filled the house with his cries. He had a cloud of hair on his skull, a mouth from ear to ear, and ears you could fold over his mouth.
>
> Forty years later, a handsome boy, of course. And the best thing about it all is that he has no notion of blaming his mother for having brought him into the world. No! All's well—why wouldn't it be? The road is stony, the chariot must be pulled; one pulls.[19]

The bizarre monologue continued. His father had had worries and doubts about him; now Georges would have had reason for optimism. Le Corbusier charted his evolution for his mother.

> In any case these forty years represent ten years of painful and unrewarded efforts. Then ten years of drifting, of hopes, and of a certain pride on the part of the parents. Then ten years of ineffable pride mixed with fear. And then at last ten years when it would have been better that the parents knew nothing of what battles were involved, what emotional situations, intense troubles, resolutions, rage, and desperate efforts which failed, ever-present hopes, etc., etc.
>
> These forty years having passed, there intervenes a salient point along the curve which I hope will continue its spiral ascent. After these groups of four decades, three of which in any case are marked by what one might call human sufferings—dreams ever and again defeated by inexorable realities—the struggle seems to be achieving, in its most effective areas, gains worth the trouble they cost. . . . Whereas during at least the first two decades, for twenty years (!!!) that struggle was so often impotent and futile.
>
> You were not sufficiently included in our joys—as was also true of the opposite—we were under great strain and it was better to keep it to ourselves.
>
> And so much for the forty years and my thanks to my chief collabo-

> rator and my deep gratitude as well to the worthy and loyal father who along with her raised us.[20]

Le Corbusier had recently been in Zurich for a "council of war" regarding the increasingly precarious League of Nations situation. He launched into a related comparison of Germany to France. Having gone to Stuttgart to work on his houses there, he was appalled by Germany in general. Its cities were atrocious; they made one physically ill. Even the most allegedly sophisticated citizens were barbarians at heart. Paris, on the other hand, was "a dazzling crystal, straight, transparent, concentrated, conditioned, human"—adjectives that constitute the Corbusean ideal. The roads in Germany were disastrous, while the minute one crossed the border at Strasbourg one was in the land of "Colbert and Napoleon: clear and distinct ideas! Straight and magnificent roads, with cathedrals of trees planted along them, already two centuries old! The whole country has proportion, measure, *style.*"[21]

Le Corbusier always categorized nationalities, inextricably linking a country's art and architecture with the citizenry that had made it. Were the largest buildings in Geneva to bear his imprimatur, they would signify the strength and independence of Switzerland; if not, if the League of Nations were to wear the tired vestiges of timid academicism, he would have to separate himself even further from the homeland he so disparaged.

6

In mid-October, Le Corbusier received a letter from William Ritter saying that Janko Czadra, Ritter's longtime partner, had died. Le Corbusier wrote his mentor, "Since my father's death, a death before my eyes, a new aspect of life has become apparent to me: that of death. And a whole cycle of ideas inevitably leading to it. Death is everywhere. I had no idea."[22]

Ritter was the exemplar of human tenderness. "I have no idea what's become of you. Dare I hope that you've grown terribly strong? You must know that your image and your presence are as distinct for me as ever—but you who are so violent of heart, what's become of you? You were all heart. That's what remains to me of you. And Janko was the object of your heart's impulses."[23]

There was a price to pay for such sensitivity. Denial was essential for vulnerable people to survive life's unbearable sadness. "My mother, I believe, is sustained by an almost alarming stoicism. It is the triumph of life. Tell me how you really are? Deliberate blindness and, luckily, daily exhaustion overwhelm us, which is how human resistance is formed."[24]

This had become Le Corbusier's own formula for survival. He believed that to manage in the face of setbacks and the inevitable tragedies of human existence one has to wear blinders and fatigue oneself in everyday struggles.

Offering condolences to the grief-stricken Ritter, Le Corbusier brought the subject back to himself:

> Remember: I owe you a lot. You are the first to have awakened me. I wanted to confide in you, in spite of everything. I say *in spite of everything,* for it is in spite of everything that life goes on and supplants disillusion and decline.
>
> I have been singularly affected the last two years by natural phenomena, cosmic events that torment me with their grim fatality, their indifference. A dramatic obsession whenever I travel and am released from the specific and intimate problems that absorb me: painting and thinking about architecture.
>
> Life opens its fan, and there is drama everywhere. At which point laughter becomes the buoy.
>
> But at certain moments you cannot laugh; laughter is only a mask.[25]

He counseled fortitude to the bereaved Ritter: "How ardently I wish you the potential of strength you need in order to go on, for there can be no stopping." Le Corbusier acknowledged his own struggles. "I'm afraid you might think me insincere, a parvenu. I am, as always, a student at the foot of the mountain. Praise terrifies me and knowledge renders me ever more timid, for there are holes that open everywhere. I have survived the worst miseries, but I have always had joy. I am still just a little bird on the branch, and today, when the elite concern themselves with my important case at Geneva (a battle of the old against a faith), I am increasingly anxious, in my innermost self, behind my closed door."[26]

To Ritter, the architect allowed his deep-seated sense of isolation and fragility: "I was a child, and the elders were above me. I felt the shadow fall over me and the horizon was limited. The duties of solidarity were revealed. Strength leads us to be conscious of the weaknesses of the young and the old, those who have fewer powers of resistance. A lonely, a very lonely situation. No support. On the contrary. People turn to you for support. Which is serious. Such moments are no laughing matter. Then come events in one's innermost self, and one realizes that life foments suffering everywhere."[27]

Le Corbusier had written Ritter frequently in recent times and been devastated to have no response. He had assumed that Ritter was not answering because the music writer had given up on him; now he realized it was because Ritter was completely distracted by Czadra's ill health. "You must have doubted me," he wrote. "I told myself: it's fate. You didn't like (or no longer liked) a life of combat. You had taken refuge within yourself. I kept thinking: 'he takes me for a lost cause.' If you knew how indifferent everything is to me, aside from the tyrannical search for perfection. And now I realize quite clearly that it becomes more indefinable every day. But I don't want to collapse into skepticism, I must avoid despair."[28]

"Ch.E. Jeanneret" ended by lambasting himself for having been so consumed with his own issues that he had misconstrued Ritter's silence. Their friendship waned with the passage of time, but William Ritter was one of the rare people whom Le Corbusier admired unfailingly. For in his music and fiction, and with his undisguised homosexuality, the writer was both passionate and brave: the essentials for a Le Corbusian hero.

7

It suited Le Corbusier to pin his failure to win the League of Nations project on bureaucratic rigidity and nationalistic competitiveness and to ignore the other factors. In November 1927, a committee assigned to review the nine schemes under consideration said of Le Corbusier, "In his desire to innovate, he unremittingly applies—to a structure that must nevertheless assume a representative role—certain formulas and procedures that, presented in so schematic a form, seem more suitable to purely utilitarian buildings."[29]

Le Corbusier disparaged such disapproval as complete moral corruption—and occasion for the sort of battle he relished. At the start of December, he wrote his mother, "The blackest state diplomacy is at work. I'm quite informed. Will such intrigues prevail against public opinion? It's all becoming very emotional. I'm flinging my last reserves into the front lines these days. We'll see! If we're defeated, it's still not over. In any case it will be a fine spectacle!"[30]

The struggle was of originality versus conventionalism, courage versus timidity, and bureaucratic rigidity versus a logical variation of the rules. He did not allow that there might be intellectually honest reasons to oppose his ideas.

While thrilling, the imbroglio was taxing, and he was contending with the change of season: "As always I dread winter, death dealer in days gone by."[31] Yet the magnitude of the controversy, the richness of the stakes, and his belief in his own rightness in a battle of good versus evil were the perfect antidote to end-of-the-year blues. "Whatever happens our defeat will ignite the powder, and there will be a great demonstration on the part of the elite," he wrote his mother on December 16.[32]

ON DECEMBER 22, 1927, the jury for the League of Nations complex rendered its final decision, declaring as the winner a scheme that had been designed by four academics: two Frenchmen, an Italian, and a Hungarian. Seventy-four-year-old Henri Paul Nénot, who for more than thirty years had been chairman of the architecture department at l'Ecole des Beaux-Arts in Paris, was appointed director general for architecture.

Le Corbusier did not give up. He and Pierre rapidly came up with a second set of plans, which they submitted in the correct ink. When those revised documents failed to sway the jury, the architect asked Hélène de Mandrot, an influential Swiss with a passion for modern architecture, to intervene on his behalf. The Jeanneret cousins were encouraged when ambassadors from five of the member countries pointed out the many flaws and shortcomings of the winning proposal. The spaces for storage and the garages were inadequate; the lighting would not work; there were problems with the design of the facade; the scale of the staircases and elevators was not correct.

The victorious architects, Le Corbusier insisted, were guilty of plagiarism, neglecting to give him the credit he deserved for the many elements of his own scheme that they had stolen for theirs and now botched. He believed that it was "incontestible [*sic*] that this joint design was directly inspired by the design of MM. Le Corbusier and Pierre Jeanneret," and asked for a further meeting of the ambassadors.[33] But for the jury the competition was over.

XXV

1

In 1927, Charlotte Perriand was a lively, svelte, flapperesque woman of twenty-four. She had a peaches-and-cream complexion, and her smile revealed a flash of pearly white teeth. Everything about her bespoke confidence and flair.

In 1925 Perriand, who was a student of design, saw the Pavilion de L'Esprit Nouveau. It opened her eyes to modernism. The following year, she left her parents' traditional middle-class Right Bank apartment for a new life. She married an Englishman, rented an old photographic studio looking out on Saint Sulpice, danced the Charleston, and marveled at "a stark naked black Josephine [Baker], her little ass embellished with a string of bananas, dancing to a wild rhythm—an authentic *femme sauvage.*"[1]

Determinedly adventurous, Perriand bobbed her straight, shining hair and wore a necklace of chrome-plated brass balls. She made her Bar sous le Toit—a daring, minimalist glass-topped unit on a truncated I-beam with a glistening nickel front—which was a hit at the 1927 Salon d'Automne. She became confident of her talent, but was unsure of what to do next.

Having read Le Corbusier's books, Perriand decided to storm the architect's headquarters unannounced. It was morning, however. Le Corbusier, as usual, was not there; he was at home, painting and designing. Pierre Jeanneret, who received her at the door, was cordial, but Perriand refused to state her case to anyone but Le Corbusier himself. That afternoon, she showed up again without an appointment, now with a portfolio of drawings under her arm. She was duly intimidated by Le Corbusier, forbidding behind his large glasses, but Perriand had moxie; when the master asked her what she wanted, she replied, "To work with you."[2]

The architect took a quick look at the fetching young woman's drawings. "We don't embroider pillows here," he snapped. He showed her the door. On her way out, Perriand told him about the exhibit at the Salon d'Automne and left her card. The next day, Le Corbusier and Pierre Jeanneret visited her stand at the salon and then wrote to offer Perriand a job.

When she excitedly told a professional acquaintance that she was going to work for Le Corbusier, he warned her not to. She would dry up, the friend insisted; to take a job in Le Corbusier's office meant becoming a drone. She never forgot the warning, but for the next ten years Charlotte Perriand remained an employee at 35 rue de Sèvres.

PERRIAND was ignited by the intense engagement of everyone in the office: "Think of that heroic period, pioneering and penniless, with access to so few resources, think of all those projects of architecture or urbanism never to be realized yet so carefully studied and planned, . . . projects in relation to humanity. . . . To create the human nest as well as the tree that would bear it. We ended by believing in it all. Enthusiastic young men from the best schools the world over came here, not only for architecture but for Le Corbusier, for his way of reconsidering all problems, for his aura."[3]

Perriand's first task as an employee was to help with furniture and revisions to the interior for the Villa La Roche, which had been begun four years earlier. Combining the concepts of Vitruvius with the latest technological advances, she, Pierre Jeanneret, and Le Corbusier worked in tandem to create seating and tables and the other necessities of comfortable living. Le Corbusier had long dabbled in apartment furnishings, but now he wanted revolution inside the house as well as outside—furniture as technically and aesthetically streamlined as his architecture.

2

Tubular steel had been introduced into furniture design in 1925 at the Bauhaus. The team at 35 rue de Sèvres worked on armchairs, chaise longues, and other pieces that employed this lightweight, tough tubing that had been invented for the construction of bicycles. At nightfall, Le Corbusier evaluated their progress. He was mocking and scurrilous, mainly in his insistence that the scale was all wrong. Perriand decided that she should make full-scale prototypes of the new pieces. She went to the enormous hardware store BHV to buy rivets and just the right springs for suspending the support of a chaise longue, got her locksmith to construct the steel frames, and located a saddlemaker who sewed hides in the style that had been perfected by the luxury saddlemaker Hermès. She used English leather, considered the best in the world, for armchair upholstery, and had cushions made with the finest goose-feather filling. With the same artisans who helped her create the Bar sous le Toit, she completed the assembly.

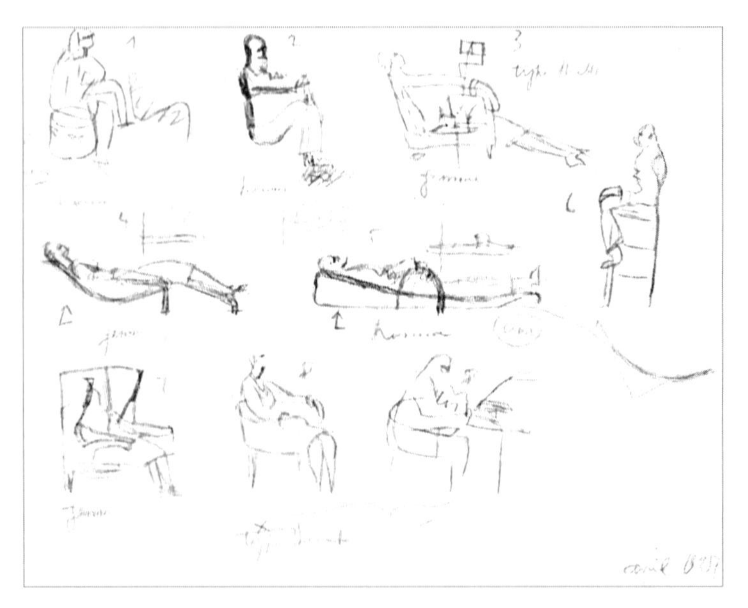

Drawing of different ways of sitting, ca. 1928

Perriand then invited her two colleagues to her studio, without mentioning that she had been making these prototypes. In that light-filled space facing the great church of Saint Sulpice, Le Corbusier and Pierre lowered their backs into the curves of the "*chaise longue de grand repos*" and stretched out their legs. They sat at attention in the visitor's chair and let the boxy armchair cradle them. "Very smart," Le Corbusier allowed.[4] The designs were ready to be built for the Villa La Roche and the interiors of his new buildings.

THE MOST INVITING, soothing, yet energetic of the threesome's seating designs was the chaise longue. Here a tubular-steel support—like a cartoon of an entire human body—is suspended above a sweeping curve. It reads like a drawing as much as a piece of furniture, as if the form of the frame had been scribed in the air. The open-armed curve of the heavy black stand underneath the seating element seems to cradle it warmly.

The chaise is a jazz-age piece of furniture—as fresh and of the epoch as Perriand's bobbed hair and the dashing window bands of the Villa La Roche. A thick pony-skin covering cossets most of the user's body, while a leather-covered cylinder cushions the neck and head. That black-and-white covering suggests the sleek speed of its source, galloping on slender, piloti-like legs. The rolling shapes invite you to sprawl and to take pleasure, to put up your feet, lean back, and feel succored. Meant for open spaces like those

LEFT TO RIGHT: *Le Corbusier, Percy Scholefield (Charlotte Perriand's first husband), Charlotte Perriand, Georges D. Bourgeois, and Jean Fouquet at the Salon d'Automne, Paris, 1922. Photo by Pierre Jeanneret*

in Le Corbusier's residences, it conjures his insistence to his parents that they take it easy in life and enjoy what they have (see color plate 3).

The visitor's chair has a simple tubular frame, armrests that resemble automobile fan belts, a minimal but comfortable seat, and an adjustable back made of stretched pony skin. Its lean form encourages a perfect mix of ease and alertness. The cubic club chair depends on its tubular-steel frame to support thick, tightly packed, leather-covered blocks that surround the user like a womb. Like Le Corbusier's architecture, this chair is a basic box form, based on the simplest vocabulary, that functions as a stage for human living.

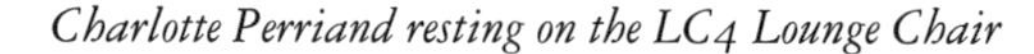

Charlotte Perriand resting on the LC4 Lounge Chair

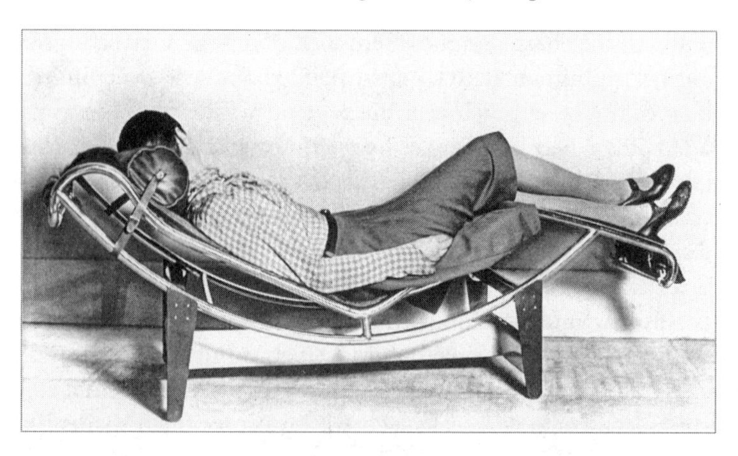

Club Chair, 1928

All of the pieces have the boldness, the balance of the tensile and massive, and the playful rhythms of Le Corbusier's houses.

IT WAS A WHILE before the new furniture found its audience. One of the places where Le Corbusier hoped the chairs, as well as some new tables, would go was the villa he was completing at Garches, but the owners chose to keep their Renaissance tables and eighteenth-century armchairs. In 1929, however, Le Corbusier and his team showed the pieces at the Salon d'Automne. It was the beginning of the slow acceptance and manufacture of these objects that today grace homes and offices throughout the world.

3

In 1906, Pablo Picasso painted a portrait of Gertrude Stein in which the writer appears physically massive and indubitably confident. The villa Le Corbusier completed in the Paris suburb of Garches in 1927 for Gertrude Stein's brother Michael and his wife, Sarah, has the same daunting, uncompromising presence.

The Steins commissioned it with their close friend Gabrielle de Monzie, formerly married to Anatole de Monzie. Even more assured than the Villa Cook, the facade of the villa at Garches (also called Villa Stein and Villa de Monzie) makes bold declarations. The entrance, with its cantilevered over-

Villa Stein–de Monzie in Garches, during construction, 1927–1928

hang, beckons us in; the garage announces the role of the automobile in the lives of the inhabitants; the lithe window bands suggest an interior full of daylight; and the large rooftop balcony invites communion with the sky.

That white block at Garches, set back from the road like a light-footed giant in its lair, is an exemplar of the tenets of Purism. So is its lesser-known garden facade. Graced by the strong diagonal of an exterior staircase and a dashing plane of pure luminous blue for the exterior ceiling created by the roof slab over a terrace, the back of the villa is an abstract composition on a par with the greatest inventions of the painters who were pushing non-objective art to new peaks at this same wonderful moment in the history of art.

Villa Stein–de Monzie in Garches, front facade, 1928

Le Corbusier achieved those aesthetic strides by taking substances of enormous weight and rendering them ethereal. The rigid steel joists and mullions and the solid concrete walls all appear to float. What Le Corbusier has done with physical

El Lissitzky (second from left on top), Mondrian (standing below, with his hand on the stairs), and other visitors to the Villa Stein–de Monzie, late 1920s

substances, he has also done with emotions. He has cloaked his own doubts and trepidations to evoke a look of positive force. With its noble design and exact proportions, Garches is unequivocally triumphant.

The man who had grown up in a world of Calvinist denial—who remained beset by anxiety—had found the means to evoke the ebullicncc and certitude that were his ideals. All that remained necessary was for his mother to picture it. He boasted to her that Garches was "a masterpiece of purity, elegance and science." This was because the three clients were "the best we have had, having a carefully established program, many requirements, but these being satisfied, having a total respect for the artist, or better still, being people who know what an artist's sensibility consists of and how much can be gained from it if it is well treated. These are the people who bought the first Matisses, and they seem to consider that their contact with Le Corbusier is also a special moment of their lives."[5]

In Le Corbusier's encomium for his clients at Garches, he described a conflict with their predecessor Cook, with himself as the Buddha of the tale: "[Cook] had fallen victim to a raging neurasthenia, stubbornly supposing that I am completely indifferent to him. We exchanged the most unpleasant words, I with glacial calm. Finally, in the face of the idiocy of such an attitude I offered peace, and now he is, in his own words, serene as an angel, a confirmation of my ideas about the misunderstandings which so stupidly manage to make enemies. Often with a well-placed word one can mend a disastrous situation."[6] No one else, of course, would have agreed with Le Corbusier's depiction of himself as the sage and diplomatic one.

Le Corbusier equated the purity and clear vision manifest in the splendid villa at Garches with the same traits in its owners. The man whom he referred to as "Le papa Stein" was on-site for hours every day. He observed everything but did not impose. Stein's assuredness was manifest in the noble facade, the graceful windows and balconies: "The house is clean and pure, far beyond anything we have done: a kind of obvious, unarguable manifesto." Le Corbusier clearly identified with the client: "Le papa Stein . . . against whom so many others struggle, denying and accusing."[7]

Just as the villa was being completed, Le Corbusier gave another lecture on the Plan Voisin. "Here in the heart of Paris, with no preambles necessary; I had the impression that I could be direct, ardent, firm, convincing."[8] He and his architecture had the same unassailable confidence.

4

"Direct, ardent, firm" was how he was about Albert as well. He wrote his mother, "It's our distinct impression that Albert was born lucky and that your continual apprehensions are entirely misplaced. I can assure you that my existence is in every way more difficult than Albert's, and you must get out of the habit of 'pitying' him. He has been very lucky, period, that's all there is to say."[9]

Le Corbusier had no doubt of his right to praise or criticize in every realm, to design other people's lives for them. When he didn't chastise, he encouraged. He let his mother know that her letters were "indispensable. . . . They bring us a breath of youth, of joy, of limpidity, of courage.

They show us that despite the fact that you are our Maman, you keep the same tempo as we do; they let us hope that perhaps like you we can remain among the young for a long time to come."[10]

But she had to overcome her mania for housekeeping. When Marie fell in her basement, he issued a sharp reprimand: "It doesn't surprise me, it was inevitable given the kind of frenzy that accompanies your domestic activities."[11] He begged her not to let her parsimony and fears about the cost of coal prevent her from keeping the house warm enough, especially since, if she became sick, she would not let anyone lend a helping hand.

Why must she live so frugally, given how many important people he knew? In October 1926, Le Corbusier had written that the duke of Württemberg had come to the rue Jacob to see his paintings; at the start of March 1927, he told her this a second time, as if the visit had just occurred. He described the grandson of the former archduke as "a young man, very refined, very gentle, tall as a grenadier, but with perfect manners. A king in exile. Actually I think he must find all this much more amusing than the throne."[12] If royalty preferred to be with him than to rule its kingdom, couldn't his mother do a better job of appreciating her son?

WHEN HE WAS NOT trying to redesign the world, Le Corbusier was revising the tomb for his father and planning the arrangement of its flowers. Like the trees on the patio at Garches, the blossoms were integral to the design. He gave his mother the task of organizing and maintaining the seasonal flowers meant to convey both the beauty and the fragility of life next to the modest but perfect monument housing the remains of the man Le Corbusier now regarded as a saint. He specified red geraniums, "a poppy of the Alps, a pansy, a saxifrage," and some modest moss, his father's favorite.[13] He sent sketches to his mother to show her where each should go.

His father's tomb, the life span of flowers, the new dog—all reflected his usual preoccupations: "Bessie has become the pretext for affective mental attitudes that are in reality destined for dear Papa. And yet life shows us how little we appreciate the time we have to live, which is constantly passing, ceaselessly concerned as we are with longing for what we don't have and so careless about appreciating what we do. How many splendid hours we might have lived in peace and enthusiasm and joy."[14] Whether this was wistfulness over his own shortcomings or advice to his mother was unclear.

Le Corbusier had become "maniacal about my time. At each second, new ideas tempt me, absorb me . . . and the years pass, wildly, alas." Fortunately, he had one constant: he kept a photograph of his mother on his desk. It stood behind his inkwell, facing him at all times. He wrote her, "I see you there often, believe me, looking just the way I most admire and respect

R 1 6 159

L'ESPRIT NOUVEAU

3 mai 1927

Ma chère petite maman.

Je pense que la tombe de papa va être achevée. Ne t'étonne pas — à ton habitude — de l'allure inédite qu'elle pourra avoir. Elle est composée pour recevoir des fleurs, et voici comment :

Dans la partie du milieu A un grand carré à remplir de géraniums serrés et hauts.

En d'autres endroits, B, C, D etc, au croisement des joints, j'ai fait réserve de poches de terre dans lesquelles tu planteras, ici un petit pavot blanc ou jaune, là une pensée des Alpes, là une androsace ou toute petite plante en mousse, modeste et timide, charmante petite fleur que papa aimait.

La tombe ainsi fleurie sera jolie, je suis certain.

Contrairement à ce que je t'écrivais, la décision du P.I.N. n'est pas encore intervenue. Il doit y avoir un désaccord terrible entre les 2 camps : académisme et moderne. Et ce doit être très grave.

C B A D

Sketch of his father's tomb in a letter to his mother, May 3, 1927

you."[15] In letter after letter, he referred to this photo, saying it made him feel as if she were present and he was actually speaking to her. The most celebrated and disparaged architect in the world wanted his mother to know he thought of her perpetually.

5

Le Corbusier continued to try to convince as many people as possible about the merits of the Plan Voisin. Even if, privately, he wanted it entertained only as a concept and not a fait accompli, he pushed forward his agenda of urbanism whenever he could. He lectured at the Bourse du Travail, an organization that helped people find jobs, and in March 1927 he met with Jacques Arthuys, a militant nationalist who, with Georges Valois, had founded Le Faisceau—the French fascist party. He wrote his mother, "The other day I was received by one of the two leaders of the Fascist Party. Arthuys. Received with open arms and much cordiality and yesterday I was sent a Fascist pamphlet of 60 pages ending with a chapter on the heart of Paris—on my version of it—with irrefutable developments and a clear proposition to appoint me minister of urbanism and housing. In short, you can bet your life I am not involving myself in politics. What saves me from any absurd or dangerous haste are my morning pictures, one each morning, where the confrontation is complete, the difficulty total, basic, overwhelming. Thus half the day I say the hell with everything and everybody and work out a problem whose solution does not exist, since it escapes with each step forward."[16] Now resigned to the idea that the League of Nations project was buried, this avoidance of political engagement and retreat to his own painting were his formula for personal balance.

In mid-March, Le Corbusier went to a masquerade party at Albert and Lotti's to celebrate the birthday of Lotti's daughter Brita. It furthered his sense of equilibrium. Albert was now back in Paris, having rejoined his wife and her daughter, and the event for the extended family at the Villa Jeanneret made his architecture serve its ideal function—as a setting for human joy and connectedness. "What must be acknowledged is people, things, events in their specific character," he wrote, "and what must be properly valued is that diversity which is the very thing that makes life agreeable: that adds, that accumulates, that constitutes a certain capital of appreciation and measurement; that embellishes, that furnishes existence. This is the whole joy of life: to know how to open one's eyes, to marvel, to recognize positive values, to bypass negative ones and not collide with them. Everyone lives among pluses and minuses. When we can respond to the pluses, that is happiness. That's all there is to it."[17]

Half a year later, however, Le Corbusier's emotional pendulum was swinging in the other direction. "I ask for nothing more than sun, sun for God's sake, by which to see clearly and be happy. Wretched winter which begins so cold!" he wrote his mother in November.[18] He had played basketball with Albert, but most of life was pointless.

An event hosted by one of his publishers exemplified the silliness and pretentiousness all around him: "On Saturday I attended a great banquet given by Editions Crès on the occasion of their new building. The building? O publishers of Le Corbu! And the most stupefying asininities. There were three speeches, and one heard not a word, not one! That was a minor deficiency, and we giggled about it, but the whole phenomenon was a madness."[19]

The more worldly "Le Corbu" was, the more he regressed as Charles-Edouard Jeanneret. He continued, "Dearest Maman, I am going beddie-bye with the following nighttime equipment: a flannel nightcap, a wool sweater. Stretched out on my back, immobile, above all not breathing. Make a note of it, dear Maman, that's how you get rid of colds, but this one couldn't be nipped in the bud the first night nor the next. In the train it assumed gigantic proportions. Affections from your Ed."[20]

In her reply, his mother only groused about the heating system in Villa Le Lac: "Here only to return (but meeting Mme. Mathey at the station), I found a freezing house and since Le Corbusier had done nothing, I summoned the plumber to find out if I dared turn on the heat and whether nothing unfortunate had happened during my absence. This lasted a long time and when I could finally get a cup of hot coffee from my neighbors, I had reached the point where my teeth were chattering and my whole body shivering." Having visited her cousin Marguerite in Zurich, she "decided not to leave the house during winter any more; it's too risky and coming home too melancholy." Her solace was the puppy: "Bessie is wonderful. I went to pick her up Monday and it was touching to see her transports of feeling. . . . I'm pretty certain now that she's sterile, as Sara [another dog] was, and that there won't be any consequences to her debauchery."[21]

Marie Jeanneret was deeply concerned about her fragile Albert now that he was again helping with household tasks while trying to run a small music school, but she made no further comment or inquiry about the life of the son who had "done nothing" to correct the problem of her freezing house.

6

As winter settled in, Le Corbusier had a recurrent dream. His father was alive, but soon to die. Each time he had the dream, he woke up and had a brief moment of thinking it was reality. Afterward, fully conscious, he was struck by the idea, as if it were totally new, that only two years earlier Georges had still been drinking in the pleasures of life.[22]

The architect was assuming a paternal role to the painter André Bauchant, a talented "naïve" artist, somewhat along the lines of "Le Douanier" Rousseau, who asked Le Corbusier to be his executor for all of his paintings. Bauchant had recently begun to win prizes and commissions, but even now,

Pierre Jeanneret, André Bauchant, Yvonne, and Le Corbusier standing with a painting by Bauchant of the four of them, early 1930s

the artist explained, his parents, friends, and everyone else laughed at him. Le Corbusier was the sole person who might do justice to his work after his death and who had the aesthetic judgment as well as the financial acumen to sell his paintings for the best value, thus to assure the well-being of Bauchant's wife, who suffered from cerebral amnesia. Le Corbusier was touched by this confidence from an artist who exemplified innocence and rare truthfulness and was "animated by an extraordinary fire." On December 17, they signed their contract. It was another moment when Le Corbusier felt he had found the balance that made it possible to survive life's defeats and the ultimate reality of death; he wrote his mother that Bauchant was the exemplar of the Jeanneret family motto: "The moral: do what one must without flinching. Neither fame nor blame has anything to do with it. Believe in what one is doing and do it well."[23]

7

The League of Nations debate resumed at the start of the new year. Le Corbusier's scheme still had its ardent partisans, with journalists and even some of the jury members entering the fray.

In February 1928, Frantz Jourdain declared the treatment of Le Corbusier's design "a second Dreyfus Affair."[24] The comparison to such a monumental incident of prejudice and scapegoating was especially startling given Jourdain's stature. This champion of modernism, a friend of Emile Zola's, had joined Zola's fight against the brutal persecution of Alfred Dreyfus and its defenders. By invoking the name of the Jewish colonel, Jourdain was depicting Le Corbusier's foes as the architect himself did: as the propagators of the vilest form of evil, deeply entrenched within the ruling establishment.

The outside support encouraged Le Corbusier and Pierre to write an appeal demanding that the Council of the League of Nations overturn the decision of the five-person jury. "There is a lot of wind in the sails. And also a lot of concealed withdrawal in my mind. The *tête-à-tête* is the great gain I have made in the last few year," he wrote his mother in mid-February.[25]

Shifting back and forth between a hard-line aggressive approach and his insistent fatalism, the architect was resigned to letting the chips fall where they would. On March 3, he wrote Marie, "We have done the best we could with what was within our means. Now once again the imponderables will function. Conscience mollified by work well done, I await with a smile the coming yes or no. And I will not be discomfited if it is no. That will be the proof the thing is not yet ripe."[26]

The warrior had again become a buddha. Or so he tried to convince himself, until an article called "Les idées de M. Le Corbusier. Maisons et Cités de demain" by Paul Bourquin appeared in two parts in *L'Impartial,* a daily newspaper in La Chaux-de-Fonds. Its content demolished Le Corbusier's calm; there was no more feigning the equanimity he was trying to maintain over events in Geneva. This was one onslaught he could not bear, because it was read by his mother's friends.

Bourquin began by accusing Le Corbusier of "certain distinctly communistic tendencies, an arrant materialism, the abolition of thought and the triumph of action. Everything is organized around these three concepts." His take on Le Corbusier's domestic architecture was: "Le Corbusier's vision of the world manages to find a model of beauty in the humblest rabbit run. One trembles to think of the lot of the poor wretches condemned to live in such houses which a wicked joker once called—quite accurately moreover—suicide crates . . . the great specialty of the architect Le Corbusier whom the Germans seem to hold in special esteem are the thickly planted terraces, pergolas and verandas he lavishes everywhere. On one terrace I notice built-in Swedish gymnastic equipment; in one bathroom hangs a punching-bag. I shall not conceal from our eminent compatriot that certain of his inventions have somewhat astounded me. Why for example make the main entrance to a house through the cellar? As for those shoulder-high reinforced-concrete barriers separating the bedrooms, they seem to lack a certain intimacy."[27]

Bourquin's article followed the line of thinking put forward by Swiss architect Alexandre de Senger in an essay in *Le Bulletin technique de la Suisse romande,* which, in turn, had been picked up by the *Gazette de Lausanne.* De Senger's text, which echoed the official reasons given for rejecting Le Corbusier's League of Nations project, was yet another frontal attack: "Thus Le Corbusier—any polyphony wearies him, overwhelms him, exhausts him. He complains, 'The moon is not round, the rainbow is a fragment, the network of veins in marble is disturbing, inhuman.' Exasperated, he exclaims: '*Nothing in nature attains the pure perfection of the humblest machine.*' . . . And to escape this dreadful torment he adds: 'Nature is geometrical.' Architecture, too, diminishes, torments, maddens this exhausted man. Only the simplest forms such as cubes and prisms are available to his comprehension; he delights in them because they deliver him from the superabundance of nature. And Le Corbusier, who believes himself to be an architect at bottom, is merely a sectarian for whom any organic development is synonymous with disease."[28]

Le Corbusier wrote the newspapers that these attacks were not simply a matter of aesthetic disagreement but were full of lies. He told his mother he was "in a violent rage"; it was "a scandal, a dirty trick." What upset him above all was the anguish this critique would bring her and Aunt Pauline, as well as the insult to his father's memory. "Corbu is denounced as an element of disorder and materialism, as the negation of art, of thought," he lamented. Switzerland itself had betrayed him: "Three years of struggle (committee, council, and general assembly of the League of Nations), and the details of this affair certainly represent for us the blackest, most desperate tribulation that can affect honest consciences. It was cruelty personified. From the beginning, the city of Geneva maintained a hostile atmosphere toward us." But, Le Corbusier assured his mother, he was tough enough to survive it all. It was "a vehement and, I repeat, odiously dishonest attack. Apart from that, dear Maman, smiles all the way. Spring is coming, the weather is fine and everything else follows."[29]

8

In 1928, an organization called the French Appeal was formed to try to convince the League of Nations jury to reverse itself and select Le Corbusier and Pierre Jeanneret's design, and the architects themselves published a pamphlet stating their case. Marie Jeanneret wrote Albert and Lotti, "Edouard tells me there is wind in his sails. What splendid optimism! But this morning, receiving the dignified communication from the President of the French Appeal from Jourdain, from Elie Faure, etc. etc. . . . I remain impressed and moved by the quantity and especially the quality of the signatures attached to the notion. What would our Papa say confronted with this admirable testimony of faith. He left us too soon! Sensitive as he had become to the consideration granted to his sons, this would have caused him, coming from such men, a sort of immeasurable joy. Alas! In spite of everything, I do not believe in the reversal of matters with regard to the Palais des Nations, and as with this hard Nennot [*sic*] Le Corbusier will seem strange to many. Who will yield, the young man or the old one? But this affair will waken or reawaken consciences, and as a demonstration it is almost American."[30]

Marie's caution was warranted. On May 5, 1928, the jury considering the Jeannerets' League of Nations appeal decided definitively in favor of the team to be directed by Nenot, with totally new requirements for the building. Again, Le Corbusier and Pierre protested. And, again, modern architects from various countries, journalists, and professional organizations chimed in on their behalf. But the affair ended disastrously. As Le Corbusier, still smarting, described it fifteen years later, "Fair-minded people, along with the intellectual elite in every country, demanded that justice be done. Nothing of the kind occurred. The Academy and politics finally triumphed in this memorable affair, this unprecedented scandal."[31] The only solution was to move on.

XXVI

1

Following the brutal slap of the League of Nations, Le Corbusier was heartened to be endorsed on other fronts.

In June 1928, CIAM—the Congrès Internationaux d'Architecture Moderne—was founded, with Hélène de Mandrot its main patroness. The new organization was launched at the Château de la Sarraz in the canton de Vaud, of which de Mandrot, already a Le Corbusier supporter, was the chatelaine. A painter, architect, and interior designer—and descendant of a grand family—de Mandrot was a strong, imposing woman in her midfifties who wore her hair in a chignon and dressed in lavish ball gowns or expensive tailored suits and large hats. The eleventh-century structure where this colorful heiress graciously received twenty-five modern architects, as well as industrialists, politicians, critics, and artists, was a multiturreted affair with a valuable collection of furniture and paintings, a perfect place to combine old wealth with new art.

Le Corbusier was responsible for the program of CIAM's first meeting, which tried to codify advances in building design all over the world. The major issues of architecture were to be addressed: the nature and potential of modern techniques, the relationship of the state and corporations to building programs, the value of standardization, and questions of urbanism, economics, and education.

CIAM's ideology called for a redistribution of land and the sharing of profits between owners and the community. At a time when Le Corbusier was already under attack, this fueled the rumor that he was a communist. He was as interested in making a luxurious new home for his hostess as in accommodating the masses, but once people got a whiff of what could be construed as socialism, there was no convincing them otherwise.

IN JULY, Le Corbusier and Léger went to the villa at Garches, where the renowned painter was completely "*estomaqué*"—one of Le Corbusier's favorite words—and told the architect that the house was a masterpiece.[1] Then Le Corbusier's burly colleague offered an even more significant endorsement. After a visit to the architect's studio, the generous-spirited Léger, whose canvases were selling for forty thousand francs, proposed an even exchange of paintings.

Le Corbusier was on a high. He had recently taken an inspiring trip to Spain, and was working on urban plans for Tunis and Buenos Aires as well as on several houses. He was now prosperous enough to treat his mother and Albert to an eight-day holiday together in the mountains, planned for September.

But try as he might to restrain his fury over what had happened in Geneva, he could not obliterate it. Thanking his mother for a letter she had written to comfort him, he continued,

> I have a furious rage against these bastards for what they have done and permitted to be done, and I am profoundly outraged, and perturbed by the blinding desires for "justice" by means of which the comedy has been rigged. That I will not swallow. And when I think of the problem itself, handsome as it is; when I see, as I do this evening, for instance, the photos of the splendid site, then all over again I suffer fits of indignation, of imprecations against this huge coalition that has crushed us with weapons having nothing to do with architecture. Nothing to do with architecture. There is the entire drama.
>
> A work so majestic seems to me incapable of being achieved on the basis of so many dirty tricks, which have become flagrantly public. I do not expect an immediate vengeance on the part of heaven. But one may grant that the measure has been so forced that the evil will fall back upon itself.
>
> These people who are making the Palace are mountebanks, businessmen licking the boots of the Academy. Where is the lively, lofty, disinterested, passionate spirit that can carry out this task by an intense love of architecture? These people are "architects" in the dreadful sense of the word. And already they are fighting among themselves.
>
> Our time had not come, nor were we wanted! We were hated because we had raised ourselves to the highest degree of prominence.[2]

His one remaining hope was that his mother understood this.

2

Le Corbusier was appointed the French delegate to a conference in Prague, where intellectuals from various fields were to converge. To get there, he traveled in an airplane for the first time. He was thrilled to be at the technological frontier.

The architect boarded the great machine with its wide wings and propeller engines at Le Bourget. After a stop in Cologne, it landed in Berlin, from where he took the train to Prague. "We started exactly on time and, miraculously . . . we arrived exactly on time."[3] This was high praise from a child of the watchmaking business.

On the second evening after he arrived in Prague, Le Corbusier was out drinking with friends in a bar. The poet Vesvald suddenly stood up and shouted out, so that everyone could hear, "Le Corbusier is a poet!" The travelers and businessmen and other strangers in the bar downed their drinks in toasting this idea. "That night I had my first and my profound reward. *In vino veritas.*"[4]

On the other hand, when the Czech foreign minister, Edvard Beneš, addressed him as "*Maître,*" Le Corbusier replied, "Be careful, no nonsense, you're going to convince me I'm an academician!"[5] A poet, yes; part of the established hierarchy, never.

HE WENT to Prague because he was on his way to the recently formed Soviet Union. The people who already believed Le Corbusier was sympathetic to communism now became further convinced.

In May 1928, Le Corbusier had been asked to enter a design competition for the Centrosoyuz—the central office of cooperatives in Moscow. In July, he had submitted the design. In *L'Esprit Nouveau,* Le Corbusier and Ozenfant had periodically published articles devoted to constructivism and the work of El Lissitzky, Vladimir Tatlin, and Kasimir Malevich, the three most daring and inventive figures in the realm of art and design in the USSR. A reciprocal admiration for Le Corbusier had developed not only among leaders of the Russian avant-garde but also in the highest political ranks; as early as 1923, Ilya Ehrenburg wrote the architect reporting that "in one of his latest articles, Trotsky has spoken in highly sympathetic terms of the trends reflected in *L'Esprit Nouveau.*"[6] Architecture periodicals reproduced Le Corbusier's latest buildings. Malevich had written a magazine article praising Le Corbusier's Stuttgart houses for "having borne in mind the

On the building site of the Centrosoyuz in Moscow, 1930

needs of contemporary man" in their scale and furnishings.[7] His championship had great value, for with his brave and utterly simplified abstract paintings—and then in his return to figurative art that honored the country's ordinary citizenry—Malevich had achieved heroic stature.

Shortly after his arrival in Moscow, Le Corbusier was received at the Kremlin by the vice president of the USSR, M. Lejawa, and by Trotsky's sister, Olga Kameneva. A few days later, three prominent Moscow architects addressed a postcard to "Madame Jeanneret-Perret" at La Petite Maison with the message: "Madame, the architects of Moscow offer their affectionate respects to the mother of the world's greatest architect."[8] For ten days, he was celebrated at banquets and parties. Everyone seemed to be campaigning for the acceptance of his Centrosoyuz design. If Geneva spurned him, Moscow applauded—and gave him reason to believe that at last he would truly realize a substantial building complex with which modernism could triumph at a seat of world power.

3

In a lecture on urbanism "in the great hall of the Polytechnic Museum, the headquarters of the Association for the Promotion of Political and Scientific Knowledge,"[9] Le Corbusier presented his Moscow equivalent of the Plan Voisin. He told the large and influential audience "that Moscow was still an Asian city, which it is necessary to care for by building new pavements and demolishing old houses, yet leaving old monuments in place. It is important to enlarge our parks and gardens, shift the business center elsewhere and, by surgical elimination of all side streets, lay out new ones beside existing main streets and line them with skyscrapers."[10]

He attacked the current preference for classical revival architecture over modernism: "I find Moscow in the same trance as our Western nations. . . . It is a criminal mistake to resuscitate things of the past, for the result is not living organisms but papier-mâché ghosts."[11] Le Corbusier pitched the idea that traditional academic architecture—of the type that had prevailed with the League of Nations—was the equivalent of the czarist regime. The visual revolution he championed was as radical as the political revolution in which his audience had participated. Surely they should make the leap in aesthetics, too.

Le Corbusier worked intensely for a number of days with a team of architects who were helping him fine-tune his design for the competition. He was impressed with what he saw in their office. A lunchtime buffet enabled employees to work productively throughout the day, with minimal interruption. When the workday ended at 3:30 p.m., they congregated in clubs, performed in amateur theatricals, played sports, or simply read in an organized environment. This systematized existence appealed immensely to Le Corbusier's belief in a scheduled combination of work and recreation.

One revelation followed another. In a village a couple of hours from Moscow, the architect saw remarkable vernacular architecture where the *izbas* (cottages) were built "on pilotis."[12] A Soviet architect introduced him

With Sergei Eisenstein (center) and Andrej Burow in Moscow, October 1928

to the film director Sergei Eisenstein, whose *Battleship Potemkin* Le Corbusier considered a masterpiece. In an interview with a Moscow journalist, Le Corbusier declared, "Architecture and the cinema are the only two arts of our time. In my own work I seem to think as Eisenstein does in his films. His work is shot through with the sense of truth, and bears witness to the truth alone. In their ideas, his films resemble closely what I am striving to do in my work."[13] That goal was unequivocal.

4

One afternoon, Le Corbusier was standing on a Moscow street corner, pencil in hand, with his sketchbook open. He was immediately stopped and informed that such drawing outdoors was forbidden. A commissar tried to get him special permission, but failed. Le Corbusier could not tolerate the idea of not capturing things visually. In the following days, he concealed his notebook under his overcoat so that he managed to illustrate, hastily and awkwardly, some onion domes and monuments. But the need to be furtive astounded him. Such restrictions on human liberty were intolerable.

Nonetheless, when he officially presented his proposal for the Centrosoyuz headquarters, the Russians accorded him all the respect he had been denied by the soulless misanthropes who had pummeled his League of Nations idea. Even though he saw flaws in the economic approach—"The system lacks a stimulus, a dynamic factor. . . . Lethargy is present"—he imagined the Soviet Union as his stage.[14]

His mother did not like that idea. When Le Corbusier had arrived in Moscow, a letter from her awaited him. Following warm wishes for his recent forty-first birthday, she finally gave him some of the praise he craved, but then proferred advice—which she pinned to the existence of Yvonne and potential children. "You have been a good son, tender, respectful of the memory of a father who died too soon, generous to the mother left behind who takes great pride in your moral qualities and your intellectual gifts. You must maintain your health and not abuse it—not too many late nights, too much work. Now that you bear responsibility for a soul (and perhaps souls), you must not wear out the mechanism; the great years of youth are past; the summer is still warm and brilliant, yet autumn is approaching, filled, it is true, with marvelous promises to those who set their sights high, making every effort to realize an ideal ever held in mind, despite underhand attacks; and who will triumph because they have had faith."[15] Above all, Marie Jeanneret was worried about how he might comport himself in the

Soviet Union: "And now there you are in the vast Russia full of such alarming legends. Here, too, I trust in your lucky star and hope that the Russians, an intelligent people, their modern ideas so advanced, will find yours to their taste and will grant you their confidence in this great architectural project. Be careful what you say, don't meddle with politics, remain an artist who desires to speak solely of his art. I shall rejoice to know you are on French territory once more."[16]

When Le Corbusier answered her letter, he was able to tell her, exuberantly, that his scheme for the Centrosoyuz had been accepted. That endorsement made the Soviet Union all the more enchanting: "I am present at the birth of a new world, built on logic and faith, which plunges me into the deepest reflections. I rein in my optimism in order not to see things except as they are. O blind Europe who lies to herself in order to caress her sloth! Here one of the most explicit designs of human evolution is being realized; and what corresponds to generosity here is egoism there. I look, I see, I question, I listen, I explore everywhere this new event; people here are starting from zero and *constructing* stone by stone. I use the word *constructing* advisedly."[17]

Marie responded practically by return mail that she was "deeply moved by your letter from Moscow. Here and everywhere in our newspapers, Russia has always been represented as degraded—the behavior of the people deplorable, the family debased and childhood abused, and above all intellectuals persecuted—so that I reread 3 or 4 times the letter in which with apparent impartiality you depict that country so differently."[18]

His mother sent this letter to Le Corbusier's apartment in Paris, expecting him to have returned there. Issuing a word of caution about Yvonne, she repeated the sort of admonitions with which he had grown up: "I assume that my dear boy has returned and found peace and affection in the rue Jacob . . . and that he might *even* be cosseted and adored (to excess perhaps); I always fear that a person's character will be spoiled and distorted by such treatment. One is always inclined to enjoy such treatment, and one cannot help enjoying the comfort of being restored to one's habits, one's way of life, one's daily work."[19]

As she reeled off opinions, Marie Jeanneret voiced the blend of intelligence and ignorance with which she had reared her family: "You were understood, taken to their hearts, and I rejoice with you that your plans are prized. Bravo! Cultivated Russians have always passed for powerful minds, lively intelligences. They have always rebelled (nihilism) against an autocratic regime they regarded as monstrous. But the Bolshevist leaders are usually Jews of rather low extraction, and the various massacres they have inflicted have certainly rendered them odious. What are we to believe?"[20]

But for Le Corbusier, as long as the Soviets would let him help design their new world, little else counted.

5

At the very moment that Le Corbusier was hoping to clinch the Moscow commission, El Lissitzky wrote a scathing article about him. Allegedly about the latest version of the Centrosoyuz proposal, Lissitzky's essay was an ad hominem attack: "The Bohemianism, isolation and inverted snobbery of today's artists have reached their apogee in France. Given that Le Corbusier is an artist, he is a case in point. Like all Western artists, he feels compelled to be an absolute individualist, and to recognize nothing outside of himself, because otherwise one might doubt his originality, and because originality is the sensation that gives the measure of what is 'new.' "[21]

Lissitzky, who had visited the villa at Garches the previous year with Piet Mondrian and Sophie Kuppers, quoted a member of the Stein family who said the villa was more interesting to visit than to live in. He attacked Le Corbusier as a figure of fashion and as the epitome of western decadence: "Le Corbusier the artist (and not the constructor, the builder, the engineer) was commissioned to build a house that is designed to be a sensation, a piece of magic, and the finished product is published in women's magazines, along with the latest in fashion (cf. Vogue, August 1928)." Lissitzky described the standard Pessac dwelling as having been commissioned by a capitalist and as being "not a building to be *lived in,* but rather, a *showpiece.* . . . [H]e has designed houses that are disorienting to the user, and which he himself would never inhabit. The reason for this is the architect's antisocial nature, the great distance that separates him from the expectations of the great mass of people. He has affinities neither with the proletariat, nor with industrial capital."[22] Lissitzky was willfully ignorant of Le Corbusier's underlying sensibility. What Charles-Edouard Jeanneret had observed in remote Balkan villages at age twenty-three—the joy and contentment of the inhabitants—had helped determine his hope of harnessing the honest aesthetics of peasant huts to modern technology.

Lissitzky treated the architect as if he were simply a fraud: "In the work of Le Corbusier, the eye of the painter is everywhere present—not only in his use of color, which he manipulates as a painter, but also at the level of architectural design: he does not materialize his designs, but merely colors them in. His system involved the construction of a frame—a fact that explains why photographs of his buildings give an impression of unity even when they are upside down."[23]

Lissitzky, a gifted photographer, had shot, with closed eyes, a detail of the stairs from one of Le Corbusier's Weissenhoff houses. The image reads like an abstract composition and could be viewed in any direction without gaining or losing meaning. Besides using this as evidence of a fatal flaw, he also pronounced Le Corbusier's urban ideal as a "city of nowhere . . . a city on paper, extraneous to living nature."[24]

El Lissitzky was not the only antagonist at this crucial moment. Karel Teige, a Czech intellectual who had been a great supporter of Le Corbusier's and who had reviewed *Toward a New Architecture* in 1923, now took up the cudgels, accusing Le Corbusier of approaching architecture as if he was designing for visual reasons only, describing a recent Le Corbusier design based on the golden section as "not a solution for realization and construction, but a composition."[25] The Moscow architect Moisei Ginzburg called Le Corbusier's architecture "poorly defined and purely aesthetic in character."[26]

Le Corbusier felt, nonetheless, more welcome than attacked in the Soviet Union: "I thought I would encounter my typical adversaries in Moscow. . . . Yet in Moscow I found, not spiritual antagonists, but fervent adherents to what I consider fundamental to all human works: the lofty intentions that raise these works above their utilitarian function, and which confer on them the lyricism that brings us joy. . . . My feeling is that what interests all these Russians is in fact a poetic idea."[27] The country of Pushkin and Tchaikovsky and constructivism would, he hoped, be the place where his own poetic vision could be realized.

XXVII

1

Two days after Le Corbusier's return to Paris from Moscow, the president of the Cooperatives of Russia met with him to work out the agreement for the architect to do the Centrosoyuz. The Russian characterized Le Corbusier's design as a modern palace. Although Le Corbusier was suffering from one of his terrible colds and a headache that was to last eight days, he had rarely been as completely content.

He saw the Russians as just like him: pure, brave souls scorned by reactionaries. On November 11, he wrote his mother, "The western world has shown itself to me under a rather shabby aspect. The sort of heroism, of inevitable stoicism, which exists in Russia . . . leaves a strong aftertaste. And I have always been sensitive to pure ideas, or to the idea itself. So I am sad to see the world rise up against an idea (however debatable). And opposing this faith and this sincerity, the rather fragile structure of bourgeois morals with all their artificiality, and *injustice* and *falsehood.*"[1]

His mother, he told her, was the polar opposite of those lifeless, self-deceiving people. She and his father were pure and righteous, which is why he and Albert were the same:

> You are a model—a model of life, strength, confidence, and artistic generosity. You are certainly not a *bourgeoise,* and that is a legacy you bequeathed us at birth. To be *firm* in life yet to be broad-minded, so that such breadth is inspired by an element of kindness.
>
> Georges Dubois has written me about the photograph of dear Papa (at the clinic). That teeming life cannot bear comparison with this already diminished image. Yet I find in this portrait much of what constituted dear Papa's farsightedness—that distance he knew to take in all his judgments, that perspective which was his wisdom. Maintain your faith and your action, your precise and upright functions, as well as that freedom of appreciation which affords the heart an open road. Sunday kisses to my dear Maman.[2]

The compliments were a tactic. By praising both his parents for their broad-mindedness and kindness, Le Corbusier was not just pushing for Marie's approval of his new affiliations with the Soviet Union. He had a plan to cast aside his own heritage, and he wanted her to accept it.

2

Slowly, Yvonne was being integrated into the family—to the extent that anyone might penetrate the nuclear unit of Marie Jeanneret and her two sons. Yvonne and Le Corbusier dined on occasion with Albert and Lotti and Lotti's two daughters.

In reporting on these events to his mother, Le Corbusier commented on the difficulties of Albert being Swiss, while Lotti and her girls were Swedish. It was the lead-in to telling his mother that he thought it would be better if he and his partner shared the same nationality. He wondered what she thought of the idea of his changing citizenship from Swiss to French.

Le Corbusier knew this might not be well received. He advised his mother not to mention it to Aunt Pauline and emphasized that he wanted

With Pierre Jeanneret and Lotti Jeanneret in the late 1920s

to be naturalized not out of disloyalty for his country but for Yvonne's sake. Then he asked another bold question. Should Yvonne come with him to Vevey for Christmas? What did she think? We don't know Marie's precise answer, but he would end up going on his own.

THAT FALL, Le Corbusier began to obsess over basic housing types. He had developed a radical theory: the assumption that Neuchâtel mountain farmhouses had been designed to withstand heavy snows was erroneous. In fact, their form came directly from Armagnac, where it rarely snowed, and had been exported to Switzerland when the Albigeois from that region were exiled to the Alps around 1350.

In Le Corbusier's eyes, this proved that domestic architecture revealed that where we come from has greater importance than the requisites of climate or other external conditions in our current location, and that style derived from reasons other than efficacity. We may move from southern France to the mountains or from the mountains to Paris, but we remain who we have always been. Like the Neuchâtelene farmhouses in which he had spent some of the happiest moments of his youth, Le Corbusier was at heart French, even if transplanted by happenstance to Switzerland.

Architecture told the truth, he insisted—and he settled for nothing less. Those farmhouses proved that his origins were French, whatever others thought; this was as inviolable as his being, at the core, a modest and private artist as much as an architect absorbed in the hubbub. He wrote Ritter:

> There is no faking when it comes to architecture, there are always reasons. In any case I am somehow *comforted* to know you agree with me, for I have incessantly and passionately worked in utter good faith. And this search for purity is a need for truth. For a long time you have supposed I was lost in Parisian fads. I want you to realize that having arrived at a certain pinnacle of fame, I continue living down to earth, working away, filled with ideas, devoured by time, not talking but doing. Since 1916 no more than ten people have knocked at the door of the rue Jacob where I am every morning. Later, the office is another affair: a veritable procession.
>
> Perhaps you are unaware that since 1918 I have passionately committed myself to painting. For five years I have not exhibited, having shut my door on my daubs. Painting every morning is what allows me to be lucid every afternoon. But what battles, what dramas! And in just the last few weeks, journalists and dealers are making a great fuss about my painting. I am attempting to repress all such behavior. I do

> not want this matter to be ventilated just now. Which shows you how loyal I am to my brushes.[3]

He was, moreover, a painter in the French tradition, just as those Swiss farmhouses were quintessentially French. He was convinced the nationality he would soon make official was in his heart and blood.

XXVIII

1

Frank Lloyd Wright called the Villa Savoye, which was completed in 1930, "a box on stilts." Some observers likened it to a space capsule fallen onto an unwelcoming landscape. Today, it is an icon of twentieth-century design and has spawned countless imitations all over the world.

Le Corbusier considered Pierre and Emilie Savoye the ideal clients. Upper-class, prosperous, and cultured, the couple specified little more than that they wanted a summer house on their land in the town of Poissy, not far from Paris, where they lived the rest of the year. They had few demands other than adequate servants' quarters and a garage, and they were amenable to all of Le Corbusier's aesthetic ideas.

What he built them was, above all, a vehicle from which to savor nature. Le Corbusier's own description of the floating white container makes clear that everything was in service of the landscape: "Site: a magnificent property consisting of an enormous pasturage and orchard forming a cupola surrounded by a girdle of high hedges. The house must have no 'front'; situated at the summit of the cupola, it must be open to all four horizons. The habitation floor, with its hanging garden, will be raised on pilotis allowing views all the way to the horizon."[1] The purpose of the faceless building was access to the wonders of the universe.

2

The villa at Poissy resembles Le Corbusier's previous houses but is simpler. The sashes of the industrial windows were the most refined to date. The overall form—a perfect square, supported on pilotis—is a statement of rightness and order. The ramps connecting the stories make the activities of ascent and descent feel ethereal.

This pared-down structure, confident without being arrogant, is an eloquent statement of humankind establishing its presence on earth: a modernized Parthenon. The supporting columns have none of the details of their Greek ancestors—spare and lean, smooth rather than fluted, perfectly straight rather than tapered to simulate straightness as were the Greek prototypes—but they still lend a classical order. The color is pure Mediterranean whiteness.

From the outside, the impression is of simultaneous mass and levity, a harmony of contrasts. The round, smokestack-like forms that pop through the roof play against the square block of the house. Everything is varied but congruent: the strong horizontals and verticals, the shimmering whites and bold blacks.

Services and garage space were kept at entry level and out of sight. Today, by contrast, garages declare themselves in front of homes as if they are the main point, boasting of the cars they protect and making clear that modern living is as much about commuting as residing. The Villa Savoye, while fully acknowledging its inhabitants' dependence on the automobile with its three-car garage positioned at a convenient angle for entrance and egress, has it tucked behind the pilotis. The car serves; indeed, it charms; but it does not own its owner. Le Corbusier kept human experience at the forefront.

If you stand facing a corner of this country retreat dead-on, you experience the force of a massive minimal sculpture: an absolute, irrefutable presence. But for all its authority and precision, this building is friendly and welcoming; once you head toward the entrance, you are greeted with a wide smile.

Le Corbusier's concept was clear: "Four identical walls pierced all the way around by a single sliding window."[2] What is achieved as you approach that body and take the splendid upward journey inside is a sequence of vistas; the act of looking is encouraged at every turn. You go from one tableau to another, from a halting view of a solid black door and white impassive walls to a sweeping vista, as in a musical progression from silence to a rhapsody.

Today, Poissy is a populous suburb, and the charm of the setting is almost completely lost. But when the villa was built, the views of fields and sky were sublime. With the latest materials assembled in a neat framework, the architect had provided an experience stunningly akin to what he had tasted on Mount Athos nearly two decades earlier.

THE HOUSE AT POISSY is designed for well-being, for dining or working under optimal circumstances, for relishing life. While more space is devoted to splendid terraces and the vast solarium than to the enclosed

The Villa Savoye, shortly after construction, ca. 1930

rooms, it has an inviting fireplace and snug womblike nooks in which to keep warm; every doorknob lends charm. The blue of the bathroom tiles is the color of the Alpine sky in clear winter weather (see color plate 7). Inside and out, there are well-proportioned tables and neat seating units. These details serve life and enhance a sense of pleasure with no unwelcome distractions. The ever-present balance of the plan helps provide calm, and the graceful lines and correct proportions of the highly refined architectural elements help one breathe deeply and regularly: all to facilitate the purposes of contemplation.

The Villa Savoye is both a place to live and a temple to the sun. Most of the house, open to the sky, puts you closer to the space that surrounds the Earth. This platform for observing the universe recapitulates those Sunday outings of Georges and Marie Jeanneret and their two young boys in the snowy mountains. Everything is about the journey through whiteness, rugged and challenging in its way (neither the ramp nor the stairs are easy), offering as its reward the miraculous sky (see color plate 5).

When Charles-Edouard Jeanneret approached the Parthenon at age twenty-three, he stalled and then hurled himself ahead, prolonged the pleasure and then recoiled from it, all because the event was so overwhelming. In this athletic, balanced, vibrant, faceless building, Le Corbusier created a monument for the twentieth century of no less force and majesty than the temples of ancient Athens (see color plate 6).

3

In February 1929, Le Corbusier visited his now sixty-nine-year-old mother in Vevey. She wrote Albert that he "installed an electric light above the coal bin, a necessity in what had been such a dark hole. But his visit was not confined to such aesthetic matters . . . and we have spent two days of perfect intimacy together, reading Sainte-Beuve's *Portraits of Women,* which Le Corbusier read aloud in a very clear voice to his delighted Maman while the latter was mending the thumbs and other fingers of her fireplace gloves."[3]

At last he was devoting himself to her needs: "Edouard has now realized that not only is there the noise of the road behind the house, but on one side as well, so that I am really surrounded—he really must make sound-proof walls on all sides. . . . Edouard has also explained about Colombo's bill. Thanks to him for that—I know it costs him so much time and thought."[4]

With an improved relationship to his mother, Le Corbusier was ebullient. He was certain the Moscow project was going ahead, and he considered himself impervious to the economic downshifts that were soon to lead to worldwide depression. In April he wrote Marie, "The crash doesn't affect us. Work comes in from all sides, increasingly interesting. Actually life is enthralling." He was not blind to what was happening, just confident in his own power. "Terrible events are occurring and hard times coming! The old world must do what it can."[5]

4

To his mother, Le Corbusier could reveal his frenzy and fears as well as his braggadocio. To Yvonne, he showed his heart and vulnerability. The combination stabilized him, providing rare understanding and acceptance in a world that often pounced on him.

The good relationship of these two completely different women with each other became essential to Le Corbusier. That spring, Marie Jeanneret visited Paris—as she now did periodically—to see Albert and his family and Charles-Edouard and Yvonne. Marie had come to accept her younger son's live-in mistress, writing Albert that Yvonne was "always full of affection" and had a "really splendid countenance, the true Arlésienne type."[6] Shortly after her return to Vevey, Le Corbusier wrote her,

I have a very gay and enthusiastic memory of your stay in Paris. How I love my dear Maman! I'd have liked to spoil you, to overwhelm you with attentions, but I could only surround you with affectionate thoughts. I'm a slave to the terrible times. And if I freed myself, I should slip and fall. The kingdom of necessity! Each hour, each minute must be utilized, fecundated. The playing-field has grown so much larger. And ideas swarm, ever greater. I know that ultimately, and in spite of everything, the earth turns. But our fragile happiness, far from being found in luxury, money, worldliness, is here with me, within me, and we must be strong to help the weaker ones. Yvonne is loyal, kind, extremely attached. A constant, vigilant presence. An ever-watchful heart. What luck, simultaneous with the risks of another attempt. We must know when to stop and when to say: this is the right way. She is a little wild creature, skittish as a gazelle, and yet possessed of a very special kind of courage, a resistance, a violence I prefer to any subservience.

You were very good with her. Thank you for that. . . . Good night dear Maman. Your D.D.[7]

WHEN LE CORBUSIER wrote Yvonne during his travels, he used short sentences that resemble the text of a children's book. She was "Mademoiselle Vvon," "Petit VV," "Petit Vonvon," "Petit Von," "Petit Vvon"; while he mostly remained "DD" or "ton Dou." He never went into any issue in depth, as he did to his mother or Ritter, and simply gave a general summary of his latest activities and let her know how he was. "All the kisses on earth" was his typical way of signing off.[8]

He was rarely serious, except about money and her need to take care of herself. But under the guise of playfulness and in his telegraphic language, Le Corbusier sometimes was more direct and truthful with Yvonne than when he addressed a larger audience or tried to seem literary. On a return trip to Moscow in June 1929, he wrote, "In Russia, this is how it is: the Eskimos play under the cactuses, the pilotis make the revolution, vodka is for washing, speeches slake thirst, and the Ideal continues. It is cold, but I am warm at heart. All's well, regards and salutes from everyone here."[9]

Yvonne, from a poor family, used to financial struggles, would, he believed, understand this sense of hope about the new Russia.

THE GLOBE-TROTTING ARCHITECT and the former dressmaker's assistant were growing even closer. By that June, Le Corbusier wrote Yvonne from La Petite Maison, declaring how happy he would be to have her see the house.

Yvonne's relationship with the woman who likened her to van Gogh's beautiful dark-haired "l'Arlésienne" was also strengthening. She spent months that spring making for Marie Jeanneret a smocklike blouse decorated with a flower pattern. Le Corbusier wanted to make sure that his mother adequately acknowledged his girlfriend's efforts. Even after his mother had written Yvonne a card to thank her, he wrote back, "It was a vast undertaking accomplished with perseverance and taste. You must look charming in it. You and your flowers—it must look very pretty, at the water's edge."[10] The peasant-style blouse was probably far too youthful in style for its wearer, but Yvonne deemed it perfect for the conservatively dressed, old-fashioned lady from the mountains.

Le Corbusier enumerated his mistress's virtues to his mother. He pointed out that while he had been traveling to the Soviet Union and elsewhere, "Vonvon has had bad times alone in the house, but she has a stubborn little philosophy, and she resists. Moreover she is used to my being far away at my work. The house is charming, clean as a whistle; each time I return I'm like a fox in his lair."[11]

In a letter that crossed his in the mail, his mother had written of "how much pleasure this pretty blouse has given me and how useful it will be."[12] Coming from Marie Jeanneret, it was a major step forward.

5

Yvonne's letters to her boyfriend's mother were written in perfect schoolgirl's penmanship, the capital letters embellished with curlicues, in lines that were ruler straight. Addressing the older woman as "*Chère petite maman,*" thus making herself a member of the family, Yvonne regularly told Marie Jeanneret that every single day she was thinking of her. She referred periodically to the blouse, in one letter saying how happy she was that it fit well: "As for the bill, I am a *grande couturière* who enjoys offering the new fashion to dear Mamans as nice as you are."[13]

Yvonne provided a picture of everyday life on the rue Jacob. In mid-June 1929, she wrote that she was making two gingham dresses to have them ready for her and Edouard's departure for Le Piquey on July 15. She recognized, though—after he had made a second trip to Moscow—that the work that had piled up by the time he returned at the end of June would probably push back their travel date.

Yvonne was doing everything she could to ensure her role as a dutiful member of the family. Lotti was away, and in order to spend more time with Albert, Yvonne intended to get her driver's license, which would make it easier to get out to his house, so far away in the sixteenth arrondissement. She began writing Marie Jeanneret with increased frequency—telling her what color skirts to wear with the blouse, when to wear it puffed out, and when it should be tucked in tight—and assured her that she would like to see her. But Le Corbusier's mother did not write back. On August 10, the architect wrote her anxiously, "What does your silence mean?" After reminding her of his and Yvonne's overtures, he continued, "Your big baby Albert is no longer there to fill your days. How about a word to console the younger son?"[14]

Yvonne was, Le Corbusier assured his mother, "loved by everyone here." Now he and she, together, proposed that Marie make a plan to come to Paris to celebrate New Year's, although it was still half a year away. After all, much as he adored his mistress, his mother's position was unassailable: "I think of you every day. I expect your letter every noon. A word, a card, if you please."[15] Occasionally she replied—mainly to report on the leaking roof.

LE CORBUSIER regularly listed his achievements for his mother. Once he and Yvonne got to Le Piquey at the end of August, he told her that besides being asked to design a forty-two-story skyscraper in the United States, he swam every day and had the perfect girlfriend who allowed him to be himself. "Yvonne is the darling little elf who knows how to let me be free in my initiatives," he informed his mother.[16] Three weeks later, he added, in a similar vein, "Vonvon is extremely accommodating and nice: she makes all

On vacation at Le Piquey, late 1920s

our undertakings easy."[17] This was his constant message to his remaining parent: that Yvonne was an essential ingredient in his ability to succeed.

ON SEPTEMBER 3, Yvonne herself wrote another long letter to Marie, explaining that while Le Corbusier was in South America, where he was about to embark on a major effort to promulgate his urbanism, she would be at home sewing and embroidering, following designs he had drawn for her to work on in his absence: "Dear Maman, I've begun my bedspread, green linen with big stars sewn with different yarns, just dazzling! It's taking a long time but it's not tiresome work. I'll have plenty to do during his absence, and the time will seem shorter."[18] She was also canning cornichons and onions and trying new ideas for her makeup and hair.

It was just what Le Corbusier wanted.

XXIX

1

Le Corbusier had been invited to Argentina and Brazil to give a series of lectures and to help develop urban schemes for Buenos Aires, São Paulo, and Rio de Janeiro. On September 13, 1929, he boarded the train in Paris for the port of Bordeaux. Albert, Pierre, and Yvonne accompanied him to the Gare d'Orsay.

Yvonne wrote to Le Corbusier's mother later that day. She was sad to think of his being away for two months and was worried that he might be seasick, but Albert was coming for dinner, and she was going to make him ravioli, one of the older brother's favorite dishes. They would also have some of the peaches and pears Marie Jeanneret regularly sent to the rue Jacob; "ever so many thanks for all your kindnesses!" Yvonne wrote Le Corbusier's mother.[1]

After settling into his stateroom, Le Corbusier disembarked briefly to post a letter to Yvonne before his ship, the *Massilia,* departed. His porter had won a bet because he had been the first person to board. "Kisses all around, keep your spirits up," he wrote. "Everything promises for the best. From your dd."[2]

Le Corbusier adored the ship. With its architecture based primarily on necessity, it provided a vantage point for splendid vistas. After two days at sea, he sent his mother a letter, which would be mailed from Lisbon, in which he compared the journey to a dream. The *Massilia* was "a miracle of modern construction and organization." On this journey that cost only twenty thousand francs round-trip, there were splendid fresh flowers in the dining room, an admirable style of service he termed "*marine-française,*" and superb cooking.[3] How restful this means of travel was; how magnificent the setting! The change from his normally packed schedule thrilled him, and he relished the opportunity to get more than four hours of sleep per night. He was even happier gliding slowly across the ocean's surface than he had been soaring through the sky. His only frustration was that there was no swimming pool; while seeing water all the time, there was none he could enter.

Le Corbusier decided to work with a private trainer. He was enjoying the people he met on board—an old Argentinian minister and the wife of a great poet, left unnamed, whom he had met initially at the house of the duchess of Dato—and, except for one of his frequent colds (he kept his mother informed of the extent to which his nose was stuffed), life was perfect. He assured Marie Jeanneret, however, that he had not forgotten the problems she was having with the leaks at La Petite Maison. But he begged her to have perspective: "You must realize that life has other purposes. That so many things can change. And above all, that there's no need to fuss over situations that are immutable. This was always your weakness and Papa's: a certain inflexibility."[4]

After ten days at sea, Le Corbusier penned a second report: "I must repeat my philosophy lessons: take life as it comes, welcoming the good and acknowledging the bad as inevitable. But for yourself, in your life, *let the scale tip toward the good,*" he instructed. It was his prelude to a diatribe about the haute bourgeoisie who constituted the two hundred first-class passengers: "diamonds and fake diamonds, toothpicks at the ready, etc." Having tired of the passengers he had initially liked, he had stopped attending the nightly parties: "I am unsociable in 'bourgeois' circles. I have a sense of emptiness confronting such people, who have no thoughts or who think other people's thoughts. Impossible contacts and frequentations."[5]

What he did enjoy were the afternoon performances of "*théâtre Guignol,*" the famous puppet show for children in which the clever Guignol beats the stupid policeman, Gnafron. Anyone who could defeat a bureaucrat was worth watching.

2

With Le Corbusier away, Yvonne dined regularly with his traveling companion of his earlier years, Auguste Klipstein, as well as with Albert and Pierre. But of everyone in Le Corbusier's circle, her favorites were the couple she referred to as "M. and Mme. Léger," who invited her to their farm in Normandy. Yvonne loved drinking local milk, eating fresh eggs, and sitting in front of a large fire with these good-natured people who made her loneliness more bearable.

Once Le Corbusier was in Buenos Aires, his days were charged from early morning to late at night. He gave lectures to university faculty, had tea with the American ambassadress, and met prominent people, among them Victoria Ocampo, for whom he had begun, in Paris, to design a large house on a beautiful site on the Argentinian coast.

Le Corbusier considered Ocampo one of his most enlightened clients to date. He had met this sophisticated and well-connected rich woman in Paris after the Comtesse Adela Cuevas de Vera had written to Le Corbusier on her behalf in August 1928. Ocampo had told him that she wanted a house like his villa at Garches; she also had organized his upcoming lecture tour. The design he gave her was full of his and his associates' new furniture designs, with a wonderful large salon and dining area punctuated by columns and a form at its center that resembled an igloo, which contained the bathroom.

Le Corbusier was also developing an urban scheme for Tucumán, a small city in the north. But while Argentinian high society and selected individuals were on his side, the Argentinian government was not receptive to his proposals. His new hope lay farther away. The American ambassadress suggested that when Le Corbusier went to New York, where he had a possible skyscraper project, he visit President Hoover in Washington.

Writing his mother from the Majestic Hotel in Buenos Aires, Le Corbusier believed, or hoped his mother would believe, that this interview he expected to be granted with the new president would enable him to discuss yet again the "world city"—meaning the League of Nations.[6] Perhaps it was not too late for him to win the Geneva commission after all. And in America there was no end of potential for his ideas on urbanism.

The United States was the land of promise. The secretary at the American embassy was "an immigrant of Slavic origin, extremely intelligent, very strong, a splendid type. As for Oklahoma, I'm told that these westerners are remarkable, taking very practical views so that now there's a tremendous new development in the far west. Both of us feel that here on American terrain everything works amazingly well. Tremendous power, though lack of culture."[7]

Attracted as he was to what was raw and uncouth—and having settled on Oklahoma as his image of a place of pure unfettered energy—for the moment Le Corbusier was impressed with himself for having made it into the refined bastions of upper-class Argentinian living. He had lunch at the Buenos Aires Jockey Club—he told his mother it was the wealthiest in the world—where paintings by Corot, Monet, and Goya hung on the walls. He mocked the pretentiousness, but he was proud to be invited.

Once again, the adventurous architect flew in an airplane and wrote his mother about it: "Tuesday night [October 23], got up at 2:30 a.m., then the plane took off for Paraguay, where I had been invited. First trip made with visitors. We are ten. Average speed: 220 km an hour. This plane is the new model, making its first major flight, a crossing of 1200 km, altitude 500,

1000, and 2000 meters. Amazing trip over the center of South America. Colossal rivers widened by flooding: they seem to be bays. The experience of a virgin nature. Plains of complete silence, meandering rivers and their constant modifications. Here and there, checkerboard cities, farming, cattle. Palms, groves, herds of cows, horses. Water everywhere. Images we traverse, flying under and over. Disturbing melancholy. Mold! It's the same mold as in jam pots; no doubt about it, mold on a huge scale. Asunción, center of Spanish and Indian America. Violent red earth, intense verdure, enormous trees. Yellow and pink violets. Poetry everywhere. The houses are adorable: Le Piquey in the tropics. Le Lait de Chaux and flowers. Pink, red, and yellow facades. Etc. etc. A day and a half. Overwhelming return, pure sky, enormous America!"[8]

It was one of those moments Le Corbusier periodically experienced—when he was not demolished by anguish. Intoxicated with earthly existence, he was overtaken by a surfeit of joy. He marveled at the ultimate new product of human intellect and impeccable engineering—the airplane—but, above all, at the inestimable magnificence of nature. The exuberance eventually showed up in the best of his architecture—Ronchamp, the assembly at Chandigarh, his rooftop in Marseille.

Concomitant with that effulgence of joy, Le Corbusier hated what was visually or morally corrupt. Mas de Planta, a beach resort, was monstrous, the Argentinian equivalent of the over-the-top French resort Deauville. Yet even there, he could dive into the pure depths of clear water. The product of landlocked Switzerland compared himself, not for the first time, to a porpoise. He could always avoid the abuses of the bourgeoisie by escaping to his underwater kingdom.

3

In South America, Le Corbusier further mastered the lecture technique that he had been developing throughout the twenties in which he memorized the key ideas in advance so as to give an extemporaneous performance like a theater act. The rooms were always crowded. Le Corbusier relished the idea that they were full not only of enthusiasts but of nonbelievers who needed to be convinced; he would wake the dead.

Unrolling his large sheets of paper, explaining his ideas while sketching away with his sure and agile hand, Le Corbusier became further convinced of his own wisdom. By the end of the Latin America tour, he was so pleased by what he codified in the ten lectures he gave in Buenos Aires and Rio that they became a summa on the functioning of cities.

AT THE END OF October, Le Corbusier again wrote his mother from the Majestic Hotel in Buenos Aires. Heading toward Patagonia, marveling at the tropical climate, he was elated: "How easy my life is here, I'm received by only the highest society—young moreover—and eager-minded. Great luxury, everything comfortable."[9]

He recounted a litany of successes. Plans had advanced to organize the meeting with President Hoover and rekindle the Geneva project; the French ambassador had attended all ten of his lectures. The previous Sunday, he had been at a rural hacienda with a splendid garden and a white ceramic swimming pool into which he had dived from the four-meter diving board, "impeccably," six times in succession: "That's all there is to it: I'm a good fish. Which for me is an extremely enjoyable situation."

He would, he told his mother, be making Buenos Aires "the counterpart of New York." It was his most ambitious urban scheme to date, and he felt that in little time he would have a similar success in the United States. "People talk and know what they're saying. And one is heard. North Americans are strong and young. Simple and not tricky. For them everything is action. In architecture they are completely backward. And then, they believe. I suspect my next voyage to the United States will be an important thing."[10]

Even in remote locations, Le Corbusier was now receiving lecture fees of one hundred thousand francs. And he was traveling in style with Gonzales Garrono, a new friend who was, Le Corbusier wrote his mother, "from the oldest family in Argentina" and a descendant of a viceroy.[11] For Le Corbusier, Garrono was the real thing: an aristocrat of impeccable style and bearing, cultured and educated, who was down-to-earth and who spoke to his valet as if to a brother. Garrono took him to one of his vast plantations, which had thrilling twelve-meter-long serpents. But for all the time he was spending with the grandest families, Le Corbusier insisted his head had not been turned: "Dear Maman, I don't want this to seem like a fairy tale. I remain a modest fellow, longing for his 20 rue Jacob, his oil painting, his faithful companion Vvon; see you soon my dear Maman. If I accept this vagrant life it's because I may make the kind of money here that will allow me to spread a little comfort around me, to my dear ones who lack the same occasion to make 'big money.' "[12] The term "big money" was in English, for it was America, the land of flashy millionaires, where Le Corbusier expected to earn enough to guarantee his mother and Yvonne and Albert the security and well-being he longed to give them. Writing these words on the day of the New York stock market crash, Le Corbusier was now confident that nothing could shatter his dreams.

4

Writing his mother five days later, Le Corbusier was even more manic: "To sum up, these are remarkable countries with gigantic tasks. They build everywhere, the cities are bristling with skyscrapers, money is flowing. Each private house costs from three to eight or nine million francs. In the provinces there are whole cities to be built. Room for millions of men. They think that Argentina is smaller than France. It may be bigger than Europe. Fertile to the highest degree."[13]

Marie responded by pointing out that, because of the language difference, his lecture audiences didn't understand everything he said. She also cautioned him against being seduced by the splendid style of his new life: "My dear boy, we think of you all the time, we envision you telling a lot of things in French to these Spanish Argentines who perhaps will not understand much of what you say. Be simple and do most of it on the blackboard. . . . Yesterday morning the great happiness of your letter, your excellent letter, read and reread! So happy that this great journey has left you with such pleasant memories. . . . Why don't you write a few of your impressions of the high seas! You have a good heart, and all this luxury will not corrupt our dear child. You must be strong in order to resist; but he who yields to the soft things of life sees his energies diminished and you need all yours, by Jove, in the great battle of life."[14]

However splendid her son's reception was, Le Corbusier's mother wanted to make sure of his priorities: "My dear boy, you won't forget Europe, its inhabitants, and the little old Maman with white hair who longs for her boy and for the good news that will invigorate and reassure her."[15]

5

By the start of November, Le Corbusier had met Josephine Baker. Le Corbusier had just turned forty-two; Baker was twenty-three. She was already a legend in Paris. Four years earlier, on the stage of the Théâtre des Champs-Elysées, the same setting where Charlotte Perriand had seen her clad in bananas, the Missouri-born mulatto had appeared naked except for a pink flamingo feather as she performed splits while being carried upside down on the shoulders of a large black man. That was not the sort of thing people forget.

The poet Anna de Noailles—with whom Le Corbusier had had lunch in Paris the previous year—described her as "a pantheress with gold claws."[16] Baker was renowned for taking Chiquita, her pet leopard, for airings on the Champs-Elysées. At the Folies Bergère, she sang "in a high-pitched warble, with an unashamedly Churchillian accent" and walked backward on her hands and feet, all four limbs stiff like a monkey's.[17] Crowds loved her, and so did the men with whom she jumped into bed—among them, it was reputed, the writer Georges Simenon and, the first time she stayed in a Paris hotel, a room-service waiter. Her husband, Pepito Abatino, was not an obstacle to her freedom.

Abatino was with Baker when Le Corbusier had his first encounter with her. The rapport was instant. We know this because Le Corbusier yet again made his mother privy to his experience. On November 4, from Buenos Aires, he reported that he had just met Baker and Abatino and that Abatino had proposed that Le Corbusier design a house for them in Passy, on the Right Bank not far from the Trocadéro.[18] Abatino also discussed their intention of creating a village for orphans from countries all over the world, and he asked Le Corbusier to look for land where they might establish it. Baker, whose success had earned her a small fortune, wanted the architect to undertake a series of maisonnettes for the village. Her vision of that housing was in many ways the Corbusean ideal: straightforward in design, livable, and with a preponderance of vegetation.

Le Corbusier excitedly quoted Baker and Abatino's vision verbatim to his mother. These dwellings were to be "charming, small and without pretension, amid all the flowers and all the green."[19] With that exquisite notion and Baker's vivaciousness and allure, Le Corbusier was instantly conquered.

He described the famous dancer and singer: "Josephine is extraordinarily modest and natural. She is actually a Creole village kid, with the warmest imaginable heart. Not an atom of vanity or pose. Really a miraculous phenomenon of naturalness."[20] These were the human qualities he prized above all else. In tandem with a beautiful body, they beckoned irresistibly.

6

The man who told all, or almost all, to his mother wanted to make sure not only that she learned of his adoring friendship with the legend of Paris's naughtiest music halls but that the good Calvinist had a clear picture of her son boozing and smoking.

Some Belgian visitors to Buenos Aires who were great admirers of Le Corbusier's were thrilled to recognize him one evening in a restaurant. They asked the architect out for a drink. He turned them down politely, but when they persisted he decided he could not refuse. After the first drink, he again tried to take off, but then one of them said, "You are Le Corbusier. The founder of the Modern Movement. The apostle, etc. Being with you is one of the great days of our life."[21]

The Belgians proceeded to drink themselves close to death. They got into a brawl, and the bartenders threw them out. None of this bothered Le Corbusier, who took one of his worshippers to his hotel for a nightcap. After only three hours of sleep and with a hangover, he still managed to meet with Victoria Ocampo the next morning to discuss her villa. He proudly told his mother that by doing gymnastics and swimming laps in the hotel pool that morning, he had overcome the effects of alcohol. Garrono informed him that everyone in Buenos Aires wanted him to build for them; all was for the best. His mother had instructed him to "invigorate and reassure her"; quoting the strangers who recognized him, describing his packed life, telling her about Josephine Baker, Le Corbusier had provided the information he hoped would have the desired effect.[22]

FROM BUENOS AIRES, Le Corbusier went to Montevideo. He adored this city on a coastal hill. It was bathed in intense light and had immense beaches from which he could swim in the sea. While Buenos Aires was possessed of a "fierce austerity" and a "fatality," the joyful capital of Uruguay had a liveliness that reminded him of the three very disparate cities of Barcelona, Prague, and Moscow. The locals, who received him like a messiah, organized large parties in his honor, and he gave two lectures. The only thing that bothered him was the incursion of Germans.

Enthralling as Le Corbusier found his new audience, he retained his sense of superiority.

> One learns to breathe deeply in these countries. One meditates, one takes it in. But the inhabitants are frightened, are timid; compared to them we are tremendously bold.
>
> The prestige of the Idea is a miraculous thing. Meditation leads to kindness, to generosity, to envisaging things in the light of benevolence and courage. What counts in all these impressions is the immensity of the countryside, nature's formidable song and sign. One must either believe or despair. Better to believe.[23]

On November 9, he left Uruguay on a small plane that returned him to Buenos Aires and landed in the harbor there. The voyage was glorious, and he had the satisfaction of having gained new allies. "The departure from Montevideo was very touching," he wrote, "at the edge of the pier some fifteen architects and students. The speedboat took me with some others to the hydroplane, which had just come from Buenos Aires. Waving our arms we made somatic semaphores. Soon the pier is out of my myopic range. I raise my arm. I still see the fifteen silhouetted against the sky. The speedboat reaches the plane, which we enter through the ceiling. There are twelve of us. The propellers are turning. We make a wide circle, and then we're out of the water. We're up in the air. Down below, the pier with the waving arms."[24]

He was thrilled that the combination of plane and car reduced this journey from downtown Montevideo to his Buenos Aires hotel room to one and three-quarters hours—as opposed to the twelve it would have been by sea. "Precision and dizzying speed," he wrote his mother.[25] Now that he was on course, it was a metaphor for his entire life.

7

When Le Corbusier left Buenos Aires five days later for São Paulo, however, he again traveled by sea, and in true luxury. The ship was the Italian liner *Giulio Cesare.* As the son of a viceroy, his friend Garrano had considerable influence and had arranged with the captain for the architect to have the finest cabin on the boat. Le Corbusier explained to his mother that he was traveling in the manner of wealthy cattle barons or diplomats. He liked the treatment but hated the style: "My salon is huge in the purest fake Faubourg-St.-Antoine Louis XVI. Louis XVI! They cut his head off but he takes his revenge with a resurrection which seems to last forever!"[26]

Le Corbusier had boarded the ship with plenty of time to spare before it

With Josephine Baker aboard the Giulio Cesare *en route to São Paulo, via Montevideo, November 1929*

was to pull out of the port. Once he was settled in his lavish quarters, he went up on deck. He wrote his mother, "Josephine Baker and her husband arrived five minutes before departure, cheered by a huge crowd on the pier. Standing for about three quarters of an hour in the rain, shouting: Merci, au revoir, Madame. Merci, Madame. Au revoir, Mr. Stoll. (Mr. Stoll, as the tug pulled the ship away from the pier, uttered a tremendous 'yodel' and suddenly unfurled the Swiss flag.) Josephine wept, shouting like a little girl: Au revoir, merci, merci, Madame. She is the most authentic little Negro child, simple as an ingénue, extraordinarily simple. A simple hardworking artist in every respect. She arrives in Rio in the afternoon of the 17th and begins her first performance that evening. She finished last night at 11:30, and the ship left port at midnight."[27]

Like him, she was totally devoted to a task she loved. That dedication to an art that brightened other people's lives mattered more than anything else (see color plate 8).

8

The architect used the time on the *Giulio Cesare* to plot his return to France. He charted out his schedule as carefully as he drew a floor plan. On December 9, he would leave Rio on the *Lutétia,* which would arrive in Bordeaux on December 21. Yvonne and Pierre were to meet him in Bordeaux with a car. Still trying to get his mother to Paris for New Year's, he proposed to her that she join the party; he would pay for her train ticket from Switzerland. Then the four of them could go to Le Piquey for Christmas, after which Marie could end the year with Albert and his family.

"*This proposition is quite serious.* Distances in America make it impossible to have epistolary arguments. This must *happen:* I am writing definitively here. Life is short, *we must take advantage of it.*"[28]

LE CORBUSIER PREFERRED the *Giulio Cesare* to the *Massilia,* both for its scale and its layout. He was especially conscious of boat design because of his own work that year on the "Floating Asylum" project for the Salvation Army. This eighty-meter-long barge resembled a freighter. Its three equal rectangular blocks with industrial windows housed dormitories with rows of 160 beds. The boat was to be parked each winter in front of the Louvre to "shelter the derelicts whom the cold drives far from under the bridges."[29] In the summer, it was to be moored on the outskirts of Paris and serve as a camp for children.

The asylum was more of a floating building than a vessel intended for long voyages, but some of the principles of nautical design applied. The project enabled Le Corbusier to replicate the tight spaces, the need for buoyancy, and the purposefulness that enchanted him on the *Giulio Cesare.* For a man who liked to make buildings that were elevated above the ground on pilotis, here was one that was literally afloat.

Drawing of drinking Neuchâtel wine, Rio, Copacabana Bay, 1929

9

> Why does Baker's backside rock the continents? Why have throngs of men been roused and even women's jealousy is disarmed? Why of course it's because it's a laughing backside.
>
> —GEORGES SIMENON

In planning so carefully for his return to France, Le Corbusier had neglected to mention a factor that was probably more than a coincidence. Josephine Baker was also going to be taking the *Lutétia.* Baker and Le Corbusier had been seeing a lot of each other on board the *Giulio Cesare,* when he made the decision to be on the same boat as her for a far lengthier crossing.

These details concerning the architect and the stage performer are knowable because of the letters Le Corbusier continued to write to his mother. On their first sea journey together, from Buenos Aires to São Paulo, he reported to Marie Jeanneret, "Tonight Josephine, ill in bed while Pepito pastes stamps in his album, explained the Bible to me: In the beginning God created Adam and Eve. Americans are red because American soil is red and God made men out of the soil. Jesus Christ is a divine man. Religion is good because it teaches love, loyalty, and a kind heart. Jesus did not like priests; he chased them out of the temple. And then she picked up a tiny guitar and sang all her Negro songs. Wonderfully sweet, tender, pure: 'I'm a little black bird looking for a little white bird.' She acknowledges only what is noblest in the Negroes. Outraged by the caricatures. She wants to show white people the greatness of the Negroes. From head to foot this woman is nothing but candor and simplicity; she led us down into the third-class hold to see a cat that had had five kittens; she couldn't tear herself away. After the 'intelligent' women of Buenos Aires society, I recognize truth here. Josephine reminds me of Yvonne. They have the same conception of life."[30]

Like his Monegasque girlfriend, the woman who danced in feathers was to be appreciated not just by him but also by his mother.

IN SÃO PAULO, the novelist Oswald de Andrade told Le Corbusier, "We study you, along with Freud and Marx. You're on the same level and just as indispensable to the study of the present social movement and to the establishment of a new community organization, etc." Naturally, he quoted this to his mother, to whom he explained the significance and potential ramifications of his lectures to important audiences: "Actually a lecture is a real creation, like a successful drawing. It begins with a few sketches scribbled on paper. And the idea develops, is expressed, connects, makes its way, its quality of expression varying with the audience that hears it. There is a tension, a flux of ideas in the lecturer's mind, and their choice and arrangement becomes his creation. When it's all over, you realize, by the strange fatigue that overcomes you, that you have made an effort."[31] It was as if he were an outsider wanting his mother to join him in observing the phenomenon they had both created.

The charismatic architect also had more to tell his mother about the gorgeous mulatto entertainer who, like him, was conquering large crowds. In São Paulo, he attended her performances. "Josephine Baker is performing here, flanked by her Pepito," Le Corbusier wrote. "She sang, a revelation: she is a very great artist. I almost wept, so pure was this art, so full of touching generosity. Her voice, her countenance, her gestures are an intense, total creation. She is lost in a stupid, brutal milieu. Pepito is somewhat aware of this. He would like to reach her level, but he is at the bottom of a hole. Josephine has gained an enormous respect for 'Monsieur Le Courbousher.' She gave me a little lead elephant, telling those present at Andrade's after my lecture: 'Mr. Le Courbousher is not like other men; I have complete confidence in him, I am at ease, he is a great friend.' I myself feel that she is an artist of a pure and intense sincerity. A true child. She said in Andrade's salon: 'I shouldn't be here, I should be at the hotel mending Pepito's socks. He has no socks for tomorrow, poor dear!' Tomorrow she's singing at the prison for the convicts who have given her a jewel box made with their own hands."[32]

Pepito was in the same category as Yvonne: the sweet and loyal soul of a lower order who needed to be taken care of. Le Corbusier and Josephine Baker required such partners. But they also craved their equals in imagination and intensity.

10

By November 27, Le Corbusier was in Rio de Janeiro. Blaise Cendrars had advised him to get in touch with the commission that was planning a completely new capital city for Brazil; what interested him even more was a variety show in which Baker sang "I Can't Give You Anything But Love, Baby." The song had been written the previous year for *Blackbirds of 1928,* the longest-running black musical of the epoch. Dorothy Fields's lyrics set to the music of Jimmy McHugh emphasized the value of warmth over money. The smiling and beguiling Baker brought that idea to life as she chanted. "I can't give you anything but love, baby. That's the only thing I've got plenty of, baby." The unguarded sensualism of that heart-filled performance moved Le Corbusier to the brink of tears.

Within little time, she was singing to him with no one else there.

WHEN JOSEPHINE BAKER was on the stage, Le Corbusier believed that what he was seeing and hearing was in many ways the equivalent of the new architecture to which he had been devoting himself. The singer was ravishing to the eyes. Her performance was as unfettered by tradition and as honest as his designs. It was possessed of the bravery and effrontery of Le Corbusier's houses and of his writing.

Baker's dancing and singing had the blunt force and the constant rhythm he sought in his own work. The legs that could jump and do splits and fly through the air embodied the synchronicity of all systems in perfect working order. Physical beauty and impeccable mechanics, heart and intellect, were here allied.

As a youth in Vienna, Le Corbusier had been happier in opera houses and concert halls than at shows of the Secession. He now considered jazz on a par with the masterpieces of Puccini and Wagner: "In this American music that comes from the Negroes there is a lyrical, contemporary quality so invincible that I see in it the basis of a new musical feeling capable of expressing the new epoch and capable also of outclassing the European ways, just as in architecture the European ways outclass those of the stone age. A new leaf turned. A new discovery. Pure music."[33]

ON THE RETURN TRIP from Rio de Janeiro to Bordeaux, Josephine Baker and Le Corbusier were alone in his first-class cabin of the *Lutétia* when she again picked up a child's guitar, more a toy than a real instrument, and sang, "I am a little blackbird looking for a bluebird." Critics of her public concerts described her voice as "lilliputian" and compared it to a cracked bell with a clapper covered in feathers; but Le Corbusier had no such criticism.

Strumming her toy instrument in the privacy of Le Corbusier's stateroom, her sleek bangs curling over her forehead, her large eyes sparkling, her smile wide and radiant, Baker sang,

I'm a little blackbird looking for a bluebird,
You're a little blackbird and a little lonesome too.

I fly all over from east to the west
In search of someone to feather my nest
Why can't I find one the same as you do?
The answer must be that I am a Houtou.

The next verse that she sang in her lighthearted and playful but deceptively serious cadences seemed written specifically for Le Corbusier.

I'm a little jazzbo looking for a rainbow too
Building fairy castles the same as all white folks do.
For love of crying, my heart is dying to keep on trying
I'm a little blackbird looking for a bluebird too.

When Le Corbusier wrote his mother about Baker singing on the *Giulio Cesare,* he had made the main lyric "I'm a little black bird looking for a little white bird." He had thought it was about him.

WHILE THE SHIP glided across the Atlantic, Le Corbusier did a number of drawings of Baker in the nude. She faces her viewer head-on, totally at ease, smiling radiantly. In one image, she has grabbed her knees with her hands in a sort of Charleston movement. But unlike the flapperesque women who specialized in the Charleston, their figures flat as boards, Josephine Baker, in Le Corbusier's drawings, even more than in real life, has an exceptionally sturdy, full bosom and large buttocks. Her hips jut out like those of Matisse's *Blue Nude* of 1907. Much as Le Corbusier liked Baker as she was, he transformed the exotic sorceress according to his own taste and made her his ideal woman (see color plates 23–25).

In another rendering, Le Corbusier gave Baker a truly primitive face, like the images Picasso and André Derain made resembling African masks. It is not a particularly good drawing. The undistinguished sketch, the cliché of a female savage, makes clear that the man who could be so utterly restrained and neat in his building facades—who could, when he needed to, put everything in its correct place down to the last centimeter—had another side that craved total abandon and wildness: in human behavior, in himself, in women. He abandoned his artistic judgment in the process. He reported a lot to his mother, but at least he didn't send these drawings to Vevey. Rather, he kept them in his private sketchbook.

Le Corbusier also outlined a libretto for a ballet for Baker. There were nine scenes, including one calling for a modern man and woman and New York, represented by a skyscraper, to dance a one-step until a cylinder

In Indian army uniform, with Josephine Baker in whiteface at his left at a costume party on board the Lutétia, *in December 1929*

slowly descends on the stage and Baker emerges from it, dressed as a monkey. She then changes into a dress and sings until the gods rise. Finally, an ocean liner takes off to sea.

The architect kept the drawings to himself, but he and Baker were very public on board the ship. A committee of first-class passengers had made plans for a costume ball, and Baker and Le Corbusier had decided to go to it together, in spite of the possible embarrassment for Pepito Abatino. Le Corbusier made some sketches for their costumes. In a photo of the two of them side by side—at a lavishly set dinner table with a starched white tablecloth—the architect is in blackface; Josephine appears white. He wears the boldly striped uniform of an Indian army guard; Baker is in a clown's costume. Le Corbusier sports a polka-dot bandanna. His usually meticulous hair is combed forward in bangs that reach the top of his trademark eyeglasses, making him a total rogue. Baker, with her heavily made-up eyes, is seated on his left, enjoying an offstage moment of unmitigated pleasure.

That the earnest, hardworking architect, normally clad in his dark suit and white shirt, wanted, in his fantasy life, to be a pirate—a cad, a thief, or a con artist—is no surprise. This was just one more mask; he was used to wearing public faces. But a large part of his pleasure had nothing to do with a disguise. The woman at his side had brought him unprecedented happiness.

11

When Le Corbusier later referred to Josephine Baker, he always emphasized that she remained uncorrupted by fame or fortune. The singer was the rare genius possessed of true innocence and kindness. "Josephine Baker, known the world over, is a little child, pure and simple," he said. "She slips through the cracks of life. She has a warm heart. She is an admirable artist when she sings, she is out of this world when she dances."[34]

Josephine Baker wrote about Le Corbusier in much the same way. Her vision of him was like his of her. She found him a pure and gentle soul, enormous fun, and a very serious artist, indeed a genius. She depicts Le Corbusier with a warmth and affection expressed by few other witnesses. But her version of their shipboard romance is played down, with her singing for him occurring in public rather than private: "In Rio we boarded the Lutétia. On board, the architect Le Corbusier. He's been on a lecture tour. A simple man and gay; we become friends. I amuse him with my little songs, which I sing for him as we walk around the bridge. His architecture of the future seems so intelligent: on the ground, gardens for pedestrians, and the cars up in the air on elevated highways. . . . But he also says 'the city is made for men, and not the contrary, Josephine!' At the masquerade ball when we crossed the equator there were two Josephine Bakers, me and . . . him. He put on blackface with a feather boa! He's irresistibly funny. Oh! Monsieur Le Corbusier, what a shame you're an architect! You'd have made such a good partner!"[35]

BAKER'S ADOPTED SON, Jean-Claude Baker, has a particular slant on her affair with Le Corbusier: "For her, sex was a revenge. In those days in America you were a colored person from the Negro race, and all those pretty black girls in show business slept with white men at night. Josephine was very angry with white people, and especially white men." The origin of that rage, her son explained, is that Baker had a white German father whom she never met. Moreover, "white men jumped on these black women—especially on Josephine and on Maude de Forest, because she was the darkest. The men went gaga; it was confusing for those young people."

Jean-Claude Baker maintains that these motives, rather than pure attraction to Le Corbusier, underlay Baker's involvement: "She preferred women, because she had been abused as a child. For her, sleeping with men—beyond the revenge—was a way of getting a little security." As for the men, "They fell in love with the spontaneity and lack of education that she had."

With Josephine Baker on board the Lutétia

Josephine Baker, her son points out, was beloved in France. She, in turn, enjoyed the respect accorded her by famous French people and the chance to know some of them: "She met Colette and slept with her. She was open, and willing to absorb like a sponge from everyone. Le Corbusier was successful . . . adventurous, open to the different faces of the world." In blackface at the party, "he was almost mocking the treatment of black people in America." The setting was perfect: "A boat is a private island, a floating paradise."[36]

There were special points in common. Baker had "built a platform for her bed in her suite in Montmartre," her son reports. Le Corbusier, too, had high platform beds—as if to put the act of sex on stage. The ship's bunk suited them well.

12

While Le Corbusier was getting to know Josephine Baker in Rio, Yvonne was growing increasingly impatient awaiting her lover's return. By the end of November, she had already begun to count the days until December 21. "Poor Edouard, he must be so tired," she wrote Marie Jeanneret.[37]

Yvonne was adapting to life as Le Corbusier's unofficial wife. She continued to visit the Légers often and to spend a lot of time with Pierre. She, Pierre, and the Légers went to the Salon d'Automne together. Here, for the first time, the furniture designed by Le Corbusier, Charlotte Perriand, and Pierre Jeanneret was presented publicly. With Le Corbusier in Rio, she served as a surrogate.

In her lover's absence, Yvonne painted the kitchen and entrance of their little apartment. She embroidered the stars he had drawn on their bedspread, and she organized a big winter cleaning. Like a diligent housekeeper reporting to an absentee employer, she frequently wrote to Le Corbusier's mother about these activities.

On December 19, Marie Jeanneret went to Paris so that on the twentieth she and Pierre and Yvonne could go to Bordeaux to greet the *Lutétia*. Yvonne was happy that the weather had calmed down. It meant that Le Corbusier would have a smoother passage. "His arrival is near, so now I sing all day long," she had written her lover's mother.[38]

ACCORDING TO CHARLOTTE PERRIAND'S autobiography, when the *Lutétia* docked at Bordeaux, she was also there to greet Le Corbusier. She claimed that her employer strutted off the *Lutétia* arm in arm with Baker. "Corbu was conquered," Perriand observed.[39]

It makes a great story. However, given that we are certain that Yvonne, Pierre, and Le Corbusier's mother were at the dockside, it begs plausibility. Numerous letters written about plans revolving around the arrival of the boat, as opposed to Perriand's memoirs published nearly seventy years later, attest to the details. There is no mention of Perriand being there. Perriand, once the others were all dead, used what she knew of Le Corbusier's truth to enliven her story, adding her own presence, but it was a falsification. Not that Perriand was alone; a slew of characters would, in retrospect, want to make it sound as if they had been more a part of Le Corbusier's life than they were.

13

Besides the chaise longue, the armchairs, and the visitors' chairs designed by Perriand, Le Corbusier, and Pierre Jeanneret, the display at the Salon d'Automne also included a revolving metal armchair. Here, the leather cushion is a perfect circle resting on a steel framework that spins freely on elegant, lithe legs. The back seems to grow organically from the base. The support is minimal: a curved cylinder, basically half a circle, made of thick cushioning, covered in leather. Light and taut, the chair provides all that is needed to hold a human being comfortably and not an iota more. Stools—simply the base of these chairs without the back support—were also produced.

A large table, meant for dining or as a big desk, was as simple as possible. A thick, wavy, semiopaque piece of glass rests on suction cups and devices like oversized screws on a minimal but sturdy frame. A series of smaller tables have simple tubular-steel vertical supports and a light steel frame holding clear glass; this concept was developed as both a square coffee table with short legs and a higher rectangular one of multiple uses.

This new furniture was akin to the designs being developed at the same time by Mies van der Rohe and Marcel Breuer, but the Le Corbusier–Perriand–Jeanneret designs still startled their audience in 1929. They are lighter and seemingly less serious than their German counterparts. With their deceptive appearance of weightlessness, they have the charm of a well-executed dance step. They add pleasure to the simple acts of everyday life in ways that eluded the designs made by others. They gave modernism unprecedented elegance.

INITIALLY, LE CORBUSIER and his team had offered their furniture designs to the Peugeot bicycle company, in the hope that, since Peugeot already mass-produced objects of tubular steel joined with rivets, they would want do the same with furniture. But Peugeot turned them down. The designers next approached Thonet, a company that had a new interest in tubular steel. Thonet had already mass-produced a lot of bentwood furniture—including chairs that Le Corbusier often used in his interiors—and had financed the room of furniture at the Salon d'Automne. An agreement was reached for them to produce the new pieces.

However, although these designs appeared in Thonet catalogs into the early thirties, they were not made in any quantity. The world was not yet ready for the flippancy of this furniture. It was to be a long time until those pieces began to appear in thousands upon thousands of public and private spaces all over the world, where we find them today.

14

In 1928, Le Corbusier and Pierre Jeanneret had also designed a car. It was not manufactured, and the design was not published until 1935. In its compact shape and the overarching curve from the top of the windshield to the rear fender, the buglike vehicle, called the Voiture Minimum, was the forerunner of the Citroën Deux Chevaux; its rear engine would be echoed in the Quatre Chevaux and the Volkswagen Beetle. Its simple shell-like form was more aerodynamic than was the norm at the time, and it was also relatively lightweight. The car had the efficiency and straightforwardness of Le Corbusier's most rudimentary housing units.

The idea for the interior was similar to the insides of his buildings: unencumbered space and a lot of glass allowing light to pour in and provide the inhabitants with maximum visibility. The placement of the engine at the back would decrease vibrations, noise, engine heat, and fuel smells. Concerned with the issue of storage, as he always was, Le Corbusier provided considerable luggage space in the front.

This inventive, high-spirited design became another source of resentment. Le Corbusier later believed that the automobile industry stole the idea of his little car. He could never prove the point, but some three decades later when a new Citroën was photographed at Ronchamp, Le Corbusier triumphantly denied the company the right to publish the photos.

XXX

1

Le Corbusier and his clients were, for a brief while, among the few who continued to ride the crest of the wave following the stock market crash of 1929. The architect was besieged by commissions to create luxurious residences.

In 1930, he designed a beach house in Chile for Eugenia Errázuriz, a rich, seventy-year-old patroness of the avant-garde. The former Eugenia Huici was an heiress to the fortune her father had made mining silver in Bolivia before civil war there had driven him, his Bolivian wife, and their two daughters back to his native Chile. When she was twenty years old, Eugenia had married José Tomás Errázuriz, "whose father and grandfather had both been presidents of Chile."[1] They honeymooned in Venice, where John Singer Sargent painted the bride's portrait, and lived in London, where Augustus John and Walter Sickert also painted her. The heiress became known for her "minimalist vision of the decorative arts" and her taste for what was "very fine and very simple—above all, things made of linen, cotton, deal, or stone, whose quality improved with laundering or fading, scrubbing or polishing." Cecil Beaton said "that the whole aesthetic of modern interior decoration, and many of the concepts of simplicity . . . generally acknowledged today, can be laid at her remarkable doorstep."[2]

Jean Cocteau introduced Picasso to Errázuriz, and the adventurous heiress became his great patron and supporter, replacing Gertrude Stein in Picasso's life during the world war, when Stein and Alice Toklas left Paris to drive ambulances. It was Errázuriz who convinced Picasso to go to Rome to work with Cocteau on *Parade.* She amassed a collection of his Cubist work, and when the artist and his new Russian wife, Olga, spent their honeymoon and most of a summer at a house Errázuriz had rented in Biarritz, Picasso frescoed some of the walls with naked nymphs and lines of texts by Apollinaire. Fortunately, Errázuriz's son, who had more money than she did, eventually bought the house for her.

Eugenia Errázuriz had other walls of that Biarritz villa whitewashed and used terra-cotta tiles on the floor so that it resembled a peasant dwelling.

Cecil Beaton described a detail that could have been on Mount Athos: "A long wooden shelf, scrupulously scrubbed, ran the length of the wall; and on it . . . she placed a still life of hams, huge cheeses, and loaves of bread."[3] She had Le Corbusier's sensibility before she even knew his name.

"Throw out and keep throwing out," Errázuriz instructed. "Elegance means elimination."[4] When Blaise Cendrars introduced the architect to his future client, he was putting soul mates together. Le Corbusier admired both his patron's taste for rough, natural materials and her well-cultivated visual judgment; the tempestuous heiress and exacting architect got along splendidly.

2

Le Corbusier's house for Eugenia Errázuriz was to face the Pacific Ocean. In drawings, its roofline is a broad V, resembling two unequal wings of a gigantic bird in flight. The off-center spine at the low point of the roof creates a gully, from which the expanses sweep upward. Le Corbusier had never before tilted a roof in this way. A bold gesture, well suited to the site, it was a breakthrough from the flat roofs of the 1920s and a predecessor of the fantastic canopied ceilings that were to follow. The architect was moving toward organic form and the appearance of motion.

What was equally unusual about this house for adventurous art collectors in the rural splendor of Chile were the rustic materials: the architectural equivalent of Errázuriz's preferred rough linens. Le Corbusier specified and sketched fieldstones for the floors and irregular, large stone blocks for the exterior. Coarsely cut tree trunks were to be used for the inside columns. Brick-colored, cylindrical tiles were to cover the roofs. It was a significant shift to what was local and biomorphic.

The project never materialized; Eugenia Errázuriz ran through her money. Her fortunes changed to such an extent that Picasso secretly had to buy back some of his work from her so that she could stumble along. After the war, when she was in her eighties, she was robbed of all of her jewels at gunpoint; the sale of the one Picasso painting she had retained saved her from being completely destitute. But when she died in Chile, she still had the fantasy of Le Corbusier's marvelous unbuilt dwelling for her where mountains and oceans meet the coastline of the Pacific.

The project altered the shapes and materials of Le Corbusier's architecture and introduced him to the possibility of building in a landscape that recalled Mount Athos, with the vertiginous drop of the mountains onto a sea presenting a vast horizon. In years to come, he grew to know such settings even better, overlooking the French Mediterranean.

LE CORBUSIER'S design for Eugenia Errázuriz's beach house was surreptitiously copied on the other side of the world. In *The Complete Work,* the architect writes, "We have had the pleasure of discovering in the *Architectural Record* for July 1934 a number of illustrations reproducing the very pretty house built by *M. Raymond* outside of Tokyo in Japan. The reader must make no mistake: these are photographs not of our house, but of a creation of *M. Raymond*'s!"[5]

In Japan, the house was clad in wood and the roof covered with grass, but this was irrefutably Le Corbusier's idea stolen and transformed. In an extensive text, he professed that he was flattered by the copying, that this fit into Japan's wonderful tradition of domestic housing, and that Raymond's project was admirable. But what fascinated him above all was the deceptiveness. Yet again, he was the victim of the forces of corruption.

3

Le Corbusier also began a project in 1930 for a penthouse apartment for Charles de Beistegui on top of an apartment building on the Champs-Elysées. De Beistegui, the heir to a Mexican silver fortune, was a bon vivant and socialite who befriended the Surrealists. Unlike the house for Eugenia Errázuriz, his apartment was completed, although it no longer exists today.

El Lissitzky might have made his assault even more ferocious had he known of this elegant folly. A confection of minimal forms on top of an old-fashioned apartment building, the penthouse was designed primarily for visual drama. The main floor had large glass walls facing the Arc de Triomphe; the crowning element was a tidy lawn that served as a rooftop solarium overlooking the wide Champs-Elysées and enclosed by the simplest of plaster walls. The solarium had a rococo fireplace, in front of which stood, in a haphazard arrangement, a couple of traditional and ornate wrought-iron garden chairs, in a dreamlike assemblage that was truly Surrealist—in spite of Le Corbusier's disapproval of Ozenfant's infatuation with the movement founded by André Breton.

Downstairs, there was a library drawn according to the golden section, starkly modern, save for a spectacular Venetian glass chandelier that punctuated its austerity. A winding staircase, coiled like a corkscrew, did not quite reach the landing above—contributing to the dreamlike ambience. Climbing up the staircase, one would for a split second walk over a void, just before landing safely on the solarium floor. The start of the descent was even more disconcerting, with the slight feeling of alarm, as if one were about to go over the edge of a cliff.

On the roof level, besides the solarium, a dining terrace floated above Paris. It looked more like the setting for a dance performance than a dining room, with its carefully sculpted garden plantings, pruned and trimmed into robotlike presences.

This penthouse for a decadent aristocrat, unique in the body of Le Corbusier's work, became the ultimate chic. In a 1934 spoof of *Vogue* and *Harper's Bazaar* and of the world those magazines invoked, E. B. White wrote, "It is the magic hour before cocktails. I am in the modern penthouse of Monsieur Charles de Beistegui. The staircase is entirely of cement, spreading at the hem-line and trimmed with padded satin tubing caught at the neck with a bar of milk chocolate."[6] It was one report Le Corbusier did not send home to his mother.

4

At the same time that Le Corbusier was designing for the rich, he went to the Soviet Union for a third time. There primarily to work further on the Centrosoyuz, he had also been asked to consult on a new "Green City" on the outskirts of Moscow. In spite of the Russian authorities' hope that he would become involved with this expansion that would have essentially created suburbs, he opposed it, disparaging any plan to dilute the strength of a densely packed city center.

Le Corbusier did not mince words: "The principle of disproportionate urban extension is a sentimental heresy rooted in the devotion to garden cities, whose effect is to isolate the individual, and to force him to perform wearisome tasks and believe he is happy . . . the garden city is a narcotic; it shatters the collective spirit, its initiatives, its galvanizations, and atomizes human energies into an amorphous, impalpable powder. . . . 'Disurbanization' amounts to the annihilation of urban energy. If we wish to create a short-sighted people, let us disurbanize; if, on the other hand, we desire a people with strong, dynamic, modern ideas, let us urbanize, concentrate, build."[7]

For central Moscow, Le Corbusier came up with a transportation plan with several railroad stations, a subway, and a landing strip for airplane taxis on the roof of one of the train terminals. Cars were to be used outside the complex. A network of elevated walkways led to schools, clubs, and athletic facilities. What he considered the ideal new world was of no interest to the Russian authorities. Le Corbusier was accused of disregarding the new realities of the Soviet system and of having created a plan better suited to capitalism.

5

In 1930, Le Corbusier published *Details Concerning a Present State of Architecture and of Urbanism*—the book for which the 1929 South American lecture tour had been the catalyst. In it he explains that architecture is often "pretentious and deceitful, motivated by human vanity," while at other times "it embodies the Truth Spirit of Le Corbusier, and is resoundingly honest."[8] To achieve that purity, the Plan Voisin could be realized immediately in Buenos Aires; replacing the city's complex of narrow streets with new buildings on pilotis, including a group of two-hundred-meter-high skyscrapers on the waterfront, would create open spaces with access to the sky and the sea. Le Corbusier devoted the rest of his life to trying to realize this vision of urban utopia.

For a while, in spite of the rejection of his transportation scheme for Moscow, he continued to see Russia as the place where that "Truth Spirit of Le Corbusier" might take hold. On his last weekend there, luxuriating in a czarist-style hotel room, he wrote his mother:

> Sunday. Moscow–March 1930
>
> I have just won a complete victory in the big committee settling the life-or-death question of our facades, that question which overwhelmed me in Paris. I have found the people here remarkably intelligent.
>
> What lies are told, what lies! Resisting to the best of my abilities, remaining as distant as possible, I observe with astonishment the creation of a new spirit. *Esprit Nouveau.* On the social level I note the reorganization that seems so urgent everywhere. Here, in everything, an enormous forward impulse. This year is a year of fulfillment. Russia is building now, after having demolished. One must be honest, one must be able to acknowledge; I have not advocated an architectural reformation to remain unaffected by this unanimous impulse. The new world

> is being made here. And I say, very coolly, without passion, that our people who calumniate this world as they do are liars and deceivers. Moreover, theirs is a wasted effort: power explodes here within the general will. Does this astonish you? Yet *so it is.* One would do better to resign oneself rather than to play the ostrich.
>
> Arrived Wednesday morning, have not stopped working since. My Centrosoyuz affairs were settled this afternoon. There are sides one must take.
>
> Lodging: I am in a luxurious bedroom of l'Ancien Régime, surrounded by every possible comfort.
>
> Here one feels how splendid it is to move.[9]

Le Corbusier then made an extraordinary comparison. The Russians, he said, had come up with forms of housing that evoked some of the best qualities of the monastery at Ema, which had remained the supreme example of architectural clarity for him ever since he had first seen it twenty-three years earlier: "The Charterhouse of Ema is a model of housing, and the Muscovites come close to it without imitating it in their new housing program."[10] There could be no higher praise.

Fortunately, Marie Jeanneret had already received a letter he had written her a few days later when he was back in Paris. There he declared, "As for proposing myself as the apostle or defender of the Russian regime—no such thing. One must be prudent. I myself have as yet no opinion on the whole affair."[11] Had she not read this assessment first, she might have feared that Edouard was attracted even more than he was to the land run by "Jews of rather low extraction." What ultimately counted for Le Corbusier was not a country's leadership or its political system, but its hospitality to his ideas, and unless he received major commissions in Moscow, she need have no fear.

6

That April, after Le Corbusier's return from Moscow, he was in high spirits. Yvonne was over her cold, and they spent most weekends at Léger's farm in Normandy; he was delighted by how well she got along with his other friends, who were also houseguests. The office was busy; among other things, Le Corbusier was exploring the possibility of doing a villa in Florida for the wife of the newspaper magnate William Randolph Hearst. He was painting a lot, which kept him calm amid the hecticness. In mid-May, he

With Fernand Léger at Léger's farm, Normandy, late 1920s

wrote his mother, "The days are full. Madly full. The further we go, the more I undertake."[12]

Le Corbusier either was informed or believed he was informed that he would, after all, be doing the League of Nations. He may have been delusional, but he was in one of his phases of being confident about everything: "You cannot imagine how my activity displaces or places me—on unexpected sites. I crystallize around such ideas certain groupings that seek prominence. And on the left as on the right I am incorporated: here by communists, there by fascists, here by royalists, there by international organizations. Thought spreads like a drop of oil, touching many realms. For me there is, these days, an irresistible crescendo. Increasingly, therefore, I act with speed, with precision, and seize each gesture of my day. New enterprises everywhere, of all kinds, and always that safety measure: painting. And Yvonne happily consenting to be present when necessary and to be ever my good companion. At least my simple hearth is calm and good-humored, a real solace. I call this a priceless boon."[13]

His only annoyance was that his mother had been frugal on a trip to Florence he had funded, and she had returned the money left over. He sent it back to her, with instructions to buy phonograph records and take boat trips on the lake.

The architect himself had made a giant step away from Swiss parsimony. After sixteen months of paperwork and red tape, he learned that his naturalization as a French citizen was finally certain to come through.

TOWARD THE END of July, Le Corbusier went to Spain with Albert, Pierre, and Léger, while Yvonne stayed behind at Léger's farm with the art critic Maurice Raynal. Anticipating the trip, Le Corbusier told his mother that, if disaster struck him, he had a valuable art collection that would guarantee her economic well-being. Marie could now depend 100 percent on the same son who had a decade earlier destroyed his parents' life savings. Lipchitz and Léger, along with the gallery owner Jeanne Bucher and his friend Christian Zervos, director of *Cahiers d'Art,* would help her sell off the work at good prices. There was also cash in his bank account, and she needed to know that de Montmollin and Raoul La Roche would assist her in managing her finances if he was no longer there to do so. He had written his will so that she, Yvonne, and Albert would all be beneficiaries; Pierre was also named, but for a smaller percentage than the others: "My intention is not to cross the Rubicon, still less the Styx. But there are my many journeys, risk, chance, etc."[14]

Le Corbusier's life plan was working. In August, from Le Piquey, he sent his mother sketches of himself with the physique of a god, diving into the ocean with perfect form—his arms and legs taut, his body as firm as a knife blade. He was again convinced he would win the League of Nations job following a fourth round of deliberations. Other commissions were flooding the office; his advice was perpetually sought; he was designing houses and cities; he was lecturing and publishing.

Only his mother gave him trouble. One Sunday night at the end of September, Le Corbusier wrote her an eight-page letter that pitted her values against his, Switzerland against Paris. He had just been with her in Vevey; the visit had ended on a sour note. Following conversations about her refusal to hire household help, Yvonne, and his change of citizenship, that he considered "melancholy, grotesque, caricatural," he had departed in a huff. "Setting foot in Paris again, the atmosphere immediately changes: occasions for meditation and appreciation appear at every step. Here there is the whole dramatic spectacle of life. . . . In Switzerland, providentially sheltered from storms, there are things you do not know and will never know. And your judgment is limited."[15]

Speaking for himself and Albert, Le Corbusier continued: "You, you were a great worker and a model of moral strength. You were endowed with a powerful instinct rather than a meditative mind. For us you remain a magnificent image, and your example is present every day in our labors. You have instilled in us a sentiment of energy. You and Papa have endowed us with a judgment independent of public opinion. We are free men, and we act—virtually—as free men. Must we see you, then, at the age when everything should be at peace, swallowing the public opinion of this parcel of land deplorably populated by the bourgeoisie? So that by virtue of habit, without any real motivation, you subject your life, and your former liberty, to the enslavement of ambient foolishness?"[16]

Le Corbusier wanted his mother to change her attitudes both for his sake and for her own:

> You have shuttered your universe too closely. You no longer take adequate views of the outside world. You must not think so often of yourself, and never of your misery, but of your happiness. Remember that you are our model!
>
> You are a tyrant. You want everything to coincide with your conception, your idea, your way of doing things. When I call you a tyrant, I mean petty tyrant, yet you persist in imposing your way of seeing things, even on your sons who are over 40![17]

That said, Le Corbusier presented himself as the diplomat who could broker peace even with this impossible despot:

> My dear Maman, let those storms which broke the other day serve as a warning to us: beware!
>
> Take advantage, I implore you, of this occasion which has furnished the warning. For unfortunate things were said and we must stop short here and see the situation clearly for what it is. My dear Maman, you see how right Papa was to tell me to look after you. It is I who am the elder now, the wise man. I give this advice with tenderness and love. We want you to be happy. You can be. But you must take responsibility for being so. Do you realize that you add to our worries if we must think of you as disarmed? You must be an armed woman, you must be vigilant, you must resist.
>
> I count on you, in Papa's name, whose daily life for so long (40 years) was so gray and so dim. I say to you: you can live a happy woman.[18]

For himself, he assured her, he had what it took for such happiness. His apartment was not as spacious as the places where she and Albert lived, but it suited him. There was room to write and paint. He sketched in trains, boats, cars, waiting rooms, or wherever he had a moment to spare. Albert, too, was productive and composing seriously. Le Corbusier had learned that the worst obstacle to personal joy, if one was otherwise fortunate, was oneself; he was determined that his mother see this.

7

In mid-September, on a Sunday when he was plagued by a particularly nasty cold, Le Corbusier ran five and a half kilometers without stopping. Later in the month, he went to Venice, where the beauty intoxicated him as always. But by mid-October, his spirits began to flag. He wrote his mother, "I feel I am abandoning you at this season's end, when rain, wind and dead leaves spread an invincible melancholy. And you're alone there, confronting nature." With winter approaching, sunlight was no longer coming through the windows on the rue Jacob. The cure was clear: "As long as we give due battle, we are active, and being active we are impervious to melancholy."[19]

He wrote his mother, "I become ever more certain of the causes of happiness: inner life. With this realization, the horizon widens, deepens, we are drawn toward it; every minute is useful, used. . . . We are filled with desires and we *ourselves* are entirely capable of satisfying them."[20]

Le Corbusier and Maître André Prudhomme, a lawyer ("*avocat à la cour de Paris*") who was a professor at the Sorbonne, had created a thirty-six-page legal claim concerning the League of Nations project. Officially, the document was "not received"; the league declared it could not respond to protests from private individuals. Even then, Le Corbusier did not give up. With Le Corbusier and Pierre having come up with a construction estimate of twelve and a half million francs, for this project on which the ceiling cost had been stipulated as thirteen million, the league was now maintaining that the scheme would have run to at least double the cost. "Thus the League of Nations embarked on the problems of building a home for itself by a deliberately premeditated act of injustice," Le Corbusier insisted.[21]

In September 1930, following the failure of the legal claim, the architect wrote a letter to Nicolae Titulescu, president of the eleventh assembly of the League of Nations, that was published immediately. He again maintained that his and Pierre's ideas were at the core of the winning scheme, and that if they had been kept on the architectural team the end results would have "become a pure and effective work."[22] But there was no response.

He was generating a lot of paperwork for another purpose as well. On September 19, 1930, Charles-Edouard Jeanneret—as he still was for legal purposes—was naturalized (his preferred word for it was "*intégré*") as a French citizen. The reason he gave was that, in mid-December, he was to marry Yvonne Gallis.

IT WAS a good moment for giving up his Swiss citizenship. Within a year, Le Corbusier would have to recognize, this time definitively, that all of his efforts in Geneva had been to no avail. He would hire another lawyer, Philippe Lamour, but nothing helped, and the only result of his continued efforts was to further his reputation for audacity and insolence. When the Secretariat was completed in 1936 and the Assembly Hall in 1937, their neo-Classical architecture was that of second-rate public institutions everywhere.

Today these pale and lugubrious structures are a sad reminder of what was once the League of Nations. The columns and Palladian porticos intended to evoke stateliness and power convey instead the weight of failure.

The shimmering assemblage of glass and steel and concrete that never got past the drawing boards would have honored the optimism of the new international organization and served its many purposes impeccably. Alas, the saga of the idealistic vision Le Corbusier hoped would advance world peace and the moribund structures built instead was like the fate of the League of Nations itself.

8

The emotional cycles that in Le Corbusier's early years had each been of many months' duration now sometimes occurred within the span of just a few minutes. Following the League of Nations disaster, the architect wrote his mother of his "invincible melancholy." Proposing hard work to combat his despair, he responded instantly at the mere thought of his self-prescribed cure on the next page of the same letter: "Everything seems easy, the world turns a smiling face, events themselves favor us."[23] His sketches from Athens and Italy and France had been requested to illustrate a special edition of Paul Valéry's *Eupalinos,* and his *Journey to the East* was now going to be published. (In fact, neither book came through as planned.) He had been invited to go to America (or so he thought; it was to be five years before he went there), and he had been commissioned to show the Plan Voisin in two important expositions in London.

In his exuberance, Le Corbusier was further refining his concept of the ideal city. "I am quite tempted to call these studies 'the radiant city,' for in such a site everything would be joy, activity, health and peace," he told his mother, using, perhaps for the first time, the term that became a staple of the vocabulary of modern architecture.[24] The worsening economic conditions worldwide made him all the more optimistic that this city could bring unprecedented well-being to the masses.

Usually impatient with his office staff, Le Corbusier was now so content that he declared them "a magnificent team." These people who diligently helped him achieve his dearest goals were true kin: "It's a family—I have a great big family!"[25]

The day following his forty-third birthday, he gave Marie Jeanneret one of his status reports on himself: "My ideas are expanding. As I see it, this is the beginning of maturity. For work and achievement are becoming joy."[26]

LE CORBUSIER was keenly aware that his mother suffered from psychological shifts like his own. "Very glad to hear you have overcome this wave of depression," he wrote her in late autumn.[27] He offered her the consolation that Lac Leman was beautiful even in foul weather, while Paris in the rainy season was melancholy and difficult.

Nonetheless, he did not spare her discouraging details about an infuriating dinner in early November when he and Yvonne had dined at Albert and Lotti's house. Le Corbusier had invited a friend of his, a Soviet architect, to join them at 10:00 p.m., following the meal. After the visitor arrived, Albert and Lotti treated him as one of those "terrible men from Moscow."[28] Rather than ask a single question about life in the Soviet capital, Albert put disks from *Rigoletto* on the gramophone. Le Corbusier launched into a diatribe against his brother as a dilettante who had willingly missed the opportunity to learn something new and enrich his mind. He insisted that their mother recognize this, at whatever cost to her tranquility.

9

Charles-Edouard Jeanneret and Jeanne Victorine Gallis were wed in a modest civil ceremony on Thursday, December 18, 1930. That evening, they celebrated at a traditional country inn thirty-five kilometers outside of Paris. Albert and Lotti, the Lipchitzes, Christian Zervos, Klipstein, the Raynals, Pierre Jeanneret, and the Légers all journeyed to the half-timbered,

"Yvonne Le Corbusier,"
ca. 1931

With Yvonne's parents in Monaco, ca. 1930

double-gabled Auberge St. Pierre at Dampierre-en-Yvelines in the Vallée de Chevreuse.

None of the bride's relatives came up from Monaco for the festivities. The groom's mother was not there either, but the newlyweds and all their guests signed a card for her. Her new daughter-in-law was thrilled by the beautiful flowers Marie had sent that day, and before the night was over she wrote to report on the simple but happy celebration. The bride and groom intended to go to Vevey immediately.

Alas, Yvonne's passport did not come through. This meant that she could not leave France. Less than a week after the wedding, therefore, Le Corbusier went home for Christmas without her. Heading off to Switzerland by car, he had Pierre at his side as far as Lausanne and then drove the rest of the way alone. Yvonne spent the holiday solo, except for the cat.

Le Corbusier was, however, back with her by New Year's. They traveled together to a farm in the Landes for the sort of quietude he loved as a respite from the full flurry of work. To the extent that world events would permit, the structure of his life was now in place.

XXXI

1

His domestic life organized, his professional life was torn asunder.

Three editorials in a La Chaux-de-Fonds newspaper berated Le Corbusier for his collusion with the Soviets and accused him of taking French citizenship for unpatriotic reasons. The day that he received the articles, he cried. His father's spinster sister—wonderful, religious Aunt Pauline—still lived in the horrible city, and he could not bear her suffering the ignominy of her nephew's bad publicity. Then Le Corbusier's books were banned in Germany, where they were declared to be Bolshevik, and the League of Struggle for German Culture labeled Le Corbusier "the Lenin of architecture."[1] The league's Nazi affiliation did not mitigate the sting.

Regardless of these attacks and his change of citizenship, the Swiss government forgave Le Corbusier and hired him to design its pavilion at the Cité Universitaire near the outskirts of Paris. And he accepted invitations to

With Léger and Pierre Jeanneret, motoring in Spain, July 1930

travel to Sweden, Norway, and England to lecture and meet with people about urbanism. Le Corbusier also took a long trip to Spain, Morocco, and Algeria with Pierre, Albert, and Léger.

He loved Marrakech especially, but developed terrible dysentery on his way home. His mother wanted to treat him with "a milk diet," a concept he later wrote about even though it failed. What fixed his Moroccan malady, he was convinced, was a civet—"burnt black"—and "wine almost as black" that he and Yvonne consumed on a peak in the Jura.[2]

LE CORBUSIER was further heartened when he was one of the twelve architects invited to submit a scheme for the Palace of the Soviets. Erich Mendelsohn, Walter Gropius, and Auguste Perret were among the others; for once, he respected the competition. Le Corbusier's concept evoked soaring confidence and imagination. It called for an enormous and sweeping concrete arch, with the roof of a fifteen-thousand-seat auditorium suspended from it. Perpendicular to the arch, at the other end of the building complex, were five right-angled buttresses resembling oversized angle brackets. A flurry of cylinders and rectangles, vastly different in scale from one another, contained, among other spaces, a second auditorium—for nearly six thousand people—and two theaters. Some of the surfaces were opaque and solid, others translucent. Graceful curves, rigid verticals, gentle horizontals, and long sloping angles, each the by-product of the demands of the interior circulation, combined to give a fantastic energy to the overall result.

The team at 35 rue de Sèvres slaved away at the project. For three months, all fifteen of them stayed at their drawing boards most nights until 2:00 a.m., sometimes even until dawn, and worked every Sunday, too. Le Corbusier considered the teamwork a "beautiful collaboration," with everyone aware of what everyone else was doing.[3] Finally, he insisted that no further modifications would be permitted, and forty meters of plans went off to the Soviet embassy three days before Christmas 1931. From there, they went to Moscow in a diplomatic pouch.

Once the project was complete, Le Corbusier slept until one in the afternoon three days in a row. Exhausted but happy, he wrote his mother, "With all this, a deep inner joy: creating."[4]

IN THE MIDDLE of trying to wrap up the Moscow design, Le Corbusier was asked to give a lecture at the Salle Pleyel, one of the most prestigious concert halls in Paris. The event was organized by Architecture d'Aujourd'hui—an organization devoted to progressive building theories that published a review of contemporary architecture in which Le Corbusier was often the subject or author of articles. Le Corbusier used the occasion to talk about the need to plan buildings from the inside out—and to blast those who violated that principle.

One hundred and thirty students of the Beaux-Arts had been invited, but more than five hundred showed up and shouted throughout the lecture. Le Corbusier believed the insurgents were there at the instigation of his old foe Lemaresquier—the man who had called attention to his League of Nations proposal not being penned in China ink—who was one of their professors. The proponents of the belief that buildings required traditional facades regardless of what happened behind them so hated Le Corbusier's viewpoint that at subsequent lectures numbered cards were distributed individually to the attendees, and the Ecole des Beaux-Arts was not invited. Modernism now required security measures.

2

At least he had his loyalists. Le Corbusier was working in this time period on a compact luxury villa in the isolated countryside between the mountains and the sea near Toulon, in the south of France, for Hélène de Mandrot. The heiress, who, in addition to her Swiss château, had a house in Paris not far from the Invalides, was now looking for a smaller modern getaway.

Le Corbusier addressed Hélène de Mandrot as "*Chère amie.*" He told her he put himself in the category of "men of action and ideals. . . . We are professionals, prevented at every step from expressing a pure conduct. . . . Politics? I have no particular identification, since the groups attracted to our ideas are the Redressement Français (bourgeois militarist Lyautey), communists, socialists, and radicals (Loucher), League of Nations, royalists, and fascists. As you know, when you mix all colors you get *white.* So there is nothing but caution, neutralization, purification and the search for *human* truths."[5] That openness about his innermost feelings was a mark of respect, but to his mother, Le Corbusier put a different slant on his wealthy client. She was, he told Marie Jeanneret, "as disagreeable as you are."[6] He was thrilled with the house he designed for her—"remarkable, new, strong, solid, splendidly incorporated into the landscape"[7]—but "the chatelaine is seriously stricken with client disease: acute crisis and lack of sang-froid."[8]

De Mandrot had reasons to be upset. Made of local rocks applied to a

The Villa de Mandrot, near Toulon, ca. 1931

reinforced-concrete structure so as to resemble old-fashioned stone walls, the sequence of interlocking geometric forms fits into its setting with grace and harmony, but, like his mother's house, it leaked. Shortly after the elegant villa was completed, de Mandrot phoned Le Corbusier in a state of high anxiety. She described "a lake" that had formed on her living-room floor during a recent downpour.

Le Corbusier quickly boarded a train to Toulon. When he entered the luxury villa—his suit and bow tie as impeccable as ever—he did not appear the least bit bothered as he viewed the pool of water. He asked de Mandrot for a plain piece of paper. The architect took the white sheet and carefully folded it into a simple toy sailboat. He set the boat down in the large puddle and watched it float. "You see, it works," he told his client.[9]

Le Corbusier then studied the construction of the windows through which the water had seeped. They had not been properly fit. He addressed the befuddled aristocrat: "Hélène, you're an architect. How could you have permitted the builders to get away with this? You were on site. Now, really, get the mistake corrected, and please don't ever again disturb me with my busy schedule in Paris about something of this sort."[10] He left, and returned to the capital as quickly as he had arrived.

3

In the spring of 1931, Le Corbusier took Yvonne to her birthplace. He reported to his mother, "She's had a childish delight to be back in her Monaco. And everywhere she went she was made much of by good, simple people."[11]

With Yvonne, Le Corbusier then made the first of many visits to Algiers. Initially, the intense sunlight, the hills surrounding the city, and the lush vegetation there made him oddly uneasy. He wrote his mother, "I've had too many struggles and misfortunes to be able to contemplate these gardens in Algiers without a certain uneasy feeling. Such radiant harmony and such perfection have a crude aspect wounding to a sensibility hungry for reality; these gardens plunge you into a convention of happiness, they are a stereotype of the beautiful."[12]

After Algiers, Le Corbusier and Yvonne went to the Côte d'Azur and then drove back to Paris. The Easter holiday made it nearly impossible to find places to stay overnight, but his wife was an agreeable travel companion. He explained Yvonne's nature and his strategy for dealing with it to his mother: "once one learns to maneuver around her basic nervousness, which is considerable, she offers the most perfect and delightful good humor. And I have the impression that ever since the mayor officiated, she's infinitely calmer. As dear Papa would have said, 'All's well that ends well.' "[13]

4

Le Corbusier and Pierre Jeanneret were in this time period also making designs for a museum of contemporary art in Paris. They were so fascinated by their idea for this project that they decided to pursue it even knowing there might never be anyone who would support it. Le Corbusier explained the concept in a letter to his friend Christian Zervos. It was to start out as a building without facades, with a single exhibition space, fourteen by fourteen meters, which could be built for the modest sum of one hundred thousand francs.

The visitor was to enter via an underground tunnel. The walls would be membranes, some fixed, some movable, to allow for indefinite expansion in the form of a square spiral growing outward around the core. The issue of what one saw from the outside was virtually irrelevant. Additions could be built at any time; with one mason and one laborer permanently employed, the museum would be in the process of perpetual enlargement.

Le Corbusier assumed that rich donors would underwrite the cost so the people at large could benefit.

> The donor of a picture can give the wall where his picture will be hung; two posts, two cross-beams, five or six joists, plus a few square yards of partition. And this tiny gift permits him to attach his name to the hall which houses his pictures. The museum is built in some suburb of Paris. It rises in the middle of a potato field or a beet field. If the site is magnificent, so much the better. If it is uglified by factory chimneys and the dormers of wretched housing developments, that doesn't matter: by the construction of partition walls we will come to terms with . . . factory chimneys, etc., etc.
>
> My dear Zervos, such is the concept of our museum, which I have hitherto shared with no one. I'm giving it to you. Now it's in the public domain. I wish you the best of luck.[14]

Willing as he was to donate his architectural fees for something he believed in, Le Corbusier was furious at the manner of the bankers who in the same time period caused problems with his Immeuble Clarté in Geneva. The architect's first apartment building, with forty-five two-story dwellings, the Clarté had cantilevered terraces, industrial windows, stovepipe stair railings, and no ornament whatsoever. Built by Edmond Wanner, an enlightened Geneva industrialist, it quickly became as popular as it was radical. But even after every apartment had been rented, the skeptical bankers who financed the project questioned whether the inhabitants of the building would still be happy there after twenty years. "The bank seems to be claiming that ordinary methods are doomed to an indisputable perpetuity, while everything progressive—and in this instance a particularly far-reaching kind of progressive—is doomed to certain death," wrote Le Corbusier.[15] Nonetheless, the building is still standing today.

5

At age forty-three, Le Corbusier began to dispense expertise even more vociferously than before. "Advance an argument, defend yourself, do not capitulate. Triumph!" he advised his mother, after telling her she must consult professional doctors and stop depending on natural medicine to deal with her frequent bouts of grippe. When Albert complained about the time constraints in completing a musical score, Le Corbusier informed their mother, "I told him: that's what life is. And that's how things get done. Someone who creates something always dances across a perilous tightrope. Man is capable of sublimating himself."[16]

For Le Corbusier himself, the feeling of walking on a tightrope was increasingly real. Alexandre de Senger was determined to prove that for Le Corbusier architecture and urbanism were merely a pretext, that his main objective was to preach communism and that his buildings were an attempt to further the Bolshevist cause. De Senger published a book, *The Bolshevist Trojan Horse;* the horse was Le Corbusier.[17] Auguste Klipstein gave Le Corbusier a copy shortly after it was published.

De Senger attacked *L'Esprit Nouveau* as "one of the most important magazines of Bolshevist propaganda," pointing out that the review was read in Russia.[18] Willfully misquoting Le Corbusier, De Senger claimed that in the magazine the architect had referred to the Gothic, Baroque, and Louis XIV styles as "veritable corpses." In truth, Le Corbusier had criticized the appropriation of these styles but not the styles themselves.[19] De Senger also wrote that Le Corbusier had declared rainbows less beautiful than machines—a deliberate misrepresentation of a comparison between rainbows and geometric forms that made no qualitative judgment.

Failing to mention that Ozenfant, too, was responsible for *L'Esprit Nouveau,* De Senger wrote, "The editor of this magazine was Le Corbusier, from La Chaux-de-Fonds. His most important collaborators are the Jews and freemasons Walter Rathenau and Adolf Loos. Most of Le Corbusier's other collaborators are also collaborators of the major Bolshevist newspaper *Le Monde,* edited by Henri Barbusse. Le Corbusier is known for his frequent trips to Moscow where he has received important commissions."[20] It was all either false or misleading, but de Senger's followers willingly subscribed to his diatribe.

In May 1934, de Senger was to publish an article called "L'Architecture en peril" in the periodical *La Libre Parole.* Here, too, his means of denigrating Le Corbusier was to accuse him of complicity with Jews: "The allies of international Jewry continue, despite the crash, to intrigue under different titles and programs in order to increase their fortunes and retain their influence."[21] This time, there were no tears. Le Corbusier wrote his mother that he felt honored by de Senger's diatribes. Such opposition put him on the level of Diderot, the organizer of a revolution, and recognized his influence. For a self-anointed martyr, opposition was the most effective incentive to continue on the path of rightness.

6

> Algiers (together with certain other privileged places such as cities on the sea) opens to the sky like a mouth or a wound. In Algiers one loves the commonplaces: the sea at the end of every street, a certain volume of sunlight, the beauty of the race.
>
> —ALBERT CAMUS

From the Hotel St. Georges in Algiers, Le Corbusier wrote his mother at the end of March 1931: "This is a splendid country where the fraternal beauties increase with every feature, from lovely sea to snowy mountains and to the desert. A charm, a light, and the endless attractiveness of the Muslim races. Here, more than ever—as at Rio—my heart is won and takes root." For fifteen days, he had studied the city of Algiers from every possible angle. "What Paris is in despairing lethargy, this land of colonization is in strength, in needs, in urgency of achievements. . . . How beautiful the world could be if we brought it into harmony! . . . Already I feel myself at one with this country; Le Corbusier the African."[22]

After returning to Paris, Le Corbusier got word that he was being asked to undertake urbanism in Transjordan. It was a "crescendo";[23] work was coming from everywhere. Mies van der Rohe and Walter Gropius invited him to show the Plan Voisin in a major exposition in Berlin. He was painting, with an exhibition planned for the fall (again making specious his claim of keeping his painting under wraps). He was also writing articles for *The New York Times* and working away on *The Radiant City*—a new and thrilling exegesis on urbanism.

Yvonne gave grace and balance to his domestic life. While the architect readied himself for a second trip to Algiers, she made another blouse for his mother out of assembled fabric samples. She was obsessed with finding all the right pieces and tested them for shrinkage. She cooked Albert his favorite ravioli. Le Corbusier wrote his mother, "I am entirely content. Our life flows by in order and good humor."[24]

The difficulties were with Marie Jeanneret and his health. As usual, Le Corbusier begged his mother for more mail, accusing her of saving her energy by writing to Albert and not to him. His repeated attacks of sinusitis and chronic nasal congestion exacerbated his irritation, and he became even more upset when his mother began to complain about her house while still refusing to hire a maid. By midsummer, Le Corbusier cracked: "You have always brought passion into these matters. Proclaiming your rights, charging others with bad intentions, nastiness or incapacity. This does not make the work easier; it creates a painful atmosphere. My stays at Lac Leman, ever since the house has been there, have been consistently tormented by this strained atmosphere. It is much more painful than you think. You don't realize how explosive you are with me, precisely when I need 24 hours of relaxation, you know what I have to deal with every day of my life. If you could give the situation some thought that would be a good thing. You must know I don't let things slide, but at the same time I don't try to make everything into a drama. What really annoys me is that in this whole business, from A to Z, I'm the one who receives your reproaches and Albert gets treated as a fine fellow. Believe me I'm not jealous, far from it. But consider the situation a little more carefully and you'll see what I mean."[25]

After all that, he instructed her, "But try to realize that life must be taken with as much serenity as possible."[26]

HE NEVER KNEW when the next onslaught would come from either her or Yvonne. In a spell of bad weather, Yvonne again became tired and nervous. In his next letter to his mother, in mid-July, he quipped, "Maman is always seething and . . . *arbitrary,* like all temperamental women."[27]

In August, he returned to Spain on his own, in part to escape both his torturers. The sights and people in Almería, Andalusia, and Málaga quickly restored his high spirits: "In everything here I sense the awakening of the Latin races, full of strength, health, the intelligence of accurate feelings." Reflecting about her from afar, he recognized that Yvonne was the essence of the type. On his way to Valencia, he characterized his wife to his mother as "like a little child, devoted, loving, loyal, and very dignified, but morbidly fierce."[28]

From Spain, Le Corbusier traveled on to continue his work in Algiers. It was, he claimed, fifty-four degrees, but even though he felt he was "dead from thirst"—so he wrote on a postcard on which he drew a skull and crossbones—he was thrilled to be in a place he loved and away from the two women whose crankiness and disapproval weighed on him more than all the critics and academies and architectural juries put together.[29]

LE CORBUSIER always had one current undertaking that was the ne plus ultra—a project that would allow him to realize his philosophy in its totality and change civilization. Now it was his major city plan for Algiers, on which he was going full throttle in the steamy North African city that August.

Then, just as he was about to set sail back to Europe, he had some devastating news. Marie Jeanneret's beloved dog, Bessie, had been run over. After the initial shock, he did his best to summon his sense of perspective: "Dear Maman, you must not interpret the effect of what was a pure accident as a stroke of fate. You must be aware of events, and sensitive to them, but not weak." He did not, however, trivialize the importance of a pet dog. He told his grieving mother that he had recently come to realize, "I've always met my dog's eyes with my own: dogs are a kind of mirror of tenderness and trust."[30] He craved constancy and affection wherever he could find them.

7

When Le Corbusier turned forty-four on October 6, he received greetings from all over the world; more important, this time his mother did not forget. He responded to her greetings by sending her a summary statement of his life. First, she should know the extent to which he suffered from stomach problems and colds; he was susceptible to sickness because of all the travel and "an intensity of work that knows neither schedule nor calendar. . . . People who live a clockwork life are more likely to be given a more regular bulletin of health."[31]

That reflection prompted one of his anti-Swiss diatribes: "Once over the border one returns, in France, to the country of *liberty.* What relief, what benign welcoming dust. Switzerland has placed itself under orders I cannot accept, for I am concerned with other things. A Vauxdois customs officer is a monument of brutal rigor and stupidity."[32]

Le Corbusier continued his overview: "Life here is calm, agreeable, productive. At forty-four, one needs one's lair with its hideouts and its *raisons d'être.* Then everything can flow without a hitch. Yvonne continues to be the understanding accompaniment to my life. That is serenity for me."[33]

His mother, however, impeded that serenity. Marie, now seventy-one and still living alone, had fallen down the stairs that led from the new room Le Corbusier was in the process of putting on the house. He implored her to change her ways and hire a maid—which was precisely why he had built a maid's room there. Le Corbusier considered the accident a result of her intractability and her deliberate resistance to living joyously.

He lashed out at both her refusal to have help and her suggestion that she might have to move:

> These dreadful threats are a distortion of your spirit. When we were kids, I remember you always made light of housework, relatively

speaking, and concentrated your energy on giving lessons, from which you obtained something for our own upbringing as well as a lively contact with your students. These threats, aside from your personal feelings, are a barrier you deliberately raise against us, thinking (what an illusion!) you could impose your concepts on us, though in such situations they are of no use to us whatsoever.

The Swiss mania for order annoys, disgusts, chills, and scandalizes me.

So all your efforts of persuasion are entirely futile.

And the consequence of this mental distortion is your feverishness, your terror of not being ready, your haste. . . . And you fall down the stairs.

I know I'm being harsh, and I make no efforts to mask my thoughts. No, this is an unfortunate aspect of your character that I implore you to turn your attention to. Pedantically, may I remind you of Jesus's remarks on the subject of Martha and Mary.

You see that the case has existed for a long time.

But you who read the Bible and can find something else in it besides Protestant points of view, take a lesson from it for life. There is a choice to be made in life—of the *important* things most of all. And you, your life, your image, what other people seek from you, is your artistic power, your freedom of mind, your personal, individual interpretation.

Life, life, life. That's what we all love.

We your children and their friends and companions have oriented our lives in this direction. *We have found our earthly happiness there.*

You will find yours there as well. Come back to it, the truth is here, and the atmosphere of the lake will be poignant with intensity, clarity, personality. Understand what I am saying: you make threats.[34]

Dressed as a cleaning woman, on holiday at Le Piquey, ca. 1930

THE ARCHITECT was becoming as discouraged about the state of the world overall as about his mother. As the end of 1931 approached, he believed now more than ever that completely new solutions were required if civilization were not going to continue its downward spiral.

His belief that society barely functioned was exacerbated by a bitter dispute concerning the enlargement of La Petite Maison. The head of public works in Lausanne had written Marie Jeanneret demanding that construction work stop because the necessary permits and permissions had not yet been organized. Rarely had the regulations and silliness of authorities infuriated him more. He wrote the official in Lausanne saying that everything had been done according to the rules, that he had personally met with the necessary people in Lausanne more than a year earlier, that it was impossible to stop construction in mid-November, and that his mother was a white-haired lady who had the right to be left in peace and not to have her health compromised.

Le Corbusier probably had not conformed to the letter of the law in planning the expansion of La Petite Maison. He still believed in his inalienable right to follow his own rules—especially in his capacity as his mother's protector. In this instance he prevailed, and the alterations to La Petite Maison were completed.

8

Le Corbusier always dreaded the way Christmas and New Year's threw life off course and led to "communal stupidity."[35] Now married a full year, Yvonne's expectations for the holidays only made matters worse; having grown up with few comforts, she was both childish and needy. The architect's greatest problem at the year's end, however, was knowing that his completed work was in that diplomatic pouch. The thrill of creation was over.

Nothing more was expected or needed, but Le Corbusier could not stop himself. For the next two months, he continued to send documents concerning details of the building. The architect made note of experiments he had undertaken with light waves in order to evaluate the acoustics, and he provided explanations for the reason that flat roofs on top of hot-water pipes were an effective means of melting and draining snow.

Le Corbusier then came to believe that his project for the Palace of Soviets had been "favorably received in all circles in Moscow, . . . [and] declared suitable for construction" and that it was to be the pinnacle of the current Five-Year Plan.[36] He was completely disconnected from reality. On February 28, 1932, a short list of three was announced, and he was not on it.

In *Izvestia,* the leading Moscow newspaper, Alexei Tolstoy wrote that the "Le Corbusiersianry" resembled "a strongbox—a latter-day feudal fortress—

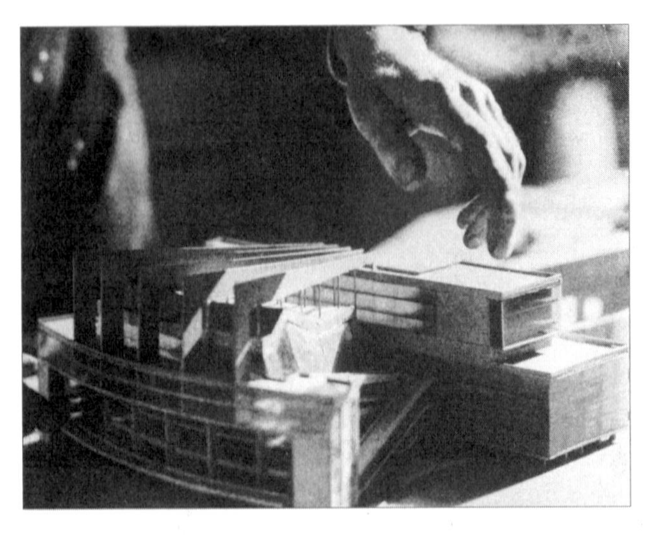

Manipulating the roof of a model of the auditorium of the Palace of the Soviets, in the office at 35 rue de Sèvres, 1934

Lecturing in Barcelona about the manifesto sent to Stalin following the verdict of the committee in Moscow concerning the construction of the Palace of the Soviets. Le Corbusier is speaking to, among others, Walter Gropius and José Luis Sert, March 29, 1932.

the home of a bandit protected by impregnable walls of gold. This is the ultimate devastation, a refusal of reality, a submission to materials, the cult of materials, fetishism; it is only one step away from the primitive condition of the psychological troglodyte."[37]

The winning design, by Ivan Zholtovsky, resembled an Italian Renaissance city, complete with a piazza and Roman-style coliseum. Le Corbusier declared, "We were expecting from the USSR an example of authority, edification and leadership, since such an example expresses the noblest and purest judgment. . . . There is no more USSR, no doctrine, no mystique, or anything else!!!"[38]

Then, in April, Le Corbusier drafted a telegram to Stalin calling the jury's decision an act of "criminal thoughtlessness." The scheme chosen for the palace, he subsequently informed the Soviet leader, "turns its back on the inspirations of modern society which found its first expression in Soviet Russia, and sanctions the ceremonial architecture of the old monarchies. . . . [T]he Palace of the Soviets will embody the old regimes and manifest complete disdain for the enormous cultural effort of Modern Times. Dramatic betrayal!"[39]

When Le Corbusier was then informed that Stalin had deliberately determined that architecture for the proletariat should be Greco-Roman, he decided to sever all ties with the Soviet Union. Although a version of the Centrosoyuz was built, Le Corbusier's flirtation with the new way of life in Moscow now came to a full stop.

But the controversy surrounding his travels and work in Russia was just beginning.

9

On Monday, March 14, 1932, in the Salle Wagram, a large Parisian auditorium, Gustave Umbdenstock, an architect who was a professor at l'Ecole Polytechnique and head of the studio at l'Ecole des Beaux-Arts, lashed out against the leader of the contemporary style that deprived human beings of the joy and optimism for which tradition in architecture was imperative. Umbdenstock accused his unnamed foe of making shoe boxes and vilified him for his use of concrete and his ideas about automobile circulation.

Le Corbusier considered the address an act of war. In response, he wrote *Crusade, or the Twilight of the Academies.* The small book, which appeared a few months after Umbdenstock's diatribe, amplified Le Corbusier's theory that a major campaign against modern architecture was being financed by large building companies, whose management felt threatened by the new technology he advocated. Businesses that specialized in slate, tile, zinc, and wood—rather than reinforced concrete—had joined forces against him and his allies. There was, Le Corbusier was convinced, a complete conspiracy determined to prevent him from realizing his ideas.

THE ATTACKS CONTINUED in a series of twelve articles that appeared in *Le Figaro,* the most widely read of Paris's many newspapers. Under the title "Is Architecture Dying?" they were written by Camille Mauclair—a poet, novelist, and critic whose real name was Séverin Faust. He linked *L'Esprit Nouveau,* the Bauhaus, and other modern movements to Bolshevism and declared Le Corbusier a Bolshevik.

The diatribe inspired a pleasant surprise. One of the people who came to Le Corbusier's defense was Amédée Ozenfant. Ozenfant wrote the paper a letter characterizing his former colleague's Russian engagement as a demonstration of French influence "on people who are looking to find a way," not as an adherence to anything Russian.[40]

Yet nothing compensated for the pain inflicted by the fate of Le Corbusier's design for the Palace of the Soviets. The architect had to deal not only with his own disappointment but also with that of the fifteen draftsmen in the office who had worked so diligently on the project. He felt that they had addressed the fundamental issues of circulation, acoustics, and ventilation, only to have these essential matters completely overlooked by the jury. Le Corbusier did not mind the attacks against him in Switzerland and France so much as he regretted the failure of the new Russia to understand the magnificence of what it was refusing.

10

Le Corbusier made his own rules for social behavior. One evening, at about six o'clock, he invited Charlotte Perriand to the construction site of the Swiss Pavilion. The architect pointed out corrections that needed to be made to the emerging structure, and Perriand took notes. Suddenly, Le Corbusier stopped in his tracks and, out of the blue, asked Perriand, who had been divorced two years earlier, how her life was going. She answered that all was well.

Then Le Corbusier blurted out: "Do you love women? I could understand that."

Sketch based on an Etruscan fresco he had seen in Tarquinia, drawn from memory, June 11, 1934

Perriand's reply was instant: "Of course not, what an idea!" To this, Le Corbusier replied, "In my studio, there's a tall boy, Pierre, who dreams about you night and day. Think it over."[41] Then the architect continued the working walk through the site as if nothing had been said.

A few days later, Perriand asked Pierre Jeanneret if Le Corbusier had told him about their discussion. He said that he had and asked Perriand how she felt. She told him she liked her freedom; he replied that he liked his.

Perriand eventually decided to continue the conversation with Le Corbusier. He cut her off right at the start, announcing, "I'm not your nanny."[42] Nothing was ever the same between them again.

11

The Swiss Pavilion, on the outer edge of Paris on the campus of the Cité Internationale Universitaire, has as its core an elegantly cantilevered rectangular slab that stands on graceful, anthropomorphic pilotis. The south facade is a pristine glass curtain wall, the north a clear composition of concrete blocks punctuated by minimalist square windows. Inside and out, there is a medley of sheer curved walls.

Le Corbusier made this vanguard structure, which was completed in 1932, despite spite of being hampered by severe budget constraints. Only three million francs were allotted for it, whereas similar buildings on the same campus were given twice that. He considered his creation of "a veritable laboratory of modern architecture" with such élan, in spite of the parsimony of his resources, a deliberate act of revenge at Swiss miserliness.[43]

On a curved wall near the entrance, there was a mural of photographs. They showed enlarged images of microbiology and micromineralogy, testifying to the combined wonders of technology and nature. As one proceeds through the building, Le Corbusier's ability to transform the ordinary is evident in the imaginative lamps and radiators and the energetic arrangement of hot-water pipes; it's as if he had taken dry, characterless Swiss bread and turned it into a brioche. Through his graceful manipulation of rudimentary components, the students' spartan bedrooms are light and amusing. White linoleum becomes fresh and mirrorlike; neatly integrated shelves, cupboards, and counters come to life like music.

But it was not well received. Le Corbusier himself was quick to point out that the naysayers were calling for something that more closely resembled a traditional chalet. He compared the inauguration ceremony to a funeral. Following a prosaic speech by a renowned Swiss mathematics professor, the audience had responded with complete silence. The overall style, and the photographic mural with its unusual content, shocked critics.

After World War II, the architect wrote, "In my innocence, I had been guilty of praising the wonders of nature, the glories of Almighty God."[44] "Fortunately" the mural had been destroyed by the Germans, who occupied the building in 1940. Edouard might tell his mother to accentuate the positive, but he still periodically played the role of Sarcasm.

12

The mayor of Algiers gave Le Corbusier free rein to redesign his city. With such a supportive client, Le Corbusier set out to create a plan that could revolutionize urbanism all over the world.

Le Corbusier proposed building upward. Skyscrapers would create space for two hundred thousand or more inhabitants within the city core. The Casbah would remain, but next to it there would be a new financial district, as well as a civic center with a courthouse and other public buildings. A second residential neighborhood would consist of skyscrapers built into the hillside and vast apartment complexes constructed on a 108-hectare property currently covered with vineyards. This plan allowed for the landscape of hills and valleys on the outskirts of town to remain undisturbed, still available for agricultural purposes, while also accommodating swimming pools and parks for walking and sports.

Le Corbusier believed that Algiers could be the fourth and final point of the star that already included Barcelona, Paris, and Rome. His efforts to realize his dream there would, within a decade, lead him inside the corridor of power at one of the lowest points in the history of France.

13

Le Corbusier attended the fourth CIAM, which took place in Athens from July 29 until August 10, 1933. On the day of his departure, he received an anonymous letter at his hotel, signed "X the Greek." "X" asked, "Without ornament, and with the present-day uniformity of construction materials, can the new architecture manage to express the specific character and the various sentiments of each country? I can see you eagerly answering me yes, and I am absolutely in agreement with you. You speak of geometry as only an ancient Greek could have done. You have opened my eyes, and I thank you with all my heart."[45]

"X" was responding specifically to the lectures Le Corbusier had just given, which became the basis of CIAM's *Charter of Athens*. Their premise was that the essential elements of urbanism were "the sky, trees, steel and concrete, in that order and that hierarchy."[46] That same year, Le Corbusier completed an apartment building near the outskirts of Paris that exemplified this philosophy. The seven-story structure at 24 rue Nungesser-et-Coli had floor-to-ceiling double-glazed windows front and back, so that light from both east and west flooded into apartments that spanned the entire building.

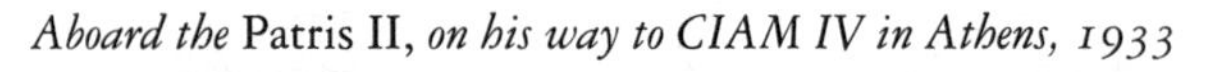

Aboard the Patris II, *on his way to CIAM IV in Athens, 1933*

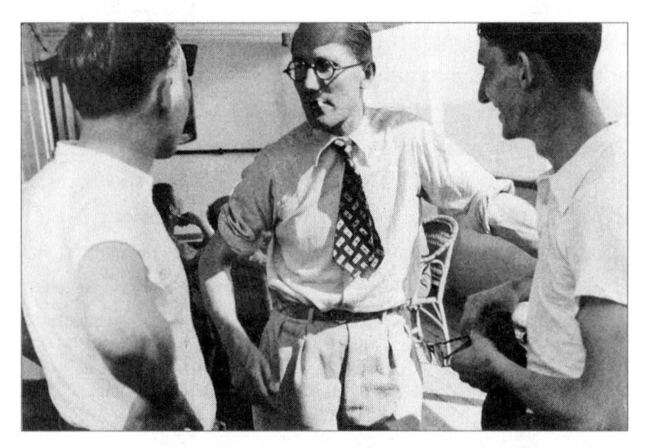

The tradition in Paris apartment buildings was to put the servants in small rooms under the roof. Le Corbusier knew these spaces better than most people, since his first Paris office and apartment, as well as the apartment in which he still lived, were initially maids' rooms of this type. On the rue Nungesser-et-Coli, he wanted to "free the servants from the frequently dreadful subjection of their rooms under the mansard roofs." He therefore put the servants' rooms on the ground floor and basement level, with the ones in the basement facing a courtyard that received ample sunlight. It was not, however, only the servants whose needs Le Corbusier was considering. The unusual distribution of space left the roof free for "the best-situated apartment in the whole house: instead of slates: lawns, flowers, bushes."[47]

24 rue Nungesser-et-Coli, 1933

Shortly after its construction, that duplex penthouse was reproduced in the latest volume of *The Complete Work.* The dwelling is shown to have a handsome modern dining room with large sliding glass doors that open onto a terrace with lovely plants and a garden chair. It also has an unusually high and austere platform bed on tall and lean stovepipe legs and several large paintings by Léger, as well as one by Le Corbusier himself. There is a cavernous studio with a brick wall and an efficient, shipshape kitchen in which a shapely dark-haired woman, wearing a blouse with wide ruffled lapels and short sleeves, is on view taking something out of a cabinet; she is the model of domestic perfection.

In another shot that presents the boldly geometric streamlined fireplace and the wide-open space of the living and dining areas, the same woman appears, this time from behind, on the balcony; now she is accompanied by a man, also seen from behind, in a robe. They look like the perfect urban couple from a film of the period: elegantly at home, happy together, impeccably dressed in their chic surroundings. What the photo captions fail to mention is that the woman is Yvonne and the man Le Corbusier himself. At the end of April 1934, they had moved from the rue Jacob to this penthouse.

14

It had not been an easy transition. Le Corbusier had found it hard to pack up and organize all of the papers he had accumulated over seventeen years. Yvonne was unhappy to give up St. Germain-des-Prés and leave the neighborhood where she knew the shopkeepers and could walk to her favorite cafés. For Le Corbusier, the vast amounts of space, the vistas, and the satisfaction of living in one of his own designs were worth the inconveniences. For her, it was Siberia.

Of course, there were some compensating amenities. They were again on the seventh floor, only now they could reach it by a small elevator. The duplex apartment was large and airy, and every last niche had been thought out carefully. Hinged walls that served as both doors and closets, and built-in shelves and cupboards were positioned ingeniously. The clean geometry of the straightforward plan, the bold planes of the floors and ceilings, and the lively staircase made the apartment a place of refreshment amid the complexity of Parisian life.

The textures of the apartment provided interesting juxtapositions: wood and plaster, marble and cane. The presence of water was also unusually strong. The bathroom, rather than being separated by a door, was open to the bedroom, with the bidet conspicuous as a piece of bedroom furniture. The sink was also in plain sight. Le Corbusier did not conceal the scenes of everyday ablutions in the usual manner of western designers; nor did he hide the water pipes. This most urbane of men never wanted to lose touch with the raw and vital elements of nature (see color plate 14).

Le Corbusier and Yvonne at 24 rue Nungesser-et-Coli, ca. 1935

The apartment gave Le Corbusier a superb studio, two stories high, full of daylight. With its curved ceiling and rough brick wall, that studio had aspects of the barn to which, in his youth, he had so happily retreated on the outskirts of La Chaux-de-Fonds. It was like being in the country in the city, and it made painting the central act of his life at home. If now the office that was formerly a ten-minute walk away required about an hour's travel time, whether by taxi or Métro, he did not mind. Le Corbusier would live at 24 rue Nungesser-et-Coli for the rest of his life.

15

Le Corbusier traveled to Algiers regularly. One evening there, he went to the Casbah to sketch in the light provided by streetlamps. Shortly after midnight, he was returning to his hotel along the narrow, empty streets when he was attacked with an expert maneuver called "*le coup du père François*."[48] While the origins of its name remain uncertain, this ancient technique involves one assailant addressing the victim with a question while an accomplice strangles him from behind by pressing hard on the jugular vein or carotid artery.

Le Corbusier was left unconscious. An hour later, when he began to come to, he instinctively asked himself who he was. Once he grasped what had happened, he knew how exceptionally lucky he was not to have been killed. Fascinated by the proximity of death, he recorded his impressions: "The ambience—in the depths of my unconscious—seemed to me a sort of shimmering golden puddle. Experts say all that gold and all that light are characteristic of moments of passage from life to death."[49]

Focused on death and danger following that attack, just before Le Corbusier and Yvonne moved to their new apartment, he wrote to the prefect of police to report a series of strange events that had occurred three doors down on the rue Jacob. At number 14, two renters had died of tuberculosis in 1927. In 1930, another resident had died of the same illness; so had a husband and wife in 1932. They had owned a boutique in the building, and now the wife of the new owner also had died from tuberculosis. All of them were hearty country people from the Auvergne. Since another couple was coming from the Auvergne, Le Corbusier alerted the prefect that they would die two years hence. The outcome of his prediction is unknown, but Le Corbusier had no doubt of his knowledge that a space could have a terminal impact on its inhabitants.

16

Winnaretta Eugénie Singer-Polignac, born in 1865—in a vast granite mansion called the Castle, overlooking the Hudson River in Yonkers, New York—was the twentieth of the twenty-four children of Isaac Merritt Singer, the tall, brawny, foulmouthed son of a German immigrant who, in 1850, had borrowed forty dollars to make a prototype for an improved sewing machine. He managed to get a patent, although it essentially copied someone else's idea.

Singer had begun fathering children when, at age nineteen, he married a fifteen-year-old. Winnaretta's beautiful mother, Isabelle Eugénie Boyer, half French and half English-Scottish, said to be Bartholdi's model for the Statue of Liberty, was the fourth woman to give him progeny. In 1863, she was seven months pregnant when she married Singer—although two other women claimed to be his wife, one as Mrs. Singer and one as Mrs. Merritt—in his large Fifth Avenue town house.

At about age five, Winnaretta was alone in her room at Brown's Hotel in London when it began to fill with smoke; the stranger who rushed in, threw her on his shoulders, and carried her to the street was Ivan Turgenev. She grew up in the English countryside in a hundred-room, four-story house called the Wigwam. Her father, whom she adored, died when she was ten years old, leaving her some nine hundred thousand dollars. For the rest of her life, she treated the anniversary of his death as a sacred day, saying she never recovered from her grief; sixty years later, she wrote, "the one thing I had, I lost then."[50]

When Winnaretta's mother remarried, they moved to Paris, and the girl became consumed by a passion for both art and music. Her stepfather had a title, but he also had a hunger for the Singer fortune. Winnaretta, at age twenty-one, decided to take her inheritance in her own hands and have it managed by Rothschild's bank. She began to indulge her own interests, buying a bold Manet from the artist's widow and a Monet from the painter himself.

At age twenty-three, the sewing-machine heiress acquired a large mansion not far from the Trocadéro. She married Prince Louis-Vilfred de Scey-Montbéliard, an aristocrat passionate for the hunt, at a ceremony from which her mother and greedy stepfather were conspicuously absent. On her wedding night, she stood on a wardrobe and threatened her husband with an umbrella, saying she would kill him if he touched her. That marriage was annulled, freeing her to marry, at age twenty-eight, someone who preferred his own sex as she preferred hers. The fifty-eight-year-old Prince Edmond de Polignac was a penurious composer who descended from a family high in the court of Louis XIV; the couple entertained creative geniuses like Jean Cocteau and were patrons of Gabriel Fauré and Diaghilev.

The prince didn't live long, but the former Winnaretta Singer honored his memory by being a great supporter of modern music. She added Stravinsky to the list of beneficiaries of her largesse, and on May 17, 1917, she had been, like Charles-Edouard Jeanneret, in the audience at the Théâtre du Châtelet when the Ballets Russes performed *Parade,* the collaboration of Picasso, Cocteau, and Satie that had inspired Apollinaire to use the term "L'Esprit Nouveau."

In 1921, after Marcel Proust encountered Winnaretta at a party in honor of the duke of Marlborough's marriage to another rich American, he described her as "icy as a cold draft, looking the image of Dante."[51] One wonders what Le Corbusier thought when he met her five years later. He had, after all, sculpted a likeness of Dante when he was fifteen.

In 1926, when the Salvation Army set out to buy and restore a large building as a women's dormitory, Winnaretta embraced the cause. One blustery winter night, she saw Salvation Army officers dispensing aid to a miserable group of society's outcasts, and she was moved to action. The commissioner of the army, Albin Peyron, then asked her if she would contribute to an addition to the existing Palais du Peuple, which was to house up to 130 homeless people. Her reply was positive, but with strings attached. Having been an early subscriber to *L'Esprit Nouveau,* she was fascinated by the links Le Corbusier made between architecture and music. Additionally, Albert Jeanneret was a friend of her friend Fauré. The princess told Peyron she might indeed fund a substantial part of the construction costs of the new building, but only if she could replace the army's chosen architect with Le Corbusier, who, in 1926, was working on a design for a villa for her in Neuilly-sur-Seine.

In June 1926, Le Corbusier went to the site of the Palais du Peuple and was deeply impressed by the work being done there. He wrote the princess that they might build a modest, stripped-down structure onto it, where he would orchestrate bold forms with impeccable proportions. He assured her the results would be magnificent.

The addition to the existing building was never constructed, but in 1929 the Salvation Army decided to create the Cité de Refuge, a shelter for up to six hundred people, at a cost of six million francs. Whereas most people whose money had American roots were substantially wiped out that year, the princess's fortune, which depended on a Canadian trust and was managed in Paris, flourished, and she offered half that money, again with the stipulation that Le Corbusier be the architect.

On June 24, 1930, the heiress laid the foundation stone. Eventually, she had to add more than a million francs to her gift when Le Corbusier went over budget, but, when the building was inaugurated by the president of the republic, Albert Lebrun, on December 7, 1933, her name appeared only on a small plaque over the entrance door saying "Refuge Singer-Polignac." This rich woman's modesty and generosity impressed Le Corbusier immensely. Heart, intelligence, and tenacity combined were his ideal.

17

The structure that opened on December 7, 1933, to house the homeless and provide a way station for immigrants was, in its heyday, a monument to visual inventiveness, technological advances, and, above all else, human dignity.

In the past, triumphant symbols of arrival, like large porticos and grand staircases, had belonged mainly to buildings associated with vast wealth. They demonstrated power—whether of the church, a monarchy, a strong government, or a giant of mercantilism. Now a new form of architectural welcome lifted the spirits of people who felt estranged from such institutions. A cubicle-shaped portico tiled in bright colors, a bridge, a vast rotunda, and a shimmering expanse of glass sheathing and mosaic bricks greeted the ex-convicts, unwed mothers, and tramps who previously had taken shelter underneath the bridges of the Seine. The sparkling sequence of geometric forms gave hope and dignity.

Today, our urban homeless burrow their way into basement soup kitchens and sleep in shelters. They are downtrodden by the message that their lives merit nothing better than cheap construction standards and shoddy materials. But when the Cité de Refuge opened its doors, it elevated the spirits of all who entered. For a very different clientele than at his luxurious villas, Le Corbusier had again succeeded in positively transforming human feelings through the architectural environment.

LIKE THE MONASTERIES of Ema and Mount Athos, the Cité de Refuge was meant to provide all the necessities of life for a large group of people living collectively. The program for the new building called for places for the residents to sleep and eat, with public assembly spaces and a range of support services including kitchens and a laundry. The entire structure was to be airtight, with a climate-control system that purified the air as

Facade of the Cité de Refuge, ca. 1933

it heated or cooled it; this was among the first structures in France to be air-conditioned.

To achieve all that was not easy; from start to finish, there were disputes revolving around building codes. Pierre Jeanneret and Le Corbusier tried to bend laws, circumventing regulations concerning the height of the structure and the construction of the glass-and-steel curtain wall. The Cité de Refuge took longer and cost more than anticipated.

But when the pioneering structure for the homeless was inaugurated on that raw December day at the nadir of an international economic depression, many people's spirits soared. In his signature bow tie, Le Corbusier beamed in the company of President Lebrun, the minister of public health, and other government officials and dignitaries. Harsh criticism was expected for a building that violated tradition so audaciously, but there were those who instantly grasped its fresh and optimistic spirit.

The day following the opening, an anonymous journalist in *Les Temps* wrote that the "architects, Messrs. Le Corbusier and Jeanneret, whose fecund originality we already know, have given the edifice the appearance of a beautiful ship, where everything is clean, comfortable, useful, and gay." The critic recognized the transformative powers of architecture, saying that at the entrance counter "unhappy people will come to deposit their misery like the rich deposit their valuables at the windows in a bank."[52]

18

The dormitories of the Cité de Refuge filled up quickly. Soup was soon being ladled out free of charge. But not everything was as it was meant to be. The climate-control system, so radical in concept and execution, was a problem. Residents claimed to be suffocating from their inability to open windows at night when the ventilators were turned off. A doctor complained of treating children deprived of adequate oxygen. The temperature inside reached thirty-three degrees Celsius.

An intractable Le Corbusier refused to perforate the glass curtain wall with windows. He summoned Gustave Lyon, the expert who had, among other things, installed the air-conditioning at the Salle Pleyel, and Dr. Jules Renault, an authority on child care, to the site, and they both issued reports disputing the claims that necessary ultraviolet rays were failing to reach the children through the airtight membrane. Le Corbusier claimed the problems could be remedied by adjustments to malfunctioning machinery. But in January 1935, the Seine Prefecture condemned the Cité de Refuge for code violations, and the police ordered the installation of sliding windows within forty-five days.

Le Corbusier was desperate not to comply. He managed to get government officials to give some time to the engineers he employed to find another solution. Then Le Corbusier proposed drilling tiny holes in the glass wall, saying that the holes could be covered in the winter. But by the end of the year, he was forced to put in the new windows.

The problems did not stop there. By 1936, tiles had begun to fall off the rotunda. Children were deemed at risk of being injured when they went out to play. The tiles had been applied with mortar directly to the reinforced concrete, a method that failed in extreme heat. The architects and contractors together had to pay for half of the cost of repairs.

Le Corbusier never accepted blame for any of these problems. "The City of Refuge is not a fantasy; the city of refuge is a proof," he declared. Its users "make a fuss and argue in perpetual confusion between their psychological reactions and their physiological reaction. They don't know at all what they're talking about; they are obsessed by fixed ideas and it is this obsession that is the cause of their protests. We have the obligation to ignore this and to pursue positive and scientific work with serenity."[53] The words were almost identical to his retorts whenever his mother criticized him for the leaks at La Petite Maison.

OVER THE YEARS following its construction, the concrete at the Cité de Refuge developed numerous cracks. Windows broke, paint peeled. But not all of the damage was the fault of the design. On August 25, 1944, the last day of the liberation of Paris, the Germans dropped a bomb directly in front of the building, shattering all the remaining glass in the facade.

On one visit to the Cité de Refuge when repairs were being made shortly after the war, Le Corbusier was shocked to discover that his pure concrete columns in the interior had been papered with materials imitating wood and marble and that an ornate and garish mural had been painted over his wall of glass bricks. In 1948, he oversaw a complete restoration free of charge, with Pierre taking on the bulk of the details. Today, some elements reflect their original concept, but a lot has been altered. The current Cité de Refuge is a ghost of the original. The structure on the edge of the thirteenth arrondissement was ultimately rebuilt so disastrously that Le Corbusier later announced, "The building can no longer be thought of as architecture."[54] What was built optimistically still stands as a symbol of hope and genius but also of decay, disrespect, and failure.

19

In spite of its flaws, the Salvation Army building won Le Corbusier an invitation to receive a Legion of Honor. The day after the inauguration, on December 8, 1933, he wrote the faithful Frantz Jourdain his response.

> You offer me, with a generosity of heart I find deeply touching, the red ribbon that consecrates so many efforts. Your entire life having been devoted to the struggle for what is good, you do not forget that others follow in your footsteps and, having arrived, yourself, at the pinnacle of honors, you turn your solicitude toward them as a spiritual father. I hope my response to your offer will not be taken as that of a naughty boy, nor as that of an embittered man, nor as that of some sort of nihilist. Yet I must tell you that my attitude in life has always been a matter of a fierce liberty, and that *at the present time,* when good and evil are confused in a dangerous mixture, I owe it to myself—and to those who on all sides have acknowledged my efforts as a useful direction—to keep apart from all such consecrations and to remain the man of my idea: a man still at the beginning of his investigations.
>
> I have twice already refused the Legion of Honor. On the occasion of

the L'Esprit Nouveau; and then on the occasion of the Palace of the League of Nations. That time, scandalously enough, it was Lemaresquier who offered it to me: an exchange, a bargain!

Today, my dear friend, the atmosphere is different. You have made a gesture of friendship and esteem. Such is my reward! Remember that in 1922 I was without resources and you allowed me to produce the panorama of the "*Contemporary City.*" Eleven years later you consider that I have deserved further support. Here is another reward. I receive this consecration from you with a deep satisfaction and with a certain pride. Thank you from the bottom of my heart. And let this consecration remain between us without ribbon or a certificate. That way I am happy and satisfied. In the present state of my existence, the author of "The Twilight of the Academies" can no longer accept the Legion of Honor. This is a simple and direct decision, between the two of us. It is not a manifesto; it is an inner manifestation of my own state of mind—nothing more.

Here in Paris, and in Moscow as well, *L'Humanité* accuses me of being vulgar bourgeois. *Le Figaro* and Hitler denounce me as a Bolshevist. I am and desire to remain *an architect and an urbanist* with all the consequences which that may involve.

And I desire above all to remain in possession of your esteem, quite simply, as before, by the effect of my efforts which I seek to pursue in all simplicity and strength.[55]

Eight days later, he wrote Anatole de Monzie, the minister of education:

Maître Frantz Jourdain has made (he tells me) a formal request for me to be awarded the ribbon of the Legion of Honor.

It is with some embarrassment that I must reject this disinterested initiative, for it is my desire not to receive the Legion of Honor. I have informed Frantz Jourdain of the fact, but he seems not to understand me.

You will greatly oblige me by willingly acceding to my desire and above all by being willing not to consider my gesture as a pretentious manifestation. On the contrary, what is involved here is an attitude dictated by an inward, entirely individual state of consciousness, one exclusive of all publicity. My entire life being devoted to an effort which finds the academies constantly in its path, I have no choice but to remain apart from a distinction that would oblige me to enter the rank of certain people with whom I am in acute disagreement.[56]

20

As Le Corbusier was building, the world was moving in horrific directions. By October 1934, the writer Carl von Ossietsky had been in concentration camps for twenty months. He had been incarcerated the day following the burning of the Reichstag and imprisoned in Sonnerburg and Esterwegen. A committee was formed to protest this act. Von Ossietsky's main offense seems to have been that, as a newspaper editor in Berlin, he had protested the budget of the Third Reich. Among those who joined the committee and signed the letter of protest were Thomas Mann and Le Corbusier.

Still, Le Corbusier had no clear ideology or political stance. In this same period, through Pierre Winter, his new neighbor on the rue Nungesser-et-Coli, he grew close to the fascist organization Le Faisceau. Winter wrote newspaper articles extolling the merits of Le Corbusier's housing and stated that Pessac was a concept well suited for the ideal fascist state.

Philippe Lamour, the lawyer who had represented the architect with the League of Nations, joined Winter in forming the Parti Fasciste Révolutionnaire; Mussolini was one of their heroes. Le Corbusier worked with Lamour on several publications and even tried to have Lamour's new magazine take over *L'Esprit Nouveau.* Le Corbusier remained friendly with Lamour throughout the next decade—apparently unbothered by Lamour having gone to Germany in 1931 with Otto Abetz, a head of the paramilitary organization Reichbanners, to create a German cell of the Front Unique.

Le Corbusier was similarly unfazed by the rise of fascism in Italy. Adriano Olivetti, the director general of the typewriter company that bore his name and another of those rare businessmen whom Le Corbusier admired as a form of modern hero, was an irresistible lure. Olivetti invited Le Corbusier to come to his offices near Turin to discuss issues of urbanism, and Le Corbusier engaged in a series of projects for Olivetti, although none of them were completed. Italy was welcoming; in 1934, the architect gave lectures in Venice at the Palazzo Ducale and began negotiations in Turin about a factory for Fiat. He imagined that the country of his early inspiration would become the land of his support—so much so that, by the end of the decade, he happily anticipated that one of his backers would be Benito Mussolini.

Yet Le Corbusier could join forces against Il Duce as readily as he would work for him. In 1933, the architect and Pierre Winter, François de Pierrefeu, and Hubert Lagardelle created two reviews: *Prélude* and *L'Homme Réel.* The agendas of the publications were unclear, but the heroes included Nietzsche and Gandhi, and their editorial pages protested Mussolini and fought fascism, while supporting Spanish anarchists and republicans. When Le Corbusier had written his mother and Hélène de Mandrot that he had faith in no one political system, he had been telling the truth; he would support or oppose almost anyone or anything, since the sole issue that counted was who would let him promulgate his ideas and build.

XXXII

1

> On the other hand, in America, in the Republic, one must waste a whole day in paying serious court to the shopkeepers in the streets, and must become as stupid as they are; and over there, no opera.
>
> — STENDHAL, *The Charterhouse of Parma*

The Museum of Modern Art in New York organized an exhibition of Le Corbusier's recent work that was to start on October 24, 1935. At last the architect went to the United States. Following the exhibition opening, he was to go on a lecture tour. He had agreed to lower lecture fees than he wanted—between seventy-five and one hundred dollars per engagement—because he was so curious to see North America and hoped to encounter clients there. He conceived of the United States as a gold mine, which made him irritated about the fees but optimistic that this was the land of unparalleled opportunity.

Le Corbusier left Le Havre on October 16, ten days after his forty-eighth birthday. Sailing first-class on board the *Normandie,* the legendary French liner, he wrote down English phrases he expected to need in the upcoming weeks: "inside street not exposed to rain, snow, or sun," "swimming pool," "people who bore me," and "here's looking at you," written next to a drawing of a martini glass in the form of an exclamation point.[1]

As soon as he arrived, he got off to a rocky start with the American press. A *New York Herald Tribune* article bore the headline "Skyscrapers Not Big Enough, Says Le Corbusier at First Sight," and smaller headers declared "Finds American Skyscrapers 'Much Too Small' . . . Thinks They Should be Huge and a Lot Farther Apart."[2] *The New York Times* also put a negative spin on Le Corbusier's initial impressions with the headline "Venice 'Best City,' Le Corbusier Finds" and the statement "he feels the average city leaves much to be desired."[3]

Finds American Skyscrapers 'Much Too Small'

Herald Tribune photo—Acme

Charles Edouard Le Corbusier, the famous French architect, with a model of his Villa Savoye, which he recently designed

Skyscrapers Not Big Enough, Says LeCorbusier at First Sight

French Architect, Here to Preach His Vision of 'Town of Happy Light,' Thinks They Should Be Huge and a Lot Farther Apart

Charles Edouard Le Corbusier, most vocal and most controversial of the prophets of the new architectural era, saw New York City for the first time yesterday. After a cursory inspection of the modern Babylon he gave a simple recipe for its improvement.

"The trouble with New York," he said, "is that the skyscrapers are much too small. And there are too many of them."

M. Le Corbusier arrived on the French liner Normandie to preach his doctrines in America under the auspices of the Museum of Modern Art. His old dictum "a house is a machine to live in," did much to sprinkle Europe and the United States with concrete and steel "functional" dwellings, and he hopes that his new one, "a town is a tool," will persuade the local citizenry to rebuild their cities by the Corbusier plan.

The leader of the sternest school of modernists described his scheme for the city of the future at the Museum of Modern Art, 11 West Fifty-third Street, where he will lecture at the opening of an exhibition of his work on October 24. Yesterday there was no sign of the exhibition, but the show of Fernand Leger's strange, mechanistic paintings made an appropriate setting for M. Le Corbusier, whose eggshaped head and face, bisected by a pair of thick spectacles with a heavy black frame, make him look like an up-to-date prophet. He was wearing an orange shirt, a black necktie with red spots and a gray suit. He complained of a headache, but he was able to talk volubly.

City All Right as Far as It Goes

"New York is the most beautiful manifestation of man's power, courage, enterprise and force," he said, "but it is utterly lacking in order and harmony and the comforts of the spirit which must surround humanity. The skyscrapers are little needles all crowded together. They should be great obelisks, far apart, so that the city would have space and light and air and order. Those are things that men need, just as much as they need bread or a place to sleep. Those are the things that my Town of Happy Light does have."

He described his "Town of Happy Light" in rapid Swiss French. He knew only enough English to be able to complain bitterly when one of the amateur interpreters translated him wrongly. He never was satisfied with the translation of the name for his town, which is called "Ville Radience" in French.

As he explained it, it is based on a series of calculations of the minimum light, air and circulation requirements of the average human being. His first problem, he said, was to accommodate these requirements to the new need for communal living. He hates the garden city idea, for he feels that it spreads a town so thin that the inhabitants lose their collective force. Thus he figures on an occupancy of about 2,400 persons an acre.

But the people will live in very tall apartment houses, built on the ribbon plan, and supported on high piers, like stilts, so that the whole ground space is left free for circulation. He believes that the apartments need cover only 12 per cent of the available space, leaving the remaining 88 per cent free for parks and playing fields. The ground would be reserved for strollers and pedestrians. Rapid transit would run beneath it, and automobiles would travel from one huge apartment house to the next on highways fifteen feet above the ground.

Idea Includes Five-Hour Day

The highways would connect most of the apartment houses, and each house would have a large parking space. A roadlike corridor would run down the middle of each floor in the houses, and on either side would be apartments. Sports would be concentrated at the bases of the houses, so that a man coming home from his five hours' work would find recreation waiting for him, and on the housetops are to be big sun decks.

"You see, my plan makes a town a tool for human use," said M. Le Corbusier. "It came to me several years ago when I was lecturing in Buenos Aires, and when the Russian government asked me to do a plan for an enlarged Moscow, I developed it in full technical detail. It has all been published in by book, 'Urbanisme.' I have worked it out since for Barcelona, Stockholm, Geneva, Algiers, Nemours, which is a new city in North Africa, and the City of Zlin, where the Bata shoe factory is."

M. Le Corbusier hopes that his plan will be put into effect in Zlin and in Nemours. Moscow turned him down, because, he said, the Soviet government had taken a lamentable artistic turn to the right. He is not very hopeful of seeing many 'Towns of Happy Light' during his lifetime, for he says frankly that the present structure of society is not favorable to their establishment.

"In a century of the machine age we have made wonderful things and a fearful disorder," he said. "Man is the slave of the machine now, but man can do such miracles that if the problem of man in modern society is once solved man can make the machine do his bidding. The central problem is housing. Housing is a matter of mass production today. The old technics are completely dead. My town is the town of the future."

Finds Americans "Chic Types"

He has hopes of making America see this, for he finds Americans "chic types," intelligent, generous, courageous and large of view. His five-week tour will take him as far as Kalamazoo, Mich., and Madison, Wis. He feels that in this country more than any other the machine age has had its full expression, and he believes that here before anywhere else machines will be mastered.

"I do not care how or where they are mastered, though," he said. "I do not care if it is Communism or Fascism that puts up my cities, or something else. I know that here I have made a plan for human happiness. I have arranged so that men can enjoy for the first time the fruits of their own labors, and whatever form of society puts my plan into effect is the right form of society."

"Skyscrapers Not Big Enough, Says Le Corbusier at First Sight," New York Herald Tribune, *October 22, 1935*

Believing that the skyscraper was a miracle of modern urbanism and the machine age, the architect was disappointed with the examples he found in New York. He thought a building of great height should be large enough to contain up to forty thousand people, and that if it was that size it could stand alone and face nothing but the cosmos: "The true splendor of the Cartesian skyscraper: the bracing, stimulant, optimistic, radiant spectacle offered from each office through the limpid windows opening onto space. Space! This response to the aspirations of being, this release offered to the respiration of the lungs and the beating of the heart, this effusion of vision from afar, from on high, so vast, infinite, limitless. The total sun in a pure, fresh air afforded by mechanical installations."[4] He felt that New York's skyscrapers did not put their inhabitants in direct connection with the wonders of the universe, were too small, and were too numerous and too close together, forcing people to look directly at the windows of another building rather than over the landscape or toward the sun.

He considered the city's tall buildings the manifestation of the selfishness inherent in capitalism. The craving for personal financial gain mattered more to their developers than did the benefits to humankind. The many small-scale skyscrapers of New York were the direct result of human competitiveness gone unchecked.

The press was not going to give him an easy time about this or much else. Le Corbusier's solution to the needs of the city—the Ville Radieuse—was translated in the *Herald Tribune* as "Town of Happy Light." It is thought that the anonymous journalist responsible for that misnomer was Joseph Alsop, who spoke French perfectly but had little use for modernism and happily belittled it. Alsop mocked "M. Le Corbusier" as someone "whose egg-shaped head and face, bisected by a pair of thick spectacles with a heavy black frame, make him look like an up-to-date prophet."[5] It was not the welcome Le Corbusier had anticipated in the land where he hoped to realize his boldest aims.

Even though Le Corbusier quibbled over the size of America's skyscrapers, they were a revelation to him. He was inspired by these buildings to abandon his usual stance against architectural historicism and the use of decorative elements on building exteriors. Having always declared his distaste for the architecture of the High Renaissance and his belief that new buildings should be completely modern in appearance, he now reversed himself on both fronts: "So it was in New York that I learned to appreciate the Italian Renaissance. You might think it was *real,* it was so well done. . . . The Wall Street skyscrapers—the oldest ones—add on to their summits the superimposed orders of Bramante, with a clarity in the moldings and the proportions which delight me."[6]

Before he took the trip to the United States, Le Corbusier had imagined its skyscrapers constructed of steel, which he pictured as the dominant material of New York and Chicago. He was shocked to discover that many were clad in stone instead. Rather than having this unexpected use of a possibly inappropriate material mitigate his pleasure, here, too, he found himself happily surprised: "I must admit that this stone is lovely under the seaboard skies of New York. The sunsets are moving. The sunrises (I've seen them) are admirable: in the purplish mist or the dim atmosphere, the solar fanfare explodes in a salvo, raw and distinct on the side of one tower, then on the next, then on so many more. An alpine spectacle which illumines the city's vast horizons. Pink crystals, of pink stone."[7]

Focusing on what Le Corbusier disliked rather than what he admired, the journalists missed the way the world-famous architect still had the soul of that twenty-year-old who had succumbed to the colors of Siena.

2

Three days after the *Normandie* docked in New York, Le Corbusier gave a radio address from the RCA Building. He was introduced to his audience as "the artist-architect whose influence is recognized in all parts of the civilized world" by a Mrs. Claudine Macdonald, who explained that he would speak in French and she would translate.[8]

Le Corbusier described to the audience the vision he had just before his arrival, when the *Normandie* had stopped for quarantine, required at that time: "I've seen rising out of the mists a fantastic, almost mystical City. 'Here is the temple of the New World!' But the ship moves on, and the apparition has turned into an image of an unheard-of savagery and brutality."[9] Standing there in his impeccable suit, the architect continued,

> This is certainly the most apparent manifestation of the power of modern times. Such brutality and savagery by no means displease me. This is how all great undertakings begin: by strength.
>
> At evening, in the city's avenues, I have come to an appreciation of this population which, by a law of life all its own, has managed to create a race: fine-looking men, very beautiful women.[10]

Le Corbusier declared, "I have brought into my realm of architecture and urbanism, with the simplicity of a professional who has devoted his life to the study of the first cycle of the machine age, certain propositions which appeal to every modern technique but whose final goal is to transcend mere utility. This indispensable goal is to give men of the machine civilization the joys of heart and health."[11] Here, the celebrant—the robust athlete and lover of women—and the manic architect who worked to make concrete and superhighways the frank vocabulary of modern life were one and the same: possessed by a supreme reverence for the magic of existence.

LE CORBUSIER walked through the rest of the RCA Building with Fernand Léger, who was also having an exhibition of his work at the Museum of Modern Art. At the top of the seventy-story-high stepped tower, he was riveted by a large red needle; it was a second hand turning in a large clock that showed the passage of each minute in a circular frame marked one to sixty. To the side of this clock there was an hour clock. He said to Léger, "The hours will return tomorrow. But this first dial, of seconds, is something cosmic, it is time itself, which never returns. This red needle is a material witness of the movement of worlds."[12]

"Time belongs to architecture," he told his radio audience. "Today the city of modern times can be born, the happy city, the radiant city."[13]

The United States, where stodginess was not as embedded as in Europe, was where such a birth could happen. "America, in permanent evolution, and in possession of infinite material resources, and animated by an energy-potential unique in the world, is indeed the first country capable of achieving this task today, and in a condition of exceptional perfection. It is my deepest conviction that the ideas I am setting forth here and which I am offering in the phrase 'Radiant City' will find their natural terrain in this country."[14]

In the upcoming weeks Le Corbusier explained his concepts to anyone who would listen and searched for the clients who might transform them into reality. He gave lectures in Connecticut at the Wadsworth Atheneum in Hartford and at Wesleyan and Yale Universities; in Poughkeepsie, New York, at Vassar Collage; and in Cambridge, Massachusetts, at Harvard University and MIT. Then he headed south to the Philadelphia Art Alliance; north again to Bowdoin College in Brunswick, Maine; and then south once more to Princeton University, where he gave a sequence of three lectures before proceeding to the Municipal Art Society of Baltimore and returning to New York to speak at Columbia University—all this before heading off for a week in the Midwest. He was like a tireless politician on the campaign trail, energized by his faith in himself and his mission.

3

He had imagined audiences would embrace him as a messiah. The students and museumgoers who attended his talks were less than he hoped for, but there was one person who accorded Le Corbusier total understanding.

Marguerite Tjader Harris, a bright and lively American writer, was the daughter of a Swedish inventor and sportsman and an American heiress. She had a mesmeric smile, her father's well-defined Scandinavian features, and her mother's wealth. Married in 1925 to Overton Harris, a prominent New York attorney, in the early 1930s she had left her husband in hopes of finding a happier life in the Alps with their three-year-old son, Hilary.

In Vevey, when she wasn't skiing or mountain climbing, the blue-eyed, red-haired Tjader Harris looked ravishing in her stylish clothes. She favored turban hats and sported a coat with an oversized leopard-skin collar and cuffs that matched her toddler son's overcoat. She was quietly at ease in the world; in the sailing season, she did not hesitate to reveal her capable and athletic body.

One day early in 1932, Tjader Harris was out walking near Lac Leman. She gave in to her curiosity about what lay on the other side of the wall surrounding the garden at La Petite Maison and rang the bell. The diminutive, white-haired Marie Jeanneret appeared. Tjader Harris was instantly captivated by the older woman's African slippers. Embarrassed to have disturbed her, the heiress faltered and then asked if the house was for rent. Le Corbusier's mother explained that it was not, that her son had built it for her to live in year-round. When Tjader Harris then expressed her admiration for the design and for the slippers, Marie Jeanneret invited her in.

Marguerite Tjader Harris sailing, Long Island Sound, 1920s

About a month later, Tjader Harris met the son who had designed the house. They began to see each other whenever he visited his mother. Soon enough, they were driving through the vineyards above the lake, discussing where she, too, might build a house designed by him. Le Corbusier assured her that the terrain was perfect and that it would be an interesting project. She quickly warned him that they could not start until she knew more about her current financial situation, which was changing because of the Depression and because she was in the process of a divorce. It would also depend on how her mother, who lived in Connecticut, felt about the project. Nonetheless, by the end of April, Le Corbusier had made plans; he told Tjader Harris that this was his way of expressing his gratitude for her kindness to his mother.

At the same time, Tjader Harris had written to warn him that she was skeptical about her ability to proceed. The heiress had learned that her family was in dire financial straits—at least by the terms of the rich—and that she would have access to only a fraction of the funds she would need to build. In error, she addressed the letter to the rue de Seine rather than the rue de Sèvres. The letter was therefore delayed, and Le Corbusier had already sent her his ideas before receiving the warning.

Tjader Harris then decided that she could consider building a much smaller house if Le Corbusier could come up with a budget of between twenty-five thousand and thirty thousand Swiss francs. She also wrote the architect that she had seen his mother again and greatly admired the older woman's "splendid gayety of mind."[15]

At the start of May, Tjader Harris received several neatly executed bird's-eye views of the revised house. Ecstatic, she took an apartment near the beach in Vevey in hopes that she would be able to start the building project nearby. She wrote Le Corbusier that his design was "the realization of my dreams which you have crystallized so perfectly."[16] Ostensibly she was just discussing architecture and a house, but her tone had all the portent of a romance in the making.

The project had summoned a burst of energy. Le Corbusier's design had two wings built on pilotis that interlocked in a bold central space with a third, shorter wing shooting out from the middle and supported by taller columns that elevated it above the other two. There was also a semicircular extension that resembled a Romanesque apse. The agglomeration of terraces, ramps, and gracious living spaces was a plastic manifestation of unmitigated ecstasy.

NOTHING FURTHER HAPPENED with the house project, but Marguerite Tjader Harris and Le Corbusier remained sporadically in touch. In 1934, shortly after her marriage was officially terminated, the divorcée sent Le Corbusier some photographs she had taken of La Petite Maison, for which he thanked her warmly.

As soon as he was in New York at the Park Central Hotel, he wrote her again. By now he was addressing her simply as "*Amie.*" Tjader Harris was at her mother's house in Darien, Connecticut, an hour's train ride north of New York's Grand Central Terminal. He gave his complicated schedule—with the key information that he would be free from 11:30 p.m. on the coming Thursday until noon on Friday. A series of letters followed in rapid succession, simply to tell her even more precisely when he would be available. Because of professional obligations, the best moment would be starting at midnight.

They saw each other sooner, however. On the weekend before the Thursday to which he referred, Marguerite Tjader Harris drove into the city. In 1984, Tjader Harris wrote a "Portrait of Le Corbusier" that has never been published. In it, she describes Le Corbusier's first Saturday in New York, five days after his arrival. She and he went to the top of the Empire State Building, the Chrysler Building, and the RCA Building so that he could observe the city from above. This is another case of a discrepancy in different accounts of Le Corbusier's life. In *When the Cathedrals Were White,* the book Le Corbusier wrote in 1937 about his American trip, the architect describes going to the top of the RCA Building on his third day in the United States—only hours before his opening at the Museum of Modern Art a few blocks away—and makes it the occasion of his observing the clock needle with Léger. Tjader Harris's recollections have him first reaching that sweeping view of New York two days later. It seems likely that Tjader Harris's account is the more reliable, and that when Le Corbusier wrote his memoir of the trip three years later, he made Léger his companion because he had reasons to leave her out of the scenario.

Le Corbusier and Tjader Harris took the subway down to Wall Street and up to Harlem: "He was like a horse, fretting against the bridles of his many activities. . . . Already, he was trying to formulate some form of urbanism that could bring order into the confusion he saw. . . . You could feel how his brain registered every impression, visual and audible; one minute he was enthusiastic, the next, disgusted."[17]

That evening, Le Corbusier and Marguerite Tjader Harris went to Connecticut. The small and exclusive residential enclave on Long Island Sound was almost entirely the bastion of rich white Protestants, a "restricted community" where neither Jews nor blacks owned property and where Tjader Harris was among the few Catholics. She lived with her six-year-old son and her mother in the family's Victorian mansion.

They also owned a beach shack nearby, on a small island. A simple and straightforward *cabanon* with a fireplace and a deck that faced the sea, it could be reached easily by rowboat. Le Corbusier and Tjader Harris went out there that evening. He impressed her greatly when he removed his glasses and dove into the bracing saltwater.

For years to come, the architect and the American divorcée reminisced about their subsequent hours in the shack, their romance at the edge of the sea. When Le Corbusier ultimately built his getaway in Roquebrune-Cap-Martin, it strongly echoed the place where he and Tjader Harris spent that October evening.

4

New York remained Le Corbusier's base camp during the upcoming weeks as he gave his lectures to the north and south of the city. This served well for trysts with Marguerite Tjader Harris. Besides meeting in the middle of the night, the two went to jazz clubs in Harlem and toured the region.

The automobile figured in their romance. Le Corbusier's urban schemes featured highways as central elements; vehicular circulation and parking facilities were pivotal concerns. Beyond recognizing the growing reality of cars, the architect had also long reveled in their capability and the power and fun they afforded their users. He loved to drive from Paris into the French countryside with Yvonne or on his longer trips to Spain or Switzerland. Now he was in the country of Henry Ford and the assembly line and of highways that allowed higher speeds. With Tjader Harris in that autumn of 1935, he experienced the pleasures of driving as never before.

Marguerite Tjader Harris owned a brand-new Ford, a powerful V8 painted a sporty tan.[18] Six-year-old Hilary was happy in the rumble seat, and the three of them took to the road. The weather was ideal, the days crisp and bright. Le Corbusier marveled at the noble bridges spanning the rivers surrounding Manhattan. The George Washington Bridge struck him as the most beautiful in the world. Taking its giant step across the daunting width of the Hudson, it was marvelous with its steel cables and its height that permitted large ships to pass underneath. Le Corbusier felt that suspension bridges were "a spiritual feature," and that the G.W. was "the sole site of grace in the disheveled city."[19]

When they left Manhattan through the dramatic darkness of the Holland Tunnel and crossed the marshlands of New Jersey, Le Corbusier was likewise exhilarated. Without indicating who his traveling companions were, he later described the experience in *When the Cathedrals Were White.* He wrote, "This afternoon I crossed the Hudson through the Holland Tunnel, then took the 'Sky-Way', so-called for the way its enormous length rises high above the industrial districts, the coastal bays, the railroad lines and highways, on its arches or its pilotis. A roadway without art, for no thought of that was taken, but a prodigious tool. The Sky-Way rises above the plain and leads to the sky-scrapers. Coming from the flat reaches of New Jersey, it suddenly reveals the City of the Marvelous Towers."[20]

That elevated roadway was the realization of many of the architect's most cherished dreams. It provided direct contact with the sacred space of the sky, and it stood on pilotis that enabled it to float ethereally over the earth. It did so as the result of intelligent forethought that harnessed the potential of modern materials. To experience these wonders in the company of a beautiful, worldly, dynamic woman who was his lover gave him new faith in his own ideas for urban circulation.

ON THE EVENING of Thursday, October 31, the divorcée compliantly came in from Darien and went up to Le Corbusier's room at the Park Central Hotel, as specified, shortly before midnight. The architect had just returned from dinner with twenty-seven-year-old Nelson Rockefeller, a member of the Junior Advisory Committee at the Museum of Modern Art, and the architect Wallace Harrison, who was related to Rockefeller by marriage. Le Corbusier saw Rockefeller and Harrison as perfect stepping-stones to his own success, although in time he realized that the woman who appeared in his hotel afterward was his only real loyalist.

For the rest of Le Corbusier's visit to America, Marguerite Tjader Harris met up with her lover as often as his schedule permitted—sometimes at the hotel, at whatever hour he designated, and sometimes in Darien. There they would sit in the evening by the fire with Tjader Harris's mother, whom he likened to his own, and her dog, whom he compared to Pinceau, his and Yvonne's schnauzer. Hilary, whom everyone called Toutou, was also on the scene. During the days, Tjader Harris and Le Corbusier often repaired to the shack on the small island in the sound.

Unlike the other women in his orbit, Tjader Harris had a rare combination of intellect, passion, and steely self-control. The independence he generally eschewed in women were part of what made the athletic, elegant Nordic redhead desirable. These halcyon escapades of 1935 were only a beginning.

5

The lectures Le Corbusier gave in America focused on La Ville Radieuse and his recent domestic architecture. Robert Jacobs, his translator on the tour, who stood at the architect's side, was nicknamed "the faithful shade."[21] The lectures were often accompanied by a silent film that showed the Villa Savoye and the villa at Garches, accompanied by a recording of music composed and played by George Gershwin.

Le Corbusier's favorite lecture venues were at the East Coast colleges and universities attended mostly by upper-class youth. These enclaves of stone buildings and gracious lawns, reserved primarily for the elite, fascinated him. In the midst of the Depression, one generally had to come from a moneyed family to be at one of the Seven Sisters or at an Ivy League university for men. To Le Corbusier, who had had no experience of anything remotely like them, Columbia, Yale, Harvard, and Princeton were each "a world in itself, a temporary paradise, a happy stage of life."[22]

Vassar College, with its impeccably manicured grounds and old-fashioned brownstone buildings, reminded Le Corbusier of a luxurious club. At this "joyous convent"—the architect's term once he learned that its entirely female student body was there for four years—he was captivated by the young women onstage when he attended a student play shortly after arriving on the campus. He leered at them whether they were "in overalls or bathing-suits. I delight in observing these splendid bodies, braced and purified by physical training."[23]

Later that same day, six hundred of these fine female specimens filled an auditorium to hear Le Corbusier lecture. Looking at the sea of privileged, well-brought-up women, his first thought was "good blood." He was surprised to discover that they all understood French, which further confirmed their distinction.

The Vassar students were his most attentive audience to date. In the course of speaking that afternoon, he came to believe that they would be his "best propagandists." When he was done telling them about new cities and unprecedented ways to live, they stampeded toward the stage. His new devotees feverishly cut up his large drawings so that each of them could take home a small fragment, like a holy relic. "One piece for each amazon," he recalled.[24] They begged him to sign the pieces of paper, which he willingly did.

This felt like a real start at convincing the most influential people in the most influential country of the world to take up the concept of the Ville Radieuse. Surely those young women would promulgate his agenda for an architecture and urbanism that integrated the pleasures imperative to human existence with modern materials and a new vision. According to his own proud calculations, he made, in the course of this seminal trip, two tenths of a mile of drawings: six rolls of paper, each fifty meters long. As he gleefully watched the undergraduates tearing apart some of the sacred scrolls, his confidence soared: "The Vassar drawings were the consequence of an especially good mood. The amazons reduced them to shreds!"[25]

Once the onslaught was over, the students asked him intelligent questions in impeccable French. They revealed impressive knowledge of sociology, economics, and psychology and a keen concern with the serious problems then confronting the world. Faced with their earnestness, he assumed a humility that had a phony ring to it: "I never felt so stupid. 'But, Mesdemoiselles, I know nothing about the problems you envisage; I am merely an urbanist and an architect and perhaps an artist. Mesdemoiselles, you overwhelm me, you are too serious, I shall leave you and join those who are munching cookies!' "[26] Today, students would boo or storm out; in the mid-1930s, they were charmed.

Following the question-and-answer session, Le Corbusier went to the house of an art-history professor and began to drink whiskey. When "a superior student" told him she was studying Caravaggio, the architect responded that he disapproved and asked her to explain "the source of the strange power in this equivocal man." He imperiously asked the student, "Do you too suffer from repression?"[27]

It was beyond him that a young woman would devote her time to the blatantly homosexual Italian painter. Le Corbusier attributed the student's misguided taste to an essential problem of America's unwise preoccupation with the facets of the human psyche best kept private. Given his closeness to

William Ritter, it isn't that he condemned homosexuality. Rather, the architect joined a handful of other influential modernists—Josef Albers, the Bauhaus professor who had two years earlier begun teaching many of the leading young artists of the next generation at Black Mountain College in North Carolina, was another—who were rankled by the American taste for autobiographical art that deliberately revealed the psychological issues of its maker. These purists disdained all fondness for Duchamp and the Surrealists. They preached an adherence to the tenets of pure geometry and clear-headed design and an avoidance of issues they believed were extraneous. Le Corbusier reflected, "Caravaggio, rising out of the past, slakes a certain thirst of the American soul; furthermore the 'surrealism' of today has conquered the USA, the USA of the timid and the anxious."[28]

Still, he had great hopes for the twelve hundred women of Vassar College. The architect came to a conclusion that was remarkable in light of the woman he had chosen to marry: "In American society, woman exists by means of her intellectual labor."[29] These women of the new world could achieve great things.

The day after his lecture, Le Corbusier's admiration for the egalitarian spirit of these female undergraduates increased when he boarded the train to return to New York. It was a Saturday morning, and a group of students was heading into the city as well. They flocked toward the smoking car. Not only were the young ladies undaunted that their fellow smokers were muscular male dockhands and factory workers, but they relished the men's company. Le Corbusier wrote about that sight: "Democratic spirit. At Vassar I detected hints of communism in this wealthy circle. It's a familiar experience: the 'good society' of the *intelligenzia,* rich and eager to spend money, looks forward to the 'great revolution' with a touching ingenuousness."[30] His tone was snide, but he loved the warm spirits and good heart.

6

The lecture tour also gave Le Corbusier his first exposure to American football culture. Princeton had a winning team that year, and the visiting architect was impressed that sports rivalry could serve as "an intense springboard of solidarity and enthusiasm."[31]

The architect considered Princeton and the other institutions with fine grounds and Gothic buildings as erstwhile attempts at Eden in their removal from ordinary reality. But he questioned the merits of the isolation imposed by these enclaves. He recognized the idyllic aspect of four years in an artificial paradise but wondered if it would be better at this seminal moment of development to have "the total expanse of life, with its flaws, its poverty, its anguish, its greatness?"[32] When he was the age of these undergraduates, after all, he had been sojourning independently from one European city to the next, taking part-time jobs and seeking apprenticeships.

After Ema and Mount Athos, the rural villages of the Baltic, and the workers' clubs in Moscow, Princeton presented a form of group living Le Corbusier had never before encountered: "These rugged boys—all of them athletes—this security of material life, this simple joy of camaraderie . . . these are the master trumps in America. . . . Across the USA, the student tribes form their *de luxe* encampments."[33]

Le Corbusier preferred the independence required of students at the Sorbonne, who lived on their own: "I'm drawn by the pathos of life and its dangers; much less by the assurance of these spoiled daddy's boys, so well-fed, well-scrubbed, well-groomed."[34] Those sons and daughters of privilege were deprived of important things. The nature of their physical surroundings, too elegant and too isolated, was complicit in the problem.

LE CORBUSIER greatly admired the energy of President Franklin Delano Roosevelt and of the building campaign recently undertaken by the Works Progress Administration. An intermediary tried to arrange a meeting between the two men. As with Roosevelt's predecessor Herbert Hoover, Le Corbusier was to be disappointed. When word came back that Roosevelt did not have time, Le Corbusier blamed the all-consuming 1936 election campaign for the president's missing something far more important than politics: "From my brief experience of the men in government, I should say they are not well-informed. They haven't time to inform themselves and to meditate."[35]

But most people were excited to meet the architect, and his lecture became part of the legacy of each institution where he appeared. At Bowdoin College, it is still remembered that at dinner at the president's house, when a guest asked the famous visitor for his views about city planning, he pushed away the dishes, got one of the female guests to give him her lipstick, and sketched in brilliant red all over the tablecloth.

The lecture audiences were invariably attentive and excited, with no protests like those in Paris. On the other hand, the dean of the Harvard architecture school, where Le Corbusier spoke, labeled the visitor "a much over-rated individual." *The Christian Science Monitor* disparaged the architect by reporting that he "never attended school, not even primary school."[36] At a formal dinner in Philadelphia, guests were appalled when he tried out certain new English expressions like "son of a bitch."

Among the people Le Corbusier offended at that dinner was the cantankerous art collector Dr. Albert Barnes. As a result, Barnes denied him the privilege of going the next day to view his extraordinary collection of Cézannes, Seurats, and Renoirs. Le Corbusier did not accept the collector's refusal to open his doors. Since *L'Esprit Nouveau* had, in 1923, published an article by Maurice Raynal about Barnes and his collection and educational theories, the architect felt he had earned the right of entry. He dispatched a note to that effect.

Barnes replied that Le Corbusier would be allowed to visit after all. The collector, however, specified a day well after the architect's scheduled departure from Philadelphia, and he also stipulated that nobody from the Philadelphia Art Alliance, the organization where Le Corbusier had lectured, could accompany him. Le Corbusier replied that while he was "infinitely respectful of pride and wealth," he could not wait "four days on the Barnes Foundation doorstep." He signed the letter, "The founder of *L'Esprit Nouveau* who from 1919 to 1925 fought the good fight for the artists you buy."[37]

The maneuver failed. After he returned to New York, Le Corbusier received a typewritten reply, unsigned and in French, a language he knew Barnes did not speak. It was addressed to "Maître Corbeau, dit Le Corbusier." Barnes wrote, "I've heard that you were quite drunk last Friday at the Sausage Alliance in Philadelphia; I presume you were in a state of similar intoxication when you scribbled your remarks. In any case, Maître Corbeau now knows that Maître Renard has no respect for clowns nor for the Nitwit Alliance that employs them." The missive was signed "Maître Renard, known as 'Albert C. Barnes' founder since before 1910 of the New Spirit which seeks to differentiate the true from the false in art and culture."[38]

Le Corbusier responded calmly. He suggested that two people who loved the same things and shared certain passions should not feud and said that the three whiskeys he had consumed at the Art Alliance dinner had not made him drunk. Taking the upper hand, he wrote Barnes, "I enjoy a good fight in life, and I engage in such combats without fear. But in this instance I believe hostility is useless." It was time for "the duel to come to an end."[39] The letter came back unopened. In large circular handwriting, Barnes had written "*Merde*" on the sealed envelope.

Le Corbusier recounted the feud and quoted extensively from the exchange of letters in *When the Cathedrals Were White,* with the conclusion that "it testifies to the crude satisfactions of the men who in one, two, or three generations have 'made America.' If you like, it is a sort of 'cowboy' story!"[40] The word "cowboy" was in English in the otherwise French text.

He was eventually to be more flummoxed by those cowboys than he ever could have imagined.

7

In the third week of November, Le Corbusier began to make his way westward toward Chicago. Near Detroit, he visited the Ford River Rouge plant, one of the largest assembly-line buildings in the world. Watching the production of six thousand cars per day, he felt he had entered the modern world at last.

That efficient, state-of-the-art automobile factory exemplified the ideal political state: "With Ford, everything is collaboration, unity of outlook, unity of goals, perfect convergence of thought and action." By contrast, the practice of architecture in modern Europe struck him as inefficient and problem ridden: "With us, in the factory, everything is contradiction, hostility, dispersion, divergence of views, assertion of opposing goals, marking time."[41]

Ford's production techniques convinced Le Corbusier that the traditional practice of architecture had not yet caught up to the possibilities of the modern world. He decided, as if he had never known it before, that architecture must make human well-being its primary goal as assiduously as Ford devoted itself to producing automobiles. Studios and factories alike must utilize modern techniques to achieve that objective with maximum efficiency. The assembly line demonstrated the possibilities of realizing the dream of allowing individual liberty and collective effort to thrive in perfect tandem with each other.

Not since the monastery at Ema had Le Corbusier been as excited by an architectural prototype as he was in that facility near Detroit. The vast factory with its cacophony of sounds and its production of the vehicles essential to everyday life in a vast and powerful country had a similar effect to the fifteenth-century retreat devoted to the contemplative life on the outskirts of Florence. It was neither the first nor the last time in his life that Le Corbusier had fallen for a false god. His vision of the core of American capitalism helped pave the way for what soon was more than a flirtation with the forces of fascism and repression.

8

In Chicago, Le Corbusier came to admire the buildings of Louis Sullivan but disparaged both the poverty of the slums and the spread of America's second-largest city horizontally into suburbs. Insufficiently connected with an urban core, isolating families on little plots of land, these communities were the antitheses of Le Corbusier's ideas. He told his Chicago audiences that American production techniques had led the way in what he termed "the first machine age civilization"—the century from 1830 to 1930—but that now capitalism was destroying American cities by producing architecture not in the best interest of urban planning.[42] He still believed that the United States had the potential to lead the world in facilitating a new urbanism—if only the country would listen to him rather than continue to cluster its skyscrapers and expand its suburbs. Le Corbusier showed his own work—the Swiss Pavilion as well as unbuilt projects like his art museum and the Palace of the Soviets—as examples of what public buildings should look like. He also pushed his urban schemes.

Le Corbusier's hosts tried to organize a meeting between him and Frank Lloyd Wright, who lived a couple of hours away. It made perfect sense for two of the greatest names in modern architecture at least to shake hands. Along with Mies van der Rohe—who was soon to move to Chicago but

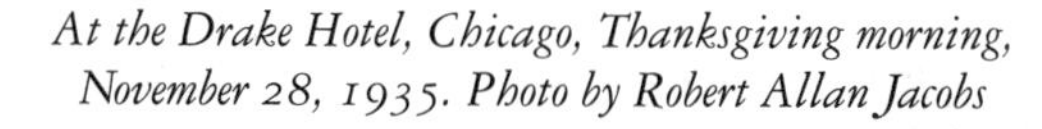

At the Drake Hotel, Chicago, Thanksgiving morning, November 28, 1935. Photo by Robert Allan Jacobs

who had for the time being remained in Berlin following the closing of the Bauhaus under pressure from the Nazis—and Alvar Aalto, in Finland, Le Corbusier and Wright were the gods of the field. But Wright declined to make the journey to meet the visitor from Paris, let alone to hear him lecture. To the Chicago-based architect who had invited him, Wright wrote, from Taliesin, in Spring Green, Wisconsin, "I hope Le Corbusier may find America all he hoped to find it."[43]

A more successful encounter was arranged on Le Corbusier's behalf with a prostitute, procured for him by his translator. When he woke up next to her on Thanksgiving morning in the Drake Hotel, the architect was in such good spirits that he took a silver-plated dome from room service and donned it as a crown, posing for a photograph in which, with his striped pajamas and trademark glasses, he resembles a circus clown. Later that same day, his spirits high, he took a TWA flight back to New York. Le Corbusier was invited into the cockpit, which he considered an architectural marvel, especially as it facilitated a smooth and quiet journey that took only three and a half hours.

9

The architect stayed in New York until mid-December. This time he was at the Gotham Hotel, an ornate building at Fifth Avenue and Fifty-fifth Street. (Today it is called the Peninsula.) Feeling that he was at the center of a universe—one that had even more potential than the inner sanctum of Argentinian high society, where he had anticipated his ascent as master builder six years earlier—he was determined to use his proximity to wealth and power to full advantage.

In those few weeks, he took every chance he could to pitch ideas to Nelson Rockefeller. Rockefeller's mother was one of the three founders of the Museum of Modern Art, and the young millionaire was closely connected to many people in the financial and political establishment. Le Corbusier imagined Rockefeller as the magician who might enable him to realize a new League of Nations proposal, a housing scheme in the New York area, a contemporary-art museum anywhere, a headquarters for CIAM in Paris, and his design for a pavilion at the 1939 World's Fair.

Once he was back in France, all these prospects came to nothing. But for those few weeks in New York, Le Corbusier believed he was on the verge of major conquests.

ON DECEMBER 6, the former child of La Chaux-de-Fonds went to a ball for 2,500 guests at the Waldorf-Astoria Hotel. The ball, given by the Beaux-Arts architects, had the theme of a night in India. When Le Corbusier had gone a few days earlier to rent a costume, he had been offered a turban and "brocaded robe" suitable for a raja or a khan. But he had other ideas: "Thanks, but no usurped titles! Not being a handsome fellow, I'll leave my anatomy in peace. Despite his protests, I've obliged the man who rents costumes to give me a prisoner's outfit, blue and white stripes, and a vermillion tunic of the Indian army (my supplier would have preferred a top officer's outfit!); I dislodged an enormous gold epaulette which I pinned on the left side. No kepi, sir, a pointed white dunce cap, please. To create a balance of colors, I attached a big blue scarf across my chest to a gold sword-belt. Damn! no pockets in my prison trousers: banknotes in my socks then, my pipe and my tobacco-pouch stuck in my belt. And to finish off, on my cheeks and forehead, three broad yellow patches of different shapes to mislead the curious."[44]

Most of the people at the Waldorf that night bowed to fashion or looked over their shoulders to figure out what everyone else was doing. Le Corbusier, as always, invented his own way. At the same time, he had outfitted himself to dance at the Waldorf with memories of Josephine Baker in his arms.

10

When Le Corbusier had set sail for America, he had expected his wildest dreams to come true. By the time he headed back to France two months later, he was devastated.

Le Corbusier characterized America's culture by focusing on the taste for Caravaggio which had initially irritated him on his Vassar visit.

> Caravaggio, a sixteenth-century Italian painter, "worked in a studio painted black; the only light came in through a trap-door in the ceiling." Stop there! Here we discover an aspect of the American soul. If we add today's surrealism, widespread in American collections, to Caravaggio, our diagnosis will be confirmed. This chapter will draw us into the dark labyrinth of consciousness haunted by young people with anxious hearts.
>
> Caravaggio in university courses, surrealism in collections and

> museums, saltpetre in the army, inferiority complexes bedeviling those trying to escape the simplest arithmetical calculations, the principle of the molested family, the grimmest spirit manifesting itself at the moment of spiritual creation—such is the unexpected harvest that filled my mind upon completing these first journeys to the USA, where I was absorbed in the study of urbanist phenomena.[45]

It's hard to fathom how a painter as wonderful as Caravaggio—whose sureness of construction, steely representation of physical space, emotional intensity, and true bravura make him more Le Corbusier's match than his opposite—should have brought on such opprobrium. But the architect could not stop ranting:

> His case is one for the psychiatrists. Young lady from Vassar, is it in the name of art that you are floundering in this sewer? I believe you are impelled to do so by an unsatisfied heart. . . .
>
> Here are sensitive, ill-constructed souls busying themselves with these splendid twilight decors. The sea withdraws; the sky bleeds to the horizon across the dark green water; ruins are heaped into cenotaphs, the clouds ripped to pieces; stumps of columns lie on the ground; by association, women's bodies cut into pieces, the black blood streaming from them, birds, a horse of decadent antiquity. Symbols, short-cuts, evocations. What is such a liturgy? What refined, moving, spectral ceremony? What appeal to the past? Is something being buried? It is the past that is being buried, all that has ceased to be. The dead are mourned. Very lovely, all that.
>
> Certainly! But the ceremony is coming to an end. The new world awaits the workers!
>
> The USA of the *intelligenzia* indulges in such rites. This country which knows only technological maturity is anxious in the face of the future. The American soul seeks refuge in the bosom of things past.[46]

In this incoherent rampage, Le Corbusier next amplified the effects of saltpeter. The substance that gave a perpetual "spoonful"—Le Corbusier's term for a nonerect penis—to American soldiers was comparable to the music and dance in Harlem in their effect on intellectuals and socialites, to the work people were forced to do in dismal skyscrapers, to "business" and a lot of other elements of American life that rendered its population, "timid" by nature, impotent.[47] His image of American soldiers—the same breed as those robust young men Charles-Edouard Jeanneret had admired during World War I—and of the country as a whole was shattered.

11

Impotence in any form was Le Corbusier's nightmare. Having thought that in the United States he would find clients and powerful patrons, he had discovered, instead, a neurotic culture of pathetic, defeated people whose lives revolved around the need to earn money. Men were working too hard to support their wives, while American women were "amazons" who dominated their beleaguered husbands.[48] These women's demands for jewelry, furniture, vacations, and other luxuries caused the husbands to die at the age of fifty. He was appalled by the ineffectiveness and timidity of all these creatures who lived as victims rather than celebrants of their existence.

Le Corbusier declared that in American design "a funereal spirit prevails, a solemnity which cannot yet be shaken off." In this land of inhuman dimensions, in spite of the attempt of Hollywood to lighten life with the comedies of Laurel and Hardy and Buster Keaton, "reality is not so funny as the films. It is serious, overwhelming, pathetic."[49]

Although everything was possible in this young country, the absence of an underlying philosophy meant that nothing had been achieved there. Le Corbusier had not disliked a place so much since La Chaux-de-Fonds.

THERE WAS, however, one aspect of American culture that had not let him down. His term for it was "the nigger music." Jazz embodied many qualities that Le Corbusier held dearest. It was "the soul's melody joined to the machine's rhythm. It has two tempi: tears in the heart, throbbing in the legs, torso, arms and head. . . . It floods the body and the heart."[50]

Le Corbusier identified the provision of pleasure through tempo and rhythm with the goals of his architecture. Not only did this American music with the power to make people dance obsess him, but so did the lives of America's blacks. Focused on both the Pullman porters and slum dwellers, he believed that, however difficult their everyday reality, black people had music that enabled them to enter "the heart's chapel."[51]

The architect had a new hero. Louis Armstrong was "the black titan . . . Shakespearian . . . alternately demonic, playful and monumental. . . . This man is madly intelligent; he is a king."[52] In Boston, he had heard Armstrong perform in a nightclub: "It was absolutely dazzling: strength and truth."[53] For all that Le Corbusier disdained in America, when the values of John Ruskin were made corporeal, he was ecstatic.

12

On December 14, Le Corbusier wrote Marguerite Tjader Harris from the SS *Lafayette,* the boat that was returning him to France. With his letter, he enclosed a sketch he had made of his lover. The drawing shows her standing on the dock, sporting a hat and a tailored suit that accentuates her impressive height, full bust, and statuesque bearing. The New York skyline is behind her; clearly this was the last vision Le Corbusier had as his boat departed. The caption underneath the drawing reads simply "*Au revoir, amie!*"[54]

He had previously sounded the themes of this letter, above all to his parents. Certain terms of adulation for his mistress echoed the praise he had periodically showered upon his mother. But a lot of what he wrote to Marguerite Tjader Harris—the woman he discussed with no one and who in turn kept their relationship secret until well after his death, and whose name never appeared in any account by or about Le Corbusier during his lifetime—reflected a degree of admiration and love he showed to nobody else.

He wrote,

> Everything was lovely, clean and careful, dignified and affectionate. Why shouldn't the heart be entitled to love where it is allowed to open, reveal itself, and receive the maximum of joy and well-being?

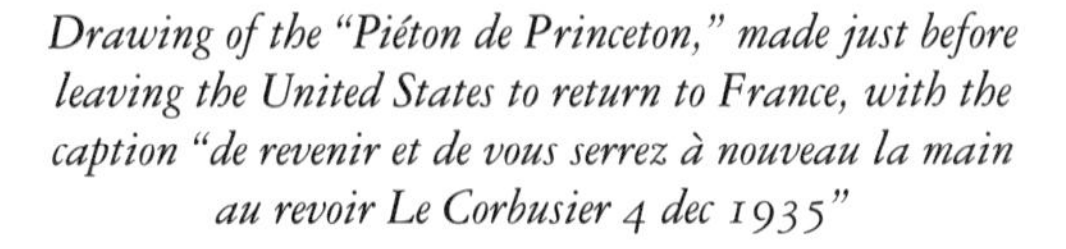

Drawing of the "Piéton de Princeton," made just before leaving the United States to return to France, with the caption "de revenir et de vous serrez à nouveau la main au revoir Le Corbusier 4 dec 1935"

Drawing of Marguerite Tjader Harris, December 14, 1935

> The road the heart takes is—step by step—precipitous, headlong, dangerous, and leads to the peaks where something of real life is visible. Why not take a look at life?
>
> I have seen you and not looked, then seen and known, and recognized. . . . You are strong, healthy, fine and fair. You are open and affectionate. Not closed. Around you the warmest feelings gather. You are strong and gay. Kind.[55]

Le Corbusier told the Connecticut divorcée that he could not imagine what New York or the entire trip would have been like without her. He savored his memories of the sea, her amiable mother, the beach shack, the Victorian house, and the roads around Darien.

> You have been the peasant-maid of New York, a little Joan of Arc for Le Corbusier rattling in the void. A sustenance.
>
> A kind blond light.
>
> Friend, I thank you. My thanks.[56]

To no other lover did Le Corbusier express himself with such respect. He had let go of his usual sense of distance; there was none of the condescension of his communication with Yvonne. For the first time, he had met a woman on his own level.

LE CORBUSIER announced his new austerity to Tjader Harris, as if he were a priest who had strayed but would now put his collar back on: "And now my life will return to its old ways, a believer's heart, vital and transparent, one I can truly respect."[57] Le Corbusier declared that he would now stop thinking about their affair. Discipline would take over; the legacy of Calvinism, of Nietzschean self-control, would prevail.

For all of his steely resolve, however, his emotions shifted constantly. As if drawn by a powerful magnet, Le Corbusier jumped from that summoning of correct behavior back to his memories of the marvelous tenderness he had experienced with his energetic, warm-spirited lover. Then, in another turnaround, he lapsed into a pathetic image of himself at age forty-eight: "The future does not belong to us. The years pass, and continue to pass. Poor old Le Corbusier, so near Autumn, though his heart is a child's."[58]

Nonetheless, the architect maintained, in secret, his connection not just to Marguerite Tjader Harris but also to her son for the rest of his life.

IN HER LATE-LIFE MEMOIR, Tjader Harris provided a portrait of Le Corbusier with observations very similar to Josephine Baker's. His lovers saw in him a simplicity and genuineness that eluded the larger public. The divorcée wrote that he "was not a complicated man, not even an *intellectual,* in the narrow meaning of the word. He lived by his faith and emotions."[59]

Both women also understood his single-mindedness and his consuming dedication to his work. Le Corbusier's American lover wrote, "His desire was to create, to work, to accomplish. Everything in him was united in this intention. If he needed a little relaxation, if he needed affection, it was to work better, afterwards. He cared nothing for a social life, nor for the hundred little subterfuges and gallantries necessary to the pursuit of women. We had found a free companionship without obligations nor demands."[60] She was as remarkable as he was.

13

On Le Corbusier's first night home after the American trip, Yvonne put a record of American jazz on the gramophone in the spacious, modern living room on the rue Nungesser-et-Coli. He considered it a perfect greeting—as if the beguiling Monegasque knew intuitively what he had liked best on the other side of the Atlantic.

He was content to be back. During the festive time of year he normally detested, Le Corbusier "found the bistros mediocre, yet the sky everywhere above the city, and the grace of proportions and the care taken in the details affords real pleasure."[61] In Paris, at least, there were no skyscrapers to destroy the street and block the sunlight.

In traveling to the USSR and the United States, Le Corbusier had visited the two most powerful countries in the world. In each case, he had embarked as a believer, hopeful to have found *the* answer and the place where he would realize his dreams of new building types and of the Ville Radieuse. What he had anticipated had not panned out. Now he had to acknowledge that neither country had adopted him as its leader and master planner.

Subsequent events only confirmed his disappointment with the United States. In the following year, Le Corbusier feuded with Museum of Modern Art authorities about unpaid lecture fees and their failure to publish an English edition of *La Ville Radieuse,* as he had hoped. He had won himself a number of fans in America, but many of the people with whom he had been closely associated there—Alfred Barr and Philip Johnson at the Museum of Modern Art among them—had found him intolerably contentious.

Le Corbusier's starting point with the United States had been a faith in utopia, the hope of perfection. He now accepted that this did not exist. On the other hand, he had confirmed his love for the woman who best understood both his heart and his genius.

XXXIII

1

After returning from America, Le Corbusier retreated to the privacy and comfort of his studio; it was his usual formula of immersing himself in the luxury of creativity on the most intimate scale whenever he despaired of his ability to change the entire world. Paintbrush in hand, a canvas in front of him, his wife just a room away, the aromas of garlic and tomatoes simmering in olive oil wafting from the kitchen, their dog scurrying around the apartment, he was content.

The moment, however, that he was beckoned to make large-scale architecture, with a chance of designing cities as part of the package, he jumped. The Brazilian government asked Le Corbusier to help develop plans for

At 24 rue Nungesser-et-Coli, ca. 1935

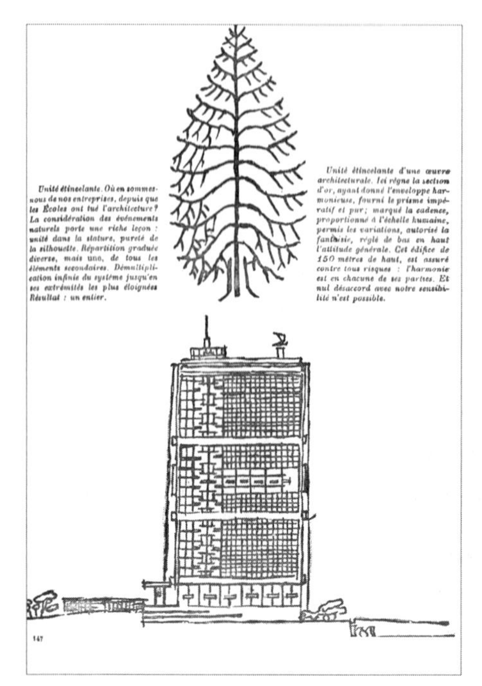

Sketches comparing the structure of a fir tree and a brise-soleil *on a skyscraper, early 1940s*

headquarters for both the Ministry of Education and the Ministry of Public Health. In July 1936, he returned to Rio.

Le Corbusier made the trip on board the *Graf Zeppelin,* a dirigible airship filled with hydrogen that took four days to go from France to Brazil. He was thrilled by the custom-fitted interior of the unusual vessel, its mechanics, and the hoopla when it landed—all the Brazilian natives rushing about to anchor the great airship.

His mood plunged when he saw the site chosen for the Ministry of Education. Then he and his clients found a more suitable setting for which he designed a vertical slab with end walls made from the local pink granite. His spirits soared, even when the minister of education told him that the plan would not work: one of the main facades faced north and would heat up intolerably in the sunlight. Le Corbusier was elated rather than discouraged by what might have been a hurdle. He had a breakthrough idea: he would use *brises-soleil.*

He had initially developed *brises-soleil* for his studio at 24 rue Nungesser-et-Coli and had then proposed their use in some of his designs for Algiers. These "sun shields" were further inventions through which Le Corbusier intended to change the way people lived and worked. The idea was to use horizontal slats to protect windows from direct sunlight. Le Corbusier believed that by observing the movement of the sun in the course of an entire year, one could fix these *brises-soleil* at the correct angle so that during the summer there would never be direct sunlight on the windowpanes, while in the winter, when it was desirable, there would be. Deferring to the ruling power of the sun, they accommodated the need for living conditions that are neither too hot nor too cold. The project in Rio would allow him to employ these splendid devices on an unprecedented scale.

TODAY THE RIO building is smaller than many structures around it, but it radiates a power they lack. The slab on tall pilotis manages the Corbusean feat of being dense and graceful at the same time. Its solid side walls have fantastic presence. But the *brises-soleil* that cover the larger northern exposure are not as Le Corbusier intended. Whereas he would have preferred all the elements neatly aligned with one another, they were immediately adjusted to various angles according to the wishes of the inhabitants of individual offices. Their differing positions give the building a haphazard look.

With his device purportedly designed to benefit a large group of people with a range of needs and tasks, did Le Corbusier truly care about their comfort above all? Or did his ability to impose an aesthetic standard, to dictate someone else's way of life and maintain authority regardless of the actual experience of his beneficiaries, matter more than anything else? The architect had himself convinced he was serving humankind; his effectiveness was debatable.

2

While in Rio, Le Corbusier was asked to design a university campus, which would include a law school, medical school, hospital, museum, sports stadium, restaurants, clubs, housing, liberal-arts departments, and other facilities. Government regulations forbade his receiving a fee for the project, but the local authorities found a loophole. They asked the architect to give six lectures, for which he was paid substantial stipends that compensated him for the design work. At those lectures, the architect proposed one of his most radical urban schemes. To counteract what he declared to be the "horrifying chaos" created by the rapid and random development of the nineteenth century—where "everything here is false, frightful, cruel, ugly, stupid, inhuman"—he designed a unifying scheme for all of Rio that honored its specific geographical situation.[1]

A second city was to be built on top of the existing one. Le Corbusier's proposal resembles a gigantic elevated ribbon snaking among the hilltops that flank the Brazilian metropolis. The undulating slab would sit on top of pilotis 120 feet high. In one direction, it faced the bay—the shape of which is echoed by the serpentine lines of the slab. In the other, this continuous line of buildings looked toward the mountains. On top of the slab, there was a divided motorway. It was one of Le Corbusier's most daring and imaginative schemes—however unrealizable.

IN RIO, he became aware that six months had elapsed since he had seen Marguerite Tjader Harris. Being back in Brazil also brought on memories of Josephine Baker.

Le Corbusier wrote Tjader Harris, opening the letter, "I no longer understand how I could sleep with black women. There are crowds of them here, some very beautiful. So much the worse."[2] Over the years, his need to tell this one woman about the others became chronic. She tolerated Le Corbusier's disregard for the effect of his confessions.

Having last been with Tjader Harris shortly before he set sail from New York, he now told her, with meticulous recall, "I haven't made love since December 13. Ridiculous. Especially ridiculous to note the fact and to assume it means something. We spoil everything with these observations of minor circumstances which are quite inexplicable. Except for arithmetic, nothing can be explained. We paddle in incomprehensible seas. . . . Lacking yours, I have these. But here we must wear bathing-suits. And a simple piece of wool is a nasty privation of great delights."[3]

Le Corbusier had recently begun to write *When the Cathedrals Were White.* He told his mistress that he could not have written it without her, and his underlying idea was that she should translate it. This was when he subtitled the travel journal *In the Land of the Timid.* These "timid" Americans, he added, were "hefty" but purposeless: "they still don't know what to do with their strength in order to have something in life to show for it."[4]

Le Corbusier had recently had his palm read and been told 1936 would be a year when he could take risks. The numbers concurred. He was forty-eight; four plus eight equaled twelve, two plus one (the digits in twelve) equaled three, and three times twelve was thirty-six. These figures all represented harmony. They gave him the reassurance and balance that, he told Tjader Harris, permitted him to face squarely the anguish of his American trip, which seemed even more disastrous in retrospect.

In contrast to New York, Rio was a virtual paradise. Even in winter, there was sunshine; the sky was perpetually blue. He swam regularly in the middle of the day, and everything was a feast for the eyes: the men who dressed in white, the "roads of love" where hundreds upon hundreds of women walked hand in hand. Le Corbusier elaborated on those roads, where prostitutes welcomed their clients: "Before 1930 the whorehouses faced the sea. The preference was for French women. Today a moralizing rigor is in force, which jars in this exuberant site."[5] He relished the liberty of reporting it all to his aristocratic, Catholic, American mistress.

ONCE HE GOT BACK to Paris, Le Corbusier received word that neither his urban plan nor most of the other ideas he had proposed for the Brazilian capital were wanted.

He was becoming increasingly skeptical, and realistic, about his ability to inspire a universal revolution. In November 1937, when his friend Elie Faure, an art historian who specialized in antiquity, died, Le Corbusier reflected, "He had to die before his work could be revealed to the public and his views circulated. Now people are looking at his texts. Tomorrow will show that he was clairvoyant. Death is the sacrament of life."[6] For the rest of his life, he assumed that he and his work would be better appreciated once he, too, was no longer alive.

3

At least the pavilion Le Corbusier was building for the international exposition to be held in Paris near the Porte Maillot later that year was a reality. It was not a master plan for Rio or a city in America, but it would actually happen.

The architect had been making proposals for the exposition ever since it had been conceived in 1932. Initially, he recommended that instead of being called "The International Exhibition of Art and Techniques" it become the "International Exhibition of Housing." Housing, he decreed, was the essential issue confronting civilization. His megalomaniacal attempt to dictate the overall theme of the exposition fell on deaf ears, however, and he later publicly complained that his thirty-six printed pages of suggestions "did not even get a formal acknowledgment."[7] Between 1932 and 1936, he had drawn up three different schemes for his pavilion—all of which had been rejected. But just after the exposition had opened, the French prime minister, Léon Blum, had been dismayed to discover that Le Corbusier's proposals had been turned down, and in December 1936, four months after the opening, Le Corbusier was offered the funds to build. The architect at first went into a public sulk and said "it was too late."[8] But having a prime minister take his side was irresistible. Le Corbusier reversed himself and agreed to erect a structure devoted primarily to the themes of town planning and Paris.

While the pavilion was being built, few people knew that, as was so often the case, Le Corbusier was afflicted by health problems. For about three weeks in April, he suffered from symptoms that suggest a flu or sinus infection or combination of the two. No specific diagnosis was given, but the architect was laid flat by headaches, congestion, and malaise. After a specialist assured him that he had no major health issue beyond the visual impairment that was a given, he became delighted with the enforced stop in his life. Yvonne took such good care of him in the new apartment that he wrote to his mother that the twenty days of illness seemed to fly. Bedridden, he had a wonderful view of the sky, and he was perpetually cheered by the optimism of André Bauchant's paintings. He could not really be all that sick, he reassured Marie, because he was well enough to smoke—news he assumed would relieve her enormously.

It was one of those moments when optimism and a sense of celebration permeated Le Corbusier's psyche as surely as pessimism and regret catapulted him downward on other occasions. Positioned with great vistas from his apartment yet with the city center in reach, he believed the reason he could feel so well while being ill signified the "victory of the *Radiant City*!"[9] Besides, he was building his pavilion and being accorded respect from both the fringes and the mainstream. In his penthouse on the outskirts of Paris, he imbibed life's bounty.

THE FRENCH COMMUNIST PARTY was organizing a conference to take place that July to address the theme of the international exposition, and the honorary committee—which included Louis Aragon, André Gide, and André Malraux—asked Le Corbusier to be one of the main speakers.

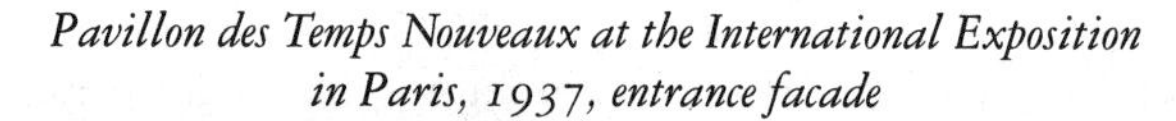
Pavillon des Temps Nouveaux at the International Exposition in Paris, 1937, entrance facade

When, two weeks after he spoke under those auspices, the Pavillon des Temps Nouveaux opened, the architect was finally decorated with a Legion of Honor. Having turned down the medal on four previous occasions, this time he accepted it in order to rebut recent attacks in which he had been declared anti-French.

His new pavilion was true to the determination of the French Communist Party to challenge and confront the old ways of doing things. Le Pavillon des Temps Nouveaux was a fifteen-thousand-square-meter space with walls and a roof made of cloth that was boldly colored in yellow, blue, red, and green. Its structure depended on tensile vertical pylons, similar to poles used to support high-voltage power lines, and on steel cables that anchored it to the ground. The temporary structure looked like a building under construction more than one that was completed. To modern eyes, it resembles a wrapped structure by the artist Christo, in particular his Reichstag encased in paper and string, as if it were a gigantic package.

Inside the pavilion, an airplane was suspended from the roof. Murals and dioramas by Le Corbusier and José Luis Sert evoked modern industry and the latest advances in technology. Le Corbusier told his mother that his intention was to create "an event, something strong, commanding, healthy, convincing. A battlefield, it goes without saying."[10]

Without some struggle, after all, how could he triumph? Le Corbusier publicly whined that "no bigwigs came to open it," but he viewed the lack of attention as directly connected to the brilliance of what he had done: "It was the boldest thing you can imagine."[11]

4

Le Corbusier showed his latest plan for Paris in the 1937 exposition. It left the French capital's monuments and city center intact but added four large skyscrapers lined up in a row on the outskirts. The magazine *ART,* referring to the eighteenth-century architect whose exaggerated classicism was a symbol of the ancien régime, called this proposal "a megalomania worse than Ledoux's, a vandalism unique in history, the dreary uniformity, vanity, and monotony of these skyscrapers . . . have been proved morally and spiritually injurious, a contempt for historic and artistic tradition."[12] Le Corbusier quoted the diatribe in *My Work;* the more pulverizing the critique, the more he reveled in it.

That year, Le Corbusier and Pierre Jeanneret also designed a stadium and open-air theatre for one hundred thousand people. At the time, it was mocked—Balthus and Picasso, both of whom preferred grand French buildings, compared the stadium to a gigantic saucer missing its cup—although twenty years later the Iraqi government commissioned a sports center for Baghdad along very similar lines.[13]

Le Corbusier's design for a monument at one of the main entrances to Paris, made for a competition organized by the Front Populaire, was, Le Corbusier himself explained, "rejected with a certain amount of nastiness. The most advanced artists, friends of Le Corbusier, castigated him for putting forward such a proposal."[14]

With all these defeats, the architect's fiftieth birthday hit him hard. To Marguerite Tjader Harris, he wrote that the official honors had been abundant, "but hatreds abound, and the struggle is as harsh as ever. For the time being, total 'depression,' no work."[15] Le Corbusier told her that an astrologist in Rio—not the same person as the palm reader—had said that at age fifty he would join the sun, Jupiter, and Venus in the most beautiful sky possible. Nothing of the sort had happened; no one in New York or Paris or Algiers was building Corbusean cities, and he felt deserted. And while he was stagnating, the bourgeoisie, the academics, and the lazy traditionalists were all thriving.

In early December, Le Corbusier and Marguerite Tjader Harris managed to organize a couple of nights together at the Hotel de la Cloche in Dijon. Afterward, he wrote her, quoting his friend Maurice Raynal as having said, "Behind that stiff facade, Le Corbusier is a tender-hearted man"; he asked her to confirm that this was so.[16] He then leaped from the issues of human personalities to the personalities of cities. He complained that Zurich, like everything in Switzerland, was "intimate"; he preferred grandeur. London had now become one of his favorite places; it was "sumptuous." "This black city" offered a panoply of rich experiences, from the traditional clubs in their dignified nineteenth-century buildings imitative of the Medicis' palaces to the beautiful merchandise in the shops, especially the woolens and leather goods.[17] On a recent visit to the British capital, its strong and powerful life struck him as ripe for romance.

He boasted unabashedly to his American mistress about a conquest: "Then a party at some gentleman's house. I had noticed the loveliest woman there. And as fate would have it. . . . In three rounds, as boxers say."[18] He was telling her this only a month after their escapade together in Dijon.

THEN THE ANSCHLUSS occurred. With Hitler's invasion of Austria, the devaluation of the franc, and the failure of the Front Populaire, human civilization seemed threatened as never before.

Le Corbusier saw both tragedy and possibility in all the changes:

"March 18, 1938: Disappointing days. Imbecility everywhere, arrogance or funk. Dilemma. Terrible risks of a nameless war. Behind all this: nothing! Words, ghosts, and even so, there are *the haves,* unwilling to accept even the possibility of a new world. They'd rather die on top of their gold. But they will make everyone else die of impotent rage. At least such terrible death agonies will be the end of the disease, the birth of a new civilization, and there will be more to talk about than chimerical vanities. What I mean is, people will share, will start afresh, will group together! We must wait and see!"[19]

In June, a Paris-based organization devoted to helping partisans wounded in republican Spain asked Le Corbusier to issue a statement. He complied by calling the fighting in Spain "satanic madness."

> Under the pretexts of points of view, blood runs, and men's bones are broken. . . .
>
> What immense and total gratitude we have for those doomed to this hell. We must sustain them with our most active love.[20]

Later that year, Le Corbusier asserted that the signers of the Munich accord, most especially the British prime minister, symbolized human evil: "Chamberlain seems to me the most dangerous kind of grim reactionary: the City, profits, money!" The invasion of Czechoslovakia in March 1939 made him even more miserable: "Then the Jews treated as no one ever dared imagine."[21]

How long he would sustain the victims of fascism with his "active love" remained to be seen.

5

In 1938, a major exhibition opened at the Kunsthaus in Zurich presenting almost all of Le Corbusier's paintings of the past two decades.

Since the inception of Purism, his painting style had evolved significantly. His still lifes had become increasingly complex, containing myriad elements in lively, animated relationships. He had also taken to making bold, oversized figures—similar to Léger's but even more broad shouldered and muscular. The effects of Braque and Picasso could also be seen in the ways human form, machine parts, and musical instruments were combined.

Like his spoken and written language, his painting style is animated by a high energy level, a deliberate complexity, and an urgent charge. But also

In his studio at 24 rue Nungesser-et-Coli, late 1930s

like his verbal communication, it occasionally lacks clarity, as if emotional tumult is more honest and valuable than self-editing.

When the show opened, there was no press coverage, and his friends remained silent—with just one exception. Le Corbusier's old pal and banker de Montmollin sent him ten bottles of Neuchâtel wine to celebrate the event—a gesture the architect would never forget. For it was a bittersweet experience. Le Corbusier wrote of his Zurich exhibition, "I couldn't have been rejected more completely. At least I've shown myself for what I am: a competent technologist, pursuing the harmonious path: poetic creation, the sources of happiness."[22] Rejection had had two effects: to show him who his real friends were and to reinforce his belief in his own achievement.

6

Le Corbusier had first overlapped with the stylish and aristocratic Anglo-Irish architect and designer Eileen Gray at the 1922 Salon d'Automne, where he presented his Citrohan house. Gray, nine years his senior, had exhibited an inventive black lacquer screen, as well as other furniture and textiles. These highly original forays in pure and vibrant geometric abstraction had made Gray's name one that everyone knew.

Two years later, Le Corbusier's friend Jean Badovici, an architect and editor, asked Gray to design a house for him in the region of Saint-Tropez. Looking for a suitable spot, Gray went far afield from the normal holiday haunts. The intrepid Irishwoman explored the wild and undiscovered reaches of the Riviera countryside on foot, with a donkey to carry her bags over the mountains. In the course of her search, she checked out a property completely inaccessible by car in Roquebrune-Cap-Martin. Having found an equivalent of the rough Irish coast, Gray was determined to build there. The natural setting was as daunting as it was beautiful: craggy, difficult to navigate, and full of precipitous drops.

Between 1926 and 1929, Gray built on that spot "E. 1027," a handsome and streamlined villa closely related to Le Corbusier's architecture of the time. Gray knew Le Corbusier's work well from having visited Ozenfant's studio and gone to Stuttgart for the Weissenhof Siedlung. The house Gray built had the identical vocabulary as Le Corbusier's villas; while it had the imprint of Gray's own design sense, it was clearly derivative. It was named E. 1027 to evoke Eileen Gray and Jean Badovici—the "E" was for "Eileen," and the "10," the "2," and "7" for, respectively, "J," "B," and "G," because of their positions in the alphabet.[23]

In the 1930s, when Le Corbusier and Yvonne were visiting her birthplace on one of their trips south, they stopped by E. 1027 for tea. Le Corbusier was astonished by the lush and rugged landscape sloping to the sea, similar in topography and dramatic beauty to Mount Athos. For all the south-of-France elegance of the general region, here one felt in direct connection with the forces of the universe, with the sea and sky as they had been for tens of thousands of years. Yvonne was delighted with the view of the coastline westward, where her native Monaco, at that time still a village, was in plain sight.

In 1938, Le Corbusier and Yvonne stayed at E. 1027 during the course of a summer holiday in Saint-Tropez. By this time, Gray, who had initially lived with Badovici, had moved out. Le Corbusier was disappointed that the fascinating Irishwoman was not there. He wrote her a fan letter about the house, applauding "the rare spirit which dictates all the organization inside and outside."[24] But for all the praise, Le Corbusier decided to improve on her design by painting murals there. Gray was not consulted.

Having become passionate about wall painting, Le Corbusier painted, both on that holiday and the following summer, eight enormous floor-to-ceiling frescoes—mostly of oversized naked figures cavorting sexually. One of the murals was on the previously spare white wall behind the living-room sofa, so that what had been specified by Gray to be a point of visual respite was now an animated scenario. In 1939, the architect was photographed working in the nude on these bacchanals.

Gray was outraged. Her biographer, Peter Adam, summed up her response: "It was a rape. A fellow architect, a man she admired, had without her consent defaced her design."[25] But the rest of his life, Le Corbusier

Painting the exterior mural at the villa E. 1027, summer 1939.
The scar was from a swimming accident.

would proudly reproduce the murals, pointing out only that he had painted them "free of charge for the owner of the villa."[26]

7

In Saint-Tropez, the architect took a long vigorous swim, sometimes two, every day in the warm waters of the Mediterranean. Shortly after the first escapade at E. 1027, Le Corbusier started a swim by diving into the water off the Môle Vert—the green breakwater. He headed toward the Môle Rouge—another jetty about 120 meters off. This was well within the range of his ability, even with the strong waves that day.

A powerful motor yacht was racing through the water. No one on board saw the swimmer stroking along, his broad shoulders and strong arms lifting rhythmically, his legs kicking in perfect sequence as he continued his daily exercise in a straight line created by the pronounced depression between two large waves. The fifty-year-old architect was about a quarter of the way toward his objective when he felt something hard hit his head. He discovered that he was under a boat. He noticed that it was as if the sunlight was trapped with him in a white and luminous cavity.

We know these graphic details because, more than a month later, Le Corbusier responded to a request from his mother for the most specific description possible of the accident he miraculously survived. In relating what happened, he diminished his own significance. He said that he rolled along

In Saint-Tropez bay, summer 1938

"like paste out of a tube" under the keel of the boat. He went its entire distance, determining that it was between fifteen and eighteen meters. While being pushed along, Le Corbusier told himself to stay calm until he reached the stern, at which point the whole unfortunate affair would be over. However, instead of emerging easily from beneath the far end of the boat, he came smack up against rapidly moving propeller blades. As he told his mother, with deliberate understatement, "The motor at 200 horsepower—a good clip."[27]

What occurred next was pure Le Corbusier. He completely suspended his emotional and physical reactions. Disconnected from his physical pain, he focused entirely on the behavior of other people—and attended logically to his immediate needs.

He reported to his mother, "After the first turn of the blades, I was thrown out of the circuit and seemed not to have been hurt. I reached the surface, and breathed *air.* I hadn't swallowed a drop of water. I saw the boat gliding slowly away. I shouted: 'Hey, wait a second, you went right over me, there may be some damage!' Quite automatically my hand went to my right thigh, my arm fitting nicely inside. I looked down: a big area of blood-red water, and half my thigh floating like a ray (the fish!), attached by a narrow strip of flesh: 'throw me a buoy, I'm badly hurt.' The yacht headed toward me, throwing me a sort of rope knot too big to be held in one hand. The side of the yacht was too high for anyone to help me. 'Throw a lifesaver.' It comes, and I sit inside it. And here are some fishermen coming into port; their boat is low, they hold out their hands, and I give them my left hand, because I'm holding my thigh together with my right; we reach the place I started from, on the breakwater; I get up on the jetty; a kind driver appears out of nowhere and helps me sit down beside him. The fisherman gets in the backseat. Hospital. They put me on the table and begin sewing me together. This lasts from six to midnight, in two sessions. I've already told you the rest."[28]

For all his mental detachment, he had recognized the imperatives of staying alive.

REPORTING THESE EVENTS through an architect's lens, Le Corbusier emphasized the factor of scale. When the people on the yacht threw out the rope with a large knot, what mattered was that the knot was too large to be held by a human hand. Then the side of the boat was too high for anyone to be able to help. Le Corbusier had had the presence of mind to recognize that he therefore needed a lifesaver and to call out for one to be thrown to him. A command of tools and a knowledge of mechanics had enabled him to survive.

Once Le Corbusier was seated inside the circular buoy, the event became more like a biblical parable. The yacht and its wealthy owners were too far above the roiling sea to help, but because the modest fishermen had a boat that was closer to the surface of the water—a vessel of work rather than pleasure, more connected to the ocean than separate from it—they provided salvation. Rather than risk trying to get the nearly dismembered Le Corbusier into their small boat, they pulled him along and brought him back to the breakwater. The heroes of the story were anonymous: the sympathetic person with a car who rushed to the scene and helped place Le Corbusier in the passenger seat next to him, and the fisherman who rescued him.

Le Corbusier later wrote Marguerite Tjader Harris that he had been "cut to pieces" during the two surgical procedures.[29] He was in the local hospital for four weeks in all. He calculated that he had two meters of stitches—a statistic he often announced—plus a hole in his head.

There was another detail he recounted to his mother as well: "On the green jetty I said to the bystanders: 'Hand me my glasses and my clothes.' "[30] He had not for a moment lost his rationalism.

8

Shortly after the accident, Le Corbusier went into the sort of rage that overtook him when he felt others had inflicted unnecessary suffering on his mother. He was more upset by the way Marie Jeanneret heard about his encounter with the propeller blades than by the event itself. For this he blamed journalists. *Paris-Soir* and other papers had picked up the story about the famous architect and reported it immediately. He was furious that the newspapers' greed for gossip had resulted in his mother's being far more frightened than if he had been the first to inform her—once he had returned to consciousness. The idea of Yvonne becoming involved in the communication seems not to have occurred to him.

And of course the papers were inaccurate. To alleviate the anxiety of his aged parent, Le Corbusier wrote her a letter from the hospital ten days after the surgery to specify the details the papers had gotten wrong, even if he had not succeeded in his goal of telling his mother first—and would have to write a second letter nearly a month later in response to her request for more precision in his report. The person for whom architectural rejection was tantamount to tragedy presented a life-endangering accident as a miracle of good fortune. He also made clear that his concern was for his wife and his mother as much as for himself.

Hospital, Tuesday August 23 '38

Dear Maman,

Yvonne and I sent you a note the other day at Evolème. Did you get it? I was afraid that the papers would have printed the story and that my accident would be revealed to you by some third party. Wretched *Paris-Soir* actually reported the whole thing. . . .

I'll try to put the whole thing on a strictly factual basis:

1. Ten days ago I was sliced up by a yacht propeller.

2. There were several ways of being killed or hideously crippled; and one way of escaping; slick as a lizard. The miracle occurred: I'm calling it the miracle of Saint-Tropez.

3. The head was the object of a special operation, in the presence of Prof. Démarets, one of the glories of Parisian medicine. It could have been serious. Nothing of the kind. Better still, it's all over today, healed, liquidated.

Thigh. Yes, the famous lardaceous tissue. But the propeller cut lengthwise and not across: no vein or artery touched. The wound is the size of the Radiant City (the book). Today is the tenth day. I don't have even one degree of fever. Baths the last four days, and the Carrel-Dakin solution has had its effect. The wound is clean, ready to be sewn up. Here, 1 doctor + 1 surgeon to deal with it. Tough customers who inspire every confidence. The hospital personnel extremely attentive and kind. Bravo, hospital, the only place to go when you're sick. This business has given me the reputation of being extremely brave. From six in the evening to midnight on Saturday the 13, I was cut, sewn, mutilated by the medicos without being put under. The doctor complimented me.

And now everything is put right. I hope to leave the hospital at the end of this week. This monastic retreat has not been without interest for me. High moments of resuming contact with the truth of things.

Yvonne of course was terribly shaken. She's with good friends who love her and are taking care of her.

So now you are well-informed. Take it in with all the serenity of your alpine vacation.

All my affections[31]

The Carrel-Dakin solution to which Le Corbusier referred was a system of irrigation for infected wounds using an antiseptic solution containing sodium hypochlorite. Le Corbusier had no idea that in little time the French surgeon Alexis Carrel, who had developed it with the English chemist Henry Drysdale Dakin, would become a close colleague.

BEDRIDDEN IN the Saint-Tropez recovery unit and unable to move virtually any part of his body while he recuperated, the architect became preoccupied with Juliana, one of his nurses. Her little acts of kindness impressed him deeply, especially as he learned Juliana's life story and became keenly aware that she was an unlucky and grief-stricken woman. Her hardships made her generosity of spirit all the more remarkable.

The Provençale nurse was the first person every morning to smile at people suffering from illness, gracing the lives of all the patients, massaging the muscles of paralytics. She always brought Le Corbusier garden flowers in a glass and placed them on his bedside table. The architect became convinced that an underpaid hospital employee who acted in this way exemplified pure charity. "Each morning's smile is an eloquent object," he wrote.[32] The commentary on Juliana's ability to give joy was both an expression of his priorities and advice to his mother.

9

Marie Jeanneret was deeply upset by all these events but full of admiration for her son's fortitude. The encounter with the yacht motor and his handling of it garnered him some of the praise he craved. On September 11, his mother wrote him,

> Thanks be to God you've left the hospital and can benefit from the good salt air following the dreadful adventures from which you have emerged wounded and further weakened by weeks in bed and so much suffering. The suffering you never mentioned: now you can claim direct lineage with the famous Spartans in their heroic combats with pain. . . .
>
> My dear boy you are a hero; you never fought in a war but had you been in the ranks of the brave soldiers of '14 to '18, you would have been cited for honors, for you have even more character than they, and strong characters are rare. . . .
>
> All of which is not to boast too much about you, but just to acknowledge those who accept without a murmur and suffer without complaint.[33]

She continued, "Make fun of your old lyrical Maman! There has been no lack of bad moments lately, and so we must praise those who warm our hearts."[34] She understood his admiration for Juliana; she also shared her son's insistence on facts and clarity: "Now before ending, I'd like to ask one more favor of you. Couldn't you tell me in detail how the yacht accident actually occurred? How you were found (fainting etc.), how the rescue was effected, things about which we are far from being informed."[35]

Meanwhile, in her suffering, Albert, she assured Edouard, was her "*compagnon fidèle.*" If she meant this to comfort him, it surely had the opposite effect.

BY THE END of the third week of September, Le Corbusier could put on his pants and shoes by himself and had given up his cane. His skin still pulled when he walked, but after more than a month of being immobilized, he was on the mend and in high spirits.

Shortly thereafter, Marie and Albert wrote jointly to Edouard. Now that he had provided the full report as requested, they replied, "Lately your description of the accident gave us all the shudders, and we have thanked God for sparing you. He will preserve you for a still higher task." Le Corbusier's brother added, "The moving account of your accident almost made me faint, but Maman's solid temperament saw her through. Certainly it reads like a page describing the heroes of long ago, whose character is not likely to be found in our period, in the tranquil ambience of present-day life . . . perhaps an ambience quite out of date."[36]

It had taken happenstance, not architecture, to get that admiration at last.

10

After writing Edouard about his accident, Le Corbusier's mother continued, "We need all our strength for future storms, for the Inevitable approaching with giant strides. Can it be possible, O Lord, that by the frenzy of one man an entire continent is being swept into the abyss? I listened to Hitler's speech in Berlin, and since then I cannot believe that so many appeals to humanity and wisdom from so many quarters will be heard! It is abominable and terrifying! Everyone here agrees about assisting those in despair because politics has forced them to accept exile in other countries. But to seek out atrocity and to wield it in this fashion denotes a man who has turned into a barbarian, an hysterical madman, a dangerous mystic. I am overwhelmed by all this, and especially for your sake, in the fiery furnace as you are. What will you and Y and Albert and Lotti do in Paris if war is declared? You know that my little house is always open to you and that you would be safe here. . . . I say this because in your present condition, my son, you cannot assist in the defense of your new country."[37]

Le Corbusier was not as worried as his mother. At the end of 1938, he wrote Marguerite Tjader Harris with the news that the plan for Algiers was moving ahead; finally, he would achieve his objectives there! Using military language—as if, like the armies of Europe, he, too, was waging war—he said that he believed that, after six years of perseverance on various fronts, he had at last conquered public opinion.

His only problem, he confessed to Tjader Harris, was Yvonne's refusal to have sex. He complained that he was living like a monk; the situation with his wife was "harsh and terrible. My nights are filled with intense imaginings." Tjader Harris, of all people, should understand how taxing abstinence was for him: "You know me well enough to know that this ascetic life I am leading is a heroic effort for me." But he was determined to resist other temptations; "If I were to yield even slightly now, I should be a ruined man."[38]

The year 1938 loomed in Le Corbusier's thoughts as the "*époque magnifique.*"[39] Tjader Harris thought so, too. From her large house in Darien, leading the life of a dutiful daughter and attentive mother, she wrote him delicately flirtatious letters. She regularly gave news of Toutou and her mother and asked warmly after Le Corbusier's mother, but most of all she missed its being just the two of them. A friend of hers adored her Le Corbusier chair; nice as that was, she longed for the architect "by himself."[40]

11

In March 1939, one of Le Corbusier's best Spanish friends was killed by a bomb. The architect wrote his mother, "One must not let oneself be overwhelmed by death. It is the most natural event in life. If life has been even normally fulfilled, I do not see how death can come as a disruption."[41] He was devastated when Franco's forces then took Madrid and Hitler invaded Poland—there would be fewer chances to make architecture when people could think only of defending what they already had rather than building anything new—but he was determined to hold the darkness at bay: "Better to occupy one's life with possible hopes than collapse into neurasthenia. Certainly this is the time for patience. France has been in crisis since 1932. No one is doing any building. And the flag must be kept flying, ready for the moment of rebirth."[42]

Meanwhile, once Le Corbusier had an idea in mind, he did not let it drop. The architect was working on "a museum for unlimited growth." The project was an elaboration of his earlier scheme for a contemporary-art showcase in Paris and of the concept he had pitched to Nelson Rockefeller. Again it was built from inside out as a square spiral and was capable of indefinite expansion, with the idea that what was an exterior wall on one day would become an interior one the next. But now it was a structure raised on pilotis, entered at its center, from underneath.

Le Corbusier wrote his mother on June 3, 1939, from Fleming's Hotel on Piccadilly in London telling her he was developing the scheme for an American client—"Guggenheim, the copper king of New York," to whom he was about to present it.[43] This was Solomon Guggenheim, the man who ultimately was the chief patron of the great art museum that bore his name when it was completed in New York in 1960. Hilla Rebay, Guggenheim's art advisor and emissary, was with him at that presentation in London. She very much liked the square spiral of ramps and the idea of entering into the core of a building that worked from inside out.

Four years later, Rebay began conversations with Frank Lloyd Wright about a museum structure to be funded by Solomon Guggenheim. The spiral that Wright designed for that patron was circular rather than square, finite, vertical, and with a large central atrium. Nonetheless, Le Corbusier's revolutionary idea for a linear presentation of modern art, with the visitor moving continuously around a central axis in a progression that broke the mold of exhibition architecture, was possibly at the root of Wright's idea, having been communicated by Rebay and by Gugggenheim, even though Le Corbusier never made the claim or tried to take credit, any more than he ever proposed that the ramps at the villas La Roche or Savoye had influenced Wright's museum design.

12

On September 3, France and England declared war against Germany. Le Corbusier was officially relieved of all military obligations because of his age, and his swimming accident and his vision problem disqualified him from volunteering as a soldier anyway, but he wrote to three different friends with high government positions seeking employment that would be of maximum usefulness to the country.

At 5:00 p.m. on the day war was declared, Le Corbusier wrote his mother, "We are—each of us—quite incapable of facing events with any sort of mastery. The unspeakable is occurring quite mechanically, with no regard for human sensibility."[44] The next day, he and Yvonne left Paris.

They first went to Vézelay, a lovely hill town in Burgundy where their friend Jean Badovici lived and that has one of the most splendid of all Romanesque cathedrals. Le Corbusier wanted Yvonne to be in a place where she felt comfortable; he figured he would wait there, too, until he was somehow called to action. Pierre Jeanneret, meanwhile, went to Savoie, and Albert and his family accepted Marie Jeanneret's invitation to install themselves in Vevey.

Le Corbusier wrote his seventy-nine-year-old mother, "Your fate may be as perilous as ours. . . . Yet I hope that Maman will be sheltered from it all. We must now see reason and realize, quite simply, that we have insufficiently appreciated all the years that were without pain." Just as he had stayed calm when his leg was severed, he was determined to make sense of a senseless world. "Impossible to speculate about the future. Will the conflict be short or long? Unknown. Whatever the case, the consequences will be crucial. Ripeness is all. . . . I've already told you where I believe the heart of the matter is: a reorganization of consciousness and a major revision of the conditions of life." Le Corbusier believed his imperative was "as much as possible, to pursue life, to create, to act, not to halt."[45]

The times were, of course, undeniably treacherous. On September 27, he wrote his mother and brother, "I am almost ready to acknowledge that the situation is so far beyond human capacities that it cannot be mastered by anyone." Yet the "almost" was key: he was confident that "the new cycle will begin. . . . One thing is certain: men will leave their shoes behind and put on new ones."[46]

Le Corbusier hated "Germany infatuated by its belligerent violence, a violence so dense and heavy it terrifies us all and must be destroyed." But he still saw the world as being on the verge of positive change and welcomed war just as he welcomed fire. Anything was better than stagnancy; destruction was always the preamble to construction: "There are great demolitions only when a great building site is about to open," he assured his mother.[47] Devastating as it was to see civilization pulverized, he was convinced that the losses would pave the way for him to design and build.

13

Jean Giraudoux was writing an introduction for Le Corbusier's *Charter of Athens.* In July 1938, Edouard Daladier, France's prime minister, had appointed Giraudoux head of the Information Commissariat, which made him responsible for French government propaganda and gave him great influence. Giraudoux believed that even if France lacked the economic or military power of other countries, it was distinguished by "the moral nature of her form of life."[48] He also had strong ideas of national self-improvement. The writer favored a firm policy concerning the physical well-being of French citizens, calling for active participation in sports and a comprehensive campaign against tuberculosis. Beyond that, he envisioned more urban planning.

To his mother, Le Corbusier described the opinionated playwright as "a sympathetic type—a splendid head, very sensitive." At the office on the rue de Sèvres, because of connections made through Giraudoux, the staff was working on "an excellent enterprise for temporary barracks, primarily for the refugee schools."[49] Requested by the national minister of education, these structures could be taken apart, moved, and reassembled as clubs, nursery schools, studios, or housing, depending on need. Le Corbusier believed that they would become prototypes for building throughout the country.

In the second week of October 1939, Le Corbusier returned to Paris from Vézelay for a meeting he had arranged with Giraudoux. Its purpose was the creation of Le Comité d'études préparatoires urbaniques. The goal of this organization was to plan the work that might occur in peacetime, once this dreadful situation was over. After the two men met, Le Corbusier wrote his mother, "The interview was really a moving one. I believe we are the left and right hands of a single body."[50]

Giraudoux invited Le Corbusier to lunch ten days later so that they could talk in greater depth. The encounter inspired one of Le Corbusier's epiphanies: "And then I felt that the way lay open and that the hour of realities was striking. . . . It was some fifteen years of preparation that were bearing fruit."[51]

Infused with confidence, Le Corbusier set about meeting other influential government officials and their aides. His movement in the corridors of power paid off; he discovered that people high up in the Education Ministry had read his work and wanted to hear his ideas: "Result: the decision is up to me. Up to me to offer these men laden with cares a clear and objective plan. Giraudoux's views are lofty—total. At last, the scope of human beings is here equivalent to the scope of events."[52]

Having secured the necessary backing, Le Corbusier said that the purpose of the new organization he would run under Giraudoux's authority was "to establish juridically, legally, the status of urbanism in France and in the colonies." His role, which he outlined with pride to his mother, was "to be the instigating, doctrinaire cell."[53] He could now put Giraudoux's lofty ideas into effect.

Jean Giraudoux considered France an "invaded country" suffering from having welcomed too many refugees; this "continuous infiltration of barbarians" was bringing the nation down. The playwright favored a draconian immigration policy that would incorporate "pitiless surveillance" and "send back those elements which could corrupt a race which owes its value to the selection and refining process of twenty centuries." Foreigners were "swarming in our arts and in our old and new industries, in a kind of spontaneous generation reminiscent of fleas on a newly born puppy." He lamented the "Arabs polluting at Grenelle," the "Ashkenazis, escaped from Polish or Romanian ghettoes . . . who eliminate our compatriots . . . from their traditions . . . and from their artistic trades. . . . A horde . . . which encumbers our hospitals."[54]

Giraudoux wanted to create a minister of race. The man whom Le Corbusier called the other hand of the same body, whose book he urged his mother to read as the epitome of rectitude and grandeur, declared—in that very book—"We are in full agreement with Hitler in proclaiming that a policy only achieves its highest plane once it is racial." Giraudoux distinguished himself from the Germans with their search for the perfect Aryan by emphasizing "moral and cultural" qualities rather than physical ones, but nonetheless pointed out that immigrants "rarely beautify by their physical appearance."[55]

Was Le Corbusier overlooking these ideas in a blindness induced by the rekindled hope that he had found the means to build his ideal cities? Now that the Swiss, the Soviets, and the Americans had let him down, was he simply convincing himself of Giraudoux's merits because he thought Giraudoux would allow him to construct on the scale of which he dreamed, or were these thoughts about other races his as well?

14

Le Corbusier stepped up the pace of his return trips to Paris. By the end of November, the arms minister, Raoul Dautry, had asked him to design a large munitions factory intended mainly to produce shotgun cartridges. Dautry gave the architect the rank of colonel and Pierre Jeanneret that of captain. In this time that was the start of a nightmare for many in France, the office staff was increasingly productive.

The onset of winter weather changed that. Since there was no heating oil available, it was impossible to keep the office open and continue staying at 24 rue Nungesser-et-Coli. Le Corbusier returned to Vézelay. Back in the Burgundian village, he painted, worked on large panels, and read English detective novels. He wrote his mother little domestic reports: "Yvonne's eyes ever dynamic: dynamite."[56] "Pinceau wants to make *pipi,* Pinceau wants to make *caca.*"[57] He also reflected on the changes he hoped to effect in France:

> The country needs several kicks in the ass. There is too much dust and dirt, too much sleep, too many false terrors and ghosts. And too much love of money. Money is over and done with.
>
> It's all coming to an end, and when it does, we shall have won back the true values and the spirit of things.
>
> Hope is in season.[58]

IN A LETTER to Marguerite Tjader Harris from Vézelay, Le Corbusier wrote that in his new job he was accepting only the salary paid to military people on the front. He hoped to sell enough paintings to provide the additional funds needed for his way of life—not easy since for seven years his architectural practice had been in what he termed a "*dépression,*" with no work at all.

Desperately, he asked his mistress in Connecticut if she or her friends could buy his paintings—abstract or figurative, gouache, watercolor, or pastel. He said he would sell them starting at thirty dollars each. Now praising Americans for sympathizing with the French cause, he believed that, if they understood his dire financial straits, they would be more willing to purchase his work. Tjader Harris did what she could to help. She looked for collectors and agreed to give up her translation fee for *When the Cathedrals Were White.* Le Corbusier regularly took his secret letters to the Vézelay postbox without Yvonne knowing what he was doing. But in his own way, he was loyal to his wife, writing Tjader Harris that Yvonne was "strong, pure, whole, clear. I have great admiration for her. She is a peasant girl, as I have told you. For me, a perfect companion. But I must remind you that I, too, am a fine fellow."[59]

15

That December, Le Corbusier told his mother that the shortage of trains would make it impossible for him to go to Vevey for the holidays. He reported diplomatically that Yvonne insisted he make every effort to get to Switzerland without her, but that was not feasible.

A week before Christmas, Le Corbusier wrote Marie,

> A good nap leads to collapse. Doctor Carrel, whom I saw last Thursday, told me as much: comfort annihilates the human race. There must be struggles. So don't take life's difficulties (whatever they may be) as catastrophes, but rather as good hygiene. It's what makes life possible. For if the contrary point of view prevails, everything seems merely disaster.
>
> We have philosophized with Carrel down to the last issue—the search for what is best for mankind, and we are in perfect agreement: the power to create, to intervene, to act is our lifeblood. Otherwise, deterioration. Carrel will work with us.[60]

Alexis Carrel, a scientist who had won a Nobel Prize and whose wound treatment had benefited Le Corbusier after his swimming accident, had published, in 1935, the best-selling *Man, the Unknown.* In it, he insisted on the most traditional gender differentiation: "The sexes have again to be clearly defined. Each individual must be either male or female, and never manifest the sexual tendencies, mental characteristics, and ambitions of the opposite sex."[61] The primary role of woman, Carrel maintained, was to bear children.

Whether he subscribed to every word of that best-selling book, this was the man with whom Le Corbusier described himself "in perfect agreement."

XXXIV

1

> A man who prides himself on following a straight line through life is an idiot who believes in infallibility. There are no such things as principles: there are only events, there are no laws but those of expediency. . . . A man is not obliged to be more particular than the nation.
>
> —HONORÉ DE BALZAC, *Eugénie Grandet*

At the start of 1940, Le Corbusier and Yvonne moved back to Paris, where there was now heating oil. Pierre and Albert also returned to the capital. Le Corbusier reopened the office on the rue de Sèvres and met again with Raoul Dautry about the proposed munitions factory.

Le Corbusier boasted to his mother that the arms minister had said, "Le Corbusier is a man of courage, and he has done something with his life." Proud to have garnered approval in the precincts of the new government, he wrote her, "You cannot imagine what perseverance it takes to offer one's service to one's country when such service means dealing with tomorrow."[1]

Dautry, like Giraudoux, was a strident nationalist whose faith in hard work and the common man appealed to Le Corbusier. For the catalog of the 1939 World's Fair in New York, the minister had written, "In France it is the peasant who holds the secrets of the race. In the harmonious construction called France, the land and its cultivation provide the fundamental economic, social and cultural foundation."[2] Le Corbusier was delighted that the author of that statement was now his main client. By mid-February, the munitions factory had evolved into a structure for three thousand workers, with temporary living facilities for one thousand.

Not only was he fulfilling his hope of being part of the war effort, but Le Corbusier also believed that he had found the cure for his perpetual foe, the common cold. "Colds," he wrote his mother: "I'll give you the prescription: from the first symptom sleep with a woolen turban or ski helmet around your head. If you do this, the cold goes no further. For years I've been victimized by these damned colds that used to flatten me several times a winter. You can understand this: at night your skull is exposed. And when the skull gets sick, we leave it out in the cold. You *must* enforce this procedure, it's a golden rule."[3]

YVONNE REDID the apartment on the rue Nungesser-et-Coli, impressing her husband immensely with her clever management of domestic life in a period when there was neither staff nor cash. The architect bragged to his mother that his wife got up before him in the morning and went to sleep after: "She does her work admirably."[4] But Yvonne was suffering from an obstruction of one of her tear ducts, which periodically had her screaming in pain. For the first time, Le Corbusier reported her in a dark mood—the product of her physical discomfort combined with their isolation in a deserted section of Paris.

In mid-March, at the first hint of spring, Le Corbusier again took up gardening—in a deliberate attempt to maintain his "euphoria under the daily threat of horrors."[5] And then the horrors came. On May 10, he and Yvonne were woken at dawn by an air alert. At 8:30, they learned over the wireless radio that the Germans had entered France.[6]

2

At noon, while waiting for a second radio broadcast, Le Corbusier informed his mother, "Such events do not discourage me; on the contrary, my temperament finds in them that movement and that struggle which alone can ultimately lead to the world's improvement. One cannot, one must not cling desperately to a dead past. Ultimately one must raise one's head and set out."[7]

At a moment that sent shivers of fear up the spines of almost everyone else in Paris, Le Corbusier counseled his mother that she should enjoy her existence and maintain a light touch. "Let a good life flow gently past, whatever follies it commits, whatever pleasures it chooses."[8]

At 1:00 p.m., he added the news that Switzerland was mobilized; Pierre, a Swiss citizen, was going to have to leave Paris. Le Corbusier was worried that Albert would have to as well.

The day was a turning point in the history of France. It was the start of the Wehrmacht offensive; within five weeks, the Germans would kill some ninety-two thousand soldiers and take nearly two million prisoners. The

French air force was inefficient and underequipped, unable to resist the German advance. For Le Corbusier, this invasion of a foreign culture, even though he disdained it, was stimulating; he was determined to flourish with the change.

ON MAY 21, Le Corbusier and Yvonne were still in their penthouse apartment. There were frequent air raids, but they felt themselves out of danger. Having mostly avoided the cellar of 20 rue Jacob during the previous war, now he was proud that the basement at number 24 was considered the best bomb shelter on the street.

Le Corbusier reported to his mother, "Yvonne is doing just fine. All the same, her ultra-nervous temperament makes her suffer at times."[9] His plan, although he did not follow through on it, was to send her to Vézelay while he would remain in Paris to work on the munitions factory, which was under construction in the foothills of the Pyrénées and was to be two kilometers long. Le Corbusier was to have the responsibility for housing its twenty thousand workers and their families; the plight of these people in the mining basin had become desperate, which meant that he could realize his ideas on urbanism as he had dreamed: to benefit the people who needed the most help.

It was a moment of opportunity, even if Hitler's power and success were horrific. He loathed the Nazi leader and his backers—"that cruel Hitler. . . . In truth the German people is stupefying in its choice of such a master. For they have chosen him"—but was determined not to crumble.[10]

"One develops a sort of hole in one's stomach when one imagines even for a second that this dreadful *simpliste*—powerful because of his simplicity, a beast for being so deliberately simple—could annihilate us here," he wrote, "before the horror of such a situation, the world comes to a realization, belatedly, as ever. It is up to us to be vigilant, to exert *strength in our turn,* once the pressure is off. There is such a thing as courage, there is such a thing as faith. But our conscience must have new motives."[11]

AS THE GERMANS advanced into Paris, government authorities urged the city's inhabitants not to panic and ordered them to stay where they were, but the plea was to little avail. Some of the people in charge fled, leaving a betrayed and resentful citizenry to follow. On many farms on the outskirts of Paris, only the livestock was left. Observing the exodus from the air, Antoine de Saint-Exupéry compared it to the sight of an enormous anthill toppled by a giant.

By June, the Germans had completed their takeover of the French capital. They were to remain there for the next four years.

CONSTRUCTION ON the munitions factory came to a halt, and Pierre Jeanneret and Le Corbusier closed their office at 35 rue de Sèvres. They and Yvonne left Paris together and went almost as far from the city as one could while still remaining in France—to Ozon, near Tournay.

Seeking a secure location now that it could no longer maintain its traditional seat in the capital, the French government, under Prime Minister Paul Reynaud, moved to Tours and then to Bordeaux. The deputy prime minister, Maréchal Henri Pétain, became its main spokesman. On June 16, Reynaud resigned in Pétain's favor, and the following day, five days after Le Corbusier and Yvonne arrived in Ozon, Pétain went on French radio to say that "with a heavy heart" he was declaring the end of hostilities.[12] Five days later, he signed the armistice, accepting the defeat of France.

To many French people, Pétain, who had played a heroic role during World War I in the battle of Verdun, seemed a savior. They believed that with the French army having succumbed to the Germans, the British now would as well. In all likehood, the war was lost, but, thanks to Pétain, at least the devastation of France would not be total.

NOT EVERYONE ACCEPTED French defeat, however. On June 17, General Charles de Gaulle, the undersecretary of the War Ministry, flew from Bordeaux to London to organize a continuation of the war effort. Le Corbusier admired the bravery but did not agree with the choice: "Now for some courage. But for me, my role is here, in this country. I will not and cannot leave France after this defeat. I must fight here where I believe it is necessary to put the world of construction on the right track."[13]

At least this is the rationale Le Corbusier later gave for working with the Pétain regime. This and similar quotations are cited ambiguously in *Corbusier Himself,* the book the architect wrote in 1960. He gives the impression that this is what he said in 1940. But there is no documentary evidence that the notion of the nobility of remaining on French soil to work was anything but an afterthought inserted into the record well after the war.

What is certain is that, on July 1, Pétain and his government established itself in assorted hotel rooms in the spa town of Vichy, in the middle of France, in the so-called Free Zone just south of the jagged border that divided France in two parts. By July 3, Le Corbusier, too, was in Vichy.

On the balcony of his hotel in Vichy, 1942.
On the reverse he has written, "à Yvonne,
pour remplacer son homme. Vichy 1942."

3

For the next two years, Vichy was Le Corbusier's main base. He stayed in one or another of its large hotels, sometimes on his own, at other times with Yvonne and their dog. These hotels, built for the visitors who came to the spa for the curative power of its waters, were one of the reasons the new government had selected the desultory town in the northern part of the Auvergne. Vacant now that people could not indulge in luxury travel, Vichy provided housing for the new ministries and instant accommodations for everyone on Pétain's team. The town also boasted an unusually sophisticated telephone switchboard.

Pétain had his offices on the third floor of the Hotel du Parc, overlooking some gardens; his second in command, Pierre Laval, was on the floor below. The Ministry of the Interior had established itself in the gaming rooms of the casino. Spaces were cramped, with people's offices in their bedrooms and bathtubs serving as filing cabinets.

The town was small; if you didn't run into someone in your hotel lobby, you might well do so on the street. This was how encounters took place and plans were made, in an atmosphere of constant gossip, intrigue, and power plays.

On July 10, six hundred deputies and senators convened in Vichy's old opera house and voted for the end of the Third Republic. The terms of the armistice with Germany charged the new government with maintaining order, thus minimizing the need for German manpower. While occupying Paris and the more populous and productive part of France, the Germans intended to maintain their latest conquest as a base for further military action and make optimal use of French resources.

Many of the French believed that Pétain was a leader who could counter the decadence that had led to their defeat. He favored a "strong, authoritarian government." By a vast majority, the National Assembly granted the eighty-four-year-old leader the role of president and prime minister combined and gave him unrestricted powers. His slogan of choice—in lieu of "Liberté, Egalité, Fraternité"—was "Travail, Famille, Patrie." It was a call for "the virtues of hard work, honesty, and respect for one's social superiors, which he imagined had existed in rural society." His goal, and that of his supporters, was "elite rule, the protection of private property, social harmony and order."[14] To that end, in October, both Laval and Pétain had cordial and productive meetings with Hitler.

With a model for a skyscraper for Algiers, ca. 1939

IMMEDIATELY AFTER the invasion of Paris, Le Corbusier had flown, under the auspices of this new French government, to Algiers for eight intense days of discussions on his renewal of that city. The trip had thrilled him—in part because of the air journey, which allowed him to go, in five and a half hours, from unexpectedly "glacial" spring temperatures in Paris to tropical heat.[15] And Algiers offered the greatest of elixirs: the prospect of work.

Le Corbusier knew that the lack of material resources put all building projects at risk. But when he arrived in Vichy two days after Pétain did, he was determined above all to move his Algerian proposals from the planning stage to reality.

4

Yvonne accompanied Le Corbusier to Vichy. Suffering from malnutrition and miserable at another dislocation, she found it hard to settle into the dilapidated spa town. "Obvious undernourishment a vicious circle, nothing to be done," Le Corbusier lamented to his mother about his frail wife.[16] The weather conditions were debilitating, and even though Yvonne was already taking the waters for which Vichy was famous, she and Le Corbusier knew that she needed mountain air instead.

She did her best to make the most of their situation. Le Corbusier proudly told his mother that his wife made herself loved by everyone. She organized their mediocre hotel room impeccably, with true artistry, and made him feel completely at home. This was high praise from one of the world's greatest designers of domestic interiors.

In these tough times, such comforts were even more welcome than usual. Food was hard to procure, and meat, normally a staple of Yvonne's and Le Corbusier's diet, scarce. Yvonne's ability to add charm to their existence buoyed his spirits in this new, uncertain life where the eighty-four-year-old maréchal seemed the one source of hope.

LE CORBUSIER gave his mother a detailed account of a significant event that occurred shortly after his arrival in Vichy, concerning his and Yvonne's beloved dog, the schnauzer Pinceau. One day when the architect was out walking him, Pinceau was spotted for his good looks and invited to breed with a bitch belonging to the son of Admiral Darlan. Darlan was almost as important as Pétain in the new government.

The admiral was a man of sharp views. He attributed France's problems to its "Judaeo-Masonic political habits" and said that, while the British had always lied to him, the Germans could be trusted. Darlan was convinced that

With his dog Pinceau I, on the roof of the Petite Maison, ca. 1935

France was destined to become part of "German Europe"—as opposed to the America-dominated bloc of countries that would be its rival. Later in 1940, he met with Hitler at Berchtesgaden, after which he declared, "My choice is made: it is collaboration. . . . France's interest is to live and to remain a great power. . . . In the present state of the world, . . . I see no other solution to protect our interests."[17] Darlan helped create the General Commissariat for Jewish Matters, which in turn initiated the "secondary status of Jews."

Le Corbusier wrote his mother about the attempted breeding. "A little farce, this week: Admiral Darlan's son wanted Pinceau as a stud for his bitch, going into her first heat. Pinceau having declared himself willing in the course of his promenades in the park. For two days, the two of them were brought together in the Admiral's garage . . . nothing was consummated! Each creature sulked in his own corner!"[18] Preoccupied with issues of potency, the architect was more bothered by his dog's recalcitrance than by who the admiral was.

5

In August, Le Corbusier and Yvonne accommodated her need for mountain air by returning to Ozon. Yvonne hated its isolation and missed both Véze-

Sketch of Main Street in Ozon with Pinceau I urinating, in a letter to his mother, August 18, 1940

lay and Le Piquey, but they had become "sealed regions" and were no longer options.[19]

In Ozon, Le Corbusier evaluated his progress in Vichy. He had made little headway with the new authorities. In his feverish efforts to establish contact with anyone in a position to give him work, his sole success was a single response from René Belin, "former secretary of the G.C.T. [Confédération Générale du Travail, a trade union]."[20] Belin was sympathetic to Le Corbusier's wish to work on Algiers and other projects, and he offered to help.

While Le Corbusier recognized that most government officials were caught up in more urgent matters, he wrote his mother, "All the same I knock tirelessly, day after day, on door after door. And perhaps someday we shall manage to serve the country usefully."[21] He assured Marie that if France in 1940 had managed a military victory, the scum would have taken over, and society would have only declined. What had happened instead was full of potential if one could take advantage of it.

Le Corbusier lectured his mother that libelous statements were too often believed by a misinformed public and that people who previously appeared to have been evil might actually help solve the recent rash of problems: "Here is what Balzac says: 'Fools employ negative discretion: silence, negation, frowns, the discretion of closed doors, true impotence.' "[22] With this rationale, as he waited for news from Vichy, he justified his "open-mindedness" about Maréchal Pétain and his minions.

MARIE JEANNERET-PERRET was one of many people who detested Hitler but did not connect Vichy with the Nazis and their atrocities. She was thrilled with her son's efforts to link himself to Pétain's regime. She wrote him and Yvonne jointly: "One is so grateful to know you are alive, and in good health, too, ready to work again, to start over, and to be one of the first active agents in the service of that France which seeks to rise again and renew herself. . . . Edouard's beautiful letter read and re-read—so true, so serious in its deductions apropos of the tragic events which have led France to surrender—fills us with hope for her future destiny, when an honest, severe direction will cleanse, will purify, will heal her wounds. . . . [T]his is an epic moment, unique for France; that she will accept it is to be hoped with relief and certainty. . . . Our thoughts here in Switzerland follow Vichy's movements and the vigorous speeches (of the old man whom some blame for letting himself be influenced by those who wield the powers of victory), admiring his robust good sense, his unflagging energy in the colossal task of renewal imposed upon him. And with pride we think of what you can contribute: your colossal work, your Swiss research, your magnificent intelligence, all in the service of the noble resurrection of a great country."[23]

Inspired to optimism by this leader who was even older than she was, Marie continued, "This old Maman nearing eighty has failed a lot; eyes and ears unsteady, frequent lassitude, legs a little less adjusted to 2000 and 3000 meters! Yet the situation is still splendid in comparison to old people of my age, and I dare say or do nothing but be eternally grateful for my lot."[24] In that dark period of France's history, Maréchal Pétain and Le Corbusier together had at last succeeded in infusing La Petite Maman with the optimism and well-being he had always urged on her.

6

On the eighteenth of August, anticipating his mother's eightieth birthday by about three weeks, Le Corbusier wrote her from Ozon.

> On September 10th you will be eighty years, proof that one is still young at such an age. Eighty years old and you remain your sons' companion, staving off the years, ever smiling and laughing.
>
> You find us closer to you than ever, for you have all our confidence, seeing that nothing daunts you, that your enthusiasm, your faith in what is good increases every day. Our family is quite small, but it is close and firm, and the vital memory of our Papa cements the fourth corner of the wall and that of dear Aunt Pauline is the fifth point of the star.
>
> There you have our accounting. Brief, but dense and positive.
>
> Let me tell you on the occasion of this splendid anniversary what I'm thinking of Albert your son attached to you by such strong bonds.[25]

From there Edouard launched yet again into an analysis of his older brother and of Albert's situation. Edouard emphasized that Albert led a less important life than he did and was too dependent on their mother. On the other hand, Edouard was grateful that Albert's presence in Vevey enabled him to continue his own work elsewhere with the knowledge that their mother was not alone.

Edouard and Yvonne could not attend the birthday celebration in this time when the authorities would not permit travel across international borders, but his writing proved a great substitute. Marie was so moved by this letter that, when a group of friends and family members assembled for the birthday celebration in Vevey, she had it read publicly. The condescension toward Albert seemed to bother no one. The listeners, she reported back to Le Corbusier, were "overcome by such filial fervor, such love for our little family."[26] Now that he was devoting himself to a cause she believed in, he could do nothing wrong.

AS SUMMER WOUND DOWN, there was nothing to do but swim every day and await further summons to Vichy. Le Corbusier decided not to return to Paris the coming winter; there would be no heat and no work. At least he had enough money to send Albert a bank draft to cover the cost of a nice meal on their mother's birthday.

For his eighty-year-old mother, Le Corbusier used words remarkably close to those he later inscribed in the windows at Ronchamp in honor of another Marie: "We shall think a great deal of our dear Maman, so glorious and radiant."[27] She had, he wrote, imbued in him his miraculous strength.

7

In the third week of September, Le Corbusier returned to Vichy—this time without Yvonne. The trip was "a journey through hell." He got from Ozon to Toulouse easily enough, but then it took him another twenty-four hours before the packed train arrived in Pétain's capital. He was astonished by the destruction of villages he saw en route and, as the congested train rolled on at its lugubrious pace, became increasingly worried about the wife he had left behind.

Shortly after arriving, Le Corbusier wrote Yvonne a letter that addressed issues he did not dare bring up face-to-face. In the infantilizing voice he always used with her, he wrote, "I have thought about you a great deal, dear Von, for I think of you often. At this moment I feel you are out of sorts, and I am very concerned. I look at you and I actually examine you, though you don't believe it."[28]

Le Corbusier told her that he had urgently consulted one of Vichy's medical specialists on her behalf. The doctor said that Yvonne was suffering from nervous agitation, exacerbated by menopause, and that her nature made her even edgier. Her difficulties, he explained, resulted from a glandular deficiency, for which she needed to take hormone replacement; he wanted her to see the best doctors and begin treatment right away.

He thought Yvonne would be happy to know that, after a tortured night of complete insomnia on the train, during which he ruminated on her situation, he had concluded, "You are wonderfully healthy you are not sick at all, what you have is simply a nervous depression. And we shall manage to overcome that. . . . Your illness comes in large part from your *will.*"[29]

They had been together for twenty years; in his restive state, he had been full of memories of her beauty. Meanwhile, she should understand that he, too, was struggling. Determined to succeed in Vichy, he was exhausted; after that wretched trip, he had to walk around for two hours before finding a hotel room, which was both uncomfortable and overpriced. Nonetheless, he exemplified the benefits of a determination he urged her to emulate.

Nothing was easy: "To conclude, I have just pitched a duck wing onto my jacket (the one with polka dots) because the knife didn't cut."[30]

AS PEOPLE WERE BEING marched off to concentration camps, the insufficiently sharp knife and the stain on his jacket disturbed Le Corbusier.

He was in bad humor in general, because he had no idea what his future would bring; nor did he know where he and Yvonne should live. In Paris, he would be without work and unable to function; Ozon was becoming inhabitable in the cold weather, but the woodstove he had put into their room was proving inadequate. Vichy seemed as good a place as any to settle, although Yvonne's condition made her unfit for the arduous journey there.

At the start of October, Le Corbusier became desperate for other reasons. For the previous two months, all mail had been blocked at the border, and the complete lack of news from his mother and Albert was unbearable. All was not lost, however; Le Corbusier assured his wife that, in the week he had spent in Vichy, he had met with a lot of people. The new authorities were efficient and capable. He admired the way the city had been cleaned up, and he imagined he could work well with these people.

Le Corbusier's spirits lifted all the more when he finally heard from his mother. While she lamented the war—"Everything seems so utterly sad, really lamentable! The newspapers can no longer be read, at least I cannot daily ingurgitate so many acts of violence, such miseries and tragedies in this pitiless war. It is the end of civilization the world over"—she still believed that Vichy was a ray of hope. "Above all we think of France, in this present state of the world! We listen to the radio and we are moved by all that she is enduring with such dignity. . . . How many are those that have sided with this restoration and general reconstruction. All true Frenchmen call for it and will loyally serve the Good Cause, the rescue of beloved France."[31]

Again Marie Jeanneret endorsed her son's efforts to work with these good people in Vichy: "I think of you continually, hoping that you will soon be called upon to move, to function! God willing, I shall live long enough to see you as one of the best workers for your country, and with you others equally qualified." Le Corbusier's mother was proud of his connection with the fascist supporters of Vichy who favored the Germanization of France. She and his older brother were bursting with pride because Albert had met "Marcel Bucard, the leader of the French *franciste* party who at the mention of your name gave a start: 'What! The great Le Corbusier. The unique Le Corbusier!' . . . It seems that this Bucard has even collaborated with you and your friends Winter and Pierrefeu." Marie commended Le Corbusier for having left Paris, with all of its restrictions and privations, for Vichy: "Properly governed, France will once again become great and strong with our best sons. Honest, reliable—long live this new and beautiful France!"[32]

8

Le Corbusier's new friends embraced many of the ideals central to Vichy thinking. Bucard's Mouvement Franciste, which the World War I veteran had founded in 1933, was a royalist, far-right organization financed by Mussolini's government. Its members wore a uniform of blue shirts and practiced the Roman salute.

Le Corbusier's old friend François de Pierrefeu had introduced him to Bucard. De Pierrefeu was a construction engineer who in the 1920s became director of major hydraulic works, overseeing the building of dams in metropolitan France, Algeria, and Morocco. In Tangiers, he had become passionate about painting, sculpture, and architecture, and in 1932 had published the book *Le Corbusier and Pierre Jeanneret.* That same year, de Pierrefeu had joined Le Corbusier and Pierre Winter on the masthead of the periodi-

In the stadium at Vichy, August 31, 1941

cal *Plans.* The following year, the three of them, together with Hubert Lagardelle, created *Prélude,* the publication of the Central Committee of Regionalist and Syndicalist Action. Throughout the thirties, de Pierrefeu was a technical and economic advisor to Le Corbusier on various plans for Algiers and Nemours; now, in the winter of 1940–1941, he took on the task, among others, of trying to help Le Corbusier do whatever it took to remake Algiers as they both desired. De Pierrefeu was working with zeal to advance Le Corbusier's cause within the internecine structure of Pétain's government; to have Bucard as a champion was a big step.

Thanks to Pierre Winter, the other person to whom Le Corbusier's mother referred in using the verb "*collaborer,*" Le Corbusier had inaugurated, in 1925, the headquarters of Le Faisceau with a slide lecture, prompting its founder, Georges Valois, to write:

> Le Corbusier's conceptions translate our deepest thoughts. Le Corbusier is quite simply a man of genius who has conceived, as no one before him, the Modern City.
>
> I do not want to set forth his conceptions here. They are of incomparable grandeur. We must request him to discuss them for a public of several million. He is a formidable figure. Our comrades' initial reaction to his slides was a moment of astonishment; then they understood and entered into a moment of enthusiasm. Enthusiasm is the word. Before the city of tomorrow—great, beautiful, rational and full of faith—they saw their own dream materialized.
>
> I then said how his grand conceptions expressed the deepest thought of Fascism, of the Fascist revolution. . . .
>
> Now, Fascism is precisely this, a rational organization of the entire national life, conceived so that the individual initiative is multiplied by ten. Le Corbusier's work expresses this with genius: this must be said and said again. It is prodigiously in advance of Baron Haussmann.
>
> Upon seeing his slides of the city of tomorrow, it occurred to all our comrades that Fascism is not the act of rioters sacking a ministry—no, it is a great constructive revolution which will give the world the cities of Light, of Joy, of Peace from which poverty will be banished. We expressed to Monsieur Le Corbusier, along with our thanks, our profound admiration.[33]

Winter took Le Faisceau to a new level in 1928 when, as chief surgeon of the Faculté de Médecine in Paris, he had helped create the Parti Fasciste Révolutionnaire. He was a passionate believer in the Radiant City, which he saw as a means of realizing his political program and the fascist agenda of revolutionary changes in the fields of science and medicine.

There is a theory that, after the end of World War II, Le Corbusier destroyed a lot of the files relating to these connections that might now embarrass him. Even if documents concerning Winter are gone, certain facts still stand out. Winter was a true military hero of the type Le Corbusier admired. He had sustained various injuries in his service for the "forty-sixth battalion of Alpine hunters." By 1930, he and Le Corbusier were close enough to write one another as "*mon cher ami.*" Winter had Le Corbusier become, at his behest, an active member of the Syndicat d'Initiative de Paris. That same year, when Le Corbusier represented France at CIAM, he counted on Winter to testify to the medical benefits of his views on "Air Sound Light." As always, the request was made with evangelical urgency: "You will greatly assist the advance of modern times."[34]

Through the period of Vichy, Le Corbusier and Pierre Winter maintained the closeness they had formed as neighbors at 24 rue Nungesser-et-Coli. Winter was a close colleague of de Pierrefeu's and Giraudoux's as well; they all had similar theories on "urbanism and biology."

Le Corbusier was convinced that these associates and the other people in charge in Vichy would effect change that would benefit every aspect of French life. They would improve hygiene and sanitation. Their regulations concerning the production and labeling of alcoholic beverages, which the new regime instigated, were the sort of bold moves that improved human existence.

About those who stood to suffer rather than thrive with all the new laws and mandates, Le Corbusier had a rationale. From Ozon, where he had returned briefly to visit Yvonne at the start of October, he wrote his mother, "The Jews are going through a very bad time. I am sometimes contrite about it. But it does seem as if their blind thirst for money had corrupted the country."[35]

On October 3, 1940, two days after Le Corbusier wrote these words, the Statute on Jews was passed. While making an exception for certain assimilated Jews from families that had lived in France for a long time, it prohibited most French Jews "from elective office, from the civil service, from teaching and journalism."[36] It established quotas in other professions as well.

The terms of the armistice demanded that German Jews who had fled to France return to Germany. This almost invariably guaranteed that they would be put to death. A decree passed the day after "the law of October 3rd" further sealed the fate of all Jews in France by requiring their internment in special camps. Then, on October 7, Algerian Jews were stripped of their French nationality.

In time, the Vichy government deported more than eighty thousand Jews. It confiscated Jewish property and sold the assets for its own benefit.

Nearly twenty-five years later, Le Corbusier gave the impression, in *Corbusier Himself,* that at the time he had been sensitive and prescient about such horrors. In truth, as long as he thought his own building program was at stake, he had ignored the plight of Vichy's victims.

9

On British radio, Charles de Gaulle had summoned the French people to fight any form of Germanization. Brave individuals who opposed the occupying forces had started to publish the newspaper that gave their movement its name—*Résistance*—and to engage in guerrilla activities within the occupied zone. In the south, there were people making determined efforts to weaken the power structure in Vichy, and on other fronts there were men and women trying to circumvent Nazi authority and help people at risk escape. Le Corbusier evinced no interest in these rescue efforts and made no attempt to join the resistance; if he was to build or plan cities, his only possibility was to stay in Vichy.

Marie Jeanneret, too, acted as if there was no alternative. To be in Vichy was "all the same preferable to what a life must be in a city where people must beg for their wretched daily bread for hours on end; where so many restrictions are enforced; where freedom is abolished for the time being. Oh! who will restore to France all she has lost in the matter of material goods! But from another point of view, how much rubbish has been swept away."[37]

She longed for her worthy son to be duly respected, high up in that new power structure, "recalled to the 'ranks' as an active, precious intelligence." Now he would rise to the stature he deserved. "How proud of you I am, my great Le Corbu!" wrote Marie Charlotte Amélie Jeanneret-Perret.[38] At last!

10

At the start of October, the war brought a new tragedy to the Jeanneret family. Albert's wife, Lotti, had a son who had killed himself—after murdering his young wife, "whom he adored and who was to have a baby at Christmas."[39] He was a career officer, recently promoted in the army, who had completely lost the ability to cope.

Lotti's son, unlike her two daughters, had apparently never figured in her

Paris life. While Lotti and Albert were, it seems, amicably separated, everyone was shattered. As if it needed to be said, Marie told Le Corbusier that not only was Lotti overwhelmed with grief but so were she and Albert. She provided an address for Lotti in Sweden, with instructions to Le Corbusier to write her a sympathy note.

Shortly after that horrific event, Yvonne's health deteriorated to such an extent that Le Corbusier, back in Ozon, took her for a consultation with a new doctor near Lourdes. She was diagnosed with a treatable liver ailment. Le Corbusier told his mother that, after following the doctor's orders for fifteen days, the volatile Yvonne had improved. He didn't specify what those orders were, but alcohol was almost certainly the issue.

During this same autumn of 1940, Maréchal Pétain met with Hitler in Montoire-sur-le-Loir. On October 31, Pétain issued a public proclamation of support for the Führer: "It is with honor, and in order to maintain French unity . . . that in the framework of an activity which will create the European new order I today enter the road of collaboration."[40]

Le Corbusier believed that collaboration could lead to good things. That same day, the architect wrote his mother, "One may presume, depending on events, that the Government will return to Paris. In that case my conduct is clear, I shall return as well."[41] Pierre Winter had already returned. To be in the French capital while it was under Hitler's control now seemed not only possible but appealing.

Le Corbusier, meanwhile, was becoming increasingly convinced that a marvelous transformation of society might be under way—and that the resistance being encouraged from England was foolhardy, its adherents at risk:

> Here is the great problem facing the French government. We are in the hands of a conqueror whose attitude could be devastating. If he is sincere in his promises, Hitler could crown his life by an overwhelming creation: the accommodation of Europe. This is a stake that may tempt him, rather than a preference for a fruitless vengeance. That is the unknown quantity. Personally I believe the outcome could be favorable. France, barring a criminal transplantation or a German invasion, is a mouthful not to be chewed, and if the problem consists of assigning each nation its role, getting rid of the banks, solving real—realistic—tasks, then the prognosis is good. It would mean the end of speeches from the tribunal, of endless meetings of committees, of parliamentary eloquence and sterility. Such a revolution will be made in the direction of order and not without consideration of human conditions.
>
> Whatever the case, the die is cast. England fulminates, Her French radio broadcasts spit out floods of eloquence, which in all sincerity

ring perfectly hollow to my ears, though dangerous when heard by those who permit themselves to be beguiled by rhetoric.[42]

The imploring voice he derided was de Gaulle's.

TWO WEEKS AFTER Pétain announced his fealty to Hitler, Le Corbusier again begged his mother to take better care of herself. He warned her not to be frugal in spite of the realities of wartime, if it endangered her health. "No criminal economies!" the architect counseled, imploring the eighty-year-old to stop raking leaves—at least on days when it was too cold out.[43] He also accused her of not heating the house adequately.

Urging Marie to spend whatever was necessary to stay warm, Le Corbusier allowed, "In these matters, I know that I am preaching in the desert. Yet you must make up your mind: A/ to spend what you must for heating. B/ realize how cold it is and leave your household in peace. Which is to say, act with common sense and with an understanding of the *hierarchy* of things. You are at fault in this matter, but my dear Maman, I fear you are incorrigible." Le Corbusier's real issue with her, however, was Albert: "Albert, less determined than I, more malleable, has been to a large degree molded by you, by your wishes, your desires, your ambitions. All this as a consequence of the noblest kind of love, of course. But who tells you—who gives you the right to tell yourself—that your points of view, your perceptions of happiness attached (alas) to the notion of 'success,' are accurate? For whom are we living? For the gallery or for the fulfillment of destinies that are anchored deep within ourselves?"[44]

Now wanting Marie to indulge his brother as a beleaguered genius, Le Corbusier lectured her for twelve pages on how she might better handle the eccentric composer—advising her to be less bothered by the lack of recognition for Albert's music.

Edouard assumed a responsibility equal to hers: "As a boy, our Albert went to war with a violin under his arm, in order to become . . . a virtuoso: a debatable point of view. Reality frustrated this undertaking. Failure of the man, or of the program? The two must not be confused."[45] His mother needed to be realistic and stop acting as if her son was the equal of Bach, Beethoven, or Satie.

Nonetheless, Le Corbusier was concerned that his brother would not earn enough money.

Where is happiness? In inner wealth, on condition that external poverty does not spoil everything. For black poverty can do that.

> On the other hand, this year 1940 is the point of inflection between a world dying and a world being born. Comparisons no longer have any legitimate application. Nothing is the same any longer. Even if success had enjoyed a material, a tangible means of manifesting itself: *money*—well, money today is damned, and will be even more so.[46]

Even if Albert had a regular job, it would not make a difference in such troubled times.

The younger son was at the pulpit: "Jesus, your great model, failed at each step of his life and by ordinary judgment deserved no better than the beggar's lot, and he took that way to the end. Which constituted his mother's enormous disappointment. It is probable that in his childhood he was promising. But the conclusion was that he did not keep his promises." Both he and Albert, clearly, were in the same straits as Jesus: truthful creatures who might never gain their warranted recognition. The essential issue, Le Corbusier concluded, was self-respect: "It is our lot to be born and to die. And on the road between, not to be too ashamed of ourselves. If we are still entitled to respect ourselves, then we have defined happiness, our happiness."[47]

11

Le Corbusier was out of the good favor he had attained by working in Vichy. Marie did not respond favorably to his diatribe on the need to understand Albert or to his repeated advice that she must recognize her relative good fortune in life. Again she complained about the house he had built for her and about his brother's inability to help with its maintenance:

> Albert and I manage to use this house, anything but solid and costing both money and effort. It is quite different from the tranquil life I lived alone for years at the lake. One must face the fact that Albert is a man, and like you little disposed to concern himself with the normal maintenance of a house! . . .
>
> But I think you should understand, you intellectuals, that nowadays life is complicated, terribly complicated for the housewife.[48]

She was determined that Le Corbusier stop minimizing her hardships: "Restrictions rain down, it's a kind of madness, and you have nothing to envy us for, because it is worse here than France! These days we need ration cards for everything."[49] And as always, there were problems with the heating system; the new furnace was not working properly.

She reiterated, however, her one source of hope: "Listening to French radio every day, we participate in the great adventure of the Reconstruction of a new France, and we marvel at everything good and fruitful being undertaken. We hope you will also have your position, in order to serve and be useful to our dear France!" And if Le Corbusier could dispense advice, so could she: "And you, dear boy, take care of your lungs, don't let yourself get too cold and go run cross-country to warm your limbs and your blood."[50]

At age fifty-three, Le Corbusier was still dealing with a mother who alternated between anger and maternal concern in rapid succession. She dispensed approval and disapproval like cannon fire.

IT WAS a particularly brutal winter. Le Corbusier wrote Marie with precise instructions on how to adjust the troublesome heating system so that she would be warm enough during the night. As for her advice on health: he proposed his own latest formula for avoiding colds. Albert should go to the lake, collect stones, heat them, wrap them in a light material, and put them in her bed. If she slept with the warm stones and a wool cap, she would ward off illness. With a watchmaker's precision and the resolve of an engineer, Le Corbusier now added the detail that it is around 4:00 a.m. that the head becomes cold, which in turn causes illness.[51]

He was writing this from Vichy. The minister of the interior had summoned him from Ozon back to Pétain's seat of power on November 25.

12

The minister, Marcel Peyrouton, had been appointed two months earlier. Le Corbusier had first met him in Algiers in 1932, when Peyrouton had a high government position there, and they had further discussed town planning when Peyrouton had been stationed in Tunisia. Now, Peyrouton appointed him as one of two experts on urbanism who would be responsible for all construction in the devastated regions of France.

Le Corbusier was in Vichy for only a few days, but he had three long conversations with Giraudoux. The playwright intended to ask Pétain and others in his cabinet to attend a public lecture, planned for December, on urbanism: Winter would speak on health, Le Corbusier on architectural technique, and he, Giraudoux, on civil spirit. Le Corbusier told Giraudoux he was sure that the government officials would be too preoccupied by other matters to sit still in an auditorium but said he would gladly return if the lecture became a reality.

It would not be hard, for with a higher position Le Corbusier intended to live in Vichy on a more permanent basis.

MARCEL PEYROUTON was a colleague of dubious merit. Just after he had been appointed minister, he had become so concerned about the Jewish "problem" that he developed a scheme to send two thousand Jews to Madagascar; the enterprise was halted in part because the Ministry of Finance deemed it too expensive.

In 1943, Charles de Gaulle had Peyrouton arrested; after the war, he was put on trial. On that occasion, Pétain's former minister declared, "I did not pose questions. I repeat: I am a Republican, I am not anti-Republican. I am an agent, a functionary."[52] It was in that capacity that Peyrouton had summoned Le Corbusier.

13

Le Corbusier had to wait in Ozon for a while until his new position in Vichy was formalized. He continued to admire his wife's comportment in exile. Yvonne rose early, kept their simple accommodations impeccably clean, filled their room with flowers, sewed *broderies,* and made them feel at home in a setting that otherwise would have seemed alien. He told his mother he was impressed

> by her never abandoned discipline to be always impeccably right about herself however varying and unexpected. While I get myself copiously criticized for my careless outfits, my wrinkled trousers and my slovenly hair. The daily round has the effect of leaving my body free and my mind cheerful. Which is a great thing.
>
> She also takes her medicines with an impeccable discipline, follows her diet, and has given up her *apéritifs.* This girl who seems so free and capricious is actually quite methodical: everything is done, everything undertaken according to rule with songs along the way.[53]

THEN, SHORTLY BEFORE the year was out, Le Corbusier got his marching orders. Just after New Year's, he and Yvonne went to Vichy together. It was another arduous journey from Ozon, this time by car. Because of exceptional snow and ice that blocked the roads around Limoges for ten days, what should have taken a couple of days required fourteen. Regardless, when they arrived in Vichy in mid-January, Le Corbusier was delighted to be there.

Although the cold weather intensified her ailments, Yvonne was courageous as always. She stayed at her husband's side, making their meager repasts as nice as possible while he struggled to secure his new post. Le Corbusier had difficulties because the Vichy regime considered him Swiss rather than French, in spite of his change of citizenship. Nonetheless, used to the presence of foes, he braced himself. Shortly after arriving, he wrote his mother,

> I'm doing my duty: the impossible. I'm holding fast. Sympathy shown on all sides. But there's a snake coiled around every doorknob.
>
> Yet there must be no abdicating. This is the hour of events, when sides are taken, consequences revealed.[54]

Le Corbusier decided that, if all went as he hoped, he would stay in Vichy indefinitely, while installing Yvonne back at Vézelay. Marie again encouraged him: "My fond hope is that you'll resume your march on Vichy and that you're presently in top form in all respects. . . . All of us listen tonight at 6:45 to Radio Français and its appeals to the goodwill of every French citizen. The testimonials of affection, of unanimous respect for Maréchal Pétain are very moving, and we'd like him to know of our great admiration for the endless task he has undertaken, which is surely bearing fruit already. We pray God will preserve him for many years more and allow him to see his fatherly work for our beloved France triumph over all obstacles."[55]

14

By the end of January, Le Corbusier had realized his mother's fondest hopes. The nomination that had initially been cast aside because he was the son of a Swiss father had now been accepted, and he had formally become a consultant to the government official responsible for establishing the new guidelines and regulations for construction and urbanism throughout France. He reported with unabashed pride, "My role is to orient these things so that I can provide them with the New Spirit. I am regarded as a gentleman."[56]

Not that the power struggles were over. Le Corbusier claimed to his mother that his aesthetic foes were so entrenched that he was tempted to quit even before he started; traditional architecture was still the preference in the devastated regions. Le Corbusier assured Marie he knew it was his obligation to forget his pride and persevere.

Le Corbusier was heartened when the students at the local Ecole des Beaux-Arts invited him to their studios; it indicated a new acceptance of his approach. Things began to go so well in Vichy that he and Yvonne decided, for the time being, to abandon the idea of her returning to Vézelay or Paris. They could afford to have her remain in the spa town now that Le Corbusier was receiving a modest salary and free lodging; he considered himself part of the establishment there.

Yvonne, however, disliked her long days in the hotel room alone except for Pinceau. She had a terrible cold at the end of January and was suffering from an unsuccessful operation an oculist had performed on her blocked tear duct.[57] Le Corbusier began to waver—maybe they should repair to the villa in Roquebrune-Cap-Martin where he had painted his murals, or even to Vézelay or Paris. He imagined resuming painting in one of those other locations. But "Duty" was the deciding factor.

Pétain fired Peyrouton on February 9 in order to appease the Germans by replacing him with someone more clearly committed to collaboration. But even the downfall of one of his closest champions was not enough to discourage Le Corbusier. On February 17, he wrote his mother that he was an "initiator of profound action. I cannot be deterred from the path I follow."[58]

IF YVONNE had to spend her life in a hotel room, at least it was in one of the best places, the Albert Premier. At lunchtime, she and Le Corbusier ate in a restaurant where there was only one menu, but they were happy with it. For supper, they often had a picnic on their beds—there was no alternative during the nightly blackouts—but they did not mind. Yvonne was unwilling to go to the cinema at night, for fear of leaving Pinceau alone in the room, barking. Le Corbusier took advantage of the situation to read a lot.

Le Corbusier's mother, meanwhile, was again complaining about the humidity in the walls and difficulties because of the flat roof of La Petite Maison, especially in a wet winter. While excoriating Edouard for the dampness in the house, she made his brother the embodiment of perfection: "And then there is Albert, a real sunbeam, content with his lot, free and at home in his snug little house."[59]

Marie expressed concern about Yvonne in the throes of menopause: "But it is sad to think of poor Yvonne and her health problems. I hope she can be patient, for the years preceding or following a fiftieth birthday are more or less good years for all women (without exception)."[60] In fact, Yvonne was doing better. By March, she and Le Corbusier had moved to Queen's Hotel—an even nicer accommodation with a view of the park. Yvonne's tear duct was operated on again and this time was successfully cured. She was taking the spa waters under a doctor's supervision and feeling generally healthier than she had in a long time.

Le Corbusier spoke on the state radio station on March 19, with kudos afterward, and he sold a painting to de Montmollin. Everything was looking up; he could gaze out the window and see buds on some of the trees. The willows were already green, and the plum trees were covered with white blossoms. By the end of the month, elated, he wrote his mother, "My undertaking is acknowledged and favored in the highest offices of the land." With Giraudoux as part of the team, he felt on his way to "a total victory."[61]

Moreover, he had a backup plan. Le Corbusier had been asked to give a monthlong course at a Buenos Aires university for two hundred thousand francs—with two guaranteed building projects. His loyalty to the new France was not so complete that he would decline to leave if necessary: "If Vichy were suddenly to collapse, it would be Argentina without delay."[62]

15

On March 29, 1941, Le Corbusier had an interview with an official high up in the Vichy government—"the one who has the power to regulate all construction in France." Le Corbusier's dream had come true. "To our amazement, he declares his eagerness to use our organization and to regard it as his organ of inspiration," he wrote.[63]

Le Corbusier then told his mother it was "Le M. lui-même" who looked him in the eyes and said that the architect would be supported by every available resource within the government.[64] "Le M. lui-même" was in all likelihood Pétain himself. Le Corbusier had not used his name, but "Le M." was a way of referring to "Le Maréchal"—indeed "the one" with the power Le Corbusier attributed to his interviewer.

Le Corbusier used one of his ultimate expressions of joy: "The horizon is clear."[65] At last he would achieve what he had been trying to do for twenty years. His incessant vigilance was bearing fruit; important work and great buildings were imminent. Everything would now happen as he hoped. André Boll, the press officer of the new committee, would make sure the whole country learned, through newspapers and radio, about the latest building plans. The necessary laws and regulations would follow. The rejections, the waiting, the problems of December and January were behind him, and the future would now be as he hoped, even if it included inevitable challenges.

Le Corbusier concluded this encomium to his mother, "Everything is just beginning. Proofs will have to be given. Difficult days lie ahead."[66] Nothing excited him more than a worthy battle.

16

That spring, Le Corbusier developed an idea for small buildings that he termed "Les Murondins." (In French, *mur* means wall, and *rondins* are circles of wood or debris.) He wrote a thirty-six-page book, comprising sketches and text dedicated to this idea of a universal form with many applications.[67] It called for rudimentary adobe dwellings, related to Mesopotamian architecture and befitting nomads.

First, a simple trench was excavated and filled with concrete to prevent moisture from rising. Then, blocks measuring twenty by twenty by forty centimeters, composed of sand, gravel, lime, and mud that had hardened in the sun, were assembled as slabs, framed in timber. The slabs were made to stand like walls and placed at right angles to brace one another. A roof was made of branches and logs of uniform length culled from the forest at the side of the road; if there were no trees around, bituminous paper and turf or corrugated iron could be used. With the Vichy government behind him, he believed that this form of housing, inexpensive and viable in a range of settings, would quickly proliferate.

"THE SKY HAS TURNED BLUE. The trees green," he wrote his mother on April 22; it was not just a report on the weather.[68]

She wrote back bursting with "the happiness of knowing you are happy, understood, and involved in this magnificent restoration of men and things which is now in the air almost everywhere, and particularly in French territories." But he must not forget the flaws of the house he had built for her: "Repairs cannot be made in this constant wet weather, and nothing is happening in the little house. Everything remains to be done."[69] She was, she reported, losing an abnormal amount of weight in spite of eating a lot; perhaps it was the fault of his architecture.

17

On May 27, 1941, Maréchal Pétain signed the law that officially put Le Corbusier in charge of the creation of the "committee studying problems of habitation and construction."[70] Two days later, the declaration was published in the state journal.

Then, like the regimes Le Corbusier had encountered first in La Chaux-de-Fonds and then in Geneva and Moscow, Vichy had in its ranks individuals who effectively opposed him. A man Le Corbusier identified only as "the director in charge of general construction and production" maintained that he would under no circumstances work with the architect.[71]

Le Corbusier had one key supporter, however. "Our president is a noble prince who places the respect for human values above all else. It was precisely when he had been asked for a measure of abandonment that he showed his allegiance to us," Le Corbusier wrote to his mother. The forces against him still had to be reckoned with, but, assuming that "*notre président*" referred to Pétain, the Maréchal's backing heartened him to believe that now he was in the right place at the right time. "The enemy is ignorance itself—a phantom: everything which does not exist, from which one makes a mountain . . . but if, at last, we can be established where we have prepared a place, the work will be firmly based on thirty years of meditation."[72]

DAY AFTER DAY, Le Corbusier walked through the formal gardens of Vichy and passed the grand hotels and elaborate spa buildings where, since Roman times, people had drunk the local springwater to cure their livers, stomachs, intestines, and kidneys. Trying in that bizarre setting to gain support for his commission and goals, he periodically met with members of Pétain's team.

Again, he and Yvonne moved. Having had to go to an inferior establishment, they now returned to Queen's Hotel, where the music from the birds in the park outside their windows struck him as exotic. On his walks with Pinceau, "day after day, I have seen the buds and the leaves and the flowers, everything created, orchestrated by a talented gardener who has specialized in rare species. How beautiful the trees are!"[73] All was for the best again.

18

Le Corbusier had to create a lengthy document in accordance with the regulations of the Vichy government. It proved his qualifications to serve.

Entitled "Request for a waiver according to the law of July 17th 1940," it was an elaborate c.v. that distorted the facts at will, particularly in its emphasis on Le Corbusier's Frenchness. The architect gave his name as "LE CORBUSIER (Charles-Edouard)." He came "from a family of French origin, proscribed during the wars of religion." He stressed his French naturalization and all the important official positions and honors he had had in France, Sweden, Britain, the USSR, and Czechoslovakia. In 1927, he won the "first prize in the construction competition for the Palace of the League of Nations"—but he failed to mention that it was never built. Le Corbusier declared that in 1934 he was "called to Rome by a decree of Mussolini in order to discuss theses of urbanism and architecture for union delegates."[74] He cited his work in the field of urban development in Moscow, Brazil, Smyrna, Chile, Algeria, Barcelona, Buenos Aires, and Amsterdam, from 1928 to 1939—without pointing out that nothing ever came of any of these projects.

Le Corbusier's self-promotion includes a list of publications, translations, reviews, and work as an editor. In a summation of his career, he wrote: "Has never had political involvements, but was alternately accused, as necessity commanded, of communism and fascism."[75]

THE VERY SAME DAY that Le Corbusier completed this document that would allow him to work with the new French government, the second Statute on Jews, the law of June 2, 1941, was passed. Its contents helped realize the goals of Admiral Darlan and others high up in the Vichy regime. Now all people considered Jewish were forbidden to work in banking, the stock market, journalism, publishing, or teaching, except at the lowest levels. Five days later, Jews started to be required to wear a yellow star. The following month, "the law of July 22nd for economic organization" dispossessed Jews of their furniture, their apartments, and most other worldly goods and forbade them to go out between 8:00 p.m. and 6:00 a.m. It also prohibited them from owning bicycles or telephones, entering public places, or changing residences.

Just as the second statute was going into effect, Le Corbusier wrote his mother that within a week he would know whether everything would happen as he hoped. With all the political turmoil in France, he was still managing to publish, and he was optimistic that his work was moving ahead.

Marie Jeanneret-Perret, as given to dark moods as her son, was now ebullient, even if the horrors of war meant that former allies were now enemies: "I have regained my spirits, thanks to my beloved son. . . . Yet there are other enormities that are of the order of the day, unfortunately! The French soldiers in Syria at war with their former brothers in arms and fellow citizens. My God, what will happen to them all. . . . Edouard's wonderful, detailed letter, received on Saturday, June 7th, brings us up to date with the situation of Vichy's good soldiers. We think of them with ardent love and constant sympathy as we hope for a happy outcome. We can do no less for the new France! Courage, hope, faith!!"[76]

19

Two weeks after saying he might head to Buenos Aires if Pétain's government did not employ him as he hoped, Le Corbusier took a six-hour flight from Vichy to Algiers. It was a mission he deemed of critical importance, a harbinger of the ultimate victory of his ideas. And he was undertaking it on behalf of the new regime.

In Algiers, he ate better than he had in ages, writing his mother that there were entire legs of lamb. Everything felt like a holiday. He returned to Vichy feeling reassured that his great urban plan in North Africa was still alive. The architect then learned that he was being sent on a mission to Switzerland; accorded a rare visa for the trip, it meant he could see his mother.

Then setbacks came. The trip was postponed. François Lehideux, Minister of Industrial Production, rejected Le Corbusier's role on the new habitation committee. The weather in Vichy was horrible that summer, with cold winds and heavy rains. Rather than taking an August holiday, he and Yvonne waited it out at Queen's Hotel, with Le Corbusier one day imagining expatriation in Argentina and the next day believing Algiers would be his to do and he was about to take the promised journey to Vevey.

At least he was still in his mother's good graces. She wrote him from the side of Lac Leman,

> Stretched out on my *chaise-longue* I read with the profoundest inner peace, your beautiful and magnificent work on the reconstruction of Paris, the destiny of Paris.

> How clear it all is, so limpidly expressed! I am overcome with admiration and so proud of my great son.[77]

Marie Jeanneret was even happier when Le Corbusier finally made it to Switzerland during the first week of September. His journey back to Vichy took fourteen hours by train, with a long delay as the Germans, whom he referred to as "Les Fritz," questioned him "aggressively," but at least he had seen his mother again.

Then, on September 12, he delivered Yvonne to Vézelay. The demarcation line would now separate them, but the move was imperative, for life in the spa town had become untenable for her.

Once he was back in Vichy, Le Corbusier's days were more of a waiting game than ever. In spite of his head scarves and other preventives, he again suffered from a nasty cold, forcing him to remain cooped up in his room at Queen's Hotel. He profited from the time to write but became convinced that his enemies had now taken over the important committees in Vichy, reducing his potential role to next to nothing.

Still, Le Corbusier would not give up. After a year of waiting, he was willing to grasp at straws.

20

On September 14, Le Corbusier's mother wrote him, "You laconically report that you have worked a lot, that this has been acknowledged in high places, and that your contribution to French National Reconstruction has been appreciated at its true value." Even as she mocked his manner, she apologized for her previous harshness: "As you tell me, I know and believe in your inviolate filial love; for my part I regret the excessive language I have used when speaking in anger. Perhaps we shall never see each other again! That is why I cherish the beautiful love of the past, so precious to my heart, intact and complete."[78]

When she wrote two weeks later, in anticipation of her son's fifty-fourth birthday, she referred to herself in the third person. "Your Maman thinks of you, alone as you are all the time, she thinks of your work, and of the powers that you lavish upon it; she hopes such undertakings will ultimately take their rightful place among the great labors of a renewed France." Then, going into the first person, she offered marital advice: "I think, too, about your separation from Yvonne and your isolation there. And Yvonne herself must suffer so, even surrounded as she is by good friends . . . for a loving friend never replaces a husband, and for a man it is worse still, since it is his wife who creates a loving ambience."[79]

Marie Jeanneret was softening up. She concluded, "My dear son, courage, good health, robust morale—such are the wishes I make for you with a loving heart. Be assured of our love."[80]

TWO DAYS AFTER his birthday, the architect was operated on for a hernia. "It's really a trifle," he had assured his mother before the procedure.[81] Afterward he proudly told her that the surgeon, after removing the staples, told him he had the skin of a baby. He considered the days in the medical clinic in Vichy "a sojourn in paradise"—time when he could read and meditate in silence, for long hours.[82]

Ruminating there, Le Corbusier had concluded that Vichy was looking less and less like a base for changing the world. But he had other irons in the fire. On November 1, the new president of the Municipal Council in Paris asked him to take charge of a condemned housing block, "number 6." After requesting authorization from the Germans to travel to the capital, Le Corbusier received word that he would have to wait until the third week of December. But the important thing was that he was returning to Paris to work for authorities other than those associated directly with Pétain.

He was ready for the change. "I feel like burning down my 20 cities and my 400 villages, as I've already said, and turning over a new leaf," Le Corbusier wrote his mother. He could no longer bear to wait for developments to unfold when he had no control of them. "What's really hard is being a bird in flight with no resting place. Waiting, watching the fatal slowness of developments and measuring the fatality of the miseries that are gathering on the horizon and that will implacably fall upon us in their inevitable, unremitting order."[83]

21

From Geneva, where he had detoured on his way to Paris, Le Corbusier warned Marie Jeanneret that it would be impossible to reach him once he was in the occupied zone. Yvonne had tried to write him in Vichy from Vézelay, but her letter had been returned. The only correspondence that could pass the demarcation line were official documents. The same would be true with mail from Vevey to Paris. All was "terribly harsh and premature."[84] But, as always, one had to make the best of it.

Le Corbusier counseled his mother, "Take note of the season." Like him, Marie suffered from serious winter blues—worse now that she had gone deaf in one ear and was losing her eyesight. Moreover, the maintenance problems in the house grew more difficult at this time of year.

Le Corbusier was in Paris from November 10 through November 12. Then, another of his terrible head colds forced him to Vézelay, where Yvonne and Pinceau greeted him ecstatically. By the twentieth, he had recovered sufficiently to return to Paris, where he checked on the condition of Raoul La Roche's and Albert's houses. Except for a water leak in Albert's stairwell, for which Le Corbusier could handily blame the war, all was fine. Léon Perrin was monitoring the apartment on rue Nungesser-et-Coli.

Le Corbusier met with the female janitor there, who was so plagued by the occupation that she was imagining voices. When the architect gave his mother a report on the French capital—in a postcard he was able to mail only after returning to Vichy—that reference to the janitor's hallucinations was his sole acknowledgment of the German presence: "All the same Paris is a beautiful, powerful city and appears so when you have been gone for two years [*sic*]. It is here, after all, that we find the creative spirits, and it is here that the present drama is unfolding. I shall figure out a way to obtain a permanent pass which will permit me to travel back and forth."[85]

Madame Jeanneret had received a handwritten letter on official stationery from André Boll—at the Ministry of Industrial Production and Labor of the "French State," as the Vichy government called itself. Boll was writing to reassure her that he had excellent news from Le Corbusier, who was still in the occupied zone but was about to leave it. Boll had been asked to let the architect's mother know that his health was good, as was that of his wife, whom he had visited in Vézelay.

DURING HIS FEW DAYS in the occupied capital, Le Corbusier worked feverishly "liquidating old things and preparing new," but nothing came either of the project to rebuild the housing block or of an agreement he had hoped to sign to become the advisor to one of the largest French companies.[86] By the end of November, he was back in Vichy, completely confused. He wrote his mother, "One's head is so full of For and Against, of arguments and debates over unknown quantities, that nothing can be easily explained. One confronts a situation, one builds a scaffolding, one prepares a line of conduct."[87] Now he was dubious about having his proposal for Algiers endorsed.

All that Le Corbusier knew with certainty was that resilience and flexibility were imperative: "I had no desire to be specific in a letter, since tomorrow changes everything. It is on such matters that people exhaust themselves; yet this is precisely where we must remain intact and confident and ceaselessly focused on the work."[88]

22

Le Corbusier spent an evening in Vichy listening to two men and a group of women sing for three hours. They intoned marching songs and folk songs dating back to François I: "Astonishing poetic treasure, full of brilliance, light, clarity, and lyricism; perhaps the most intense manifestation of the French soul there is, yet no one knows anything about it."[89] These honest and simple forms of human expression, pertinent for everyone and close to the heart, were an essential element of human civilization. More than ever, Le Corbusier deplored art that belonged uniquely to the domain of the elite. It was worthless compared to his beloved Balkan pots, the singing of Maurice Chevalier, and the dancing of Josephine Baker.

But there was another aspect to this taste for popular culture. The adulation of the "honest, healthy, robust nature" in those traditional French marching songs could also fuel a lethal patriotism. To people like Giraudoux, Darlan, and de Pierrefeu, such patriotism encouraged a sense of superiority over the members of society who were considered less fit, and in a more extreme form it called for the extinction of those deemed lacking the national soul.

LE CORBUSIER decided to stay on in Vichy. The opposition against him was plain to see, but he also knew he had allies.

The material deprivations were difficult, but his mother sent provisions from Switzerland. While he declined further chocolate and coffee, he was grateful for anything with fat in it and wrote her that he constantly craved sausage. He also desperately missed tobacco—until he dined with one of the most important tobacco producers in France, who gave him some as a gift; there were always solutions to problems.

Even with Algiers on hold, he still had sufficient faith in Pétain and his subalterns to make him want to tough out the problems. Le Corbusier explained to his mother on December 15, "for the moment, everything is spiritless: reaction triumphs everywhere, fear, weakness, backward glances. Yet we are an army of the righteous, but it must be reinforced. Only the Maréchal is young."[90]

23

"What a business!" Le Corbusier wrote his mother toward the end of 1941. "This time we're losing our footing, things make no sense any more, good only for liquidating a collapsing civilization. Then will come the internal squabbles, the most agonizing of all. What scores to settle! It seems to me that international hostilities cannot go on forever. Those who have no music, art, or thought are pitiable, the rest of us redeemed by what we have. Courage then! Here in this insipid and ill-heated Vichy we are bored to death!"[91]

Le Corbusier saw his own actions as redemption—as if he were clinging, in this shipwreck of Europe, to art and music as he had held his own leg when the fishermen pulled him to safety in Saint-Tropez. His tenacity finally paid off. By the end of the year, he was using the official stationery of the Ministry of Industrial Production of the French state. Le Corbusier had become a legitimate part of Pétain's government.

Everything was again for the best. His mother had sent andouilles for Christmas. Yvonne was in Vézelay while he was in Vichy for the holiday—Le Corbusier calculated that in the twenty-one years they had been together, she had never spent Christmas with him, except for the previous one in Ozon—but all the privations were manageable now that he was truly at the seat of power. Le Corbusier wrote his mother, "I dearly love my little wife; she is all loyalty and dignity."[92]

24

After their years of close partnership in Paris, Pierre Jeanneret and Le Corbusier had been sundered by the war. Charlotte Perriand later suggested that Pierre, like Le Corbusier, had not been strong enough against the forces of collaboration, but there was a substantial distinction: Pierre never went to Vichy. When he was living near Le Corbusier in Ozon, Pierre had worked with him on ideas for prefabricated housing for workers and engineers and on a youth program that Le Corbusier was going to present to the minister of youth in Vichy, but the quieter cousin soon went his own way.

In this period at the end of 1941, when Le Corbusier had finally established himself in Pétain's government, Pierre wrote him from Grenoble, "I haven't a clue where you are . . . in South America? In Algeria? . . . but not in Vichy."[93]

Pierre knew perfectly well where Le Corbusier was; he had addressed the envelope to a Vichy hotel. It was an odd ploy—presumably Pierre's way of expressing shock. But he kept his disapproval veiled: "Your silence doesn't surprise me, I'm not complaining about it, I deserve it, for I write so little. I have my reasons. I don't like to write when I can't express just what I want to say. Besides, what I'd like to say to you might be very complex. Fortunately material matters are simple, and in writing that is the only aspect I adopt." Pierre was clearly disappointed by Le Corbusier's move to Pétain's power base but was not so disgusted as to give up on the relationship. "It's over a year that we've been working, each on his own. At the time of my departure I wanted to organize an effective collaboration with my friends from Grenoble. You, Le Corbusier, always opposed such a notion. You had your reasons. Nevertheless each of us works, I believe, with courage and pleasure. Being able to see each other in a favorable atmosphere remains for me a luminous hope."[94]

Pierre Jeanneret was one of those people for whom, no matter what, Le Corbusier belonged to another category of human being, heroic in spite of his flaws: "In any case, my dear Le Corbusier, you remain for me the great exemplar of architecture, specifically the perfect explorer of the Modern Aesthetic and all its consequences, thanks to your clear, sharp mind and a profound and discriminating analysis of the past." Pierre accepted his position as acolyte to a god: "Despite your onslaughts, justified or not, my esteem, my gratitude, and my friendship remain great."[95]

Trying to survive in tough times, Pierre, too, was trying to hold steady even if he could not have countenanced doing so in Vichy.

> I try to preach elementary principles now and then in order not to lose my way in a dingy world. . . .
>
> What will become of the New Year? Do you think the world will overflow its banks? For obsessed individuals like ourselves, we need merely plunge into our work as effectively as possible—design, perfect, and prepare fine things for the year to come. By then the great problems will be (I hope) vast and harmonious.[96]

Many years would need to pass, however, before they would again work together. Pierre was not inclined to voice his disapproval, but he never fully forgave Le Corbusier for working with Pétain. It was to take a major turn in history before the man who was considered a partner in the firm was again willing to cross the threshold of 35 rue de Sèvres.

XXXV

The most powerful men have always inspired the architects; the architect has always been influenced by power.

—FRIEDRICH NIETZSCHE

1

By the end of January 1942, Le Corbusier had again lapsed into a period of unbearable restlessness. He wrote his mother, "My Vichy patience is at an end, and I am packing my bags. This is an administrative city that has replaced a resort where the bilious sought cures. An unbreathable atmosphere, impossibility of making contact with people so different from ourselves, at the antipodes, entirely given over to administrative tasks, which is to say officious, frightened, inassimilable. Nothing here will move unless it receives a kick in the ass, either from the masses or the elite, at which point the flow of ideas will be clarified. Now I am twenty years in advance of the rest, which represents a certain gap."[1] What troubled him had nothing to do with compliance with the Germans, only with the inertia that was preventing him from building.

His eighty-one-year-old mother was unhappy about how he looked in a recent picture she had seen in the newspapers; she had not seen him in person for half a year: "I'm not really fond of the photo. You look tired, bitter, disabused, for all the stylishness of the suit and the necktie."[2] She disapproved of the dandyishness that prompted him to pay too much attention to details of his wardrobe and not enough to himself.

TWO WEEKS AFTER announcing that his bags were packed, everything had changed. On February 12, still in Vichy, Le Corbusier wrote his mother, "Here the situations are singularly improved. I'm being sought out!"[3]

Again, he thought his moment had come and his patience had paid off: "I can tell you that the Maréchal's cabinet—both: civil and military—has definitively sided with me and is organizing a movement on my behalf, to be made manifest by real and singularly eloquent facts."[4] He expected to have another important audience—if not with Pétain himself, then with one of his closest associates—in which he would be officially asked to lead a mission to deal with family housing. Additionally, thanks to efforts made on his behalf by Pétain's office and by the Ministry of Youth, he was being interviewed increasingly on national radio. When, in late February, he again received clearance to cross the demarcation line and go to Paris and Vézelay, he was determined to be back in Vichy within two weeks.

The journey from the new capital of France to the former one took longer than he anticipated, but its purposes made it worth the time. One of Le Corbusier's reasons for being in occupied Paris was to sign a contract with Ugine Electrochemical, a private business. As their advisor, he was to design a factory building and propose housing for their employees in Savoie. But a far more grandiose concern had captivated him. The authorities in Vichy intended to put him in charge of the reconstruction of the place he still considered the center of civilization. Little could be better, he wrote Jean Berthelot, secretary of state for transportation under Pétain, that February: "Paris is extraordinarily stimulating. Great and beautiful, a splendid city, powerful and upright. I shall be concerned with its immediate destiny."[5]

People were beginning to return to Paris. The areas within a comfortable radius around the place de la Concorde were safe again; only the industrial zones on the periphery were still dangerous. The rue Nungesser-et-Coli was too near those outskirts for Le Corbusier to stay there, but he had been able to return to 20 rue Jacob, where Pierre had taken over his old apartment, and sleep there during his visit.

Le Corbusier spent a total of sixteen days in Paris and an equal number with Yvonne in Vézelay. He was concerned about his wife; she had palpably suffered from five months of solitude and was tired because of her liver problems. But the place he considered a springboard for action beckoned, so by mid-March Le Corbusier was back in Vichy. It was the start of spring, and the architect was as excited as he had been discouraged two months previously: "Since the 7th of February a page has been turned and everything is turning out differently for me. . . . I quickly adapt to an exceptional situation," he told Marie.[6]

2

Near the end of March, Le Corbusier wrote his mother and brother to say that he had news that would fill them with joy. A decision had been made "on the highest level" that was truly one of the peaks of his life. None other than the office of the Maréchal himself and the president of the Municipal Council of Paris had announced that Le Corbusier would be a member of the committee that he had "scaffolded." With the Vichy gift for long-winded titles, it was called the Committee for the Study of Habitation and the Urbanism of Paris.[7] Giraudoux was on the committee, as was Gaston Bergery.

Bergery's close access to Pétain had impressed Le Corbusier from his earliest days in Vichy. A former radical, socialist, and left-wing dissident, Bergery had shifted course by supporting the Munich accord of 1938—the agreement whereby Chamberlain and Daladier granted Hitler all he wanted in Czechoslovakia. Previously, Le Corbusier had railed against that agreement; now he was more than happy to have one of its supporters as an ally. In July 1940, just before Pétain was granted his fullest power, Bergery had published a profascist declaration calling "for collaboration with Germany, and the organization of a new authoritarian order in France."[8] He actively supported a German-style youth movement.

Another of Le Corbusier's fellows on the committee was his acquaintance of three years' standing, Alexis Carrel. In November 1941, Carrel had, under Pétain's authority, created the Foundation for the Study of Human Problems, an organization comprising mainly medical specialists whose purpose was to "study the most appropriate measures to safeguard, improve and develop the French population." Carrel espoused the idea of "reconstructing mankind" as part of Vichy's campaign for "national renewal." This meant that boys were to be brought up as part of a "virile elite," while women were to assume their domestic roles as wives and mothers to serve men and the home. That development would reestablish the " 'natural' sexual order" essential to the eradication of current French decadence.[9]

In 1936, Carrel had written, in the preface to the German edition of *Man, the Unknown,* "In Germany, the government has taken energetic measures against the increase of minorities, criminals, and the insane. The ideal situation would be that each individual of this kind be eliminated once he has shown himself to be dangerous."[10] This was consistent with Carrel's recommendation, initially made in that widely disseminated book, for the "creation of euthanasia establishments provided with appropriate gas." The doctor continued to advocate that concept as an essential element of the Foundation for the Study of Human Problems.

Le Corbusier's idea of destroying the most decrepit parts of cities echoed Carrel's concept of extermination. There was, to be sure, a fundamental difference between buildings and people, but each believed in total razing, a cleansing of what they considered decadent or useless. Le Corbusier owned Carrel's seminal book and annotated his copy copiously.

From Queen's Hotel in Vichy, Le Corbusier was in close touch with Carrel, who maintained his residence in Paris at 20 rue de la Baume, in the eighth arrondissement. In February 1942, Carrel sent Le Corbusier a letter to thank him for having sent *On the Four Roads,* his book of the previous year that addresses the issue of how the human race moves—in relation to the four elements of earth, air, iron, and water. Carrel congratulated him on the energies he had consecrated to the issues of urbanism and architecture, and voiced his belief that he and Le Corbusier were thinking in a similar vein. He wrote the architect, "Among its diverse activities the French Foundation for the Study of Human Problems proposes to clarify certain rules for habitation, and I attach, as you know, a very great importance to the influence of milieu on human beings. The present time poses numerous problems, and we must study them thoroughly before administering indispensable remedies."[11]

Having recently met with Carrel in Paris, Le Corbusier had written to say how pleased he was that Carrel had promised the committee he was trying to form "the collaboration of your Research Institute and your personal sympathy."[12] When Pétain made the committee official ten days later, Le Corbusier was thrilled to have the maniacal doctor among the members.

AT THE END of March, Le Corbusier proudly described the mandate of the new committee to his mother, "From Paris our mission will spread to other cities and the French countryside and to the empire." Accordingly, he was about to return to Algiers, where, in spite of his previous skepticism concerning its political stability, he would meet with the governor general in the course of a monthlong visit. He was realistic about his potential effectiveness, writing that in Algiers he would wage "the first serious battle of modern urbanism, and I believe I shall be defeated. All the same, acting as leader for a month, one may hope to advance."[13]

Every day in Vichy, at 12:30 p.m., Maréchal Pétain left the Hotel du Parc, the nerve center of his operation, and went for his daily promenade. Underlings who were sufficiently in favor would join him. Strolling past closed movie theatres, they would bend their leader's ears with their ideas. Le Corbusier now knew that some of those proposals to Pétain were in support of his and Alexis Carrel's ideas for the improvement of the French population and for the new cities in which these healthier, more robust people would live and work.

3

Le Corbusier was on a manic high. He proudly told his mother that, beyond this new appointment, he was remaining an advisor to Ugine Electrochemical, which he termed "one of the finest French industries."[14] He gave Marie the pivotal information that the head of the company was an intimate friend of Pétain's; everything was going forward.

In Paris, he would reopen the office on the rue de Sèvres; it would become an architectural mecca. He looked forward to hiring many individuals trained under the auspices of the Propagande de la Jeunesse, headed by Georges Pelorson. Pelorson, an eager proponent of "the New French State," had organized volunteer teams of youths in the occupied zone into "a single youth movement swearing total obedience to the Maréchal."[15] By the time he embarked for Algeria, Le Corbusier thought of Vichy with a new appreciation, for the people there who had helped him and shared his goals: "farewells filled with a comforting friendship, and a confidence in the future."[16]

The Committee for the Study of Habitation and the Urbanism of Paris represented a whole new life for Le Corbusier. He felt that it would be the means to achieve the aims of *L'Esprit Nouveau* and to sponsor a publication similar to it. He was fulfilling, at last, the vision he had read in his horoscope of 1937. Beyond that, it was a beautiful spring, rich with sunlight. In his euphoria, Le Corbusier instructed his mother, "Try to allow the coming summer to crown your beautiful life with peace and quiet—it is a life which inspires your son with such admiration and filial love."[17]

At this same moment, French Jews were being deported in increased numbers to concentration camps. On every front, the Allied troops were imperiled. But for Le Corbusier, it was a rare period of hope for humankind. Adding to his joy was the realization that, again, his mother was brimming with pride and approval. She wrote him, "We were delighted by your good news, which sounds so promising. What happiness to know that you are occupied so intelligently, so willing to be useful to your adopted country with all your generous nature and all your talents."

She was apprehensive, however, about his returning to Algiers: "You're about to leave for Algiers when the sea is filled with engines of destruction and disaster can come so quickly. May God protect you, my dear boy, and may you return from this dangerous voyage intact and content in these uncertain times. . . . [B]e careful, don't take unnecessary risks, don't venture too far into the famous Casbah, once is enough!!" His mother also had marital advice: "And then you'll doubtless take Yvonne back to Paris with you, and that will be the end of her isolation in Vézelay, and so much more normal for both of you."[18] Marie Jeanneret had no doubt, however, that at last her gallivanting son's risky life and the impositions he made on his wife were for a worthy purpose.

4

After flying to Algiers on April 1, Le Corbusier immediately began to work with the governor general and other officials to create a committee along the same lines as his Parisian one. Three days later, he received a letter at his hotel, the Aletti, that made him so proud that he wrote, in the margin, the precise hour of its arrival, 10:00 p.m. It had come by special post, and it was on the official letterhead of "Le Maréchal Pétain chef de l'Etat." Pétain's personal secretary had written to say that the Maréchal had received *On the Four Roads* and wanted his thanks conveyed to Le Corbusier. The note credited the book with addressing issues essential to the existence of the country and focusing on positive solutions to the reconstruction of cities and the transformation of urban life. Pétain also wanted it known that he supported Le Corbusier's creation of the new committee in Algiers and hoped that the architect's urbanism would advance there.

Not all the attention Le Corbusier received was as pleasing. Struggling to avoid what he termed the "malignant eyes" of local journalists, he employed a strategy that he proudly explained to his mother: "I cut short their indiscretion by declaring I would not say a word." The issue at hand was rumblings of major turmoil in Vichy. Le Corbusier wrote his mother, "Patiently I weave my web, eternally I wait. These are hard times in Vichy. The government will be changed. And then?"[19]

He answered the question himself. "The news from Vichy seems to be bearing, as far as I'm concerned, the seeds of destruction. Everything may be swept away. So much the worse! I'll go back to painting."[20] Not that he believed what he was saying. If one side of Le Corbusier imagined that he might return full-time to making pictures in solitude, the other still believed that he would work within Pétain's inner circle to reconstruct France.

5

François de Pierrefeu, who continually tried to advance Le Corbusier's cause in Vichy, wrote the architect:

> Received your letter just when Baudry [Jean Baudry, the man responsible for architects and urbanists in Vichy] was showing me your report of the 14th to the civil cabinet. . . . As for your questions:
>
> Everything is still extremely fluid, no one can make any prognostications concerning the role of the civil cabinet in tomorrow's organization. This cabinet was discrowned the first day of the crisis by the necessary resignation of du Moulin [Henri du Moulin, director of the civil cabinet of Pétain from July 19, 1940, to April 13, 1942]. Lavagne [André Lavagne, head of Pétain's civil cabinet] and the other collaborators remain at their posts, at least temporarily, at the request of du Moulin, after having offered their resignations. According to circumstances unforeseeable today, they will remain or surrender their portfolios. Lavagne, overwhelmed by the task of succeeding his chief, is and remains invisible, but Baudry keeps him informed of what concerns us, and he is disposed to spend the time remaining to him launching the Paris committee once he knows who the ministers will be (Interior, Education).[21]

De Pierrefeu provided details on who was talking to whom and what might happen. Le Corbusier marked one passage in particular: "Baudry has had occasion, during a lunch, to inform the head of state about his studies concerning the Paris committee. The Maréchal was extremely interested in this initiative of his cabinet and greatly encouraged Baudry to bring it to a successful conclusion."[22]

De Pierrefeu was a perfect aide-de-camp. He advised, "You should therefore remain in Algiers as long as it seems strictly indispensable for your success in creating the Algiers committee or in correcting the overall plan. But if things turn out badly, take a plane and come back."[23] He pointed out that Le Corbusier would profit from the time in North Africa to gain some weight.

Le Corbusier's mother had already used the related verb, but the letter from de Pierrefeu was the first to use the noun "*collaborateurs.*"

DE PIERREFEU wrote again at the end of the month. He had spared Le Corbusier a day-by-day account of the "constant fluctuations of our affairs in Vichy" but wanted to assure him "that the new government has determined to preserve all possible continuity with the old one, at least with regard to administrative rather than political affairs such as ours. On the other hand, it must be acknowledged that the solid footing represented by the old civil cabinet for this matter, which it had thoroughly studied, has been replaced by a new arrangement of which we know nothing and in which certain interests, like those of the former committees of reconstruction or urbanism, may eventually press certain claims or manifest certain fears; this is all the more likely because our committee, according to the texts prepared, would have a jurisdiction extending initially to Paris but in principle to all of France. . . . If our texts pass, you will be immediately supported by your membership on the future committee and by its jurisdiction which, as I have told you, will extend from Paris to the entire country. . . . Till soon again, my dear old friend; telegraph the date of your return and make provisions for your health—life in Paris will not pass without a struggle and without difficulties until our work produces a favorable resonance in people's minds."[24]

6

When Le Corbusier returned to Vichy on May 22, there had been so many changes within the power structure that he felt as if all his work had been to no avail. He wrote his mother, "During my absence the splendid results I had obtained entirely evaporated during the changes of government. We must begin again, new persons having intervened in the circuit. Whatever happens, the struggle is henceforth in Paris. Here in Vichy it will be to no avail. Moreover Paris appeals to me; the two visits I have made there have shown me what splendid intensity Paris has, what a magical place it is. So now you understand the situation."[25]

The architect remained in Vichy for one more month. As he had with the League of Nations, he continued to grasp at straws long after it would have been better to resign himself to defeat. Then, on June 12, the Municipal Council unanimously rejected his Algiers master plan, the seventh one he had developed. They declared that his concepts would destroy the entire city. For twelve years, Le Corbusier had tried to orchestrate a metropolis that melded Muslim and European cultures in a way he considered "the manifestation of the spirit of an epoch." Now, he declared with resignation, "Some inventors have ideas and receive a kick in the behind."[26]

On July 1, finally convinced there was no hope for any of the other projects he had tried to achieve with the Vichy regime, Le Corbusier left the spa town for good.

7

That summer, Le Corbusier and Yvonne returned to Vézelay. A twenty-year-old architecture student at the Ecole des Beaux-Arts, Roger Aujame, was staying there as well. He quickly noticed that the most famous architect of the era was in the small inn, but he did not want to disturb him.[27]

One morning when Aujame was strolling around the village with his friend Pierre Guegin, he encountered Le Corbusier walking Pinceau. The architect was unmistakable—dressed completely in white from his cap to his espadrilles, with his shirt, pants, and belt all perfectly matched. Against all that white, Le Corbusier's salt-and-pepper hair was a perfect foil to the dog's black coat.

When Guegin, who knew Le Corbusier, said that Aujame was a student at the Beaux-Arts, Le Corbusier exclaimed, "Huh. You're one of them!" Welcoming the chance to convert a member of the opposition, the architect invited Aujame for coffee at Jean Badovici's house.

At 2:00 p.m., the student nervously rang the bell. When he walked into the living room, he recognized most of the people present from their photos in magazines or newspapers. Besides Le Corbusier, Guegin, and Badovici, the poet Paul Eluard, Eduard's wife Nusch, Christian Zervos, and Zervos's wife were also there. Le Corbusier launched into a half-hour-long lecture on architecture, using a copy of his *Complete Work* to show illustrations. He noticed that Aujame was a good audience and invited the student to join him for a walk around Vézelay.

On the steep, narrow streets of that Burgundian hilltop village, Le Corbusier pointed out the vernacular architecture. For Aujame, whose training to date had been to draw classical columns, it was a revelation. Le Corbusier got him to see the merits of anonymous, allegedly styleless, generic stone houses.

The walks became regular events. On one or two occasions, they ventured into the countryside and went down a long flight of wooden steps to a river. The moment he reached the riverbank, Le Corbusier stripped and dove in.

Aujame followed suit and began to do the backstroke. Le Corbusier was fascinated. Having never seen or tried the stroke before, he quickly learned it.

It was the start of a warm working friendship. The young architects Le Corbusier considered responsive gave him joy and hope, and Aujame, whom he hired the next year, was one of his favorites. Many such acolytes would eventually join the crew at 35 rue de Sèvres. Like Charlotte Perriand, they felt they were exposed on a daily basis to true genius and unequaled creativity. It required forbearance to work with someone who was at times excruciatingly difficult, but they knew he was giving the world something it had never had before.

BY OCTOBER, Le Corbusier was back at 24 rue Nungesser-et-Coli. It was a very different Paris from the one he had left. The French flag had been banned and replaced by large black swastikas set against white backgrounds. These Nazi flags were flying throughout the parks and along the streets, and on official buildings and hotels, even atop the ultimate symbol of Paris, the Eiffel Tower. The motto that dominated the French capital was "*Deutschland siegt auf allen fronten* [Germany wins on all fronts]."

Shortly after arriving, Le Corbusier received a letter from de Pierrefeu in Vichy making clear that Pétain's new "chef de cabinet" was opposed to his committee. "This is extremely regrettable from your point of view, which is that of a man regarded as a master by a whole generation of professionals and who sought solely to give his country his experience and his teachings and the doctrinal influence that would ensue," his great champion wrote.[28]

De Pierrefeu reported, however, that Le Corbusier had a key supporter in Robert Lallemant, a cabinet member who had told the others how strongly Maréchal Pétain had advocated to have Le Corbusier in charge of urbanism on a national scale. Even if Le Corbusier never built for the Vichy regime, Lallemant was to help him make his next step forward.

PÉTAIN'S GOVERNMENT began to lose its power during the course of 1942. When the Allies landed in North Africa, the Maréchal ordered French troops to resist them, but Admiral Darlan, on the scene, disobeyed. The French army soon rejoined the war effort on the side of the Allies, and Pétain and his minions faced an inglorious repudiation.

Because of his decision to disobey Pétain, Darlan became beloved by the American president, Franklin D. Roosevelt. De Gaulle, on the other hand, could not overlook Darlan's previous activities. Winston Churchill, out of deference to Roosevelt, "forbade de Gaulle from criticizing Darlan publicly," but everyone knew that the general despised the admiral.[29] When

Darlan was assassinated in December 1942, a twenty-year-old royalist fired the gun, but conspiracy theories still abound about the death of the man whose son had thrilled Le Corbusier by choosing the architect's dog to mate with his own.

On November 11, the Germans moved into the Free Zone. The French population was less and less inclined to accommodate them; a new atmosphere was sweeping over the country. The improved military situation for the Allies, combined with the increased hardships incurred under German and Vichy dominance, were nurturing powerful forces of resistance. To side with Vichy was no longer to be part of the winning team. Le Corbusier had gotten out just in time.

XXXVI

1

Le Corbusier and Yvonne did their best to settle back into the airy penthouse on the rue Nungesser-et-Coli, but the food shortages continued without reprieve, and during the frequent air raids they had to scurry into the cellars at night. Yvonne was now losing her patience: "Women (all of them) are overwhelmed and overcome by everyday difficulties. I myself stand firm," Le Corbusier reported to his mother on December 22.[1]

Although Le Corbusier had left Vichy, he was still working in compliance with its ruling powers. On January 8, 1943, he completed an agreement with Lallemant to open a studio that would be free for students from the Ecole des Beaux-Arts—the institution whose values he had claimed to hate. The students would, according to Le Corbusier's proposal, have the opportunity to be awarded a "diplôme Le Corbusier."

Le Corbusier's idea, which the minister supported, was the fulfillment of a dream he had had ever since working for L'Eplattenier in La Chaux-de-Fonds: architecture would be taught in a new way. Having never received a diploma himself, he now wanted to make it possible for others to do so according to unprecedented principles. In the document he prepared for Lallemant, he wrote,

> 1. in the last twelve months, young architects from the various studios of the Ecole des Beaux-Arts de Paris had asked LC to open a free studio at the school.
>
> But examination of the conditions under which the architectural diploma is awarded has shown that such a studio would confront the students with a cruel dilemma: studying architecture as they had hoped but being unable to obtain the architectural diploma and, consequently, under the new legislation, being unable to practice.
>
> 2. The question is to decide whether the state diplomas, according to today's legislation, will be of an exclusively official and academic tendency. This question deserves to be asked if there is to be any future

for architecture in France and if an imminent rebellion of the candidates is to be avoided against those regulations that would satisfy only one aspect of architectural training.

3. LC has lately settled, for a certain period of time, the question of his studio's location at 35 rue de Sèvres. These premises will be put at the disposal of the students who desire to work under his supervision. But aside from these young architects, others who already possess their diploma have stated their desire to benefit from LC's instruction.[2]

The Vichy authorities were in accord. On January 19, the chief of the cabinet wrote to the minister and secretary of state for national education to confirm that Le Corbusier could open this studio. The chief informed the education secretary, "M. LC has shown me the invitation given him to work up a dossier of qualification for the architectural diploma. It seems highly desirable that such a theoretician and builder, from whom virtually all present-day architects, even the most official and most traditional, have borrowed their general ideas of architecture and their style, should be welcomed to the rank of Architects without indulging in polemics that would merely cast discredit, to a large degree, on present-day French Architects and that, in France's current situation, would merely lower her prestige abroad by depriving her, in an unprecedented manner, of one of her most ardent workers."[3]

The answer on February 12—from the minister's office in Paris at the Palais Royal—crystallized the plan. Le Corbusier had at last gained official approval for a radical way of teaching. The education secretary wrote that "the free studios have the same characteristics as the official studios except, with regard to these latter, for their leader's appointment by the minister and the use of premises in a state establishment. The pupils of either studios undergo the same tests and are judged by the same juries. . . . It is important to emphasize, finally, that no distinction of principle has ever been made between the respective value of these two kinds of studios."[4]

On March 8, Robert Lallemant, in turn, sent Le Corbusier a note and provided copies of these letters. It was under these auspices that the studio at 35 rue de Sèvres reopened. In Maréchal Pétain, Le Corbusier had at last found someone in the inner sanctum of power to sanction his way of practicing architecture.

2

Life was looking up for the whole Jeanneret family. Le Corbusier was happy to learn from Swiss friends that his mother and Albert had performed together at a party at Christmastime, and again there was heat in the apartment on rue Nungesser-et-Coli. Yvonne, Le Corbusier boasted to his mother, became "heroic, alone, without a cleaning woman."[5] She was making marvelous meals with virtually no ingredients, delighting her husband after what he termed his eighteen months of starvation in Vichy.

Like many people that winter, Le Corbusier and Yvonne were obsessed with food. They felt saved by the parcels Marie Jeanneret sent from Vevey. After thieves twice stole Le Corbusier's beloved salami before it reached him, he furnished his mother with packing instructions as detailed as building plans, in order to thwart further robbers.

Le Corbusier saw nourishment and housing as the universal issues that were at the heart of his consuming desire to redesign all of human habitation. One thought chased the other. In March, he wrote his mother, "Yvonne struggles hard without help (virtually not to be found) to make three meals a day, standing in lines, doing the dishes, and cleaning the rooms. She is occasionally exhausted. My effort concerning architecture and urbanism is daily reaffirmed."[6] One of his greatest goals would be to make both food preparation and cleaning easier universally.

IN LATE WINTER, four young students from the Ecole des Beaux-Arts—Roger Aujame among them—started work under Le Corbusier's guidance, in accord with the arrangements worked out with the Vichy regime.

Aujame was with Le Corbusier when the architect entered his old headquarters on the rue de Sèvres for the first time in three years. The long corridor, which had not been heated since 1939, was bitterly cold. Papers, books, and writing instruments were scattered all over the floor. Le Corbusier showed no marks of distress. "Let's roll up our sleeves. . . . This goes here, that there," Aujame recalled the master saying as the young architecture students sorted through lithographs by Picasso, Gris, and Braque, the deluxe edition of *L'Esprit Nouveau,* canvases by Bauchant, photos of Josephine Baker, and masses of blueprints and architectural drawings.

In little time, they were at work on the projects that had been called to a halt when Le Corbusier and Pierre had rushed out of Paris four years earlier. The students were on their own in the mornings, and every afternoon, like clockwork, Le Corbusier appeared in the office. There was no coal or wood; they burned newspapers in the one stove to stay warm. The students plied Le Corbusier with questions about the state of architecture, and he responded with long, passionate commentaries.

Le Corbusier had the young people do studies of how human beings lived in their abodes—the way they habitually navigated in the kitchen and bathroom. Aujame quickly understood that "man was at the center of the architect's preoccupations" and that human needs, rather than columns or capitals, were what counted. To Aujame, it seemed that Le Corbusier "was the only person who had ever insisted on this point." He "was always practical. His questions were, 'Why do it at that height? How will people reach it? How do you walk in?' "[7]

The atmosphere in the neighborhood was dramatically different from how it had been in the old days. German officers were living less than half a block away in the Hotel Lutétia. People who were seen to enter, in order to be interrogated, were sometimes never to leave. But Le Corbusier, to a remarkable degree, had resumed his former way of life. He was painting again and took a philosophical approach to the overall situation: "If the burden of events in general did not weigh so heavily on each of us, life (for me) would be adequate and fulfilled."[8]

3

Le Corbusier's letters to his mother provide a vivid historical record of weather conditions in France throughout the course of World War II. In 1943, Paris had a beautiful, dry April. The idyllic spring weather renewed him, and he was cheered all the more because the *Charter of Athens* was finally published by Plon, with an "introductory speech" by Giraudoux.

Le Corbusier met at this time with the sculptor Arno Breker, a Nazi whose greatest patrons were Albert Speer and Adolf Hitler, over dinner at the historic bistro Chez Josephine, on the rue du Cherche-Midi, only a short walk from the studio. Le Corbusier and the carver of muscular marble and bronze figures meant to represent the spirit of the Nazi party had a fruitful discussion "to exchange insights on urbanism and the future."[9]

By June, Le Corbusier reported to his mother that he was "very busy with a major effort to establish a building doctrine in France, an organization that absorbs all my time." Writing about "this atmosphere of uncertainty that plunges the world into breakdown," he assured her that, while the situation was demoralizing, life back in his apartment was "bracing from morning to night."[10]

Yvonne, meanwhile, had become painfully thin. In mid-June, her weight was down to fifty-one kilograms. Le Corbusier, as usual, was consulting specialists. The latest had diagnosed the source of her problem as "a distortion of the thyroid (hypertension)," although Le Corbusier continued to put the blame on menopause. The care packages of condensed milk and Gruyère from his mother were a lifesaver, without which his emaciated wife would have wasted away to nothing.

Le Corbusier was nonetheless savoring his own existence. Deprivation always had its positive consequences for him. At a time when there was no fuel for cars, the air in the city was better than usual: "an extraordinary dryness for Paris, the air is so pure in and out of town that one's vision is transfigured by it, one breathes magnificently—no more gasoline, no more dust."[11]

When Le Corbusier designed cities pierced by four-lane highways and grouped human living in towers clustered in one sector while keeping business and government separate in others, it was in part because he wanted to offer others that same sensation of communion with the elements. He sought for all humans the well-being that comes with a healthy connection, physical and emotional, to the universe. Ironically, better living and an appreciation of the natural world were the goals of the man who was so disconnected from the emotional truths of his frail wife and a collaborationist government. If the contradictions were apparent to others, they were not to him. Wanting the best for humanity, he sometimes chose the worst.

4

Le Corbusier's Paris routine was back in full swing by the summer of 1943. With La Chaux-de-Fondian precision, at 7:15 every morning he performed a quarter of an hour of gymnastic exercises while listening to Radio Paris. He was aware that while Yvonne was suffering from a wretched summer cold—"fierce rheumatic pains"—he felt himself to be "an eternal cab-horse, I trot cheerfully enough."[12] In spite of his own medical issues, he saw his role as that of the healthy one married to an invalid.

Yvonne's symptoms worsened, and by October the doctors had determined that she had an illness related to her nervous system. She was advised to abandon all "muscular efforts" for the time being. While she had to remain sedentary, Le Corbusier, with his daily exercise program, took a Darwinian approach to his own superior fitness: "We have a tendency to believe that human beings are alike. Now even on the physical level it is clear that there are separate classes."[13] The person to whom he could express this sense of his own elevated position, was, of course, his mother.

Le Corbusier was firmly convinced that he could control his state of well-being by taking care of himself and being positive even in the face of difficulties. It had been a year since he had smoked; he kept track of the date as carefully as he did his lovemaking, noting that it was on April 15, 1942, that he had had his last cigarette—in Algiers. He did not lament his eye problems, frequent colds, hernia, or the aftermath of his accident.

His campaign for his own well-being was enforced by Marie Jeanneret's remaining a model of good health. Shortly after his fifty-sixth birthday, he wrote his eighty-three-year-old mother another homily: "Your example gives me courage: I tell myself I still have 27 years ahead of me in which to achieve your present stage. And if I kept your lucidity I should then be quite capable of undertaking some plan of a great city or of an enormous edifice. Your predecessor Michelangelo built the dome of St. Peter's at 90!"[14]

These were, he acknowledged, hard times: "Newspapers and radios sing fantasies, and nothing is believable."[15] Nonetheless, he was determined to make the most of what had been a fallow period: "For ten years now, individuals and events have prevented me from undertaking anything at all. This exclusion from the circuit of action has somewhat the effect of appearing to be an unavoidable destiny. And yet I feel myself to be still a beginner, actually a student, though all my present efforts, among people of all ages and the most varied characters, indicate that as a matter of fact I am not quite the greatest fossil of them all. The question is not to continue on the previous level but to locate yourself, by decision and action, on another infinitely more advanced level. I consider that these 4 years of meditation have afforded me an exceptional situation. It remains to be seen whether my personal conviction can serve as an encouragement to others."[16]

Without heat or a telephone at 35 rue de Sèvres, Le Corbusier and the students were working away on ideas for postwar reconstruction. Le Corbusier started a new organization to develop standardized dwellings and to address issues of architecture: ASCORAL—the Association des Constructeurs pour la Rénovation Architecturale. The goals of ASCORAL were not unlike what Le Corbusier had been trying to establish in Vichy; but what he had tried to achieve for France under Pétain he would next attempt under the authority of Charles de Gaulle.

5

Le Corbusier had begun to develop the concept that was to obsess him for the rest of his life: the Modulor. This unit of measurement, two meters and twenty centimeters high, was derived from the standard height of a man with his arms raised, as measured from his feet to his fingertips. Its potential application to all of architecture was enormous.

The idea was the result of Le Corbusier's ongoing attempt to apply to architecture the ancient notion, articulated by Protagoras in the fifth century B.C., that "man is the measure of all things."[17] Others put the emphasis on God, or the gods, subjugating human beings to a higher force; Le Corbusier believed that men and women should always be the ultimate point of reference, glorified rather than reduced. Gerald Hanning, one of the young architects in the office, and Elisa Maillard, who was a mathematician and worked at the Musée de Cluny, were devoting almost all of their time to developing the device to honor that precept. Hanning carried out much of the research, while Maillard verified the numbers. As with the furniture designs, others played major roles in the collaborative process, but the end result is usually credited to Le Corbusier alone.

LE CORBUSIER, meanwhile, had not yet completely severed connections with the stragglers from Pétain's regime who still had authority. Toward the end of 1943, the architect was proud to accept Alexis Carrel's request that he become technical advisor to his French Foundation for Human Research, with its goal of cleansing society of criminals and the insane. Carrel also asked Le Corbusier to be one of the "technicians of value" for the French Foundation for the Study of Human Problems, to assist with the specific task of creating guidelines and regulations that would improve sanitary conditions in factories, locker rooms, showers, and medical centers all over the country.[18]

But for all the committees and titles and the panoply of rich ideas the architect developed between 1940 and 1945, not a single concept from those years made it to the stage of bricks and mortar. The most impressive, had they been built, were the law courts he developed for Algiers. The buildings as sketched conjure a triumph of civil reason; the bold, geometric assemblage of cell-like units raised on pilotis brings to mind the majesty of a high judge in his robes. A residence he wanted to build on an agricultural domain in Algeria would also have been remarkable. The construction was to have been in wood, local stone, and hollow bricks that could easily be made by local laborers in an era when there was little access to anything else. It would have fit in harmoniously with the landscape around it and was meant to please the local population with their preference for folklore and ancient building styles. When Le Corbusier was working in a setting he liked, both for its natural beauty and the authenticity of its citizenry, he envisioned some of his best architecture.

But, like most people, he needed the war to be over before he could really get back to work.

XXXVII

1

At the beginning of 1944, Albert had one of his kidneys removed. Le Corbusier was concerned mainly about their mother, who was left alone for a month in the badly heated house during the harshest period of the Swiss winter, while Albert recuperated in a clinic.

To relieve her loneliness, Le Corbusier wrote "La Petite Maman" regularly, always signing Yvonne's name as well as his own. He used those letters to declare his latest theories on his role in the grand scheme of things. Le Corbusier believed without question that the elite should make decisions for the many, that rare individuals like himself should establish the master plans. It was his responsibility to provide external circumstances that brought maximum joy to all of humanity.

At this bleak moment of history, Le Corbusier, in an oblique way, seemed to be reflecting on where that sense of his own mission had led him during the reign of Pétain.

> Ours is a decisive epoch when countless sufferings classify people as selfish or charitable. I often think that Papa would not have had sufficient resistance to survive a period as fantastic as the one which began five years ago. Day after day, we see the implacable deliberation of events with endless consequences. And men's hearts, or their minds, do not know exactly toward which poles to orient themselves. This great mutation exceeds our understanding, solutions are only provisional, incriminating generations to come. A man's life no longer involves, as in stable periods, the gesture of sowing in order to reap. Sowing and reaping will extend over generations, and an individual man can live without having anything to harvest for himself. . . .
>
> Moreover the human reason for living remains quite mysterious. And without a deeply rooted ideal, human beings become poor wrecks.[1]

He saw himself as having maintained a consistent ideal throughout the epoch of Vichy. The behavior of others, however, incurred his wrath. The care packages that arrived at the rue Nungesser-et-Coli, lovingly put together in Switzerland, continued to be pillaged. As before, the salami was the thieves' prime target, but now chocolate and cheese were also stolen, leaving only the condensed milk. In the course of 1944, Le Corbusier developed anger toward his mother's grocer that was comparable to the invective he usually reserved for academics or bureaucrats. He flew into a tirade at the man's idiocy and wastefulness in failing to pack things as instructed. Inefficiency enraged him far more than the thievery.

Meanwhile, in spite of all that was patently wrong in the world, his cause was making progress through ASCORAL: "I am achieving this task of establishing a healthy doctrine of construction with the impassioned contribution of people of all kinds and all ages. Everything advances regularly, like a carefully seeded plant which when spring comes will flourish."[2]

While the spring of 1944 was a troubling time for most of humanity, Le Corbusier felt "the certitude of enormous fundamental changes. Only the first act is ending at this moment. The curtain will rise on the second. It requires vast provisions of patience to envisage with some serenity all that is imminent. But it is encouraging to realize that the evolution will be in the direction of the good."[3]

2

On May 28, 1944, Pierre Jeanneret opened his own Paris office with his colleague Georges Blanchon. Le Corbusier claimed to be pleased with the development; he had come to find his cousin too meek as a partner. He admired Pierre's physical prowess but felt that his mental attitude did not match it.

At least this is the slant Le Corbusier subsequently gave to their breakup. The few known facts suggest another scenario. It was only on November 4, slightly over five months after Pierre opened his office ten minutes away, that the quieter Jeanneret even called on Le Corbusier to say hello. He had learned how to endure the master's rages, but the alliance with Pétain was more than he could tolerate.

Le Corbusier, meanwhile, was now trying to disassociate himself from his efforts of the past three years. That spring, he resigned from the projects with Carrel, saying that this approach no longer appealed to him. He willingly joined the momentum toward a new France. In April, just after the second anniversary of his having quit tobacco, he said that his days were flying as fast as cigarette smoke. Vichy, too, could disappear into thin air.[4]

3

On June 6, 1944, the Allied forces landed on the coast of Normandy. On August 15, additional French and American troops began their advance from the southern coast up the valley of the Rhone. Ten days later, Paris was liberated.

Le Corbusier described the spectacle to his mother. Reading his letter in the serenity of her quiet living room, with Lac Leman lapping the shore only a few meters away, she would, he hoped, be able to imagine the scene in all its operatic glory.

> Here, from my roof, there was a month of preamble, then the violent realization of the liberation of Paris. And suddenly Paris was rid of them! What a moral sensation! Then came the shortages: of water, light, gas, and the closing of the Métros for a month. This inevitably occurred precisely at the time of a minor famine, since no further provisions arrived from the countryside. As always, the sly ones—prudent, as they are called, and they may still be the unconquerable egoists—have long since hoarded their supplies. . . .
>
> The dogfights of planes in the sky, the bombardments, day and night, of railroad stations and bridges, the munitions depots exploding in the distance, close by, even 100 yards away—all this going on 24 hours a day, the sirens sending us to the cellars several times day and night. It was a busy everyday existence gleaming in the brilliant sunlight of the dog days. No elevator for months! . . .
>
> Saturday August 19th, at six o'clock in the evening, I see for the first time in years a French flag on the gun platform of the DCA [Défense Contre Avions: cannons for defense against air attacks] of the Lycée La Fontaine. It vanishes half an hour later, and it is only the following Friday that we went to the Bois de Boulogne to see the parade of the French army and the American army, which had arrived in the majesty of new vehicles and new uniforms, proving that a page has been turned. The next day came the parade down the Champs-Elysées and the hail of bullets from Notre-Dame. At midnight the enemy had returned; the American DCA is located in the Bois all around us, spitting an inferno of racket and luminous shells; the alcohols of the Halle aux Vins are burning. And coming down from our bedroom, we observe through my studio window an intense red light. Yvonne

exclaims "Paris is burning!" she faints! That was the only time her senses failed her.

What a life for women these last 4 years here! Crushing tasks—demanding, meticulous, endless! Above all, it is this absolute of the everyday which is so pernicious. There can be no doubt that these years have defeated many people. But let this scrap of narrative not persuade you that we are so damaged as to think only of ourselves. On the contrary. There is good reason to think of others—of the people and the country and very often of you![5]

LE CORBUSIER was convinced the time was ripe for his ideas to be realized. Maximilien Gauthier's book *Le Corbusier; or, Architecture in the Service of Mankind*—the title was Le Corbusier's own invention—was about to be published by Denoël. ASCORAL intended to publish more of his writings—if they could find the paper to print them on. The architect uttered his familiar cry with more enthusiasm and optimism than ever before: "A veritable swarm is forming around my ideas. A decisive battle is being fought which must see them triumph."[6]

Claude Laurens, son of the sculptor Henri Laurens, had carried Le Corbusier's letter about the liberation of Paris to Marie. Henri Laurens exemplified, in Le Corbusier's eyes, the human qualities he held most dear. He was "the sort of man whose life is exemplary, indicating where true happiness abides: within—in the human heart, an inexhaustible treasure."[7]

No one could have convinced him that Maréchal Pétain had violated that principle. But Le Corbusier was well aware that, following the liberation of Paris, Pétain was tried and sentenced to death—although he was spared execution because of his age and senility. Some ten thousand collaborationists were executed. Eleven thousand civil servants were dismissed—although many of them were reinstated within a few years. As recently as a year and a half earlier, some of those people had been Le Corbusier's chosen colleagues.

In April 1945, Le Corbusier was appointed urbanist counsel of the city of Saint-Dié. The position called for him to develop a plan for this city in the Vosges that had been heavily bombed on December 8, 1944. He wrote his mother that "Saint-Dié was systematically destroyed in 3 days. A splendid problem."[8]

The demolition of Saint-Dié and the need to rebuild it signified to the architect that he would at last undertake the postwar reconstruction work he had hoped to perform since July 1940. "My long retreat of 5 years has borne its fruits," he wrote with unabashed satisfaction on a postcard to his mother.[9]

Le Corbusier was awarded the assignment in Saint-Dié thanks to Jean-Jacques Duval, a prominent cheese producer in the region. The previous year—in a period when most cheese makers were, to the architect's horror, forced to produce cheeses with no fat content whatsoever—Duval had sent him four full-fat cheeses. Le Corbusier rated the plan to rebuild Saint-Dié as a similar triumph: "It appears as the peremptory sign of France's will to live."[10]

His idea was a prototype he believed could be re-created all over the world. Its components included a civic center with a skyscraper to house the city administration, an elevated roadway on pilotis, under which pedestrians could safely pass in areas reserved for them alone, the same spiral museum he had always wanted to build, and housing near the outskirts that could accommodate ten thousand people. The architect considered it nothing less than "an architectural melody . . . an opulent symphony . . . a plan of modern times."[11]

4

After the Nazi concentration camps were liberated, Le Corbusier wrote his mother,

> May 8th, 1945. Darling Maman, peace will be proclaimed in a few hours. Five years ago, the Germans overran the west. Now we discover all the horrors that pride and overweening vanity can produce: the charnel houses of the camps!!! Paris is filled with sunshine. We are happy but actually unconscious of the value of the signature that was scrawled yesterday at Reims. Will our energies be kept united long enough to construct peace? I know there [is] a new war to be waged against money and sloth. I am armed and ready, filled with courage. Brazil—by the magnificent publications of New York and London—reveals to world opinion its astonishing effort of construction since 1936. L. C.'s "Radiant City," people say, acknowledging it, and everyone is struck by the harmony launched by my 1936 trip to Rio. Received yesterday Albert's undated card (stamped 4/26/45). The Lake Villa repainted? Fine. The same day a card from W. Ritter whom I thought was dead. Courage, hope, and joy in doing what one owes it to oneself to do.
>
> Tenderly from Yvonne and Le Corbusier[12]

Were the "pride and overweening vanity" his own? Did he have a moral compass after all, or was he blind to the connection between what he thought would be the positive solutions of Nazism and the monstrosity that had engulfed civilization?

Or was all that counted the effect on his own work? In late May, the architect received a letter from an assistant editor of *Les Cahiers du Sud,* a monthly literary review in Marseille. François Le Lionnais, its chief editor, had, during the war, been arrested by the Gestapo and deported. Now Le Lionnais "has just returned from Buchenwald. So our work will resume and soon be completed. Publication cannot be long behind."[13] Le Corbusier scribbled on the letter that the editor's liberation from the concentration camp meant that his article on proportions could now appear.

5

In *Le Corbusier Speaks,* orchestrated during Le Corbusier's lifetime although published only afterward, the crafty text jumps from third to first person, but in either case the message is mainly one of hardship and sacrifice in wartime: "During the Occupation, from 1940 to 1944? Le Corbusier, at that time separated from his cousin and associate, Pierre Jeanneret, received no architectural commission, his material situation remained precarious, despite unfortunate and fruitless efforts made with the Vichy authorities with whom he stayed in contact for a long time, he received no official commission. . . . I did not want to leave France after the defeat. I put my energies into the battle where I believed it was necessary to do so in order to put the process and possibility of construction on likely terms. For four years I was excluded from all commissions, and no work was entrusted to me. During the previous twenty years I had constantly been accused of being the advocate of Bolshevism. Darnand remembered. During this period when I lived under the threat of real material indigence, the French ambassador to Argentina sent invitations to come to Buenos Aires on dazzling financial conditions and give lectures on urbanism and build various structures; these offers were renewed for a whole year. I declined them and refused the golden bridge proposed; I judged that my duty was to remain in France, believing my battle was there and not abroad."[14] It was a strange choice to evoke the name of Joseph Darnand, a hero of the Great War, ten years Le Corbusier's junior, who, in 1941, had created a paramilitary movement, which was actively anti-Semitic and endorsed by Pétain. Darnand had joined the Waffen SS in 1943, and had been condemned and executed in 1945. Le Corbusier may have hoped that since Darnand had accused him of Bolshevism, he would be seen as a victim of collaborationist evil.

In *Corbusier Himself,* the architect distorted history shamelessly by reporting only that he bravely challenged Nazi authorities during the German occupation of Paris. When an exposition of Léger's art was forbidden by the Germans, Le Corbusier allegedly insisted on an audience with Lieutenant Heller, director of intellectual propaganda, to protest the cancellation. Heller told him, "Everyone tells me you're a Communist," ending the interview;[15] the implication is that Le Corbusier was too far to the left to have possibly had a sympathetic hearing from someone high up in the Vichy regime, even though the architect had bravely approached the man anyway. Le Corbusier allows that he met Arno Breker, but leaves out that they had a constructive discussion over a leisurely dinner; rather, he proudly suggests that he infuriated Breker by saying that the greatest two artists of the era were Picasso and Léger. And he describes how a M. de Precigout, a friend of a friend, who had spent an afternoon with him at 24 rue Nungesser-et-Coli in 1943 and had bought six canvases and eight gouaches, had subsequently been arrested by the Gestapo. He gives no reason for providing this information, although clearly it is to point out the horrors of the epoch and link himself, by implication, with a victim of Nazism.

Whether any of this happened is not certain. But there is no question that, decades later, this was all that Le Corbusier wanted people to know of his behavior during wartime.

MARÉCHAL PÉTAIN'S trial in August 1945 relied heavily on the Vichy's leader's own words. The prosecutor of the republic, André Mornet, quoted a radio pronouncement from the early period of Pétain's rule in which the Maréchal had said, "All our miseries have come from the Republic. . . . The responsibility for our defeat lies with the democratic political regime of France. . . . A strong state is what we wish to erect upon the ruins of the old, which fell more under the weight of its own errors than under the blows of the enemy. . . . You have only one France, which I incarnate."[16] The arrogance of that sentiment helped convict a despot, but for three long years it had convinced both a desperate architect and his determined mother that they and the government at Vichy were on the right path.

Le Corbusier justified his behavior between 1940 and 1942 with a simple explanation: "Here for the first time in my life was the occasion, since I had always been rejected by the administrative centers and consequently deprived of administrative data, of being able to know the general elements of the national plan and therefore of being able to conceive urbanism on a level hitherto inaccessible to me."[17]

For the rest of his life, he was savvy enough not to let his enthusiasm for Pétain and people like Carrel be public knowledge. Remarkably, no one publicly pressed the point. But some of those who knew never again felt the same about Le Corbusier.

6

Charlotte Perriand was among those who perpetually disdained her former hero's alliance with Vichy. When she returned to Paris in 1946, after having spent the war years in Indochina and Japan, she contemplated resuming work at 35 rue de Sèvres, but she could not forget what she considered a betrayal of decency.

Perriand did, however, agree to meet Le Corbusier at the café Les Deux Magots. She reminded herself that, in 1936 and 1937, he had written to Léon Blum about the Ville Radieuse; he would as easily have worked with Blum as with Pétain. Le Corbusier had tunnel vision; he saw only the distant light, not what was going on, in close proximity, all around him.

Charlotte Perriand did finally return to the fold, but with an awareness that, as focused as Le Corbusier was on the privileges of human existence, he was irreparably disconnected from certain truths.

XXXVIII

1

Charles de Gaulle led a victory march down the Champs-Elysées on August 26, 1944. From the moment he had gone to London on June 17, 1940, de Gaulle, a junior defense minister with a special knowledge of armored warfare, had challenged the legitimacy of the Vichy regime. Now it was clear that he was the person who could lead the country after the war. For much of France, after four years of darkness, the charismatic leader was the epitome of triumphant leadership, an irresistible symbol of decent values and intransigence of the best sort. He had never for a moment failed in his devotion to maintaining democracy in France or considered courting the Germans.

With de Gaulle at the helm, France was resurrected. Le Corbusier was as excited as if he, too, had never toyed with the policies of the leaders of Vichy. No one was more eager to help with the reconstruction of the country than the architect for whom France had offered personal salvation after the mundanity of Switzerland and the torpor of Germany. After all, to build for its people had always been his objective. When he was summoned to meet the general, he needed no persuading.

LE CORBUSIER long remembered the precise details of that first command to meet de Gaulle. The previous night, he had returned home shortly before midnight. His spirits were low; he was exhausted from a sixteen-hour train journey from Lausanne following a visit with his mother and irritated that people working at the train station in the Swiss city had given him the incorrect departure time. Casualness about time invariably sent the architect into a rage; like lateness, it was a violation of the order and precision imperative to a fruitful existence.

At about 11:30 p.m., just as he was entering his building, the mayor of Warsaw got out of his car a few meters away. They greeted each other and, standing under the gas streetlight, had a conversation on the sidewalk. The encounter restored Le Corbusier's spirits because he knew that the Pole had considerable influence with the new French government. He considered it a natural sequence of events when, the next day, he received instructions to go immediately to the Atlantic seaport town of La Rochelle to meet with General de Gaulle and Raoul Dautry, the first minister of reconstruction.

It was a Friday; Le Corbusier scrambled unsuccessfully to find a car or a train that would get him there right away. In the aftermath of the war, transportation was limited, and for many hours Le Corbusier could not figure out how to get to this vitally important meeting. Then he was notified by the air minister that a plane had been arranged for him. The architect left Paris Saturday at 4:00 p.m. and was in La Rochelle an hour and a half later.

Having momentarily felt important, he then waited for a day and a half. The idle time recalled Vichy. The architect chatted amiably with anyone he encountered but did not see de Gaulle. In his own office, Le Corbusier was imperious over the slightest delay; here he had no choice but to be patient. Then, on Monday, at noon, he shook de Gaulle's hand.

That was the extent of their meeting. That night, Le Corbusier took the train back to Paris. Even though the meeting with the head of the new France had been nothing more than a handshake, he felt it was immensely significant.

WITHIN A COUPLE OF DAYS, Dautry approached him with a proposal that changed Le Corbusier's life—and the course of architecture worldwide. The minister asked Le Corbusier to design a large apartment building in Marseille.

L'Unité d'Habitation would change forever the concept of how humanity could house itself.

2

Today l'Unité d'Habitation is a Marseille landmark, signposted simply with the name "Le Corbusier." But initially most people were skeptical about Le Corbusier's revolutionary vision and ridiculed the apartment building, which burst the boundaries on every front. Its form and structure were without precedent, its facades inconceivable to anyone but the man who made them. Its interior corridors, the layout of its apartments, and the design of their fittings were all so new as to seem preposterous. More than half a century later, however, even those who do not admire the building accept its importance, and more and more people succumb to its beauty.

Primary colors dazzle the eye inside and out. The roof garden brings the high drama of ancient amphitheatres into the precinct of everyday domestic architecture. At last afforded the opportunity to evoke the ferocious energy, as well as the clarity, of Greek architecture, Le Corbusier used the materials and techniques of modern engineering to do so.

After l'Unité d'Habitation, no apartment building has ever quite equaled it. On the other hand, it has propagated thousands of clones. Imitations in distant lands sometimes improved living standards markedly but at other moments emerged as cold and lifeless developments; even Le Corbusier's own subsequent l'Unités lacked the magic of the original. But for better or worse, Le Corbusier's building in Marseille became the village of the twentieth century.

3

Le Corbusier often spoke in units of five. He habitually said that he was about to achieve the objective for which he had been slaving for the previous ten, fifteen, or twenty years. With the Marseille commission, using the verb "*potasser,*" which translates as "to cram" or "to bone up," he gave fifteen years as the warm-up period to this monumental building in the second-largest city of a new and vital France.

He became ecstatic about everything. Visiting Vevey, he found the eighty-five-year-old "la Petite Maman" especially well; afterward, he allowed, "Maman so careful not to turn her nose up at this dirty Le Corbusier, Albert so attentive." Now that the war was over, he was "happy to rediscover France with her grand handsome landscapes and that enormous task which we must now attempt to perform."[1] Civilization was being reborn that summer. Le Corbusier was content to eradicate the past, especially elements of his own previous five years, as if with a fire or a bomb. With the Unité d'Habitation, he was to succeed in putting this manic joy, the power of the sun's rays, into plastic form, transforming steel and concrete into the substance of euphoria.

4

In March, Yvonne had broken her femur at midcalf. She had spent three months in a plaster cast that extended from her navel to the end of her foot, and she had been unable to emerge from her horizontal position for the entire time. Fortunately, Le Corbusier was able to get a maid who had helped in Vézelay to come take care of her. While Yvonne had broken her leg falling down drunk, Le Corbusier told his mother that it was the result of "decalcification."

Although at the end of June Yvonne began to get around the apartment using a side chair as a walker, there was no thought of a summer holiday. In August, she suffered another "attack of cruelly painful neuritis" that again completely prevented her from walking.[2] Le Corbusier was content to be working, going back and forth to La Rochelle on the night train to develop a new plan for a fishermen's port built around the natural gulf. At the office, his young crew was busily working on details of this project and the plan for Saint-Dié.

Initially, the scheme for Saint-Dié was applauded—"Msgr. the Archbishop had found it very attractive. The industrialists were delighted"—Le Corbusier reported euphorically. But then local authorities, members of the Association Populaire des Sinistrés, an organization opposed to the idea of any new solution to Saint-Dié's urban issues, rejected Le Corbusier's project definitively. As usual, Le Corbusier saw the defeat as evidence of human stupidity and willful ignorance. A complacent bourgeoisie had managed to annihilate the efforts of the messiah: "This is a plan for modern times. A man sitting in an armchair has managed to cancel it!"[3]

The martyr did not stay down for long. Dautry submitted a contract to him for the Marseille project, to which Le Corbusier agreed only under the condition that he get a special dispensation from the usual rules about how the design team would be formed. His demand was met, and he hired a slew of younger architects for the office, among them André Wogenscky, who had worked in his studio between 1937 and 1939 and who now became his "assistant-architect."[4]

His spirits soared. His latest treatise on housing, *The Three Human Establishments,* sold out an edition of six thousand copies—an extraordinary response for a book in 1945.[5] The book introduced the idea of "the industrial linear city"—to be installed on such a scale that it would cross national borders. Le Corbusier claimed that, at dinner in the presence of André Gide, Léon Blum called the book " 'the most remarkable he had ever read.' . . .

The statesman who had spent his entire life on propositions to no effect suddenly discovered the new paths leading to actions and enterprises relieving crises and creating 'Tomorrow.' "[6]

That fall, Le Corbusier's and Yvonne's beloved black-haired schnauzer, Pinceau, died at age eleven. Beyond being their roommate in Vichy, Pinceau—whose name means "paintbrush"—had been their constant companion since 1934. When he was one year old, the puppy had nearly died of pulmonary congestion. Yvonne had sent a telegram to her husband care of the Museum of Modern Art in New York City to say that Pinceau was in the clinic and that there was "little hope."[7] But he had survived and been an integral part of the couple's existence.

Le Corbusier proudly kept the pedigree that named Pinceau's parents, Graal du Paddock and Irma von Wartberg, and traced his lineage back to his eight great-grandparents. The architect was often photographed with the sweet and sympathetic creature with his long, floppy ears, unkempt hair, and large eyes.

After Pinceau died, Le Corbusier, at great expense, had the dog's body skinned and tanned. He also had his skull preserved, with a spring mechanism in the jaw. The services were provided by "naturalists" with offices a short walk from Le Corbusier's old digs on the rue Jacob. This was probably the skin used to cover his old copy of *Don Quixote*—extant to this day—but what he did with the skull is unknown. Entrances fascinated Le Corbusier; at Ronchamp, he was to create incredible doors. Perhaps that dog's mouth, able to open and close with his manipulation, became an inspiration.

To Le Corbusier, death, like war, was a source of transformation. Saving bones, reconfiguring his dead dog's skin and skull, he tried to control the next stage of existence according to his own terms.

5

De Gaulle's government, through its Ministry of Foreign Affairs, had created a Mission on Architecture and Urbanism to examine how other countries were handling those areas. Le Corbusier was appointed chairman. A grander version of the task he had been given as a young man in La Chaux-de-Fonds when L'Eplattenier had commissioned him to study the latest developments in modernism, it made him an architectural ambassador—on a global stage—for a client who would presumably listen. He was euphoric to be doing exactly what he wanted for the government in power at a turning point in history.

One of his first tasks in the new position was to return to America, the hotbed of progress and new ideas. On December 22, 1945, Le Corbusier boarded the cargo ship *Vernon S. Hood,* which had been refitted after its use for the transport of war materials, as one of its twenty-nine passengers. The voyage, which took twenty days, gave him the chance to be with a new friend, Eugène Claudius-Petit, the beginning of an alliance that was to last until Le Corbusier's death. The trip also provided him with the opportunity to elaborate on the idea of the Modulor with his office colleagues Justin Serralta and André Maisonnier. While crossing the Atlantic, they developed the spiral that was a central image to the Modulor idea. This semiabstract rendition of a human being provided an empiric method to harmonize all the measurements used for the construction of a building.

When Le Corbusier arrived in the United States, all of his clothing was, by his standards, unacceptably wrinkled and full of holes. Paul Lester Wiener, José Luis Sert's partner, who was there to greet him, lent him a jacket and trousers. In his published accounts of the time, Le Corbusier depicted himself as not having eaten for four years and, with his skeletal physique, being unable to fill out the new clothes.[8] Focusing on himself as an emaciated Christ-like figure and on his own shabby suit, he seemed oblivious to the worse problems others had suffered during the war.

Wiener soon took the architect to meet Albert Einstein at the Institute for Advanced Study in Princeton so that the great scientist could give his view on the Modulor. Wiener served as translator. Le Corbusier's report of the encounter emphasized their comparative states of nutrition and appearance more than any aspect of the discussion: "Einstein had eaten normally, I had not. Which demonstrates the method leading to underdeveloped countries. The Swiss gentlemen arriving in Paris after the liberation found it dirty (no paint on the façades, no wax on the parquet floors), and the French in a lamentable state: those cheeks, those bellies!"[9]

What was Le Corbusier saying? The mockery of Swiss arrogance and insensitivity to the wartime suffering of the French is clear, but was Le Corbusier also deriding himself as part of a culture that might think the state of the wax on the parquet really mattered? Or did he only see himself as being among the downtrodden victims of recent history?

A photograph of Le Corbusier and Einstein gives a totally different impression than the architect's plaintive depiction. Le Corbusier looks fit and elegant. His bow tie is as straight as a steel beam. He is sporting an impeccably tailored, double-breasted navy blazer; the triangle of his white pocket handkerchief emerges in starched perfection, its proportion just right. His trousers are neatly creased, and there is a shine to his shoes. He walks in a brisk gait that suggests the peak of health. Einstein looks every bit the refugee, his trousers crumpled, his sweater fitting poorly, his expression awkward and worn. The evidence of that photo only adds to the bizarreness of Le Corbusier's notion of his own deprived body and sorry clothing.

After their meeting, Einstein wrote Le Corbusier a letter about the Modulor with a pronouncement that the architect quoted forever after: "It is a range of dimensions which makes the bad difficult and the good easy."[10] The reduction of complexity to simplicity was a mutual dream of both these geniuses.

With Albert Einstein, Princeton, 1946

The dapper Le Corbusier, as he walked around Princeton with a disheveled Albert Einstein, might well have discussed the scientist's summer getaway with him. Before he left Germany, Einstein had, in the small town of Caputh, where a path through the woods overlooked Templiner Lake, built a simple wooden house where he and his wife could escape Berlin and his existence as an internationally famous figure. Einstein had initially wanted solid logs, and while he agreed to a less expensive structure sided in planks, he rejected the modernist look that had been proposed to him and opted instead for architectural ordinariness and the functionalism of a monk's cell. He shocked visitors by greeting them barefoot and in his sailing shirt. Le Corbusier's own choice of a getaway for himself and his wife, and his way of life there, was to be nearly identical.

6

Le Corbusier started his New York stay in a shabby third-rate hotel, but after three days his trip organizers moved him to the Carlyle. He considered the lithe and elegant tower on upper Madison Avenue the most beautiful hotel he had ever seen. He proudly wrote Yvonne that a room cost two thousand francs per day—which was fine because he wasn't the one paying the bill.

The architect traveled to Washington to meet the French ambassador and from there went on to the Tennessee valley to see a spectacular dam. On his return to New York, he visited the Museum of Modern Art and was delighted to see one of his own paintings hanging in the permanent collection alongside masterpieces by Matisse, Picasso, and Léger. He returned to France by plane on January 29—his longest flight to date, requiring a change in London and taking nearly an entire, marvelous day.

Jerzy Soltan, a young architect who had recently started work on the rue de Sèvres, described the master's return: "Le Corbusier left for the United States highly excited over what would happen in New York. We expected that he would be absent a long time. But suddenly, a couple of days later, the door opened and Le Corbusier entered with a small suitcase. He was obviously coming directly from the airport. Keeping his coat and hat on, he zoomed to the Modulor table. The short sojourn to the United States revealed to him a blunder in the Modulor reasoning. The Americans were tall and the United States intensely industrialized; one had to recognize these facts. The Anglo-Saxon measures—the foot, the inch—are far more human than the metric system's meter, an arbitrary segment of the equator's length, or the centimeter, an arbitrary part of the meter related to it only by decimal order. A six-foot-tall man should be the starting point of our anthropometric considerations. Le Corbusier was enchanted by this new development, and he left me with the new computations. Soon he was on his way back to New York."[11]

In fact, someone standing at six feet with his arms at his sides was not so different from Le Corbusier's previously established standard of two meters twenty centimeters for someone with his arms raised, but in his mind Le Corbusier had made a profound discovery in America.

LE CORBUSIER had planned eight Unités d'Habitation for Saint-Dié, none of which were constructed, but one building did come to life there. This was a factory for Jean-Jacques Duval, which had its proportions based on the Modulor and provided Le Corbusier a chance to push color to a new extreme. Against the neutral background of rough concrete, strong reds sung from the ceilings and from the plumbing and heating pipes that were blatantly revealed. That frank celebration of the guts of a building was a precedent that was to affect modern architecture to an astonishing degree; today we take for granted this approach that was radical in 1946.

Duval's manufacturing plant reflects Le Corbusier's keen awareness of the everyday needs of its employees. It stands on pilotis that permit an airy and useful courtyard to exist as the transition between the outside world and the inside, with a large bicycle park at ground level that protects bikes from rain and snow without requiring their users to deal with doors or stairs. The sidewalls are faced with sandstone indigenous to the Vosges mountains and scavenged from the remains of old local buildings; their texture is warm and rich. There are other poetic touches rare in an industrial building, such as the large photographic enlargements of Le Corbusier's own paintings, which add color and vitality to the offices. Lively tile work on one of the roof-garden walls injects color, rhythm, and lightness into the daily existence of the executives who are invited there. Built-in shelves have a jazzy rhythm. In the following decade, this innovative emphasis on art and nature as essential elements in the workplace influenced corporate architecture all over the world.

SHORTLY AFTER the Saint-Dié defeat, Joseph Savina, a talented cabinet-maker from Brittany, asked Le Corbusier if he could make sculpture based on the architect's paintings. Le Corbusier jumped at the idea; he and Savina

At 24 rue Nungesser-et-Coli, late 1940s

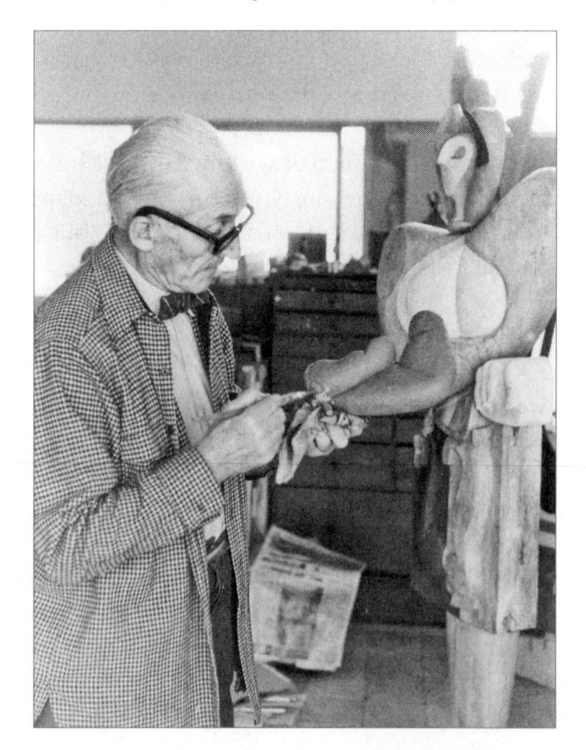

proceeded, with the understanding that the architect himself would color the work. With the move into sculpture, a new life opened up before his eyes.

Other things did not change, though. At the opening of an exhibition, Le Corbusier suddenly found himself face-to-face with Amédée Ozenfant. Ozenfant made the first move, attempting to shake hands. "We were two idiots," said Charles-Edouard Jeanneret's former soul mate.

Le Corbusier did not smile. "I see that one of us still remains so," he answered, and walked on.[12]

Le Corbusier told the story without regret.

XXXIX

Arrange things, Marguerite. Give orders, leave a key, give me instructions. You're the mistress, you'll do it. And I'll have the key!

—LE CORBUSIER TO MARGUERITE TJADER HARRIS, 1946

1

On March 24, 1946, Le Corbusier informed his mother that he had been waiting to write her until he had confirmation of some news that should make her happy. It was the identical sentiment he had voiced three years earlier, after being appointed to the government commission under Pétain. Referring to himself in the third person, he told her that, the previous evening, the newspapers had announced that Le Corbusier had been named by the French state as its architect in the planning of the recently founded United Nations, to be constructed in Connecticut. The project was to start immediately: "For here, in the midst of this architectural squabble, is the victory of the antiacademic camp. Moreover everything is advancing with giant strides. . . . The modern world is born, shifting its center, revising its values, etc. Everything is shaken up."[1]

As if he were observing someone else, Le Corbusier applauded his own steadfastness. He had stuck to a worthy program, and now it was paying off. To his eighty-five-year-old mother he explained time and again that his appointment to the UN project was the ultimate validation of the nobility of his behavior.

The subtext was a justification of his time in Vichy. For if no internal guidelines were telling Le Corbusier how slimy his involvement had been, the trial of Pétain and the executions of collaborators forced him to examine the choices he had made, at least to the person who had enthusiastically supported them. Sewing everything up neatly for his mother, he was also assuring himself: "Amid this confusion I did not flinch, not having responded to solicitations and flatteries, having always been where the battle was fiercest, and I powerfully advanced my theses, my doctrines, installing them everywhere, keeping my distance, assuming a certain superiority. And I can say that I am bequeathing a healthy doctrine, uncertain only whether it will bear its fruits now or later."[2] When his old admirer Marcel Bucard was found guilty of high treason and executed that same year, both Marie Jeanneret and Le Corbusier presumably had little recollection of how proud and excited she had been a decade earlier when Bucard raved to her about her son.

Le Corbusier told his mother that any day now he would receive a telegram that would send him off to Orly Airport and on to New York for two months. Delighting in the many simultaneous pulls on his life and the sense of urgency, he summarized his current activities. He could live serenely off his painting but didn't have time to do it at the moment. Dividing his days between work in Marseille, the Pyrénées, La Rochelle, and Saint-Dié, where the municipal council now wanted to see another design, he often slept on trains. He was also one of six members of a government committee for architecture and urbanism—they were an "army of the mediocre," but at least he had a voice.[3]

"Here I go, speaking only of myself!" the architect then wrote, following his long exegesis on the international ramifications of his success. He knew his mother never approved of that focus. Yvonne, he now reported, had spent her birthday with another broken leg. Now blaming his wife's situation on the deprivations of the war, he said the recovery process was an enormous struggle for her. He became solicitous of Marie Jeanneret herself. His mother could now see with only one eye; he coached her on how to adapt to this limitation, with which he was so familiar. Dutifully, he went over minute maintenance details of La Petite Maison and some repairs he wanted to make there.

He also gave advice about Albert. Albert was trying to get a ballet produced; Le Corbusier offered to help get it performed in America if Albert would revise it, but the ballet was flawed because Albert tried to moralize rather than divert. The world in this postwar moment needed "sun, spring, courage, hope, relaxation (at last!!), nourishment, clothes, etc."[4] He hammered on about how Albert should be making recordings of a children's orchestra; Le Corbusier regularly proposed this idea, which would be popular regardless of the nationality or class of the audience.

Le Corbusier was determined that his mother recognize that, in a time period when he was flourishing professionally, nothing concerned him more than his family. What mattered the most about the United Nations was the joy the news should bring Marie Charlotte Amélie Jeanneret-Perret.

2

Le Corbusier's greatest difficulty that spring was one he craved: an excess of work. A book devoted to his painting and sculpture—with 250 pages of reproductions—was under discussion with a New York publisher (although it was never realized). His ministerial committee met every Tuesday morning. The office at 35 rue de Sèvres was full of work, even if low on cash. He had now been asked to give advice on urban plans for Warsaw, Tunis, and Bizerte, also in Tunisia. There was going to be an international conference in Italy to debate Le Corbusier's ideas against Frank Lloyd Wright's: "these two theses of urbanism and even of ethics and social discipline."[5] In May he accepted yet another Legion of Honor, now as an "officer." Most important of all, there was the United Nations. Le Corbusier was perpetually waiting for the telegram.

To his mother, he emphasized the precariousness of things and the fortitude demanded of him: "The goals I pursue are intense and delicate, even perilous. One must keep a close watch, study continuously and do battle without respite."[6]

Marie Jeanneret replied with the information that she was thinking of selling La Petite Maison. He told her it was out of the question, an act of madness. But when she then proposed altering certain details to suit her own taste rather than his rigorous aesthetic, he did not quibble. He regretted that his busy schedule made it impossible for him to come to give her a hand, but she should do with her house as she wanted, even though her alterations, he let her know, would damage his reputation.[7]

Le Corbusier asked his mother to send him and Yvonne some bed linens. They needed sheets and plain white pillowcases, absolutely without decoration or a scalloped edge, for large, square pillows. He emphasized that they never used bolsters—as if bolsters were the devil. Marie could live as she wanted; he would not compromise *his* style.

Le Corbusier had doubled the size of his studio on the rue de Sèvres in order to make the first studies for l'Unité d'Habitation and work on La Rochelle, now that his initial proposal for its port had been accepted. Writing his mother and brother about his new prosperity thanks to the success of his books and other work, he was soaring.

Then, at the start of May, the long-awaited telegram arrived. Le Corbusier jumped at the call to leave Paris immediately. He booked a night flight for Saturday, May 4. It would get him to New York twenty-two hours later, following a stopover in Iceland, at half past noon on Sunday. He would remain in America for the next two months. If others thought he would be merely an equal part of the United Nations team, he intended to be its mastermind; there could be only one primary designer for the single most important building complex in a newly unified world, and there was no question about who it had to be. For while he had not yet developed his scheme, he was confident that designs he had already made provided ideal prototypes.

His conquest in mind, all was for the best. Yvonne was courageous, and France was waking up with a new creative spirit. The day before he departed, Le Corbusier wrote his mother, "Aching, exhausted, my mind overwhelmed, yet I am filled with calm and joy and certitude: everything is working. Everything has worked. From these enormous trials all of us will draw a powerful new life."[8]

In advance of the trip, Le Corbusier also let his mother know that he had received a charming letter from Mrs. Tjader Harris. The tall, handsome woman Marie Jeanneret had introduced to Le Corbusier in 1932 wanted news of her. As Le Corbusier headed back to the United States to work on this project, the charming and intelligent divorcée, in whose Ford he had explored that part of the world a decade earlier, would not be far away.

3

The initial intention was for the United Nations headquarters to be built on untouched land, which would become an entire city. Besides an assembly hall and offices, there would be housing for the international population of delegates and their families, as well as schools, shops, and other support facilities.

The plan to have the new complex in Fairfield County, the same part of Connecticut where Marguerite Tjader Harris lived, was not, however, definite. One of the main tasks of the UN Permanent Headquarters Commission was to evaluate five different sites, all in or near New York City, while determining the organization's requirements in greater detail. The other four potential locales were the Palisades, alongside the Hudson River in northern New Jersey; Flushing Meadows Park, in Queens; suburban Westchester County; and Rockefeller Center, without the ancillary buildings.

Le Corbusier objected to all the sites proposed. He was adamant that proximity to the heart of New York was vital, but he also insisted that it should be on the edge of Manhattan rather than at the center. At least this was how he subsequently presented the history, claiming that from the start he only wanted the current site on the East River in Manhattan and never considered anything other than those seventeen acres which, with his usual mathematical calculations, he said was 1,500 times smaller than the 26,500 acres of the forty-square-mile parcel in Fairfield County in Connecticut preferred by others.

Le Corbusier was less personally responsible for that choice than he later made it seem. He had in fact drawn a proposal for the Connecticut site. Moreover, he was just one of many people who were enthusiastic about the property that was eventually chosen, which was then owned by William Zeckendorf, a New York City developer.

Then Wallace Harrison, the American architect Le Corbusier had met in 1935 with Harrison's relative Nelson Rockefeller, had the idea that John D. Rockefeller Jr., one of the richest men in America, should buy Zeckendorf's seventeen acres and give the parcel to the UN. Le Corbusier was pleased, but he did not anticipate the power that Harrison would assume concomitantly.

ONE OF THE FIRST THINGS Le Corbusier wanted to do after arriving in New York was to change the constituency of the architectural steering committee. He proposed that Alvar Aalto, Walter Gropius, and Mies van der Rohe be added. It was exceptional for him to include other architects who would have demanded equal footing rather than bow to his taste. But Harrison rebuffed this idea of a collaboration of the master modernists.[9] A vision that might have yielded extraordinary results was scrapped. Problems had begun.

Worse yet, Le Corbusier's lover was not there. He had written Marguerite Tjader Harris to alert her that he was on his way and could hardly wait for them to get to her *cabanon.* Once he arrived in New York, he phoned her house in Darien. Alas, she was in California, working on a screenplay.

Knowing that she was part of a circle of writers that included Ayn Rand, Le Corbusier immediately wrote to ask her to tell Rand how much *The Fountainhead* interested him. The novel that depicts architecture as a world of good versus evil—the hero a purist of relentless independence, the villain a weak academic of the Beaux-Arts style—hit home. But eager though he was to have his mistress give messages to Ayn Rand, he wanted even more for her to be at his side.

On May 17, Le Corbusier sent Tjader Harris a second letter from the Roosevelt Hotel to say that, even with his charged schedule, in his quiet moments back in the room he missed her immeasurably. As he planned the institution he hoped would transform and unify humankind, his thoughts constantly returned to the vibrant woman who brought him such joy: "America without you is a mutilated country. No, I correct: New York, that frantic city, is for me a wounded bird without you."[10]

He continued: "I've been told you've become serious. So have I, but with needs for connection." He followed "connection" with "violent," which he then crossed out, replacing it with "imperative." The next words were: "in order to commune in a few seconds of harmony: man and woman. And with age I, a man with grey hair, submit to the rule; a woman in spring."[11]

Le Corbusier let down his guard with Tjader Harris as with no one else. Although he still addressed her with the formal "*vous,*" he confessed that he hoped "that you would direct me to one of those bodies containing a solid heart, the sort you were so optimistic about in those days when you had not yet become serious."[12] He told her that both Albert and Louis Soutter, a painter who was his cousin, spent their lives dreaming of women without acting on their fantasies and doing what was, in Le Corbusier's eyes, "necessary." Le Corbusier analyzed their plight: society got in their way, and the circumstances of their lives were not favorable.

In this uncensored narrative of his thoughts, he then wrote, "I seem to remember that a book exists by an important author, about an aging man who needs to penetrate young, healthy, laughing flesh." Then the same conscience that had overcome him in the presence of prostitutes came into play, and Le Corbusier justified his need for pleasure: "From a certain point of view, my life is overwhelming, the life of a man sacrificing himself. . . . Ah, this *quotidian*!!! The ideal site for courage and sacrifice. Quotidian, *i.e.,* banal, regular, constant, with no vacation or relief: every day, every hour. Ever vigilant."[13] He told her that his endurance was that of Jesus, stripped and flagellated. The image gave him a charge.

In the midst of the battles of his life, how he craved sex. He told Tjader Harris that the intensity of his desire peaked especially in New York,

> where the potential of machine society makes its racket, emits its waves, its overwhelming electricity—such action calls for its sanctuary, its retreat, its profound vital juices: a naked body one can look at and love.
>
> And all this is worth nothing, indeed does not exist unless the secret is kept, unless no one is told, for then everything becomes stupid, and the sacred turns to gossip. It is only you my friend, to whom, being in New York, one can in all simplicity say such things and ask for help.[14]

4

In this secret relationship with the radiant woman he had first begun to love more than a decade earlier, Le Corbusier did what he could do with no one else: he acknowledged need. He implored her to return from California to New York as soon as possible. He told her he had a key to an apartment that was both intimate and unoccupied. She must join him there in "Calypso's cave."[15] The moment she told him when she would be back east, he would provide the details.

Ten days later, Le Corbusier was desperate. He wrote again. Of course she must realize that he was dreaming of the little beach in Connecticut and the romantic shack on the rocks. Couldn't she meet him "for one or two weekends? Arrange things, Marguerite. Give orders, leave a key, give me instructions. You're the mistress, you'll do it. And I'll have the key!"[16] Begging her to take charge in any way, just so long as the plans brought them together, he told this extraordinary woman how much he longed to hear her "Amazon voice." In his mind's eye, he was seeing her as she looked on the dock when his boat pulled out of New York harbor eleven years earlier.

By the end of June, Tjader Harris still had not returned to the east. The architect was falling apart. He wrote her that he was calling Darien regularly. He had to leave on July 8; he reiterated precise instructions on how she could get a message to him at the Hotel Roosevelt to organize a rendezvous before then. He urged her to phone at any hour—if necessary, at 2:00 a.m.; "I adore that. . . . Do what's needful so that a film of time or of miles does not separate us once again like the width of an ocean."[17]

To his other intimates, Le Corbusier proffered advice. Only Marguerite Tjader Harris had him pleading.

As his days in America drew to a close, Le Corbusier warned Tjader Harris that if she wrote him in Paris, she must realize that his secretary often opened his letters. Surely they could see one another before their privacy was invaded.

5

The work at the UN that spring went far better than his attempts to lure Tjader Harris. Le Corbusier proudly wrote his mother about his role in the site selection and building program: "I am fulfilling a delicate mission of considerable importance, representing France as a pioneer of the modern spirit." Seven new books about him were in the works—three in New York, and one each in Algiers, Buenos Aires, Paris, and Zurich. "The Le Corbusier star is rising in the firmament, and this time the barriers may be knocked down. Life flows along with uninterrupted intensity," he wrote. For fifteen years, Le Corbusier had built nothing, but he had kept conceiving ideas. Having "prepared a tidal wave against the ossified creatures who thought they could hold me back," he believed now it would all pay off.[18]

Le Corbusier became friends with the Italian sculptor Costantino Nivola and his wife, Ruth, spending Sundays in their apartment on Eighth Street and carrying on only about what was wrong with the sculptor's work. The Nivolas, the Serts, and Le Corbusier often ate at Greenwich Village restaurants, and the Nivolas regularly invited Le Corbusier for summer weekends on the far end of Long Island. That summer, the fifty-eight-year-old Le Corbusier improved his swimming, telling his mother he had made "amazing progress. I swim like a gentleman, even crawl!"[19]

Water obsessed him much as the sun did: "My mouth waters just thinking of it and as I send my elementary thoughts toward you, Albert, and your blue lake. I see myself diving! For the moment I am behind my broiling studio windows. But New York has given me some idea of cooking. . . . What a terrible furnace! You can be in water over your head and still sweat!"[20]

Le Corbusier saw the perpetual movement of the ocean and its shifting tides as analogous to the perpetual flow and alterations of his own emotions. "The mind and the heart do their work, but in waves," he reflected to his mother in July, before instructing her, "Spend a lovely summer at the lake. DON'T WORRY!"[21] In the villa he had built her, overlooking the oceanic mirror of light as if one were on a ship at sea, she should know only life's magic.

6

Le Corbusier had a grueling return to Paris at the end of the second week of July, with his plane held up for thirty hours in Newfoundland. Once he was back in France, he immediately had to take the train to Marseille to consider the details of l'Unité d'Habitation on-site.

The urgency thrilled him, but the architect could not delude himself that everything in life was perfect. Yvonne was deeply upset that he had rushed to Marseille so soon after returning from America. She reminded him that they had had no vacation together since 1939. When, six weeks after his return to France—in the course of which he had been away from Paris as much as he was there—Le Corbusier went back to New York, Yvonne felt abandoned.

THE FIRST HINT that Le Corbusier began to see Marguerite Tjader Harris almost as soon as he arrived in America was a letter he wrote to Yvonne in which he emphasized the silence and solitude of his room at the Hotel Grosvenor. He provided a profusion of details, with the zeal of a criminal declaring his false alibi.

After checking in, he unpacked his recent watercolor sketches of Vézelay, Ozon, and Paris and put them on a pedestal table. An ink drawing—"beautiful . . . elegant," he told Yvonne—disappeared on the first day.[22] He summoned the chambermaid, and that night, it was back on the table. Le Corbusier believed that this uneducated woman's having tried to steal it was a mark of his artistic success.

Le Corbusier was as solicitous as he was chatty, asking his wife about the effect of her latest series of injections, addressing her as "little Von, brave girl, light of the Le Corbusier hearth."[23]

Bedridden with sciatica, Yvonne, in turn, made it her task to keep La Petite Maman and Albert apprised of what Edouard was doing in New York. She stressed that Edouard had been away for nearly six of the first nine months of the year and that she missed him terribly.

Le Corbusier's mother, in fact, knew more about what was happening in America than Yvonne could have imagined. The architect was sending missives directly to Vevey with information he certainly did not send to rue Nungesser-et-Coli. He was eager for his eighty-six-year-old mother to know that he was seeing a lot of Marguerite Tjader Harris that fall. At the start of November, he informed Marie that he had visited the divorcée and her son "several times on her estate," and that Tjader Harris often asked after her.[24]

ON NOVEMBER 6, Le Corbusier presented a report to the United Nations secretary-general with his master plan. It called for two skyscrapers, each a lithe rectangular slab on pilotis at right angles to one another, with lower structures between them accommodating public spaces. He had achieved his goal of becoming the dominant voice of the building committee, and *Time* magazine and others embraced his scheme, but he was not completely confident he could retain his full authority and convince the governing body of the UN itself. Between November 21 and 28, Le Corbusier went from New York to Philadelphia to San Francisco to Boston and back to New York, campaigning for his proposal. Exhausted, he then decided to return to Paris.

The main pull on him was Yvonne. Just before going cross-country, he had written her that a letter in which she referred to herself as "the poor little cripple" had brought him to the edge of tears. He told her she was "the poor little cripple I love so much, respect so much, who is the very soul of my hearth and home. Poor child, poor child." She needed to understand, however, that he, too, was struggling—as the object of ferocious attacks because of his UN ideas. One witness, the architect Abel Sorenson, said that a report to the design commission by Le Corbusier, calling for the UN to be in "Manhattan . . . a fabulous fact," as opposed to the suburban setting preferred by the commission, "landed like a bomb at the General Assembly."[25] The embattled Le Corbusier insisted that his lonely wife limping around their isolated apartment grasp his own suffering as he waged the war of architecture at the seat of power: "My nerves are at the breaking point. I have to control myself to keep from spoiling everything, letting everything go. I was fiercely attacked last Saturday, an incredible affront." Le Corbusier wanted her to see their struggles in tandem: "If I stop now I'm a coward, and it will be the enemies who triumph. Little Von, will you be brave?"[26]

On November 25, he wrote from San Francisco that it would take him only a couple more days to wind up his affairs and fly back to France. Pierre Jeanneret was scheduled to be in New York by the time Le Corbusier returned there; they had reconciled sufficiently for Pierre to have agreed to help. How glad he would be to head home!

On December 1, however, Le Corbusier was still in New York, writing his mother to say that he hoped to leave in ten to fifteen days. He was postponing his departure because Nelson Rockefeller, as influential as Le Corbusier had imagined him to be, had now heeded Harrison's advice and persuaded his father to donate $8.5 million to acquire the Zeckendorf site on the East River in the Forties. The UN leaders worked out an agreement with the city of New York, and it became definite that the new complex would be built at the location for which Le Corbusier had campaigned.

In a letter to Dr. Eduardo Zuleta Angel, chairman of the Permanent Headquarters Commission, the elder Rockefeller wrote that it was "a source of infinite satisfaction to me and my family to give the property to the United Nations since New York was a center where people from all lands have always been welcomed and where they have shared common aspirations and achievements."[27]

BEYOND THE UN, Le Corbusier had another reason for delaying his return. On December 3, he wrote Marguerite Tjader Harris,

He who has entered
Into life must seek
To remain as long as
Pleasure makes it endurable.

LUCRETIUS *(De Rerum Naturae)*[28]

On December 16, Yvonne was awaiting instructions as to whether to go to Orly in two days with friends who had a car. Le Corbusier's latest bulletin had scheduled his arrival for the eighteenth. In an exceptionally cold December, with no coal, the activity of getting the apartment ready for his return was the only thing that kept her warm. By the time he left for Paris on the twenty-first, Le Corbusier knew he would not make it to Vevey, as he had promised his mother, but at least he and Yvonne would have one of their rare holidays together.

7

Le Corbusier had hoped for a quiet and calm Sunday following his morning arrival back in Paris. But the moment he saw Yvonne at Orly, the rare tranquility he had enjoyed on the flight—this time a mere eleven and a half hours, nonstop—was over. His wife was in tatters. With her worsening alcoholism, she didn't stop berating him all day long. He reported this to his mother, emphasizing the inconvenient effects of his wife's condition on his own busy life but adding, "Yvonne has been heroic, much more than anyone imagines or carelessly acknowledges."[29]

The wife of the former French president Léon Blum invited the architect for Christmas dinner at the official state residence, with André Gide as the only other guest.[30] No one even considered the possibility of Yvonne attending. But Le Corbusier was happy enough, reporting to his mother that the main subject of conversation was his project in Marseille. The next day, he met with the director of urbanism, then with the minister of reconstruction.

The hectic schedule, a relief during the usually slack period between Christmas and New Year's, was possible, he informed Marie Jeanneret, because he was in perfect health. But what he wanted her to know above all was that he had escaped the shackles of his upbringing. "Bravo!" he concluded. "Will life relax its ordeal of trials now? When I think of our youth and how we felt obliged to consider ourselves unhappy or dissatisfied!"[31]

JUST AS THE SUN was going down on New Year's Eve, Jerzy Soltan, a young architect in Le Corbusier's office, brought his wife and their new baby, born two days earlier, home from the hospital. The Soltans had only a few francs to their name. Watching the splendor of limousines with people in evening clothes cruising along the boulevard St.-Germain, they could hardly afford groceries and were facing the evening in their small apartment with a nearly empty larder.

Shortly after they had begun to settle in with their infant, the doorbell rang. It was the building superintendent. He delivered an enormous package of holiday food, including a magnum of champagne and a colorful papier-mâché rooster. The card said "from Yvonne and Le Corbusier." The Soltans asked the super who on earth had delivered the package on New Year's Eve. He answered that it was a tall white-haired man with round eyeglasses and a bow tie.

8

From the moment 1947 began, Le Corbusier regarded it as the year when he would turn sixty: "For God's sake! After sixty, one is on the downward slope." He felt "thickened, with heavy, creaking joints where everything should be swimming in oil."[32]

That January, the UN General Assembly officially designated Le Corbusier as one of the ten architectural consultants for their new building. Secretary-General Trygve Lie had opposed Le Corbusier's appointment—it's unclear whether the issue was his personality or aesthetics—but he was named nonetheless, thanks largely to support from Wallace Harrison, who had been appointed head of the planning office.

Oscar Niemeyer, the *chic garçon* who had done drawings for Le Corbusier's project in Rio in 1936, and Vladimir Bodiansky, an engineer who was on staff at 35 rue de Sèvres, were on his team, and he was delighted to consult with both. But he was so eager to initiate the UN design process on his own that he decided to rush back to New York two months ahead of the date when all the experts were scheduled to start work.

In his usual psychological pattern, Le Corbusier saw himself as not just triumphant but resurrected. After arriving in New York at the end of January, he wrote his mother, "For the last 10 months I've been fighting a desperate battle. Now, total victory: the World City will be built in New York according to my ideas." But after all his years of crushed hopes, he was both unequivocally confident and fearful that the victory might be pyrrhic:

"March '47 will see the Le Corbusier Explosion everywhere. This must be written in the stars, for it will be a kind of symphony. I don't like to prophesy results, for each time Fate sneers and produces her own version."[33]

He amplified on the "Explosion": *When the Cathedrals Were White* was to come out in America with the publisher Reynal & Hitchcock. The fourth volume of his *Complete Work* was to appear, as was *The World City.* There were to be further publications and exhibitions devoted to his painting and sculpture. Le Corbusier then added, "Dear Maman, I'm boring you with all this. I think of you often and even occasionally talk about you." And, he continued, "Marguerite Tjader Harris also speaks of you when I occasionally visit her seaside estate. I'm working like a dog."[34]

Le Corbusier went on to say that he was painting at night and on Sundays and that the New York winter was "extraordinary . . . a cold dry sky: stimulating climate." The freezing temperatures were bearable because the heating at the Hotel Grosvenor was "fantastic."[35] Even if he knew that there was still no coal available at 24 rue Nungesser-et-Coli for poor Yvonne, Le Corbusier could not contain his own happiness.

9

In the middle of March, Le Corbusier interrupted his UN activities to fly back to Paris for ten days. The rapidity of Yvonne's decline was horrifying.

Le Corbusier became enraged at both the Swiss and the Americans for their blindness to the tragic deprivations suffered by those people who lived where World War II had actually been fought. In Paris, he was stupefied by the American abundance that had so recently enchanted him. The standard of living on the other side of the Atlantic seemed outrageous, while he and Yvonne still had no heating fuel. Yvonne managed to put together her miraculous meals with scant ingredients, but there was not enough food; there was not even soap.

The hardships shattered people's nerves. "My poor wife is a tragic example of the phenomenon," Le Corbusier wrote his mother; Yvonne's weight was down to forty kilograms.[36] He now attributed her limping and chronic exhaustion to vitamin deficiencies.

He had hopped back to Paris in part to check up on his wife but mainly to make sure that everything in the office was up to speed. There were now thirty-five employees. Among them were Charlotte Perriand and Pierre Jeanneret, who could not resist when he told them that the office was engaged in actual building, rather than simply theory and research. André

Wogenscky was studio head, while Bodiansky, even if he was temporarily in New York, was technical director.

When Le Corbusier arrived at the office each afternoon with the sketches he had made at home that morning, he would first sit alone at the worktable of one of the younger architects assigned to the current project and begin revising his subaltern's work. Jerzy Soltan described the process: "Now, all of a sudden, Le Corbusier wanted a piece of charcoal. I found a forgotten stub in a drawer. He started sketching with a deliberately shaky hand. He stopped for fractions of a second. He went on. Meanwhile he succeeded in erasing half of what he began with. The charcoal stub was ridiculously small in his big fingers. He stopped again. He returned with a light, jittery line to the spots that had already been drawn and erased. The new line was almost the same—almost. He barely looked at the drawing. His eyes were 'turned inward,' attending to his subconscious. Finally, he stopped. He looked this way and that at the drawing. He pondered it, and then he said, 'Maybe it's worth retaining?' He pulled out his own pen, an old Parker 51, and traced with a slow movement on top of the charcoal the final (for the time being) version of the concept."[37]

Le Corbusier had recently reconfigured the office, so that the open space, where everyone had talked freely with everyone else, had been chopped up into little cubicles, with a corridor that led the employees to Le Corbusier's own office, which felt like the summit. The hierarchy was clear.

The office ran like clockwork. If anyone returned from lunch a minute after 2:00 p.m., when collaborative work with Le Corbusier was scheduled to begin, the architect issued a strong reprimand: "Exactitude is a necessity. It is a mark of respect for others. To be exact is merely to be polite. The excuses of modern life, or of Parisian life, are merely foolish pretexts. How can you command, how can you be a leader if you have no notion of the time of day, the very meaning of exactitude? Even a joke is a question of timing! Beforehand, out of the question. Afterwards, too late. In my own case, I find that I must wait very often for others, for I'm usually on time. I've always been and am still a punctual and exact fellow."[38]

In those afternoons of clockwork precision, Le Corbusier had one imperative for the resultant architecture: "It has to be beautiful!"

10

The main project on the drawing boards during the ten days' return was the building in Marseille. New techniques of prefabrication guaranteed a breakthrough in the construction process there, and Le Corbusier declared it the greatest housing idea anywhere in the world. La Rochelle, he was confident, would be another triumph. He also had his Paris team working on the UN, which he felt would be the most extraordinary and magnificent building built in centuries.

When Albert urged him to come to Vevey, Le Corbusier chided him for even proposing that such a deviation from his schedule could be possible. And he was out of patience with their mother's recalcitrance: "The line of conduct is clear: Maman must no longer serve, but be served."[39] If she would not hire domestic staff at home, she would have to move to a pension. Le Corbusier said he would arrange to rent out La Petite Maison to generate income and told her exactly what objects to take with her.

He lectured his aged parent by mail, "I beg you to consider your troubles in their true proportions. I know that the everyday irritations are a veritable wound. Have the wisdom to take prudent and useful measures. . . . You're at peace in your labors and healthy in body and mind, in a magnificent country beyond the horrors of war. And you're religious into the bargain! What more do you need?" In the pressured state brought on by this brief return to France, he then let loose: "If our two women, Maman and Yvonne, had had the brains to reach some kind of agreement instead of each trying to bring the other around to her own point of view, both would have enjoyed being together. You've missed the bus, and that is the bitterest remark I can be led to make."[40]

Having found Yvonne in such a wretched state, Le Corbusier blamed his mother. Marie Jeanneret could either have gone to take care of her daughter-in-law or invited her to Vevey. He urged his mother to think of "poor Yvonne sick and stoical, *alone* in the world, and distributing to a whole group of good people around her, all that overflowing heart of hers she gives to her *true friends:* those who understand."[41] He made clear to his mother that he adored Yvonne's generous, fragile soul and could not forgive Marie Jeanneret for her coldness.

His mother's response was to tell Le Corbusier that she would act toward Yvonne as she wished. Moreover, she refused to move to a pension. He, in turn, instructed her to respond "*graciously*" to people who wrote to her. He advised his mother and brother to try to be "a little practical on this occasion." They should also consider his busy schedule; they were wasting his time. "Try to take events as they come: with good humor and without getting all upset," he counseled.[42]

If he couldn't change his mother's attitude toward his wife, there was no point in further discussion: "All right, everything's for the best and heading for the better: it's spring." He signed off, "your son who does what he can.

Ed."[43] Underneath that nickname reserved only for her and Albert, he wrote a single word: "affection."

ON THE TWENTY-ONE-HOUR flight back to America, Le Corbusier had a dream worthy of recounting to Yvonne. "A 'Bastard' " was painting the bottom of Le Corbusier's pants with rustproof red paint. Le Corbusier ran after the culprit, who stole his jacket at the same time.

Le Corbusier also reported to his wife that, before landing, "I shaved, washed, shat." He then explained to her that he was writing this account naked. Lying on his stomach on his hotel bed, he had a thermometer in his rectum for ten minutes: "The thermometer somewhere = a sentimental situation!"[44] He was measuring his fever because of an infection in his arm, but the swelling had gone down. He continued the letter from the bathtub, again providing a graphic description of his physical situation at the moment of writing.

Anyone who could be coated in rustproof paint must be made of iron; on the other hand, in all these images, Le Corbusier wanted Yvonne to see him as completely vulnerable.

There was another reason for all the intimate details. They made Yvonne feel that she knew every last thing about his life. They were combined with the information that he was going to Long Island to see the Nivolas. It was all a perfect ploy. For what was left out were the increasing journeys to the little beach shack in Connecticut.

11

"It's a sure thing: Le Corbusier architecture victorious one hundred percent," Le Corbusier wrote his mother on March 27. It was a complete triumph; he might even make some money. "The page is turning, has turned. This is the architecture of tomorrow."[45]

On April 18, Le Corbusier announced at a meeting of the board of design consultants that this would be a collaborative vision: "We work as a team. . . . Each helps his neighbor. . . . [W]e are united . . . the World Team of the United Nations laying down plans for a world architecture. . . . We are a homogenous block. There are no names attached to this work. As in any human enterprise, there is simply discipline, which alone is capable of bringing order. Each of us can be legitimately proud of having been called upon to work on this team; that should be sufficient for us."[46] There is a charm to the architect claiming to espouse the tradition of the Gothic cathedral—architectural creation as a joint effort—but in truth he could imagine only himself as the designer of the new headquarters dedicated to international understanding. In the drafting room where all the design consultants were working together, on the twenty-seventh floor of the RKO Building, Le Corbusier told Geoffrey Hellman of *The New Yorker,* "I am in complete calm here. I think God has come down to earth. I don't even mind working in a room with other people. An architect shouldn't be alone. . . . You develop ideas when you have an audience. And anyway, you don't have to listen to what the other man says."[47] That last sentence was key.

During lunch with the other designers at an Italian restaurant, Del Pezzo's, near the office on Forty-seventh Street, Le Corbusier was observed to pay little attention to what other people were saying.[48] To Yvonne, on April 22, he wrote that he was in a "period of deflation"; architects inferior to him were trying to have their say.[49] The problem was that he did not have the power to ignore them.

The "one hundred percent" victory of Corbusean architecture about which he had written his mother less than a month earlier was no longer certain. In the moments when Le Corbusier thought he was changing the world unimpeded, the universe had been in perfect order, but now that he knew his power was not absolute, he was miserable. As the architect George A. Dudley, who took notes that served in lieu of minutes for the "forty-five meetings of the Board of design for the United Nations Headquarters in 1947," observed, the main issue revolved around a scheme for the UN that had been developed by Oscar Neimeyer: "The comparison between Le Corbusier's heavy block and Niemeyer's startling, elegantly articulated scheme seemed to me to be in everyone's mind. As different as night and day, the heaviness of the block seemed to close the whole site, while in Niemeyer's refreshing scheme the site was open, a grand space with a clean base for the modern masses standing in it."[50]

Le Corbusier wrote Yvonne, "On the road there are so many insignificant details! Unimaginable!! I can tell you one thing: those who pursue an ideal, struggling on its behalf, must be made of tempered steel." Although he publicly voiced approval of Niemeyer's concept, to Yvonne he treated it as a rejection of his own—and tried to take the long view about the architects who were opposing his ideas: "This will pass, such things are merely human nastiness."[51]

There were still beautiful things in the world. He was astonished by an exhibition of modern masterpieces at the Museum of Modern Art, where a Bonnard and two Matisses moved him far more than the Légers and Picassos; he was fascinated that Matisse, the artist whose work he had disparaged as a young man, now seemed greater than the artists he had expected to prefer. He also relished an hour on a Saturday night in mid-April when he met Charlie Chaplin; not only did Le Corbusier joke with the great comic, but he did so in English.[52]

Le Corbusier continued to calibrate his image of the denizens of the nation where he had once believed he would do everything he had ever wanted: "Ah, Americans are funny people! Their ways are different from ours! . . . I tell you, these people are kids."[53] When he became so sick that wintry spring that he spent twenty-four hours in bed without eating, he wrote Yvonne that his inadvertent fast didn't bother him because he felt good about his ascetic self compared to the Americans all around him, stuffing themselves and becoming as fat as pigs. But his wife had to realize that he did not have things too good. While she had a new maid in Paris, he was leading "a dog's life" on the other side of the Atlantic and in pain because he had to leave her alone.

Le Corbusier also told her he was now furious at Pierre for disagreeing with Bodiansky. Disloyalty to the rule of Le Corbusier was bad enough from the outside; from the inner camp, it was not to be tolerated.

12

Geoffrey Hellman had written a two-part profile of Le Corbusier for *The New Yorker,* with the second installment appearing on May 3. Someone else might simply have been pleased to enter the inner circles of American culture—*The New Yorker* had unequaled cachet at the time—but Le Corbusier was enraged at this biography he could not control. In October 1946, the *Biographical Encyclopedia of the World* had decided to include Le Corbusier in its "Who's Important in Government" section rather than "Who's Important in Art." This was the level of respect he liked—as opposed to *The New Yorker*'s irreverence.

Each part of the magazine profile had a witty sketch of the architect. The first, by A. Birnbaum, emphasizes Le Corbusier's perfectly round eyeglasses with their thick dark frames—as boldly geometric as his architecture—along with his furrowed brow, slicked-back hair, and trademark bow tie. A cruciform skyscraper and a bold grid pattern appear across his chest, suggesting both the crux of his urbanism and a dapper tattersall shirt. The second portrait was by Saul Steinberg. It shows Le Corbusier in profile, with the eyeglasses and grim cast of his face again dominant. Here Le Corbusier personifies the American concept of stylish French living; although he is clearly at work—besuited and with pencil in hand—he is sitting at a table with a bowl of fruit, a wine bottle, and an espresso cup.

The *New Yorker* writer calls Le Corbusier "one of the most revolutionary, controversial, and vociferously influential architects and city planners in the world" but devalues that assessment by saying, "Except, perhaps, for Frank Lloyd Wright, no living architect has been more widely discussed, by others or by himself." While crediting Le Corbusier's significance as a founder of the International Style, Hellman continues the subtle mockery, pointing out that the architect "has, as far as he is concerned, no first name." He adds that "this unusual circumstance has bewildered or misled a number of persons, including the editors of the Encyclopedia Britannica, who list him as 'Le Corbusier, M.' possibly for Monsieur." Hellman says the architect was called "Charles Edouard" until he could no longer put up with it. Such trivializing rankled Le Corbusier. So did Hellman's description of his "boulevardier air, . . . egg-shaped head . . . [and] heavy-framed spectacles that make him look like an owl."[54]

After explaining *L'Esprit Nouveau,* Hellman describes Le Corbusier's feud with Ozenfant and the various editions of *Toward a New Architecture.* According to Hellman, Le Corbusier had boasted, "The fellow thanked me for the dedication. He didn't realize that by printing it I had prevented anyone from thinking he'd written the book."[55] Hellman also cites Ozenfant as claiming that the original authorship had made people think that he, Ozenfant, had a mistress named Le Corbusier.

Hellman peppers his text with half-truths and innuendo that make not only Le Corbusier but other family members seem ridiculous. He says that Georges Jeanneret took up mountain climbing because his flute playing was not of the same level as Marie's piano. He claims that young Charles-Edouard Jeanneret had started manufacturing bricks because so few clients could walk up to his seventh-story office in Paris, and reports that Le Corbusier made plans for rebuilding Algiers, Paris, Stockholm, and other cities "more for the hell of it than in the expectation that anything practical would come of them." He also informs his readers, "Le Corbusier's Calvinistic censoriousness and his relentless air of martyrdom have not endeared him to his critics, and this may account for a certain amount of their censure of him."[56]

Hellman also tells in detail a reported incident concerning the architect's desperation to be photographed when he arrived in America in 1935. And he reports that, during the same trip, although his host had picked him up in plenty of time to give a lecture at Columbia University, Le Corbusier had insisted on stopping at a delicatessen on the way, making himself half an hour late for the lecture and still eating a baguette as he mounted the podium. Given Le Corbusier's punctiliousness, the story is unlikely.

On the other hand, Hellman serves Le Corbusier's purposes by completely leaving out the two years in Vichy and giving the impression that Le Corbusier had simply toughed out the war as best he could.

HELLMAN does accurately evoke what Le Corbusier sounded like. When speaking to his colleagues on the UN project, "His voice is low, gentle, insistent, and musical." In lectures and conversations, Le Corbusier is characterized as having "a fluent, incisive, mordant, staccato, rhetorical, Gallic literary style."[57] There is a tender moment with the architect reporting his admiration for the structure of melons.

Le Corbusier's direct statements to the writer have the ring of authenticity: "This is a funny country. Your hospitality is Draconian, and your convictions are too tied up with finance. Money is ferocious here. . . . But the country . . . is *alive,* and everything is possible in it."[58] To Hellman, Le Corbusier laments the lack of cafés where friends could chat in a leisurely way over aperitifs. Instead, the architect points out, America has only anonymous cafeterias. He goes on to say that even in Paris he was not among those who had time for those same cafés he missed in New York. It is accurately Corbusean: to purport to know what humanity in general needs and then to distinguish himself as different.

Le Corbusier tells Hellman, "I'm the only man here who climbs stairs two at a time." He says escalators are "undignified." Le Corbusier also remarks that the light of New York is "red . . . the color of blood and life. Everything in it arouses both enthusiasm and disgust; it reflects God and the Devil."[59] The architect emerges as he was: robust, intoxicated with human energy, thinking only in extremes.

LE CORBUSIER wrote Geoffrey Hellman ten days after the second piece was published. The letter is an exemplar of how he dealt with conflict. He starts out laudatorily, saying that the articles are well written and amusing and will interest a range of readers; the writer's lighthearted attitude toward issues of major importance has a certain charm. Still, he is shocked, as are his friends, by the "lies, virtually calumnies."[60]

Knowing that the pieces might eventually be republished in an anthology, Le Corbusier demands that the story about his having begged to be photographed on the *Normandie* be either removed or given a footnote rectifying it. He also insists that changes be made in the text about Ozenfant and the authorship of *L'Esprit Nouveau.* If Hellman did not do as requested, Le Corbusier would take action through his lawyer.

He then puts his velvet gloves back on: "I must thank you for the friendly attention you accorded my own person in this affair. I say 'friendly,' for I'm convinced that your lines testify to sympathy and not the contrary. And I'd like to report the pleasure I took in your style, which has a true journalistic flavor. I'll always be a partisan of what we call '*la petite histoire*' as produced by writers of talent like you, on condition information is exact and not contrary to the reality of facts or to psychological reality."[61] Like everything else about Le Corbusier, his condescension was quintessential.

13

The avant-garde French composer Edgard Varèse was then living in New York; he invited Le Corbusier to hear part of a new work. The architect wrote his mother that the combination of choir and "*batterie*" was "absolutely remarkable, powerful, a grand style sung, spoken, cadenced, pounded out, sometimes overwhelming." He also considered American brass bands "amazing, so rhythmic, so intense, so new."[62]

He had hoped that with music he could awaken his mother to his existence, but, in the first week of May, he wrote Marie Jeanneret on United Nations stationery to say that he was intensely irritable because neither she nor Albert had written him in a long time. In spite of being an architect of inestimable importance, he had been trying to help her with her house issues; how could she be so patently ungrateful? She had such an easy life, surrounded by flowers in springtime, while he was locked inside an office on the twenty-seventh floor of an air-conditioned skyscraper; couldn't she have found the time to send a single word?

"I am engaged in a considerable project, which may become the cornerstone of modern architectural evolution," he informed her. The workload was so oppressive that he would start a letter and put it down, then take it up again five days later; every day was a matter of "doing battle and never leaving the line of fire."[63]

He told her that on those rare occasions when he did escape the office, he was a celebrity. Restaurant waiters treated him deferentially. Strangers in the street said hello to him. Everyone admired him, he explained—except for the one person to whom he had to wave the flag of his success.

WHILE LE CORBUSIER was long-winded and often prickly at the meetings of the UN Board of Design, which at the start of May were practically daily events, he and Bodiansky and Niemeyer were all essentially in agreement on the overall scheme for the complex. The main differences to be sorted out were the precise shape of the General Assembly and the means by which it would connect to the Secretariat, as well as questions of spacing and scale. Nonetheless, in letters home, Le Corbusier presented their vision as if it was his alone, and he calculated that one third of the other architects on the commission were hostile even if the rest were distinctly favorable. By mid-May, he was sensing serious jealousy from Wallace Harrison. After being confident less than two months earlier of "a sure thing," he was rapidly losing faith that the new UN would be his creation.

Having assured Yvonne he would fly back to Paris quickly, Le Corbusier now let her know that he could not yet return. He was optimistic, however, that things would be resolved by June 9, when they would end their work with "a banquet Rockefeller," and then he would come home.

Yvonne had fallen again. She described the event in vivid detail to Marie Jeanneret. She was bending to pick up the dog's cushion and thought the window behind it was open. The glass was so clean, Yvonne explained, that light didn't reflect in it. Bending down, she banged herself hard against it and landed flat. At least the glass was solid, she added.

The heat in Paris was so bad that Yvonne slept on the lower terrace, miserable in her solitude. Suffering the aftereffects of the fall, she could not get out easily; she felt completely isolated on the rue Nungesser-et-Coli. But she accepted her situation. For "Edouard" had his battles to fight and could only be admired for his strength.

Le Corbusier wrote his wife that he longed to be alone with her in the countryside, to escape his "dog's life" in muggy New York. He did not mention, of course, that he had ample respite on the Connecticut coast.

14

> Those who want to assist the people and their affairs and who help faithfully are thanked as the world is accustomed: it kicks them and wipes its shoes on them. . . . Therefore learn to recognize the world; you will not make it different; it will not direct itself according to you; above all other things learn and know that the world is ungrateful.
>
> —THE LUTHERAN BIBLE, *passage underlined by Johann Sebastian Bach in his personal copy*

LE CORBUSIER returned to Paris during the second week of July. One of the first things he did was write his mother about how esteemed he felt in France. At an exposition at the Grand Palais, the president of the republic had visited a stand devoted to his Marseille building. Yet another radio broadcast about him was scheduled. He instructed Marie to benefit from his prosperity and spend his money more easily. Le Corbusier also told his mother that on his return he had found Yvonne virtually incapable of leaving the apartment, although he gave no reason why and was not particularly upset by the fact. "Paris is so *magnificently human*! After the catastrophe of New York!"[64]

He had used the word "catastrophe" because the UN situation was now deteriorating. Again a project that had felt like the dawning of a new era was turning into sand sifting through his fingers. The injury was a mixture of what Le Corbusier believed to be deliberate misattribution and plagiarism followed by debasement. His initial idea was not merely stolen but transformed into something criminally devoid of heart and soul.

Le Corbusier's view of what had happened was that, having come up with the initial building concept and then fine-tuned it with others in New York and Paris, and having been confident at the start of 1947 that his design would be used as he intended, while he was back in Paris for his ten-day junket in March, he had been fundamentally betrayed.[65] This was the occasion when Oscar Niemeyer, having only just arrived in New York, worked on an independent proposal at the request of Wallace Harrison. Even then, Le Corbusier claimed to remain amenable to a degree of give-and-take, the architectural teamwork he had discussed publicly. In that vein, at the end of August he wrote Wallace Harrison a letter, which began, "The first round is won, the round of modern architecture." He assured Harrison, "I have no personal ambition but to continue as strong as we knew [*sic*] in the spring." But the letter included a startling diagram indicating what the work process should be from then on. Le Corbusier now gave Harrison the role of " '*architect en chef*,' responsible for relations with the U.S., New York City, and the banks, and for supervision of construction and financial matters," while naming himself as "*chef d'atelier—mandate par l'U.N.*" and stating that the task of doing the final drawings would be his.[66] This was not an allocation of power to which others would agree.

Once Harrison did not consent to have him do the final drawings, Le Corbusier realized that he was losing control of the building. Soon it was changed beyond recognition. Harrison, José Luis Sert, and Max Abramovitz, Harrison's architectural partner, were among the many people who always credited Le Corbusier with major aspects of the initial concept, but it would not be long before most of the world would largely forget that he had anything to do with the UN.

15

Because of a meeting of CIAM in London in September 1947, Le Corbusier knew he would be unable to go to Vevey for his mother's eighty-seventh birthday. He made clear to her, however, that even while he was trying to rebuild the world and was working in Paris that August because he was too busy to take a holiday, he had not neglected his family.

In New York he had actively pursued the idea of Albert conducting and recording a children's orchestra. His brother's indifference to his efforts infuriated him. Le Corbusier wrote their mother and Albert jointly: "He is obscure as well as laconic. Observation of the younger brother: I believe that when one writes one takes the trouble to focus one's attention for 15 minutes on the person being addressed. . . . A little precision, Albert, some effort of realism, out of *pity for others*!" He was also enraged that his mother had not taken his advice about the length of her summer holiday: "I deplore the fact she has not extended her stay. 10 days hardly count."[67] The denial of both her pleasure and his authority was intolerable.

He stopped his grousing, however, for birthday greetings: "All my affection, all my admiration, all my encouragements. Good holidays, happy holidays your *Ed,*" he wrote, with Yvonne adding, "Dear Maman, a big kiss for you on the occasion of your birthday. Bravo, dear Maman. Edouard had tears in his eyes when he told me you were as happy as a lark. At your age it's magnificent."[68] Even if Yvonne still used the formal "*vous*" for her mother-in-law, Le Corbusier was pleased at their civility. But by November, he was again in a state of "rage and upset." Winter was coming; the latest round of strikes in Paris irritated him; above all, "In New York apparent kidnapping of the Le Corbusier UN project by USA gangster Harrison. Yes New York 1947 imitates, with variations on certain aspects, the scandal in Geneva 1927."[69] To the beat of time, a neat two decades later, evil in the hands of the powerful was again prevailing over truth and virtue.

Enemies could be conquered, though; at last the cornerstone had been laid at Marseille. In the two and a half years since the project had been launched, he had, he told his mother, "traversed five ministries and escaped six torpedoings," but now work had actually begun. The usual list of successes followed, but his anguish over the UN managed to cast a pall over everything in his life. Le Corbusier had visited the Villa La Roche; the house had survived the war, "but frigidaire and co. in the dining room; the soul was missing. The USA banal types hang out there." Since 1939, Raoul La Roche, under the domination of a nasty housekeeper, had only used the living room, turning the rest of the space over to Americans—those heathens who had stolen the United Nations from his clutches. All this made 1947 the "ninth year of war."[70]

So long as he had battles to wage, it made no difference to Le Corbusier that the world was enjoying overall peace: "You need the endurance of a plow horse, the tenacity of steel, and a lot of good humor. Shit is everywhere, but the sun is ready to shine on a lovely civilization."[71]

At least, on the first page of an important magazine in Bogotá, he was named among the most influential people of recent times—the equal of Marx, Freud, Einstein, and Picasso. He quoted the precise text to his mother and brother: " 'The old master' has entered his final stages, he's joined the trinity of the 'young.' Picasso, Matisse, Le Corbusier, a youth which adds up to over two hundred years." At sixty, Le Corbusier was the youngest. Picasso was then sixty-six, and Matisse seventy-eight. But what mattered the most was that, unlike the other two, the architect still had a living parent. With a mother who was the paragon of youth, he had a different perspective than the other geniuses, he assured Marie Jeanneret. "I've not yet concluded my studies and feeling as if I were taking my first steps in life," he wrote her.[72]

XL

In my architectural exegesis, I speak only of music. I don't know the notes, but architecture, like music, is *time and space,* an art of successive sensations brought into a symphony.

—LE CORBUSIER TO HIS MOTHER

1

A photo of the journalist Hedwig Lauber alongside Le Corbusier shows a young, vibrant professional with a radiant smile. She was the same physical type as Marguerite Tjader Harris: broad shouldered and sturdy but not stocky. Wearing smart black-and-white sandals with two-inch heels, the fit and healthy woman is nearly Le Corbusier's height. She looks blissfully happy in her career-woman suit, her gloves in her hand, a portfolio under her arm, while Le Corbusier, in a double-breasted pinstripe suit, his bow tie unusually askew, has the mischievous look of a little boy up to no good.

Besides photos, the evidence of what went on between them is found in a few letters. While staying at the Grosvenor House in London in May 1947, Le Corbusier addressed a letter to an architect in Lima referring to "Mlle. Hedwig Lauber, a very good friend of mine and a talented journalist" and asking his colleague to help her with her research on an upcoming trip to Peru.[1] Two months later, Le Corbusier wrote Lauber—addressing her as "*Chère Mademoiselle*"—instructing her never to write him—the demand is underlined—saying that he has a phobia of letters, that he prefers to have memories in his head only. He alerts her that writing things down might prove "fatal." He goes on to say that he had instructed their mutual friend Justine Fuller to write her; if she insists on writing, she could do so to 35 rue de Sèvres but to no other address. His final instruction is "Don't be angry with me. I have great esteem for you"; the word "*amicalement*" is inscribed below his signature.[2]

But, having tried to distance himself, Le Corbusier could not let go of the

With Hedwig Lauber in the mid-1950s

bright and good-looking Lauber any more than he could accept defeat in an architectural project. Lauber periodically reappeared in his life. As Yvonne, increasingly emaciated and crippled, became more difficult and bitter, the journalist gave Le Corbusier the unequivocal admiration he craved, even if he had to work to keep it secret.

2

In 1945, in Marseille, Le Corbusier had met Edouard Trouin. Trouin, ten years his junior, owned one million square meters of land in rocky terrain near the Mediterranean in Sainte-Baume, about halfway between Marseille and Toulon. Trouin was Le Corbusier's sort of character: "descended from Saint-Malo sailors and pirates and from Provençal peasants." A beefy man who sported a beret, Trouin spoke with a Marseille accent and had, according to Le Corbusier, "a vitality of 'God's thunder.' "[3]

Trouin was determined to save the countryside from development and had resisted repeated offers for his land from builders of holiday houses. He wanted instead a structure for meditation and worship that would do justice to the natural setting. He decided that Le Corbusier had the enthusiasm, originality, and eye that made him, without question, better qualified than anyone else for the task.

Mary Magdalene had allegedly lived on Trouin's property, in a cave halfway up the vertical sweep of a spectacular rock face opposite Mont Sainte Victoire. The entrance to the cave was a black hole in the jagged cliff. Le Corbusier believed, or said he believed, that "every morning the angels came for her in front of the cave, and carried her two hundred meters to the top of the mountain known as Le Pilon, where she would pray." There was, nearby, a basilica, "where they keep in a golden tabernacle the skull of Mary Magdalene, extremely beautiful."[4]

In 1948, Le Corbusier designed, at Trouin's request, an invisible basilica to be built entirely within the rock. The subterranean structure was to run from north to south, through the mountainous ridge, from the entrance of Mary Magdalene's cave to the other side of the rocky cliff, "opening suddenly onto the brilliant light of a limitless horizon toward the sea to the south."[5]

This was the Corbusean ideal: a feat of engineering that allowed the worship of the sun, the sea, and the distant horizon in all their glory. The cave-like basilica was to be flooded with light, incorporeal and uplifting. Pouring through its northern and southern exposures, sunshine would also radiate through wells cut into the rock. There would also have been electric light.

Had the meditation hall been built, it would have been one of the architect's most extraordinary achievements. Le Corbusier's imagination, his true religiosity that extended beyond any concept of traditional religion, in combination with his knowledge of materials that enabled him to make radical concepts into plastic reality, had led him to conceive of a physical space unprecedented in its form and emotional power.

But, again, one of Le Corbusier's greatest projects was not to be. The officials of the Catholic Church responsible for that jurisdiction rejected it unanimously. They must have known with whom they were dealing; they even specified in advance that no appeals would be considered.

3

The failures were now tempered by successes. At the start of 1948, Le Corbusier informed his mother, with the words underlined, that he was on the National Economic Council, to which he been named by a decree of the president of the Council of Ministers, and that his title was "*representative of French thought.*"[6] As contemptuous as he was of government authority, he became excited the moment he was officially anointed, and he boasted to his mother about a dinner of the council at which he had been seated next to Frédéric Joliot-Curie, a famous scientist married to the daughter of Pierre and Marie Curie. He also told her that the council's esteemed members were paid almost as much as parliamentary deputies: "the National Assembly, the Council of the Republic + us."[7]

Beyond that, he had begun work on a new book, *The Poem of the Right Angle*—a luxurious volume for the great publisher Tériade that gave him a chance to combine his euphoric sense of language, painting, and architecture. And there was a new book about him in which he was praised by none other than "the Americans." These people who gave him so much trouble now credited his painting and architecture with having given birth to "a new notion of space in which calm, limpidity, and clarity prevail, affording a certain contrast with the spikiness of Fauvism and Cubism, and the decompositions of post-war Surrealism and Expressionism."[8] If that analysis was beyond Marie Jeanneret's grasp, he still quoted it to her verbatim.

HE NEEDED SUCH BOOSTS, for he had embarked, yet again, on "the battle for the United Nations. The Americans behave like gangsters: ambush in the woods, murder and pillage of the victim. However I manage to reply with sang-froid and considerable strength."[9]

What gave Le Corbusier that will to fight was his belief that the French government was intervening on his behalf. The backing of the country where by choice he had become a citizen was pivotal. He needed nothing less to counteract the way America was trying to push its own architects. " 'The nation of the timid' takes its revenge and seeks to dominate the world. Today: superiority complex."[10]

4

In contrast to the moral corruption and greed of human beings, Le Corbusier's pets offered immense solace. They were also the mutual terrain of his relationships to his mother and Yvonne. He reported to his mother that his new dog, Laky, would go for a thirty-minute walk and, only after returning to the apartment, would scratch to be let out on the balcony to "piss and shit" at long last; Le Corbusier was more amused than annoyed.

Le Corbusier counted thirty sparrows who depended on Yvonne to feed them three times a day. It was Yvonne's instinct to be generous in illogical, eccentric ways that Le Corbusier proudly reported to his mother. Whenever anyone showed up at the penthouse apartment, be it a delivery person or someone to make a repair, she offered the stranger cigarettes and, depending on the hour, a glass of wine or an aperitif. And then there was Le Corbusier's and Yvonne's adopted fly. Le Corbusier wrote his mother, "During December and the first days of January, Yvonne has raised and fed Titine, the only fly to have survived; dying of hunger and thirst, she visited our plates at every meal. We gave her powdered sugar and poured out a little lake of water onto the table. At every meal Titine is there, but she must have split lately through the balcony door."[11]

LE CORBUSIER now told Marie Jeanneret that architecture was like music. His profession depended on timing and weight and rhythm, much as hers and Albert's did. She should realize that he was the equal if not the better of his brother in having taken after her professionally, even if Albert was the one living with her.

But the battles he was forced to fight required his being constantly on the run. The official architects of the French Academy—those who had a diploma awarded by the "Beaux-Arts"—had tried to put a complete stop to all activity on the new building in Marseille. They were convinced the design would destroy the Marseille skyline; for similar reasons, his old mentor and friend Auguste Perret had "declared LC public enemy number one."[12] His foes were everywhere: "America *über alles,* your money or your life!!—or: your life or your money!"[13] Marie needed to understand that this was why he was so frantic and could not spend more time at her side.

On June 11, he flew to and from Marseille in the same day to be on the construction site of his new building; during the few hours he spent there, he sent his mother a postcard: "I'm very proud, and received like a lord."[14] In mid-August, when most Parisians were on their annual summer holiday and Le Corbusier was still in the office, he wrote her, "All the humans here are like ants, very busy—or imagining they are! For me, life is pitiless and I drink deep." While most people were scurrying around to no good purpose, he was changing the world: "It's an enterprise which, in principle, is linked to the Middle Ages, a vast and rigorous Cartesian enterprise each detail of which is an ineluctable part of the whole."[15] Having conceived the Marseille project, he now had to consider every detail down to the door handles.

His able crew was working so hard on the large apartment house in order for 1,600 people in the south of France to look at the mountains in one direction and the sea in another. Their new dwellings would enable these lower-middle-class people to live, like Yvonne feeding birds on the terrace, with access to the cosmos. Le Corbusier wrote his mother, "Already from the first apartments, extraordinary landscapes appear, animating each room. This will be a great, magisterial work. We are laboring here, 30 technicians in the rue de Sèvres, with complete faith."[16] She of all people should understand the symphonic effort to give access to views that recalled the mountaintop outings of a mother and father and two little boys.

Le Corbusier followed this encomium by saying, "From the exterior, the Academy, the Society of Architects, the Ecole des Beaux-Arts are attacking with a violence that is quite simply scandalous, shameless. They are in their death agony, we are on our way to victory. But what an atmosphere of continuous contention!"[17] Opposition was, of course, a requisite in the life of a martyr.

5

"Every day Yvonne is exhausted, overcome," Le Corbusier wrote his mother that August. In the absence of a maid, she struggled to clean and do errands, and her "dragging foot" bothered her even more in the brutal heat. Le Corbusier then hired an Annamite to help at home, telling his mother these Indochinese were "serious people."[18] He also let his mother know that he was having de Montmollin send her extra money so that she could hire the best possible maid for herself as well.

His wife's and mother's everyday chores obsessed him. "It is absolutely essential that women be freed from the domestic drama (which involves so much discomfort for men). . . . But Marseilles is the *solution of modern life,*" he wrote Marie Jeanneret.[19] In his design for l'Unité d'Habitation, housekeeping tasks would be simplified and streamlined. Women—it did not occur to Le Corbusier that married men might cook—would be able to prepare food in the presence of their families, with a minimal number of steps required to serve it. The open kitchen he designed has become so universal today that it is hard to recognize how innovative it was then.

FOR NEARLY TEN YEARS, Le Corbusier had been sporadically consulting with authorities in the ancient Greek city of Smyrna—now in Turkey and called Izmir—about an urbanization plan. He finally went there in October 1948. Officially, it was the realization of a long-held dream; in private, it was a hardship.

On October 7, from what he called Smyrna, he wrote to Marguerite Tjader Harris, "How stupid life is and how hard!"[20] On Tjader Harris's last stopover in Paris, they had had only ten minutes together. Now she was again in France, but because he was in Turkey he was missing her completely. He recognized this as the price of success, but it stung.

The pull in every direction was, however, Le Corbusier's intoxicant. Now designing tapestries to be made at Aubusson, he reveled in the foray into another medium. As he created oversized images of robust figures composed with woven thread, he felt a new burst of creativity. He would make large wall hangings for many of his major buildings of the next decade; in their nonstop rhythm, these colorful tapestries add vitality and exuberance to his interiors, even if they lack the subtlety and refinement of his architecture.

6

In the fall of 1948, there was another official attempt to put a halt to l'Unité d'Habitation, this time from the Council on Hygiene. Le Corbusier was convinced that the council was a part of a cabal and was using hygienic problems as an excuse; the real reason for their demanding the cessation of work was the style of his building.

Yet his ideas were finding wider acceptance. In 1948, he published the first volume of *The Modulor.* Le Corbusier's standard in it is the six-foot-tall man he had observed in America: he calculates that, with his left arm fully extended upward, the distance from the man's navel to the soles of his feet is 113 centimeters, from his navel to the top of his head an additional seventy centimeters, from the top of his head to the fingertips of his raised left hand a further forty-three—adhering to the anthropomorphic principles developed by Matila Ghyka in 1931. These measurements are, he explains, to be applied to all of architecture and in particular to l'Unité d'Habitation.

The focal points of the human body chosen by Le Corbusier suited his personal hierarchy. The essential element was the navel: the link of nourishment between the embryo and the mother, a perpetual reminder of the attachment to the female parent. The top of the head suggests the greatest achievements of the human mind. The bottoms of the feet represent the physical basis of our positioning on the earth. As for the fingertips, with one's arm shooting upward, these are as close as one can get to the sun, linking Le Corbusier's universal creature to the miraculous core of the solar system that is the primary source of human energy and growth.

The book was the result of more than four years of collaborative effort, with some of the participants having worked full-time, but Le Corbusier published the book in his name alone.

IN HIS FIFTH VOLUME of *The Complete Work,* which covered the years 1946 to 1952, Le Corbusier proudly wrote about the findings of the Congress on Divine Proportion, an assembly of mathematicians, artists, and architects held at the Milan Triennale in September 1951. The names under discussion included Vitruvius, Dürer, Piero della Francesca, Leonardo da Vinci, Alberti, and, with no one in the void of the four intervening centuries, Le Corbusier. The architect was elected president of a new organization that grew out of the conference and was called the Provisional International Committee of Studies of Proportion. Le Corbusier summed up his achievement by declaring, "At a given moment in the threat of disorder, certain ideas may reach the level of a principle."[21]

Over the years, the many images Le Corbusier painted and sculpted of the Modulor make clear that his objective was to ennoble man, to make him strong and broad shouldered, standing erect on muscular and sturdy legs with his arm raised in a gesture of victory. His illustrations divide the figure into a bold red and a light-infused blue that convey pure vitality. For Le Corbusier, who struggled for optimism even when feeling defeated, the Modulor fixed man forever in a state of confidence and empowerment.

7

In December 1948, a session of the United Nations took place in Paris at the Palais de Chaillot. Le Corbusier invited the delegates, as well as selected journalists, to a cocktail party at 35 rue de Sèvres. The architect had violated his own role of keeping the atelier off-limits so that he could publicly give his version of the history of the UN project and his own seminal role.

Le Corbusier showed his audience photographs of a maquette he had constructed to demonstrate his original scheme for the complex in New York. It was, he explained, a natural outgrowth of projects he had done in Geneva, Moscow, and elsewhere over the previous twenty years. He also distributed to his guests a sheet of paper, printed front and back, that presented the UN building complex as he had initially designed it—elevations and bird's-eye views—with a text explaining that these drawings were evidence of the role he had played designing the building now attributed to Wallace Harrison and Oscar Niemeyer.

For the rest of his life, Le Corbusier believed that the origins of the UN as it was built could be traced back as far as his 1922 City for Three Million, which he had subsequently improved in other projects. But the crux of his anguish was not the lack of credit; it was the absence of aesthetic quality and life force in the end result.

On future trips to New York, whenever Le Corbusier looked at what he called "my skyscraper," he felt palpably violated. Yet within the next decade, he was to succeed, on the other side of the world, in making a spectacular "General Assembly" and "Secretariat" exactly according to his own design. The martyr was to find his pulpit.

XLI

1

In February 1949, during a brief stopover in New York on his way to Colombia, Le Corbusier wrote Marguerite Tjader Harris, asking her to organize a meal in a good restaurant. His instructions were specific. The event should be planned by her, but he would pay, and he did not care what it cost. The restaurant could be Italian, French, or Spanish. The following women should attend: herself, Helena (for whom he gave two addresses but no last name), Barbara Joseph, and Mitzi Solomon. He had, he explained to Tjader Harris, met them all in 1946 and 1947.

Anticipating the event, he explained: "Life and hell and paradise are the walls in which there are sometimes doors, keyholes, openings, and sometimes the door itself opens. . . . So in the difficult life I lead, the entrance to consolation may open to me."[1]

He told Tjader Harris that while the UN had thrown him into despair, she and these other women represented "the great New York I love."[2] His haremlike rendezvous should occur at the start of March, when he would be stopping in Manhattan on his return to Paris from Bogotá.

Le Corbusier was ebullient because he had signed a contract with the Colombian authorities for a pilot plan for Bogotá, then in a period of rapid growth with its population jumping from half a million to one million people. He planned to divide the Colombian capital into distinct sectors, fulfilling his dream of designing an entire city with a unifying, modular element as its basis. He was more the product of La Chaux-de-Fonds than he acknowledged. Having grown up in a grid of neat blocks, he was now trying to impose its rationalism and systematization on a more exuberant metropolis. Importing European civilization into a distant territory, he had the mentality of a conqueror.

Le Corbusier commuted to Bogotá until April 1951, when the completed plan was officially accepted. That victory sent him into one of his upward swings. With Bogotá on top of Marseille, he became convinced that, finally, his patience had paid off. This time he declared that the duration of his waiting period had been forty years. He also felt he was making strides in his painting.

The only area in which victory still eluded him concerned his mother and Albert. He urged them to spend ten days in the mountains—he would pay—but they refused. Offering gratuitous advice to a stubborn eighty-eight-year-old, he again instructed Marie Jeanneret to enjoy herself more and reminded her that life would pass quickly. Then on July 18, the architect wrote his recalcitrant mother and brother on the official letterhead of the Conseil Economique—for which the sole address line was "REPUBLIQUE FRANCAISE LIBERTE EGALITE FRATERNITE." His tone was huffy. He had written them ten days previously, to say he would be in Bergamo—in northern Italy, not so far from the Swiss border—between the twenty-second and the thirtieth, and he wanted to visit them for a couple of days. They had not, however, had the simple courtesy to respond.

Le Corbusier told them he was enraged by their silence. If they did not signal that he was welcome, they would miss their chance to see him for a long time, since during his summer holiday on the Côte d'Azur, he would be meeting with Sert and Wiener about Bogotá and would not possibly have time to break away to Vevey. "Answer. I am in the grip of a very active life. A simple word, if you please."[3]

THERE WAS AN ENCLOSURE with the vituperative letter. It was a copy of a translation of a letter from Pedro Curutchet. Curutchet, a doctor who lived in La Plata, Argentina, had commissioned Le Corbusier to build him a private house. It had been a long time since Le Corbusier had worked on a luxury villa, and he wanted his mother and brother to know what was being said about the plans he had made.

Curutchet admired "the graceful and transparent structure" and "the harmonious continuity everywhere." The aesthetic perfection of the spaces was not all the doctor praised.

> But after this first impression I look more closely and in each detail I discover a new interest, a new mirror of intellectual beauty. Henceforth I realize I'll be living a new life, and later on I hope to assimilate completely the artistic substance of this architectural gem you have created.
>
> People I have shown the plans to have been enchanted. I know this work will remain a kind of lesson of contemporary art, of your avant-garde mind, and of your original creative spirit. My duty will be to see that everyone makes use of this lesson to the benefit of his own culture and in gratitude to the great master.[4]

The house for Dr. Curutchet is one of Le Corbusier's most spectacular luxury residences. To build a private palace out of reinforced concrete was audacious; so was the lively and irregular plan. The house is an exciting jungle of terraces, interior gardens, courtyards, large rooms, and great cantilevered roofs, with *brises-soleil* and pilotis at every level.

Curutchet, another of Le Corbusier's ideal clients, was, in his own field, as independent as the architect was in his. A doctor who performed home surgery in a rural region nearly four hundred miles from La Plata and Buenos Aires, he was obsessed with the idea that a surgeon's hands needed to be in their most comfortable and functional position for a successful procedure. To this goal, he developed special instruments for what he named the "aximanual" technique—in comparison to the "crucimanual" technique, in which the doctor's hands were cramped in order to cope with awkward, old-fashioned tools. Not only did Curutchet have in common with Le Corbusier an abiding interest in the human hand, one of the greatest of all mechanical devices, and a wish to use modern technology in new and unexpected ways, but the erudite doctor wrote long books to explain his theories with references to people ranging from Bach and Delacroix to Stravinsky and Valéry.

Wishing to move back to La Plata to live in a combination of house and surgical clinic, Curutchet had acquired a small building site opposite a park. Once he decided that Le Corbusier should design it, he had his sister, Leonor, and their mother meet with the architect in Paris. Following that meeting in September 1948, Le Corbusier came up with a design for a 531-square-meter house to be built for about $32,000. With Amancio Williams as the site architect, the house was completed in 1954, and although Le Corbusier never actually saw his own creation or met his client, the project had served a wonderful purpose by providing the adulation that he could forward to his mother.

2

Le Corbusier's mother and brother failed to encourage him to visit from Bergamo. He let his mother know that, therefore, instead of going to Vevey at the start of August after attending CIAM, he made the short trip across northern Italy "in order not to see any more architects and to get a whiff of that great, real-life poetry which is in Venice."[5]

On August 1, from his *albergo* near the Piazza San Marco, he also wrote

Yvonne, who was alone in Paris. Le Corbusier wanted her to understand that he was away on this date when most French husbands started their family vacation only because of the obligations of his work. But even the glories of Venice did not distract him from his highest of all personal priorities:

> The true site of my happiness is my home, which you illuminate and make so beneficial by your presence. *Guardian of the hearth.* Your magnificent gift of remaining young and beautiful by means of the profound character within you.
>
> Everyone says of you the best that can be said and of 24 N-C that it is a unique site.[6]

Sitting near the spot where, when he was twenty years old, the sunshine following seven inclement days had suddenly opened his eyes to the miracles of architecture, the sixty-one-year-old had another moment of revelation: "My life often transports me into glories to which I am indifferent and into the realm of imbecilities that drive me mad and wound me. When I return to 24 N-C, I return *chez moi, chez nous.*"[7]

Le Corbusier assured his wife that, if she had been at CIAM with him, she would have been loved by his colleagues. But the trials and tribulations of the trip would have been untenable for her. Consoling her, he reminded her that they were about to spend a month in her home territory in the south of France.

AFTER ONE NIGHT in Vézelay and the next in Avignon, Le Corbusier and Yvonne reached Menton—not far from Nice—where they stayed at the Majestic Hotel. Almost as soon as "M. et Mme. Le Corbusier" checked in to their grand hotel at the seaside, Sert and Wiener arrived, and Le Corbusier began to work day and night on plans for Bogotá. He did, however, manage to swim twice every day, once at noon and again at 6:30 p.m. Then, after Sert and Wiener left on August 22, Le Corbusier started to restore the murals that had so upset Eileen Gray in E. 1027 in nearby Roquebrune-Cap-Martin. The murals had been damaged during the war by the occupying army, and Le Corbusier worked on them for the next nine days.

The heat was terrible in the south of France that August, but Yvonne was happier than Le Corbusier had seen her in ages. At lunch and dinner, the couple ate without fail "in a casse-croute 15 yards from the villa, a pleasant new building run by a good sort, patronized by campers and hitchhikers etc. . . . a simple and honest and humorous humanity, a friendly intimacy and a real match between *Panam* and *Midigue* [slang for Paris and the south of France]. Hilarious contests, sometimes lasting hours. This couldn't be better for us. And from this shed an extraordinary view of Monaco, night and day."[8] The term "casse-croute" meant a simple shack or lunch stop where people ate straightforward local food, which Le Corbusier described with relish to his mother and brother. He advised that they, too, take advantage of the time of year at the edge of a vast and beautiful body of water.

LE CORBUSIER was portraying the very spot that was to be his definition of earthly paradise for the remaining sixteen years of his life. The restaurant was l'Etoile de Mer. The "good sort" was Thomas Rebutato, who with his wife and son were to be the saviors of Le Corbusier's and Yvonne's later years. That lunch stop would be the place where Yvonne would get her six dozen sea urchins a day, where the two would drink their pastis together and look over the sea toward the land of her birth.

THOMAS REBUTATO, who had been a plumber in Nice, had bought a parcel of land near E. 1027 in 1948. Where he had opened his simple restaurant, mainly to serve grilled local fish to students, he also built a couple of modest *cabanons* for vacationers.

One day, when Rebutato was sitting on the terrace at l'Etoile de Mer, a

At lunch with Yvonne and others at l'Etoile de Mer, late 1950s

man came up the hill from E. 1027 and asked the restaurateur if he could provide lunch for twenty people. If the lunch went well, he said, he would ask Rebutato to do the same on various occasions in the upcoming days. After the repast, a great success, the man identified himself as Le Corbusier.

The former plumber, his wife, and their twelve-year-old son, Robert, were among the rare people who could get along equally well with Le Corbusier and Yvonne. Rebutato spoke with the thick southern accent of the villages that dot the Mediterranean coast. He stood for hours each day behind the bar of his little restaurant in the summer heat, one hand often placed firmly on the wooden counter, the sleeves of his baggy white shirt rolled up to reveal his darkly suntanned arms, his shirt buttons open to the navel. He sported a beret at jaunty angle even in the warmest weather. Invariably he had a cigarette clenched between his teeth, with an ash dangerously close to falling. His personal style made Le Corbusier and Yvonne totally comfortable.

Le Corbusier soon gave Robert a model of the Modulor and began discussions with the boy. Within a couple of years, Robert decided to be an architect; a decade later, he wound up working in Le Corbusier's office. Yvonne was very maternal with him; she loved to tell Robert stories, and he sang to her.

In time, Le Corbusier and Yvonne lived on this hillside in a structure that resembled a mountain hut—or one of the single monastic dwellings located in the wilderness on Mount Athos. It had everything the architect wanted—the bare necessities for living and working, and a large window opened to the vast horizon. This was where, until Yvonne's death, they slept at right angles in their single beds, hers elevated on a base that contained storage bins, his only a mattress, with a low square table, also providing storage space, in the void between them. Le Corbusier stayed on, summer after summer after Yvonne died, and he moved to her bed.

Writing his euphoric letter from the modest seaside restaurant in 1949, Le Corbusier was also within view of the spot where he would ultimately join himself to the sea and the universe. But there was still much to do—and a chance to impress his mother.

3

José Luis Sert let Le Corbusier know that Picasso wanted to visit the construction site in Marseille. Le Corbusier wrote the Spanish painter, "With pleasure: you give the orders. The sooner the better, as I'm always at the mercy of unexpected problems."[9] He asked Picasso to send a letter or telegram in care of l'Etoile de Mer because there was no telephone, and advised Picasso to meet him at the Roquebrune-Cap-Martin train station on any morning he proposed, as early as 7:00 a.m. This was the sort of scheduling of which he had once dreamed.

ON SEPTEMBER 11, Marie Charlotte Amélie Jeanneret-Perret, who was born in 1860, would, it was said, turn ninety. Only nine years earlier, she had turned eighty. With his passion for round numbers and his impatience to have his mother reach one hundred, Le Corbusier had moved the clock ahead. There is no sign that she argued with the idea.

The architect drew a schema to suggest the perfect divisions of his mother's life as she reached the harmonious sum of decades. It was a vertical figure poised on a horizontal line. Two ascending lines curve upward in opposite directions, crisscrossing at the thirty-year mark, then diverging again, meeting a second time at sixty, then veering away again, and joining up for a third occasion at ninety. The ninety is a summit, a moment of harmony and union.

The loyal son explained the drawing in a letter sent on September 7, 1949: "Now three cycles of life have ended, each as complete and pure as the next: nothing has failed. A splendid ascent. All my respect, all my admiration. It is the third one that you have achieved ahead of any of us. It seems to me that in our family one grows young."[10]

On the previous Sunday Le Corbusier had been with the seventy-nine-year-old Henri Matisse, "pink-faced, entirely white hair." The architect was deeply impressed by the way Matisse, "nailed to his bed for ten years," was using a three-meter stick with a charcoal at the end to design the interior of the chapel at Vence and managed to cut forms out of colored paper and arrange them rhythmically. "He has found the key," Le Corbusier wrote about this artist he failed to understand as a young man. For two hours, Matisse regaled the architect with "a whole heap of stories, all of them gay and playful."[11]

Le Corbusier added that nearby, in Golfe Juan, the sixty-seven-year-old Picasso had just had a baby girl. Le Corbusier, too, was feeling revitalized, thanks to the role model to whom he was writing: "And following the example of his mother, at sixty-two [*sic*], at a time when all other comrades are falling out of the race, Le Corbusier begins a new thirty-year cycle."[12] On September 11, she would, he reminded her, begin her fourth cycle; she must live to be 120.

He would not actually attend the birthday celebration—Marseille beckoned; work had its priority—but he enclosed a newspaper article as a reminder that "the younger son has finally taken his worthy place on the track."[13]

4

In late October, Le Corbusier told his mother that he had been filmed for two days on the construction site at Marseille "as a kind of 'star' with Jean-Pierre Aumont" and that the building there was beginning to take shape; the skeleton of the fifty-six-meter-high structure was in place even if the walls and the rest of the superstructure still had to be added. A new "association for a synthesis of the fine arts" had been created that year of which he had been appointed the first vice president, "which is to say, the man in charge," and he was planning a show at the Porte Maillot devoted to this coming together of the visual arts. He had also just finished the factory at Saint-Dié, where he had manifested that unity of the arts by incorporating his own painting and sculpture within his architecture. But then he observed to Marie Jeanneret and Albert, "My dears, here I am again chattering of egoistic matters," and went on to discuss the new automatic heating system he had installed in the house in Vevey as if it were the most important thing of all; his mother had not yet mastered it, and must do so before the onset of cold weather.[14]

Le Corbusier closed by telling Marie that he would be writing to Marguerite Tjader Harris, for she had remembered his birthday a few weeks earlier.

AS THE WINTER of 1949–1950 approached, the man who was working with state-of-the-art engineers to develop climate controls to combat extreme heat and cold in vast apartment complexes now set out to accomplish the more difficult task of teaching his own mother how to work her furnace. He was determined that she master the new system both for its effectiveness and for the attitude to life its radical technology represented. He concluded his instructions and encouragement, of which every sentence had an exclamation point: "Moral: seize the happy hours as they pass and close your eyes to the others!"[15]

Not that Le Corbusier followed that advice himself. He did not dissemble about his rage over recent events in America, where President Truman had laid the cornerstone of the UN without in any way citing Le Corbusier as the source of its design. "It's amazing! That skyscraper is mine," he wrote his mother. The architect was now constantly barraging Trygve Lie, the UN secretary-general, about the injustice: "Indeed this is an historic event in the history of architecture. I am not letting up. I have all the trumps in my hand. They have robbed me, there must come a day when they admit as much and pay. In what coin? I couldn't care less!"[16]

Then, two days after he accompanied twenty journalists via train to the construction site in Marseille, the cinema news, radio, and newspapers all began fulminating against his radical design for the new apartment building. The main problem, he asserted, was that the negative voices had reached his mother and she was upset. He encouraged her to realize it was only the old problem of journalists: "Etc. etc., gazette, late news, press press press!!!"[17]

She should know that he was walking 1,500 meters every morning, and even though Yvonne was too unwell to write, she was sewing. He advised yet again that one must look on the bright side.

5

One of the press photographers assigned to take shots of Le Corbusier in that time period was Lucien Hervé. The moment the architect saw the younger man's pictures, he told him, "You have the soul of an architect."[18]

Hervé, who worked with Le Corbusier for the next fifteen years, was not impervious to the architect's cantankerousness, even brutality, but also saw the generosity. At their first meeting, Hervé had extolled the mixture of abstraction and realism in one of Le Corbusier's paintings. Three years later, the doorbell of Hervé's Paris studio rang at precisely 8:00 a.m. He knew it had to be Le Corbusier—his only acquaintance who ever came precisely at the hour, never a minute earlier or later, and never having telephoned in advance. Le Corbusier handed the large canvas to Hervé as a gift, saying he knew the photographer had always liked it.

There was only a single exception to the 8:00 a.m. rule. One day, Le Corbusier telephoned Hervé far earlier in the morning and demanded that the photographer come immediately to the rue Nungesser-et-Coli. After hearing Yvonne's usual complaints about being so far from the center of Paris, Hervé learned what was on Le Corbusier's mind. The architect was consumed by anguish over news of the proposed exploration of outer space. "He could not understand the interest in space when there was so much misery on the earth."[19] At that early hour, he talked about human values gone astray, the idea that by the year 2000 it would be impossible to drive or park in Paris, and his own determination to help its poor population, who he felt were underserved. He told them that Einstein had said the Modulor could prevent evil from occurring in the world, a goal far more urgent than what the astronauts were doing.

6

As the war-torn decade drew to a close, people eagerly anticipated New Year's Day 1950. Le Corbusier, however, was, as usual, doing his best to avoid the holidays; he reminded his mother to leave Christmas to children. Besides, Marie Jeanneret had more important things to worry about: she had fallen and broken a bone. The architect begged her to hire an aide, for whom he would gladly pay, but once again she resisted the idea of the domestic help Le Corbusier considered one of life's necessities.

He then raised the issue of her Christmas present. He had given each of his draftsmen a proof of an engraving he had recently made and had also found presents for their children, but he could not settle on a gift that he was certain would please his mother: "For dear Maman doesn't like her younger son's works of art, she thinks it's ugly, she once declared 'I'll never have such painting in my house'!! Andalusian temperament!"[20]

Worse still, she had no end of admiration for his brother's music. Le Corbusier ended this pre-Christmas letter to the alleged nonagenarian, "And then, both of you, go listen to those cantatas, the works of Albert the Great. Then happy holidays to you both, and to dear Maman a good year."[21]

His conclusion for a Christmas present was to give her *The Modulor.* It was, he assured her, the latest rage, even though the ink was not yet dry. But he let her know he held scant hope that reading it would afford her comparable pleasure to listening to Albert's music.

7

On December 30, Jean Badovici wrote Le Corbusier that the architect's "vanity" concerning the murals in E. 1027 had inflicted great pain and that the pure and functional architecture of his villa had called for a complete absence of paintings: "With your worldwide authority, you have been lacking in generosity toward me. A correction by you seems necessary to me, otherwise I shall be forced to make it myself and thus to reestablish the original spirit of the house by the sea."[22] Badovici then reiterated his love for Le Corbusier, recalling their long history and expressing his hope for a resolution of their problems and wishing the architect and Yvonne happiness in the new year.

Le Corbusier did not bother with any such sentiments in the response he wrote on New Year's Day. He simply demanded "formally" that the murals be photographed before being destroyed and then accused Badovici of being incomprehensible, which was to be expected since he had never in his life succeeded in writing in a way that others could understand.

Badovici supplied the photos; Le Corbusier's answer, in its entirety, was "My dear Bado, received your photos of my paintings. Your photographer is a donkey who knows neither values nor cropping nor filters. Couldn't be worse. I hope he's not ruining your finances. Best to you, Le Corbusier."[23]

He could be as devoted as he could be furious. In 1949, when the Galerie Charpentier, one of the most important in Paris, mounted a large exhibition of André Bauchant's work, Le Corbusier showered praise with a reach of enthusiasm that was his alone. He wrote the painter, "The soul of the Parisian is in you, consisting of the original soils of each of us and of the fundamental aspirations of the complete man: the love of nature, the forest, the fields, the streams, the need of history, which is the foundation of existence and the love of legends, and your work is full of goddesses, of heroes and sirens, and of God as well. You are a peasant, but in your veins flows aristocratic blood, the miracle of France, where the nobles and gentlemen knew the shepherdesses."[24]

His own building in Marseille was to be the architectural equivalent of Bauchant's paintings: a sylvan ideal that would allow the worship of a sacred landscape. And he was determined that a sense of mythology and pagan worship should course through the bold and colorful structure.

Le Corbusier identified with Bauchant: "You have worked hard, like a man possessed: from dawn to dark." Bauchant had endured a "heroic struggle in solitude and the mockery of those around you."[25] Even the champions of Henri Rousseau had initially considered Bauchant one step too primitive. That changed only when the dealer Jeanne Bucher saw the Bauchants in Le Corbusier's apartment, after which she organized exhibitions in her gallery and sold the work to museums worldwide.

The sheer animal naturalness and kindness Bauchant and his work embodied provided relief from the tumultuous disorder of the architect's own mind. Le Corbusier delighted in being someone else's savior.

8

The drawings Le Corbusier made for the civic center of Bogotá emanate energy and efficiency. The lithe slabs that would have made up the center of that South American city befit elegant Latin government officials running the affairs of state with verve and élan.

The two main buildings, set perpendicular to each other, are the ultimate exemplar of the right angle, an homage to the sheer panache of two straight lines juxtaposed at ninety degrees. One is basically a calm, horizontal, rectangular block, resting with tapered vertical rectangles at either end; the other is a skyscraper. Yet strong as the architecture is, it is impressively modest in relationship to the landscape; it does not impose itself but respects the mountainous setting, being above all a vehicle for looking out at the earth.

When Le Corbusier flew to South America to try to advance this project, he made it his routine to go via New York. On a stopover there in February 1950, he was incensed by the latest developments. After arriving in Bogotá, he wrote his mother and Albert that he had visited "*my* skyscraper, very far along but giving every evidence of Harrisson's [*sic*] ignorance and lack of imagination. There are horrifying mistakes." The sight of his great conception—its authorship stolen, its quality compromised disastrously—rendered him almost senseless. He continued, "I've touched on so many facts and circumstances . . . that I've conceived a tome (yes, unfortunately!) that will be powerful: 'The end of a world,' 'deliverance.' "[26]

The "tome" to which he referred was a treatise he had written in his own defense. Published in 1947 by the Reinhold Publishing Corporation, it was called *U.N. Headquarters.* In the course of its rampage against Americans in general, he mocked the trend for building shelters against nuclear fallout.

"Looked at Harrison's skyscraper," he reported to Yvonne. "Poor fools. To massacre such an enormous thing! . . . N-York is a terrible city. Everyone is quite crack-brained! They're all abominably scared of being bombed. It's revolting to see such a strong people showing themselves to be so crazy."[27]

But Colombia was different. The port city of Barranquilla, on the Caribbean, asked him to execute a design similar to what he had done for Bogotá, with Sert and Wiener again collaborating. It was a working relationship Le Corbusier prized. Sert and Wiener were "two *perfect* teammates. We work together to an astonishing degree." His mother and Albert, to whom he wrote this, knew how rare such a felicitous collaboration was.

"The exactitude of these transcontinental journeys is of a magical order," he also wrote to those family members who well understood the merits of clockwork. And Bogotá had a lot that New York lacked. "I am regarded as a Gentleman!" he declared to his mother, while describing his thrill at seeing, so far from Switzerland, portraits by Victor Darjou—the same painter who had immortalized his ancestor Lecorbesier at age eighty. "Life strikes me as either magnificent or stupid," Le Corbusier concluded.[28]

Yvonne, however, needed to know that he was not having fun. "What a dog's life! At my age!"[29] He complained that the altitude in Bogotá made him feel tired and caused him to have terrible headaches and bizarre dreams. If she thought she was suffering in her solitude and isolation in Paris, she must realize that he was working from 8:30 in the morning until late at night, speaking Spanish, English, and French in a combination that exhausted him. He spent the whole day visiting cities and factories; the workload was without respite. There were good moments—he had had a meeting with the president of the republic and had also enjoyed dinner next to two toreadors, excited that each of those little men with notably small hands had killed two bulls—but he hardly had a moment to himself.

But for both women he had the same rallying cry. Each must find a good maid. This was Le Corbusier's solution to women's woes.

9

Yvonne was in better form that spring once Le Corbusier returned from Colombia. Albert came to stay with them on the rue Nungesser-et-Coli, and the three occasionally dined in restaurants with old friends like Léger, Pierre, Charlotte Perriand, and Winter. In spite of Le Corbusier's professed objection to socializing, there was a cocktail party at 35 rue de Sèvres, where the young staff sang folk songs. Albert wrote to La Petite Maman, "Yvonne makes very funny remarks when she's in company, and everyone loves her."[30]

In mid-May, Le Corbusier made arrangements for Marie to go to Marseille. The trip was possible now that the elevator, which would allow her to reach the roof, was working. Albert was to accompany her. Le Corbusier had organized their travel arrangements in meticulous detail: tickets for the sleeping car on the train from Geneva to Marseille, use of an apartment there for two days, a visit to the construction site. With the aid of his office staff, he had planned every meal, right down to the coffee ice cream that was his mother's passion.

Then it all had to be scratched, because construction work at l'Unité was behind schedule. Le Corbusier switched the departure date from the end of May to the end of June and reengineered the identical journey. His instructions were explicit: his mother need only take along something to sleep in—"No suitcases, no change of clothes."[31]

Then Marie Jeanneret fell from a ladder and gashed her face above her eye. She was not able to travel; Le Corbusier wrote urging her to "give up climbing ladders . . . out of consideration for her progeny" and put off the trip until she was fully recovered, while stressing that nothing was to stand in the way of her seeing his greatest achievement to date.[32]

10

At the beginning of August, Le Corbusier and Yvonne took a holiday in Roquebrune-Cap-Martin. They rented a bedroom in a shoemaker's house under olive trees down below l'Etoile de Mer. The hot, sultry days and all his swimming helped Le Corbusier sleep better than he had all year. In high spirits, in a single day he painted a lively mural on a wooden panel along the front of the bar at l'Etoile de Mer. Called *Saint André des Oursins,* that colorful testimony to the pleasure of summer is a tableau of underwater life, dominated by a smiling sea urchin surrounded by eels, langoustines, flatfish, and starfish, with a self-portrait of the artist as a jaunty sea bass with a pipe coming out of his mouth and a little bowler hat on top of his head. It fit easily into the setting, with assorted glasses and bottles of pastis and whiskey and wine sitting above it.

A couple of days later, Yvonne stumbled and hurt her knee. It became so swollen that to walk up the steps from the shoemaker's to the shack was hard for her, but Le Corbusier, in a humor where nothing could damage his sense of the beauty of life, simply profited from their immobility by reading Henri Mondor's life of Mallarmé. The architect fit Mallarmé's life into a numeric scheme, concluding that, while Mallarmé had been the greatest poet of the nineteenth century, in 1900 the change of century turned him into a madman. This was one of Le Corbusier's greatest stretches ever, since Mallarmé had, in fact, died in 1898.

Refreshed by good nights and by days of reading, swimming, and eating fresh seafood, in the middle of August Le Corbusier was off to Marseille before returning on the twentieth to Paris, where most of his office crew was still on vacation. Then, on the twenty-sixth, he would fly on to New York for a two-day stopover en route to Bogotá.

From New York, Le Corbusier used his mother's impending birthday to

"A 91 ans Marie Charlotte Amélie Jeanneret Perret règne sur le soleil, la lune, les monts, le lac et le foyer entourée de l'admiration affectueuse de ses enfants. 10 septembre 1951."

write her, saying that, since she liked compliments now that she was getting older, he wanted her to know that she fascinated all his friends. But then he let loose. The architect informed her that she had always been ferocious and readily cruel—either from genius or from ignorance—because of the way she had been raised. He credited her for his having the heredity of a lion, although, unlike her, he was not a lion but a bird.

Le Corbusier said he owed her almost everything—which, since he was often in life-threatening danger, included the fortitude to survive events and circumstances that would have killed others. He attributed that strength to a mutual bullheadedness, pointing out that the four Jeannerets were all alike, especially in their unwillingness to open themselves to other points of view.[33] In this uncensored explosion allegedly written as a birthday congratulation, there was no distinction between mother and son.

DURING THAT STOPOVER in New York, Le Corbusier was even more horrified than before at the fate of the UN. He poured out his anguish to Yvonne: "The architectural spirit in even the slightest details = a grim, dim and insipid flop. Such icy, heartless work leaves us cold."[34]

He also emphasized the need for Yvonne to gain weight, telling her what a marvelous surprise it would be on his return if she could become "round as a ball."[35] From Bogotá, he continued his counsel by writing, "Smoke and don't eat, for my sake," as if the sarcasm might yield results.[36] However, when he advised her that if she needed money for tobacco, she should ask Paul Ducret, his perpetually helpful office manager, he was being perfectly straightforward. After all, Yvonne gave away even more cigarettes than she smoked.

When a woman in Colombia had asked for news of Yvonne and he reported some of her problems, the woman had been dismayed that Yvonne did not take vitamins. Le Corbusier quoted the subsequent dialogue to his wife: " 'Unfortunately, Madame,' I replied, 'my wife doesn't believe in doctors, nor in what I advise her to do; she doesn't want to take care of herself.' "[37] But, six thousand miles away, he was racking his brain to find the right way to cajole her to health, short of being at her side or moving her to where she might have been happier.

Le Corbusier wrote Yvonne every four or five days on that trip. He found some new pills for her that had been recommended by an Australian who took them every day and was in great health; these would be her salvation. When he learned from one of the watchdogs in his office assigned to look in on Yvonne that her health was improving, he was euphoric, writing, "I hope you've grown fat as a pork sausage."[38] Meanwhile, he was pleased to have trimmed down a bit; back in New York after Bogotá, he wrote, "You can see in the photo that I've grown thinner. The stomach still makes a little hump, but on the other hand, if I go hunting the rabbits can easily escape between my knees! And I used to be so proud of the weight it took me 60 years to gain!"[39]

He went on to instruct his wife to have Luan, the Annamite houseboy, cut up raw carrots. They would give vitality—the energy and verve essential, equally, to people and buildings and missing in the UN, he explained in one of his soliloquies where the human physique and the nature of a building were inextricably linked.[40]

11

In October, after he returned to Europe, Le Corbusier was again seeing Hedwig Lauber. The woman whom he had instructed to cease writing to him was now allowed to do so as long as she sent the letters to the office and marked them "personal"; Le Corbusier alerted Lauber to his secretary's habit of opening his mail otherwise.

The architect arranged to see her in Zurich. He planned the evening carefully, opting for a quiet dinner in her flat: "I should like to speak to you in peace and quiet. I want no one else to be present, especially intellectuals. No one. And I do not wish such a meeting to take place in a Swiss restaurant."[41] He said that he would pay for the wine and sausage and slices of ham and would ring at 8:00 p.m.

The bright and attractive journalist was another person who made Le Corbusier happy to be who he was. In his letters to her he described himself as "*la bête noire des conformistes*"—the autodidact who left school at thirteen, never went to architecture school, never received a diploma, and led "a dog's life"—whom she put at ease.[42] Throughout the fifties, the two saw each other when they could. Their plans often suffered from missed opportunities, however. He could not get her to India when he tried to; she went to Roquebrune-Cap-Martin when he was not there. They had a number of happy meetings, though. Lauber was blond—her hair color an obsession for Le Corbusier, who had spoken about it to Paul Wiener in Bogotá—and she was spirited and happy. She called him "*mon cher petit grand Corbu*": small and large, human and great, at the same time—exactly as he wanted to be.[43]

THAT AUTUMN, there were problems not only with leaks in Vevey but also with the roof of the apartment on rue Nungesser-et-Coli. Le Corbusier was determined that his mother recognize that, even if her villa had rainwater coming in and so did his and Yvonne's penthouse, he had been asked to build for the world. He was doing an urban scheme surrounding l'Unité in Marseille; plans were under way for a second Unité d'Habitation, in Nantes; he had also been asked to design a chapel in a small mountain village. Le Corbusier continued the litany: in addition, he was working on a hotel in Roquebrune-Cap-Martin and on a different project for Sainte-Baume—this time a building with two arches to suggest the form of a boat for the arrival of Mary Magdalene. He was entering the second phase of the Bogotá plan. His new title was "architectural government advisor. . . . And that's only a part of it," he boasted at the end of November. She must, therefore, accept the leak: "I repeat: All over the world there's an outbreak of physical disasters (storms and hurricanes) and moral and political catastrophes. To some degree inescapable! Be happy as the Seraphim!"[44]

Her response was further complaints about her roof. The man who was housing hundreds of families in Marseille could not stand it: "I hope that the moral catastrophe of the leak has evaporated from dear Maman's heart. When you see what water can do the world over, this year. . . . And the other elements into the bargain."[45] The only solution left for him was moral superiority.

12

Le Corbusier was determined to use the exposition scheduled for 1952 at the Porte Maillot, on the periphery of Paris, to realize the dream that had preoccupied Ruskin, William Morris, the founders of the Bauhaus, and all the other aesthetic pantheists who had tried to marry painting and architecture and design.

He designed a pavilion that would present the latest contemporary painting, sculpture, and architecture in combination. A bold concept, it was open to the elements on the sides, with a roof that looked like oversized beach umbrellas. The contents were equally audacious: in theory, the pavilion was intended for work by other artists, but in fact it had nothing but Le Corbusier's own painting and sculpture. It was his ultimate fantasy: a solo Le Corbusier museum displaying his achievement in all the arts, at the bustling entranceway to Paris, visible from his perch on the rue Nungesser-et-Coli.

The project never got past the drawing boards, but the architect was about to realize his urbanism, his building designs, his tapestries, and his sculptures on the scale of which he had long dreamed.

XLII

1

One morning in the summer of 1950, a letter arrived at 35 rue de Sèvres from the government of the Indian region of Punjab. The brief document announced plans for a mission, in which two men of rank were to visit Europe in search of a team of architects for a completely new capital city.

India, a British territory since the second half of the seventeenth century, had gained its independence from England in 1947. With the partition that year of the former British colony into India and Pakistan, Punjab, a province in the north, was divided: its eastern part remained in India, while its western part became West Pakistan. (Part of the old province of Bengal became East Pakistan, which in 1971 became Bangladesh.) Since Lahore, the historic capital of Punjab, was now in West Pakistan, the Indian section needed a government headquarters of its own.

It was decided that Simla, the former summer capital of the British regime, immortalized by Rudyard Kipling, was too isolated and too close to the new border to assume this function. The site chosen instead was slightly south of that Victorian city. Two hundred and forty-one miles north of New Delhi, in view of the Himalayas, it was on a vast plateau between two wide rivers that were dry for all but two months of the year. The highway that linked it to New Delhi was a two-lane road that, to this day, feels, along the entire route, like the main street of a crowded and dusty village, flanked by tin huts, fruit and vegetable stands, and ramshackle shops. Making the journey, one stops constantly for hordes of people or cattle crossing.

The name of the new capital, Chandigarh, came from one of the seventeen preexisting villages on the site, where there was a temple dedicated to Chandi, the goddess of power. Chandi is one of the forms assumed by the Hindu Shakti—a symbol, always female, of energetic transformation and a presence required for all important events. It was the perfect avatar for Le Corbusier.

BY THE TIME Le Corbusier was approached, the new project already had a cumbersome history. Initially, an American, Albert Mayer, had been selected to be the overall planner of Chandigarh. Mayer, an MIT graduate, was a civil engineer who had been stationed in India for the U.S. Army during World War II. The Siberia-born Matthew Nowicki was to be responsible for the architectural design. Both men had visited the site, and Mayer had worked out a plan to do most of the design work in the United States and be paid in American dollars. Mayer proposed that Indian government officials travel to Europe and America to get ideas for the look of the buildings—a suggestion that quickly upset people in a country trying to escape the shackles of western imperialism.

Then, on August 31, 1950, Nowicki was returning from Chandigarh when his TWA Constellation crashed near Cairo. It was a moment when the exchange rate between rupees and American dollars was particularly unfavorable to the Indians. Looking for an excuse to drop Mayer, the government used Nowicki's death as a reason to consider changing teams. This was when P. M. Thapar, the administrative head of the capital project, and P. L. Varma, the chief engineer of Punjab, were dispatched on the four-week trip to the United Kingdom, Holland, Switzerland, Germany, Italy, Sweden, Belgium, and Paris.

The Indian delegates were seeking a new architect willing to move to India for three years and accept an annual salary of not more than three thousand pounds, or about $50,000 today. Eugène Claudius-Petit, the French minister of reconstruction and urbanization, whom Le Corbusier had met while crossing to America in 1946, had recommended the architect—in spite of his notoriously difficult personality and the unlikelihood that he would agree to their terms.

IT WAS A COLD and gray November day when Thapar and Varma, both nurtured on warm sunshine, entered the offices at 35 rue de Sèvres. The sixty-three-year-old Le Corbusier did not greet them enthusiastically.

The dapper architect immediately told the two emissaries that he would not consider relocating and that their new city would have to be designed in the heart of the very old city of Paris. Even before coming face-to-face with Le Corbusier's imperiousness, Thapar and Varma had other reasons to be skeptical about Claudius-Petit's recommendation; they had already visited l'Unité d'Habitation in Marseille and doubted the value of its underlying ideas for India. Now they were even less inclined to hire the Swiss. They traveled on.

In London, the two officials met the husband-and-wife team of Edwin

Maxwell Fry and Jane Beverly Drew, both members of CIAM. They asked Fry and Drew to take on the task of implementing Mayer's basic ideas. However, Thapar and Varma, for all their trepidation and misgivings, had also seen the fantastic potential of Le Corbusier's inventive design sense and groundbreaking urbanism for their project. They asked Fry how he would feel about working with Le Corbusier and making it a team effort. The Englishman replied, "Honour and glory for you, and an unpredictable portion of misery for me."[1] Like Thapar and Varma, however, he was one of the rare people willing to endure the misery to achieve the possible rewards.

On December 8, Claudius-Petit spent two hours at 35 rue de Sèvres. The minister continued his attempt to persuade Le Corbusier to undertake the project that he had initially treated with such skepticism. Two days later, Fry and Drew joined Thapar and Varma in Paris for a meeting with Le Corbusier, who then signed a preliminary contract. That momentous event occurred at 9:30 in the morning on a Sunday—a fact Le Corbusier relished; he loved India in part because, unlike France, it was a country where one worked seven days a week.

THE COMPLETE SOCIETAL and historical change that underlay the new project now thrilled Le Corbusier. More than six million Muslims had left India to move to Pakistan, while some seven and a half million Hindus and Sikhs had moved across the new borders into India. Ever since Punjab had lost the beautiful, romantic Lahore to Pakistan, the new capital was urgently needed to administer a state that, from the start, had a major problem deriving from the influx of refugees. Those tensions and necessities required him to build a brave new world. Architecture had to fulfill a burning human purpose well beyond the basics of housing.

2

An entirely fresh start requiring an unprecedented solution was the Corbusean ideal. When Chandigarh was selected in March 1948, Prime Minister Jawaharlal Nehru had said the site was "free from the existing encumbrances of old towns and old traditions. Let it be the first large expression of our creative genius flowering on our newly earned freedom."[2]

Equally befitting the Corbusean vision, the location had been chosen by airplane reconnaissance. The two seasonal rivers, Sukhna Cho and Patiala Rao, and abundant underground water nourished its 8,500 fertile acres sufficiently that there were groves of mango trees. The chosen terrain was close to sources for sand, cement, and stone. At an altitude varying from 304 to 365 meters above sea level, Chandigarh had two rainy seasons, one from June to August, the other in January and February. Temperatures ranged from freezing to forty-five degrees Celsius.

Le Corbusier informed Thapar and Varma that Pierre Jeanneret's involvement was a further requisite to his taking on Chandigarh. His clients agreed, as they did to Le Corbusier's laying out the new city, planning its neighborhoods, and designing its main official buildings in the heart of old Paris. An agreement was drawn up for Fry, Drew, and Pierre to become senior architects on the project, spending most of their time on-site, for which each would earn three thousand pounds per year. Le Corbusier was to be the architectural advisor, with a salary of two thousand pounds plus transportation and thirty-five pounds per day for expenses while he was in India, as well as a fee of 4 percent of the cost of any building he designed in Chandigarh.

The financial rewards were not commensurate with what any of them would otherwise have earned; Fry was giving up a lucrative practice of forty thousand pounds a year. But the idealism and commitment of Thapar and Varma moved the westerners. After his hesitant start, Le Corbusier announced that he would give himself over with all his heart and soul to the new project.

Le Corbusier then told the others that once they had all gone to India, they would have to change Mayer's plan and "begin from the beginning."[3] Unlike the American, the Swiss intended to honor Indian culture—the way of life practiced by the peasants for the past thousand years, as well as the geometric beauty of the Hindu temples constructed in carved stone. When Nehru got word of Le Corbusier's intentions, he was delighted. The architect's wish to make architecture that was "neither English, nor French, nor American, but 'Indian,' of the second half of the twentieth-century" was exactly as the prime minister had hoped.[4]

3

It was one of Le Corbusier's moments of apotheosis. On November 29, 1950, the ecclesiastical authorities had given their final approval to his design for the new chapel he had been discussing in the little village of Ronchamp in the Haute Saône, in the Franche-Comté region. The archbishop of Dijon signed the contract on December 8—the very day that Claudius-Petit had persuaded Le Corbusier to undertake Chandigarh.

In reporting all this to his mother and describing events at the Indian embassy, Le Corbusier, as always, listed his latest triumphs. He had signed books in a bookstore. He had been on television; she would have seen the programs were it not for her unwillingness to bother to meet people in Vevey who got TV reception from Paris. Le Corbusier implored his mother that, while he was so busy and upbeat, she should stop continuing to fuss over the leak into her living room—which he still hoped to resolve. After pages in which he reiterated his importance and quoted the people of rank who regarded him so highly, he wrote, "And dear Maman? Those gutters, those workmen, those dead leaves, etc., etc.: I hope that the danger is past and that calm has been restored. Be sensible; what the hell can it matter if the water occasionally leaks somewhere? Aside from that, doesn't the house manage to perform a certain function?"[5] He and Yvonne had also had the painters in their apartment for a month, he reminded her. These things happened.

Then, on December 19, Le Corbusier walked through the gardens of the Indian embassy in Paris—not far from his old workplace for the Perret brothers—and entered its elegant offices, where he signed the final agreement for Chandigarh.

TWO DAYS AFTER that ceremony, he wrote his mother that—in between trips to New York, Bogotá, and India—he would send her detailed drawings for a new facade that would fix the problem of water getting into La Petite Maison. She and Albert must be sure to specify the same sheet metal that was on the side facing the water. This would finally stop the leak.

Following this, Le Corbusier declared the contract with the Indians "a triumphant business."[6] He enclosed a translation of part of it—spelling out his role of "architectural advisor." It meant that he was to design the city, determine the overall style, and lay out the main road, squares, public gardens, and water system.

He also enclosed numerous press clippings and let his mother know that, by the end of the year, there would be major coverage on him in newsreels that would be shown in cinemas all over France. The French and American press was requesting interviews as well. He was so busy—with Ronchamp, Marseille, Nantes, and now Bordeaux—that he had neglected to listen to a half-hour broadcast about himself on national radio.

Le Corbusier asked for assurance that his mother and Albert had eaten their roast chicken for Christmas. He also told his elderly parent that he had had such a bad headache that he had the doctor come. The cause was only fatigue and was not dangerous, and she should know that it was not preventing him from dealing with her roof and the south facade, for even in his exhaustion he would not forget what mattered most to her.

4

Chandigarh was the summons of a lifetime. All of Le Corbusier's ideals might at last become the everyday reality of a city built for five hundred thousand people—and that in less than half a century would house well over a million. Through design, he could give daily existence the qualities of rightness and morality he held sacred. He could apply the ideas of urbanism he had developed but not been given the chance to execute in Paris, Algiers, Bogotá, Stockholm, and a range of other cities. Here, Le Corbusier would fulfill his dream of subdividing a city into regions for business, administration, and housing. He could lay out a transportation network, erect individual buildings of monumental value, and redesign the life of everyone from the highest government official to the poorest worker.

"I realize the enormous responsibility I've taken on, from the technical as well as the architectural point of view. Esthetic and ethical responsibilities equally dominate," he wrote.[7] The man who had demonstrated that his only political philosophy was opportunism had, as the objective of his wish for any government, a consistent goal: the greatest good for the greatest number. In keeping with the principles that had swayed Charles-Edouard Jeanneret in Ruskin's "Lamp of Truth," his favorite of *The Seven Lamps of Architecture,* at Chandigarh Le Corbusier was to evince an honesty in materials, clarity about form and ornament, and a respect for nature that gave harmony and hope to human existence.

5

While Yvonne stayed cheerful by feeding her forty sparrows—the number had grown—on the balcony at 24 rue Nungesser-et-Coli, Le Corbusier began to plan a trip to Punjab. He was also in a frenzy of publishing. His *Poetry on Algiers,* which had been written in 1942 but could not come out during the occupation, now appeared.[8] He brought out a volume on La Petite Maison, with fifty photos.[9] Even if he was still trying to resolve its leaks, at least he could present it as a beautiful building.

But the leaks were not his only problem. Bogotá had now been put unexpectedly on hold. Even more painfully, a book called *Le Corbusier,* essentially a diatribe against his proposals for Algiers, was published in Florence by Electa. It was written by Alazard d'Alger, an art critic from the south of France who specialized in Italian Renaissance art and was also a curator at the Museum of Algiers. Le Corbusier wrote his mother that d'Alger was "the latest of the treacherous bastards to sling some mud at us."[10]

In mid-January, after hearing a song about a nurse, Le Corbusier wrote his mother urgently requesting details of his own birth. Had he been sent right away to the country to a farmer's house, without having been given mother's milk? He asked Marie Jeanneret to let him know exactly how long he had taken cow's milk.[11] He wanted precise answers, which, he said, were for his private and personal use. He was preoccupied with issues of physical health and resilience; to Albert, who was turning sixty-five, he wrote, "Dear chaps: we're on the other side of the fence now! Courage and Optimism!"[12] In an effort to stave off age as best he could, on most mornings Le Corbusier jogged the few blocks from home to Roland Garros Stadium, where he ran laps.

Loping around that track on the outskirts of Paris, the architect decided that if there was going to be a third world war, as he feared, it was because the Americans did not know what it was to suffer. The excessive and intolerable buildup of arms and military force was, he was convinced, occurring because, to save its postwar economy, the United States was selling arms to the world. Le Corbusier believed the Russians, too, had become imperialists, but at least they were "bearers of the principle of the just distribution of consumer goods."[13]

While railing against America's economic motivations for warmongering and its willful ignorance of human suffering, did Le Corbusier have so much as a fleeting thought that this stadium where he was jogging had, less than a decade earlier, been used by the Germans as a makeshift prison for dissidents—"we called ourselves the cave dwellers, about 600 of us who lived beneath the stairways of the stadium," recalled Arthur Koestler—while he was in a hotel room in Vichy?[14]

6

Before leaving for India, Le Corbusier again set out to resolve the problems of La Petite Maison. Now he decided that for the siding they would use aluminum, rather than the originally planned sheet metal, to halt the leaks;

the price difference would be negligible. On February 12, he went to Vevey to check on the work being done and to say good-bye to his mother; then, after returning to Paris on Monday, February 19, with Pierre Jeanneret, he took the train to Geneva so that the following morning he could begin his first journey to India.

On the Sunday before his departure, the architect looked at a recent photo of his mother that he was taking along. He wrote a farewell letter:

> How touching your image is, with those huge pupils shining through your glasses, your eyes so vivacious and actually *laughing.* You are gay, and I'd be your worthy son in gaiety if the profession didn't turn me into a howling dog. Your cheeks are like no one else's (all that country health mounting guard around a solid nose).
>
> No pessimism. I believe in a noncatastrophic outcome to this stage of evolution, of revolution throughout the world.[15]

XLIII

1

When the Jeanneret cousins left Geneva that Tuesday morning, they flew first to Cairo. From there, they took an Air India Constellation to Bombay, continuing on to Delhi, where they arrived in the middle of the day on Wednesday.

Le Corbusier was transformed. "I've never been so tranquil and solitary, absorbed by the poetry of natural things and by poetry itself," he wrote Yvonne after reaching the site where the new capital was to be constructed. "We're on the terrain of our city, under a splendid sky, in the midst of an eternal landscape."[1]

The villages he had gone through on the road from Delhi were so old that no one knew when they had begun; he felt himself linked to the origins of the world. It was a terrestrial paradise in perfect accord with the entire cosmos; he marveled at the way myriad forms of life were intertwined, with men, women, children, donkeys, cows, buffalos, dogs, all functioning with a kind of unity: "Everything is calm, slow, harmonious, lovable—everyone addresses you in low, modulated tones."[2]

Moreover, everyone was on his side. Varma, a Hindu and the son of a peasant, was an easy collaborator. Le Corbusier raved to Yvonne that he and Pierre were at last working "*without pedants.*"[3] Driving in a jeep over rough terrain where there were no roads, tackling the concept of the new city, living at first in a tent, getting little sleep, he was exhausted—but hardships only contributed to his exhilaration. Besides, there were lots of servants to help out, and the food was great. As in Bogotá, Le Corbusier drank only water and was perfectly happy without wine or liquor—or so he told his alcoholic wife.

In his tent, Le Corbusier marveled at a life where there were no locks on the doors, where everything and everyone had a true openness. He would plan and build, and earthly existence was beautiful. He wrote Yvonne, "I think I've been very lucky to have a wife like you. You've protected my soul from banality."[4] Le Corbusier was in his most euphoric state yet.

Visiting Punjab in India in the early 1950s

NOT THAT the architect could suspend awareness of a lashing defeat simultaneous with this wonderful leap. The Sainte-Baume project was definitely rejected by municipal and church authorities, who claimed it did not adhere to irrefutable guidelines. Le Corbusier wrote Claudius-Petit that what would have been "the work of a man of action and a poet"—he was referring to his patron, Edouard Trouin—had required "nothing of the public powers but a waiver of the most idiotic and criminal regulations. . . . Truly we are, with horrifying insistence, under the rule of boors."[5] Again comparing himself to a beast of burden, Le Corbusier said he felt "muzzled." But in India, he would achieve poetry in the sunshine—at last without the impediment of the interfering and blind bourgeoisie.

2

During his first week on the subcontinent, Le Corbusier completely redesigned Chandigarh. Now he was certain that Albert Mayer's plan was as much of a mistake as he had initially suspected. On Tuesday, February 27, the new scheme was completed. Le Corbusier had filled thirty-two pages of a large sketchbook with the main concepts, while the other three architects—Pierre, Fry, and Drew—hashed out the details. The objective was clear: "The last touches have been put to the plan of what will become a city unique in the world, to be realized here in simplicity and the joy of living. To do such a thing, we had to come to India!"[6] He wrote this to Yvonne, whom he still imagined as the person who would understand his dreams.

VARMA, who completely backed Le Corbusier's ideas, was the perfect intermediary to the local people. And for their realization, Pierre Jeanneret was the ideal second in command. Pierre shared Le Corbusier's "horror of the past, horror of the bourgeoisie."[7] At the same time, Pierre recognized that his own self-doubt limited him, and he willingly ceded to his more confident, domineering cousin—rather than struggle for an equality that would have been impossible.

In work as in marriage, a collaboration without a hierarchy was impossible for Le Corbusier; anyone who wanted to maintain a connection with him had to accept the self-anointed martyr's position of superiority. The only person who remained close to him without allowing him to dominate was his mother, but anyone else knew that to challenge him meant rejection. Pierre recognized whom he was dealing with: "Our collaboration became possible because I remained very flexible with Le Corbusier who conceived himself as the absolute master."[8]

Le Corbusier put more of a spin on his relationship with Pierre, while carefully skirting the issue of Vichy: "Between myself and Pierre Jeanneret there has always been an unlimited, total confidence, despite the difficulties of life, despite the inevitable divergences. If our characters, over the years, have taken different directions, our friendship remained. My architectural work exists only because a certain teamwork has existed between us. It is work shared, until the moment when the circumstances of life (and of good friends) have separated us. . . . Pierre Jeanneret has been my best friend. His modesty and perhaps the grumpy side of '*Père Le Corbusier*' have occasionally kept us from communicating more closely. Pierre was a comrade. . . . He knew how to reassure me. We have been closely united. That is what friendship is. And it is friendship that matters in life."[9]

IN FACT, Pierre Jeanneret's survival technique was based on conscious gamesmanship: "My position with regard to him necessarily involving a constant hypocrisy, I feigned submission, the sort that naturally suited his personality, but ironically my doubts remained all the stronger in every case."[10]

Charlotte Perriand credited herself as the intermediary who got Pierre to make that trip to India in spite of those uncertainties. According to her account, when Le Corbusier initially asked his former partner to go to Chandigarh, Pierre refused. Even the intervention of Claudius-Petit could not persuade the gentler cousin to work with the man who had tried to prevail in Vichy. Le Corbusier phoned Perriand to say that he could not understand what Pierre had to do that was more interesting in his life than this. Pierre would have unprecedented freedom in his new job and would be in charge of 150 people.

Pierre had told Perriand he was too busy with other projects in Paris and that, furthermore, Florence Knoll, head of a major new design company, had invited him to New York to work on furniture. He did not want to take on the difficulties of working with Le Corbusier and moving to India; nor did he want to give up the life he was enjoying in Le Corbusier's old apartment on the rue Jacob. Perriand replied that to work with Le Corbusier in India was the opportunity of a lifetime—and that he could keep the apartment for return trips. It was with this coaxing that he finally consented.

In India, Le Corbusier and Pierre would collaborate more harmoniously and effectively than ever before. Pierre had the craft to take his more inventive and dynamic cousin's ideas, where the obstacles to their execution were "almost insurmountable in the technical and ethnic context of the country," and make them succeed.[11]

THE DAY BEFORE he completed the plan for his new city, Le Corbusier wrote Yvonne, "I'm telling you, Von, I'm making here, at last, the crowning work of my life, among these Indians who are extraordinarily civilized people." Everything was colluding toward his feeling possessed. The sky was "extraordinarily gentle," and the temperature was "delicious."[12] The flowers were beautiful, especially in the gardens of the maharajah of Patiala, which he and his amiable colleagues had visited one evening. He was now full of admiration for the same Pierre who had previously infuriated him, and credited his own wisdom in taking him to India, for Pierre's demeanor reminded him of the good things his father had said about Pierre's father.

In his ebullience, Le Corbusier wrote Yvonne that a yellow towel she had packed among his toiletries had a red stain on it, "difficult to identify, for a man alien to the secrets of an intimate toilette, to my minister, my chief engineer and to the ten servants who preside over my private life night and day, from emptying my toilet to changing the little bouquet of pansies and maidenhair fern for my buttonhole, as well as serving my breakfast, luncheon, dinner, etc."[13] This and all of his letters, he instructed, should be sent to his mother.

Le Corbusier had organized the Ducrets and Wogensckys to take care of all Yvonne's needs in his absence and to keep a watchful eye. He assured his wife that he would be back in Paris in time for Easter: "My dear Maman will be there, and my big brother, and you can shed your light on your kingdom, seated on your throne."[14]

3

The Jeanneret cousins went from Chandigarh to Simla, which was functioning temporarily as government headquarters. The lovely old colonial town with its rambling Victorian buildings is at the foothills of the Himalayas. The dramatic zigzag ride there from the plain of Chandigarh had exhausted Le Corbusier, but he was happy to be in the cool mountain air, at an altitude almost equal to Bogotá's. Less than two weeks since his arrival on the subcontinent, he and his colleagues were now ready to present their new urban plan to the governor of Punjab and his cabinet.

Yvonne shunned most discussions of architecture, but Le Corbusier counted on her to understand the human element of his work: "For, dearest Von, in eight days, we have created a complete, prodigious plan of urbanism which rediscovers the great Asian traditions and which will provide the most beautiful architectural solutions. We have wiped out the American who would have imported to India the American ideas I condemn." She would also understand his joy over both the bounteous nature and efficient, docile staff: "Never have I worked under such favorable conditions and in an atmosphere so propitious: calm, solitude, mute servants, etc., etc."[15]

ANSWERING A LETTER from Yvonne, Le Corbusier wrote back, "Received yesterday your excellent letter of March 2"—it being only the seventh, he was delighted as always by the power of air mail—"the handwriting perfect, optimism in every line, a permanent freshness and youth in every word."[16] The encomiums continued; he was convinced that she was thriving and surrounded by friends. Thapar was proud of their work; the governor of Punjab was content.

In the cold air of Simla, though, "it would have been a fine occasion to provide more than the shorts and briefs, which barely conceal my charms."[17] In the mountain town, crowds of monkeys were always jumping around and embracing one another along the roadsides; Le Corbusier deduced that the grilles on the windows were protection against them, since, he claimed, one night an old Englishwoman had been raped by a curious monkey. He was obsessed with monkey life. To his wife he described the monkeys' red rectums, characterized one of them as a Don Juan, and imagined scenes of jealousy and recrimination. He also drew splendid pictures of himself in the bathtub and self-portraits in which he was skipping around like the monkeys—nude except for his trademark glasses.

As always, when Le Corbusier was happy about his work, he was thrilled by everything.

4

Only one source of anxiety threatened Le Corbusier's ebullient state: his mother was to visit Yvonne in Paris during his absence. He wrote Marie Jeanneret, "I'm sure she's delighted to have you there, after a life of 30 years spent with me in the most total harmony, her role having been never to have smothered me. Praise to her for that!"[18] He was determined that his mother respect his uneducated wife for having so perfectly adjusted to his needs.

He tried to mastermind Marie Jeanneret's visit from afar. He warned his mother that the door latch to the bedroom balcony was difficult to operate, instructed her to look carefully when crossing the street, and cautioned her to rest a lot. He advised that Yvonne should invite Brigitte Trouin and Germaine Ducret to visit.

Le Corbusier also told his mother that he had had to scrap a poor plan made by "an American imbued with his own culture. . . . But Corbu, inventor of the Radiant City and of 3-dimensional urbanism, triumphs utterly when, in such a theme, the terrain is totally free—a limitless plain reaching to hills and the Himalayas in the distance. We delivered a knockout blow to the American."[19] And now the authorities were trying to schedule a discussion between him and "*le pandit*" Nehru. How proud Marie Jeanneret should be of her Edouard—designing a new city in concord with the highest powers of the land.

5

On March 19, Le Corbusier left New Delhi to fly to Ahmedabad, a large city in the region of Gujarat, which for the last thousand years had been one of the most important textile centers in India. India was according him one victory after another: he was there for discussions with new clients about what were to become two masterpieces, the Millowners' Building and a villa for a wealthy widow, Manorama Sarabhai.

On the tropical subcontinent, in unimaginable heat, in a society of rare spirituality, with problems and charms totally new to him, the child of La Chaux-de-Fonds had found a support system and salubrious working conditions beyond his wildest hopes. He was determined to give to that new world buildings of equivalent greatness.

THE INDIAN ARCHITECT Balkrishna Doshi, who had joined Le Corbusier's office the previous year, accompanied him on that trip. Doshi had decided to apply to work in the office on rue de Sèvres, even though he had been warned that Le Corbusier was a difficult person. It was required that the application be filled out by hand—a quirk of Le Corbusier's that no one dared question. He was known for his eccentricities— like always having a heavy Brazilian coin in his pants pocket and treating it as an icon, although it regularly tore holes, which a furious Yvonne then had to sew up.

The first time Doshi entered the office, Le Corbusier was seated in a room that was an exact square, 226 centimeters on a side. Everything was painted black. There were only two lights; one was beamed on a sculpture, the other was on top of the master's worktable. The arrangement revealed an individual who had definite ideas about details, brooked no compromise, and treated light and mathematics as both scientific and spiritual.

For his first eight months there, Doshi did not get paid, but at least he regularly got invited to 24 rue Nungesser-et-Coli for free meals. At one of his first dinners, he began to eat his soup, and as he raised the spoon to his mouth, drops of the hot liquid cascaded onto the table and his lap rather than into his mouth. Yvonne had played one of her favorite practical jokes, which was to encase the bowl of the spoon tightly with plastic wrap. She also used fake sugar cubes that floated in the coffee rather than dissolved.

Once they were in India together, both in Chandigarh and Ahmedabad, Doshi observed Le Corbusier's work habits with fascination. The architect often went off to think in solitude. He would forgo lunch in order to meditate. He told Doshi that defeat was a regular part of his life but that he had a method for dealing with it. "The one thing I've learned in life is to take revenge from defeat by working twice as hard," Le Corbusier explained.[20]

He weathered challenges on his own terms. Years later, when the mill owners who had commissioned Le Corbusier to design their headquarters complained that the doors to the toilets were only seventy centimeters wide, the architect replied, "Gentlemen, you will realize that a pregnant woman with two suitcases walks easily along the corridor of a railway wagon which is never wider than 70 cm; so I'm very sure that this door is not too small for you, fat though you are."[21]

ON THAT FIRST TRIP to India, Le Corbusier remarked to Doshi: "I'm surprised at your Indian cows—they have such beautiful eyes and horns, yet they're so gentle. When you go to America those cows have no horns at all, but they're very fierce and ugly."[22] The local cows, as Le Corbusier saw them, had the attributes of the local people: strong but mild mannered and gentle.

Le Corbusier immersed himself in Indian art, especially the miniatures, and when he worked on his own painting there, he proceeded with a new spontaneity. India let him embrace his instincts, to be receptive rather than to premeditate. When the architectural historian Sigfried Gideon wrote asking Le Corbusier how he could build in the heat so far from his beloved San Marco, he replied by saying he was making architecture for the mountains.

At the same time, he exercised control over everyone in his orbit. When Balkrishna Doshi, anticipating conflict, commented on the mediocre quality of Fry's and Drew's design sense compared to Le Corbusier's, Le Corbusier replied, "Don't worry. I'm going to create hills here so that we will not notice them."[23] He actually constructed mounds of earth, odd clumps that mimic the shapes of the distant mountains and blocked out the English pair's designs.

There could, after all, be no question of who was at the helm. Le Cor-

With Telly Tata in Bombay, mid-1950s

busier flew from Ahmedabad to Bombay, where he met with Bhabha Tata, a steel magnate and a major shareholder in Air India, who he felt might entrust him with even more major commissions. Then he circled back up to New Delhi, where he was received in the presidential palace on March 25. He then made the rugged trip to Chandigarh and returned once more to Delhi. The moment he was back in Paris, on April 2, he set out to orchestrate his new cast of characters as carefully as he planned a city. He declared, "I believe Fry is a good man, but he's an islander, and his lyricism is of a different kind. He too likes to be in command. Bravo!" As for the staff in Paris: "The team is of the highest quality, but each man projects his own universe with such egoism that the place becomes a psychiatric clinic. Life is hard."[24]

To Pierre, who had remained in Chandigarh, Le Corbusier instructed, "My dear Pierre, write a little, a matter of relaxing, deflating, not business letters but letters of free friendship. Don't stiffen up in your sublime but dangerous isolation. Tell yourself that the priests invented confession to save people morally and physically!"[25] Even to someone who had needed to be coaxed back into the fold, Le Corbusier had no qualms about dispensing advice on how to conduct his life.

THERE REMAINED one situation he could not master, however. The aluminum siding and other repairs had not done the trick at La Petite Maison. His mother now had her own ideas on how to deal with rainwater and melting snow, which naturally offended him. At the start of May, Le Corbusier wrote her: "When it rains, everything softens, and in the desert they call that a benediction. If you want to extend the spout to 25 centimeters it's all right with me. I'm amazed by such finicky preoccupations!!!!"[26]

At age sixty-three, Le Corbusier then resorted to the child's device of diverting a parent from anger. He tried to get her sympathy. He wanted to return to the United States, but it appeared that the Americans were not going to grant him a visa because of his stance on the UN. Persecuted by a powerful government, he counted on Marie Jeanneret to know it was finally time to let up.

6

Contrary to Le Corbusier's expectations, the visa came through so promptly that four days later he was on his way back to New York, en route to Bogotá. He was ecstatic in the anticipation of triumph in Colombia—so should be his mother. Avoiding the subject of the leak, he wrote her from New York, "The cherry-tree is in bloom, the house is brilliant. . . . Dear Maman, take advantage of this lovely spring. . . . Observe, appreciate."[27]

Then, when he was in Bogotá, the new government, under President Laureano Gomez, conservative and authoritarian, rescinded the approval of his pilot plan. The chambermaid in Le Corbusier's hotel told him, "The people are furious. They would kill you if they caught you!" And yet the idea that he considered "the fruit of the Radiant City which is human and in the service of the people" was focused on the poor![28] Le Corbusier was attacked by the people in power for failing to accommodate the rich; at the same time, the press, like the general population, laced into him for being an aristocrat too focused on the rich.

The double-barreled fusillade threw Le Corbusier back into doldrums. So did the idea that this plan, which had been legally ratified, could now be stopped. The weather only made things worse; he wrote his mother about the "austere and persistent rain over a grim and grave countryside." He stooped to tawdry sarcasm: "It's politics. The newspapers accuse me of being an aristocrat and a conservative! Everything's fine!"[29]

When the world was beyond his control, one of the solutions to which he had long resorted was to focus on the details he could handle. From Bogotá, he wrote his mother to ask her if she would like a high-fidelity sound system. Just as he had tried to educate her on the new heating system, he explained that this was an arrangement of a gramophone and a radio, connected, where one could put one disk on top of another. Determined to give her the machinery that would enable her to hear long-playing records, he described these miraculous vinyl disks where, for example, ten Debussy preludes were all on a single side.

AS ALWAYS, Le Corbusier fought to the bitter end. He spent two hours with the president of Colombia explaining yet another notion of new government buildings and a palace of justice that would be in harmony with the old cathedral and the existing capitol. But this was to be his last trip to Bogotá. The Colombian capital was, after all those years of effort, the scene of nothing more than another near success in Le Corbusier's life.

Like a lover who cannot quite accept the end of an affair, he continued to maintain glimmers of hope—still thinking, months later, that the commission for a new presidential palace might come through, believing that he and Sert and Wiener might somehow prevail with the urban scheme on which they had worked so diligently for so many years. But Bogotá had now definitely joined the League of Nations, Algiers, Saint-Dié, and the United Nations as another of Le Corbusier's great unrealized fantasies.

7

By June, Le Corbusier had roughly conceived the main buildings of Chandigarh. The High Court, the most important structure in the capital complex, was to be massive and noble, with an entrance as dignified as that of the Parthenon—the totality a simple and powerful presence against the profile of the mountains.

An enormous blocklike form, the court was to stand assuredly on flat ground, doubling its apparent size through its reflection in the adjacent lake. Its effect was of force and ethereality at the same time. The scale and grandeur of the entrance columns—while simpler than the pillars of the Parthenon, they were equally suggestive of godlike strength—gave the building, even when it was only a simple pen-and-ink drawing, a glorious voice. The idea of justice, the rule of law, and the possibilities of human wisdom deserved nothing less.

Le Corbusier always included distant peaks in his Chandigarh sketches. The relationship of the building to its natural setting was an imperative; this was as true in India as it had been on the coast of Uruguay, the outskirts of Paris, or the shores of the Mediterranean. As he planned structures to be constructed on the plateau facing the Himalayas, he focused on the crests and dips of the ever-present mountain ridge.

The Secretariat was to be a skyscraper, lined up with the highest of all the nearby mountain peaks and echoing its form. The General Assembly, the Governor's Palace, and a large sculpture of an open hand were to be carefully spaced between it and the High Court. Over the next few years, Le Corbusier and his team were to develop all the details of these structures; those that would be completed within the coming decade would alter the possibilities of architecture worldwide.

Delighted with all that was sent to him on-site, Pierre Jeanneret began to tinker with the High Court and other structures to accommodate them to their actual location. And on the rue de Sèvres, the joy of creativity and collaboration induced such optimism in Le Corbusier that he even convinced himself that confirmation was soon to come for the presidential palace in Bogotá.

Then, in a letter to his mother, he launched into the diatribe against Americans quoted at the start of this book. Something about Albert Mayer's lifeless scheme for Chandigarh, even though he had been able to defuse it, rekindled his rage over how the main United Nations skyscraper had turned out. Not only had he been hoodwinked out of a project that should have

Comparing his model and the final result for the UN headquarters in the early 1950s

been his—a violation of decent human behavior—but the finished building, a travesty of architecture, was possessed of the same evils as the people who had built it. He wrote his mother,

> At the UN in New York, the skyscraper is an event in the sky. The annexes (great hall + committee rooms) = soap box! I've concluded:
>
> No head
> No heart = Harrison
> No balls = American
>
> This amazing country is a machine out of control, gigantic, titanic: a runaway horse. Dangerous.[30]

Immediately following "dangerous," Le Corbusier wrote, "This word to wish you: a good calm summer of repose. You only live once! Special affections to dear Maman, who will think up her comment while mending 50-year-old sheets, with love, respect and patience."[31]

8

From Paris, Le Corbusier was directly in touch with Nehru on a regular basis. The implementation of his decision to scrap Albert Mayer's original concept required diplomacy, and he incrementally sent the prime minister sketches of his ideas. Then negotiations over the changed design came to a head on June 15, 1951. Mayer met Fry, Jeanneret, Varma, and Thapar in Simla. The others bluntly explained to the American the deficiencies of his concept and the reasons for replacing it.

Le Corbusier succeeded in making his plan the one that would be used. Its most radical elements included the complete separation of locations for living, working, and recreation; the subdivision of an equally isolated communications system, which allowed for different forms of traffic; and the inclusion of sun, space, and greenery in urban life. These were ideas Le Corbusier had been developing for more than a quarter of a century but had never before realized.

There would be, in his ideal Chandigarh, one roadway for buses alone. Other, separate roads would exist for private vehicles. A great avenue, one hundred meters wide, would rise to the magnificent complex of capitol buildings he had already sketched. The new design also allowed for a number of sectors, each of which functioned as a small and independent village. These sectors mixed—and here Le Corbusier and his cohorts departed completely from Indian tradition—the poorest people and those with the most money, "proposing social contacts which can only be educational."[32] Each sector, 800 by 1200 meters, contained everything necessary to daily life and would house between five thousand and twenty-five thousand people. To this day, when one meets residents of Chandigarh, they tend to declare their sector number as if naming a village—with pride in the particular community.

In addition to a "Green City," there were to be open green spaces, markets, and a "Valley of Leisure Activities." In that open space, Le Corbusier was determined for others to enjoy a relaxed interaction and relief in their routines that were alien to him personally, except for his occasional walk or jog. Even as he remained the outsider to most people's notions of leisure time, he cherished recreation as an essential component of human existence. By changing the course of the existing river, he would create a low ground—below the level of most of the town—that would accommodate "all the sites and localities necessary and useful for leisure activities, such as: improvised theater, public speaking, dancing, open-air cinema, pedestrian promenades in the cool of the evening. It is here that everyone can meet in those friendly and numerous contacts the Indians adore when they create those grand morning and evening promenades in their villages."[33]

The closest that Le Corbusier had come in his own experience to equivalent promenades was in the old spa of Vichy. But he did not make that comparison now that he was pursuing his romantic vision of human happiness on the Indian subcontinent. He had observed and valued village life ever since he and Auguste Klipstein had traveled through the rural reaches of the Balkans. In South America, he focused on how large groups of people lived with their markets, festivals, and daily rites. In Moscow in the 1930s, he had been fascinated by the prospect of combining work and pleasure and the integration of physical exercise with healthy human existence. He had been formulating his ideal community for a long time.

Le Corbusier was now determined to provide the possibility of a rich and balanced everyday life for the masses in Chandigarh. While respecting the different factors that came with the locality, referring to himself in the third person, he wrote, "The responsibility is Le Corbusier's. Here began a great architectural adventure with means of extreme poverty, a labor force unaccustomed to modern technology, a climate which in itself is a considerable adversary, and a native population whose ideas and needs must be satisfied rather than imposing western ideas and ethics. The problem is also expanded by other givens: the sun is the imperative or imperial factor in these regions. It is with the sun that a new Indian society must deal in its modern economy; for the sun is so violent that, hitherto, the habits of repose, of siesta, and of indolence were virtually obligatory under local architectural conditions, which permitted no work of any kind to be performed at certain seasons and certain hours. The rainy season also raised a series of problems extremely difficult to solve. In the general imbroglio of information gathered by Le Corbusier, the latter could hope to make progress only on condition that he create, here, too, a 'Climatic Grid' applicable to extreme conditions and permitting the problem to be posed for each of the cases envisaged. The 'Climatic Grid' has been created at Studio 35 [his nickname for 35 rue de Sèvres]. . . . Thanks to this grid, it is possible for the first time to spread out on the drafting table the complexity of the real conditions imposed by a climate which is difficult, imperative, and constantly changing during the twelve months of the year."[34]

In his "Climatic Grid," Le Corbusier had tried to find the means of mastering one of the major, insoluble issues of his life: the effects of weather change. Adequate protection against the variables depended on *brises-soleil* to provide the functions of both the umbrella and the parasol, creating simple shelter against rainfall and baking sunlight. Like his father, Le Corbusier had long been obsessed by fluctuating temperatures, the impact of extreme cold or heat, and the range of sky conditions. He believed deeply in the direct influence of climate on one's work and emotional state. With his new device, he had used the order and systematization of his childhood to cope with extreme conditions in India.

9

In much of Chandigarh today, the geographical flatness, the sameness of the architecture, and the division into sectors create an overall regularity. The intense heat and the arrangement of blocky buildings make it seem similar to the vast suburban sprawls of Texas and southern California—except for its extraordinary public buildings, which are without equal.

The comparison to American suburbs belongs to the eyes of an outsider, however. Indians who come from Chandigarh or who choose to move there (of whom there are many) feel for the most part that it is the promised land. From the moment Le Corbusier set foot on the terrain of his future city, he had a spectacular vision for it, and to most of its inhabitants that dream has become reality.

Le Corbusier's Chandigarh resulted from goals which he articulated, at the start of that first trip, in a letter to Yvonne that he intended to be read by his mother as well: "Chandigarh will be the city of trees, flowers, and water, of houses as simple as those of Homeric times, and of some splendid edifices of the most extreme modernism subject to mathematical rule and a proportion to be verified in everything here by the poor as by the prosperous."[35]

In this place he associated with both ancient Greece and the vanguard, nature's marvels would exist in all their glory. By utilizing modernism in its purest form and relying on the best available technology, he would realize human habitation in its most rudimentary and elegant sense, both as a shelter that provided life's necessities and as a platform for worship of the universe. What he gave the Indian population was, in those respects, exactly on a par with the way he housed himself and his immediate family.

From the start of that first trip to India, Le Corbusier woke up in sunshine; the air was fresh; the birds were singing. This was what counted. He was in a state of total ecstasy. Fry was "a fine man." Varma was "an angel of gentleness." Everyone he encountered was blessed with humility—"quite touching in contrast to the arrogance of Wall Street."[36] The sophisticates of the world, the powers of the UN, could all be damned.

XLIV

1

In August 1951, Le Corbusier and Yvonne returned to Roquebrune-Cap-Martin for their holiday. He and Yvonne again slept in the small house surrounded by olive trees a short walk from l'Etoile de Mer. "Mr. and Mrs. Le Corbusier" were so happy that they hardly ever left the premises. Twice a day, Le Corbusier walked down to the ocean for a vigorous swim, but otherwise they lived between their modest room and the restaurant. The architect's schedule on holiday was as orderly as it was unpredictable during the rest of the year.

The location could not have been more perfect for him and Yvonne. The land sloping down to the sea was covered with thick vegetation. Although Monaco and Monte Carlo were visible across the vast inlet, the property was as rough and savage as that tiny principality was built up and manicured. The spot had some of the barren simplicity of Mount Athos. The ocean was perpetually in view, the rocks and flowers and dense foliage fixed by a crystalline light. The Mediterranean coast was both Le Corbusier's and Yvonne's nirvana—his because it was everything he loved in contrast to his childhood, hers because it recalled the joys of her youth.

Jean Petit, a young architect at 35 rue de Sèvres, had become Le Corbusier's Boswell, recording every statement and trying to retain the master's words for posterity. Le Corbusier told him, "Over the years, I've become a man of . . . everywhere. I've traveled across the continents. I have only one deep attachment: the Mediterranean. I am, intensely, a Mediterranean man. The Mediterranean Sea is the queen of forms and of light. Light and Space. . . . Mountains I probably grew to dislike in my youth. My father loved them to excess. They were always there: heavy, stifling. Then, too, they're monotonous. The sea is movement, endless horizon."[1]

At Roquebrune-Cap-Martin, Yvonne spent her days happily on a chaise on the veranda of the little bistro or in the shade at the shoemaker's. The shoemaker's wife kept chickens, rabbits, and a goat. To the noise of this menagerie and the shoemaker's many daughters, she and Le Corbusier slept especially well, just as they had the previous summer.

Every day, Robert Rebutato, now fifteen years old, brought Yvonne six dozen sea urchins he had fished out of the sea. In the winter, the boy had taken to writing to her often—in neat schoolboy script, not so different from hers. His respect for the couple approached worship. That Easter, at Robert's request, Yvonne had been the patroness of a light Easter meal for the local children. With his work habits and her drinking, Le Corbusier and Yvonne never seem to have considered having children, but at l'Etoile de Mer they enjoyed a connection with a child that fulfilled a need in them. Now more than ever, Le Corbusier was determined to make this spot an integral part of his existence.

2

Henri Matisse's chapel in Vence, a forty-five-minute journey by car from Roquebrune-Cap-Martin, had recently been completed. Le Corbusier would not have been pleased if he had known the history of its construction. In 1948, when Matisse had undertaken to do the art and windows and liturgical garments for the small church, the enlightened Dominican father Marie-Alain Couturier had proposed that Le Corbusier be its architect. Matisse had refused; he chose Auguste Perret instead, claiming, "He'll do as I say"—which the painter knew would certainly not have been the case with Le Corbusier.[2] Knowledge of that piece of history would have prevented Le Corbusier from going to see Matisse's chapel that August 1951, one of the few times he left his retreat during the holiday.

The building had been consecrated two months earlier. The plain structure with Matisse's black-and-white mural, bright abstract windows, and boldly refined crucifix and other fittings was even better than Le Corbusier anticipated. He now reversed himself even further about the artist's work. After the visit, he wrote Matisse, "I visited the chapel at Vence. Everything there is joy, limpidity, youth. The visitors, by a spontaneous triage, were dignified, delighted, and charming. Your work has given me an impulse of courage—not that I am lacking in that department, but at Vence I renewed my supply. The little chapel is a great testimonial—of truth. Because of you, once again, life is beautiful. Thank you."[3]

Originality, creativity, and honesty were his own goals as well. On August 27, the architect wrote his mother, "Forgive the vacuity of this letter. Happy men tell no tales. And my notion of a vacation is to make things which are difficult to invent."[4] This was his time to escape the rat race, to allow himself the void that facilitated being creative rather than reactive, and to use his imagination to its utmost. He had taken his painting and sculpture in unprecedented directions.

Then architecture beckoned. On September 2, Le Corbusier and Yvonne took the train for Marseille. At last, they could sleep on the site of his new apartment complex. Staying overnight within the walls of his creation, he was more convinced than ever of his own magic.

3

The only thing he believed was still missing in his life was sufficient attention from his mother and brother. When Le Corbusier returned to Paris in September, there were business letters to read and answer, visitors calling on him in droves, and endless telephone calls. The barrage of communication was because people needed him all over the world, yet there was not a word from Vevey.

As important as he was globally, he always found the time to write his mother and Albert long letters. This was more than they did: "And you—do you write much? Not that I know of. I have the feeling I write more than you do—and do you have any idea of the work I have on my plate?"[5] He provided his mother and Albert with a numbered list that included the projects in Nantes, Marseille, Chandigarh, Ahmedabad, and Ronchamp, various villas, a house for the industrialist André Jaoul, a tomb for a general in Caracas, and the urbanization of Bogotá (as if that project were still alive). He also summarized the books he was planning to write and let them know he was preparing a major exhibition of his work to be held in New York at the Museum of Modern Art in 1952 as well as an important show of his paintings at the Musée d'Art Moderne in Paris the following year. He would probably receive a significant commission for UNESCO in Paris, and had met with Claudius-Petit in Strasbourg to plan the construction of eight hundred dwellings. Not that his mother and Albert could have been ignorant of any of this information, which Le Corbusier had repeated time and again to them, but he wanted to emphasize the juggling act by which he concerned himself with the most minor details of their lives while they neglected him totally.

They must know the ordeals he had been through and the horrible people with whom he had to put up. They had, after all, seen the "snotty nose" of the "mayor of Marseille's *chef du cabinet.*" Le Corbusier had been forced to take the government official and the adjunct mayor around the construction site and explain himself to them—which made him feel completely "done in: that kind of asshole digs perpetually deepening ditches under my feet. Such creatures are stupid, fatuous, cowardly, disgusting."[6] At least "this callow fool" had said that he had never seen a woman of the caliber of his mother, a compliment Le Corbusier was happy to pass on.

His workload was "crushing," he repeatedly told his family members. "But the work under way is assuming an unheard-of proportion, linked to the great moments of the history of architecture as a revolutionary social phenomenon, opening paths beyond the present methods of east or west. A spiritual conquest that scares some and brings tears to our eyes time and time again. We're achieving something truly superior!"[7]

Not that the conquest would be total. Strasbourg was yet another project that would fail to materialize. The studio had drawn 120 meters of plans for two rectangular housing slabs that between them contained eight hundred dwellings; with its park and swimming pool and appealing housing that could be built at an unusually low cost, it had unparalleled charm for a new city. But Le Corbusier, allowed only eight meters on which to present the project to the jury, was forced to overlap the drawings and blueprints in thick bunches. The jury of twenty, ten of them architects, said it could not even be considered. Le Corbusier was convinced that the perpetrators of this crime had conceived of the size restriction and then caused the consequent rejection of his scheme as a deliberate act of vengeance, at a cost to his studio of five million francs.

The seesaw of success and defeat within Le Corbusier's mind caused him in the next breath to instruct his mother, "Ultimately, happiness is within, in ourselves, so that dear Maman need not offer the Villa Le Lac to her guests as anything more than it is: a living-space with endurable faults."[8]

4

As Marie Jeanneret approached what was now claimed as her ninety-second birthday, Le Corbusier drew her another vertical graph. The scheme is divided in units like a thermometer, with each horizontal dash across the spine marking a decade. Le Corbusier shaded in the area above ninety, making it clear that one hundred, a perfect globe at the top, the essence of roundness and symmetry, was not so far away (see color plate 10).

Alongside the diagram, Le Corbusier wrote, "Dear Maman, as you proceed one step farther into the high attitudes, your children congratulate you, surrounding you with their admiration and their affection and wishing you a wonderful and simple life." Then he proffered some of his usual advice: "Look ahead and above. And learn to love the weeds (which the Good Lord made as well as the flowers!)."[9] He had not cut a thing out of his own garden since 1939, he explained.

He continued with the botanical analogy. As she approached her centenary, his mother should be less judgmental, forgive him for the leaking roof, and accept him and Yvonne as she did Albert—the first seed of her garden. She must embrace all that was natural, even if it was not tidy and orderly.

5

Le Corbusier returned to India that fall. This time, he was stationed in a luxurious hotel suite in Simla, looking out on the mountains. At an altitude of 2,600 meters, he had a glass veranda, a large bedroom, a boudoir, and a spacious bathroom. He could see the higher reaches of the Himalayas toward the north and, to the south, the foothills sloping down toward Chandigarh. Every day, starting at 6:00 a.m., the sun shone brightly in a cloudless sky. The architect savored the good mountain air and complete silence that made his "hermit's life" ideal for hard work.[10]

On the site in Chandigarh, construction was under way. The radiant city was, at long last, going to become reality. Pierre, Fry, and Drew were working well together. The Indian crew was splendid. And a powerful government was endorsing it all.

Even if he now claimed himself as a Mediterranean man, Le Corbusier wrote his mother, from Simla, that he remained guided by the lessons of his childhood. He never allowed himself to procrastinate; to postpone any task would have violated the maxims on which she had raised him. "But dear Maman's precepts do not attain the peaks of her bright young cheeks and her smile, so magnificently confident, total, and optimistic," he added, in his voice of unequivocal adoration.[11]

ON NOVEMBER 22, Le Corbusier had an appointment in New Delhi with Prime Minister Nehru. The meeting was scheduled for 11:00 a.m. The architect respectfully arrived at 10:30. He paced back and forth for fifteen minutes and then could no longer restrain himself from approaching the office. In the waiting room, he had glanced at the day's newspapers and discovered that there had been a plane crash in Calcutta the previous night. A number of leaders of industry and government officials had been killed. It did not even occur to Le Corbusier to dissemble when describing his reaction to that tragedy. "Now is my chance," the architect thought.[12]

Plunging in—at least according to his account, no one tried to stop him—Le Corbusier immediately offered Nehru his condolences, in the best English he could muster. After the prime minister invited him to speak French, he continued, "May I present my respects and declare that I bring and shall bring all my intelligence and also all my sensibility and my heart to this task which delights me as the crown of my career: in humility, even in poverty, to free architecture from its dead crust, to express it and give it the greatness of youth."[13]

The Swiss architect, his receding white hair brushed back from his forehead, stood confidently in his white linen suit and bow tie before the distinguished world leader. He continued on the theme of life and death, announcing that the tragic deaths that had just occurred made it an opportune moment for resurrection and that architecture was a living force that could replace the unexpected void. He urged Nehru to make his colleagues' fatal accident further reason to do the unprecedented and start fresh. Le Corbusier considered building a process of birth. It was the solution to all hardship—the means to overcome torturous rejection of the type he had experienced, even by his own mother—and a compensation for death.

With Nehru in India, mid-1950s

The architect continued, telling the prime minister that Thapar and Varma were both excellent at their jobs. He also reminded Nehru that he had declared that "Chandigarh should be a symbol of the Freedom of India, unfettered by the tradition of the past."[14]

If Le Corbusier's report is to be trusted, Nehru looked at him gravely when he urged that a sculpture of an open hand should stand at the edge of the city, in front of the Himalayas. The architect told the prime minister that "with the modern world flowering into limitless intellectual and material riches, the hand must be open to receive and to give."[15] Nehru's serious expression was transformed into a gentle smile, and the two left the office together in a spirit of complete rapport, the prime minister en route to his colleagues' funeral.

Le Corbusier was certain that he had touched Nehru. He may have been delusional, but to an unprecedented extent he believed himself completely understood and welcome in the halls of power. At last, Le Corbusier had found a world leader who—unlike Mussolini, Stalin, Pétain, the heads of the League of Nations and the United Nations, and the president of Bolivia—had hired him to do the job.

6

Le Corbusier returned to Paris on Thursday, December 6. The following Tuesday, he was on-site in Marseille. The crew was already at the point of working on the roof lighting. The mock-up of that illumination was, he wrote his mother, "a great song"—remarkably like the lights that were to flood the night sky over the Cour Carrée du Louvre fourteen years later.[16]

One of the purposes of his trip was to determine the illumination at the entrance level. He reported to his mother that, underneath the pilotis, "the lighting was 'rarefied.' I say rarefied because everything here requires, demands of us a deeper search: the structure is becoming magnificent, the roof is an acropolis. All this amid struggles. But also amid the sympathy of the workmen and the foremen."[17]

His professional life, he assured Marie Jeanneret, was progressing miraculously, in spite of the inevitable hurdles. Father Couturier had proposed that he design a convent near Lyon; this was like having gold fall from the sky. But then came the counterpoint. The United States had vetoed Le Corbusier's participation in the project he had expected to undertake for UNESCO in Paris, saying he was a communist. He intended to wage a defense campaign and take legal action at the embassy against these "dirty tricks."[18] And his colleague Jean Prouvé told him that Auguste Perret had voted against a second Unité d'Habitation in another French city, even insisting that the idea shouldn't be considered.

The checks did not faze him anymore, Le Corbusier told his mother. He would no longer bow to the opposition—even for a minute.

LE CORBUSIER and Yvonne went to Roquebrune-Cap-Martin for Christmas and New Year's. Since he had to be in Marseille at the start of January, it would be nice for Yvonne to celebrate her birthday so close to her birthplace. When they arrived, Le Corbusier slept sixteen hours a day for six days in a row—or so he claimed. On December 31, he drew, on the corner of a table at l'Etoile de Mer, the plans for a small *cabanon.* The following day, he gave them to Yvonne as a birthday present (on January 4, she would turn sixty), along with the declaration that he would construct the little house alongside l'Etoile de Mer, "on a spit of rock pounded by the waves."[19]

It took him three quarters of an hour to make those plans. Le Corbusier had evolved to complete simplicity. For the public, he was multiplying regular units by the thousand; for his own purposes, and those of his wife, he had made one modest room.

In both instances, the framework was solid and simple to facilitate focus on the essentials. A balanced life did not require complicated trappings. The holiday *cabanon* was to be as lean and purely functional as possible, devoid of bric-a-brac or unnecessary objects.

The Modulor provided the proportions; a lifetime devoted to a consideration of what it takes for people to live in their houses determined the rest. In making a birthday present for the ill, nervous, fragile, and good-hearted but vituperative Yvonne, his wounded bird, Le Corbusier had, simultaneously, created his own ideal.

7

Le Corbusier was now guiding the building in Marseille toward completion. In mid-January 1952, he wrote his mother that the project was "astounding. A crescendo."[20]

Yet the other side of martyrdom was present as always. Although the office was bustling with activity, Le Corbusier's enemies still plagued him. In the same letter, he complained, "Nasty guys have played dirty tricks and robbed me of important commissions." As much as he was having his way about l'Unité d'Habitation, control eluded him on other fronts: Marie had agreed to have four meals per week prepared for her but protested the idea of his covering two of them, with the bills going directly to de Montmollin. Albert was equally obstreperous; he had failed to send music that Le Corbusier wanted to have performed and published. Le Corbusier told his mother he'd like to come visit them for a day, "But such trips are exhausting in the long run. And I need a little *calm*."[21] The final word was underlined twice—to emphasize how miffed he was never to experience it with her and his brother.

Then, in the third week of January, Le Corbusier returned to India. To Yvonne, he wrote: "Your husband swims through the air like a fish through water. Airplanes are fabulous!"[22] Swimming and flying were his ideal states: swift, effective, and purposeful.

First, he met with his client Mona Sarabhai in Ahmedabad; then he was driven in Thapar's car on the long journey north from Delhi to Chandigarh. India again filled him with unequaled joy. He was thrilled to be with the likable Thapar and happy to return to the same splendid room in Simla, which Pierre had now personalized with knickknacks and photos.

One Sunday, even though it was a workday for the natives, he simply stayed in bed. He claimed to Yvonne he had not done this for thirty years. Nostalgic for that period when they had first met, invoking the nickname she then used for him, he wrote her, "I remembered that now immortal rue Jacob, where you would emerge from the bed or the bedroom, tits to the wind, shouting 'Dou! Dou! Dou!' "[23]

At the start of April, the architect sent his mother a copy of a letter from Thapar reporting that Nehru was extremely pleased with all the construction in Chandigarh and was requesting another meeting with Le Corbusier in Delhi. He enclosed a translation of a letter Nehru had written about Chandigarh to the Planning Commission of India, in which the prime minister identified "Mr. Corbusier" as "perhaps the world's greatest architectural authority." Nehru praised Le Corbusier especially for not copying a foreign style and for "taking into account our particular climate and other consequences," marking a radical change from the colonialist tradition of imposing a style from the outside.[24]

Nehru saw Le Corbusier as the embodiment of a truly democratic spirit of architecture. The new city would provide affordable housing that was a miraculous improvement over the squalid living conditions it was replacing. Nehru wrote, "Nothing is more horrible than the housing for 'peons' or 'servants,' the standard type of which arrived with the British and have continued, with certain variations, ever since."[25] Le Corbusier presented a refreshing alternative to the small and dark rooms in which the workers had previously lived, providing each dwelling with a shower or a water closet or a kitchen. If there was no chance of all three, the presence of running water was itself a miracle.

8

In 1952, between trips, Le Corbusier did a series of exceptionally large paintings and began making cartoons for tapestries measuring nearly five by three meters. The spirited work features voluptuous women with immense breasts and hips. It has spirit and vigor but lacks the quality or originality of Le Corbusier's architecture. Nonetheless, those paintings and tapestries, as well as the architect's sculpture, figured in all the exhibitions and publications in which he had a hand. Le Corbusier succeeded in coercing editors and curators to accord his nonarchitectural work the stature of the buildings.

There was no aspect of the visual world that did not intrigue him, no detail he didn't consider both visually and symbolically. He was obsessed, for example, by his pajamas. He wanted them solid colored, dark, cuffless, and, imperatively, with no white piping. When the best shirtmakers on the Left Bank did not have what he required, he protested that what they sold was unbecoming and looked like theatre costumes, and was annoyed to be informed "we always do it that way."[26]

Whatever Le Corbusier wore fit impeccably and was of the highest quality. For work, he usually opted for dark business suits, occasionally double-breasted but mostly classically cut, the only hint of dandyism being his signature bow ties and bright pocket handkerchiefs. In the tropics, he switched from navy pinstripe to crisp white linen suits. When he painted at home, he often sported a bold plaid lumberjack shirt, and for walks in the Bois a leather bomber jacket. His choices were jaunty and emphatically masculine.

On one of his transatlantic crossings on an ocean liner, Le Corbusier lamented the drabness of the usual male evening wear: "I asked the purser for dinner clothes with some color: the stewards dressed in vermilion are in keeping with the pomp of the ship; at dinner the rest of us are like people at a country funeral; the beautiful women seem like flowers in the splendors of their gowns. It is a curious end result of civilization that men who used to wear ostrich plumes on their heads, rose, white and royal blue, a vesture of brocades or shimmering silk, should no longer know how to do anything but thrust their hands into the pockets of their black trousers."[27]

In clothing as in architecture, it was time for a totally new approach. Le Corbusier longed for greater color and playfulness in everyday wear: "The question has to be reconsidered, and the transformation of masculine costume is necessary. It is as difficult as changing the ethics and institutional state of a society. Costume is the expression of a civilization. Costume reveals the most fundamental feelings: through it we show our dignity, our distinction, our frivolity, or our basic ambitions. Though standardized, masculine dress does not escape individual decision. But it is no longer suitable. From what persists, we have proof that the machine-age revolution has not reached maturity."[28]

Le Corbusier lectured a group of male architecture students that they should consider expressing more flair and optimism in how they dressed: "Nowadays people are unaware of the power of color as it was used in Doric or medieval times. They know nothing of the clarity or glitter of golds, or mirrors, or silks, or brocades, or of Louis XIV, and Louis XV felts. The strength, health and joy of aristocrats in other times strike our grocer types as lacking the necessary degree of refinement. That revolution of consciousness belatedly emerging now after having too long burdened society, will one day even affect our dress. Women have already taken the lead. Their styles and fashion are bold, sensitive, expressive. Just look at the young girls of 1942. Their hair styles reflect a healthy and optimistic outlook. They go forth crowned in gold or ebony. But in the reign of Louis XIV or during the Renaissance, you boys are the ones who would have been as radiant as archangels with hair like theirs, and strong as Mars and handsome as Apollo. But the women have stolen your thunder."[29]

Always interested in what Yvonne and other females wore, Le Corbusier made some women's clothing designs, which he felt were breakthroughs. In 1952, Henri Cartier-Bresson, who had just photographed the architect for *Harper's Bazaar,* encouraged him to submit the designs to Lily van Ameringen, his editor there. Le Corbusier described his concept to van Ameringen as "a woman's costume for actual life (which sacrifices in no way feminine charms) . . . not a fashionable creation but a new mode of dressing." Le Corbusier had already patented both the idea of this outfit and his description of it. "I would like to earn a fortune in dollars in the States," he wrote van Ameringen, while explaining that his goal was to see these garments made in a range of materials. He felt they would give "a modern woman a free and easy comportment and a charm that is a direct result of physical allure (when it exists)."[30]

The architect made three drawings. The first shows a loose-fitting V-neck blouse with three-quarter-length sleeves and a diaphanous pleated skirt. In the second, the blouse is removed, showing that the skirt is the bottom of a dress with a tight-fitting, low-cut, short-sleeve jersey as its top. The third is the same dress worn folded to be shorter. He drew these combinations on bodies that look like Greek statues except for their hairstyles, which resemble those of the prostitutes he had admired on the Métro thirty years earlier.

Le Corbusier considered his concept "more durable than ephemeral." He explained that the loose top was basically a poncho to be removed. The second sketch revealed his idea for a "tea gown," with its clinging top and flowing bottom. In the third drawing, the pleated skirt had been pulled up a few inches, gathered at the waist, and secured with an elastic belt, to make it easier for the wearer "to walk, work, move, get in and out of carriage, a bus, etc." The outfit was shown with "dainty sandals convenient for walking. These sandals have a good-size heel but not the high heel which is disastrous (though most charming . . . but alas!). Corns, which so often haunt stylishly shoed ladies, will disappear. Nylon stockings will no longer be a good bargain; they are often a hindrance even though they look so well." The wearer could, in bad weather, put her sandaled feet directly into thick boots: "The contrast between a thick boot, easy to put on, and the feminine exquisiteness is an asset. Exit nylon stockings, enter thick boots: from a certain point of view the last items can perhaps replace the first."[31]

Like his housing types, Le Corbusier's clothing idea had universal application and served multiple purposes. The garments could be made of the cheapest Indian cotton or of "priceless wools and silks." The architect credited himself with having considered all human needs: "This costume is made for a living creature with a skeleton, muscles and flesh, necessary plumpness and slimness. All these essential feminine characteristics have been considered by the gentleman who, although an architect and a painter, is not blind and can appreciate what is always agreeable to be seen and what is best to hide some times, leaving to circumstances the occasion or the pretext to certain delights of discovery."[32]

9

In December 1950, Yvonne had written Albert and Marie a year-end greeting pointing out that 1951 would be her sixtieth year. The frail Monegasque told her in-laws that Le Corbusier always compared her to a six-year-old. In his messy script, he had written on her neat missive that "she has kept the soul of a child."[33]

There is a wonderful group photograph that includes Picasso and "Yvonne Le Corbusier," and that shows her at her most relaxed. A patch of bright sunlight makes a triangle across Picasso's face, virtually blinding him, but he doesn't flinch. Yvonne has her usual scarf tied tight around her head. They could be members of a large Mediterranean family on a Sunday afternoon—content to be together, but each lost in a lazy reverie, even though other people are trying to talk to them. It is clearly very hot out; the

With Pablo Picasso and Yvonne at l'Unité d'Habitation in Marseille in August 1949

painter has the sleeves of his white shirt rolled up a couple of notches, and the shirt is open practically to his belt buckle, in a swooping V that reveals a mass of gray chest hair. Yvonne, looking earthily sexy in spite of the visible ravages of illness, is in a short-sleeve flowered blouse. She seems very feminine and strong willed; he is markedly masculine and powerful. These are tough, vibrant people, stolid and sensuous at the same time, in some way very much at home with who they are in the world. Yvonne may have maintained "the soul of a child," just as Picasso regularly said he aimed to do, but she bears the weathered looks of someone who has lived long and hard.

The setting is l'Unité d'Habitation in Marseille. The event was Picasso's visit to the site in 1949. Le Corbusier guided him through it, and the painter was fascinated by all the surprises. He spent an entire day exploring Le Corbusier's complex and found it admirable in all its details as well as its overall form. If Balthus was telling the truth when he said that he and Picasso had both mocked Le Corbusier's abstract modernism of the thirties, now that Le Corbusier was building for the masses in a style that celebrated complexity, Picasso had reversed his opinion.

Le Corbusier proudly referred for the rest of his life to how much Picasso loved the building, even in its unfinished stage. From Le Corbusier's point of view, there were few people whose endorsement mattered more: "There's nothing to say about Picasso because Picasso is inexplicable. Picasso does his work. The result is greatness. You like Renoir? Then go see Picasso and discover that Renoir becomes anecdotal. Picasso is not a bluffer. He's not what we call an *artiste-peintre.* He works, calls everything into question, searches for new answers. He's a creator in the biggest sense of the word. There's no 'Picasso case.' There's a man who has never stopped."[34]

A couple of years later, Picasso invited Le Corbusier to construct a wall at his villa in Golfe Juan. According to Paulo Picasso, the artist's son, the architect misunderstood what his father wanted, which had been transmitted in a message rather than in a face-to-face conversation. Le Corbusier simply provided a couple of practical suggestions on construction technique. Of the many unrealized projects in Le Corbusier's life, one of the most intriguing to contemplate is what he would have made if he had collaborated with Pablo Picasso.

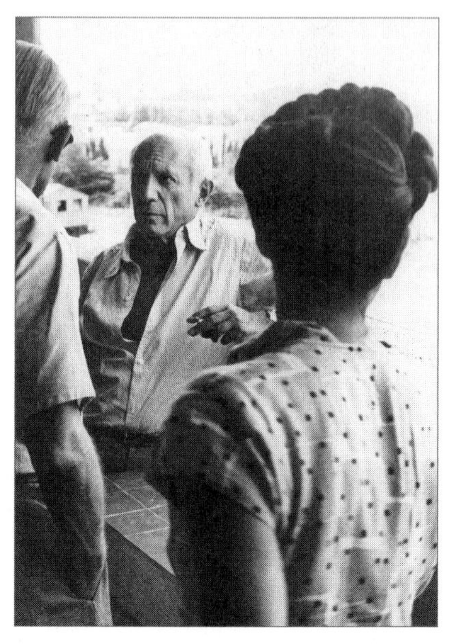

Visiting the building site of l'Unité d'Habitation in August 1949 with Pablo Picasso and Françoise Gilot

10

One of the many things Le Corbusier and Marguerite Tjader Harris had in common was a fealty to their aged mothers. In June 1952, Tjader Harris wrote that her mother had died that February. Le Corbusier had first come to know the older woman seventeen years earlier, in her house in Connecticut. It was a habit for the lovers to dine with Mrs. Tjader and Toutou before leaving the grandmother in charge of the little boy when they went off to the beach shack.

When Tjader Harris wrote Le Corbusier with the news, she added, "She died, as she lived, a Saint, 'filled with truth and grace.' " The divorcée had, to the end, been living with her parent on the family estate, Vikingsborg, in Connecticut. Le Corbusier wrote her there immediately, "I'm terribly sorry about your mother's death. I know nothing about things of the Beyond except for the Gate of the Beyond, the only geographical site known to us ordinary mortals."[35]

The daughter was candid about the financial consequences; beyond the large house and half of the property, she had inherited a great deal of money. She instantly had an idea about how to spend some of it. Le Corbusier could design either two or four small houses on the land next to her Connecticut mansion, all one-story dwellings like La Petite Maison, which had first attracted her to his work and thus led to their meeting in Vevey. The houses would face the water and fit in with the large rocks and trees there. She would create an artists' colony, lending or renting these modest residences to worthy people.

If only Le Corbusier could come to America, just for a couple of days, to make a master plan. "You know that I'm a person of action, and this time I have the money to realize those dreams," his lover assured him. It was a good investment; she knew young architects who would help; it would be a "little project, gay and simple and good."[36] Her brother, who was converting the larger of two garages into his own house, agreed to the idea.

Tjader Harris would fund his air ticket so that he could come right away; it was no problem if he used the free trip for more important matters: "May God guide your response and may all creation be made by Him and with Him and for Him."

LE CORBUSIER was amused by Marguerite Tjader Harris's proposition but could not entertain it. "You Americans are extraordinary, men and women both!" he responded. He had ideas for these houses but had constant travel ahead and too much work in every direction as it was.

On the other hand, how could he refuse her even if she lived in the greediest country on earth? With one of his usual barbs at America, Le Corbusier declaimed, "I'd be delighted to draw up these plans for you if such a project didn't depend on the future collapse of your dear country's industrial stocks, i.e., a depression whose effect would be to stick us with the same damn collapse over here! Once again, I'm at your disposal if you give me the time I need, i.e., at least a year."[37] He also suggested that she approach José Luis Sert about the project and advised her to tell Sert she had little money.

Unaware that this was merely his recommendation for a tactical maneuver, Tjader Harris wrote back that he must have misunderstood what she said, since she could easily afford the four houses that, to use his word, would enable her to construct a "Unité." "On the contrary, I have so much money now that I can't imagine how to do anything reasonable," she wrote.[38] Moreover, like him, she had lost faith in the capitalist system; therefore she did not want her funds in investments.

Tjader Harris was willing to wait for the moment when he might come, however briefly, so that they could realize the dream with which their relationship had been initiated in the early thirties: "I'd like them to be *Cor-*

busier houses . . . 4 little houses at one with the site: the rocks, and the sea in front of them—like the little house which you imagined for me among the vines of Lake Leman, and which never saw the light of day."[39] If he was en route to South America, she would fetch him from the airport in New York, so he could spend at least two days with her. If it were in September, the sea would still be warm, the large house nearly empty.

Le Corbusier replied that he was developing a housing prototype in Roquebrune-Cap-Martin that might serve her needs. Perhaps they could find someone who could execute the idea in America—"and keep whoever it is from robbing me all over again!"[40] Her response was to insist that he at least glimpse the actual setting in Connecticut. Even if he could give her no more than a couple of hours, even if it was not until next spring, nothing would thrill her more.

11

A film was in the works about Le Corbusier's building in Marseille; he wanted Albert to compose music for it that was possessed of the inventiveness and spontaneity with which he had tried to imbue the building. Everything was to be approached in a fresh way; when Le Corbusier's friend and gallerist Denise René had no idea how to title some of his drawings in an exhibition, the artist, deliberately insouciant, proposed that they select titles from the telephone book. They named the work with street names that appealed phonetically.

Le Corbusier now wrote his mother of Marseille, "It's triumphant and triumphal. Besides, the wind is shifting and we're entering a period of enthusiasms, the opposite of the dirty tricks that have been our constant lot." Once he was in this state of mind, everything else followed. Galerie Denise René had a show of tapestries by twelve artists, with one by him, and he told his mother that "everyone claims mine is the best."[41] More books by and about him were coming out right and left.

That July, Le Corbusier went to Corsica, where he had a meeting in Ajaccio to discuss a project along the lines of the one in Marseille and the second Unité d'Habitation he was designing for Nantes. Again he wrote Yvonne to convince her of his devotion, while begging plaintively that she go easy on him: "I'm writing this letter with all my heart. . . . You still don't realize how deeply you've been anchored in my heart all these years—my guardian angel. You're constantly in my thoughts—at home or away. Each time I return home I find you as beautiful as ever—or even, as we grow older, more beautiful still. There's something extraordinary in your face. You know perfectly well—I keep telling you—that I discover it anew each time, and I look for your wonderful smile, sometimes hard to find. Why should that be? You must smile, my darling, and smile at your man who is a soldier on the battlefield from morning to night and all his life long. I'm overwhelmed by all I have on my mind, and all I must do, the commitments I've made and the duties I must fulfill with regard to others. I must constantly give and produce, I'm not allowed to fail."[42]

Le Corbusier wanted her to appreciate his having stopped to work on their getaway at Roquebrune-Cap-Martin before going to Corsica, but it wasn't easy to placate a wife who was now completely fed up with his absences. With another of his bizarre analogies, he reminded her that for thirty years he had always returned to Paris, "like the cab-horse to the manger, galloping and (silently) whinnying for joy."[43] Never over all those years had she seen him look regretful when he was with her. Now, with their new house, he hoped she would start smiling again.

Beyond struggling to appease an unhappy wife, Le Corbusier was also battling to salvage his role in the UNESCO project. He wrote his mother that August was "the Lamp of Sacrifice!"[44] It's unlikely that she understood this reference to John Ruskin, but she was meant to appreciate his martyrdom.

12

That August, the *cabanon* came into being. At last, Le Corbusier could compensate Yvonne for her loneliness on the rue Nungesser-et-Coli. Here, she could have her husband all to herself and drink her pastis in view of her birthplace. He had built a low-cost masterpiece that honored her innocence and simplicity and her affinity for nature. The joy was immense for both of them.

After Le Corbusier had made his sketches in those pivotal forty-five minutes on December 31, 1951, he had taken the plan back to 35 rue de Sèvres. Those first renditions for the *cabanon* look like late Mondrian sketches more than architectural blueprints, but the abstract flurry was not hard to translate into something that could be built. Minimal lodging had always been an obsession of Le Corbusier's; here, he took it to a new extreme, with exterior walls that would simply be pine planks nailed onto a wood frame, with a roof constructed of tiles of "fibro-cement."

Le Corbusier had the main elements prefabricated in Ajaccio—another reason for the trip to Corsica—and dry-mounted on-site. He had arranged with his friend Claudius-Petit to have all the materials brought by special train, routinely making the last leg of the journey between 2:00 and 4:00 a.m., when the tracks were free from normal use. Locals did the simple construction and electrical work. Thomas Rebutato put in the plumbing. The architect delighted in that rudimentary process as much as in the straightforwardness of its product and the low cost.

When Le Corbusier and Yvonne moved in on August 5, 1952, the expenses had totaled four hundred thousand francs—or approximately $6,800—for the perfect human dwelling.

13

At a glance, Le Corbusier and Yvonne's getaway in Roquebrune-Cap-Martin looks like a run-of-the-mill summer-camp cabin. The split pine logs that encase the rectangular box belong on a Swiss mountain hut or beside a Scandinavian lake. Le Corbusier had chosen them at the last minute, a replacement for the siding he had initially planned. This rough sheathing is not what one expects to find at the edge of the Mediterranean.

For Le Corbusier, it must have felt like home, but for the visitor it is startling. Nothing prepares you for its utter simplicity. Most people expect glistening surfaces, jazzy ramps, and bands of windows framed in taut steel. Having arrived in the town of Roquebrune, they take the footpath—the only means by which the *cabanon* is accessible—imagining at least some kinship to the known classics of modernism. They discover that the architect of the Villa Savoye, the modern palace at Garches, and the monuments of Chandigarh himself lived in the equivalent of a solid pup tent.

Tucked into the hillside where the sound of the surf is continuous, the deliberately rough and austere *cabanon* appears completely lacking in design. The chestnut door seems haphazard in relation to the split pine logs. But the coarseness and randomness befit the task of the house, which was to confront the demands of earthly life.

Basically, the *cabanon* was an add-on to the Rebutatos' little restaurant, to which it was joined by a doorway. It was a highly unusual living arrangement, as if Le Corbusier were annexing another family's daily existence. By building his getaway so that it shared a wall with the restaurant, the architect was joining himself to a place where they could have lunch and dinner every day, where they could even shower. With the complicity of the former plumber and his wife, Le Corbusier was also guaranteeing a degree of caretaking for himself and Yvonne as he was for the house—a private "assisted living" arrangement. This, too, was a way of facing the truth.

If we did not know that the *cabanon* was made by a world-famous architect at the peak of his power and international success, it would not seem so profound and moving. But this bare-bones dwelling, perfectly encapsulating the essence of human needs—with a consciousness and deliberateness so bold as to be perverse—is completely poetic.

THE SUNSHINE that August was superb as Le Corbusier and Yvonne settled into their dream house. The property Rebutato had sold them was dominated by an enormous fig tree that kept it cool in the shade; everything was perfect. "Our seaside *cabanon,* 3.66 meters by 3.66, is a masterpiece," Le Corbusier wrote his mother on August 20.[45] With its height of 226 centimeters, it corresponded perfectly to the dictates of the Modulor.

When Le Corbusier and Yvonne were standing outside of the *cabanon,* the only sound they could hear—unless there were people dining at l'Etoile de Mer or the Rebutatos were cleaning up after a meal—was the sea lapping on the rocks below. Most of the time, a coastal breeze wafted through the open windows and the cracks between the boards. The garden contained cacti, cypress trees, and lemon trees, their blossoms giving off a pungent smell.

It was a tough walk down a narrow path to the pebbly beach. There were train tracks only twenty meters or so away from the *cabanon,* but even the cars clanking by did not bother Le Corbusier and Yvonne. In this pocket of nature, the architect may have enjoyed a reminder of Alfortville and of steel and speed. And if the walking was difficult for his lame wife, for him it demanded the physical vitality essential to healthy living.

LE CORBUSIER had seen similar structures ever since he had stayed in hikers' shelters with his father, brother, and mother on their Alpine outings. When he traveled on Mount Athos, he had come to know the crude dwellings for those monks who wanted solitude while facing the infinite horizon separating sea from sky. Now, on his own modest parcel of land, Le Corbusier designed a structure where, similarly, you entered with the sea behind you. Then you turned around in the living room and faced the view through a large window.

It's debatable whether the proportions and placement of the other windows represent complete eccentricity or a strong sense of purpose. These openings vary from thin vertical slits to perfect squares. They are all of a simple type known as "*summer-banin,*" consisting of glass panels, framed in wood, that open outward and are hinged on one side while having a large latch on the other, with wooden shutters for protection against winter storms. Some are as small as peepholes, others ample.

To be inside the *cabanon* is like being in a monk's cell; there is denial, a call to work, and also one to contemplation. The minimal furniture announces life's essential activities as writing, eating, washing, sleeping, and, perhaps above all else, thinking. There are no soft surfaces.

The fittings are as functional and purposeful as those in a train car or boat cabin, or on board an airplane, even if the space is not quite as tight or compact. The cabinets, shelves, and drawers are built in, and there is suitcase storage abutting the painted ceiling. The stainless-steel sink is determinedly small, and the simple light fixtures are frankly purposeful. The plain bunk that served as Yvonne's bed has the toilet enclosure right next to it—separated not by a wall but only by a red curtain. That red is the scarlet of a theatre curtain, as if to announce a spectacle on the other side. The wall next to the plain white porcelain toilet is a vibrant green. These bold colors—the floor is painted a golden yellow, the ceiling panels in bright hues—confront the neutral tone of the rudimentary plywood of which the room is made.

The rigor and the deliberate economy and sparseness provide a rich experience—akin to that offered by an apple, the unadorned fruit of the earth with its delicious flavors and textures made only by nature. Along the south wall—the front of the *cabanon,* its side nearest the sea—the table for writing and eating juts out as a simple plane at a right angle, clearly stating its purposes like the energetic dining tables at Mount Athos. It is supported by one leg, a miniature piloti. Its top made from olive wood, a tribute to the splendors of the Mediterranean forest, has the sort of low-cost opulence that Le Corbusier interjected even in the most austere of worlds (see color plate 13).

Details within the simple *cabanon* encapsulate various sides of Le Corbusier's creative life. The door handles suit a factory—his streamlined, straightforward, practical, industrial aspect. The entrance door, only seventy centimeters wide, reveals his infatuation with trains and ships. His Rabelaisian side also looms large. The modest dwelling, after all, was a love song to his wife and to male/female sexual magnetism. There is the powerful presence of sex, although it is relegated to the wooden window shutters, which are painted with figurative imagery and decorative patterns that are a mix of bawdy humor, Matissean joy, and Picasso's painterly evocation of the libido. The subject of one is mainly a penis, the other a vagina. They bring sensualism into the monastery; if the act of sex was no longer practiced within the house, those murals put the pleasure of cavorting in broad sunlight and give it primal power rather than make it illicit.

Abutting those colorful murals, hinged to the shutters as their other wings, are mirrors: the vehicle for looking at one's self physically and a metaphor for psychological exploration. The house is all about the act of looking—intensely and with maximum clarity—at nature, at the fundamentals of human habitation, at the organs of human reproduction, at the self. But above all else, the getaway provided a calm communion with the splendors of the earth and cosmos.

This simple hut is surrounded by exotic trees called *caroubiers.* The air is redolent with honeysuckle. If the murals suggest Adam and Eve, this is the garden of Eden.

14

Fifteen meters from the *cabanon,* Le Corbusier eventually built a little shed for work. It was simply a construction shack covered in rolled roofing. Le Corbusier put it in place in 1954, after receiving the pieces from the Dordogne. Following the opening of an exhibition of his painting in the grand and imposing Kunsthalle in Bern, Le Corbusier flew to Nice, and then, with a young architect from his office, erected the prefab units. He wrote to his mother and brother ecstatically that August to say that this two-meter by four-meter structure was his "ideal studio royally arranged by the miracle of proportion."[46] The bigger and grander the scale on which he was building worldwide, the more modest his own needs became.

Inside the little work space, Le Corbusier had a drawing table, a stool, and a wastebasket. He also had a collection of bones lined up on shelves: some came from animals, others from human beings. The sea breeze drifted in through the two windows and the slots underneath the roof. He wanted nothing more. Here, he could focus on the essentials of habitation.

IN THE *CABANON* and this work shed less than a minute's walk away, Le Corbusier had created his dream compound. Stripped down, devoid of cushiness, the living and working spaces were a reduction to diamond-hard truths.

In spite of the total disparity of scale, Taliesin West, the elaborate village in Arizona where Frank Lloyd Wright spent the last years of his life, reflects many of the same desires. So did the small lakeside house in which Alvar Aalto ended his days in central Finland. These very different masters of modern architecture all sought proximity to pure nature, to what was universal. Their chosen environments offered uninterrupted views of spectacular geological formations, of the earth as it was carved by melting glaciers.

Le Corbusier belongs to the tradition of complex thinkers who ultimately wished to pare down the ingredients of their own lives. Palms and lemons, the sea and the sky, what one needs to live and nothing more: this was what counted. The architect's legacy would be pretentious white villas in East Hampton, Long Island, and other chic watering holes—the antitheses of this simple *cabanon.* But the rudimentary dwelling overlooking the Mediterranean indicates who he really was and what he cared about.

Here one feels the perpetual presence of the sun in all its life-giving power. By day, this force that does not change or alter its position, the sun, is there as the giver of heat and light; at night, it lingers via the moonlight and the reflection of that light on the water. The deliberately simple architecture of the *cabanon* recedes before Le Corbusier's deity. And because the austere hut does not distract or conspicuously announce its presence, it serves to facilitate contemplation, reverie, and joy.

Few people could dare to pare things down so extremely, to return to the scale of childhood. Sartre in his small apartment, Giacometti in his plain studio—these existentialists partook of this same drive to get to the essence of life and to divest themselves of all that is superfluous. Like Le Corbusier, they also enjoyed being perceived for their deliberate rejection of bourgeois comforts. The refutation of majority values, the self-conscious alliance with peasant life, was intentional. Le Corbusier called the *cabanon* his "*château*" or "*palace*"; he was making a point.

Looking out of the small windows or standing on the modest terrace in front of the *cabanon,* facing the large bay or the open sea, one has the sense of being nearer the cosmos, of being part of what has been here for ages and should be here ages from now, whatever other changes have occurred on earth. Even with the views from the terraces and roof at rue Nungesser-et-Coli, one cannot forget the frantic getting and spending of the city as one can here on the Mediterranean. The man obsessed with urbanism always saw the importance of connecting to the eternal beauties.

15

At Roquebrune-Cap-Martin, four miles from her birthplace, Yvonne could spend her time joking with the Rebutatos or bantering with the local fishermen, who also spoke with her rough Monegasque accent. She enjoyed the *rougets, dorades,* and the inevitable sea urchins that had been the greatest luxury of her youth.

Yvonne became famous in the region for her eccentric generosity. She and Le Corbusier periodically dined at one of the nearby seafood restaurants, more upmarket than l'Etoile de Mer, where she invariably doled out packets of cigarettes to the uniformed busboys and waitresses and the maître d'hôtel; this was her trademark quirk wherever she went. Back in her element, she gave signs of her former colorful self. Compared to his frugal, pious mother and Aunt Pauline, Yvonne, with her heart-shaped lips and jet-black hair, her Monegasque swagger, her bawdy jokes and flirtatious quips, and her insistent need to make gifts, was as exotic as the hibiscus in their garden.

LE CORBUSIER developed certain routines during that first summer in the *cabanon* that he was to follow for the rest of his life. From time to time, he went into the bustling principality of Monaco—often in the company of a visitor, like his new admirer Jean Petit. Le Corbusier did most of the talking, holding forth on his history as an architect, and then interrupting himself to savor the beauty of one or another old yacht in the harbor. He and Yvonne and their visitors periodically spent afternoons in Roquebrune, at the base of Mont Agel, and walked around the grounds of the historic château where Le Corbusier particularly admired the large roots of an ancient olive tree: "Le Corbusier was interested in everything," he wrote of himself. "He kept observing, always seeking some wonder of Nature, which would constantly leave on his path a lovely rock, a root, or else, on the beach, a pebble different from any other pebble."[47]

On one occasion, when Jean Petit accompanied him to the post office, they had to wait for an urgent piece of mail that was late in arriving from Paris. Le Corbusier sat down and began to chat; on holiday, he was far more relaxed than when confronted with similar tardiness in Paris. He began to observe everything: the people coming in and out of the post office, the details of the architecture. He turned to Petit: "Look: on the floor of this little hall there's a medley of all kinds of stones that just delights me. The mason who made this was an artist: the pattern of the stones changes in every direction. To make such things we must return to the sources of the Mind (and of play), regardless of the artifices of professional artists who usually reveal the trappings of pretension or affectation."[48]

He preferred this, of course, to any hint of the academy or stifled bourgeois taste.

16

The photographer Brassaï visited Le Corbusier during his first summer in the *cabanon.* Twenty years earlier, Brassaï had called on Le Corbusier and Yvonne on the rue Jacob. On that occasion, Brassaï had "expected to find an ultramodern apartment with huge expanses of window and bare, brightly lit walls, an apartment similar to the ones he had designed for the millionaire Charles de Beistegui, the painter Ozenfant, the sculptor Lipchitz, and many others. Imagine my surprise when I entered a fairly messy apartment crammed with odd pieces of furniture and a weird collection of bric-a-brac."[49] Now that he was entering the *cabanon,* Brassaï mentally reviewed the history of Le Corbusier and Yvonne and their homes.

The photographer remembered Yvonne with tears in her eyes explaining why they were leaving that cluttered love nest: "Corbu has finally had enough of all the sarcastic remarks people make about it. . . . [H]e wants to live in a Le Corbusier building." After seeing the rue Nungesser-et-Coli apartment for the first time, even before moving there, she had lamented to Brassaï, "You can't imagine what it's like! A hospital, a dissecting lab! I'll never get used to it."[50]

Now, even though Yvonne was surrounded by marvelous trees in Roquebrune-Cap-Martin—aloes, acanthus, mimosas, eucalyptus—and living in what Le Corbusier hoped would be her paradise, she still groused. The moment their old friend arrived, Yvonne greeted him by exclaiming, "Brassaï, you're a witness, just look at the cell my husband keeps me in . . . just look! He makes me sleep on the floor in a bathroom next to the washbasin. . . . I wonder how I've managed to live for twenty years with this fanatic and put up with all his crazy notions."[51]

Le Corbusier, on the other hand, was as proud of the prefabricated wooden building as of Chandigarh or l'Unité d'Habitation. He quickly told Brassaï that he had taken out a patent on it. He had, he said, first had the idea for it on a steamship, where he had had a cabin of the same dimensions. He had replicated the two beds, the folding furniture, and the utilities.

Le Corbusier was especially pleased with the handsome washbasin in the middle of the room and the toilet arrangement. He pointed out to Brassaï that there were vents on opposite sides to evacuate odors. He demonstrated how the mirror next to the washbasin opened to a long vertical slit of glassless window, a further way of letting out bathroom smells.

After Le Corbusier showed Brassaï around the tiny house, the two walked down the path to the shore so they could take a swim together. Afterward, they sat on the rocks, chatting to the sound of the pounding waves. The sixty-four-year-old Le Corbusier was proud of his good health. He told Brassaï that a few weeks earlier he had run one hundred meters in twenty seconds. Le Corbusier was delighted that, when he had boasted of this to his doctor, the doctor had told him he was mad.

The doctor had reminded Le Corbusier that his arteries were not the same as when he was eighteen. Le Corbusier quoted the medical professional saying, "If you strain them, you'll explode. You have to come to terms with your age."[52] Le Corbusier believed, on the other hand, that, like his mother, he was different from other people. They were both heartier and unaffected by the vicissitudes of time.

Then, in a change of humor, the architect told Brassaï he would face reality. He would treat his arteries like water pipes in a building, as part of the machinery that had to be maintained. Out of respect for that machinery, he had now given up all other sports except for swimming, which he confined to half an hour per day.

Le Corbusier was scribbling while speaking. On sheets of paper that Brassaï treasured ever after, the architect noted the key events of his life, giving prime importance to his visit to Ema in 1907. He termed the Italian monastery "a harmonious synthesis of individual and group." Le Corbusier also used the occasion to qualify his myths. He told Brassaï that the expression "machine for living" had become "somewhat distorted. What did I mean by 'a machine for living'? Simple: the optimum return in terms of function and furnishings."[53] Even as he moved full speed ahead, Le Corbusier was determined to sum up and edit his past.

RELAXING ON THE ROCKS, Le Corbusier was in a reflective mood: "You asked me if I was a contented man," he said. "Yes, I have managed to make some of the ideas I most valued into reality, but think of all my plans that have never been realized. All my life, I have had to struggle very hard. Often, I was literally crushed! Even now, almost every one of my plans arouses some violent reaction. I'm insulted, I'm treated like a barbarian, a madman, a dreamer, a man without heart, an iconoclast, an antichrist. I am denounced either as a tool of Lenin or a capitalist lackey. In either case, I'm a destroyer."[54]

Le Corbusier told Brassaï that architects were the most competitive and rivalrous people on earth, worse than all other professionals: "You've no idea of the intrigues, the baseness, the outright cruelty. They'd strangle you with their bare hands to get a commission. Because it always entails a great deal of money. I know what I'm talking about!"[55] Le Corbusier was more convinced than ever that the greed for financial gain was the source of much of the evil in the world.

This led him to the issue of the UN: "The Americans did everything they could to exclude me from its actual construction so that they themselves could derive all the moral satisfaction and material benefits from its construction . . . today world public opinion attributes my plan to the American architect Wallace K. Harrison."[56]

Then, as the sun began to set behind the rock known as the "*Tête de chien,*" above Monte Carlo, and a cool breeze wafted in from Corsica, Le Corbusier and Brassaï walked back up to the *cabanon.* Le Corbusier ended the conversation by saying, "I'm so comfortable in my *cabanon* that I'll probably end my days here."[57] It was one plan no one else could foil.

XLV

You can gather together all the words in the world, all the pretty colors and dappled lights, all the finest and fittest people, every good and noble intention, and you can place this assemblage on a page or a stage, but that is technical, that is craftsmanship. I need the introduction of the heart; I need to see and to feel some blood; I need to rub against some warm flesh. In the name of God, touch my heart. At that point, there is art.

—LE CORBUSIER AS PARAPHRASED BY TENNESSEE WILLIAMS[1]

1

As Le Corbusier's mother approached her supposed ninety-third birthday on September 11, 1952, her younger son assured her that even if she and he barked at each other, in the end they loved each other. In early October, just prior to his own sixty-fifth birthday, he told her that when he recently went to Venice for the first international arts conference organized by UNESCO, thirty people greeted him at the train station, and the auditorium was packed when he gave a lecture. Afterward, he returned to Roquebrune-Cap-Martin, where Yvonne was in the "miraculous *cabanon.*"[2] Life was perfect.

The crowning glory would be to have his mother and brother in Marseille for the official opening of l'Unité. Marie Jeanneret had never gotten there after falling off the ladder, and Le Corbusier anticipated the opening as one of the ultimate moments not just of his life but of hers, as if she was personally responsible for the new apartment building. He wrote, "Maman and Albert: I'll be proud to show you around Marseille, but this will be above all a testimony to our loving solidarity, a proof of our mutual effort in life."[3]

The official invitation was addressed to Albert and his mother as "Monsieur et Madame Jeanneret"—as if they were a couple. Yet even if Edouard was the outsider, what a joy it would be to have them with him in the spotlight.

2

Le Corbusier's idea of the ideal human habitation was centered on the idea that women were responsible for food, and food was the essence of a family's existence. He had made a design in which food preparation, cooking, and washing up could be done within a space measuring two meters by two meters, so that "the housewife's legs, at the end of the day, will not be swollen with fatigue." He conceived of the home as a haven in which that kitchen was central: "One has come in from the world outside . . . to find the ancient 'fire,' the 'hearth' of all traditions. The housewife is at her oven preparing the food: the family surrounds her, father and children. All of them are around the 'fire' spending that time of day which consecrates the very institution of the family: mealtime."[4]

His ideal also called for a living-room space open to the outside and filled with sunlight. This would be possible thanks to his *brises-soleil* . . . "this portico, this loggia, this sun-screen." He linked its design to Socrates, crediting it with "connecting the most modern architecture to the most ancient traditions" and permitting "the inhabitants of the house to enjoy the pleasures the Good Lord dispenses to mankind . . . coolness in summer, warmth in winter."[5] Everyday domestic spaces were to be chapels to facilitate the connection with nature.

L'Unité d'Habitation was to be but one example of this housing type that Le Corbusier termed a "Virgilian dream." He believed its application was universal. Since it fulfilled basic human needs—"sociability, mutual assistance, protection, security, economy"—it could serve almost any location.[6]

To illustrate how his ideal housing units would be connected, Le Corbusier sketched a pair of six-story buildings on pilotis. There are trees in the foreground, foliage on the roof, birds flying above, mountain profiles behind, and the sun smiling on the assemblage. He wrote that whereas post-war housing had already become "the monstrosity of tentacular concentrations represented today by the cities of machine civilization," this "vertical commune" created the alternative possibility of a "village" built according to human scale.[7] Roads would be for cars only; there would be other paths solely for pedestrians.

Le Corbusier's vision was romantic and utopian. With "the friendly soil . . . [b]ody and mind . . . will flourish in the sun, in space and in greenery." The new network for transportation and walking was "a system of blood vessels, a lymphatic system, a respiratory system."[8] He amplified in detail his notion of walkways and highways, streets with shops, and multiple vertical villages linked by roads, which he compared to the routes that connected villages in ancient times.

The new homes concurrently proliferating in American suburbs were, by contrast, "that great extravagance of modern times." Le Corbusier believed that the American model burdened housewives twenty-four hours per day, requiring excessive driving and causing a "great diffusion of panic."[9] The architect credited his own concept with bringing people together and providing a physically close community, while at the same time establishing a vital link to the natural world.

DURING ONE of his visits to the site in Marseille, as he put the finishing touches on, the engineers told him that the design for the roof of the gymnasium was flawed and that it would develop cracks. The architect replied, "What would have happened if God had done this and the cracks appeared?" He explained that if there were cracks, they could conceal them with paint; "things will always go wrong some place, but we can always find alternatives. If you have an idea, you must pursue it." Of his ideal housing types, he explained, "It is God who has brought them into the world."[10]

3

Marie and Albert Jeanneret did not make the trip to Marseille, but one of Yvonne's few public appearances was for the opening of l'Unité d'Habitation. The long-awaited event took place on October 14, 1952. Le Corbusier's sixty-fifth birthday, eight days before, had been an easier passage than usual for him, because of the impending occasion.

The invitation to the official ceremonies was as pioneering in its graphics as the building was in its architecture. A swirling, tiptoed abstract form—an amalgam of a Modulor drawing and the interlocking ovals Le Corbusier had drawn for the start of his mother's fourth decade—dominates the card. Its ascending, steamlike twisting ribbons give a sense of the future being born. The text is set in a light, contemporary typeface—a squared-off sans serif—arranged on the page as imaginatively as bookshelves in a Le Corbusier house or the balcony railings he made for Ozenfant, similarly using only a few simple elements to create a lively, delightful rhythm. It also organizes visual information so that it drives home its message. The date—and nothing else—is in bold type, declaring the day a major historical event.

L'Unité d'Habitation in Marseille, ca. 1952

At the appointed time, five hundred guests assembled at street level. Many came from Paris; arriving in the city that opposed Henri IV and infuriated Louis XIV for its "impulses of independence" and knowing Le Corbusier's daring, they expected the act of rebellion they would find. All of Le Corbusier's office staff was there to observe the results of their years of labor.

What appeared on the boulevard Michelet that Tuesday at 10:00 a.m. was a turning point in the history of how human beings live. The triumphant building was unlike anything that had ever existed before. Its north and south facades were as complex as the moment when every instrument is heard simultaneously in Charles-Edouard Jeanneret's beloved Tchaikovsky symphonies, the mix of notes creating a harmony and force that pushes aside reason and intellect and reduces the listener to a state of sensuous absorption. The great horizontal mass of concrete, with its staccato march of vertical supports, its seemingly infinite openings of varying sizes, and its complex visual sequences, is as alive as anything that has ever been created out of a so-called inert material (see color plate 11).

It was, in some ways, the natural descendant of the facade of 25 bis rue Franklin—the Perret brothers' marvelous 1902–1904 testimony to the stunning variety that could be achieved with reinforced concrete. But the energy of l'Unité and its sheer size put it in a completely different league. It is distinguished by the absolute modernism of its appearance, derived

The pilotis at l'Unité d'Habitation in Marseille

entirely from functional and structural elements. Except for engraved images of the Modulor, there is not an iota of naturalistic ornament or decoration—at the same time that there is a total connection to nature itself. Why imitate or offer a facsimile of what is at the core of a building's being?

For all of its mass, the apartment building in Marseille stands easily and lightly on its graceful legs. The pilotis elevate it with acrobatic skill. One becomes aware of air circulating not just above and around the great structure but also beneath it. Le Corbusier had created the quality of one of those ocean liners that had intoxicated him as a young man. L'Unité is a self-contained floating city that appears as if it has just arrived and could take off instantly.

Le Corbusier had experienced physical love most ecstatically surrounded by sea and sky—not tethered to the earth in the confines of a city. The shack in Darien, the *Lutétia,* and the aeries that he had initially known with Yvonne—atop 20 rue Jacob or overlooking Paris on rue Nungesser-et-Coli—were the settings of his own peaks of aliveness. These were places where gravity was briefly transcended. The haunting passage of time seemed momentarily to halt; sensuous pleasure subsumed all other feelings. This was why music remains the perfect metaphor for Le Corbusier's work: weightless, charged, and orgasmic.

4

At the opening ceremonies, Eugène Claudius-Petit, the government minister who had made this possible, gave a speech, as did the architect. Le Corbusier felt impelled to justify his creation. He might have, for a brief moment, simply allowed himself to relish what he had done. But this was not his style; he resorted, as always, to a fusillade of words.

The architect insisted that those attending the inauguration ceremony on that bright October day see the building rising before their eyes not merely as a celebration of positive forces but as the end result of a prolonged battle against opposition and oppression. He characterized himself, as usual, as the workhorse, the beaten beast of burden. If Le Corbusier had simply contemplated his achievement and said nothing at all, he might have recognized that at last he had united people with the seminal elements of the universe and have enjoyed himself in silence. For the building placed its inhabitants, in their everyday living, in direct harmony with the sea and the mountains and in as straight a connection as possible with the sky and the sun, the source of all life.

Instead Le Corbusier talked: "I want to thank the workers and contractors who have collaborated with me; my gratitude to all those who have helped us and not to those who have behaved badly. The work is here: '*Unité d'habitation* of appropriate size' built without regulations—against disastrous regulations, and made for men, made on the human scale."[11] Like a rebellious child, he wanted the world to know that he had broken the rules.

As Apollinaire said of *Parade,* that pioneering ballet of which he had attended the premiere thirty-five years earlier, this was truly "*l'esprit nouveau.*" Le Corbusier had married imagination and discipline, and, with a beat as sure as Satie's and a mastery of materials as absolute as Diaghilev's dancers' control of their limbs, he had broken all boundaries.

5

From a distance, l'Unité reads like bits and pieces of bright-hued laundry hung out in a strong wind. While irrefutably stable, it thus resembles the monastery of Lavras that Charles-Edouard Jeanneret had viewed on Mount Athos more than forty years earlier.

Then, as one approaches, one sees, to the side of the facade, Modulor figures with their raised arms stacked one on top of another. Even the person uninitiated in the thinking of Le Corbusier and unable to understand their precise meaning realizes that the main intent of all this reinforced concrete is to honor human beings.

Le Corbusier wanted people to enjoy daily pleasures; every detail of this vast apartment complex was planned with that objective. L'Unité provided families of low income with magnificent views, splendidly workable kitchens, graceful accommodations for congregating and sleeping, even a school and playground on the roof. It also used architecture to impart joy; Le Corbusier's belief in the wonder of earthly existence is palpable as one stands before the pilotis. The regular beat of those noble legs, their flawless geometry and scale echoing columns at the Parthenon, and the vibrant colors animating the neutral, whitish color of the basic shell, all in the brilliant sunlight of Marseille, are a celebration of life.

AFTER THE OPENING CEREMONY, the five hundred people present ascended the fifty-six meters to the roof in a mere thirteen minutes total. The roof is in every sense the crowning touch. Its chimneylike forms resemble gigantic exclamation points and express the unadulterated pleasure of drumrolls and leaping dancers.

Once on the roof, one walks out into the fresh sea breeze, under a sun that seems nearer and stronger than in many other places in the world. Gulls soar around your head and swoop beneath you, toward the sea. In that salubrious setting, there is an amphitheatre for theatre performances or concerts and a wading pool, surrounded by a gently curving structure of tiles decorated with anthropomorphic forms, that is an idyllic setting for children to frolic. Stairs go everywhere on this roof—the way they do in paintings by that other liberated Swiss, Paul Klee—inviting the pleasures of ascent and descent without particular purpose.

A curving sculptural chimney has wavy sides that grow wider as they ascend, with an esplanade of tiny square windows underneath its lively cap. It looks as if it has just belched an explosion of smoke.

The center tower of the roof comprises concrete units that resemble wooden logs with deeply incised graining. They by no means imitate such logs—that would have violated every principle of Ruskin's. Rather, they create a new variation of concrete. The kindergarten is composed mainly of shapes that appear like sea stones, also formed from concrete. Elsewhere, there are plain, bold, structural concrete blocks. Bright-red banisters and elevator doors and vibrant yellow water pipes animate this otherwise plaster-colored universe.

The bold, rectangular nursery is raised above the roof on especially narrow pilotis and is faced in a Byzantine pattern of vibrant mosaics. The hut-like exercise room resembles a sort of prehistoric dinosaur. There are graciously curved, seemingly organic benches scattered about, as well as free-form sculptural masses with holes punched in them; melted Bronze Age–style megaliths, they serve no purpose other than the one Claudius-Petit had pointed out in his speech: musical luxuriance.

The roof is like a wild tropical garden where, in keeping with Le Corbusier's horticultural advice to his mother, nothing has been weeded out. Everything, however unusual or unexpected, has been allowed to thrive. The myriad elements perpetually combine, move apart, and recombine to provide a sublime sense of well-being.

In reinforced concrete, a material that endures and withstands all change, Le Corbusier had evoked the glorious and otherwise fleeting aliveness of youth—and he had provided vitality and sheer fun for the inhabitants of the great and singular city below.

On the first floor of the building, there was a so-called commercial street, with a coiffeur, sauna, a small grocery shop, a butcher shop, a bakery, and a pastry shop. On the upper floors, along the corridors, which Le Corbusier also called "streets," the apartment doors and mailboxes are painted in vibrant primary yellows and blues and orangey reds, accented in bold dark greens, with no predictable pattern; what could be ordinary is intensely animated. Beside each door there is a box for milk, bread, and the daily newspaper; rather than sitting weightily on the ground, this simple vessel for morning deliveries is cantilevered off the wall, opening on the other side directly into the apartment. Le Corbusier has imbued the details of daily existence with charm and cheerfulness of unprecedented form.

6

It is from the residents that one best understands, today, the value of Le Corbusier's building in Marseille. The effect it actually has had on the lives of its inhabitants and the sense of personal connection many of them feel with its creator, more than half a century after he designed their homes, testify to its success.

Gisèle Gambu-Moreau, who was born at l'Unité just after it opened, grew up with the knowledge that Le Corbusier had volunteered to be the godfather of the first baby born there. Since she was that baby, he was part of her legacy—although they maintained no direct connection, and Le Corbusier told his mother that Gambu-Moreau's mother, the wife of a military pilot, had asked him to assume the honor, not the other way around. Regardless, in the summer of 1965, when, at age twelve, she was on the roof, running around the wading pool in her bathing suit and playing with her friends, and she heard the news of Le Corbusier's death, she was as devastated as if he had been a family member.

When her parents moved in, the building was officially a "*habitation à loyer modéré*"—a low-rent building for people with moderate salaries. It instantly provided them with living spaces that were far more capacious than they had dared dream. Their apartment was unimaginably splendid, as were the building's facilities. The children in l'Unité were perpetually in the youth club, playing Ping-Pong and basketball. People like Gambu-Moreau's parents were regulars at the cinema club. They often attended events in the large hall that was available to residents for big parties and weddings, and they used the small hotel on the lower floors of the complex as accommodations for visiting relatives. It was miraculous to have all of this accessible under one roof.

By the time Gambu-Moreau was a young adult, the building had changed and become more of a midprice-range building. In better economic circumstances herself, she decided the setting was so ideal that she would bring up her own children there. In turn, one of her daughters took an apartment in l'Unité at the time of *her* marriage. Shortly thereafter, the daughter gave birth to the first of the building's fourth-generation residents.

Gambu-Moreau talks animatedly about the wonder of "people living together. . . . It was and is paradise for children because they feel safe and the parents feel safe."[12] As a child, she felt sorry for friends with wonderful villas elsewhere in Marseille because they needed permission to go out. "We could get together all the time," she recalls. At night, if two couples wanted to play cards, rather than hire a babysitter, they would take their children along and have them fall asleep in their friends' apartment, knowing that, whatever the weather, it was only a short walk home indoors with the sleeping children. "When two old ladies became widows, they did not feel lonely as they might in some other place; for people of every age, this was the utopian ideal of community living," she said.

LIKE ALL THE APARTMENTS in l'Unité, Gambu-Moreau's home is a duplex. In hers, the downstairs is oriented to the west and faces the mountains, while the upstairs faces east, toward the sea. With Le Corbusier's design of interlocking spaces, the reverse is true in half of the apartments. Both landscapes feel near, not as views but more as if they are joined to the interior through the glass walls protected by *brises-soleil.*

The floors of the apartment are all oak, the walls white, the trim, in keeping with Le Corbusier's original scheme, varied and bright. Gambu-Moreau is pleased with all the details. Every apartment has a diaper-changing station; there are two sinks in the children's bedrooms; sliding doors between the bedrooms have blackboards on them. The storage units under the sink basins and other details of the kitchen, all designed by Charlotte Perriand, have a rare charm.

Gambu-Moreau does not gloss over problems. She is aware that many of the subcontractors were skeptical about "Le Fada"'s building. In the fifties, especially, many people considered it ugly because of its stilts and quibbled about problems like the interior surfaces of the double-glazed windows, where there was dust that could never be cleaned. But for Gambu-Moreau's extended family, the apartments, with light coming in from both directions and everyday needs beautifully accommodated, have provided inestimable well-being.

7

This, anyway, was the view from within l'Unité. The reputation of the building abroad was less laudatory.

Americans had followed the development of the pioneering residential skyscraper through the mainstream press, especially *Time* magazine. In 1948, *Time* had reported that the French government had lifted rationing on concrete and steel for the seventeen-story structure because the building was to be a national model. Although the magazine said the building would be a "happy hive," much in the article makes Le Corbusier sound crazy. He is quoted as saying, "Men are so stupid, I'm glad I'm going to die." "Should we burn down the Louvre?" Roman architecture was "the damnation of the half educated." "Skyscrapers are veritable prisons. They suffocate their inmates, deprive them of sun and air." He allegedly claimed, "There will be no quarrels between neighbors and no divorces in my house."[13]

Two years later, when the magazine gave an update now that there was a furnished apartment at l'Unité, it called the apartment "cramped" and echoed a Marseille paper in reporting that the building for just over three hundred families was to cost more than what it would have taken to construct six hundred "nice little private houses." Le Corbusier sounds like a complete crackpot discussing the everyday existences of the residents of the three-million-dollar project: "Why do you want sunshine in the bathroom when you are in it only in the morning and at night? . . . What's wrong with the smell of food if the cooking is good?"[14]

Le Corbusier is cited as having motives of which few readers would have grasped the significance. "My mother was the slave of the little house," he said. His new apartment type was its alternative, fulfilling his wish "to make life as luxurious as a first-class cabin on an ocean liner." No reader of *Time* in 1950 would have realized that in essence what the architect wanted was to have his mother in the setting he had shared with Josephine Baker.

Seven months later, in yet another article on the building, *Time* took to mocking French living in general. The cramped quarters and prevalent cooking smells are emphasized, the windowless kitchens deemed a problem for housewives who, according to the magazine, had the habit of throwing their garbage onto the streets. And the lack of wine cellars in the apartments is cited as "the most serious flaw of all."[15] On this subject, Le Corbusier is quoted as saying that the tenants had a grocery where they could buy their wines each day; he proposes that if they were dissatisfied, they could "go and live elsewhere."[16]

Such was the general perception, at least in America, of l'Unité d'Habitation: an unlivable, too costly folly built by an arrogant despot for people in a decadent, unruly civilization. It was pretty much what Le Corbusier had come to expect from the out-of-control country on the other side of the Atlantic.

8

The morning after the ceremonies in Marseille, Le Corbusier and Yvonne returned to Paris.

Le Corbusier was not yet falling into the blues that beset him after each pinnacle. The depression was to come later, once the critics had a go at him. For now, he needed to make sure his mother, after not making the journey, at least understood her seminal role in his triumph.

In an almost perfunctory way, Le Corbusier wrote, "Returned this morning to Paris. Yesterday a great day. We missed you terribly. It was very beautiful." That telegraphic opening style led him to proclaim with characteristic frenzy that the building was, quite simply, "one of the great works of architecture (of any period)—moving by day and magical by night."[17]

Le Corbusier went on to describe the ceremony. For once, a public event was everything for which one might have hoped: "perfect, noble, affecting,

Albert and Marie Jeanneret playing music together at the Villa Le Lac in the late 1950s

stirred by emotion and sensibility, pride and dignity." The minister had made a beautiful speech. What mattered above all was that "in his very first words he told me that the origins of my art were revealed by the dedication of the 'White Cathedrals': '*to my mother.*' It is Mme. Jeanneret-Perret's music which accounts for the art of L-C."[18]

To Le Corbusier, the word "music" meant not just the qualities of mathematical orderliness and rhythm and melodic charm. Beyond that, in her piano teaching and playing, Marie had demonstrated the ability of sensory and aesthetic experience to impart profound pleasure. Greater still, his mother's "music" was the act of having brought him into the world. All that was needed now was for Marie Charlotte Amélie Jeanneret-Perret herself to enjoy both her son's success and this public acknowledgment.

Le Corbusier painted a vivid picture for his mother of the festivities that followed the speeches, the rush of compliments, and congratulatory telegrams from all over the world: "When the festive wines flowed, one woman after the next came to embrace me: the tenants of the building. I went with them to see how things were going several times, it was amazing; the men all bless me saying they're in paradise."[19]

The building looked spectacular lit up at night. The park on the roof was splendid, the gardens sublime. But the joy of the people living in it was what thrilled Le Corbusier above all: "Evenings and all through the night the house is magical: down below, up above, on the walls, with three windows lit. It is absolutely prodigious. The park has the splendor of noble times. And human beings are living in it as if in a mirage. The silence is complete. . . . Already the children have understood this future life under the sign of gaiety, of warm hearts."[20]

He wanted his mother and Albert to take a sleeping car from Switzerland and come see the building when conditions were calmer. Meanwhile, she could see it on the French news.

At the same time, he continued to defend his uneducated wife to his puritanical mother. "Yvonne managed to be wonderful with everyone, but especially with the workers!—a fine tribute."[21]

9

While Le Corbusier was contemplating his second, larger Unité d'Habitation in Rezé, on the outskirts of Nantes, Claudius-Petit, having given up his position as minister for reconstruction and town planning and been elected mayor of Firminy, had now commissioned a third Unité for two hundred inhabitants. All of these plans were put in jeopardy on December 15, two months and a day after the opening in Marseille, when the Seventh Correctional Tribunal of Marseille tried a case initiated by the Society for Overall Aesthetics in France.[22] Le Corbusier and the people who had hired him were accused of not having respected the most elementary rules of building construction: they had not even had a correct building permit and had violated the regulations for hygiene.

The usual rage and despair followed. However, for once, the opposition lost. The tribunal ruled against the litigious society. During the same time period, Le Corbusier was elevated to the position of commander of the Legion of Honor, and accepted.[23] Now even his enemies could not stop him.

XLVI

1

By the time Le Corbusier got the news of his victory in the lawsuit in Marseille, he was in India. He had returned to Chandigarh following the inauguration of l'Unité.

Yet again, this meant a long separation from Yvonne, who remained sequestered in their apartment. They had by now been together for more than thirty years, married for twenty-two of them; in all that time, the event in Marseille had been the only occasion of her going with him when he traveled for work.

From India, Le Corbusier wrote to her as if to a beloved child: "I hope you're having a wonderful time in that sumptuous warm apartment looking out on the snow in the street. You're a lucky girl! You can do your embroidery, read detective stories, be at peace, write to your kid [presumably young Rebutato]. In other words, freedom and happiness!"[1]

In Chandigarh, mid-1950s

Knowing Yvonne would never see the actual work in India, Le Corbusier sent her sketches of the major projects. While most photographs of Le Corbusier's High Court and other monuments focus on the buildings alone, in his quick study of it for his wife, the architect drew a number of stick figures in proximity to the form he identified as the High Court. These represented "teams of women dressed in the wildest colors, carrying in baskets on their heads the earth of the foundations and relaying each other in a chain that was like a hallucination." The drawing was in black ink, but Le Corbusier wanted Yvonne to picture the "the loveliest fabrics dyed brilliant colors."[2]

In the sketch, the famous entrance columns of the great court are no taller than those women bearing their loads. The physical reality was otherwise, but that distortion of scale was Le Corbusier's psychological truth. He did not see architecture as something that should diminish human life and impose itself as a representation of authority—as was often the case with the academic Beaux-Arts buildings he loathed. Rather, he considered building design an integral part of earthly existence that not only respected the natural setting but, equally important, accommodated rather than diminished the ordinary inhabitants of villages and cities.

2

This time, rather than commuting from Simla, Le Corbusier was living in the middle of all the bustling activity in Chandigarh. He was staying in an "extremely pleasant house" in the temporary camp for engineers and architects in the new city.[3] He wrote Yvonne about "evenings, [when] everyone sleeps under a thatch of reeds supported by two low walls, and at night the whole place fills up with children and men. This all happens on the site itself, in the dust, among bags of cement, bricks, etc., naked kids running around everywhere. The women never have a place of their own. These people are nomads."[4] Five thousand people were at work on the construction. They worked twelve hours per day, he pointed out to both Marie Jeanneret and Yvonne—reminding both his mother and wife, whose complaints tortured him, of their good fortune.

Le Corbusier imagined Yvonne's response to these local women with no place to live. " 'At least they can laugh!' says a charming woman I know in a seventh-floor walk-up," he wrote her, conjuring the good old days on the rue Jacob. He signed off with "a kiss to the loveliest girl on earth."[5]

Le Corbusier wrote Yvonne about Varma: "my friend. A broad mind, a smile: calm, precision, order. In me he finds calm as well, and I can now say:

mastery. A life dedicated to such themes has given me that. In contrast with my men here—Pierre and Fry and Drew—how fully I feel in possession of my thought."[6] Yet even if he considered himself one notch above, he was delighted with the progress his less-assured cousin had made. Pierre, who was in charge of a team of young Indian architects, was well liked. Thapar was enchanted with him. Since Le Corbusier's own house was only ten meters away from Pierre's, where there was a cook and a valet, he took his meals there.

In the past, Le Corbusier had, at the start of each major project, been totally convinced that he would change the world with it. Now, after years of reversals, he was, to his mother, more skeptical: "The work, which is all my own: the city (urbanism) then the Capitol (five palaces) will be a link in the chain of history . . . if we come to a good end, without the breaks and catastrophes which have accompanied all my undertakings."[7]

Yet the hardships that might have troubled other westerners in this hot and foreign country—the changes of food and diet, the terrible roadways, the crowds, the dirt and dust—were of no note. He had a large office with a view of cows, amiable bulls, and a well-irrigated esplanade of flowers and trees. He loved the way things were done: "All this is accomplished in an administrative calm that delights me."[8]

The sky, consistently blue, gave him confidence. And he was again—it was often the case—rereading *Don Quixote.* "One of the finest, healthiest and most masterful books that was ever written," he wrote his mother about Cervantes's magisterial portrait of a dreamer.[9]

In that mood, he wrote one of his most reverent and, at the same time, critical remarks to his wonderful, infuriating mother: "I see dear little Maman, a lioness in her lair, her face pink and glowing with joy, torn between the moon (the Moonlight Sonata) and the glorious sun of the next washday!!"[10]

FROM CHANDIGARH, Le Corbusier posted his mother a copy of a letter he had recently received. The first time he sent it was at the start of December. The document was a "Strictly Private and Confidential" declaration from the Royal Institute of British Architects that he had been unanimously elected its Royal Gold Medalist for the coming year. If he would accept the honor and if royal approval was granted, the ceremony would occur on March 31, 1953.

This was all top secret. But Le Corbusier sent it to Vevey nonetheless, with a few lines scribbled on the bottom telling "Petite Maman" he knew it would make her happy. He also underlined the word "confidential."[11] On two subsequent occasions, he mailed her identical copies. He kept sending it until he had some response.

IN MID-DECEMBER, the architect went from Chandigarh to Delhi to start work on a project he was never to realize: the National Museum of India. He then flew on to Bombay.

There, more than in the north, Le Corbusier was dumbfounded by the serious food shortages and other problems posed by population density. At a lunch gathering of people in important positions, the architect predicted that in ten to twenty years there would be seven hundred million Indians and widespread famine. Another lunch guest commented that it was essential to suppress hormones, to which Le Corbusier, livid over the imperiousness of anyone suggesting that the masses would be better off with less sexual drive, retorted, "It is hypocrisy that must be eliminated."[12]

From Bombay, the architect caught a direct flight to Paris. Landing at Orly on a Saturday, he maintained his breakneck schedule with meetings all day Sunday. On Monday, he worked at the office until the last possible minute before taking the train south to spend the Christmas holiday at Roquebrune-Cap-Martin with Yvonne. In the midst of it all, he suddenly realized that he had committed a great oversight. He had forgotten to give de Montmollin instructions to transfer the funds for a turkey for his mother and Albert to eat on Christmas Eve.

That failure was a signal: he was overworked and exhausted. He now confided to Marie Jeanneret that he would probably turn down the request for the British honor. Work and his mother's needs had to be priorities; there was no time to waste.

3

Back in Paris after the winter break in Roquebrune-Cap-Martin, Le Corbusier renewed his frantic pace. His busy life was possible thanks to his great physical fitness, about which he became increasingly diligent. He began working out with a private trainer named Doyen, who came to the apartment every morning at 7:30 for half an hour; Le Corbusier liked his company and the way he felt after the exercise. His morning routine now consisted, first, of serving Yvonne her morning coffee in bed; then she lay there while the house shook with his calisthenics. Her limp had worsened, and she now had difficulty walking even with a cane, so she waited for him to come back before getting out of bed.

In February, he decided to accept the medal in London after all. To his mother, he feigned modesty, insisting that the applause did not interest him; while four banquets were planned, he agreed to only one. But of course he wanted her to be impressed. The architect wrote the widow a description of Queen Elizabeth: "She's quite sympathetic, this little woman."[13] He didn't bother with more description; for a man of his importance, with such a great mother, seeing the nice "little woman" was a routine event.

The architect Berthold Lubetkin was given the task of showing the honoree around London. Lubetkin asked Le Corbusier what he would most like to see; the answer was the corner of Oxford and Regent streets. The gold medalist cared less for architectural monuments than for being at the crossroads of a bustling metropolis and feeling its pulse; nothing by Christopher Wren or Inigo Jones interested him as much as the heartbeat of urban life.

WHEN HE RETURNED to the Paris office, Le Corbusier began to finish up his projects for Ahmedabad, which now included a museum in addition to the Villa Sarabhai and the Millowners' Building.

Work was moving ahead on Ronchamp, and construction on Nantes was to begin April 1. Marseille was garnering further praise, and Le Corbusier had progressed with what had become two splendid houses for André Jaoul in Neuilly and was giving further consideration to the convent near Lyon, the project that would evolve into the magnificent La Tourette.

Fired with confidence, Le Corbusier imbued his mother with the flair and force he was feeling himself. On March 1, he wrote her, "Your letters are (always) a ray of sunlight. You have a happy soul, playful and strong. For us it is a blessing to see you cock a snook at the coming century with such a youthful heart: Madame centenarian. Ordinarily old age makes us tough. You know how to see the sun where it is and the blue sky and the lake. You're tough only for housework—work, work, work. And really, what does that matter? All of us forge our own chains, which establish the frontiers of our action."[14]

Now in his midsixties, questioning how he would manage the ultimate phase of his existence, Le Corbusier was evaluating his own capacity for life and its pleasures. His mother's longevity thrilled him, but he knew it had little bearing on how long his own biological clock would run. She was his role model for energy and work ethic, though—the main difference being that the compulsion to do well had her at the washbasin and him at the drafting table.

4

In March, one of Le Corbusier's dreams came true. His mother agreed to go to Marseille to see his building. She would be accompanied by Albert.

Le Corbusier organized the details of the voyage. He bought second-class train tickets from Vevey to Paris, with a departure scheduled for April 5. He would be at the station waiting for them. After about a week in Paris, Marie and Albert would take a sleeping car to Marseille, where they would spend a day at l'Unité before returning the following morning to Geneva. He drew diagrams to show the logistics of the trip.

That was plan A. With Marie Jeanneret, nothing was ever simple. A week after the initial proposal, Le Corbusier's secretary wrote to say that she could travel "*3ème classe*" if she absolutely insisted, but that she really should not hesitate to pay the supplement to travel via "*2ème classe*" to be more comfortable and in order to have lunch in the dining car. Now a friend would drive them to Marseille and, afterward, from Marseille to Vevey—so that Marie could be spared a complicated and exhausting train journey on the return. The secretary concluded, "M. Le Corbusier hopes this plan is to your liking and is delighted to be seeing you again."[15]

All was in order. But just before his mother embarked on the journey, Le Corbusier scribbled off a word of warning. Yvonne had "a nervous condition"; her hyperthyroid imbalance made her occasionally violent. "So, dear little Maman, you whose blood also occasionally acts up, be a good girl now and a grown-up. Yv is a little girl, utterly devoted, correct and generous. But she's sick now, as well as suffering from very painful rheumatism + her lame leg. So: no lectures about hygiene, no reflections or animadversions about tobacco or drinking. Yvonne is stubborn, nothing you can do about it, don't even try. All of us must follow our own path, our own destiny, our own instinct."[16]

His two worlds were again about to collide. With his mother, at least, there was some possibility of control.

THERE IS NO KNOWING how things went between "Vonvon" and "La Petite Maman," but photographs testify to the successful visit of Le Corbusier's mother to the building in Marseille. The white-haired lady from Switzerland can be seen beaming in the modern skyscraper that was so totally different from the world in which she had nurtured its architect. His perpetual wish for her to be proud and happy was, however briefly, again realized.

5

After the triumph of Marseille, there was no stopping Le Corbusier. In the early spring, he wrote his mother, "I lead a dog's life here, very difficult. Or a cab-horse's, as I said in my London lecture at the end of March." He was further exhausted because of the shots of anticholera vaccine he had to take to prepare for his next trip to India, as well as by struggles over the Unité proposed for Nantes, where he was battling "bastards (at the top of the profession)"—the underlining reflecting his usual rage at the practice of architecture. But the Tate Gallery had bought his most recent painting, magazine articles about his architecture were appearing all over, and a large catalog was in the works for a major exhibition in Paris that fall. He told his mother about all of it and more, while tempering his glee: "Dear Maman, I'm bothering you with all my troubles. You know what kind of a life I must lead. Everything becomes harder and harder: responsibilities and *the* Responsibility."[17]

While he was beleaguered by obligations, Marie Jeanneret, at least, should free herself of the shackles of domesticity and enjoy the liberation he intended to give all women. Le Corbusier linked his own mental state to hers: "You mustn't lead such a life 'at the lake'—housework and laundry, etc., along with everything else. I want Maman to let herself go!!! For God's sake!"[18]

HIS SIX WEEKS in India at the end of May and into June were a welcome respite from his frantic life in the west. His spirits were raised even more when he got word that the French minister had agreed to the project in Nantes, which transformed itself into an outburst of warmth toward his mother. Le Corbusier attributed his success to her, writing, "You are a great woman, worthy of the great historical periods."[19]

The heat in Chandigarh was oppressive that spring. This prompted Le Corbusier to draw for his mother a remarkable self-portrait to illustrate an Indian bath. The technique was to take a bucket of water that came out of the faucet at forty degrees Celsius and throw it on his body with a metal ladle. Le Corbusier's sketch shows his balding head, with beaklike nose and glasses. The image of him dousing himself is full of life and humanity. It is also

An Indian bath: self-portrait drawn for his mother, 1953

astonishing. For in this self-portrait drawn for his mother, his sagging testicles are clearly visible in profile, as is his penis, with a drop falling off its tip.

TO COUNTER the Indian heat, Le Corbusier would cool himself with a fan, then drink boiling-hot tea, and, at night, down a whiskey under the mosquito net on the lawn in front of the house; he had changed his stance on alcohol. He wrote his mother assuring her that what he was achieving in India was going to be a sensation. It was "raw concrete, as sharp and clear as Egyptian or Greek architecture: a great step forward." Adding to his joy, he had a recent picture of his mother with her "lovely nostrils," which he looked at all the time.[20]

Everything was for the best. Pierre was happier than he'd ever been; Le Corbusier even convinced himself that Yvonne was fine. Although she could no longer leave the apartment, he had organized someone to come in and play the accordion for her. If one made the effort to focus on joy, it could always be had.

6

Le Corbusier returned to Paris from India on June 21. The following day, Douglas Dillon, the American ambassador to France, awarded him "the rosette" of the American Institute of Arts and Letters, with a diploma naming him as an honorary member for his service to architecture. The induction ceremony at the American embassy might have been the beginning of a reconciliation with the United States. However, five days later, the United States and England definitely vetoed Le Corbusier's design for UNESCO. It baffled him to be turned down by the two countries from whom he had recently received official honors. "Reign of the mediocre and triumph of the timid," he wrote his mother, to whom he had proudly sent a newspaper clipping about Ambassador Dillon.[21]

The summer, however, was more restful than usual. Le Corbusier and Yvonne left for their hideaway in Roquebrune-Cap-Martin on July 17 and settled there for an unprecedented six weeks, in which the architect swam, caught up on sleep, and painted twenty watercolors for a new project with Tériade. Twice every day, he and Yvonne repaired to l'Etoile de Mer for their pastis and seafood.

Then, in September, Le Corbusier left Roquebrune-Cap-Martin for Paris with such a bad cold that he traveled via train in a sleeping car rather than fly or drive as usual. The illness turned into severe pneumonia; for six days, he had a fever of forty degrees Celsius. Too sick to read or work, he passed the time lying in bed and listening to the radio.

The radio was almost dead—he had great difficulty getting reception—but, with much effort, he managed one afternoon to tune in to the Wagner opera *Tristan and Isolde.* In his feverish state, he wrote to his mother about hearing "the indefatigable duet and the orgasm. Then I said to myself: I'll send dear Maman a note to tell her what tremendous emotion I experienced hearing this music you so love and respect and that I admire and 'consume' for reasons different from yours: yours are those of a musician and mine of the life experienced precisely where communion is possible between two human beings. If all the reasons were put on the table, it would be apparent that you and I are in perfect agreement. For in that half hour of Wagner everything is in order and reaches a conclusion. And so, dear Maman, while you're telling YOUR Albert: 'Don't listen to your brother, he's luring you away from your proper (musical) path.'—for Albert will have received my letter from Cap-Martin—make a new listing for your son on the first page of the New Year: *'architect-sculptor-swimmer-diver,'* fundamentally a musician *par excellence* and inventor of the Modulor, that eminently musical creation. And moving on to the circumstantial kisses." Le Corbusier signed off, "To Dear Maman, young as she is with her magnificent smile, all our best wishes, our affection, our admiration, our gratitude. And thanks too for all the wonderful nourishment you managed to get inside us all along."[22] How clear it was: a Wagnerian duo, an orgasm, him and his mother.

It was the height of Le Corbusier's career: Chandigarh was proceeding at a clip, applause was still reverberating for Marseille, Ronchamp was nearly complete, and there were projects galore in the office. Yet lying there in his fever delirium, he was still determined to achieve one further victory: the dethroning of Albert.

7

On October 7, 1953, Chandigarh was to have its opening ceremony. Two and a half weeks prior to that event, Le Corbusier prepared a letter in English for Nehru.

> Your Excellency and Friend,
>
> I think you should be acquainted on the day of the Opening Ceremony of Chandigarh—a halcyon day full of lightheartedness—of the sad financial plight of your Architect, your Town Planner, Le Corbusier, *the animating spirit of the town.* He is in debt of several millions because:
>
> 1°) the Punjab Government had not yet payed [*sic*] him,
>
> 2°) his wealthy Ahmedabad clients (the Municipal Corporation, the Millowners' Association and several private and very rich clients) have not yet payed [*sic*] him.
>
> *Since two years and ten months I have devoted nearly the whole of my activity to India* thereby neglecting to undertake more profitable surveys. Despite all my efforts I have not yet succeeded in being paid. Who is the real responsible? Since June last, my Creditors have become exacting and I have been obliged to leave off paying my draftmen in my architectural office. At 66 [*sic*] years of age I have never been in such a desperate financial plight.
>
> Meanwhile, all over the world, the public opinion praises Chandigarh, India and the Indians.

I will say no more. My grief is immeasurable. I hope this letter will be handed over to you on October 7th.

I remain,

ever your most truly,
LE CORBUSIER

P.S. Repeatedly Chandigarh has asked me to send innumerable plans for the Governor's House, the Assembly, the Capitol Park and the National Park, the Monument, etc. How am I supposed to pay my draftmen?[23]

WHEN THE CITY of Chandigarh was inaugurated on the day after Le Corbusier's birthday, the press called it "The hour of Le Corbusier," but the architect himself was not present.[24] He probably could not have paid the airfare.

There were other reasons as well not to travel. Le Corbusier was suffering from rheumatism in both ankles, especially the left one, because of decalcification. He enjoyed the cure—eating masses of meat—but there was no clear course of action for Yvonne, whose right knee was terribly swollen. Her diagnoses included decalcification worse than his own, fluid retention, and other causes, with the doctors still submitting her to endless X-rays and testing. Of course, the main problem was that she kept falling down drunk.

In addition, she was anorexic. Le Corbusier wrote his mother, "She can't eat because of some obsession or psychysm or other." Deeply upset as he tried to figure out how to get nourishment into her, he admitted to Marie Jeanneret, "It's extremely depressing to see this splendid girl chained to the unknown."[25]

His mother, on the other hand, was his solace, the equal of the greatest force in the universe. "You're my sun," he wrote her.[26]

8

A month after the inauguration of Chandigarh, Prime Minister Nehru laid the foundation stone of the new Secretariat. Again Le Corbusier was absent from an event he should have attended.

Nonetheless, the prime minister's presence gave incomparable glory to the architectural milestone. Nehru landed at 8:30 a.m. by jet at the Ambala airfield, near the new city. Some twenty-five thousand people greeted him.

At the ceremony, Nehru emphasized the need for peace between India and Pakistan. Lamenting a recent incident in Calcutta when "some unknown person foolishly . . . fired at the building of the office of the Deputy High Commission of Pakistan," he declared the future Secretariat a symbol of peace and unity.[27]

The prime minister was also determined to counter the strong criticism uttered in many precincts about Le Corbusier's architecture: "A city without a soul would be a heap of mud and mortar. . . . A city built must have a soul and provide a spirit to its inhabitants based on our old traditions." Attacking "the few cities built by the British Rulers in their days for their own convenience," Nehru urged the public to be open to a new style, admirable because of its lack of reference to European tradition, and to recognize that the residential bungalows to which they had become accustomed had been designed to suit the colonialists rather than the Indians.

It was as if the absent Le Corbusier had written the prime minister's lines. Nehru continued, "Probably one who is accustomed to looking at ugly things is not accustomed to objects of beauty." It was the spirit of *L'Esprit Nouveau* come to life. At last a person of far-reaching power echoed the precepts of Ruskin and disparaged weak traditionalism as vociferously as Le Corbusier: "The houses built by a particular type of rich people . . . were more marked by their vulgarity than by anything of taste." By contrast, "the foreign architects" who had designed Chandigarh "get full praise from the Prime Minister." He told the audience that, for the first time, the foreign press, especially in Europe and America, was heaping compliments on modern architecture in India, saying that Chandigarh should be a model for cities all over the world. It was a great source of pride—the opposite of Calcutta and Kanpur with their huge skyscrapers overpowering "the hovels in which the poor laborers live there."

This architecture in which everyone was to be housed decently was part of a new social order. Its ultimate goal was the disappearance of the caste system, under which the servant class had previously been relegated to inadequate accommodations. The prime minister assured his audience that this new Secretariat, planned so that it would take only forty-five seconds to go to the highest story in spite of the enormousness of the structure, would be the symbol and embodiment of this revolutionary equality.

The Ambala *Sunday Tribune* reported that, accompanied by his daughter, Indira Gandhi, "the Prime Minister was in a very bright and jovial mood throughout." A group of girls from a local school sang the "*Jana Gana Mana.*" After laying the cornerstone, which was positioned by electrical machinery, "he jumped up to the dais to take back the baton which he had forgotten to carry with him when he went to press the electric button which lowered down the simple and sober bronze plaque bearing Pt. Nehru's name in the socket below." With the Punjab governor, Indira Gandhi, and Varma, the great leader toured the new city in an open truck and "ascended to the top of the club building in Sector twenty-two to have a clearer view of the houses built around."

In Paris, Le Corbusier read the newspaper account eagerly. On his carefully cut-and-pasted clipping, he circled one key sentence: " 'The old methods do not suit the new age of Democracy,' said the Prime Minister."[28] At last, Le Corbusier was understood.

9

The opening of Le Corbusier's major exhibition of his work at Le Musée d'Art Moderne of Paris, in the eastern wing of the Palais de Tokyo, in November 1953 was for him one of the most significant moments of his life. The Palais de Tokyo was only a few blocks from the Perret brothers' offices, where Charles-Edouard Jeanneret had shown up forty-five years earlier as a hesitant young man with the portfolio of Italian sketches that landed him his first job. It had models and photos and plans of Le Corbusier's architecture, as well as drawings, paintings, sculpture, books, houses, and urban plans. It presented the full body of Le Corbusier's work as a unified entity.

Le Corbusier believed this presentation demonstrated "a single and constant created manifestation devoted to various forms of the visual phenomenon."[29] The initial reaction was, however, a stinging disappointment. The architect's own account of the opening took to a dramatic peak the pain he invariably felt when snubbed. Now more than ever, he saw himself as an exile and castaway—and the people in power as evil incarnate. He wrote in his diary, "November 17th, 1953. Paris: Opening of the Le Corbusier Exhibition at the Museum of Modern Art. 11 o'clock, official visits. 3 o'clock, journalists. 9 o'clock, invited guests . . . 11:45, 11:30, 12 . . . Minister of Education and Minister of Fine Arts, Secretary of State for Fine Arts, Director-General of Arts and Letters, Director-General of Architecture . . . all absent. When telephoned, one is busy with the budget, another can't make it, the others the same. These are the four leaders of the arts in France. The Le Corbusier exhibition is an important event, properly scheduled. I sent out invitations to the dinner myself. They don't come. I'm not the loser. The game was played correctly. According to the rules. If they're satisfied, so are we—even more so."[30]

His mother and brother also had failed to show up for the opening events. Le Corbusier wrote them to emphasize only what they missed, not the other absences. Between two and three thousand people had attended the opening, he told them. It had become necessary to organize, on the spot, a system whereby the crowd went through the show in an orderly progression. It was so mobbed that it was impossible to see the art.

"Enthusiasm and anger," Le Corbusier wrote his family about the public response.[31] The critics had unanimously tried to outdo each other in nastiness, while the attendance broke records. Three hundred and fifty visitors had gone through on the first Saturday, 620 the next day. During a recent Léger show at the same museum, there had been 1,700 in all, 1,200 at a Klee exhibition; his totals would be far larger, and 12,000 visitors had walked through an exhibition of his work in Stockholm. The officials and his family had ignored him; the journalists had slammed him; but the numbers were on his side.

10

The continual financial problems in India and the boycotting of his Paris opening were not all that was plaguing Le Corbusier. Yvonne had become so difficult that he could no longer resist confiding to his mother and Albert. At the end of November, he wrote them, "Yvonne wavers between confidence and rebellion. She has a damn hard little head. But she obeys—secretly—all our orders and suggestions."[32] Le Corbusier went on his own to Vevey for Christmas with "M. et Mme. Jeanneret." Then he doubled back to Paris to take Yvonne to Roquebrune-Cap-Martin for New Year's.

The weather was bitter cold, and Le Corbusier had a relapse of his pneumonia, requiring penicillin. Then Yvonne broke her right leg in another drinking binge. The injury was complicated, with fractures in three places, including a broken tibia. She was put in a cumbersome cast that made the return to Paris exceptionally difficult. When the architect went back to Chandigarh at the end of January, his own energy was depleted. He wrote his mother, "My health suddenly improves and I gain weight in just a few days, then everything collapses with the heavy burden of events."[33]

Le Corbusier arrived in Delhi in a storm, with heavy rain and surprising cold. On his first few days in Chandigarh, he suffered repeated nightmares. But his spirits quickly revived. He was impressed with what Pierre had achieved, both architecturally and diplomatically, and was delighted with the quality of the concrete used in his various buildings. Le Corbusier also enjoyed the feeling of being "respected and considered and accommodated"—words he delighted in spelling out to his mother.[34] He spent an hour with Nehru in New Delhi and felt that the meeting served to make the governor of Punjab that much more amenable to his ideas. There was no further reference to his fee.

From India, Le Corbusier wrote his mother that he had decided that his wife's main problem was malnutrition. She was "completely decalcified"—to such an extent that he used his most gruesome adjective yet: "Buchenwaldized."[35] But he also reminded his mother of why he had married Yvonne to begin with. Her good spirit, intrepidity, and simple kindness were what had lured him, and they counted still.

He begged his mother to recognize that he had done everything possible to help his wife—even if he had failed. "So I scolded, organized gastronomic events, and exerted moral pressure at every moment, on this child that she is, who ended by 'psychologizing' herself in reverse."[36] It was another battle Le Corbusier could not win.

11

After two weeks in Chandigarh, Le Corbusier went south to Bombay for three days. While he was there, the largest Bombay newspaper published a piece by a reporter who had visited his site at Marseille. The residents had said that because of the sunscreens they froze in the winter and died of the heat in the summer. The journalist predicted that the use of the *brises-soleil* in Chandigarh would be a disaster.

By now, Le Corbusier was accustomed to this sort of criticism. This time, though, a head of state was on his side. The money problems about which he had written Nehru did not matter as much as the prime minister's strength in dispelling the usual forces arrayed against him. Le Corbusier had found his place in the world.

The journey back to Paris at the end of February took twenty-six-and-a-half hours, but it was comfortable. "Nothing is more ideal than the airplane. I usually get a real joy from flying," he wrote his mother and brother.[37]

Yvonne's state upon his return was worrisome, though. She was not able to greet him at the airport as usual. The day after his arrival, he wrote his mother and Albert, "She is a lot thinner, living like a recluse far from daylight, fresh air, and sunshine. Her husband, as you know, is the man who discovered SUN, SPACE, GREENERY, the raw materials of urbanism."[38]

With Pierre Jeanneret in Chandigarh, shortly after they were reunited following the schism that occurred between them during and following World War II

WHEN AUGUSTE PERRET died just after his return, Le Corbusier was asked to speak at his former mentor's funeral. In public, he was appropriate; to his mother, he was blunt about yet another of the people he had once deified but had come to loathe: "Perret was a violent adversary, neither pleasant nor correct. I tore him out of my heart long ago."[39]

Le Corbusier's personal worries were mounting. Yvonne was out of her cast but now required an apparatus to keep her leg straight. That spring, his mother had bronchitis and needed to stay in a nursing home. He assumed all the costs, but, given her age, her condition was a real concern.

Professionally, however, he was at a high. Le Corbusier was completing one major project after another. He was very pleased with the quality of construction in Nantes and with the helpful role of Claudius-Petit. Jane Drew and Maxwell Fry left India in the middle of the year, leaving Pierre in charge, which suited Le Corbusier; it enabled him and Pierre to work, unencumbered, toward the opening of the High Court in November. Even if India was now three years in arrears on his architectural fees, he had come a long way from the errant son who depleted his parents' life savings.

XLVII

1

For the first time in thirty years, most of what Le Corbusier was designing was getting built. Girders were rising in two cities in India, at Ronchamp, and at La Tourette.

But, just as the League of Nations headquarters and the United Nations buildings had tortured him, so did his bridesmaid's role in the UNESCO headquarters in Paris, where, having been ruled out to design it, he was now on the selection committee. While Le Corbusier had envisioned a building

Meeting with Balkrishna Doshi on the site of the Millowners' Building in Ahmedabad, ca. 1955

of concrete and glass that would use *brises-soleil* to optimal advantage, a very different structure went up, designed jointly by the Bauhaus-trained Marcel Breuer, the Paris-based Bernard Zehrfuss, and the Italian Pier Luigi Nervi. Le Corbusier was among those to ratify that choice, but was still furious not to have been the architect of this important building not far from his office doorstep.

A continent away, however, Le Corbusier's architecture was triumphant. The Millowners' Building opened in Ahmedabad.

The Millowners, an association of owners of cotton mills, was the sort of upper-echelon client Le Corbusier adored. Rich and distinguished, its members belonged to one of the highest castes in Indian society and were reputed for their generosity and public-spiritedness. They totally respected Le Corbusier.

Ahmedabad had a population of about one million people. Mahatma Gandhi, who had had a modest compound on the riverbank on the city's outskirts between 1915 and 1930, had been instrumental in establishing a connection between the cotton mill owners and their workers. Now their organization, which consciously strived for a spirit of goodwill and mutual betterment, wanted a place to assemble that would echo the human harmony they advocated. Desiring a natural setting for their meetings, they had acquired a site overlooking a river. In March 1951, the president of the association, Surottam Hutheesing, had commissioned Le Corbusier to design their headquarters.

From the start, Le Corbusier conceived of a structure with the aura of a private palace. But rather than house royalty and facilitate pomp, this streamlined equivalent of Versailles was to be a place from which people could savor "the highly picturesque spectacle of the dyers washing their cottons and drying them on the sand, accompanied by herons, cows, buffaloes and donkeys half submerged to keep cool."[1] The building was intended as a platform for viewing; its external appearance was a secondary consideration. Le Corbusier designed the main elements of each floor as frameworks for the panorama. Architecture would organize and compose the myriad elements of the vista and create glassless picture windows for the benefit of the building's staff as much as for the distinguished mill owners, who would periodically meet there.

Essentially, the form of the building is a cube with complex subdivisions inside it. There are no doors or windows, only openings in the walls. Fifty percent of the interior space is empty, with neither function nor furniture; birds fly across it, and one feels that the building exists for their benefit as much as for that of its human visitors. It is a stunning sculptural object, a lively and rhythmic monument in which gray concrete is intensely animated. As he had in Marseille, Le Corbusier breathed life into inert materials; the

Millowners' Building, interior, ca. 1955

ramps and *brises-soleil* and outdoor staircases and protrusions of every sort give the concrete structure in Ahmedabad fantastic energy.

These elements were all designed to accommodate the vicissitudes of the local climate, and the building was deliberately oriented toward the prevailing winds. The *brises-soleil* of both the east and west facades were "calculated according to the latitude of Ahmedabad and the precise solar positioning."[2] As a youth, Charles-Edouard Jeanneret had learned to position his body on Alpine mountaintops so as to have maximum stability, and he still had his consuming respect for nature.

Le Corbusier saw to it that people could stay as dry as possible during the rainy season, thanks to both the parking spaces right up against the front and the long and gentle ramp running from the more distant parking area to the building entrance. Even if, in Europe, his roofs sometimes let in the rainwater, in Ahmedabad the architect was reverent in his subservience to local conditions.

IT IS an extraordinary experience to arrive at this visual oasis. Inside and outside are intertwined; architecture defines space in unprecedented ways.

Traffic-clogged and noisy, Ahmedabad teems with women in bright saris, with camels and goats and wagons and beggars. Wares are for sale everywhere, and the sights of tin shop signs and feverish industry are constant in the blistering heat. Reaching the haven that Le Corbusier built, we instantly slow down. The noble entrance ramp changes our pace and breathing, no matter how many horns are honking simultaneously in our ears.

The moment we set foot on that ramp, we have arrived in the sacred precincts of a modern temple. Right angles of reinforced concrete become as soothing as the courtyards of a Moorish mosque after the helter-skelter activity of the medina. The oversized *brise-soleil* of the west facade, which we see right away, has a hypnotic effect, like a machine in repetitious slow motion.

It cools and diverts us with its mesmerizing form. By some miraculous act of transformation, the raw, unfinished concrete provides a gentle welcome at the same time that it bespeaks a tough reality (see color plate 17).

Once we walk in, that resonant opening note is tempered by wooden struts of further *brises-soleil* and sheet metal on some of the walls. The uniquely Corbusean composition of textures works like the progression of a symphony as the various instruments simultaneously sound their high and low voices. The floors and nonmetal walls are made of Morak stone, brought from Delhi, which provides a delicious coolness against the higher pitch of the wood and metal.

Although we are inside, the many openings make us feel as if we are in a lush park. The surrounding trees and the nearby river are constantly visible. Nearer to us, the bright red, yellow, and black metal walls are like flower blossoms that are the colors of fire and coal. The elegant, graceful architecture forms a dreamscape of surprises.

The empty spaces defined by impeccably crafted shapes provide immense calm in the heart of a teeming city. The voids, some of them vast, are odes to light and space, established by an unprecedented architectural vocabulary in union with the riverscape beyond it.

Every step inside the Millowners' Building offers a different visceral thrill. Walking along, periodically stopping to take in the constantly shifting elements, we progress from moment to moment on a course of subtle emotional shifts.

Inexplicable pleasures give way to occasional instances of terror. The open stairs indicate a constant possibility of danger and injury. They demand alertness; what would not have been permitted in a western country with stricter building codes here provides an existential experience. Le Corbusier was able to give the visitors a series of tough, challenging, awakening encounters.

The intensity is relieved by moments of calm; in the garden on a balcony, for example, we feel as if we are on a ship on a smooth sea—or studying the horizon from the terraces at Athos. Fluted columns of reinforced concrete rise from the roof terrace, where there are two gardens and a water basin. The columns are an homage to ancient Greece rather than an imitation, respectful of the past but not enslaved to it. They, too, provide a respite of calm and order.

ABOVE ALL, the Millowners' Building is about the air it encloses. Although built for assemblies and the congress of people, it has few specific functions. There is very little furniture. The walls serve mainly as containers of emptiness; architecture carves out forms in the atmosphere. What a luxury this is—all this openness, this celebration of what is always there but is so rarely sanctified: oxygen and space. Within a crowded and cramped city center, this use of air as an element of architecture is revelatory.

Le Corbusier, fully in power, has assumed his preferred role: leading others into a wonderful territory of artistic pleasure. At one moment we face red stone, then a mass of concrete. Then, suddenly, we luxuriate in a view of the river or confront a black metal wall. The total experience is a wild fantasy designed by conscious plan.

2

On this journey of surprises Le Corbusier has charted for us, we eventually arrive at the chapel. Officially, it is an assembly hall, but the space is holy. This really cannot exist on the earth as we have known it until now. The concrete ceiling swoops down like a billowing sail, giving us the sensation of being tiny mortals under the wings of a gigantic angel in a gesture of benediction. The curved walls are composed of rows of simple slats, made of molded plywood, stained dark, arranged so that they acquire dynamism and energy. The excitement generated by these undulating panels mounts the longer we look at them.

Light seeps in from the clerestory, as in the Gothic cathedrals Charles-Edouard Jeanneret had discovered in his early travels. Just as we are becoming overwhelmed by the throbbing walls, that narrow band of light provides relief. It moves our vision upward, and again we are hypnotized by the ceiling that reverses the roofline of a Mughal tent. The sagging concrete seems on the one hand weighed down, ready to collapse on our heads, only to soar heavenward on both sides to top the playful windows high above. In Ahmedabad, the sunlight is so powerful that it needs only these tiny openings to stream in brightly; in a larger quantity, it would blind us.

This building that calms and terrifies has the sum effect of being invigorating. It testifies to artistic genius and technical ingenuity, to the marriage of creativity with the discipline of mathematics. It is a mix of knowledge and feeling, each in its extreme. Le Corbusier, whose own inner life was so complex, had the astonishing ability to celebrate and reflect that complexity and his own imposing humors in his architecture.

BALKRISHNA DOSHI had made the initial drawings for the assembly hall. The young architect had proposed a standard auditorium, basically a rectangle with a fan shape at one end. Le Corbusier said it was fine, and Doshi had worked away at the details for two weeks.

Then Le Corbusier reviewed Doshi's work. He told his young colleague to imagine coming into the space so that one would know immediately where the speaker was. Equally, Doshi had to give visitors the feeling that they could sit in the back and exit quickly. "Every time he drew," recalled Doshi, "he would speak about how people live. It had nothing to do with a machine for living; it was a celebration of life. His whole phenomenon was connected with behavior. He knew the psyche of the people. He knew what emotions could catch you. He was a combination of the sensual and the psychic, touched internally and externally simultaneously. When he drew a column, he would talk about the thighs of a woman and how you touch them. When you caress a column, a shiny round column, a voluptuous column, then you must touch the body. Beauty was always there for him. He was on the one side very sensuous and on the other very compassionate. The hen and the cock."[3]

During visits to the site when the building was under construction, Le Corbusier cast his eye everywhere in order to ascertain truth, rather than turn from sights others might have deemed disconcerting. He took in the details of the local animals and looked directly at the slum dwellers of Ahmedabad.

> He looked into the beauty of the eyes of the Indian woman, the gentle eyes of the Indian cows, the big bosom and body of the Indian woman, the hump of the bull: he would see beauty everywhere.
>
> There was a lot of glory that he saw in the slums—the eyes of the women and children—always he had fascination. He would ask why they were made the way they were made. He believed in eternity in a very different way. He asked questions. Real poverty was the poverty of the mind.[4]

One day, while looking at some of the natives of Ahmedabad, Le Corbusier said to Doshi, "Americans have big bodies but no brains. Frenchmen have large heads; Americans have pea-heads."[5] Doshi believed that the forms Le Corbusier made in India could not have come about unless their maker had this fascination with scale and connected physical attributes to qualities of intelligence and wit—however lopsided and eccentric his vision was.

While Le Corbusier oversaw the big concept, Pierre tended to the details, making admirable lamps out of the metal bowls the women carried and fashioning chairs out of bamboo. But, able as he was, Pierre lacked Le Corbusier's visionary flair, and Doshi noted that Pierre, for all that bothered him about the man who had gone to Vichy, adored Le Corbusier like a guru. The practical aide willingly served the mystic creator.

3

Le Corbusier operated in another realm of existence. Observing the architect, Doshi recognized the way that the creation of the Millowners' Building and the other structures in India was an organic, instinctive process; at the same time, it was the result of a subjugation of self to a higher force.

> Le Corbusier never theorized about his buildings. He never justified them. Le Corbusier referred to himself in the third person, which is very Indian. It was as if he were saying, "I am not this body." His approach was very spiritual. When it came to creative work, it was the soul working.
>
> When he did these buildings, Le Corbusier must have discovered that nature has systems, but not identical ones. They are similar, but there are exceptions. Le Corbusier was always playing the game of multiplicity—putting things together in counterbalance. He and his architecture reflect a Hindu temperament, like a Buddhist temple. You can only work with your soul when you've detached your body.[6]

Le Corbusier took the otherness of India completely in stride. For all the differences of dress, diet, climate, and language, he had in common with its culture both a spirituality and a strong sense of family. His ease and comfort are manifest in the magnificence of the work.

4

In the periods of 1954 when he was not in India, Le Corbusier was busy dictating 150 manuscript pages of volume two of *The Modulor* to his secretary. The first volume had by now been published in five languages, as he made sure his mother knew.

Le Corbusier's mother was now in her midnineties. Her famous son wrote her that he thought of her every day and that her capacity to absorb new experiences was "magnificent." He credited her with having imbued him and Albert with the same quality, making them full of life at a time when many of their contemporaries were beginning to give up. Having previously called her "Andalusian" to honor her fiery side, he now wrote her that his book about La Petite Maison was his "homage to the mother and to the powerful woman you always were for us: in other days *Spanish y Perez,* today Lioness! Le Corbeau embraces you very tenderly."[7] In the accompanying self-portrait, he depicts himself with an enormous beak.

TO LA PETITE MAMAN, Le Corbusier expressed himself in a language as singular as the feelings it attempted to convey. In late September 1954, just as Ronchamp and Chandigarh were keeping hundreds of people busy under his steely rule, he wrote, "My dear Maman, you are happy by nature and by will. It is a joy to see you. (And when we are face-to-face . . . we scold each other!!) Life is a crazy thing! There is, around our thoughts, the network of nerves performing its seguidilla. And the nerves emit waves! As we now know! When it's the radio that howls, we carefully make the proper adjustment. When it's men and women, static! Well, let the static go on!! It's of no more consequence than the discomfort of a storm (more waves!)."[8]

Meanwhile, Le Corbusier wanted to provide Albert with funds that would enable him to cut back on some music teaching he was now doing and to have time to record some of the music he had composed for children. Uncertain if Albert could be coerced to accept the money, Edouard asked their mother to serve as the go-between; he used the reverse tactic when he implored Albert to persuade their mother to hire a maid. As with architecture, willpower and diplomacy were requisite to win the results he craved.

5

Le Corbusier checked various building sites and made a quick trip to Vevey in the summer of 1954, because he knew he would be immobilized in October by a major operation for varicose veins in his leg. In a letter to his mother and brother, he drew diagrams, labeling his veins A, B, and C; he anticipated the surgery as a feat of smooth engineering that would be a solution to a problem that had plagued him since 1930.

After the procedure took place on October 17, Le Corbusier wrote his mother: "Seventy centimeters of veins as fat as a pencil were at last removed,

Facing the High Court building in Chandigarh, mid-1950s

put into a glass tube, and then thrown into the wastebasket. It was a 'big boo-boo.' "[9] He had to stay at home afterward and could not go to the office, although his staff came to him, as they always did when he was ill.

He recuperated so rapidly that on November 10 he was back in Chandigarh. It was the ideal season to be there; the flowers and birdsong were sublime. Pierre was hospitable and helpful. The "Open Hand" monument, still unrealized, was under discussion with the authorities. Le Corbusier immediately went to his "palace"—the High Court—in the moonlight at midnight; he was eager to see the building's surface, which had been formed by having the rough concrete shot through a cannon.

He wrote his mother, "This note to tell you that the Palace of the Supreme Court, where some 1000 workmen and women and donkeys are preparing for the inauguration of January 3 '55, is quite simply extraordinary—an architectural symphony that exceeds all my hopes, exploding and developing under the sun in an inconceivable and tireless fashion. Close to and far off, it is a surprise and a provocation of astonishment."[10]

Yet again, he was reborn. He wrote, "Dearest Maman, this present letter, free of any worldly modesty but filled with pride, I send so that you may know that at last the architect, the urbanist, the painter and the sculptor have here given birth . . . to *poetry*—the *raison d'être* and the reason for living of those who are well born!" He needed to imagine her experiencing equal pleasure: "Be happy all this day. I see you in my mind's eye waking up in the morning, eyes glistening and lips stretched in a smile."[11]

A month later, when Le Corbusier was flying between Delhi and Bombay on the start of his homeward journey, the person seated next to him was reading a magazine. The color photo to which it was opened caught his eye. He asked, "Do you know who that is? It's my '*petite mère.*' "[12] Two days later, on a plane from Bombay to Ahmedabad, the flight attendant showed him the same publication, an issue of *Esquire.* On his flight to Cairo on the sixteenth, the stewardess offered him yet another copy. From the stopover in Egypt, he reported to his mother these incidents of her fame thanks to him, embellishing the details and also making a rapid sketch of the magazine image, accentuating her mane of white hair and her noble face. How much clearer could Le Corbusier make it that her glorification accompanied his own?

6

When Le Corbusier arrived back in Paris, Yvonne was in even worse shape than when he left. Beyond being completely housebound, she could hardly function within the confines of the apartment. The accordion player was little compensation. Le Corbusier wrote his mother that he would have liked to have gone to Vevey to be with her for the holidays, but it was impossible; with Yvonne immobilized, he could no longer leave her on her own for Christmas, as in the old days.

They could not even go to Roquebrune-Cap-Martin; beyond Yvonne's situation, he was swamped with work. But Le Corbusier arranged for his mother and brother to have chicken, cakes, the best wines, and flowers for the holidays, and on New Year's Eve he managed to get Yvonne to a restaurant. It was the first time she had gone out for dinner in four months.

It was during this time period that a beggar began to appear regularly on the rue Nungesser-et-Coli and hold out his tin cup to passersby. Having observed him from a front window on a couple of occasions, Yvonne called out one day and told the beggar to take the elevator to the seventh floor. She handed him some cash and urged him not to bother to continue panhandling on the street. Instead, he should simply come up to see her every Wednesday and could depend on receiving his payments on a regular basis.

Jacques Hindermeyer had taken charge of Le Corbusier as well as Yvonne. At the end of January, the doctor insisted that the architect go for complete silence and solitude in Roquebrune-Cap-Martin to recover from the exhaustion induced by the combination of Yvonne's health problems, the bitterness and anger he was feeling over the UNESCO debacle, and general work fatigue. Moreover, Le Corbusier had had further surgery to treat varicosity, this time in his femoral vein.

Once the architect was on his retreat, in spite of the rain and February cold, he unwound completely and slept, he wrote his mother, between eighteen and twenty hours a day. In his few hours of awakeness, he read fiction; Albert had sent him a novel by Ernest Hemingway that he found "magnificent and sympathetic, simple and without fussiness."[13]

In his solitude, Le Corbusier found that the *cabanon* and the studio were ideal for living and working; at last, he had in his own life the "perfect refuge" he had long been trying to create for others.[14]

In high spirits, Le Corbusier wrote his mother, in anticipation of the end of winter, "In a month's time you'll have sunshine. That will be the vernal equinox. You'll open your laughing eyes of a fifteen-year-old peasant girl in your bed one morning, and you'll smile at life."[15] He was back on a high; Roquebrune-Cap-Martin was proof that good architecture in combination with nature was the perfect medicine.

XLVIII

1

Nothing more came of Marguerite Tjader Harris's dream of her lover creating a little colony for her on the Connecticut coast. But the idea was reincarnated in a surprising way. Nearly two years after approaching Le Corbusier about her wish to build a small artists' community, Tjader Harris again booked herself into the Hotel Lutétia, a minute's walk from her lover's office and halfway across Paris from his and Yvonne's apartment. She was there in part to discuss her financial support for a development of holiday dwellings Le Corbusier wanted to create up the hill from l'Etoile de Mer.

The initial agreement had been established by a formal proposal prepared by Le Corbusier's office. It referred to a meeting held at 35 rue de Sèvres on May 3, 1954, in the presence of M. Ducret, the office administrator. Le Corbusier was to construct five holiday dwellings on land belonging to Rebutato. The total costs were estimated at 15,700,000 francs—about $350,000. Tjader Harris was to provide those funds with an interest-free loan. The five units were to be offered for sale before July 1, 1956.

In return for his design services, Le Corbusier was to own one of the five dwellings, with the other four sold to buyers of his choosing. One of those four was to be reserved for Marguerite Tjader Harris. Thus, in their old age, the couple that had seen each other periodically for two decades would be together, living modestly at the edge of the ocean, albeit in separate digs and with Yvonne living with Le Corbusier in their *cabanon* only a few meters away.

Marguerite Tjader Harris had opened a special bank account in Le Corbusier's name to facilitate the arrangement. On June 8, 1954, the heiress and the architect signed a document in which she agreed to write to her banker that "M. Le Corbusier is my silent partner in this matter."[1] They scheduled payments first for the purchase of the property and then for the construction costs, with Tjader Harris providing 14,130,000 francs and Le Corbusier 1,570,000 francs.

E. C. Llewellyn, at the Hanover Bank near the Ritz Hotel on the place Vendôme, acted on Tjader Harris's behalf in the transaction. The undertaking had the ingredients of a Henry James novel: an elegant banker, a rich American heiress, an artist, and intrigue in the heart of Paris.

Problems soon arose. André Wogenscky, who was the liaison in Le Corbusier's office with Llewellyn, was notified in December that Tjader Harris was not going to make payments until construction actually began. Le Corbusier, who had been in India, then returned to Paris and tried to smooth matters over by writing her warmly and assuring her that he was achieving miracles in the subcontinent.

At the start of January 1955, Tjader Harris wrote him to say she would immediately authorize payments once she was sure they were for bricks and mortar rather than for something still only on paper. Meanwhile, her son had married a woman she very much liked, and all three of them wanted to go to Roquebrune-Cap-Martin. Tjader Harris voiced her hope that Yvonne was doing better, and that Le Corbusier's beloved mother was in form, too. They were like an extended family.

2

During his period of solitude in Roquebrune-Cap-Martin in February 1955, Le Corbusier wrote a long, sprawling letter to his "*Chère amie de Darien Connecticut.*" Le Corbusier was, he told her, living alone and in total silence, exhausted by "the harbingers of the 'nervous breakdown' so dear to Americans." He was mostly sleeping, he claimed. "20 hours a day my ears ring with the racket of the grasshoppers," he wrote her.[2] Le Corbusier observed that both he and she were next to the sea, if on different continents.

He was eager for her to picture his life in detail. He told her with pride how he had built his shack. Tjader Harris was the soul mate who would understand the pleasure the boxy enclosure afforded him: "I work here like a prince, but in possession of my freedom (hence happier than a prince)."[3]

Le Corbusier assured her that construction would proceed rapidly on the holiday dwellings, which he called "Rob" and "Rog." Their completion "required the presence, the action, the perseverance of a creature like me. Years of preparation, of focusing. Now everything's in order. I'm prepared to make a minor masterpiece on that wave-battered rock." The architect proffered one of his grand conclusions: "Dear friend, I'm blooming or fructifying (as you choose). I prefer blooming. Blooming like an apple tree in spring. For this is just what's happened: if you live your life severely but strongly, youth comes to you, everything blooms. Not a maturity, a harvest, but an authentic *flowering*. Of course, this doesn't keep my hair from falling out."[4]

The future was bright because "you'll be there. What a blessed creature you are. . . . There is no nationality but beings of flesh and blood with a brain and a heart. Be careful! Make no promises. Don't commit yourself to anything!"[5]

Following that window to his unique mix of faith and confusion, his sincerity and sarcasm in tandem, Le Corbusier signed off by saying, falsely, that he had never before written such a long letter. When he added, however, that with her everything was different, he was being truthful.

3

Marguerite Tjader Harris responded by return mail. She was now vacating the Connecticut mansion to turn it over as a convent for the sisters of St. Birgitta and would keep for herself a modernized studio in the garage.

A week later, for unknown reasons, Le Corbusier abandoned their plan in France. He asked Ducret to repay, from the account in Roquebrune-Cap-Martin where Tjader Harris's loans had been deposited, the full amount to the Hanover Bank. This was, he had decided, the wise course. He was not in the least bit bitter: "In life one must know how to keep one's eyes and ears open when it matters and be able to turn the page when that seems important. In any case I want you to know you have all my gratitude and my friendship on the occasion of the gesture of trust you've made to facilitate our undertaking."[6] Le Corbusier's only request of Tjader Harris was the counsel he had given to more than one woman: that she be sure to write him at the office and not at home.

The American was gracious and understanding in response, regretting the turn of events but telling Le Corbusier that it made her life simpler. She assured him she was writing and swimming and proposed that he take a vacation with her in Connecticut. Even if they were not working together, they could enjoy each other's company.

THE FIVE HOLIDAY houses were completed in 1957, but there is no evidence of Marguerite Tjader Harris ever having visited them, and her name appears nowhere in the publications about them. The units are distinctive mainly for their economy and austerity; they comprise a bare-bones retreat hardly distinguishable from other campgrounds. Their romance and charm lie mainly in their history.

But Le Corbusier did give each of these simple dwellings isolation, a view, direct sunshine, and the requisite shade. He achieved those modest goals with simple construction techniques, utilizing aluminum, and he built each standardized unit as a 226-centimeter cube. Putting this low-income housing with rudimentary materials not far from Eileen Gray and Jean Badovici's luxurious villa, he also had the last word in an ongoing feud—the result of his having painted, unbidden, those murals nearly two decades earlier—by making a statement of moral superiority through architecture.

THE MOST LIKELY REASON that Le Corbusier removed Marguerite Tjader Harris from the project when he did is that he recognized how unrealistic he was to imagine her holidaying there with Yvonne nearby. After Yvonne finally went from her wretched alcoholic state to death in 1958, Le Corbusier would, however, manage to see his lover at least one more time in Paris.

XLIX

1

At the start of March, his mother fell in an accident caused by her cat. Le Corbusier did not, however, go to Vevey, since on March 15 he had to leave for Chandigarh for the inauguration of the High Court. This was one ceremony in India he could not miss. Having initially telegraphed to say that he would not be attending unless the many millions that had now been owed him for fourteen months were received before the event, he made the journey.

PRIME MINISTER NEHRU once again presided. Almost the entire population of the new city turned out to greet the popular leader as he arrived from New Delhi, with thousands of children lining his route for nearly two miles and waving multicolored flags. Once Nehru was in front of the new building, Le Corbusier made a speech linking his architecture with social change and defending his designs for Chandigarh against their critics, who, he told his audience, were too cowardly to accept progress. Then two thousand visitors watched as Nehru "pressed an electric button and the doors of all the court rooms opened automatically" to reveal Le Corbusier's tapestries and his and Pierre's furniture.[1]

The building was the first monumental structure completed in the controversial new city. The Indian papers referred to the roof of the structure as an "inverted umbrella" and its overall appearance as "cold and rugged."[2] But what was at first startling to wary journalists and a skeptical public was given a rare boost by having the public endorsement of a beloved leader, and soon enough the building's intrinsic splendor helped dissipate the initial resistance to its many surprises. The unprecedented composition of rough concrete quickly assumed the status of a monument of modern architecture.

THE HIGH COURT encourages faith in government and the possibility of true justice. Authoritarian without being arrogant, this completely original building has a nobility of form and emanates a wonderful energy and optimism.

When you first see it, from afar, it draws you in, like a magnetic force, the way the Gothic spires of Chartres summon you nearer. Part of that pull comes from color. While it was under construction, Le Corbusier asked everyone with whom he was working if they should put color on the three great columns. Without exception, the other architects and engineers said no, the forms themselves had such majesty that the addition of hue would be an unnecessary distraction. Le Corbusier listened attentively. Nonetheless, day after day, he continued to pose the same question. The negative response was unvarying. Then he went ahead and had the colors of the Indian flag applied to the columns anyway.

Le Corbusier may have initiated the consultation in earnest, convincing himself that he cared about what the others would say. But his decision making came, as always, from within himself and from some vague source of inspiration. It was as if his art happened to him, and he was merely the agent. In that vein, once he had received the impetus and executed its directives, he was unequivocal; as M. S. Sharma pointed out, this was the same person who said of his paintings, "If you like them, very nice. If you don't, forget it."[3]

The columns are painted, from left to right, in vibrant pastel tones of green, yellow, and salmon pink. As you face these pillars and look up, generous amounts of blue sky come through wide openings between the building and its roof, which is like a flapping canopy, so that the blue, too, becomes an element. To the left and right as well, color is everywhere—showing up through further openings and the windows—and is always changing and surprising you. But for all that fury of hues and forms and sense of reckless abandon, the columns support the roof with impressive strength and muscular grace. The color is not overkill; rather, it gives music to the concrete. In the bright sunlight, the green, yellow, and salmon are as bold in spirit as the robust cylinders they cover.

The three entrance columns have the lasting power of a force of nature, like a mountain peak or a giant waterfall. Yet they declare themselves as having been constructed by man. Those great stiltlike legs are monumental in the same way as the buttresses of Notre-Dame, manifesting their builder's capability. The High Court at Chandigarh is different in scale and purpose from the cathedral, but like that great edifice, it has both a grandeur and the quality of not diminishing the viewer. Like Notre-Dame, Le Corbusier's court makes you feel tall and strong; its radiant energy enters you.

The fenestration of the High Court is one of Le Corbusier's finest abstract compositions, precisely orchestrated to suggest randomness and improvisation. The well-organized complex network of interior ramps that lead visitors to courtrooms and offices is equally dynamic. In its framework, it is comparable to the human skeleton; in its ongoing motion, it resembles the human circulatory system—the miraculousness of which Le Corbusier was particularly aware, having sketched the varicose veins that had only recently been removed from his own body. Nature, after all, is the greatest architect ever.

2

Most photographs show the High Court brand-new. In those images, it might as well be a building model, rather than the living and breathing entity it has since become. For a virtual village has developed at its feet, and the building itself has acquired signs of age and use.

As a sculptural object, the High Court is a fine amalgam of forms, with rhythmically charged verticals and horizontals and a perfect balance of small and large elements. But half a century or so after its completion, while it remains a virtuoso visual performance, it is richer still. For not only does the High Court connect harmoniously to the plateau that surrounds it and to the distant mountains, and relate to the adjacent buildings in view, but it also interacts with the people perpetually entering and leaving it.

As you approach the looming structure, you walk amid women in brightly colored saris, many of them sitting on the ground and selling peanuts; half-clad children milling about; old men stooped on walking sticks; and judges and lawyers and their clients pacing purposefully toward the courtrooms. You hear the composite sounds of the assembly of people, and the justices in their black robes speaking both Hindi and Punjabi.

The High Court seems to succor them. All these unexpected elements—the people selling their wares, the piles of faded legal documents visible in the windows of the offices and courtrooms—are at home in Le Corbusier's creation, rather than intrusive on a pristine design. The building is a setting for justice and life-altering decisions in the same way that a Gothic cathedral is a vehicle for religion and faith.

IN JANUARY 2000, the building entrance was partially obliterated by all the cars of Indian officials parked in front. The interior was appallingly filthy and decrepit. There was a distinct lack of maintenance—apparent in dirt, crumbling plaster, faded paint, and, on the roof, a pile of discarded tires and inner tubes.

But for all that, what force! And what a new way of thinking about the role of justice and the ability of color and form to add confidence and joy to the minute-to-minute experience of human beings.

3

Inside the High Court, there is a tapestry designed by Le Corbusier that is 144 square meters. It was woven over a period of five months by the men in Kashmir who had also made the 64-square-meter tapestries he designed for each of the eight smaller courts. The woolen hangings absorb noise, mitigating the resonance of the reinforced concrete and making the acoustics comfortable. They also give energy to the judicial proceedings. Bright abstract forms play against somber ones, while depictions of lightning, sun, clouds, and stars are present. Like work by Kandinsky and Miró, to which they refer, the tapestries evoke the entire universe.

Shortly after the High Court was put into use, Le Corbusier heard from Pierre Jeanneret that some of the justices had removed his tapestries from their courtrooms. The chief justice, however, had kept his, and was enthusiastic about it.

Le Corbusier wrote to Nehru. He began by obsequiously heaping gratitude on the prime minister for the commission of the new capital. Then he got to the point. He asked how these "subalterns" could possibly have the right to make such a decision. What gave them the temerity to countermand the taste of the person who, because of Chandigarh, had become "the first architect of today's world?" While apologizing for his conceit—"a thousand pardons for the lack of modesty"—Le Corbusier said he would not tolerate the maneuver.[4]

Subsequent details are lost to history, but the tapestries are back in place.

4

Balkrishna Doshi had a particular perspective on this building, starting with its political implications: "His bow to democracy lay in not placing his buildings on a pedestal—both the Assembly and the High Court do not have flights of steps. They're not imposing that way. He put them on the ground—perhaps he didn't want to change the level, he felt that in a democracy you do not put buildings on platforms."[5]

Of the billowing roofline of the High Court, Doshi observed, "As always, silhouette was important for him. You see these shapes, almost like an umbrella, but look at the negative space and it's like a dome . . . so he had this play of positive-negative, of floating form against the light."[6] Doshi recognized that the reason for this form was that it was essential for Le Corbusier that the sky actively penetrate his buildings. Earlier, this had been through geometric vistas, as in the Villa Savoye; now it was through a more organic interaction.

This desire for a connection between solid structure and the amorphous gases surrounding the earth was not always easy to realize. While Le Corbusier intended the shells in the High Court to be very thin (like the roof he was concurrently designing for Ronchamp), the realities of engineering did not permit this. They had to be redesigned as a heavier slab that in turn was curved and cantilevered.

The architect also had, yet again, a problem with the realities of the climate. His mother's and Hélène de Mandrot's leaking roofs and windows represented a difficulty that was endemic to his work. At Chandigarh, the beating rain during the season of heavy showers made it necessary to build an arcade in the High Court that had nothing to do with Le Corbusier's original plans. His accommodation to the rain at the Millowners' Building had been a rarity.

The roof constructions and the arcades were not the only instances of Le Corbusier's idealism and aesthetics obliterating practicality or a full concern for the client's needs. Doshi also witnessed the judges' displeasure because, in spite of the architect's intention to work with the local culture and Nehru's praise of him for having done so, the High Court did not function according to Indian tradition: the courtrooms were too public. It was "a building that doesn't work."[7] Modifications were necessary.

But Balkrishna Doshi still thought it was "magnificent." The High Court had two sides, just as Le Corbusier did. The building design turned its back to certain truths and was wide-open to others.

5

Balkrishna Doshi was one of Le Corbusier's favorite young architects and was accorded the exceptional treatment that went with that position. He was invited to lunch when others were not, and he and Le Corbusier took long walks together, during which the older man liked to tell stories. Le Corbusier sent his young colleague to a doctor when he needed one and helped him get a fellowship from the Graham Foundation.

When Le Corbusier gave Doshi and his bride a drawing as a wedding present and Doshi did not look sufficiently pleased, Le Corbusier immediately took it back. That evening, he went to Doshi's house for dinner. In addition to another drawing, he gave the young man five hundred rupees. On the envelope, Le Corbusier wrote, "This is a small token to add grease to the wheels of life. I'm sure you will break many dishes on each other's heads but you'll survive all that with joy and pleasure."[8]

Le Corbusier interacted with people according to his own terms. Doshi was present at a party in Chandigarh at which Le Corbusier conspicuously refused to shake hands with the judges and said, "You don't dispense proper justice."[9] Sometimes he acceded to his whims; at other moments, he strategized. He cautioned Doshi never to send all the photos of a building model to a client; one was enough. It would give the client some idea of the proposal but would help avoid sources of disagreement. Similarly, Le Corbusier advised Doshi to let the client pick a single color to be used in a house but then to save the other choices for himself. That way, the client would feel he had made a decision and would thus be kept happy, but the architect would maintain control of the quality.

THE YOUNGER MAN was as impressed by Le Corbusier's adaptability as by his craftiness. Le Corbusier also had a remarkable ability to improvise. If, in India, contractors had only two of the three sizes of stone that he had designated, he would have them cut one of the two existing sizes to make the third—all corresponding to the Modulor—and then, with characteristic frugality, would use the residue in floors or window panels or sunscreens.

6

Balkrishna Doshi also saw Le Corbusier at his most humane: "He gave the ordinary man dignity. It was as if he were looking at men and God together—no human being was really ordinary. Since he was not involved in politics or economics, he tried to give man dignity through his dwelling." Le Corbusier used scale so that "no man felt less than a king in his house."[10]

15. Self-portrait as a crow delivering Christmas presents, in a letter to Yvonne, December 1953

16. Sketch in a letter to his mother and Albert, August 31, 1955

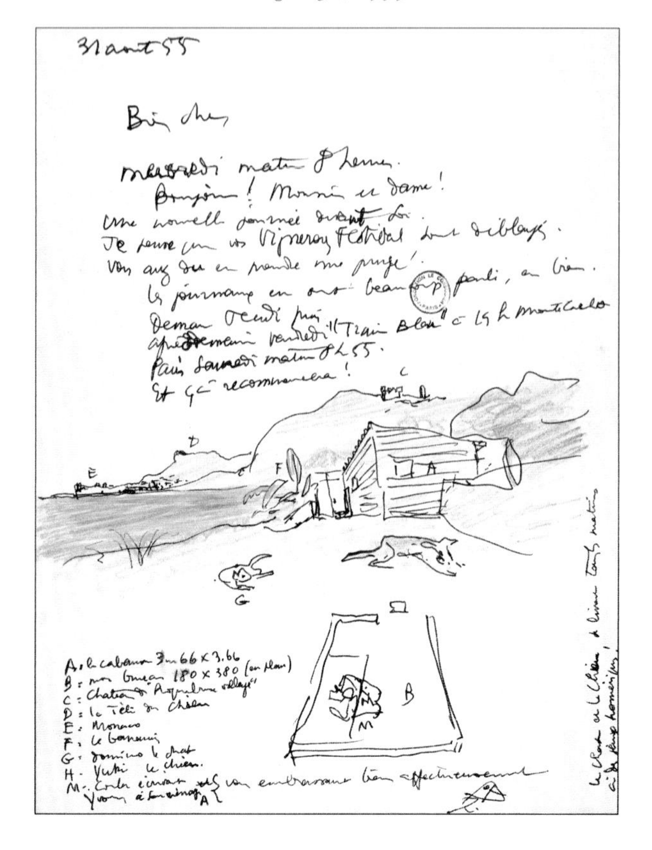

17. Entrance facade of the Millowners' Building (1951–1956), Ahmedabad

18. Ronchamp, interior, view from the altar
19. Ronchamp, interior, wall of painted glass windows

20. *Interior of chapel at La Tourette*

21. *The light cannons at La Tourette as seen from above*

22. *The Assembly Building in Chandigarh, late 1950s*

23. Josephine Baker, watercolor, 1929

24. Josephine Baker, watercolor

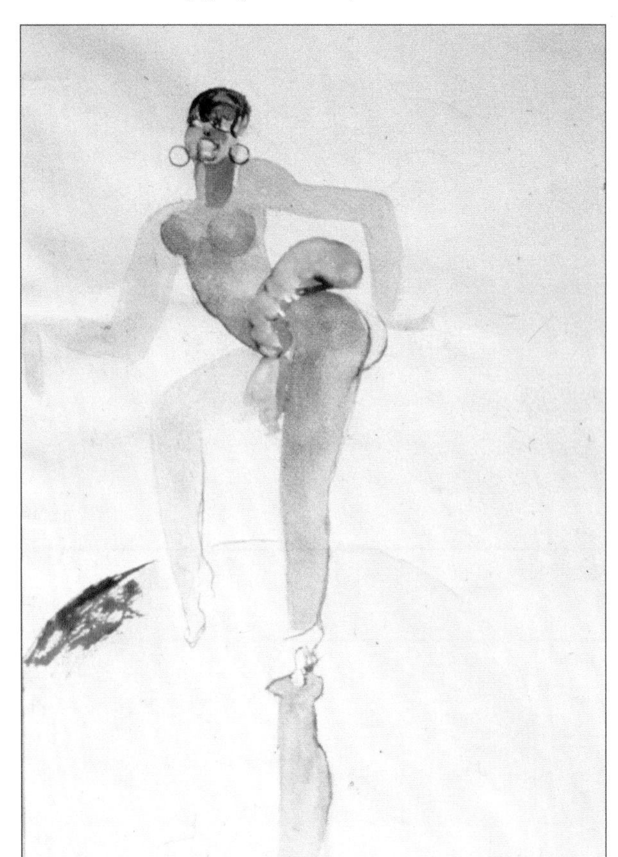

25. *Josephine Baker, watercolor*

17 juin 58

Bien chers tous deux !

Rentré dimanche matin, d'une semaine passée à Roquebrune cimetière pour construire avec Bertocchi (le maçon dont le fils était filleul d'Yvonne) la tombe d'Yvonne.
Nid perché à 300 m plus haut que notre cabanon. Pour transports il faut une mule, puis les épaules (les charges) d'hommes.
De lundi matin à samedi midi, Bertocchi a fait les travaux de fouille, fondation et ciment apparent.
C'est bien !

La tombe.

26. Sketch of Yvonne's tomb in Roquebrune-Cap-Martin, in a letter to his mother, June 17, 1958

Doshi was struck by Le Corbusier's fascination with steamship cabins, train berths, and the shacks that poor people lived in. These small-scale spaces reflected very different economic means but had in common that they were composed of tight, shipshape units. When Doshi took the Swiss to see old six-foot-wide shacks in the slums of Ahmedabad, rather than recoil in horror Le Corbusier stretched out his arms in admiration. "My God, look how these people can live," he declared, more with respect for their ingenuity in dire circumstances than sadness at their paucity of resources.[11]

Le Corbusier was so interested in sensuous experience in India that when eating meat he put big pieces of salt on some of the food and none on other pieces. "It seemed as though he always wanted two dimensions—thin and thick, tall and low, rough and smooth, light and shade. There was always this kind of counterbalance," wrote Doshi.[12] Such attention to the details of life and the will to alter its components were part of the refinement of his vision.

Often comparing his work to a fugue by Bach, Le Corbusier understood that change and difference, jumps in scale inside and outside, alteration of thick and thin lines, and variables of rhythm and balance are what make things work.

AFTER A WHILE, Doshi felt so resented by others as the master's pet in Chandigarh that he got himself sent to Ahmedabad, where he replaced Jean Véret, one of the main architects in the Paris office, as Le Corbusier's chief site architect.

There, Doshi saw Le Corbusier's musical sense of composition at work as they were detailing the private house that Le Corbusier made for Surottam Hutheesing. Le Corbusier was displeased because he felt that the pattern was too rigid. Doshi proposed using rectangular columns instead of round ones: squared-off columns could serve as walls and storage spaces as well. Le Corbusier liked the idea and ran with it: "Within two hours he had made a miracle out of the sections by just adding a little beam here and a slab across and putting a circle there to open it up."[13] He had interjected the rhythm that brought it to life.

This exquisite villa—which Hutheesing sold to another mill owner, Shyamubhai Shodhan, before it was completed—demonstrates the results of Le Corbusier's flexibility. A wonderful rough concrete shell with multiple openings and terraces, it includes a spectacular hanging garden. Inside, with its surprising juxtapositions of scale and unpredictable twists and turns, complete with staircases that seem to float in midair, it looks like a composition by Piranesi. Outside, the Villa Shodhan is a particularly luxurious Corbusean statement, with its ambient rough concrete punctuated by boldly painted, sparkling yellow and green panels, and its large, round swimming pool, with bright-orange ladders around the concrete perimeter, blending industrial toughness with a euphoric approach to color.

BEFORE HE LEFT INDIA for the last time, Le Corbusier invited Doshi to select another drawing for himself. The young acolyte made his selection, and Le Corbusier told him that he had picked the right one, so now he should pick another, and the process went on until he was given four in all.

That generosity was in the same proportion as Le Corbusier's acidic toughness. Doshi accepted the apparent contradictions or inconsistencies as balanced sides of the same person. Once, when Le Corbusier was going to travel by car from Chandigarh to New Delhi and Doshi asked him for a ride, the older man gruffly replied, "No. No. No." He then immediately said that if Doshi really wanted to go along, he could of course do so, if he was punctual. They were leaving at 6:30 the following morning. Doshi was there at the appointed hour, and Le Corbusier treated him as a cherished traveling companion for the next several days.

First, he insisted that they stop en route in the village that had his favorite restaurant for Tandoori chicken. Le Corbusier emphasized that he loved it because this was a true "mountain chicken," tough muscled, more flavorful and full of character than a city chicken. In Delhi itself, Le Corbusier was equally definitive about everything he saw. He spent a lot of time studying Indian miniatures in the museums; he loved their intertwined figures. On the other hand, he thought Edwin Lutyens's much-touted British colonial architecture was merely "okay."

"The sense of eternity was very important to him," wrote Doshi. "Counterbalance. Uncertainties. Conflicts. The dialogue that goes on within one's self. The battle between one's self and black paper. Some force is coming—the light. The idea of a pact with nature. A building and nature must merge."[14]

L

1

Hutheesing's house was not the only villa for a rich client living in seclusion and luxury in Ahmedabad. On his trips to the great textile city, where he was building a local museum, Le Corbusier took on the task of creating a private, modern palace in a lush tropical garden for Manorama Sarabhai. For all the modesty of his taste in his own dwelling and the egalitarianism of his housing complexes, the architect relished the task of building her an exquisite and opulent retreat.

The Sarabhais were a prosperous textile family—cultivated, intellectually avid, and international, while remaining grounded in their local culture. Prominent in the Millowners' organization, they had been instrumental in bringing Le Corbusier to Ahmedabad initially. For generations, they had had a family compound, called the Retreat. While geographically near the center of the bustling metropolis, this lush garden with family mansions offers the privacy and seclusion of a private park.

Manorama Sarabhai's husband, one of the heirs to the family fortune, had recently died. Her brother, Chinubhai Chimanbhai, was the mayor of the city. This woman, connected to two important dynasties, was faced with the daunting task of bringing up her children on her own. She had definite theories about the house in which she would do so. She and her husband were both Jains, a sect whose belief system is based on respect for the natural world and the wish to leave it undisturbed. Sarabhai wanted a new residence that would maintain a strong connection to its environment; she also intended it to reflect western modernism. Completely atypical for her generation, this sophisticated young widow had taken her children to New York for two years, where she installed them at the Waldorf-Astoria Hotel; with equal audacity, she was now hiring a Parisian architect.

In the enchanted garden of the family compound, Le Corbusier placed her villa in such a way that the structure is scarcely visible through the trees that surround it. The ground floor is open to the outdoors, the only semblance of walls being wooden-slat rolling blinds controlled by ropes. The large-scale living spaces and many terraces provide the rustic luxury of an expensive safari camp. The architecture recedes, completely subservient to the natural setting, providing luxuriousness but not flaunting it.

While Le Corbusier was working on the house, he became close to the Sarabhais' young son Anand, then about ten years old. Ever eager to swim, the architect borrowed Anand's school shorts to wear as swim trunks in the pool of the family's old mansion. Anand Sarabhai had a favorite book, *Fatty-puffs and Thinifers*—about fat people and thin people. Its author, André Maurois, gave the skinnier creatures beds that extended and catapulted them through holes in the floor into their bathtubs every morning. It became a fantasy of Anand's to do the same, and Le Corbusier decided to realize the boy's dream. He built a marvelous slide that goes from the bedroom floor of the villa directly into the swimming pool one story below. Water flowed down the slide; Anand could start his days with a refreshing dip. This device was also a means of air-conditioning for the house; the water on the slide was recirculated from the cooling system.

The main units of the Villa Sarabhai are in the style of Catalonian vaults, an architectural form Le Corbusier had come to admire in Barcelona. Half cylinders of rough concrete, they are covered on their tops by earth to form a lawn and roof garden. Unlike normal roofing materials, that sod serves to cool the inside of the house, even when the Indian heat rises to 120 degrees Fahrenheit. The insides of these vaults, meanwhile, seem like capacious caves; the barrel-shaped enclosures make the innermost chambers of the house dark and deeply romantic.

However cavelike within, these bays are completely open at the front and back. This has its hazards when it is raining, rendering the villa "very nice to live in, although impractical in many ways."[1] But the house accommodated the client's wishes for a direct proximity to nature and also for flexibility of space; Le Corbusier designed a structure that could change as Sarabhai's use of the place did. In keeping with her request, any wall in the middle could be removed.

Even if a bit of rain gets in through the ends of the bays, the villa coheres in such a relaxed way to its natural surroundings that when you see, on a downspout, a cobweb with a blossoming weed coming through it or a chipmunk running down the pool slide, they become part of the integrity of the experience, not intrusions. This villa built with constant awareness of water and the sun has wide-mouthed downspouts that evacuate the rain. They are big enough for torrential tropical downpours. The sod roof also accommodates rather than fights nature. Le Corbusier was delighted to build for the rich, but what he gave them, while immensely comfortable, was completely lacking in the sort of artifice so often associated with financial wealth. Rather, open to its tropical surroundings, working in concord with the sun, it is reverential of wonders that money cannot buy.

2

Once the villa was complete, Manorama Sarabhai found her new home equally suited for sumptuous family get-togethers or quiet moments reading in a corner. For affluent people in the tropics, Le Corbusier had achieved much the same thing as at the modest house in Vevey by making the exterior and interior interact. Here, too, there is constant rhythm and a vitality to the forms. One of these celestial residences housed an austere piano teacher living at the edge of a cold lake, while the other was for an international arts patron with bright-green wild parrots in her garden, but the values were consistent.

It was the specifics that were different. Le Corbusier had applied himself to the task of Sarabhai's villa with a keen awareness that he was constructing in conditions unlike those for any of his other houses except for Hutheering's. This was one of his few private residences where he did not also have to factor in the need for heat in cold weather. His primary goals were coolness, shade, and the ability to capture air currents; the heat of the sun had to be minimized or avoided. Since mosquitoes were a significant factor, he incorporated screens and netting.

Knowing that a glass wall could become an enemy in the summer heat, Le Corbusier again utilized *brises-soleil.* He also situated the house so that it would be traversed by the prevailing breezes. He used bricks and rough concrete, the latter often coated in white to induce coolness, both physical and psychological, with bright colors creating elements of joy. The results were salubrious.

From the start, however, Le Corbusier's relationship with his client was contentious. After the initial contracts had been signed in the summer of 1953 and plans were under way, the architect found it necessary to have Ducret write to his patroness to say,

> I beg to insist quite particularly on the character of the role taken by M. LE CORBUSIER.
>
> M. LE CORBUSIER is not a businessman. He is an artist and, the world over, he is regarded as such and surrounded by consequent respect.
>
> It is extremely disagreeable for him to discuss questions concerning the rates of remuneration for his services, and he is especially unhappy to have received the impression that he might be regarded as attached to financial considerations.[2]

Le Corbusier had by then made several trips to Ahmedabad. His draftsmen had done considerable work on the plans, and he had commissioned expensive surveys requiring him to lay out considerable funds. He had received only a pittance in payment. His office manager insisted that the architectural fees and travel costs to date be paid immediately.

During the construction process, relations improved. The architect collaborated quite easily with Manorama Sarabhai, acceding to her views on many issues. He shifted from a black stone for some of the walls to a lighter-toned brown, as she requested. However, when Sarabhai requested a reduction in the size of the swimming pool, Le Corbusier made it clear that he had gone as far as he was willing to go. To make the pool any smaller would put Anand at risk of losing his life by striking his head on a pool wall. "I'd look like an idiot if I made a pool 24′ by 24′ at the end of a slide 46′ long!" the architect wrote his client.[3] Here, he prevailed.

WHILE THE BUILDING PROCESS was taking place between 1952 and 1955, Le Corbusier visited Ahmedabad every November. When he returned in the spring of 1956, the house was complete. This was when the trouble really began.

The architect was furious at Manorama Sarabhai's treatment of his creation. He wrote his client, "You've got a lovely house. But you can Kill it!" He informed her that the work of her gardener, along with her old furniture and decorative, tasteless art objects "will have soon annihilated the ambiance, the atmosphere, the spirit of the house."[4] While couching his critique in polite language, Le Corbusier warned Sarabhai that she had better take care; she needed to make an effort to keep from disappointing visitors. He suggested that Doshi, who was at this time in Ahmedabad and had his full confidence, could help rectify the mistakes she had already made.

Sarabhai justified some alterations as being for her son's sake. Le Corbusier replied that the boy, while charming, was still young and had not seen a lot of the world. It was a grievous error to pander to his whims. Instead, she should tell Anand to make an effort to adapt to the spirit of his new home. If handled accordingly, Anand would adjust.

Sarabhai was intensely annoyed. She let Le Corbusier know that, while she had fulfilled every point of their contract and had followed his advice by painting the upper floors and doors his chosen colors and had been a good sport when she had problems with one of the open arches during the heavy rains, he still had not done his promised garden layout or designed any of the customized furniture she wanted. This is where their correspondence ended—with both parties feeling wounded.

3

Le Corbusier spilled out some of his problems with the Sarabhai commission to Taya Zinkin, a journalist from the *Manchester Guardian Weekly,* whom he met at a party in Bombay. Zinkin's account, which was published only after the architect died a decade later, has entered the Le Corbusier mythology, but it is of questionable validity.

The writer says that when she was introduced to him, she knew only that he was a "tall, handsome, elderly" Frenchman who was standing by himself drinking cognac, and that he spoke no English. This was a fallacy: by then, Le Corbusier was able to converse in English and often did so in India, as in the United States and Britain.

Zinkin wrote that Le Corbusier was in a rage because he was having trouble transferring funds paid him by Sarabhai to France. He was, the journalist claims, on his way to Delhi to urge Nehru to intervene. She says he also told her that Sarabhai had implored him to install railings or a low wall around the balconies of her villa. Zinkin quotes Le Corbusier as saying, "The good woman was afraid that when her sons get married their children would fall off and kill themselves, as if I cared. As if I, Le Corbusier, would compromise with design for the sake of her unborn brats!" Zinkin also quotes Le Corbusier as calling Yvonne "pretty stupid" and saying, "Madame wants children! She keeps pestering me for children. I *hate* children. She already has a little dog, that should be good enough."[5] In spite of *The Guardian*'s reputation for the highest journalistic standards, a lot of this is implausible. Le Corbusier was not publicly disloyal to Yvonne, and he had many successful connections to children even if he had none of his own.

Zinkin had an apparent reason for wanting to skewer Le Corbusier. The day after they met, they were on the same flight to Delhi. She claims that, as they were leaving the plane, he asked what she was doing that night. When the journalist replied that she had a train to catch, he said, "Pity. You are fat and I like my women fat. We could have spent a pleasant night together."[6] She claims not to have been offended, and when, a few days later, she was given the chance to interview him in his office in Chandigarh, she eagerly accepted.

She arrived for that meeting armed with questions about his work. Before she had even asked the first one, Le Corbusier said, "We are not going to discuss architecture. I hate talking shop to a woman." He told her to come the next night to his room at Maiden's Hotel in Delhi and said he would give her her choice of his drawings of bulls. "Now run along, don't stand there wasting my time," he then instructed her.[7] She walked out, never to see him again.

This, anyway, was Taya Zinkin's report on their relationship, published for all the world to know, becoming one of the staples of the architect's reputation in his dealings with women.

4

Though he locked antlers with the rich and imperious Manorama Sarabhai, in Chandigarh Le Corbusier got along well with his client base. What he built brought delight and pride to the hundreds of thousands of people who were flooding into the new city. The thousands involved in its construction were also, in general, content. The workers considered Le Corbusier demanding but respectful, aloof but amiable. He was a visitor from the west who, rather than impose his ways, responded to theirs. And he was admired for the courage and genius that resulted in such remarkable architecture.

One of the people who worked closely under Le Corbusier, M. S. Sharma, was among the many who found the architect unlike anyone else he had met. Part of what struck him was the architect's essential unknowability: "Nobody knew Le Corbusier in all his aspects. The only one who might possibly have known most sides was Pierre Jeanneret." What Sharma did know with certainty was what it meant to work for Le Corbusier. "He was a very hard taskmaster. Each time he came, people were eagerly awaiting, and didn't know what to expect. He himself didn't have a moment to spare and expected everyone else to be very serious."[8]

One day, the younger man had a meeting to discuss the new Post, Telegraph, and Telephone Building with top officials in the telecommunications industry. The project was to be the tallest in the city center, eleven stories high. Sharma was to take the bus to the site. Le Corbusier, noticing that Sharma was late to leave for his appointment, told him the hour—three times, in rapid sequence. Georges Jeanneret's punctiliousness was inviolate.

Le Corbusier's sheer brilliance, however, made Sharma feel it was a privilege to do as he beckoned:

> He was the most observant man I've ever seen. Always with a small sketchbook and pencils bound in an elastic. Wearing a khaki safari jacket with big pockets. A most elegant person; at meetings, he had

> his bow tie and impeccable suits. And when he sketched a bull that was just outside his office window, it was a very elegant bull.
>
> Except for Leonardo and Michelangelo, I've never known of anyone so deeply immersed in life—and so versatile. Everything has the master's touch. Every work he did reflects his greatness.[9]

SHARMA OFTEN HAD DINNER with Le Corbusier and the other architects and builders at Pierre Jeanneret's house, where they drank Pierre's homemade wines. Le Corbusier talked nonstop, dashing from subject to subject and addressing minute details and major philosophical issues in the same breath. One never knew in what direction his discourse would go. He would be carrying on about one subject while clearly thinking of something else, formulating an answer while speaking about an unrelated matter, as if he could operate simultaneously on two different levels. Sharma was once aware of the master digressing completely from the theme at hand for a full seven minutes, only to return to the initial topic and provide a precise answer to the question that had been posed.

One afternoon, Le Corbusier had a small seashell in his pocket that, for no particular reason, he gave to Sharma's four-year-old son, Manu. "Do you see how beautiful it is?" the distinguished architect asked in Swiss-accented English. Manu Sharma, more than forty years later, still has that small shell as a precious relic.

For Sharma, Le Corbusier, despite his occasional cantankerousness, remained an idol: "He walked straight. He talked straight. His attitude was so masculine. There was nothing feminine about it. This was not a man who could be humbled by any power. He was the embodiment of the spirit that Lord Krishna preached—Karma theory—you have to work for any achievement. Deep concentration on the work at hand, devotion to a building project, was akin to worship, to religion."[10]

5

Le Corbusier knew that the "Open Hand," the monument that would be the crowning element of the capital, still required Nehru's endorsement. P. M. Thapar advised him on the best moment to turn to Nehru with the proposal for this gigantic thick-fingered hand—its form simplified and generalized but still recognizable, elevated on a sort of stand, symbolizing a new, more generous approach to human existence. Le Corbusier set up a meeting in Delhi during a visit in the late 1950s, when Chandigarh was well advanced.

To persuade the prime minister, Le Corbusier told a cautionary tale. He explained that at the World Congress of Peace Supporters, six years earlier, the judges of a design competition had made the mistake of rejecting his proposal. Le Corbusier provided Nehru with a document, as well as its translation into English, presenting his philosophy on politics. Nations and their differences, he explained, were minor issues by comparison to certain universal needs.

Le Corbusier informed Nehru that not only was this document of great intellectual value, but it had led to a development of even greater importance than the words themselves: an open hand floating over the horizon, symbolizing the universality about which he had written. It would reach a height of twenty-five meters, would be built out of "enameled wrought iron," and would move according to the wind.[11]

Le Corbusier told Nehru that Varma, the chief engineer of Punjab, was already prepared to build the Open Hand. The architect also informed Nehru that he had presented the concept to the Cabinet of Ministers in November 1954 and had completed all the technical studies to make the monument work. Two French manufacturers were willing to make it; Le Corbusier cheerfully let Nehru know that he was "stupefied" at the bargain price they offered.

Le Corbusier finished by declaring that if the prime minister authorized the building of the Open Hand, he would be making a major step toward the achievement of world peace: "I am certain that by raising the 'Open Hand' in this location, India will be making a gesture which will confirm your decisive intervention at the crucial moment of machine-age evolution and its dangerous implications. . . . I shall end these remarks with that declaration I made in one of my books: 'Architecture is the expression of the spirit of an epoch.' "[12]

The monument was to be positioned precisely in the center of the most public part of Chandigarh, with an adjacent amphitheatre where the public could sit and face it. The architect made a plaster maquette of the form, with its large thumb thrust at a right angle, slightly resembling a flying bird. The three middle fingers, stubby and of equal length, were a sort of cockscomb, and the wide pinkie, angled backward, the tail. The finished work was to be made of metal and enameled in bright red, white, green, and yellow. Le Corbusier issued further statements about its importance, saying it represented abundance and was open to receive the bounty of the earth and to distribute it to the people of India and other countries. It affirmed the beginning of "the era of harmony."[13]

However buoyant and optimistic the monument's spirit, it required all the hyperbole and justification because it failed without them.

In spite of the propaganda campaign, the Open Hand fell into the category of Le Corbusier's unrealized dreams; Nehru did nothing about getting it constructed. But unlike the League of Nations and a range of other projects, it eventually rose after its designer's death. Today, it floats over the land amid the architectural masterpieces of Chandigarh. Although it lacks the force of those buildings, one imagines that Le Corbusier would only have been pleased.

LI

1

During one of his visits to the Sarabhais, Le Corbusier was on his way one morning to the local airport when he saw the vast power station of the Ahmedabad Electricity Company. Its monumental cooling tower had the form of a grain silo but with all the surfaces curved and stretched. Le Corbusier was riveted by the gigantic elastic structure. He was just then developing the General Assembly at Chandigarh, and he imagined how this shape might be applied to the entirely different domain of civic architecture. He immediately began sketching.

Anand Sarabhai was in the car that morning. The architect's unique ability to see what others would fail to notice, and the fancifulness that accompanied his perceptiveness, were striking to the boy. At the airport, where there was a tiny restaurant, Le Corbusier fixated on the orange and green of the plastic salt and pepper shakers, moving them back and forth like chess pieces, staring at them. Everywhere he looked, color and form affected him.

In little time, a short, seemingly open-topped structure—concave around its entire surface and resembling the cooling tower—rose from the roof of the General Assembly. The base of the assembly is a Corbusean rectangular block, a lively amalgam of pilotis, *brises-soleil,* and exterior spiral stairs. The anomalous form emerging victoriously from its flat roof, serving as its main auditorium, the meeting place of the Punjab Senate, has the triumphant energy of birth itself. It was a public space entirely without precedent (see color plate 22).

Le Corbusier had utilized not only the appearance but also the structural properties of cooling towers. He had visited such structures at night, when he could observe them freely, and spent considerable time checking their acoustics, sometimes banging two wooden planks together to hear the echoes. He then applied the principles of these industrial forms to the hyperbolic shell of the assembly, which is consistently one meter and fifteen centimeters thick.

That sheath has been molded in a form that maintains its tensile

The roof of the Assembly Building in Chandigarh, late 1950s

strength. At its top, the tower culminates in an oblique, angled section—as opposed to a flat, horizontal roof. That unusual roof is buttressed by an aluminum framework that is—Le Corbusier delighted in providing the explanation—"a veritable physics laboratory destined to deal with the play of natural light and with a degree of artificial light, with ventilation, with the electronic-acoustic machinery."[1] This "laboratory" was a rational and orderly structure intended not to impose an impossible order on the natural havoc of life but, rather, to serve and honor complexity.

"Furthermore, this cork will lend itself to future solar festivities, reminding men once a year that they are children of the sun (a fact entirely forgotten by our extravagant civilization, crushed as it is by absurdities, particularly with regard to its architecture and its urbanism)," he wrote.[2] The juxtaposition, in a single sentence, of all-consuming sun worship with the absurdities of a civilization deprived of its instincts reveals the simultaneous hope and tragedy inside the perpetual cacophony of Le Corbusier's mind.

The interior of the hyperbolic cylinder of the Assembly has thrilling physical properties. Part of it reflects sound, another part absorbs it, to allow for ideal acoustics on ground level when the deputies meet. The shape serves the purposes of air-conditioning by allowing cool air to enter several meters above the level of human congress and descend to breathing level, while the warmer air rises to the level of a mechanical apparatus that removes it. The form that, from the outside, is startling and discomfiting, is, within, accommodating and succoring.

The cooling tower also gave Le Corbusier a chance to link architecture

The Assembly Building in Chandigarh, late 1950s

with the reigning political philosophy. Nehru had established "a five-year plan whose primary aim was to develop industry and produce electricity on a large scale. Thus, the cooling towers of an electric power plant must have seemed to Le Corbusier a particularly appropriate symbol for expressing the social and political aspirations of this friend and patron. . . . Gandhi's philosophy of rejecting technology and focusing on the importance of agriculture, handicraft, and cottage industry finds many direct and indirect references in the Assembly. The hand-made quality of the *béton brut,* the folk imagery on the ceremonial gateway, the wall decorations based on imprints made by the workmen, and the juxtaposition of the oxcart with the building in one of Le Corbusier's sketches all attest to a world view that shared a great deal with Gandhi's own. For Le Corbusier, Gandhi's philosophy of rural rejuvenation offered a felicitous balance to Nehru's technological bias."[3]

Le Corbusier saw himself as possessed of the power to understand the validity of such overarching ideas even more clearly than world leaders like Gandhi and Nehru did: "Life has placed me in the position of an observer, giving me incomparable—and exceptional—means of judgment. I believe that this order of thought is not available to political leaders and that they live *in* the problem and hence do not see it."[4] He believed that his architecture, more than the ideas of any world leader, whatever his or her philosophy, was the salvation of humanity.

2

Because of security regulations put into effect after a bomb in front of the nearby Secretariat killed sixteen people in 1995, it is now difficult for laypeople to obtain permission to go inside the General Assembly. If as a tourist you do manage to get in, you must carry nothing and empty your pockets completely; you are not even permitted to have a paper and pencil in hand. The absence of a camera or note-taking capability has its benefits, for you concentrate on an unforgettable unfolding of events. You do nothing other than look and absorb the sequence of astonishing experiences.

From the vast entry hall bathed in cathedral-like light, you proceed through a wide corridor that feels like a promenade, a glade in a forest: man-made architecture that conjures very tall trees with sunlight filtering through the foliage above. This space, which Le Corbusier planned for deputies to pass one another and meet for informal conversation en route to or from their assembly hall, encircles you in quietude and calm.

Then you enter the great meeting room. At first, it is frightening, like a weird cave. A visitor from the west could well wonder if this is suddenly the effects of the antimalaria medication or of the scorching Indian sun. The space is a hallucination. The ceiling soars in a myriad of directions. There are relief sculptures plastered onto its crazy ziggurat of forms that resemble

The Hall of Parliament in Chandigarh, late 1950s

shapes by Jean Arp animated and gone berserk. One cannot possibly fathom everything going on. Nothing has prepared you for the play of light and dark, the explosion of deep colors, the nonstop choreography of ostensibly inanimate materials.

You are used to art as seen in museums: paintings on the walls, sculpture in the round. This time, you are inside the work of art. If you can imagine being totally enveloped by one of the great abstractions of Wassily Kandinsky or Jackson Pollock, being surrounded by its elements as if it is a vast tent, you approximate the life force and energy of this auditorium. But you are also in a functional space, a meeting hall where rational decisions are made, a place where the acoustics and air-conditioning work efficiently. Tough events take place inside this work of art, and people engage in conversation, however disputatious, and exchange ideas. In spite of the taxing exigencies of politics and nationalism and the divisive religious differences that dominate discussions here, it is a setting where human beings achieve congress.

It has been reported that when the senate first tried to assemble in Le Corbusier's new building, logical debate and productive communication were impossible. The architecture was too distracting, the effect on everyone's mood too tumultuous. That disturbance is understandable. But once the politicians became habituated to the stimulus, dialogue flourished. Just as Le Corbusier had dreamed, a generosity of space, a spirit and energy in the physical surroundings, and a charge of visual rhythm were salubrious, infusing human beings with energy and opening their souls.

ARE WE INSIDE a vast human heart, having entered through an aorta into its throbbing chambers? This space, unlike any that has been made before, inscribed with unique forms, represents an apogee of imagination and courage. Standing at ground level with that whirlwind of shapes above us, we have no doubt that great art is at the edge of madness. The sheer unabashed courage evident in this hall, its Wagnerian emotionalism, the will to do what no one has ever done before are both wonderful and terrifying.

For all of his defeats and bitterness, Charles-Edouard Jeanneret had never lost an iota of his youthful intensity. Here, encouraged and supported by Nehru, welcomed by a culture completely different from his own, he expressed all of his rapture. He gave from the same depths with which he responded. Now that he could let loose, everything flowed in a torrent, cacophonous yet coherent.

Le Corbusier managed, on his own, what few people would dare to consider: the expression of psychological complexity in tandem with the logic, precision, and practicality of the sharpest engineer. He found the means to construct a sound and functional being that represents havoc and clarity at the same time. He showed unstinting generosity in making happen for others everything that occurred inside his own fabulous imagination. No wonder the architect was so often arrogant or impatient. How could someone of such breadth be expected to tolerate academic stodginess, bureaucratic obstacles to life, bourgeois timidity?

Speaking of Le Corbusier's Assembly, the architect Louis Kahn remarked to Balkrishna Doshi, "I have never met a man in my whole life who can freeze his decams."[5] That invented term suggested the power of a rotating cam multiplied by ten. To harness, encapsulate, and generate force was the miracle of this building.

3

Le Corbusier's enormous office building—the Palace of the Ministries, known generally as the Secretariat—opened in Chandigarh in 1958, five years after Nehru had laid its foundation stone. Initially, the architect had hoped to make it a true skyscraper. The prototype was a structure he had designed for Algiers in 1942, which had not gone beyond the drawing board. That form had in turn led to the ideal secretariat he had designed for the United Nations, which had been kidnapped and disfigured. Le Corbusier hoped that Chandigarh would at last afford him the opportunity to realize his dream.

It was not to be. The engineers and Indian architects on-site told the architect that there was no local concrete strong enough to bear the vertical load of a skyscraper. So Le Corbusier simply turned the form on its side as a great horizontal slab. When the necessity for compromise had technical reasons, rather than being the result of human ignorance, no one could be more accommodating.

Again, one should not picture the building as it appears in many photos: as a purely aesthetic object gently doubled in size by its own reflection in the pond in front of it. The experience of the Secretariat is, rather, quite unsettling. To enter, one has to go through security checkpoints, facing a plethora of machine guns and rifles. Soldiers spit and belch while rejecting the credentials of most would-be visitors. And if photos suggest an orderly appearance to the grid of the facade, in actuality, up close, what is contained in that rectangular block is a frenzy of forms.

Yet there is a system to the madness; the surface and structure of this office building intended to serve three thousand employees is based on the

In front of the Secretariat and the High Court in Chandigarh in March 1958. Photo by Pierre Jeanneret

Modulor. Issues of climate and sunlight are addressed by deep *brises-soleil* to provide shade, floor-to-ceiling window glass to permit maximum light, and narrow metal "aerators" with copper mosquito screens. The facade has rhythmic regularity, like the beat of the metronome atop his mother's piano. It also depends on the mastery of materials and craft essential to his father's livelihood, as well as the responsiveness to the sun and direct confrontation with the sky that marked the Sunday outings that were such a feature of family life.

Balkrishna Doshi was witness to the process whereby Le Corbusier came up with the design of this building front. Initially, he had designed the Secretariat to have balconies that stretched across the entire facade. But these long spans were so heavy that they needed to be cantilevered and required supporting elements that were not part of the plan. The contractors and site architects could not figure out how to conceal the necessary armature. Doshi reports, "Everyone wondered where the solution lay, and a lot of work was put in. One fine morning Corbusier arrived at the site, took a look at what was happening and said, 'No, no, no, not like that. Let the columns go straight down breaking the sun breakers. Don't make changes in design. Just let them go through.' "[6] As is often the case with easy solutions to complex problems, no one else had thought of this idea of keeping the armature visible.

These bold, continuous columns on the exterior of the building, blatantly there to provide support, had, Doshi observed, an aesthetic consequence as well: "The sun breakers changed and a totally new pattern emerged, most interesting and very beautiful because you never anticipated the strange rhythm that would occur. Le Corbusier was always able to give us the unexpected. In his desire to be formal he got into difficult situations in which there was no alternative but to land in a mess. But like an acrobat, he always managed to emerge unscathed."[7]

Le Corbusier spoke about what he had done with the building's circulation system in his most straightforward language: "The two large ramps in front of and behind the building, connected to each floor, are also made of raw concrete. They provide the three thousand employees an attractive means of circulation (morning and evening). The mechanical vertical means is provided by banks of elevators, in addition to a double staircase set in a vertical spine rising from the ground floor to the top of the structure."[8]

Depending on whether employees arrived by foot, on their bicycles, or by bus, they approached the Secretariat from either the Boulevard of the Waters or the Valley of Leisure Activities. Amusing vestiges of his early romanticism, the terms reflect Le Corbusier's attempts at poetry, which might have better suited a retirement community. In spite of those calm descriptives and the ordering role of the Modulor, the building itself is intensely animated. Both the southeast facade reflected in the water and the northeast side, which one approaches from the large area of land defined also by the High Court and the assembly, are highly charged.

Each facade is an amalgam of solid and void, of closed and open shapes. There are even more ins and outs and unexpected twists and turns than the Perret brothers' building at 25 bis rue Franklin had had. These facades are completely asymmetrical, each as impossible to absorb or understand in full detail as the workings of a human mind, conjuring Kandinsky's statement, "There is always an 'and.' "[9]

4

The roof of the Secretariat is even livelier. The forms that rise out of the flat terrace atop the building resemble plants growing out of the sea bottom. Perhaps Le Corbusier was indirectly influenced by what he saw when he was swimming in shallow water along the Mediterranean coast. Or maybe, like the cloudlike reliefs floating around the ceiling of the Assembly, these organic shapes are simply the product of the architect's imagination. Whatever the source, a Corbusean playground of forms teeters on madness. Antonio Gaudí's Casa Milà and Church of the Sagrada Familia are among the few architectural equivalents to this multidimensional free-for-all.

As on the roof of l'Unité d'Habitation in Marseille, on top of the Secretariat Le Corbusier has put you under the hot sun, facing the mountains in one direction and flatness in the other. When you look from that roof in the direction of the General Assembly and the High Court, you see an architectural landscape unlike any other on this earth. But, oddly enough, the High Court, so thunderous up close, from here reads as a series of graceful arches, a bit like the calm and orderly facade of the first Renaissance building, Brunelleschi's Hospital of the Innocents in Florence. The High Court is not governed by the same precise system of equals as the Brunelleschi, but a harmony and a sense of measure and logic prevail, thanks in part to the Modulor. With Le Corbusier, however, where there is order, there is also madness. You are surrounded by a lush frenzy on this eagle's nest, and you face the assembly's extraordinary tower—as well as the completely unusual monument to the Open Hand. One understands why Doshi was so struck by the architect as a man of counterbalances.

Today, on top of the Secretariat you might find tents or colorfully dressed bakers frying pastry balls. It is a floating village—like the roof at Marseille with its nursery school and playground, a place to be used, a gathering point where people can breathe good air. As always, Le Corbusier's architectural machine accommodates endlessly varied living.

BALKRISHNA DOSHI does not dissemble about the flaws and shortcomings of the Secretariat: "Everyone knows of course that the Secretariat fails, fails totally, as an office building. It doesn't take into consideration the requirements of an Indian office. . . . The people involved were over-awed by the fact that he was a genius and also a foreigner and therefore thought that nothing could go wrong; they were hesitant to discuss functional issues with him. He didn't ask, they didn't question, so the blame lies with both. Indians are generally too subservient to foreigners."[10]

Charles Correa, another architect who built in India, points out other inherent problems, putting a very different slant on Le Corbusier's beloved *brises-soleil:* "they are really great dust-catching, pigeon-infested contrivances, which gather heat all day and then radiate it back into the building at night, causing indescribable anguish to the occupants. They are not nearly as useful as old-fashioned verandahs, which are far cheaper to build, protect the building during the day, cool off quickly in the evenings, and, furthermore, double as circulation system. Neither have the great parasol roofs (as in the High Court) proved much more useful. Was LC perhaps more concerned with the visual expression of climate control than with its actual effectiveness? In any event, his enthusiasm seemed to lie not in solving the problem but in making the theatrical gesture—assuming the heroic pose—of addressing it."[11]

To the architect Paul Rudolph, on the other hand, the Secretariat was an aesthetic wonder, whatever its flaws: "In every way it opposes the mountains; the angled stair way, the ramp on the roof . . . all these angles are obviously and carefully conceived to oppose the receding angles of the land masses."[12]

Finally, there was the evaluation of Nehru: "It doesn't really matter whether you like Chandigarh or whether you don't like it. The fact of the matter is simply this: it had changed your lives."[13]

5

The Governor's Palace was never built, and the Open Hand rose only later, but most of Le Corbusier's buildings, as well as his overall scheme for Chandigarh, had come into being as he intended. In March 1959, Prime Minister Nehru declared, "I have welcomed very greatly one experiment in India, Chandigarh. Many people argue about it, some like it, and some dislike it. . . . It hits you on the head, and makes you think. You may squirm at the impact but it has made you think and imbibe new ideas, and the one thing which India requires in many fields is being hit on the head so that it may think. . . . There is no doubt that Le Corbusier is a man with a powerful and creative type of mind. For that reason, he may produce extravagances occasionally but it is better to be extravagant than to be a person with no mind at all."[14] Because Nehru considered the architect a demigod in his lifetime, appreciating and supporting his creativity—even if he did not construct the Open Hand—Le Corbusier had blossomed and made some of his finest architecture.

Almost everyone living in Chandigarh says the same sort of thing: "It is the best organized city in India." "The nicest city to live in." "We have family in Delhi, but could only live here." "Things are near to each other and easy to find."[15] Its residents are glad to be there, and if outsiders see it as a down-at-the-heels, polluted, unkempt metropolis, Chandigarh still beckons with some of the most exhilarating buildings on earth.

LII

Architecture is the masterly, correct, and magnificent play of masses brought together in light.

—LE CORBUSIER AS PARAPHRASED BY TENNESSEE WILLIAMS[1]

1

In his chapel at Ronchamp, Le Corbusier transformed rough concrete into an expression of bounteous hope. He made stone seem weightless and captured pure light as if it had mass.

When the idea for this hilltop chapel first made the miraculous leap from Le Corbusier's brain to a hasty pen-and-ink rendition, it was an act of pure creation. One can identify the influences on Le Corbusier's vision just as one might detail the genetic makeup of a newborn, but the conception of Ronchamp remains in a realm beyond total comprehension.

Le Corbusier had the vision in his very first sketches; only the means to realize it had to be found. His initial conception resembles an ancient megalith, an imaginary mix of dolmen and stone circle from the Bronze Age where so-called primitive people assembled and worshipped the forces of the universe. The finished building that opened a mere four years later on that hilltop in the Vosges remains faithful

Ca. 1950

to that image, while it is at the same time a complex structure of uniquely modern form that looks as if it has descended from the heavens. From its earliest inception to its completion, Ronchamp belonged equally to the ancient mythic past and the unknown future.

2

> The cathedral of Chartres had had the effect on me of the most terrible battle. Never say that the Gothic is serenity. It's a poignant and gigantic struggle, and of the nine towers, only two rise up into the air of the hillside. Chartres is a life of deliberate forces and demoniac optimism, of clenched fists and clenched jaws.
>
> —CHARLES-EDOUARD JEANNERET TO WILLIAM RITTER, 1917

The rural site where Le Corbusier built his masterpiece is in the hilly part of the Vosges region of southeastern France, adjacent to the Swiss Jura. It is 110 kilometers from La Chaux-de-Fonds, in a sparsely populated region of quiet, undulating hills.

"Ronchamp" comes from the Latin "*Romanorum campus,*" meaning Roman camp or field. The town, at the base of the steep hill, was near an old Roman road. A pagan temple, said to be for the worship of the sun, had been erected there. According to some sources, in the fourth century A.D. a church dedicated to the birth of the Virgin was built on the hilltop, while others date the first Christian church on the site to the twelfth century. By the thirteenth century, it began to attract pilgrims, and in the middle of the nineteenth century the ancient sanctuary was rebuilt in a form that combined an octagon and the Greek cross. In 1873, on September 8, the date on which the Virgin's birth is celebrated, more than thirty thousand pilgrims from Alsace and Lorraine, their lives changed two years before by the Franco-Prussian war that had made their homeland part of the German empire, flocked to this corner of Franche-Comté to ask Our Lady for their deliverance.

In 1913, the church burned to the ground after being struck by lightning, and in 1924 a neo-Gothic structure was built around the ruins. The new structure was destroyed in 1944 when the German army bombed it during an attack on French soldiers gathered on the hilltop, just as France was being liberated.

In 1950, two officials from the Commission of Sacred Art from Besançon, where the regional government was located, asked Le Corbusier to build a new church where all these earlier structures had existed. The architect turned them down.

As with his spontaneous rebuff of his visitors from Chandigarh, there are various accounts of why Le Corbusier said no to that first approach. Some claim that in his modesty the architect felt he was not ready for such an undertaking. Such humility, however, seems unlikely. Officially, Le Corbusier declared that what he would propose would be yet another source of controversy and would certainly be rejected. He was still smarting from the halt brought to his idea for the underground church at Sainte-Baume. Yet while he pretended to be unwilling, he would certainly have been miserably disappointed if his suitors had not continued their pursuit.

Canon Lucien Ledeur, one of the two officials, begged Le Corbusier to consider the beauty of the site. The distinguished clergyman issued an irresistible mandate: "You will be given free rein to create what you will."[2] Father Marie-Alain Couturier also implored him to consider it.

In mid-May 1950, shortly after saying no to the project, when Le Corbusier was on a train between Paris and Basel, he sketched the site and the rough form of the church ruin. He visited Ronchamp itself for the first time on June 4 and made further drawings in a little sketchbook as he sat on the hilltop for several hours. Canon Ledeur observed that the architect seemed

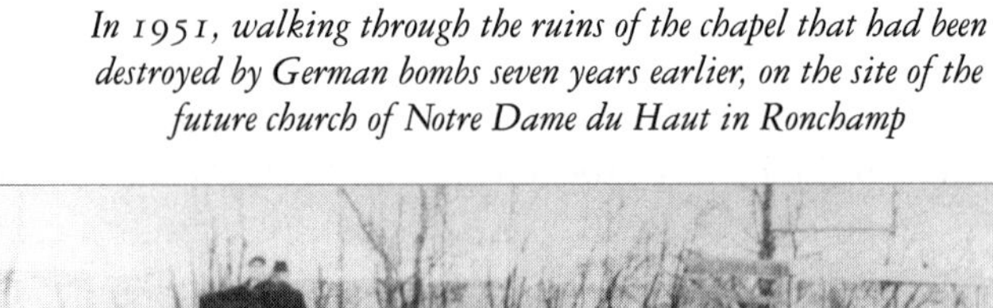

In 1951, walking through the ruins of the chapel that had been destroyed by German bombs seven years earlier, on the site of the future church of Notre Dame du Haut in Ronchamp

to feel an immediate connection to the landscape as he studied the rolling hills and looked at the views of plains and distant peaks.

This was the moment when he changed his mind. Since it was not a competition, and no jury was involved, it is hard to think that he would have done otherwise. Le Corbusier was moved not just by the beauty of the setting and the freedom he was to be given but also by "the spiritual grandeur of the undertaking."[3] The splendid site supported his faith in a higher being that went beyond any traditional notions of organized religion. A place that had been used for worship of the sun, the deity he revered above all others, was irresistible.

THE CLIENTS gave Le Corbusier a straightforward program for a church with a principal nave to accommodate two hundred people for mass, three smaller radiating chapels, and the capacity for ceremonies outside on August 15 and September 8, two annual pilgrimage days. A seventeenth-century polychrome wood sculpture that had been rescued from the previous church was to be placed in the new structure. It was also stipulated that there should be a means of collecting rainwater, because the hilltop was famously dry.

With those requirements and the setting in mind, Le Corbusier began to invent. He summoned ideas unprecedented in ecclesiastical design, just as he had broken the mold of domestic architecture at l'Unité d'Habitation and the notion of civil construction in Chandigarh.

When he was first on the site, he drew only the horizon lines and natural shapes that appeared before him. He kept himself open to inspiration, a process he described as a communion with nature whereby the horizon lines "architecturally released the acoustic reply—*visual acoustics in the realm of forms,*"[4] and "the idea is born, sways, diverges, seeks itself out"—as if it just happened like the winds of fate.[5]

Next, Le Corbusier echoed the hills in the sweeping roofline and the trees in the towers of his building design. Canon Ledeur made note of what the architect did during those hours on June 4. Le Corbusier penciled a curve mimicking the shape of the hills; this line based on nature was to become the south elevation of the church. He then quickly sketched the form of the outdoor altar. He furthered the scheme with a series of convex and concave curves and straight lines—ideas he continued to work out in his small sketchbook. Eventually, he developed the scheme to have large gables that were connected by a rigid line, like a tightrope suspended from peak to peak. Over this device, he seemed to throw an imaginary fabric; the result resembles a tent roof with its two main elements sagging under the weight of water. The rest of the forms derived both from the setting and his imagination. The building design that emerged has an affinity with its site—it looks as if it belongs there—while at the same time it boldly declares its completely unusual presence.

3

In designing Ronchamp, Le Corbusier responded to what he saw and let his natural genius for shapes and his instinctive thrill at movement through space take possession of him. The making of architecture was both a physical and a spiritual act, a conjunction of the premeditated and the spontaneous. In determining the form of this rural chapel, he plunged into his own inner depths. Various memories may have figured. There were the outings with his father and mother and brother, where, backpack on his shoulders, he learned at an early age to brave the high winds of mountain peaks similar to this one, if steeper. He had certainly had some residual memory of the ceilings of the barns that had been his bucolic retreats on the outskirts of La Chaux-de-Fonds. The immeasurable power of religious architecture as he had first experienced it before the cathedrals of Milan, Pisa, and Paris, their marvelous spires reaching heavenward as they had for centuries, had imprinted itself on his thoughts. So had his awareness of the primitive need for simple shelter and the wish of human beings to gather for the worship of God as he had observed in the male republic of Athos.

Le Corbusier referred specifically to his memories of a visit in October 1911 to the Villa Adriana in Tivoli as having given him the idea for the remote slip of light near the top of Ronchamp's tower.[6] And he also acknowledged a modern hydraulic dam he had sketched at Le Chastang in central France as a further model for the structure of its drainage and overflow.

Le Corbusier was responding again, too, to the powerful idea of a white building on a hilltop, of which the Parthenon was the ultimate example. And he let the cadences of music enter his soul as he had in the small rooms of his childhood and the vast concert halls of Munich and Vienna, where opera first moved him to tears. The chapel in the Vosges was an apotheosis that brought all of this personal history to the surface.

MORE RECENTLY, the architect had picked up a crab shell on a Long Island beach. He credited that natural structure as his main source of inspiration, saying it dictated the overall form, which then became modified by the addition of the element of time. That factor, of architecture being sequential, was central; Le Corbusier explained, "The plan is man's hold over space. One covers the plan on foot, eyes fixed straight ahead, and perception is successive, it implies time. Perception is a series of visual events, as a symphony is a series of sonorous events; time, duration, succession, continuity are the constitutive factors of architecture."[7]

In the six months that followed his trip to the site, Le Corbusier and his minions at 35 rue de Sèvres turned his concept into detailed plans. André Maisonnier was the main project architect. On January 20, 1951, Monseigneur Dubois, the archbishop of Besançon, and the members of the Commission of Sacred Art, gave their approval. To agree to something so completely unprecedented in appearance was almost as brave as to design it.

The forward-looking prelate of Besançon offered precisely the sort of support Le Corbusier craved but had found on few occasions in his life. The religious leader defended the project in its early days by publicly insisting that "in a period when art is fumbling, we must avoid all absolutism and all narrowness of judgment. We must have the courage to regard certain novelties with a favoring eye, and not hesitate to make experiments, even if they appear somewhat reckless."[8]

4

Le Corbusier remained faithful to his original concept, though perpetually modifying the design in a process he depicted as a progression from Zen-like responsiveness to a warrior's frenzy of action. "When I accept a task," he wrote, "I'm in the habit of shelving it in my memory, which means not allowing myself to make even a sketch for months. The human mind is so constructed as to possess a certain independence; it is a box into which you can pour any number of the elements of a problem. Then you let things 'float,' 'mix,' 'ferment.' And then one day a spontaneous initiative from your inner being occurs, the catch is released; you take a pencil, a piece of charcoal, some crayons (color is the key to the procedure) and you give birth on paper; the idea emerges."[9]

This making of a monument to the Holy Virgin, the woman to whom a miraculous birth was attributed, was itself a miraculous organic process. Obsessed with the person in whose womb he had grown, he, too, nourished and developed a simple seed. As the process continued, he referred directly both to the "spontaneous birth" and to the period of "incubation."[10]

AFTER HE HAD DEVELOPED the initial design scheme, the architect had to reduce its scale for budgetary reasons. The construction cost estimates made clear that to build the chapel as he had first figured it would significantly exceed the financial limitations. He willingly redesigned the building with smaller overall dimensions.

The office at 35 rue de Sèvres then made a model out of steel wire at a scale of one to one hundred. To confirm that all the curves and angles would work structurally, they took photographs of that model, which they provided to the engineers. The technical experts then confirmed that all was in order.

The measurements of the chapel were based on the Modulor. Charting his use of that sacred measuring tool, Le Corbusier wrote about himself in the third person: "The Chapel (like all of Le Corbusier's constructions, in fact) is based on the Modulor. Thus it has been possible to reduce the dimensions to sometimes extravagant figures without the spectator's thereby sensing the smallness of the work's dimensions. Le Corbusier admits that here is made manifest the plastic event he has described as 'ineffable space.' The consciousness of dimensions vanishes before the ineffable."[11] A relatively small building could seem enormous.

5

During the construction of this mountain chapel, Le Corbusier was more actively involved with all the details than in many of his other undertakings. At l'Usine Boussois, a factory in the Department Nord–Pas de Calais, he applied color to some of the stones and painted the glass windows. Le Corbusier also worked with his colleague Joseph Savina on the wooden confessionals and benches and the doors. He designated African wood for seating, an aluminum roof painted gray for the ceiling, and cast iron for the communion bench. No aspect of the building escaped his scrutiny.

On-site, he selected some of the stones from the old chapel to be incorporated into the walls of the new structure. The ones that were not suitable were carted away and piled into a pyramid at the edge of the area of grass that defined the chapel grounds. Then, when the new building was nearly completed, Le Corbusier was asked to erect a monument to the French soldiers who had been killed on the hill in 1944. The pile of discarded stones inspired one of those spontaneous events, governed both by fate and by an attitude of openness, that often occurred in Le Corbusier's life: he turned the chance pyramid into a monument to the dead.

Church of Ronchamp, under construction, ca. 1953

This bold, minimal sculpture was perhaps the first of the type of abstract war memorial that was to become a staple of late-twentieth-century design. A miniature of the great temples of ancient Mexico and Egypt, it used ordinary stones, rudimentary masonry, and the power of its sequence of ascending right angles to convey with profound simplicity the tragedy of lives lost because people fight.

The pyramid at Ronchamp is, to this day, a mystery to most visitors. There is no plaque, and no explanation is provided. The ambiguity, the sense of the unknown, suited its creator's taste and intentions.

6

During the design process, not everyone was as open-minded as Monseigneur Dubois. When a plaster model was first shown to the local parishioners, they were appalled at the bizarre form. Many urged that the ruined church on the site simply be rebuilt. The vast majority preferred the nonthreatening echoes of tradition; some sneered or laughed, while others became furious.

Le Corbusier's perpetual champion Eugène Claudius-Petit came to the rescue. He reinforced the approval already granted by the Commission of Sacred Art. But some powerful clergymen simultaneously urged that the financing be halted. The press laced into the proposed chapel as an "anti-atomic shelter," a "bunker," and an "ecclesiastical garage."[12] The full barrage of negative clichés used against all modern architecture in the early 1950s was thrown at the scheme. The local chaplain, Abbé Bolle-Reddat, however, was steadfast. Later, the prelate recalled "in what occasionally nauseating humus this flower of grace has grown"; the steadfast chaplain encountered such intense opposition to Le Corbusier's design that he considered its completion "a true miracle!"[13]

The architect, meanwhile, reacted to his attackers quite differently from his usual way. He did not assume the role of embittered martyr or fly into a vituperative rage. Rather, he calmly defended himself and his proposal against the assaults by pointing out his intention of creating something beautiful and his ideal of service to humankind. He also deliberately distinguished himself from the surrealists and many other modernists, with their intention to shock: "Not for a moment did I have any notion of making an object of astonishment. My preparation? A sympathy for others, for the unknown, and for a life which has trickled away into the brutalities of existence, nastiness, egotism, cowardice, triviality, but also into so much kindness, goodness, courage, energy, smiles, sunshine and blue sky. And the resulting choice: a taste, a need for the true. Ronchamp? Contact with a site, situation in a place, eloquence of the place, speech addressed to the place. To the four horizons."[14]

LIII

From his bed, on a sheet of paper, he had explained to me the reasons for the measurements of a monastery in the highest Dominican tradition: "Here, we walk in two rows, here we sing in two rows, here we face each other and prostrate ourselves at full length; it is just such things which condition the form of the premises: walks, chapel, refectory, etc. and their measurements." He had drawn that. Then he added: "It is for you, Le Corbusier, the finest commission you can ever have, the one which corresponds to your deepest being: the human scale."

—LE CORBUSIER

1

Father Marie-Alain Couturier had first met Le Corbusier in 1948, when the architect was working on his scheme for Sainte-Baume. He had subsequently been among the architect's defenders over the design for Ronchamp.

Ironically, Couturier was a member of the Dominican order; Saint Dominic had been engaged by Pope Innocent III to restore Catholicism to the territories controlled by the Cathars, those heretics from whom Le Corbusier so proudly claimed to descend. Nonetheless, Couturier recognized, in the way Balkrishna Doshi did, Le Corbusier's spiritualism: "Not only did we regard Le Corbusier as the greatest living architect, but also as the man in whom the spontaneous sense of the sacred is strongest and most authentic."[1]

Since 1936, Couturier had been one of the editors of *Art Sacré*—a publication that put forward his view that "for the rebirth of Christian art, the ideal would be to have geniuses who were also saints. But under present circumstances, if such men do not exist, we believe that to provoke such a rebirth, such a resurrection, it is wiser to seek geniuses without faith than believers without talent."[2] This open-minded patron had already commissioned projects by Matisse, Léger, Rouault, and Lipchitz when, in 1953, he gave Le Corbusier the task "to lodge a hundred bodies and a hundred hearts in silence" in a new monastery near Lyon.[3] The same architect who could thrill to gongs and drumrolls and to the sirens of Edgard Varèse relished such total quietude. To build a retreat for the cultivation of feeling—at a remove from the hustle and bustle of the urbanism he also loved—was one of his greatest goals. The project for which Couturier enlisted him was to prove to be his final masterpiece.

On May 4, 1953, Le Corbusier, accompanied by André Wogenscky, now in charge at 35 rue de Sèvres, visited the site where the monastery was to be built. It was another hilltop, not quite as commanding as that at Ronchamp but similarly secluded and with a view of rolling fields—near the town of Eveux, in the Rhône-Alpes, about twenty-five kilometers from Lyon. The Dominicans had acquired the property in 1943. It included substantial agricultural lands, an old château, and vast woods. Le Corbusier instantly recognized that the setting was perfect for building the sort of monastic community that had been his ideal from the time of his earliest travels. He made preliminary sketches and asked Wogenscky to question Couturier about details of the monks' everyday lives so that he could attune the program accordingly.

The reverend father, who was suffering from myasthenia, was then in the Paris hospital of Bon Secours. Le Corbusier regretted that he would have no time to visit this wonderful man himself before leaving for India, but he wrote the farsighted Dominican, "While I'm still here, since you're not going to be spending your time indefinitely in hospital, it would be a kindness, as soon as you have a little appetite, to telephone my wife and tell her you're coming to lunch or dinner. The poor girl will be delighted; she's very fond of you, and you'll be performing a pious action by going to cheer her up in her solitude."[4] He could put two good souls together.

And Le Corbusier was comfortable in the knowledge that on Couturier's first visit to rue Nungesser-et-Coli, when Yvonne had deployed her whoopee cushion, the priest had reacted with as much mirth as the hosts.

2

Marie-Alain Couturier gave Le Corbusier the freedom and the confidence essential to making his best architecture. In July 1953, the Dominican wrote him, "It will be one of the great joys of my life to have been able to persuade you to undertake this, and even now I know it will be, in its very poverty, one of the purest and most important works of our time." To this supportive sentence, written with a manual typewriter, Couturier added, by hand in fountain pen, "And I hope that you, too, take joy in it."[5]

Le Corbusier warmed to the positivity and to the mandate to make a place where, in the Dominican's words, "the poverty of the buildings must be very strict, which consequently implies that the shared necessities will be respected: silence, sufficient warmth for continuous intellectual work, areas of comings and goings reduced to the minimum. . . . Our type of life is absolutely shared by all and consequently requires no personal differentiation within groups."[6]

Couturier was Le Corbusier's sort of person: straightforward, well grounded, masculine, and professional. Clean shaven, his white hair cut very short, he was modest in his style, inevitably dressed in the same plain black-and-white robe. Whether it was a coincidence or a habit he deliberately adopted, the no-nonsense priest's only bow to modern style was that he wore eyeglasses identical to Le Corbusier's.

Once Le Corbusier considered someone a friend, there were no limits to what he might do for him. Unknown to the priest, the architect desperately sought information on a more effective treatment for myasthenia, for which Couturier was enduring twenty-five injections per day. That fall, Le Corbusier took his Chinese-medicine specialist to his new friend; the results were miraculous, and Couturier again became master of his movements while stopping the shots. But Couturier then suffered a relapse.

Le Corbusier devoted himself to pursuing other treatment options. He had an American friend, Pauline Shulman, an architect who lived in Bloomfield, Connecticut, who told him that Prostigmin, the most effective medication for myasthenia, was now available in France but should be administered only by a doctor experienced in its use. Shulman knew a doctor who in turn consulted Dr. Henry Viets, the world's greatest authority on myasthenia and an advocate of Prostigmin in Boston. Le Corbusier and Shulman organized a chain of communication from Viets to translators to French doctors to create a team to help Couturier—with encouraging information about nearly miraculous remission for certain symptoms of the incurable disease.

At the same time, Le Corbusier plunged into the monastery project. On his first visit, he had made a drawing of the road and the horizons and had studied the orientation to the sun. He treated each act concerning the position and form of the monastery as an existential experience: "In choosing the site, I was committing a criminal or a valid action. . . . Let us take the upper layer, the horizontal line of the building at the top, which will harmonize with the horizon. Starting from this horizontal line at the top, we will measure everything from there and will reach the ground at the moment we touch it."[7] The reason for starting the design with the roof and working downward was to connect the monks to the universe.

Le Corbusier also immersed himself in the rules that had been practiced by the Dominican order since the thirteenth century. He submitted completely to a program based on the many requirements of their monastic life. As much as the desires of his bourgeois clients upset him, he found the needs of these worthy monks of irrefutable merit.

3

On January 30, 1954, Father Couturier would complete an essay on Le Corbusier. After singling him out as the greatest living architect and a man of authentic feeling, Couturier continued, "We shall repeat this and insist upon it. And we shall add that it is a pleasure to say such things, in the face of the conspiracy of the mediocre (and, alas, it is sad to see included among these certain great names) which unceasingly calumniate him, spy on him, pillage him: 'they shoot us, but they empty our pockets,' as Degas used to say, fifty years ago. . . . With a very great architect like Le Corbusier, the freedom of forms and of certain audacities is a prerogative and probably a duty. His admirable rigor, the innate sense of proportion in realizations allow him a lyricism by which he completes his expression. . . . Things which are true and pure are always the dangerous things. One must run the risk, or else resign oneself to inaction. But fools must be warned."[8]

It was the last thing Marie-Alain Couturier ever wrote. Only two weeks later, Le Corbusier, who was in Chandigarh at the time, would get word that his friend and champion had died on February 9. This was one occasion of his being less resigned than usual to someone's death. Devastated, the architect immediately issued a statement:

> I've come here to Chandigarh, in India. And now a brutal telegram tells me he is dead, though both of us had believed he had overcome his sickness. Alas! It is an intense sadness we feel. Around his idea, his dream, his mission, he had gathered the adherence, the devotion, and the activity of remarkable people, those of wide-ranging views, people who, to his own youth, conferred their "youth" of a maturity rigorously conquered by perseverance, courage, invention.
>
> Father Couturier was our friend, a friend to what is most sacred to us: the faith in our art. But he was a friend of our hearths as well. His

company was agreeable, alert, and there was a certain ease in his remarks. He seemed to me a historical figure who in giant strides had traversed certain books where "men" recognize one another in conscious action, living words, an infallible trajectory—through winds and tides.

And his black-and-white robe, that majestic uniform, suited his brush-cut hair so suited to soldiers. There he was! It is very sad.

The work of Father Couturier was in full spate.[9]

LIV

1

In the spring of 1953, the construction drawings for Ronchamp were completed, and in September the excavating and building began. Because there was no road to transport materials to the hilltop, Le Corbusier had decided to construct virtually everything out of sand and cement that could be mixed into concrete on the spot. The only substantial material that had to be brought in was metal lathing to serve as joists.

The chapel walls were constructed to be nearly four meters wide at the bottom and as narrow as half a meter at the top. Those walls—each a curve, with the south facade slightly concave and the others convex—followed forms calculated for maximum stability. Rather than being perpendicular to the ground, they slope inward, like the sides of a teepee. Aside from providing a dramatic impression, that formation contributed to the structural soundness of the whole.

Ronchamp, view of chapel, ca. 1955

The design facilitated the seepage of light from above that Le Corbusier desired: "An interval of several centimeters between the shell of the roof and the vertical envelope of the walls makes possible the arrival of signifying light."[1] In that single tightly composed sentence about this unusual construction, Le Corbusier invokes music, a biomorphic parallel, the emotional security offered by neat packaging, and the capacity of light to uplift the soul—all of which were priorities for him.

In addition to its many other inspirations, the reinforced-concrete roof was built according to the principles of airplane wings, each with a structure of seven beams linked by parallel ribs. The separation between the two winglike forms was 2.26 meters, a measurement essential to the proportions of the Modulor. The beams of the two wings—each a taut canopy, watertight and with strong insulating capacity in spite of being a mere six centimeters thick—rest on load-bearing struts within the chapel walls. Impeccable engineering was essential to realize the fantasy.

WHAT A VISION had been born from that crustacean's shell transmogrified by Le Corbusier's primal instinct to heighten the experience of form and space. The soaring roof looks like a mix of a partially crushed sombrero, a ram's horn, and a bell clapper; Le Corbusier himself compared its form to a stretched bowstring. Tiny windows are scattered as if by chance in the thick plaster walls. The open-air pulpit and dramatic downspouts seem fictive. The looming towers are bifurcated cylinders with windows that resemble caricatures of noses and eyes as conceived by Klee or Miró. The interior is even more surprising than the exterior, with light arriving in a range of unexpected ways, spaces soaring heavenward just where one least anticipates them, and chapels of startling simplicity.

The concrete of this winged roof is rough and completely without tint. Its raw state declares it a structural material. On the vertical elements within as well as on the exterior of the church, however, a cement gun was used to spray concrete mortar that was then coated in gunite and whitewashed to resemble bright white plaster.

Inside, the floor slopes slightly downhill, as determined by the natural tilt of the land. Thus, after entering the chapel, one descends dramatically toward the altar, walking on cement paving between battens spaced according to the measurements of the Modulor. The altar is constructed of white stones from Burgundy, their color and texture of a beauty that ravished Le Corbusier. He used those same natural blocks for the altar on the outside of the building.

This subtle range of materials and textures is visually and tactilely enchanting. The coarse yet opulent Burgundy stone has a rich roughness. The clean Mediterranean-style whitewash and the bluntly industrial concrete of the roof play against each other. The differing surface treatments also suggest contrasting degrees of weight or lightness that have nothing to do with reality, a demonstration of the ability of art to deceive, and color and dressing to disguise physical reality.

Le Corbusier had kept the statue of the Holy Virgin on the construction site. A member of the Commission of Sacred Art suggested that it should be

Interior view of entrance wall at Ronchamp, ca. 1955

surrounded by stars. As the props that held up the wall scaffolding were being taken down once the concrete was set, Le Corbusier spontaneously instructed the builders to leave the holes where the supports had been, spaces that normally would have been filled. "Look! You have your stars! There they are!" he declared.[2]

The architect then edited the miracle. He designated which openings should remain and which should be filled, with the result that the sunlight makes a halo of bright dots that gives the Virgin in the east wall her perfect crown. This most mechanical of materials and Le Corbusier's openness to what was haphazard and unexpected thus facilitated poetry and art and religion. The wonder of machinery lay not in the technical mechanism itself but in its service to the soul.

2

On December 9, 1953, just as construction at Ronchamp was going full steam ahead, Le Corbusier sent Yvonne a euphoric anniversary card. He sketched a gnomelike figure shouldering a cornucopia of gifts. The overstuffed sack of presents on its side is perpendicular to the similarly shaped conical cap atop Le Corbusier's puffy head; the eyeglasses essential to his image are again prominent. Le Corbusier depicts himself with enormous shoulders and sturdy legs; he is a true beast of burden here, and his gait is that of one of his beloved soul-mate donkeys. He grasps at a tall and slender walking staff that is slightly tapered, wider at the top than the pointed bottom.

A number of ten-franc bills are falling out of the cornucopia, while on the top of the walking staff there is a little flag with "100" written on it. We assume that the card accompanied a cash gift. The banknotes appear helter-skelter, but, as the flag indicates, they add up to a precise and balanced total; as with the Modulor, a regulating system has been applied.

This loping self-portrait bears an astonishing resemblance to one of his sketches of the chapel on the hill at Ronchamp. The vessel of presents on Le Corbusier's shoulders and his funny hat assume the profile of the great roof of the chapel. The walking staff resembles the largest of the towers. The overall proportions are that of the church. The background of mountains and the horizon cause the figure to stand in the landscape much as Ronchamp does. By making his self-portrait the likeness of the church he was offering the world, the gift-bearing Le Corbusier revealed his personal reality. He and his creation were one.

A SECOND CARD FOLLOWED (see color plate 15). Here Le Corbusier shows himself as an enormous and powerful black bird—the ultimate crow—that is yet another image of the church under construction. As it looms over the landscape, the crow's fully spread wings resemble Ronchamp's marvelous roof in its command post in the Vosges. It flies above the horizon, looming over a vast cityscape on which thumbnail sketches indicate Notre-Dame, Sacré-Coeur, and the Arc de Triomphe. This time the gift contains two hundred units in a box tied with a ribbon and bow, suspended from the crow's clawlike feet, which have ferocious talons. The message is as sweet as the crow is forbidding: "With all my affection of 31 years of perfect happiness."[3]

The looming roof at Ronchamp with its two equal wings separated by a meticulously measured void was to many people as terrifying as this gigantic bird, but Le Corbusier here suggests a very different interpretation. Even if its face appears at first frightening, the church on the hill should be understood as the image of tenderness and as a bearer of wonderful gifts.

In the note scribbled alongside the drawing, Le Corbusier voiced his desperate wish for his wife to get healthier and happier. He instructed Yvonne, "promise your Le Corbusier, who follows your anxieties *hour by hour,* that you will wear your white shoes, that you will eat soup, that you will come every day after lunch to join me for a little stroll in the Bois, to get you used to walking again."[4]

It is a heartbreaking scenario. Le Corbusier has depicted himself as the image of virility and aliveness. At the same time that he was flying all over the world, realizing his potency in Chandigarh and at Ronchamp and La Tourette, he had to beg his wife simply to take in enough sustenance to stay alive. There was little hope that she would take the daily walks he proposed or that her legs would again function properly.

And even if Le Corbusier declared her to be the source of his unblemished happiness, Yvonne was becoming increasingly difficult. She dressed as a little girl but could comport herself as a hag. The few visitors to the apartment where she lived in seclusion were struck by her "incredible language" as "she insulted Le Corbusier" mercilessly.[5] She was hiding her liquor bottles. A true "alcoholic *exsangue,*" when she fell, she also broke her limbs without feeling the pain sufficiently to know what she had done.

What was needed above all was for her to cease drinking in order to stop the falling. That she might abstain from alcohol was unlikely, but Le Corbusier clung to the belief that her new doctor, versed in the latest advances in medical thinking, still offered hope.

3

During his retreat in Roquebrune-Cap-Martin in February 1955, Le Corbusier told Marguerite Tjader Harris about Ronchamp. It was, he allowed, "an ineffable thing! I believe it to be an apparition from 2000 years ago. From the Christianity which by grace overwhelmed Rome." Le Corbusier exulted the white inside and out of this structure "beyond dimensions, beyond measurements, alone in the landscape by the miracle of proportion."[6] In the construction shack, he was designing the windows. Again he specified that he would paint them rather than use stained glass, a material he detested. And he was completing the design of the enormous door, composed out of enamel tiles that would be baked at 670 degrees Fahrenheit to fix the colors.

To Tjader Harris, the architect associated his recent operation for varicose veins with the idea of "circulation" for the pilgrims entering or exiting the church and ascribed to different aspects of his existence the same numeric harmony he put into his building: "And in a few days, I'm going to a factory to paint in *enamel* both sides of the main door. Eighteen square meters, nine on each surface! An enamel door of 9 square meters turning on a central pivot, making it possible for pilgrims to enter and leave to the right and left. I've based the design (pentagram) on an altarpiece in the Louvre, a French primitive I fell in love with at twenty (around 1918) and since then inscribed in the depths of my affection. The other day, in the hospital, after a difficult operation, I had noticed the drawing among some photos I had put in my bag to study in the solitude of my hospital room. Foresight, since I was then *stripped of 80 centimeters* of the femoral *vein,* from ankle to anus. (I've suffered for 30 years from a painter's (varicose) vein, so-called because some painters put their entire weight on one leg in an effort of mental concentration.) Ten days later I was in India. In five weeks we'll be finishing *Nantes,* our second *Unité* (like the one in Marseille), this one completed in eighteen months. A triumph of organization and will on the part of my studio, particularly the younger members of the staff."[7]

In this kaleidoscopic letter where he lopped ten years off his age, Le Corbusier provided a sketch in which he vividly rendered the pile of discarded veins. He also boasted about the High Court in Chandigarh, calling it "a sensational building, striking and brilliant against the background of the Himalayas."[8] Marguerite Tjader Harris was still the person who could best understand both his fortitude in face of hardships and the miracles he had now accomplished.

4

Time was flying, Le Corbusier wrote his mother that March, "at cyclone speed. Evening is divided from morning by nothing more than a fugitive fifteen minutes: not even time to breathe." Now that he was back in Paris, his tasks at hand were "exhausting. Actually dangerous!" For this reason he had put an end to all social life, was seeing no one, was not showing himself, and was refusing all visitors—he specified each category of social avoidance—and was applying himself to his work alone: "I pay no attention to everything humming and buzzing around me. Silence!"[9]

The construction of his second Unité d'Habitation was soon to be finished, having been completed entirely by his office crew. In Berlin, the "Fritz"—as he continued to call Germans—were organizing an enormous housing exposition and had given him a prime spot. Then there had been the summons to Chandigarh for Nehru's inauguration of the High Court on the nineteenth of March.

In this litany of successes to his mother, Le Corbusier did not, however, mention Ronchamp. The omission of the chapel in the Vosges was curious. It was, after all, nearer to Vevey than most of his projects. In many ways, it was to be his masterpiece.

The architect had his reasons for remaining mute.

5

With the sole exception of New Year's Eve and a second restaurant outing via car, Yvonne had not gone out of the house for six months. Le Corbusier wrote his mother that he was concerned that even under Jacques Hindermeyer's care his wife was not improving. By April, however, she was benefiting sufficiently from the new treatment to travel to Roquebrune-Cap-Martin. Le Corbusier wrote his mother from the *cabanon* that Yvonne would have been happy, if only her health was better, for in their wonderful getaway, "far from snobs and futile arguments," she was beloved by all "the best people."[10] But there was no chance of abstinence from drinking.

The cold on the Mediterranean coast was so biting at first that even the beautiful sunshine did not mitigate its effects, but then the weather turned soft. The sky and the sea were perfect, Le Corbusier euphoric. Having read in the newspaper that there was snow, astonishing at that time of year, on the lakeshore between Lausanne and Vevey, he wrote his mother that he assumed she was "taking refuge with the sun, *Père soleil.*"[11]

In the small studio ("precisely 183 × 388 cm," he informed his mother), he was now working, simultaneously, on the Governor's Palace in Chandigarh and on the second volume of the revised *Modulor 2:* "My lay-out work is terribly exacting, exhausting, absorbing, as any work that is well done must be."[12] He did this work seated on one of two wooden whiskey boxes that he had collected from the sea, which had presumably been thrown overboard from boats. If in earlier years Le Corbusier had been thrilled to be placed at dinner next to people with titles and had sought out the company of anyone with power, now he could afford to deal with humanity according to his own standards and work in solitude. Decent, honest human beings like Yvonne and the Rebutatos were the architect's personal royalty, unlike the pretenders in Paris, and the monk's cell for work was all he needed.

6

Early one Sunday morning in the middle of May after he and Yvonne had returned to Paris, Le Corbusier took one of his frequent walks through the Bois de Boulogne. On a road lined by chestnut trees, a magpie had fallen out of its nest. Apparently knocked down by a high wind during the night, the wounded creature was lying on the path. Le Corbusier picked it up.

During the rest of his usual hourlong walk, carrying the magpie, he thought about what he had done. At first, he considered himself ridiculous. He did not know how he would find the correct insects with which to feed the poor creature, or what box to put it in. He was afraid that Yvonne would force-feed it. It would be necessary to protect the wounded bird from the dog and cat at home.

But then he reconsidered his action: "No, what I did was right: there are no trivial actions—that's what I realize every second of my life," he wrote his mother.[13] Half an hour after picking up the bird, he found the nest that had fallen out of a tree. His first thought was that it was not God who had organized this encounter. Rather, Le Corbusier reflected, his eyes—unbeckoned by any other source—had located that nest.

Le Corbusier observed that his soul had been preoccupied by the search for any sort of container, such as a discarded box, with which to harbor the injured bird. Indeed, before he saw the nest, he had found such a box. Then, although he was no longer aware that he was looking for anything, his unconscious mind, which a few moments earlier had been programmed for the discovery of a box, had now caused him to spot the nest. He noted all of these cerebral processes in the account he wrote his mother and Albert.

Le Corbusier put both the nest and the bird into the box. The bird opened an eye. Then, all at once, the creature flew off—only to crash into a streetlight and claw onto it for dear life.

The architect could not get the bird down from the streetlight. He went home, fetched a ladder, returned to the scene, climbed up, grabbed the injured bird, folded up the ladder, and returned home. He went immediately to the roof garden. There Yvonne had her collection of sparrows, which had now grown from forty to between fifty and sixty. Le Corbusier installed the "*piaf*" on the rooftop structure that housed the top of the elevator. Again, it batted its eyes and flew off, returning to nature.

The sixty-seven-year-old architect concluded, "This situation has its importance!" It symbolized the fleetingness of all experience and the ungrasp-

With his dog Pinceau du Val d'Or (Pinceau II) at 24 rue Nungesser-et-Coli, ca. 1955. Photo by Robert Doisneau

ability of what one thinks one has in hand. "You know the old song: time is merely an endless, terrifying leak," he wrote.[14]

What counted even more than the rapid flight of time was Le Corbusier's relationship to the bird's housing. Having tried to use a box—constructed by an alien species and made of materials completely foreign to a magpie—at least he had then had the wisdom to include elements of the little creature's indigenous housing. Nonetheless, having used every means at his disposal—his own cupped hands, the ladder—to care for the wounded animal, he had, in the long run, failed to exercise control, however well meant, and the bird had eluded him. Nature had prevailed; he was humbled by its force.

7

At the start of June, Le Corbusier made a quick trip to Ronchamp, his last before its inauguration. For two days, he was on his feet there from 8:00 a.m. to 8:00 p.m., installing the windows and altars.

When he got back to Paris, he wrote his mother that he was anticipating eighteen thousand people at the opening ceremonies. On the other hand, it was not necessary for her and Albert to attend. Le Corbusier attempted to explain why: he would not be available to them during the proceedings, and he was going to flee the scene the moment the official acts were over. He could not imagine, besides, how all those people would reach the church on the one footpath. He also advised that it was a longer distance from Vevey than they realized. He proposed that his brother and mother see the new chapel in July, instead. He would happily meet them there for such an encounter.

None of these was the real reason Le Corbusier did not want Marie and Albert on the scene.

In the same letter where the architect spun out his fatuous excuses, he continued, "One request in this matter: suppress all declarations like: we Protestants; *wir schweizer;* etc. I've made a perilous work. Rome has its eye on me. The cabals need only a spark."[15] He did not want to disabuse anyone of the false assumption that he was Catholic.

Le Corbusier became even more adamant in a letter he wrote his mother and brother on June 23, the day before he left for the opening. Reminding them that they would see Ronchamp in July, he asked, as if he could not remember, if he had already written them on the subject of their discretion. In case he had not, he now instructed, "Don't go shouting: 1. We Protestants . . . 2. We, Le Corbusier's mother and brother . . . 3. We Swiss . . . etc. Forgive me, but understand: there will be eulogies. . . . You understand, don't you, or do I have to send smoke signals???"[16]

Le Corbusier told them about an "*imbécile*" from the *Chicago Tribune* who had asked him if to build Ronchamp it was necessary to be a Catholic. The architect replied, "*Foutez moi le camp!*" On the edge of panic about what his mother and brother might reveal, he snapped, "Like the American journalists, you specialize in insolent questions!"[17]

He instructed Marie and Albert that surely they did not want to make his life any harder. The upcoming inauguration of his building at Nantes—scheduled for July 2—was bringing out the foxes and jackals; he begged for support and sympathy.

He was, he told them, in a state of exhaustion. He had been summoned by telegram to help advise on the new capital of Brazil, but it was all too much for him. Yvonne was even more unwell—too incapacitated to attend the Ronchamp inauguration. He now gave arthritis as the cause.

Two days after he wrote that entreaty, the crowd at Ronchamp cheered Le Corbusier as one of the creative giants of the twentieth century. But Charles-Edouard Jeanneret was still determined that his mother and brother recognize the difficulty of his lot in life. He was counting on them, for once, to go easy on him—and to guard their silence.

LV

I improvised, crazed by the music. . . . Even my teeth and eyes burned with fever. Each time I leaped I seemed to touch the sky and when I regained earth it seemed to be mine alone.

—JOSEPHINE BAKER, ON HER PERFORMANCE WITH THE REVUE NÈGRE IN 1925

1

On June 25, 1955, when the chapel at Ronchamp opened to the public, the event was instantly recognized as a milestone in postwar cultural history. The time had come to be receptive to modernism—to endorse what was daring and untraditional—rather than to risk being guilty of committing the sin of the famous rejections that had thwarted Manet, van Gogh, and the Fauves in their heyday. However outraged the critics and public were in private, they had now learned to act respectfully. Reading *Le Figaro*'s coverage of the inauguration of "the chapel built by Le Corbusier" over its morning café au lait, the French public now knew the architect's name as a household word that warranted respect.[1]

Under brilliant sunshine, the day's events began at 8:30 a.m. at the local town hall, where Mayor Pheulpin made Le Corbusier an honorary citizen of the town of Ronchamp. From there, a cortege formed, headed by the local band, and proceeded to the monument to the dead. A spray of flowers was placed on the impressive pyramid of discarded stones. Previously, such monuments to victims of war tended to be figurative sculpture, often with Latin inscriptions. Now the crowd stood for a minute of silence before something that resembled a heap of rocks. What Le Corbusier had spontaneously erected on the chapel grounds was the perfect physical equivalent of that silence.

At 9:30, further dignitaries arrived in their official cars at the bottom of the steep path. They walked up and joined the rest of the assemblage in the chapel itself.

Le Corbusier had asked Edgard Varèse, the composer whose work he had admired in New York eight years earlier, to produce music that would somehow be recorded in a linear way—on a ribbon or wide thread—and could be cut into morsels by a music director during the opening. Varèse had declined. Some of the music performed during the inauguration was almost as modern—"Te Deum" by Marc-Antoine Charpentier; "Apparition de l'Eglise Eternelle, les enfants de Dieu, les Bergers, Jésus accepte la souffrance" by Olivier Messiaen; "Symphonie de Psaumes" by Igor Stravinsky—but there was also the traditional "Enveillez-vous" and "Grand Prélude" by Johann Sebastian Bach.

Alfred Canet, secretary of the real-estate company that had diligently overseen the development of this unusual project, publicly gave the new building to the archbishop of Besançon, Monseigneur Dubois. The Belfort newspaper reported: "An especially moving moment, for it was the workman on the land who offered his labor to the Lord and Master of all things."[2]

The archbishop quoted Minister of Reconstruction Roger Duchet's praise of the local authorities for having had "one of the masters of contemporary architecture" replace the destroyed sanctuary.[3] Following that discourse, Eugène Claudius-Petit, General Touzet du Vigier—a member of the Force Française Libre (FFL) who had been a companion of De Gaulle's in North Africa—and Le Corbusier himself could all be seen praying respectfully. No one seemed aware that the architect descended from the sort of Protestants who during the Reformation had pillaged the edifices of Roman Catholicism.

Further officials and dignitaries gave speeches emphasizing the tragedy that had befallen the previous chapel and affirmed the wish that the new structure would serve pilgrims as its predecessor had. Canet offered profuse thanks to "the leading architect of our time who, with an exceptional team, accomplished this work he holds so dear to his heart." He ended by reciting the prayer that King Solomon had offered Almighty God on the day of the dedication of the Temple at Jerusalem: "Grant to all peoples who climb toward . . . this house we have built for You . . . in order to offer You prayers, and grant us Forgiveness, Justice and Peace."[4]

Le Corbusier repeated the realtor's gesture of publicly handing the building over to the archbishop. Man's work was being given to the representative of God. He underlined the religiosity of the chapel and the way it conformed to aspects of a traditional ecclesiastical program, while pointing out its ability to serve nonpractitioners as well: "In building this chapel I wish to create a place of silence, of prayer, of peace, of inner joy. The sentiment of the sacred animated our effort. Certain things are sacred, others are not, whether or not they are religious."[5]

The architect singled out Maisonnier and Savina—the two craftspeople with whom he had worked most closely—and praised all the other engineers, workers, and administrators who had figured out the mathematics and systems necessary for the construction of this complicated building.

Then, carefully, and with a brevity unusual for him, Le Corbusier specified the ways in which the chapel honored Catholic liturgical tradition: "Certain scattered signs . . . and certain written words express the praise of the Virgin. The cross—the true cross of torment—is installed within this ark: the Christian drama has henceforth taken possession of the site."[6]

It was an occasion for him to be humble and unassuming. Yvonne, as a Catholic, would surely have been pleased. There was no way she could have made it up the footpath to the actual scene, but he would tell her about it. Addressing himself specifically to the archbishop, Le Corbusier concluded his remarks, "Excellency, I deliver to you this chapel of loyal concrete, built boldly perhaps, certainly with courage and the hope that it will find in you, as in those who climb the hill, an echo to what all of us have inscribed herein."[7]

While the architect underlined the religiosity, the archbishop praised the modernism. Monseigneur Dubois called the chapel a "witness to the faith of new times." It was as if he had boned up on Le Corbusier's history and the goals with which Charles-Edouard Jeanneret and Amédée Ozenfant had launched *L'Esprit Nouveau* more than three decades earlier. The religious leader then declared, "*Maître,* you have performed an act of courage in creating such a work."[8] Dubois said that the new chapel honored the tradition of thirteenth-century cathedrals as "an act of optimism, a gesture of courage, a sign of pride, a proof of mastery."[9]

Dubois pointed out that, three years earlier, Le Corbusier had told Claudius-Petit he had created l'Unité d'Habitation in Marseille " 'for men.' Here, *Monsieur,* you have labored for a greater master: for God and for Our Lady. You feel this: the soul of the true 'radiant city' is here, on this hill."[10]

For a cleric to be so knowledgeable about the architect's work and intentions was unusual. His recognizing and publicly acknowledging the consistency and continuity of Le Corbusier's life's work and the extent of his dedication to the goal of making the world a better place was a small miracle on the holy site.

Mass was performed. The archbishop gave his benediction and "by special favor, grants an indulgence to those who have associated themselves with this benediction."[11]

The crowd returned to the pyramid made from the stone of the destroyed chapel. It was then officially dedicated to the memory of those who died during the liberation of France. Two generals presided; the flags of the FFL were ceremoniously placed on the monument by a group of veterans. "General Touzet du Vigier evoked, with the simplicity and feeling of a great-hearted man, the harsh battles which took place on this hill and which this monument commemorates." The general adjured, "Our Lady, take under protection those who died for France." One must never forget "those who have given their lives so that there shall be no more division, hatred, and war."[12]

A representative of a veterans' organization offered sympathy to the families of the dead, and "The Marseillaise" was sung. Probably no one present realized that, while the dead people now being honored had been fighting France's invaders, Le Corbusier had been working away in Vichy.

2

> Light acquires a transcendental quality: it is not the light of the Mediterranean alone, it is something more, something unfathomable, something holy. Here the light penetrates directly to the soul, opens the doors and windows of the heart, makes one naked, exposed, isolated in a metaphysical bliss which makes everything clear without being known. No analysis can go on in this light: here the neurotic is either instantly healed or goes mad.
>
> — HENRY MILLER, *The Colossus of Maroussi*

The morning that had started in bright sunshine turned torrid, and then the sky became stormy. But the weather cleared again, and a light breeze offered relief from the heat. Four hundred people were given lunch in a vast metal hangar erected nearby. Le Corbusier granted interviews to journalists. According to one account, "He rather disappointed us by the slightly ironic tone he gave to his answers. . . . Then he surprised us by these statements: 'I have performed my little task. . . . If what I have done is understood (apropos of the motifs decorating the doors of the sanctuary) I have succeeded; if not, it is a failure; I have in my pocket a child's drawing; I do not know what it is, but he surely knows.' "[13]

As people were finishing their lunch, the ceremonies ended with "the solemn salutation." A number of those present had made the long journey because the following day, Sunday, was to be the official beginning of "the era of new pilgrimages," one local newspaper reported. Almost everyone there was visibly moved by both the building and the words used to sanctify it. One local journalist referred to "the generosity of the faithful" that had made possible this sanctuary, "whose dazzling whiteness emerges from a nest of foliage to be silhouetted against our country's sky."[14] The architect who had designed it was just one of the thousands of people in a state of transport.

RONCHAMP ENABLED Le Corbusier to articulate the true merits of his own achievement with new authority and simplicity. While he was glib with the journalists, in his public address he had told his audience, "The premises begin to be radiant. Physically they are radiant."[15]

The architect expressed his foremost goal: his burning wish to give all people—every stranger who might enter one of his buildings at any moment—uplifting and salubrious experiences. There were "things no one may violate: the secret in each individual, a great limitless void where one may lodge one's own notion of the sacred—an individual, totally individual notion. This is also called conscience, and it is an instrument for measuring responsibilities or outpourings ranging from the tangible to the ineffable."[16]

"Ineffable" was one of the words he used time and again, because the con-

The inauguration ceremony at Ronchamp on June 26, 1955

cept of what was too great to be expressed in words, and too sacred to be uttered, was of such vital importance to him. For all of his cynicism about human greed and intransigence, Le Corbusier believed that everyone responded to visual wonder, that it opened up the heart.

However misguided some of Le Corbusier's decisions—aspects of the Plan Voisin; the attempted collaboration with the authorities in Vichy—his instinct had always been the same: to provide each and every human being with the palpable pleasures of which architecture is capable. In Ronchamp, the devices, at least as he described them, were simple enough: "curved volumes generated and regulated by straight lines . . . a kind of acoustic sculpture of nature," evidence that "architecture is forms, volumes, color, acoustics, music." In summation, he declared, "Architecture is an act of love, not a stage set."[17]

The impulse to tap into clandestine sources of spiritual feeling had inspired the shelves with which Le Corbusier had fit his brother's room in the house that had wrecked the family's finances; the ramps of the Villa La Roche; the soaring entrance at the Cité de Refuge; the colorful facade of l'Unité d'Habitation; and the amusement park of vision offered by the great public buildings of Chandigarh. At Ronchamp, the "act of love" was the most rapturous yet.

THE EVENING AFTER the inauguration, some journalists asked Le Corbusier if he was happy with the way the day had gone. Repeating one of his lines from the early afternoon, he replied, "Why happy? I have performed my little task. Today that has provoked speeches that give pleasure to those who uttered them. Probably less to those who heard them. In any case, I hope to deliver a great blow to both the detractors of my architecture and to my imitators, those who imagine that architecture can be reduced to formulas. This possession of Ronchamp by the Catholic cult was extremely beautiful, very precise. It was the most precise moment of the whole day."[18]

3

Normally, Le Corbusier wrote his mother and Albert together. On June 27, he wrote to her alone from Ronchamp. However assiduously he had encouraged her absence, he was desperate to share the thrill of his acclaim and his achievement with her. At the same time, he reiterated his warnings about the risks of anyone knowing the family's background.

The letter was both a boast and a supplication. At the ceremonies on Saturday, Le Corbusier told "*ma chère Petite Maman,*" "Everything was cheer, beauty, spiritual splendor. Your Le Corbusier was honored to the highest degree. Considered. Loved. Respected."[19]

Then he explained how delicate the situation was. For Ronchamp was a revolutionary work of architecture—radical in its approach to the Catholic rites and ritual: "By my architecture, worship is raised to the highest degree, purified, restored to the Gospels."[20] The best of the priests acknowledged this cheerfully. The opposition did not.

The architect's attitude was grounded in reality but had a paranoiac tinge. He drove home the main points to his mother as if he were depicting a Last Judgment to an illiterate child. Repeating almost verbatim his dread of the response from the Vatican, he wrote, "Everything was joy and enthusiasm. BUT, the devil must be sneering in a corner, and it is his custom not to remain idle. Rome is keeping an eye on Ronchamp. I am expecting storms. And even vile and contemptible actions. That is why I myself have been, by necessity, vile and contemptible in making my recommendations to you on these three points. But I have no right to cease being vigilant."[21]

He instructed his mother to go to Ronchamp, to open all the doors he had made there, not merely to see the interior but to enjoy her right to go behind the altar and climb the sacristy staircase. He sketched a bird's-eye view of the church plan for her, drawing arrows to indicate the path she would take.

Then, in his endless attempt to please and humor her, he reported that at the inaugural banquet he had been seated to the right of the archbishop (a title he underlined to emphasize its importance) and across from the minister when the archbishop spoke about "L-C's mother (because of the dedication to *When the Cathedrals Were White*)."[22] He was determined that this dedication—"TO MY MOTHER, a woman of courage and faith"—reside at the forefront of her thoughts.

Le Corbusier had asked the archbishop to write her a postcard, which he enclosed. On its face, it showed a detail of the dramatically sculpted rough concrete of the church exterior. A massive, eyebrowlike corner of the roof, as well as the outdoor pulpit, are in view. On the other side, in neat script, is written, "For Monsieur Le Corbusier's venerable mother, 'a woman of courage and faith' whom I had the joy to invoke this morning in the cool, bright chapel created by the heartfelt intelligence of her son"—signed by Marcel-Marie Dubois, the archbishop of Besançon.[23]

To a stalwart Calvinist, the praises from within the hierarchy of the Catholic Church may have meant little. But her son continued to try to make her proud.

4

The moment you glimpse Ronchamp from the valley below, you are drawn to it as to a powerful magnet. As you approach, the experiences multiply, with a lot happening all at once. The giant ram's horn of a roof seems audible; concrete has been given the lightness of sound. It is a holy, resonant tone. Then there are the unusual forms of the towers, like giant periscopes, and the apparent faces on the many walls. Some of the masses are anchored; others soar.

Once you have taken in the forms, you notice the shadows—as important to the appearance of the building as what is solid. The roofline imprints itself on the surrounding grass and then moves. Other shadows resemble eyes and mouths and noses, so that Ronchamp sees and breathes, and gives out energy.

The chapel has a circulatory system that connects it to the natural climate. The flow of water off the roof, down the drainpipes, and out the spouts is emphasized by the overstated nostril-like gargoyles and the catch basins that receive the melted snow and summer rain.

At age twenty-one, when Charles-Edouard Jeanneret looked out of his window on the quai Saint-Michel and gazed at flying buttresses atop Notre-Dame, those fantastic jutting protuberances represented a language of hope and possibility after the clay-footed blocks of La Chaux-de-Fonds. Now he used architecture to express faith and optimism.

Inside the chapel, the tiny cracks of light between the immense sagging roof and the tops of the looming white walls resemble the slim lines of daylight seeping through the logs of those granges on the outskirts of La Chaux-de-Fonds. He built Ronchamp out of concrete, but he also constructed it out of daylight (see color plates 18 and 19). And then he augmented the composition with color; the deep red of the walls of one of the side chapels evokes the blood of Christ, making that particular space feel like the chamber of a beating heart.

When you walk toward the altar, every step yields a change. Colors beckon you; their aftereffects come and go. Turn from one of the intense painted glass windows and then look at a massive white wall; you will see, briefly, that same red or yellow. That brief encounter with an illusory hue is the sort of psychic event Le Corbusier loved to orchestrate.

The tilt of the floor, the irregular and shifting depths of the windows, the helter-skelter pattern of some of the openings, and the roof that for all of its weight floats ethereally give a sense of sheer liberty. At the same time, there are traditional religious motifs. An arrangement of seven panes of glass refers to the seven sacraments; three windows evoke the Trinity; cruciform shapes are everywhere.

On the outside, nature changes the building perpetually. For Ronchamp is a transmitter for the cosmos, wearing a different covering with every movement of the clouds. Inside, the light shifts constantly, causing an ongoing performance. Le Corbusier has given his real gods—the universal forces worshipped in India as by the ancient Greeks—a modern temple.

LE CORBUSIER'S great admirer, Father Alain Couturier, an expert on modern ecclesiastical architecture, had understood why this was, indeed, a sacred space. Two years prior to Ronchamp's opening, Couturier had written:

> At first the extreme novelty of these forms will be surprising, but in short order . . . the sacred character is affirmed everywhere, and first of all by that very novelty, that unexpected aspect. . . .
>
> We may assert that it is in such edifices that we accede to that higher type of architecture which transcends pure functionalism and in which the dignity of functions is directly manifest (and already operative) in the beauty of the forms. In religious structures, these things assume their entire meaning: for a truly sacred edifice is not a profane edifice rendered sacred by a consecrating rite for its eventual use (as was recently written in an extremely ill-considered article); a sacred edifice is already sacred and substantially so by the very quality of its forms.[24]

Le Corbusier himself said of Ronchamp, "All I know is that every man has the religious sentiment of being part of the human capital. . . . I bring so much effusion and intense interior life to my work that it has this quasi-religious aspect, by which I mean to say that it is not an emotion of pounding drums."[25]

It is as if what Bach discovered about the direct effects of certain musical cadences on the humor of the brain—and what experts in brain chemistry have found in the realm of psychopharmaceutical medicines—Le Corbusier had instinctively recognized about the effects of movement through architectural space and the sight of certain visual leaps and turns. Color, too, had those magical abilities that he cultivated; in combination with ever-moving form, it can impart well-being.

This amalgam of Stonehenge, Noah's ark, and a spaceship, as infused by faith as the soaring Gothic cathedrals and as radical as Picasso's boldest canvases, as true to the immediate necessities of construction and shelter as a cormorants' nest on a remote island, and as sophisticated as the music of Stravinsky, evokes so many comparisons because, while being unprecedented in its architectural vocabulary, it joins them in its authenticity and force and as an embodiment of human courage.

5

Ronchamp is also a private homage made public. Inscribed into the chapel windows in large, bold script, at a low level, are the words "*la mer,*" the sea. We can also hear it as "*la mère,*" the mother.

The name "Marie" and the words "full of grace" loom largest of all. To the world at large, that name and description refer to the Holy Virgin, the mother of Jesus. But they are, equally, a reference to Le Corbusier's private Marie, his own mother, who had also borne a "Le C" who would change the world and sacrifice himself in glorious excruciating martyrdom for his cause.

6

When asked about his intentions for Ronchamp, Le Corbusier had a stock answer: "I am asked what are my secrets for Ronchamp. There are none save a harmonious research among the problems raised. The Gospel: an ethic. The site: the four horizons. The means: a crab shell. Open your eyes and perhaps you will understand. Can the writer assist a man who does not find the meaning of the sentence in the words? One must seek out finesse while preserving force. Not for a moment have I had any notion of creating an object of astonishment. My preparation? A sympathy for others. For the unknown."[26]

THE ARCHITECT WORSHIPPED the power of the sun, the wonder of conception and birth, the stupendous construction of all living beings. Ronchamp is their vessel.

He elucidated the visual miracles that many people considered holy. The most salient of these was light, the symbol of the immaculate conception with its ability to pass through glass without breaking it, the incorporeal equivalent of the Holy Ghost: "The key is light, and light illuminates forms. And these forms have an emotive power by the interplay of proportions, the interplay of unexpected stupefying relations. But also by the intellectual interplay of their *raison d'être:* their authentic birth, their capacity to endure, their structure, their boldness, the interplay of beings which are essential beings, the constituted beings of architecture. . . . I compose with light."[27]

He was also attentive to the traditional religious elements required by his client's goals. Le Corbusier gave close attention to the holy crosses within the chapel. He made them out of metal and concrete as well as the traditional wood. The symbols of Jesus's death and martyrdom have physical and psychological weight; just looking at them, you imagine how heavy they are to bear on the shoulders.

When the human-scaled wooden cross made for the altar arrived at the building five days before the inauguration ceremony, Le Corbusier believed that that was the moment when the building ceased being a construction site. He saw it as a silent evocation of the great tragedy that had occurred on the hill of Golgotha and was now being represented on the hill at Ronchamp. Martyrdom was what affected him most of all.

7

The day before the inauguration of Ronchamp, Le Corbusier had begun a letter to Marguerite Tjader Harris that he completed shortly after the chapel opened. At one of the proudest moments of his life, the architect could not get over his regret at abandoning her idea of a colony of small houses where they could have been close to each other: "I am leaving to inaugurate the Chapel of Ronchamp. It will not perhaps be as beautiful as your nunnery at Vikingsborg, which was materially and spiritually inspired by you. I had written you the day after the tidal wave at Cap-Martin. You did not reply. I think you were navigating at the time between heaven and earth. Preferably heaven! As for me I've had the most intense regret for having to take the decision I was obliged to make. But the gods wanted me to be present at the tidal wave. I lost several years of work on a theme particularly dear to me. I should consider myself a dishonest or criminal person not to have warned you and to have begun work on the site that was ready for such activity. Hence I had the comfort of your friendship and your kindness in this matter. You have a vision, and that is rare! I was sure of creating something very fine for you. But you know very well that here on earth men do not do all that they desire (nor do women); later we shall speak of this again when we meet in the Upper Regions. But meanwhile I hope to see you again on this earth!"[28]

In the part he wrote after the opening, Le Corbusier complained about the coverage of the event in *The New Yorker* for being "without proportion and without much tact." For all the praise, there were always thorns in his side: "We shall see what we shall see! The architecture of reinforced concrete has entered into the history of pure architecture, and moreover—what is even more amusing—the priests have said that this church inaugurates a new era. I am afraid that the pope is not very happy! He had sent a bishop to supervise the inauguration."[29] He hoped that, while a devout Catholic, Marguerite Tjader Harris would be more lenient.

8

A week after the opening of Ronchamp, Le Corbusier's second great Unité d'Habitation opened in Rezé, near Nantes. At that ceremony on July 2, the architect publicly addressed himself to the representative of Minister of Reconstruction Duchet: "I am 68 years old. I have achieved a position throughout the world thanks to my researches concerning the structures of a machine civilization. I have created a hearth around the mother of the family, under new conditions of child-raising; I have re-established the 'conditions of nature.' "[30]

He had not just made architecture; he had made a pact between humanity and nature. A contemporaneous newspaper pointed out that success: "These tenants, as in Marseilles, have formed an association. Their opinions? Out of 120 families questioned, only two are satisfied, 118 are enthusiastic. And these enthusiasts declare: 'we prefer to live in the year 2000 rather than vegetating in 1830.' Certainly this must be said: that everything has been admirably thought out and anticipated. Grouping 294 habitations without achieving a monstrous construction, but on the contrary a haven of peace, that is Le Corbusier's merit. The labor of the mother of the family has been simplified. A true family hearth has been recreated in each habitation. Le Corbusier distributes freedom, silence, independence, verdure and nature."[31]

This bold structure on the outskirts of the commercial capital of Brittany has a force and energy and a use of color all its own. Looming over the landscape, it is rough and impressive, an energizing amalgam of coarse stone and primary colors.

The other buildings of distinction in greater Nantes are charming factories—structures used for the making of biscuits and other butter-based confections indigenous to the region. Their architecture has the pleasurable quality of what they produce. Le Corbusier's building, with its Modulor carved into the facade and its gigantic pilotis next to which we walk on a floor of flagstones, has gargantuan strength, a crazy vitality. Looming over the flat Loire landscape, its bright panels glistening in the sunlight, its rhythmic facade in nonstop motion, it is another bold declaration of human existence. As at l'Unité at Marseille, Le Corbusier gave people a new way to live.

LVI

1

Yvonne seemed somewhat better that summer. She and Le Corbusier were eager for their annual holiday—she because she had done so little, he because he had done so much. When they arrived in Roquebrune-Cap-Martin at the end of the third week of July, the architect was very pleased because "Vonvon" was able to walk from the train station to the *cabanon*.

Three weeks into the holiday, he wrote his mother that Yvonne "has the gift of catalyzing the right values. Instinctively she avoids bores and draws good people to her." One of them, named Vincento, was another of her visitors who came to play the accordion. To his mother, Le Corbusier described his wife's companion as looking like a little monkey and having some of the same attributes as peasant architecture: "He plays like a pair of thumbs, but sensitive thumbs. How far we are from the conservatories! Pieces from the Italian hills, from the mountains, enlivened by answering voices from the audience."[1]

With all the acclaim Le Corbusier was enjoying, the rustic getaway at the edge of the Mediterranean was remarkable for its "utter purity. . . . Not one false note. Everything is natural, healthy, honest, and extraordinarily intelligent. I can't stand bourgeois performances any more, with their commentaries." In his high spirits, he read authors who shared that disdain of the bourgeoisie—Rabelais, Villon, Baudelaire, and above all Cervantes. He considered *Don Quixote* "an inexhaustible book . . . the finest of all, read and reread these last five years."[2]

What an exceptional couple they were in their one-room *cabanon* (see color plate 16). While Yvonne, in the few hours of the day when she was sober, read, at most, fashion magazines and detective fiction, Le Corbusier, in the respite from his hectic professional life, not only read those masters but also plunged into Homer's *Odyssey.*

His mother was mellowing. Marie Jeanneret sent a postcard to him at Roquebrune-Cap-Martin: "My dear boy! There you are, living in the laughing land of the sun, in peace and the joy of life, far from tumultuous

Paris. . . . Repose, yes, you've needed that for a long time." She now called Edouard a "good son and brother."[3]

Le Corbusier's spirits were dampened when Fernand Léger died that summer, but the architect accepted the loss of one of his few longtime friends with resignation. His fellow Chaux-de-Fondian Blaise Cendrars wrote him on the subject: "My dear Le Corbusier, . . . but fuck the devil! Léger just died, beautifully. He had a seizure, right there where he was standing. I embrace you, Blaise Cendrars."[4] Like Cendrars, Le Corbusier thought it was the right way to go.

WHEN HE RETURNED to Paris at the end of August, the architect put down the cornerstone of another project, the Pavilion du Brésil, and hastened to finish some large paintings. At the end of September, he believed he was about to start a big urban scheme for Berlin, putting him in such high spirits that he wrote his mother and brother, "I remain your humble and devoted Knight Errant, Quixotte [*sic*] by name."[5]

When Le Corbusier's plane landed at Berlin's Tempelhof airport, he was greeted by more than two hundred journalists and the flashing of cameras from twenty photographers. He appeared on American and German radio and was very proud of his German, since he had not spoken it for forty years.

At an event attended by Gropius, Mies, Niemeyer, and Aalto, the speaker declared Le Corbusier "the world's leading architect." As always, he reported all his achievements to his mother, adding, "Berliners have no modesty, and therefore they want me to help them realize their dream of being the most beautiful city in Europe."[6]

When he turned sixty-eight at the start of October, Le Corbusier, while pleased that his mother remembered his birthday, was worried about the handwriting in her letter. Fearful that Marie Jeanneret's eyesight was failing, he counseled her to heat the house well and not to engage in false economies. Money was not a problem; he had sold a Braque that belonged to Albert for three hundred and fifty thousand francs.

His mother had to take care of herself because Yvonne would not. His wife, he complained, refused to accept the advice of doctors. Le Corbusier himself was in much better shape for having a shot of cortisone in the knee that had bothered him for four months, but when he told his wife he had gotten better because he had listened to the doctor, she remained intractable.

IN NOVEMBER, Le Corbusier flew to Japan. There was a big exhibition of his painting and tapestries in Tokyo and the chance he would design a museum. He thought the Japanese people were extraordinary and admired the high level of aesthetic judgment in every aspect of their existence. Yet the perfection made him feel like an outsider: "Everything was plush and consideration, so much so that I finally refused to bite, for I'll never be anything but a man waking each morning the same gullible idiot as the day before."[7]

Violating his usual practice of returning to Paris between clients when he flew east, he then went on to Saigon, Karachi, and Bangkok, before ending up in Ahmedabad. On the plane from Bangkok to Ahmedabad, he began to anticipate his upcoming meeting with the Sarabhais and Shodans, writing his mother, "Tomorrow I'm stuck for two days with my Ahmedabad millionaires who, like the rich in general, are heartless and unscrupulous, quite incapable of appreciating anything."[8] He disparaged the way these clients felt themselves superior in the world because they had houses by Le Corbusier.

Then he was to spend a month in Chandigarh: "All of which is well and good, but Le Corbusier, that withered old pickle, is the odd type who'll drop dead one of these days on the line of fire." It was a strange sentiment to admit to his aged mother, but he needed her to know his fears and peeves as much as his triumphs. He was out of sorts: "The journalists, the radio, and the devil and his crew (the photographers among others) create that crazy, idiotic, disjointed atmosphere of modern times." He expected his mother to understand his need for tranquility and recognize the shallowness of others, in contrast to his own purer values: "A little while ago I saw at an elevation of 6000 meters an absolutely fantastic cloud mass. Leonardo divined such things, and maybe [Joachim de] Patinnier and Turner. Above the clouds, there is a conquest of weather meant for seasoned and sensitive souls. The rest, of course, are reading their newspapers, their magazines, their novels."[9]

2

Work is not punishment, work is breathing.

—LE CORBUSIER

The buildings in a remote part of India quickly became known worldwide through publication. Along with the projects recently completed in Marseille, Ronchamp, and Nantes and the one under way at La Tourette, they established Le Corbusier as one of the most discussed architects on earth.

His furniture designs were increasingly in demand, and his books and theories on urbanism were affecting architecture and planning everywhere. Regardless, he was not making a lot of money. He could afford his way of life in Paris and Roquebrune-Cap-Martin, pay for his mother's chickens—not just on Christmas but on every Sunday—and allow himself the finest clothes, but he was not affluent. The architect had been driving the same modest car, a six-horsepower Fiat, for eighteen years and felt he could not afford a newer model.

"People say I am rich," he wrote. "I don't have a penny, I have never had money." His lot had improved since the total penury of his first years in Paris, but he was far from enjoying the wealth of today's celebrity architects. While, he declared, "the whole world builds according to my doctrine," the remuneration was modest at best. "I am 68 years old. Architecture has left me nothing and brought me nothing."[10]

The meagerness of his income was especially noticeable because of his latest client's wealth. He was now building two houses in the Paris suburb of Neuilly for André Jaoul and his family. The Jaoul houses were large and luxurious, however meager their architect's fees.

André Jaoul was an engineer whom Le Corbusier had first met on a boat to New York. After buying property in Neuilly, he and his wife had decided to ask Wogenscky to be their architect because they believed Le Corbusier himself was too busy. The architect who so often declined commissions flew into a rage—and got the job. He took the occasion to go in yet another direction. With their rough surfaces and primitive, grottolike forms, the paired structures represented an unprecedented approach to how the rich might live.

3

The two rectangular dwellings in Neuilly are set at right angles to each other, with the main entrances on the mutual courtyard in between. Both structures are defined in large part by their gently curved roofs, which, like the cylindrical forms of the Villa Sarabhai, derive from Catalonian vaults. Unlike the Villa Sarabhai, however, they were built in a climate that required that they be completely closed off from the elements. So the vaults rest on heavy walls that suggest a small turbine factory (see color plate 12).

The architect has encircled both structures with massive bands that cap the ground and first floors. The exterior surfaces are amalgams of squares, vertical and horizontal rectangles of varying proportions, and heavy cylinders. They are frenetically energetic relief sculptures that function as walls of marked resolution and stability.

In tandem, the Maisons Jaoul constitute a haven. They accommodate a privileged life with a place for cars, a lush garden, a large kitchen, guest rooms, and ample closet space; their enveloping forms also stimulate your mind and increase your alertness. While rather unappealing in photographs, in reality these structures soothe and invigorate you.

The moment you walk into House A—the first of them as you approach from the street—you feel a marvelous enclosure and warmth. Low ceilings are juxtaposed with tall chapel-like shafts of light. Shelves float musically from the living- and dining-room walls. Corridors beckon, inviting further exploration.

Thanks to the governance of the Modulor, a person of average height can reach up and touch, with the tips of his or her fingers, the base of the dining-room ceiling vault. A person of equal height standing on that person's head could touch its summit; while no one was likely to attempt the acrobatics to put those measurements to the test, their logic and balance pervade the atmosphere.

An abundance of nature permeates the interior. Foliage high above virtually presses against the windows, while the tree trunks and lawn appear to enter the living room through the glass below; you feel as if you are simultaneously inside and outside.

In these two houses, you feel secure and happy as in a boat, filled with a sense of well-being and peace. You are coddled. But rather than feel bound or cramped, you feel emotionally elevated and viscerally released. There is both perpetual diversion and abiding harmony. Curves of plaster induce coziness. The other elements—wood, tiles, and concrete—invoke energy. And then there are the colors: concrete walls painted aqua, and other such transformations that enable what is heavy to become light.

The rhythmic spatial play is accentuated by marvelous textural events. Vertical wooden beams work against flat plaster planes and large, pure expanses of window glass. The red bricks of some walls and pebbly concrete blocks of others play off one another like instruments in a woodwind quartet. The concrete assumes the rich resonance of a bassoon; the glass floats in its tensile way like the music of a flute; the brick and the wood could be the voices of clarinet and saxophone. Each material sounds its own notes, but they also all work in unison.

HOUSE A has a little chapel in it—intended for private worship. The effect of its painted-glass windows and of a wall broken by shelves and altars is hypnotic. Elsewhere in the house, the ordinary substances of life are rendered equally religious. Because radiator pipes have been painted in bright colors, the passage of water, with its ability to heat as well as its plumbing function, is given the miraculous spirit it warrants.

On the second floor, a bright yellow slab of concrete is perched on top of a wooden cupboard under a white plaster vault. We are in a Romanesque crypt; we are also inside a late Mondrian! The concrete appears to float in the air; we are in something that no one else on earth had ever created before.

The fireplace is pure sculpture. Its recessed storage cube for wood is all red inside, with a green floor. The man who used these bold and cheerful colors was following the advice he perpetually gave his mother: enjoy and relish life. These vibrant hues are fabulously unnecessary; inside a practical storage unit, they are there only to enhance daily experience. The stepped chimney above the fireplace, with its little recesses, is equally generous—a puritan's hedonism.

MADAME JAOUL, who was in her fifties at the time her house was under construction, asked Le Corbusier what she should do with her old family furniture once she moved into her new home. The architect told her to keep it and use it. But on another occasion he balked, "It's me who decides. *Merde! Merde! Merde!*"[11]

The mother was compensated by the wonderful design details; her

The kitchen of the Villa Jaoul, Neuilly, France, ca. 1955

daughter was less happy. As a client, she felt intimidated by Le Corbusier: "On this site we always heard his raucous trumpeting voice giving orders. It was impossible to make him do anything, although he used to say, 'We'll make this house together.' To most proposals he answered, 'Shut up, little fool, I know what you need.' And yet they did really make the house together as he said. One day Le Corbusier asked me: 'What kind of a bedroom do you want, do you want to be all by yourself, don't you want to be with your brothers?' That's the only thing he ever asked me. I said, 'I want to be by myself.' And he said to me, 'All right, you'll have your bedroom, I'll show you.' "[12] He kept his word, although she was disappointed that it was shaped like a corridor and separated from her parents' room by nothing more than plasterboard, so that she could hear their toilets flush.

From a child's point of view, the impeccable aesthetics had too hefty a price. "We weren't allowed to dirty our walls. Opposite my bed was a blue wall, and I was constantly told, 'You can't scribble your drawings on the wall. Look at that blue panel, it's so beautiful the way it is!' All right, the blue was fine but . . . this house always seemed so sad to me. Very beautiful, beautiful and sad, like a museum. It's a house that lays down the law. . . . Le Corbusier was a God for everyone. Except for the children."[13]

4

At the start of 1956, Le Corbusier was invited to join the esteemed Institute of Architecture. He proudly described his response:

> Yesterday, January 3, 1956, M. X, a member of the Institute, asked me to meet him about an important matter. Fifteen minutes later he put this question to me: "Are you willing to join the Institute?" Answer: "No thanks, never." . . . The Academy is sick, it has a French disease. France has lost the line of architecture which for so long was one of its chief glories.
>
> A diploma of mediocrity is awarded to a couple of hundred fellows each year, entitling them to practice architecture. They are given examples such as the Paris Opera + the Grand Palais + the Gare d'Orsay in Paris. . . . At best a few real minds might be able to manage the history of Architecture. But not the rest! . . . Becoming a member of the Institute is not only a consecration, it's an adhesion. . . . Alas, dear Monsieur X, you must not stay on the line of fire, where real bullets are aimed at you and where life is hard![14]

He preferred to venture into new territory rather than to align himself with the architectural establishment. Junzo Sakakura, an architect who had worked at 35 rue de Sèvres in the early 1930s, asked him to design a 230-square-meter curtain in 1956 for a theatre in Tokyo; Le Corbusier worked on it in the nude at Roquebrune-Cap-Martin. "I had sought and found, but I was still quite uncertain, dubious, dubious! . . . Suddenly (like a whiplash!) I catalyzed: a new project leaped into my understanding. On August 18, I was drawing it stark naked. The Modulor afforded me splendors of organization and indisputable harmony."[15]

Following Matisse's example, Le Corbusier made a maquette of cut paper pasted in position. After sending it to Tokyo, he declared, "What delights me is that I have the feeling (modesty!) of having made a mural masterpiece, something never achieved before: a wall of 230 sq. meters in woven wool. It will spit fire and it's wildly new and grand, and entirely of today."[16] The son of the man who had only done miniatures was working on his preferred scale.

5

On February 7, 1956, Le Corbusier wrote "an open letter" to the prefect of the police of Paris to put forward his ideas on urban living. In it he lamented the fate of a city strangled by automobile traffic, the lack of available housing for young couples as well as old, and the increased number of slums. He then described a number of the solutions he had proposed over the years—among them the democratic concept of four airports, one east, one south, one west, and one north of the city, linked to the center of town by special motorways: "I happen to belong to the category of beings who concern themselves with what's none of their business: they aren't qualified by a diploma nor by any official function. In this whole business I was preoccupied. Incorrigibly curious about the human problem, the key to the problem. The human factor! I've always been concerned with the human person, whose heart is moved and curiosity awakened and mind always inclined to invent solutions by a fundamental ingenuity—that optimistic, joyous, and investigative force which leads me to building."[17]

Those of us who lament the lack of affordable housing, who have experienced the pollution, and who have sat in interminable traffic jams between Charles de Gaulle Airport and the center of Paris might well feel that we would all be better off if Le Corbusier's voice had been heard on these subjects. One of the main reasons his advice was not heeded was that what he attributed to the blindness of his listeners was often the result of his own blindness in failing to recognize how he antagonized people who might have supported his theories.

With his passion for recounting the slights against him, Le Corbusier reported on the laceration he had received from Dr. Alexis Carrel. Carrel disapproved of his urban schemes for Bogotá and Chandigarh. He quoted Carrel saying to him, " 'All in all, you build vertically like the Americans, and I've demonstrated in *Man, the Unknown* how the Americans have stuck us with a dangerous and threatening civilization.' "[18] The ever-defiant Le Corbusier had given Carrel a copy of *La Ville Radieuse,* but the doctor had completely rejected its ideas out of preference for the style of bungalow he had seen in California.

Recounting this to the prefect of police, Le Corbusier made no mention that he and Carrel had worked as the closest of allies under the regime of Maréchal Pétain, nor that the terrifying Carrel was someone Le Corbusier had cited to his mother as a source of ineffable wisdom.

The combustive quality of Le Corbusier's fury now brought out a new extreme of confused and paranoic megalomania. "I was (crudely) cheated out of my plans for the Palace of the United Nations. Sulking in my tent, I smile with a malice mitigated by altruism and playfulness, knowing that along with this Palace is incised, in the hide of a baffled New York, a juvenile graft of the 'Radiant City,' in other words the fruit of forty years of meditation and research on the way in which man himself, henceforth projected into a machine civilization, could survive in this Homeric adventure, having looked, seen, read, retained, sought, found, decided and acted, having surmounted this phenomenal adventure of machine life which Louis Vauxcelles, around 1921, in the early days of 'L'Esprit Nouveau' (our review which concerned itself with precisely this matter) declared to be a good old refrain of the pure French tradition: and he called to witness the chariot of the Merovingians, and with the strength of that insight he concluded that nothing new had appeared on the horizon ever since!"

The prefect of police may never even have read this letter, but if he reached the final paragraph, he learned that Le Corbusier divided humanity into two categories—egocentric liars and brave revolutionaries. "With this classification, and with modern means, the present problems are solved—especially with regard to authority. The impasse is surmounted. The sap flows again—it is springtime—and circulates anew. It nourishes all things. It gathers strength from its roots which are eternal and natural. The roots are not up in the air, nor the treetops underground. No! And this 'new' occupation of the territory recovers the most permanent places and paths, going all the way back to prehistoric times. These are the constants of our sojourn on this wrinkled sphere, where nothing is extravagant but the reign of lies, whose true countenance = selfish interests, fear, ignorance, petrification. Nothing is revolutionary but the act of putting the car back on the train or on the road or on the tracks, if derailed or smashed. It is a powerful gesture. And it disturbs . . . by restoring. I offer you, Monsieur Commissioner, my respectfully devoted sentiments."[19]

Convinced more than ever that the drive for personal advancement and the hunger for money were destroying the world, Le Corbusier, at such moments, was not in his right mind.

6

When Le Corbusier witnessed humanity and generosity, however, he heaped praise in the same extreme manner that he unleashed rage. In 1956, Jean Prouvé, with whom Le Corbusier had periodically collaborated on housing ideas, made a small, simple prefabricated house on the banks of the Seine. Its concrete base sat on a bed of stones. The main materials were aluminum and Bakelite; its "*bloc sanitaire,*" which contained the heating, toilets, bathroom, and kitchen, was manufactured elsewhere and lowered in place by a crane. Le Corbusier was unstinting in his admiration for the intelligence and modesty of this low-cost dwelling, calling it "the most beautiful house I've ever seen: the most perfect way to live, the most thrilling thing ever constructed."[20]

Le Corbusier still had his own hopes of improving human existence. There were more than twenty new projects on the drafting tables at 35 rue de Sèvres that year, even more in 1957. They ranged from chapels in six different locations in France, Switzerland, Belgium, and Germany to a hospital in Flers in Normandy; a hotel in Berlin; an apartment building for UN employees in New York (remarkably enough); a congress hall in Thun, Switzerland; a new plan for Les Halles; an ashram in India; a psychiatric hospital in Amsterdam; an art center in Nice; an office building for Air France in Paris; Unités d'Habitation and apartment buildings at locations all over France; and private villas from Nice to Caracas. But not one of these was built.

He now weathered most of his defeats with grace, but what happened following another conference on urbanism in Berlin devastated him. Le Corbusier was one of 13 architects, out of 151, who had made the short list for developing a new urban scheme there. His plans were then rejected. Le Corbusier was convinced they would have won had not Walter Gropius, who was to be on the jury and would have supported him, become ill. Le Cor-

Yvonne in 1949

busier no longer expected every one of his ideas to succeed, but the hope of redesigning the metropolis where he had once slaved away for Peter Behrens had tantalized him.

When he was in Paris, he painted or worked on sculpture or tapestries every single day. But Yvonne had become so difficult that the architect could never stay home for long. Then, once he was away, he became desperate. "Dearest Von, I love you more than ever . . . that's how it is!" He sent her articles about the effects of smoking and lectured in letters that all the pastis was killing her appetite. Knowing she would explode at being given any advice face-to-face, he wrote,

> Your health is in your hands. You are *amazingly healthy*—an iron constitution.
>
> You've had one bad deal: *your bones.*
>
> You don't take care of them.
>
> You've got prescriptions.
>
> You don't buy the medicines.
>
> You have no notion of the life I lead. Anyone else would have croaked long since!

So help yourself, and heaven will help you. . . . And so will I, who have retained all my affection for you and also (yes!) my admiration. You can work miracles. Do it![21]

In letter after letter as he traveled, Le Corbusier begged his wife to be kind, praised her, urged her to eat, and insisted she take better care of herself—starting with having X-rays. He referred, on April 4, 1957, to "36 [*sic*] years of perfectly happy life thanks to you."[22] Three weeks later, he wrote about "all that you've been for me: an empress's daughter giving despotic commands and a childish waif so sweet, so pretty, so full of charm, so loving (behind her grumpy facade)."[23]

Le Corbusier was still obsessed.

7

In 1957, Le Corbusier and Yvonne spent their usual August holiday at Roquebrune-Cap-Martin. Jean Petit visited them that summer and was struck by the robustness of the septuagenarian Le Corbusier. On one occasion, however, Petit was alarmed by the sight of him struggling to climb back out of the sea: "Just as he grabbed the iron ladder to climb back up out of the water, a stronger wave prevented him. Then another. Each time, he was pushed back and violently crushed against the rocks. After several attempts which I watched helplessly, he managed to get up onto land, green rather than white. After having caught his breath, he told me: 'You see, the Creator is always there to remind playboys like me that they're not much, and that's just when you have to react, when you have to fight back.' "[24]

AFTER "M. ET MME. LE CORBUSIER" returned to Paris that autumn, Yvonne began to fall even more frequently while still failing to recognize the pain of her own broken bones. At moments, however, she again started joking—overwhelming Le Corbusier with her good spirit and warm heart. When she died at four in the morning on October 5, 1957, the day before Le Corbusier's seventieth birthday, her husband was holding her hand.

Le Corbusier wrote that his wife passed from life "in silence and utter serenity. I was with her at the clinic for eight hours, watching her—quite the opposite of a nursling—taking leave of life with the spasms and mumblings in a tête-à-tête that lasted the whole night. She departed before dawn."[25]

Even if the very end was graceful after all those years of misery, Le Corbusier was devastated. To friends he sent out a reproduction of a drawing of his and her hands clasped together, but no form of memorial was sufficient to assuage his despair.

AS WITH HIS FATHER, following Yvonne's death he voiced only unequivocal love and admiration for an individual he deemed totally selfless and kind and the soul of goodness: "A high-hearted, strong-willed woman, of great integrity and propriety. Guardian angel of the hearth, of my hearth, for 36 [*sic*] years. Beloved by everyone, adored by the simple and the rich alike for the pure riches of her heart. She measured people and things by that scale alone. Queen of a tiny fervent world. An example for many, and entirely without imitators. In my 'poem of the right angle' she occupies the central place: characters E3. She lies on her bed in the guest room, straight as a tomb figure, with her mask of magisterial country bones. On this day, feeling calm, I can believe death is not a horror."[26]

The crusty and often outrageous Yvonne Gallis was, indeed, for people like the young Robert Rebutato and the fishermen at Roquebrune-Cap-Martin, every bit as decent and amiable as her husband remembered. She was as addicted to acts of generosity as to alcohol. Even when the former beauty had completely disintegrated emotionally and physically, her deep-seated kindness, complete indifference to pretension, and Mediterranean earthiness had remained intact. Toward the end, Yvonne had developed the habit of giving cartons of Lucky Strike cigarettes—the amount had expanded from mere packages—even to strangers. It was an extraordinary gesture, especially for a frugal person. Many people who met Yvonne remembered that eccentricity above all else.

Though the creature Le Corbusier had saved in the Bois de Boulogne had flown to freedom, this wounded bird had stayed. She was always at home, and her need for him was a rare constant in his tumultuous life. He had no children, but she played, in many ways, the role of a needy child. She was the one person in the world who depended on Le Corbusier completely, and acknowledged it.

In his own way, Le Corbusier had adored his wife and never failed to provide for her. In return, this kindhearted, tough, temperamental woman was a source of stability that energized him. And even though she hurled verbal abuse at him, Yvonne, unlike his mother, revered Edouard—not as an architect, but as a man.

A WEEK AFTER Yvonne died, Le Corbusier responded to a condolence letter from Pierre Jeanneret, who was in India. Thanking his cousin for the precious comfort his words had given, he wrote, "Her death revealed Yvonne in a luminous intensity transcending anything imaginable. She (Yvonne) is in the hearts of so many people. In addition to these words, I think I can report that there is no reason to be pessimistic about the concluding work on the Capitol. Someone high up is watching over the future. I have my contacts. Perseverance. It would take only a moment of inattention for a collapse into the kingdom of failure of an enterprise which, by the energy of 4 or 5 individuals, may just as well terminate with a magnificent burst of brilliance. Impossible to say just when I can get to Chandigarh. Wait for November."[27]

Not everyone would have jumped so instinctively from the subject of his recently dead wife to the challenges of making architecture. But Le Corbusier was ready to get back to work.

The issue with which he was wrestling above all others was human goodness. There were people like Yvonne who were decent and emotionally honest, and then there were bureaucrats, academics, journalists, and authority figures who applied their power unworthily. The world of architecture was full of vipers; he had needed this rare woman with whom he had no doubt where he stood. Life was a battle in which one side acted out of kindness and good intentions, the other out of selfishness and cruelty. For all their intellectual differences, for all her eventual toughness and all his errant ways, Yvonne and Le Corbusier, two strangers in the world, had been good to each other.

LVII

1

One of Le Corbusier's most provocative buildings no longer exists except in photographs. The Philips Pavilion, erected for the 1958 Exposition Universelle in Brussels, was a multifaceted structure that resembled gigantic tents impossibly interlocked, simultaneously collapsing and inflated.

Here, too, Le Corbusier had initially said no to the project. Early in 1956, representatives from Philips had approached him with the proposition; compared to all he was working on in India and elsewhere, a 6,500-square-foot space was not of much interest. Then Philips, a leading manufacturer of lighting and sound equipment, assured Le Corbusier access to all the latest technology that would enable him to integrate the most advanced sound and lighting devices into his architecture.

With that idea in mind, Le Corbusier was inspired one Sunday morning walking his dog in the Bois de Boulogne. He used the third person to describe the arrival of the idea in his mind: "He sees several notions gradually appear: light, color, rhythm, sound, image . . . psychophysiological sensations: red, black, yellow, green, blue, white. Possibility of recalls, of evocations: dawn, fire, storm, ineffable sky. . . . Measurement of time: rhythm, elegy and catastrophes."[1] It would be an "electronic poem."

Le Corbusier conceived of a carefully programmed spectacle through which visitors would walk over a prescribed period of time inside an organic structure. In ambient darkness, there would be a violent performance of colored neon lights and images projected on the walls. A sound program by Edgard Varèse would accompany the visual shifts. The total visit would take eight minutes, during which seven minute-long films separated by brief interludes of darkness would be shown in sequence.

Varèse's involvement was central to the architect's thinking. He wrote the composer, "I hope this will please you. It will be the first truly electric work and with symphonic power." Varèse replied, "I find your project superb. . . . I accept with great pleasure your offer of collaboration. . . . Like you and the Philips company, the only thing in which I am interested is to give birth to 'the most extraordinary thing possible.' "[2]

The Philips Pavilion at the Exposition Universelle of 1958

When the people at Philips voiced fear about the effects on the audience of the composer's unusual electronic score, Le Corbusier supported his fellow modernist with the loyalty he expected others to display for him: "There can be no question, not even for a minute, that I will renounce Varèse. If that should happen, I will withdraw from the project. This is a very serious matter. My reputation is at stake as is that of Philips. My life has been a succession of efforts and battles. The UN in New York was built on my plans (stolen). . . . I have written more than 40 books."[3]

Le Corbusier convinced his clients to accept Varèse's combination of percussion and the sounds of machinery: "rattles, whistlers, thunders and murmurs"—as they were eventually characterized by the *New York Times* critic, who called the building "the strangest exhibit at the Brussels World's Fair."[4] Sirens of the type used on ambulances and police cars vied with screeches that were like the cries of tropical birds on a desert island and with deep animal roars. By calling on Edgard Varèse, the architect had summoned everything he believed in: bold modernism, the timeless forces of the universe, and the spirit of the automobile, all combined.

2

After engaging Varèse and conceiving of the pavilion as a building without a facade, to be made from the inside out, accommodating Varèse's sequence of sounds and allowing for the seven films, Le Corbusier assigned much of the design process to Iannis Xenakis, one of the younger architects on his staff. Xenakis, born in Romania in 1922, had studied engineering before fighting for the Greek resistance; after his radical politics led him to flee to France in 1947, he had been hired to work at 35 rue de Sèvres. Since 1951, he had been concentrating on l'Unité at Nantes and then on La Tourette.

Iannis Xenakis's lack of formal training in architecture in no way bothered the master. Moreover, the young man, handsome in spite of a severe face wound that cost him his sight in one eye, was a great advocate of the Modulor. Also a composer, he had written the seven-minute-long "Metastasis," performed by sixty-one instruments, with the Modulor and its proportions and divisions as its basis. Xenakis wrote two minutes of music for the Philips project, to be played between presentations as one audience left and another filed in.

While Le Corbusier was in India, Xenakis came up with the scheme of the building as it was constructed, sketching the hyperbolic paraboloid forms and making a model in which he used piano wire and thread. Guided by the structure of shells, Xenakis unquestionably followed Le Corbusier's lead and accepted the idea that the requirements within the container must determine its external appearance, but then he devised shapes far from Le Corbusier's initial idea.

In July 1957, Le Corbusier visited the Philips headquarters in Eindhoven to learn more about the technical requirements for the *Electronic Poem.* During his August holiday in Roquebrune-Cap-Martin, he ruminated on it, and in September the model for the pavilion was published in the magazine *Combat.* The design was attributed solely to Le Corbusier.

Xenakis was appalled. He wrote Louis Kalff, the art director at Philips, demanding that his name appear alongside Le Corbusier's. Kalff turned him down, explaining that Philips had commissioned Le Corbusier, who had conceived and developed the plan, which Xenakis had then simply sheathed. Attribution would be given to Philips, Le Corbusier, and Varèse—and no one else. Kalff assured him, however, that articles and histories of the building would acknowledge Xenakis's role.

Le Corbusier became enraged that Xenakis, his employee, had been directly in touch with a client without his permission. The master advised Kalff to "take a panoramic glance" at the six volumes of his *Complete Work.* Kalff would discover that Le Corbusier had never "personally drawn a line on a drafting table. Consequently I authorize you to agree that it was not I who designed the palace of the League of Nations nor the Centrosoyuz nor the Mundaneum nor the World Headquarters of the United Nations in New York nor the Villa Savoye nor the villa at Garches nor the plan for Bogotá nor the plan of Meaux nor the chapel at Ronchamp nor even the apartment in which I live on rue Nungesser-et-Coli. However, the following fact will appear curious: among the 250 architects who over thirty years have formed the studio at 35 rue de Sèvres, not one has appeared on the professional horizon. . . . All this is quite troubling, don't you think?"[5]

Le Corbusier then resorted, as usual when he was piqued, to downplaying the conflict as if everyone other than he was simply being childish: "It frequently happens that the team is convinced that it is driving the carriage. Let's not give this incident greater importance than that of a violent outburst of a temperament itself violent."[6]

FOUR DAYS AFTER WRITING to Kalff, Le Corbusier decided that the wording engraved in concrete on the front of the pavilion, to appear in all future publications, was to read "Philips – Le Corbusier (coll. Xenakis) Varèse." That this would make sense to the general public is unlikely, but the master had spoken. Xenakis was sufficiently satisfied to continue working at the Philips project, on La Tourette, and then on the stadium in Baghdad.

But the affair was not over. Following the summer holiday in August 1959, Xenakis and two of his closest colleagues in Le Corbusier's studio returned to 35 rue de Sèvres to find the doors locked and their keys no longer working. Shortly thereafter, Xenakis received a letter that begins, "Modern architecture triumphs in France; it has been adapted. Today you may find a field of application for everything which you have acquired by yourself as well as through your work with me."[7]

Xenakis was shattered. A year later, when he and Le Corbusier met at the inauguration of La Tourette, in an astounding about-face, Le Corbusier asked him to return to 35 rue de Sèvres as architect in chief. Xenakis replied that he now only wanted to compose music. He never again practiced architecture.

3

At the start of 1958, the town of Poissy insisted that the Villa Savoye be torn down so a school could be constructed on the site. Since French law did not permit "historical monument" status for buildings when the designers were still alive, there were no legal grounds for saving Le Corbusier's masterpiece of the 1920s. Distinguished supporters from all over the world sent telegrams, but the bulldozers were scheduled.

In March, at the last moment, André Malraux stepped in. It was only the intervention of the influential writer that spared the twentieth century's answer to the Parthenon from the wrecker's ball.

Le Corbusier was in one of his tumultuous periods. The opening of the Philips Pavilion took place on a later date than Philips had intended because of delays caused by his incessant modifying. Then, following the official event on April 22, 1958, the pavilion was promptly closed. The *Electronic Poem* was a technical disaster.

Numerous time-consuming adjustments were necessary before the multimedia event was ready for the public. But once it opened, it was an exhilarating spectacle, even though it needed constant tinkering throughout its brief existence. The films showed the history of human civilization and addressed threats to the future of the world. There were images of prehistoric man, concentration-camp victims, New York skyscrapers, and other elements that provided an encyclopedic overview of humanity. Le Corbusier had invented a new art form that simultaneously surrounded the viewer and assaulted his or her senses head-on. It presaged the video and installation art of recent years.

The titles of the seven short films were "Genesis," "Matter and spirit," "From darkness to dawn," "Manmade gods," "How time molds civilization," "Harmony," and—the longest of all, running nearly two minutes—"To all mankind." Each segment flashed sequences of images that lasted only a second. To the sound of a gong and then Varèse's score, the shots for "Genesis" jumped from a sparkle of stars in the darkness to a bull's head to a matador to a man and bull in combat to a Greek statue to a woman lying facedown to the same woman staring into a skull. "Matter and spirit" was a rapid cascade of images ranging from a nearly naked African woman to a woman from a Courbet canvas to a dinosaur skull to the rest of the dinosaur's skeleton to a monkey. The other films had fleeting shots of tribal art, the skeleton of a human hand (single and then in duplicate), horrific corpses from Buchenwald, close-ups of Chartres, religious art by Giotto, and a Buddha. Jumping between despair and hope, between destruction and creativity, between western and eastern traditions, this imagery, in a panoply of colors, touched the extremes of existence. The haphazardness of one's birth was clear—one might as easily have been born as another species or in a totally different culture.

At the end of the *Electronic Poem,* Le Corbusier gave hope for this complex universe he had just presented at breakneck speed. The solution lay in his own work. He showed his projects for Paris and Algiers, the Unités d'Habitation in Marseille and Nantes, the High Court at Chandigarh, his plaster model of the Open Hand, and his drawings for the Modulor. As an epilogue, he presented people of all ages, with, at the very end, a baby's head next to the profile of someone we assume to be its mother, looking on tenderly.

THE EIGHT MINUTES during which five hundred visitors at a time circulated through the mélange were extraordinarily intense. While this rich subject matter flashed by, projectors superimposed simplified abstract images across it. And within the space of the pavilion, sculptural forms were illuminated with ultraviolet rays.

More than forty years after Le Corbusier had seen *Parade* and read Apollinaire's exegesis on "L'Esprit Nouveau," he had joined Cocteau, Picasso, and Satie in making a new form of collaborative performance, to which he had added the element of the latest in pioneering technology. The *Electronic Poem* was a means of combining operatic effects with modern engineering, two forms of human expression that Le Corbusier especially esteemed.

During the eight months that followed the public opening on May 2, about one million people flocked in, most of them greatly impressed, even if the theoretical points were often lost on them. Le Corbusier was pleased, deciding that the endless technical problems and delays, as well as unresolved issues concerning reproduction rights for some of the photos, were irrelevant. The masses were enjoying themselves, which was what counted.

The architect was, however, annoyed with the response of the corporation that had sponsored the undertaking. In July, he accompanied a bill with a letter to Kalff saying, "I've never received a friendly word from your Committee Director about the enormous effort I made on the occasion of your Pavilion. This is an instance of human ingratitude, pure and simple. When an architect has made a building, the client pays him a lamb chop or a veal cutlet when the work is done and gives him a little smile, even if the latter has to be a little crooked."[8]

Nonetheless, Le Corbusier regarded Kalff as one of those rare characters from the corporate world who was enlightened. The architect applauded the Philips art director as having "committed himself to this enterprise totally, calmly, good-humoredly, concealing his anxieties, standing up to the unknown, incurring expenses, taking responsibility for everything, smiling at his purveyors. I insist on informing the Philips directors that M. Kalff is one of those Dutchmen, patient, persevering, trusting, courageous, who have bestowed upon their country so splendid a history. Each of us went about his tasks with his nose to the grindstone, forgetting perhaps to appreciate the fact that someone was overseeing everything without respite."[9] If Xenakis had overstepped the limits, the man who had enabled Le Corbusier's vision to become reality was a hero.

4

The electronics company had initially considered reconstructing its pavilion permanently in Eindhoven as a corporate museum following the eight months at the fair. But the expense proved too high, and the vibrant creation was destroyed quickly by a wrecker's ball on the afternoon of January 30, 1959. Today there remains a splendid book about it by Le Corbusier and Jean Petit, a recording of the Varèse composition, and a film. The recording fails to capture the effects of the tapes and various noises projected from all around. But what remains is the composer's statement of what he achieved thanks to Le Corbusier's concept and tenacity: "For the first time I heard my music literally projected into space."[10]

Varèse also wrote, "Trust that I won't forget the expression of solidarity by one who doesn't let his pal down."[11] The composer felt as sustained by Le Corbusier as Xenakis felt betrayed.

5

While crowds in Brussels were queuing to experience the *Electronic Poem,* the architect met quietly with the stonemason Salvator Bertocchi in Roquebrune-Cap-Martin to work on a tomb for his wife's ashes in the local cemetery (see color plate 26). Bertocchi's son had been Yvonne's godchild; the mason had warm memories of her.

Le Corbusier and Bertocchi worked together for a week. The burial ground was on a hill, three hundred meters higher than the little *cabanon.* It was necessary to use a mule and human shoulders to bring in the heavy materials. Le Corbusier was immensely grateful to Bertocchi for his aid with the ancient tasks of carting and cutting.

At the end of June, Le Corbusier returned to Paris. On July 1, he went to Père Lachaise to collect the urn with Yvonne's ashes. With Ducret, now more than ever one of his favorite young architects in the office, and Ducret's wife, Germaine, he drove the thousand-kilometer journey south, across most of France, to Roquebrune-Cap-Martin. Then, on July 3, at 10:00 in the morning, Robert Rebutato and seven of Yvonne's friends, local people about her age, met in the graveyard in front of the tomb Bertocchi and Le Corbusier had made. The cover was lifted, and the urn placed inside. A single bouquet of flowers stood alongside the container with her ashes. They came from Henri, the office boy at Le Corbusier's studio, who had become Yvonne's confidant in her last years.

Once Le Corbusier and Yvonne's friends had walked back down the hill, he felt at peace. He wrote his mother and brother, "And now things are in order, the order of things. I have a feeling of quietude, telling me: She is at home now. A thousand kilometers and back: total two thousand. Le Corbusier's age 70 years!!!"[12]

The architect had more to say; he always did. Having appeared to achieve resolution with these round numbers, he used up the remaining space on the paper, filling the tiny margins, to report on his work problems.

The situation was changing in Chandigarh, he explained. Pierre had encountered enemies there—"narrow-minded bastards!"[13] Le Corbusier knew he should return there and also travel to Baghdad to work on his stadium, but the temperatures in these parts of the world in summer were ferocious.

In minuscule handwriting, Le Corbusier wrote that he would pay for Albert to go to Brussels to visit the *Electronic Poem.* Finally, he scrawled the last piece of information: next to the container of Yvonne's ashes, there was space for his own.

6

Le Corbusier went back to the *cabanon* in solitude that August. He was exhausted and in need of silence but content because he had won his battle with the engineers at Chandigarh and prevailed in having his ideas put into effect on the buildings still under construction. Nehru had again been his savior.

He wrote his mother on August 23, "We've got rid of the sons of bitches. But it was intoxicating. And ahead of you, dear Maman, crushing tasks and endless battles."[14] While Le Corbusier vacationed on the Mediterranean coast, his mother was mountain climbing and hiking to summits and glaciers. Addressing her as "worthy wife of an Honorary President of the C.A.S. [Swiss Alpine Club]," he wrote, "I want you to know of all my affection, all my admiration, all my respect. I think of you every day of my life."[15]

He also let her know that he had turned down trips to Rio, Stockholm, and Copenhagen, but he was overjoyed that he was going to be visiting her. Then he proferred strong advice: "What luck that you have your Albert beside you! A real stroke of luck. You must do as he says now and then, when you must. Dearest Maman, you used to exhort us to be good. Let me ask the same of you now. Be nice to those who serve you. Care for them. Love one another (as you deserve): the most beautiful words ever spoken." This last bit of counsel, of course, had been his father's final words more than thirty years earlier. "Above all be kind and tolerant to the people around you," he concluded.[16] The irony of those words coming from the man who would secretly change the lock at 35 rue de Sèvres was lost on him.

7

The Japanese government commissioned Le Corbusier to build a museum in Tokyo because a rich Japanese businessman, Kojiro Matsukata, who lived in Paris, had amassed a major Impressionist collection, which had been seized by the French government during World War II. The Japanese had negotiated the return of the collection with the proviso that it be housed in a new structure in the park where several major national museums already existed. Matsukata's holdings would become part of a National Museum of Western Art, with Impressionism merely the starting point. The notion of the growing collection gave Le Corbusier a chance to move forward with the design of a square spiral museum, intended for infinite growth expanding outward from a central core, on which he had been working for a quarter of a century. Constructed between 1957 and 1959, it was his first and only project in the Far East.

The building realized the architect's ideal only in part. There is a nearly square court at the center, around which a sequence of galleries was wrapped at higher levels. The Impressionist pictures were to be in the middle, and Le

Corbusier acted as if the building could keep growing, to accommodate an ever-expanding encyclopedic collection. That concept did not connect with reality, however. The result is a distinguished structure but does not allow for easy additions.

Two Japanese architects employed at the Paris office detailed the building so that it appeared somewhat indigenous in Tokyo, not like a foreign impostor. Fulfilling the same goal Le Corbusier had in India of wanting his architecture to reflect local culture, he adapted to Japanese taste by using wooden molds for reinforced concrete that looked as if it were composed of wood fibers. He also introduced tiny green pebbles into the concrete as a bow to Japanese aesthetics, and he deliberately gave the building certain Zen-like qualities. The rectangular block on pilotis recalls many of his structures going back to the 1920s, but there is a new placidness—an impressive mixture of strength and quietude. Its simplicity and grace make this voice of the west at the heart of Tokyo a welcome blending of traditions.

In his *Complete Work,* however, Le Corbusier's callousness is seen to rival his astuteness. He described the interior arrangements as "forming eaves in the shape of a swastika. The swastika keeps leading the visitors back to the central point of the museum and allows them to descend the ramp toward the exit. At each of the arms of the swastika, there are museum halls on the same level."[17] His obsession with the physical functioning of a structure and his concept of abstract visual harmony seemed to give him a special permit to ignore the hideous symbolism of the form he named three times. Even though in India, as in Japan, the swastika traditionally represented the sun, its recent associations were unavoidable. Le Corbusier's use of gravel and his harmonic design conjure the most sublime and peaceful rock gardens of Kyoto, but inside his museum he willingly sent visitors on a course of right angles that recalled the goose step.

8

The inauguration of Le Corbusier's Brazilian Pavilion, a residence not far from his 1933 Swiss Pavilion at the Cité Internationale Universitaire, also took place in 1959. At the event near the periphery of Paris, the architect and various dignitaries had to wait for the arrival of André Malraux, who was late. Once Malraux arrived, he took time getting to the podium, stopping to shake hands and chat with various people. Le Corbusier stood erect without moving. When Malraux reached him, the photographers and journalists swarmed around both of them.

As the architect and de Gaulle's appointee walked into the new building, crowded by the press, Le Corbusier was recognizably in a rage. He wanted Malraux to himself. He gripped the minister's arm and forced him into the small elevator, closing the door before anyone else could squeeze in. Then Le Corbusier stopped the elevator between floors. No one knows what was said, but there was no question that this time it was Le Corbusier, not Malraux, who had altered the pace of the proceedings.[18]

9

The aging Le Corbusier remained hell-bent on the idea of completing the sort of urban scheme that he had championed for the past forty years—even beyond the scale of Chandigarh. The will to achieve some version of the Plan Voisin and instigate his urbanism in Paris became the hope that could keep him alive now that Yvonne was gone. Two years had passed since her death; it was as if the completion of that mourning period allowed self-resurrection. And so, in October 1959, he wrote to Gabriel Voisin.

The two men had not seen each other for thirty-four years, but Le Corbusier still admired the industrial pioneer who had applied aeronautic techniques to the construction of prefabricated houses, and he addressed him as "*Mon cher ami.*" His effusive letter was specifically prompted by the publication of *The Three Human Establishments*—an elegant volume, brought out by Jean Petit's Editions de Minuit, that was a grand summation of Le Corbusier's ideas on urbanism and how people should live. Le Corbusier explained to his former patron that the Plan Voisin was the basis of many of the ideas that had flowered in his book.

Le Corbusier informed Voisin, "The sites and the working conditions of machine civilization are now appearing, and—O miracle—they emerge from contingency itself: the world is changing, the world has changed. The page will be turned; if it fails to turn, disaster. But it will turn!"[19]

Le Corbusier was not one to have forgotten a good deed any more than he ever forgave transgressions against him. He delighted in pointing out that "the Voisin Plan" was infinitely more mellifluous than "the Peugeot Plan," "the Intransigent Plan"—named for the popular French newspaper of the twenties—or "the Citroën Plan" would have been. He recalled how the industrialist had given him the twenty-five thousand francs that had made possible the Pavilion de L'Esprit Nouveau. The 1925 pavilion had been destroyed, but its ramifications had been monumental. Le Corbusier reminded his patron that this structure had also housed a residence that was the model for the apartments that had since been realized in Le Corbusier's buildings in Marseille, Rezé, Berlin, and Briey. Thus, Voisin's support had given birth to a type of housing now inhabited by 6,500 people.

Le Corbusier fervently believed that a few brave individuals had the power to change all of human history; he and Gabriel Voisin were among them. With the Pavilion of L'Esprit Nouveau, he had achieved the most perfect marriage of "efficacy" with "temerity."[20] But it and its offshoots were only the beginning. The promised era was still to come.

10

In *The Three Human Establishments,* Le Corbusier both recapitulates the ideas of a lifetime and puts them in a form that he was convinced made them more realizable than ever. The volume is an elegant, square object. Jean Petit was Le Corbusier's best publisher, his books aesthetically in concord with their contents. *The Three Human Establishments* opens with pages printed in the luminous, rich greens and blues of the windows at Ronchamp. A drawing of an immaculately designed tree, illustrating the mathematical harmony intrinsic to nature, follows. The tree is accompanied by the statement, "You must always say what you see, especially (what is more difficult) you must always see what you see."[21]

That same tree reappears in larger form a few pages later, next to a quotation from Plato that concludes, "The most beautiful and the highest of all the forms of wisdom, Diotima adds, is the one used in the organization of cities and of families; it is called prudence and justice." Le Corbusier next cites Rilke quoting Cézanne on the horrors begat by modern industry and on the destruction of the natural world: "Things are going badly, life is terrifying." Le Corbusier disagrees: "Yet life will always be the stronger. You must understand this and not proceed against life."[22]

Le Corbusier then explains that, as an alternative to the dreadful suburbs and garden cities that have wreaked havoc on the way people live, his own "Green City"—with buildings on pilotis and an intelligent circulation system separating automobiles and pedestrians—would give priority to "Sun. Space. Greenery": the essential elements of human existence.[23] Agriculture would flourish, people would work and live together harmoniously, and true unity would prevail.

Whether out of naïveté or blindness, Le Corbusier still believed he might exercise total control over all issues of human habitation and that the world would be better off with new cities designed according to his master plan.

11

On September 10, 1959, the Swiss paper *L'Impartial* did a major feature on the alleged hundredth birthday of Le Corbusier's mother. The nearly seventy-two-year-old architect, the article explains, had just arrived from India, having traveled all night to be at the birthday celebration.

"There's the young lady!" he is quoted as saying. "*La jeune fille*" was then led to the piano, where she played a few chords. Local children sang the Neuchâtelene hymn in her honor, after which her sons ran around to find tables that could be set up for an impromptu lunch. Marie Jeanneret is taciturn and droll: " 'But you still see the lake from your bed, dear Madame!' an old friend said to her. 'When I'm in my bed, Monsieur, I sleep.' "[24]

On February 15, 1960, the great exemplar of vitality and fortitude died, at what was really the age of ninety-nine. She had been ill a brief two months. The Geneva paper added that she died in her "aluminum" house built by the world-famous Le Corbusier and was also survived by her "second son," Albert—an error that must have pleased the younger brother immensely.

With his brother and his mother for what was said to be Marie's hundredth-birthday party

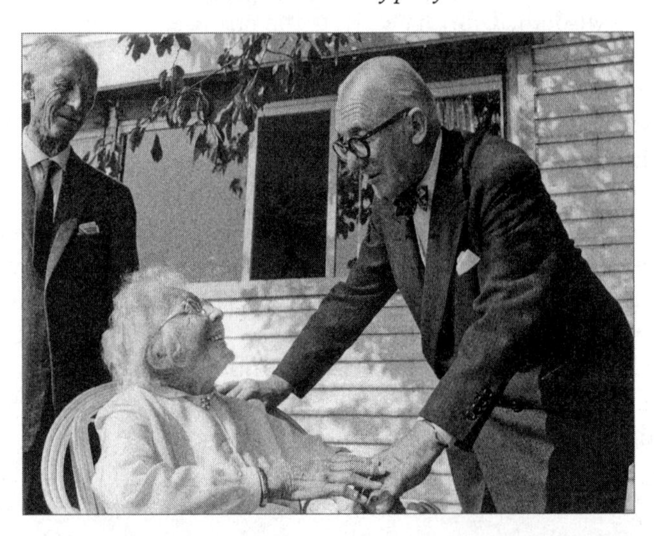

THREE DAYS AFTER the death of their mother, Le Corbusier wrote Albert a letter:

> Dear old boy. The black car covered with flowers, with rosy little Maman in her coffin inside, has left on the East Road, miraculously empty of cars, there having been a heavy snowfall, the snow now falling silently. And the hideous red "TOTAL"—the gas truck—has arrived; it had to slow down and line up behind Maman. And everything was hidden and finished in a winter silence as total as in the mountaintops.
>
> All that was simple enough. The two bare-headed brothers saw their mother departing. A mother one hundred years old whose laughter they had been hearing for over 70 years.[25]

Having been present as well, Albert was not learning anything he did not already know. But a dream Le Corbusier recounted was new to him. It took place "on the Jolimont pier, papa and I arriving in a cloud of steam, young Maman waiting for us in a pink dress and a flat pink hat bristling with artificial pink flowers. Greetings, Albert, from Your Edouard."[26]

Le Corbusier illustrated this missive to his brother with a drawing of an elegant young woman, tall and buxom, in a hat. She looks nothing like the person in the hundredth-birthday photos. Rather, she resembles Marguerite Tjader Harris as Le Corbusier drew her on the New York pier.

LVIII

We have been the ones to receive kicks and blows on the nose, the back, the head, or wherever you like. Such things occur. Much work has been done, even so, and I am certain that the next two generations, in fifty years, will have achieved something remarkable. If poetry is not in the facts, it will be in the hearts of men, or in their desire. But they will always argue with one another. There are those who make money out of their ideas, and they will always make money. There are those who put vanity into their ideas, and they will always be vain, and those who have a certain social spirit and who will try to talk together. Which is difficult, for it takes time, and such problems require a long development; they cannot be flipped like a crêpe. This entire task facing modern society is addressed to those who have the desire to give to something and for something. They will be called "dupes" by some of their friends. And "the friends of society" by others. We do not work to be praised, we work out of a duty to our conscience, which is within every man and which is there to tell him whether he is behaving well or badly.

—LE CORBUSIER, ON THE LAST OCCASION OF HIS BEING RECORDED SPEAKING, TWO MONTHS BEFORE HIS DEATH

1

Le Corbusier had clandestinely involved Marguerite Tjader Harris in the development of La Tourette. In September 1956, when construction had just begun, Le Corbusier sent a Dominican father to Vikingsborg to meet her and discuss the convent. "Of course these Gentlemen are going to talk finance to you," he wrote, "but I should like to say something so you will understand that they are doing so with complete disinterest, and I should also like you to know that the Dominicans of Lyon have shown themselves to be magnificently open to the most modern ideas (which moreover as they emerge from the Atelier Le Corbusier turn out to be ideas precisely congruent to the decisive periods of architecture's birth in the west around 1000 or 1100, at the moment when, at the instigation of St. Bernard, certain monasteries of great architectural power were built, free of any superfluous decoration and representing pure architecture, i.e., architecture only). The Dominicans have had to insure, by a loan or by gifts, the conclusion of their undertaking, that is, the final millions, which extend beyond their budget but which we cannot do without if we want to remain loyal and honest architects."[1]

Le Corbusier assured Tjader Harris that she could not possibly put her inheritance to better use. The undertaking was to realize the best ideas of both Father Couturier and himself, an unbeatable combination.

He continued the entreaty with a second missive. Le Corbusier underlined the importance of the project and the courage of his Dominican clients. He had exceeded budget in spite of all of his efforts not to do so but was loath to compromise the integrity of the building. He had agreed to create La Tourette on a shoestring, and while he had complied, they still needed her help.

Le Corbusier made his request, and gave the history of the monastery, with characteristic candor: "God knows you have Ladies and Gentlemen who come fund-raising, since the day your Maman left you more than you need to pay for lunch and dinner every day! But our friend Father Couturier was a master; it was he who got the Monastery of La Tourette going. He died very suddenly in his hospital bed two days after having informed me that he was cured of his muscular asthenia [*sic*] following the violent shock he received when Rome took her dramatic decisions against the 'worker priests,' especially the Dominicans, who had employed nonacademic methods in the practice of their convictions. This monastery of La Tourette is therefore (forgive me) a very strong, valid work to which I have devoted all my talents. I'd be happy to think that when they put fifteen centimeters of soil in which grass will grow and perhaps some tulips and narcissus, ordered from Holland, on the church roof, it will be thanks to your dollars that this smile of the earth could be addressed to the heavens. You are a brave girl. I have nothing but the best memories of you. And you know perfectly well I'm no fund-raiser."[2]

There was no chance of Tjader Harris providing financing, however. By now the heiress had paid for a chapel on her Connecticut property, which she had in turn given to a convent. The sisters were settling in, and she was moving into the garage apartment to function as their secretary. She was effusive and admiring to Le Corbusier in response, but her funds were depleted.

As always, she urged the architect to visit, but now with a new twist: "If ever you'd like to get some rest in a northern Convent, surrounded by gracious and silent sisters, come, come and find the Peace of a house of God beside the salt blue sea. (They accept pilgrims, men and young people.)"[3]

LE CORBUSIER WAITED nearly three years to answer. When he did, he acted as if Tjader Harris's letter had arrived only the day before.

In 1956, the American divorcée had signed her refusal to fund La Tourette with "all my admiring and affectionate thoughts." In July of 1959, Le Corbusier wrote her, "You kissed me off in your reply of October 9, surrounding your refusal with any number of kindnesses and favors and even inviting me to visit you as 'pilgrims, men, or [*sic*] young people,' as you put it."[4] Now he was back with a more modest and realistic financial proposition. He was attaching a document with the Dominicans' needs marked in red. He pointed out that in the previous two years, Ronchamp, which had opened its fantastic door only four years prior to his writing, had seen its annual income from entrance fees rise from four million to thirty-three million francs. The builders of the church had been penniless at the start; now their courage was paying off. He expected similar success at La Tourette.

Le Corbusier made his entreaty: "Dear Friend, money has to be good for something. If you don't want to give any, be good enough to contribute to the loan being proposed." He attached photographs and stated his case: "It's a crate of 'divine' proportions. The interior has a stunning kind of lighting. The walls are entirely raw concrete. . . . The hundred cells for meditation are oriented around a huge flat surface facing . . . the sky." And he summarized his own attitude toward money: "An excess of money is pure sterility. It's easy for me to say so, since I've never had any. And yet . . . at this very moment there is coming into being a movement for the purchase of painting by Le Corbusier all over Europe. Imagine, Le Corbusier honored everywhere after thirty years of silence! And perhaps I'll have some change in my pocket. I can assure you quite simply that the vanity of money seems to be an obscenity at this particular moment. So long as people have to fight for life such combat is licit; once the proportions change, the very definition of money is in question once again!"[5]

Marguerite Tjader Harris, surely, was one person who would understand his personal plight, his frustrations as well as his dreams, and the paramount importance of his architectural goals. "Soon you'll be taking me for a Preaching Friar; which is hardly the case," he continued. "I'm leading a terrible life, my travels criss-crossing Europe. They'll do me in, if it goes on much longer. On August 1, I'm going to see my mother who'll be a hundred next year. *P.S.* Last year in Brussels I made a devilish thing: the 'Electronic Poem' in the Philips Pavilion. I can promise you it shook out the fleas from those who saw and heard it. But it was a localized manifestation. Now I'm looking for the possibility, in my Monastery, of being able to extend certain sonorous experiments from the Philips Pavilion."[6]

Again, Tjader Harris had to turn him down, though she profoundly admired La Tourette: "Everyone is delighted by it—including your humble friend in Darien." But she was building onto the convent in Connecticut. She had a proposition, however. Le Corbusier could raise funds if he would grant her an interview for the American publication *Liturgical Arts.* Convinced that such an interview would lead to contributions from readers, the following day she sent questions and ideas for the article in a letter which she signed, "Your secretary, servant, friend . . . Marguerite."[7]

Tjader Harris offered to pick up Le Corbusier at Idlewild Airport, perhaps if he was on his way to Boston to work on the arts center he was undertaking for Harvard University. She amplified the offer with an enticing detail: "I have a shack here, quite nearby, at the sea's edge, heated and full of tropical plants."[8]

By the time Tjader Harris's letter arrived at 35 rue de Sèvres—following the celebration of that hundredth birthday he had admitted to his lover would actually occur the "next year"—the architect was back in India. His secretary acknowledged its receipt and forwarded it to him. Le Corbusier answered four months later by having the secretary write on his behalf: "Madame, M. Le Corbusier will be in India until approximately May 15. He would have liked to write you personally, but he has requested me to inform you that since the New Year began he had been leading a very fatiguing life. Having been ill in January and February, his work has accumulated, and he was subsequently obliged to make four successive trips in less than a month."[9]

Their relationship was not yet over, however. Le Corbusier and Marguerite Tjader Harris were to see each other one more time.

2

Six years after Marie-Alain Couturier died, Le Corbusier did justice to his patron's vision and completed the monastery complex.

La Tourette looms large on the hillside. Like Iviron on Mount Athos, it initially appears top-heavy. The windows and pilotis of the bold convent give the illusion of hanging loosely from a roof that is mysteriously fixed in place, like a taut curtain rod without visible supports. While in truth the vertical structure within the walls holds up the top, it appears like a religious miracle—as if what is above is floating in space independently, with everything else suspended from it.

This unusual building is exciting but discomfiting. It does not soothe or welcome. Its surface of rough reinforced concrete is cold, and its complex fenestration is challenging, full of shadows and of suggestions of what is unknown and cannot be seen. The structure echoes the rugged and somewhat secretive lives of its inhabitants.

Once you are inside, La Tourette resembles a grim high school or administrative building, with dark corridors going in myriad directions. But then you reach the church. The experience is without precedent. Like Ronchamp and the interior of the auditorium of the General Assembly at Chandigarh, this place demonstrates Le Corbusier's unequaled imagination. It reveals artistic bravery and gives courage.

The church offers the celebration born of tragedy. A tall, generous space, it feels like a small, heavenly city. Yet it is a cavern that conjures those underground refuges in which Charles-Edouard Jeanneret found safety during the bombings of 1917—deep, dark spaces with light seeping in from above. It also recalls the tall, unadorned barn at La Chaux-de-Fonds, similarly illuminated mostly from above. This stark interior like a gigantic cellar is hard to reckon with. It is unbelievable that the heavy blocks that make up the flat ceiling above don't fall and crush us. Yet they float ethereally over the narrow clerestory windows.

To look up and around and walk through the space is to have one jolt after another. The colors beneath the bands of fenestration are bold and powerful. The pitch-blackness in front of the organ suggests the power of music that will emanate through the church. The altar, again with unexpected colors, is a surprise. Compared to the Baroque church within the monastery at Ema, this is blood and guts, a raw and tough encounter (see color plate 20).

The cinder blocks and concrete are painfully honest and devoid of covering. The radiator pipes are uncompromisingly factual. The cement floor—patterned according to the Modulor, which Le Corbusier renamed "Opus Optimum" for the occasion—and the rough slate of the altar do nothing to soften the impression. But for all its brutality, the church is majestic and simple. And it emanates truthfulness.

IN THIS harshly minimalist space, dramatic lighting ushers in intense delight. It comes both from a single square skylight punched into the flat ceiling and from that ever-so-narrow band of clerestory lighting—both at the altar end. Far below, to the left and right of the altar, there are more small windows, pristinely simple openings composed of right angles and straight lines.

Because the clerestory strip has been divided into three distinct units, the light recalls the Holy Trinity. But, equally, it could represent Le Corbusier's personal holy trinity of sea, earth, and sky. The plain windows to the left of the altar, three on one side, four on the other, invoke the seven sacraments or the seven days of the week.

At the opposite end of the church, behind another altar, a vertical window is stretched to its ultimate height and narrowness. A sliver of light makes its way into the church. A more diffuse light arrives from the two chapels that jut off of each of the long sides. One of these chapels is in the courtyard of the monastery, the other on its exterior; they both are well lit from above, and their muted glow beckons you to come in from the darker sanctuary.

When we accept this summons to leave the larger sanctuary and go into the chapel growing out of the outer wall of the convent, we feel as if we are in a crypt. The crypt floor is a series of broad platforms that proceed down shallow steps, following the natural slope of the land. Each platform has its own altar, allowing for priests to celebrate individual masses. The concrete walls behind the altars are painted a striking orange-red and a celestial blue; that blue is also used for the ceiling.

Opposite those brilliantly colored walls behind the altars, a concrete wall undulates like ribbon. Convex at the top, it twists itself into concavity moving downward, while at the same time it leans in as if blown by a strong wind. Fantastically, daylight pours in from above through three circular wells—or cannons. Again, the number is holy. The inside of the first is painted white, the second red, the third blue. From the outside, where these wide cylinders emerge from the chapel roof, they look like periscopes or gigantic compressed Slinky toys. The shapes cause an ever-changing, unpredictable light and color to fall below, as if they come from a spiritual realm. The light coming in at these angles is unique in the history of building design. It has a stunning effect and gives the two candles and small crucifix on each of the altars below a crystalline majesty.

Iannis Xenakis deserves credit for these light cannons. Creating La Tourette, Le Corbusier had become increasingly dependent on others in his office. The work on the monastery began in 1953, in the heady days when the architect was also building in India and completing Ronchamp and other major projects. This was well before the difficulties over the Philips Pavilion, and Xenakis had been given the assignment of transforming Le Corbusier's quick sketches into actual building plans. In the course of that work, Xenakis had invented these new forms to illuminate the monastery chapel.

Xenakis was equally responsible for the marvel we encounter if we yield to the temptation to go off from the main sanctuary in the opposite direction—to which we are beckoned by a small opening suggesting a chamber of mysteries beyond. Proceeding that way, we enter the sacristy. This chapel

Light cannons at La Tourette, ca. 1957

has seven angled cannons of light. But whereas the ones over the crypt are round and at differing angles, these unprecedented sources of illumination have flat sides and trapezoidal cross-sections (see color plate 21).

The ceiling of the small chapel lit by these lopsided, energized forms is painted a bright yellow. Inside and out, this chapel is yet another occasion at La Tourette when celebration acquires raw force. This lurid space with its crazy septet of light sources is charged with the reality of death as much as the solace of religion. It exudes the power of our most primitive and authentic emotions.

3

> Supreme achievement and outstanding capacity are only rendered possible by mental concentration, by a sublime monomania that verges on lunacy.
>
> — STEFAN ZWEIG, *"Buchmendel"*

La Tourette has, in addition to its sanctuary, all the elements of a monastery of the type Charles-Edouard Jeanneret had initially studied at Ema and inhabited on Mount Athos. It's hard to know what to attribute to Xenakis or others on the staff at 35 rue de Sèvres and what to credit to Le Corbusier's own genius, but the complex in central France is endowed with details that cause everyday acts to waken the mind.

The corridor that provides access to the cells runs around a square interior courtyard, so that you take a quiet walk in fresh air before reaching your home base. You then enter the assigned residential unit on the side of the corridor opposite the courtyard—and proceed into a space that, at its far end, opens to a broad, seemingly infinite expanse of nature. The visual and tactile details of the cells have been carefully considered for the experience they provide. Most of the units are 5.92 meters long and 1.83 meters wide; their height is 2.26 meters. Unsurprisingly, these are all Modulor dimensions.

These rooms for solitude are welcoming and at the same time challenging. You feel that your needs are thoughtfully accommodated, and everything is clean, but the amenities are rudimentary. As you enter, a simple washbasin is on your left, backing up to a short entrance wall, alongside the door. Directly in front of you, a plain armoire forms a sort of partition, parallel to the entrance wall. On the other side of it, a narrow bed runs along the sidewall. A basic desk at the far end is placed perpendicular to the window wall and affords a sideways view outside. A modest desk lamp and straight-backed wooden chair, the remaining essentials, are in place.

The main activity in one of these rooms is lying, awake or asleep, on the cot, which is not much wider than a bench. You observe and reflect in conditions that echo those of a second-class train carriage. The rough and brutal is juxtaposed with the poetic.

Lying on the hard bed with scant adjacent space, you feel compressed, enclosed by coarse and pebbly plaster that is stark to look at and cold to touch. Its hard, deliberately ungracious surface is unadorned by pictures or decoration of any sort; it becomes a tabula rasa for contemplation or fantasy.

The green linoleum floor, surprisingly cushioned and soft underfoot, is a practical solution at the same time that its color and synthetic quality are jarring. Inexpensive and washable, this could be a surface in a hospital corridor that has to stand up to traffic; the governing force was that it was easy to maintain.

A machinelike and spare dwelling space, the cell ensconces you in silence. Its austerity is initially unsettling; there isn't a hint of luxury or embellishment, and the linoleum and rough plaster and coarse bed linens do nothing to comfort you. But then there is, as the conclusion of the space, facing the landscape, a composition made by a window, a narrow door (about eighteen inches wide) to the small loggia, shutters, and draperies. The window frames and the solid panel are yellow, the louvers orange, the other moving parts green. While the radiator pipes, underneath the window, are painted black, the wastewater pipes are cobalt blue. The colors lend charm to these assorted elements.

Moreover, lying on the bed or sitting at the narrow desk, you look beyond that composition at the offerings of the world outside. Be it night or day, fine weather or storms, you can proceed onto the loggia, which runs the

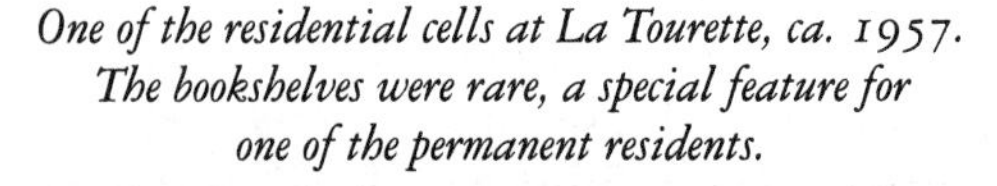

One of the residential cells at La Tourette, ca. 1957. The bookshelves were rare, a special feature for one of the permanent residents.

width of the cell and is 1.47 meters deep. Some of the cells adjoin lush woodland foliage; others open to a mountain vista. Infinity is the reward for your modest accommodations.

4

The bare lightbulbs, rough shelving, and simple sink in each room fulfill life's requirements without pandering to vanity or wastefulness. They compose a modest, unassuming stage for the great richness of observation, thought, reading, and writing. The living space that is like a splash of cold water on the face serves as a platform for the salubrious experience of nature that had always been essential to Charles-Edouard Jeanneret. He lived in a mixture of necessity, pain, and poetic abundance. The devices of his architecture combined the same elements. He achieved for the residents and visitors to a monastery the same blend of rigor and beauty he had realized in his own retreat on the Côte d'Azur.

The auditory experience at La Tourette is comparable to the visual. The sounds throughout this carpetless building complex are as harsh as those on a clanking train. In your room, even with the door and windows shut, you hear other people using the plumbing or closing their doors. The mechanical crashing reverberates in your ears. Simultaneously, from outside, there is the symphony of the birds.

5

The stairs that link the floors of the monastery complex are steep and challenging. These long flights of steps are at an unusually sharp incline; the spacing of the treads and risers is uncomfortable and physically demanding. That design forces you to get from one level to the next with maximum efficiency. Le Corbusier publicly lamented that too few people in the world walk upstairs two steps at a time; at La Tourette, he forced the reach of the legs.

There is a deliberate discord; things are at odds with one another. You go from the calm of nature and flowers, the poppies in high grass on the roof, to rough masses of concrete. You jump from the brutal candor of a metal drainpipe to a lovely and poetic play of soft colors. The kitchen door handles inject unexpected pleasure. The tough and the gentle, the factual and the charming, are united.

IN THE LARGE central courtyard, a pointed pyramid form sits on top of the square oratory. Inside this simple space are modest benches. A rough stone slab forms the altar. Pencil-thin vertical windows that penetrate the pebbly, white plaster walls are the sole distraction as one looks upward to the high ceiling formed by the pyramid. The only traditional objects are a small crucifix on one of those walls and the Bible that lies open on the altar.

The stillness and quietude here are breathtaking. The effect of the void and the leanness are infinitely soothing. Adornment would be an offense.

From the outside, the pyramid creates a visual stop, a stasis in the midst of all the slopes and curves and light cannons. It resembles a metronome and functions as a similar means of balance. Is this yet another homage to his mother, to music, to the possibility of a dependable core to counter the whirlwind of life?

6

Brother Roland Ducret was on the scene when La Tourette was being built. Forty years after the monastery opened, his memories of Le Corbusier are still vivid. Brother Ducret recalled that many members of the order had been enthusiastic from the start, while others never wanted to set foot in it. The architecture was not the only issue. While Father Couturier had the idea that the monastic life was worthwhile and that the Dominicans should return to it, others objected to the idea of being at a remote location in the countryside. Their tradition was to work in cities—as opposed to the more reclusive life of the Cistercians.

For those who accepted the principle, Le Corbusier was an ideal collaborator. If to his wealthy clients like Manorama Sarabhai he was difficult and contentious, insistent on imposing his will on theirs, to the Dominicans he was the model of cooperativeness. Told that it was a tradition to eviscerate the church, he replied, "No problem! We'll eviscerate the church." When the monastery was under construction, the brothers were living nearby in a château. The architect "thought of us as his children," giving "a very warm welcome" and making them feel "like real friends."[10]

Ducret was keenly aware that Le Corbusier had many adversaries. He felt that if others deemed the architect cold, this was because Le Corbusier was a polemicist: "His calcification was the result of people not understanding him." With the Dominican brothers, he was "very warm, very friendly, very close."[11] The architect in his top hat and bow tie and double-breasted suit enjoyed an easy rapport with the monks in their austere white robes.

Le Corbusier arrived for the inauguration of La Tourette on October 19, 1960, the day before the ceremony. He spent the night in one of the cells. Many of the Dominicans observed him that evening and the following morning, walking around alone, pacing up and down the corridors that linked the private and public areas. With a meter-long measuring stick in his hand, he busily measured everything, noting the dimensions of each small element, confirming their accuracy and speaking little.

In the morning, before the actual ceremony, Brother Ducret accompanied the architect on his first visit to the church since it had been completed. The Dominican opened the large pivoting panel that separated the church from the low-ceilinged dark corridor. The tall and cavernous space, flooded with the light of the sky, was revealed. "A wall on hinges: it is a miracle," observed Ducret, forty years after the opening, having opened and shut this wondrous device for most of his lifetime. He never forgot that, as the wall swung open, Le Corbusier looked in and simply whispered into his ear, "Bravo."[12]

THE EVENTS of the inaugural ceremonies included a high mass in which the eucharist was distributed. The Most Holy Reverend Father Brown, master of the Order of Preaching Friars, was the first speaker. Brown, an Irishman who did not know much about architecture, had been a friend of Couturier's. He thanked Le Corbusier, in simple language, for making a building in which one could study and pray: "I am not an artist, and I perhaps lack the aptitudes necessary to judge the great virtues of this house, but I am certain, Monsieur Le Corbusier, that you are giving us a monastery which can serve for many long years, can worthily serve the purposes of the Order, the apostolic purpose of the Order."[13] Others speakers followed, mainly with prayers. Le Corbusier had tears streaming down his face throughout the ceremony.

Afterward, during the repast in the refectory, Cardinal Gerlier of Lyon lectured at length. Then, he addressed a toast to Le Corbusier. The cardinal admitted that he had initially had many reservations about the architect's work. But over the years he had come to see that Le Corbusier's purpose was above all the mass that would be celebrated here.

The cardinal also allowed, "Then I discovered that you were friendly, that you could be contradicted, that you could even be teased. Yet someone had told me 'Watch out, Le Corbusier doesn't like jokes.' And I say to that person—he is listening to me now—'You are wrong.' And I am glad of that, for I have no great esteem for people who do not enjoy a joke." The cardinal went on to say that he would leave Eveux happy that day because Le Corbusier had "the worship of spirituality which gives his works their true value."[14]

IN THE COURSE of the opening, Le Corbusier acknowledged Xenakis and Gardien, both of whom were present. Although he had never apologized for the Philips palaver—or considered himself at fault—he emphasized the importance of such marvelous collaborators, while, as usual, mentioning his foes: "This is one of the joyous moments of our difficult profession: to find one's friends among those who know what they are talking about, which is to say, among those who execute, though many enemies oppose their progress, whatever it may be, even without knowing what it concerns, without having seen anything, without knowing anything at all!"

In the sanctuary of Jesus Christ, Le Corbusier's sense of martyrdom was accentuated. At least for once, however, it was in the happy context of felicitous partnership. And the hard facts of extreme financial limitations had been nothing more than an obstacle to be surmounted: "The house was built under conditions of poverty (to evoke that implacable aspect of economy), which find in me a man trained in those useful Indian gymnastics."

Le Corbusier also took up one of the elements of the monastic complex others might find problematic: its sound quality. "It is possible for poor acoustics to adapt to the liturgy," he said. "The liturgy accepts them. So many churches have such poor acoustics that we confuse poor acoustics with the liturgy itself. This creates that echoing noise, that mystery, that confusion which occasionally charms. Here you confront acoustics that are of great purity."[15]

Le Corbusier's declarations that day were a mix of audacity, crankiness, originality, and pure sacrilege: "Granted that I have, perhaps, a certain flair. . . . If you want to be kind and show sympathy to your poor devil of an architect, it is by formally refusing any gift concerning windows and images and statues, which will ruin the entire enterprise. These are truly things of which there is no need. Note that the architectural work suffices. . . . Yes, it does suffice, it suffices amply."[16] It was as if a descendant of the Cathars was avenging the conquerors.

The Dominicans had, in fact, agreed in advance to Le Corbusier's program by letting the architecture speak without the distractions of the traditional liturgical objects to which they were accustomed. Now, with unabashed boastfulness and repeatedly using his most beloved adjective to conjure a plenitude too great to be expressed, the architect told the inhabitants of this building what he had given them in return: "Proportion is an ineffable thing. I am the inventor of the expression: 'ineffable space,' which is a reality I have discovered in the course of my work. When a building achieves its maximum of intensity, of proportion, of quality of execution, of perfection, there occurs a phenomenon of ineffable space . . . which does not depend on dimensions but on the quality of perfection. That is the domain of the ineffable."[17]

Le Corbusier then looked at the cardinal and amplified on his spiritual intentions without pretending to a false religiosity. If for the opening of Ronchamp he had wanted his mother and brother to appear Catholic, at La Tourette he was known to be an atheist—or at least a nonbeliever in the Dominican sense. The public awareness of his Protestantism, as well as his own emotions that day, led him to reveal his true faith. He declared his respect for organized religion even if he did not practice it and emphasized the passionate belief system whereby he linked the acts of building and worshipping.

Le Corbusier made the connections between the tactile, the visual, and the spiritual, and he voiced his faith in the richness of the earth and his love for human beings of all cultures.

> I shall add only this word: this morning's ceremony, that ritual High Mass of the earliest days of your Order, that grandiose thing that stages High and Low, as the Chinese say, Heaven and Earth, with men and this present work, this monastery, this substantial structure, so full of finesse and so charged with sensibility to the limits of eye and hand. An encounter which for me is the joy of this day and perhaps much more still. I can say, in all simplicity: this architecture is valid!
>
> Your eminence, I thank you for having come here today. I hope that our rough concrete and whitewash can reveal to you that our sensibilities, nonetheless, are acute and fine underneath.[18]

Le Corbusier's remarks were eventually published. But there was another sentence that the architect uttered extemporaneously, that was not part of the programmed script. Roland Ducret never forgot it: "He has raised the earth to meet the . . ." At that moment, Brother Ducret remembered, Le Corbusier suddenly hesitated. "And then he stammered—he couldn't find the word—and said, 'celestial.' "[19]

7

After the inauguration, Le Corbusier issued one of his humblest public statements, as if Couturier's personality had infused his own.

> Architecture is a vase. My reward for eight years of labor is to have seen the highest things grow and develop within that vase. The ceremony whereby the Catholic Church took possession of the monastery the morning of the inauguration was a very precise and very beautiful moment.
>
> I have tried to create a site of meditation, of research, and of prayer for the Preaching Friars. The human resonances of this problem have guided our work. An unexpected adventure—like that of Ronchamp. I imagined the forms, the contacts, the circuits necessary for prayer, the liturgy, meditation, and study to be at ease in this house. My profession is to house men. Here the question was to house men of religion, trying to give them what today's men need most: silence and peace. These priests, in this silence, locate God. This monastery of raw concrete is a work of love. It does not speak of itself. It lives on its interior. It is in the interior that the essential occurs.[20]

The result of his submission to a scheme, his approach to workmanship, respect for the client, and the goal of serenity and contemplation are evident on the hilltop near Lyon.

8

An article published in the Lyon newspaper the day after the inauguration gives a vivid description of Le Corbusier: "Le Corbusier is here, anxious, timid, rather embarrassed by all the prominent figures around him proclaiming their admiration. His lucid eyes assess the quality of the volumes, the alternating hollows and swellings, the bold outline of the structures, the modulations of the lines, the cohesion of the forms, etc., etc., and perhaps he remembers that Charterhouse of Ema, already so distant, where in his youth his human vocation as a builder was affirmed. . . . In the first row of those present M. Le Corbusier had on his right M. the Mayor of Lyon, Louis Pradel, and on his left Messrs. Gardien, Xenakis, Burdin, Ducret, Brisac, Messrs. Rostogniat, president of the Council of the Order of Architects, Foch d'Hauthuille, Maître Chaine. etc., etc. . . . Le Corbusier uttered a few words muffled by emotion, and it was apparent that the impassive architect, solid and loyal as the pillars of his Unités d'Habitation, had been deeply touched. 'I have known many struggles, disappointments, attacks in my life,' he explained. . . . 'This morning I found my finest reward in discovering that my work could bring into play the High and the Low, man and spirituality, and could develop the most exalting regions of the human soul without the builder's realizing it. Behind these simple and rough surfaces there is, do not doubt it, a rather fine sensibility.' Yes! there, on the walls of La Tourette, is the human and unmasked message of Le Corbusier."[21]

The architect could not quite master his voice that day. The man who usually spoke with an arch tonality and complete assuredness was for once "a little quavery." What was evident to astute observers was Le Corbusier's "very great sense of the spiritual, or transcendence."[22]

9

In a statement he issued once La Tourette was in use, Le Corbusier was proud to point out the possible unpopularity of the design from the start and the Icarus-like risk he had taken: "You have a building . . . which . . . touches the ground as it may. This is a thing which is not to everyone's liking. It is an original aspect of this very original monastery."[23]

Initially, he had intended the cloisters to be on the roof, facing the spectacle of nature: "I think you've all been on the roof and you've seen how beautiful it is. It is beautiful because you don't see it. You know, with me there will always be paradoxes." But then he had decided that if he put the cloisters on the roof they would be so beautiful that the monks would lose sight of the real goals of the religious life. It would distract them from the hard realities of their interior lives. "The pleasures of sky and clouds are perhaps too easy," Le Corbusier had determined. Instead, he put the cloisters below, with the idea that access to the roof could be granted on rare occasions.

With that focus on the psychological and spiritual impact, he made the church steeple the highest point of the assemblage and devoted himself to the issue of letting light in below. "Emotion comes from what the eyes see, which is to say: the volumes; from what the body receives by the impression or the pressure of the walls on oneself; and then from what the lighting affords you, either in its intensity or in its delicacy, according to the sites where it is produced."[24]

10

Five years following the opening of La Tourette, Le Corbusier's body was brought to the monastery. His funeral cortege stopped at the site en route from Roquebrune-Cap-Martin to Paris. The architect's closed casket spent the night of September 2, 1965, in the austere cavern of the church.

Paris Match reported, "In the courtyard of the Louvre, in the presence of thousands of Parisians, there was the brilliance of such official ceremonies. But, on the road which the funeral procession took from Roquebrune, there was a discreet halt. This was at the Monastery of La Tourette which he had built and which today is regarded as one of his masterpieces. His coffin was set down before the altar. Yet he was not a Catholic. When asked 'Do you believe in God?' he answered 'I'm available, I'm searching.' The Benedictines [*sic*] lined up in front of the remains of this man who had built their cloister and kept watch all through the night."[25]

It was as if Charles-Edouard Jeanneret had been returned to the rustic silo where he had lived on the outskirts of La Chaux-de-Fonds as a young man. All night long, on this final visit with some of the truest devotees of his architecture, the Dominican brothers prayed around Le Corbusier's body in its sealed casket, yet again giving religion to a Cathar.

LIX

1

In the years following Yvonne's death, Le Corbusier's creative impulses declined. Their marriage would have suited few people, but his role as peripatetic caretaker had given him what he needed at home to be Le Corbusier in the world. With Yvonne gone, he began to lose his creative spark, even if he was technically very busy.

He took up painting again. He no longer had the luxury of being able to open the door of his cavernous studio on rue Nungesser-et-Coli to find his wife two rooms away crumbling saffron into a bouillabaisse or wanting him at her side for a pastis, but in his solitude, he threw himself into the making of large enamel plaques, six of them all at once. He would paint away his emptiness.

LE CORBUSIER returned to England to be anointed doctor *honoris causa* by the faculty of law at Cambridge University. For the man who had once caused his father serious worry about his schoolwork and who had never received a degree in architecture, there was a certain satisfaction in the endorsement. If the speech about him fell short of likening him to Christ carrying the cross to Calvary, it still put him in impressive company: "He shares with Cicero the view that utility is the mother of dignity. His relation to Leonardo derives from the fact that he too envisages the principles of mechanics with a painter's and a sculptor's eye. To those who seek the 'divine proportion,' he has given the Modulor, based on the measurements of a man whose height is 1 m 85. . . . Not only France but India, Moscow, and North and South America testify to his importance, so that in his regard we may cite, with some modification, this line of Virgil: 'What region of this earth is not full of the work of this man!' "[1]

His response to this praise was plain: "In order to arrive at this 'certain level,' let us suppose a level meter of a thousand millimeters, whereupon we must begin with the first millimeter, the second millimeter, etc. . . . regularly and in the order of things. You soon realize how serious, how difficult it is, how steadily you must persevere, how much confidence you must have, and energy to forge ahead."[2] The lessons of the watch engraver and piano teacher were imbued in him still: his father's insistence on effective labor and his mother's counsel always to do all tasks right away.

After the morning ceremony that required his wearing a cap and gown for three hours, he derided such academic formality as a nonsensical waste of time. In retrospect, it became "playing the fool for 3 hours."[3] The architect subsequently declined invitations for honorary degrees at Harvard University and at a new university in Brasília. But even if the ceremony at Cambridge had been three hours of nonsense, Le Corbusier was proud of the tribute and eventually reprinted it as part of his official biography.

2

His mother's death less than three years after Yvonne's had left Le Corbusier bereft and even more alone. No one could rival these women in assuaging his solitude, in making him feel that with all the unchartable variables of his quirky personality he had a true connection to someone else. Even Marguerite Tjader Harris had become so devoted to her nuns in Connecticut that she seemed spiritually as well as geographically distant.

It was not that he lacked admirers. Women, especially, still found Le Corbusier charismatic. The gallery owner Denise René was enthralled when traveling with him to exhibitions in Bern and Venice and observed that he completely mesmerized his companions by talking about the sources of the local architecture. When René was with him in Stockholm, a woman told Le Corbusier she simply wanted to breathe the same air as him: "The very elegant architect—tall, a dreamer, a strong presence, successful with women—replied by telling her to calm down."[4]

Heidi Weber, a Zurich decorator who had a gallery to show interior design, became so devoted to Le Corbusier that she swapped her car for a collage by him and then put on an exhibition of his paintings in her studio where, when nothing sold, she bought all the work herself without telling him who the client was.

His mother's passing was a fresh reminder of the inevitability of death, and Le Corbusier began to prepare for the aftermath of his own life. In August 1960, while puttering around the *cabanon,* he developed with Jean Petit the idea of a Fondation Le Corbusier. After his death, it would house his work, his collections, and even his personal possessions. It would be located in the villa he had designed for Albert and Lotti but would also preserve the apartment at rue Nungesser-et-Coli, as well as the Villa La Roche, which Raoul La Roche offered for this purpose. This organization would manage the archives the architect had long hoarded with what he termed "my old-fox order." But Le Corbusier was concerned more with young people and those who would profit from his legacy than with issues of preservation. He intended to create a travel scholarship for worthy recipients "who want to learn to see."[5]

The architect was delighted when he gave a lecture in the largest amphitheatre at the Sorbonne, with seating for 3,500, to find that a thousand students beyond that capacity clamored for seats. To the new genera-

Sketching during a lecture at the Sorbonne, February 1960

tion, he voiced his ideals, exalting the highest moral standards while using American materialism as an example of the opposite: "I want to address here the man and the woman, which is to say, the living beings who have a heart, a sensibility, a mind, some courage perhaps, and who desire to see things as they are. There are possibilities—a Cadillac, of course, that's one, but there is the other possibility—to have the satisfaction of one's own conscience."[6]

The office provided some welcome distractions after his mother's death. Le Corbusier designed a museum for Chandigarh—a large structure similar to the one he had made in Ahmedabad, a crisp container for Indian art from ancient times to the present. There were new proposals for churches, apartment buildings, an embassy, a hotel, and a factory—the majority in France and Switzerland, but some in locations from Egypt to Chad to Brasília to Oakland, California. All these projects met the usual fate, but they kept Le Corbusier and his staff busy. In 1963, the Olivetti company, with which Le Corbusier had initially tried to work nearly thirty years earlier, asked the architect to design a laboratory and factory for electronic calculators. These mathematical tools, evoking both the timepieces of his youth and the Modulor, greatly appealed to Le Corbusier, and he liked the idea of building the place where they would be developed and assembled. Moreover, although he was no longer alive, Adriano Olivetti, whose name was synonymous with the aesthetic refinement that was just then catapulting Italy to the forefront of elegant design, had been "not only an industrialist in love with beauty, but also an organizer of our epoch."[7] But nothing came of the project.

Le Corbusier was proud to be busy enough to have to turn down work, especially from potentially prestigious clients. Prince Moulay Hassan of Morocco summoned him to Rabat to consider taking charge of the reconstruction of Agadir, which had been partially destroyed by an earthquake; the architect declined, saying he was too consumed by a plan for the Meuse valley, among other urban schemes. He could refuse such offers because there was something in the air that warranted his utmost concentration. At last, Le Corbusier had—or so he believed—a major project in the heart of Paris.

This would be his first structure at the city's epicenter and thus more significant than the Cité de Refuge or the two pavilions at the Cité Universitaire. The new Paris undertaking was similar in scale to the three great buildings about which he still felt slighted: the unrealized League of Nations in Geneva, the architectural assemblage for Moscow that had been reduced to a single structure, and the stolen UN complex. He had one more chance of influencing the look of the world as profoundly as did the Parthenon, Notre-Dame, and the Milan Duomo. Again, he was full of hope.

3

The plan was for a hotel and cultural center to be built at the Gare d'Orsay, the large nineteenth-century train station overlooking the Seine on the opposite side of the river from the Tuileries. The main stipulation of the undertaking was that nothing disrupt the reigning aesthetics, but there were no impositions about the choice of materials. Le Corbusier was thrilled at the possibility of the views he would be able to provide of sights he had deemed exquisite ever since his early years in a garret—"the unexpected poem of Sacré-Coeur, the splendor of Les Invalides, the spirit of the Eiffel Tower . . . a feast for the mind and for the eyes."[8] His relationship with the city he had known for half a century was as complex as that of a child with a parent he both loves and wants to destroy, but he had come to worship the poetry of Paris's landmarks more than ever.

He was thrilled to design a place where people would gather en masse; he would give them the benefits of modern technology: "Actually what I'm talking about is a cultural center for congresses, exhibitions, music, performances, lectures, provided with all the latest equipment for traffic, for acoustics, for ventilation and fresh air, and impeccably connected with the totality of Paris by water, by Métro, by streets, and (perhaps) by the (express) train to Orly, now the main wharf of Paris, not a seaport but an airport."[9] The enthusiasm of this run-on sentence recalled the happiest days of his past.

Yet again, Le Corbusier would seize the moment: "The construction methods of modern times permit the creation of a prodigious instrument of emotion. That is the opportunity Paris has, if Paris realizes the desire to 'continue' and not to sacrifice to sentimentality the enormous historical landscape existing on this site. It is by a fervent love for Paris on the part of the promoters of this project that a goal so accessible on the one hand, but also so lofty on the other, can be attained."[10] Le Corbusier's manic ecstasy overtook him when he thought he could vanquish his enemies and give the world something unprecedented.

Not that he had stopped smarting over previous Parisian failures. "My name has always frightened Paris," he announced.[11] He would not forget, or let others forget, that his stadium design of 1937 for one hundred thousand had been summarily rejected, while now its clones were popping up everywhere. Perhaps the same ugly fate would happen with the great complex on the Seine. But for the moment he was floating on air.

THE PLAN CALLED for a hotel with twenty-five floors of rooms and a large public space for airplane companies, boutiques, and a bank. All the commercial enterprises would be in a giant slab on pilotis parallel to the Seine, with the powerful skyscraper attached to a congress hall and cultural center. The Gare d'Orsay would have been torn down.

Le Corbusier credited himself with "a spirit of absolute loyalty, of total constructive organic rigor, and with the desire to provide a decisive manifestation of architecture at the hour when Paris must be wrested from the profiteers or from the mindless."[12] So he claimed, but there are few among us who can regret that this project failed to become a reality. His proposal would have brought the worst aspects of modern Parisian architecture—exemplified today by buildings like the Tower of Montparnasse and the Australian embassy—into that magnificent region where, on one side of the Seine, some of the most charming streets of the faubourg St. Germain remain a bastion of small-scale architecture, and, on the other side, the Tuileries and the Louvre exert their quiet splendor. Not only would the scale of the structures proposed by Le Corbusier have been a disaster, but his skyscraper did not even have the charm or excitement of most of his work. It resembled a gigantic, merciless grate.

Le Corbusier's office prepared a photo of central Paris with the model of this massive block superimposed. It's not hard to understand why the city administration took the idea no further after seeing this mock-up. The shadows Le Corbusier's project would have cast over the seventh arrondissement would have committed the very offense the architect so loathed in New York skyscrapers. His towering hotel would have put people in permanent shade and deprived them of direct sunlight.

For all his genius, Le Corbusier remained completely insensitive to certain aspects of human existence. His fervent faith in his own way of seeing blinded him to the wish of people to retain what they most cherish in their everyday lives. The old Gare d'Orsay is a building of dubious architectural merit, but at least its ultimate renovation did not destroy the heart of a beautiful metropolis.

4

Not everything came to a halt. In Zurich, Heidi Weber persuaded Le Corbusier to do more printmaking and to design a villa on the lake; intended mainly for the display of his graphic work, it was completed in 1967. The architect also had some amusing forays in the design world. One of his tapestries was hung in the great London fish restaurant Prunier, for which he also designed china.

In 1961, Le Corbusier overcame his ambivalence about official accolades sufficiently to travel to New York to receive a doctorate at Columbia University and to go on to Philadelphia to be awarded the gold medal of the American Institute of Architects. The advance directives from the dean of the Columbia University School of Architecture, Charles Colbert, must have afforded the architect some satisfaction, given his previous slights in America. They stated that events "will conform entirely to [Le Corbusier's] wishes, which we will determine upon his arrival."[13] At Columbia, the architect was to receive honors and speak "with the entire audience anticipating your words of direction and wisdom."[14] Le Corbusier circled "direction" and "wisdom."

When Le Corbusier arrived at Idlewild Airport on April 25, he was greeted by the entire student body of the architecture school and taken by limousine to the Plaza Hotel. Then, at the magisterial campus on Morningside Heights, he was awarded a doctorate *honoris causa.* The statement read: "Charles Edouard Le Corbusier, eminent theoretician, profound architectural innovator, inventor of the skyscraper-studded park, you have resolutely proclaimed Man's right to an environment of increased amenities. Through your architecture you have sought to bring Man and the Forces of Nature into beneficent accord. In a technical age you have endeavored to produce a Universal Man, a concept designed to give unity and validity to creative achievement in those broad fields of the Arts upon which your abundant energies have been so productively expended."[15]

AS ALWAYS, however, there were areas of conflict. In 1962, Pierre Jeanneret wrote Le Corbusier that Hindustan Machine Tools, a large Indian company, wanted to create an "industrial city" next to Chandigarh. It was to go between the Punjore Gardens, a lush outdoor space, and the main cement factory.

Enraged, Le Corbusier wrote to Nehru. Knowing that the prime minister was busy because of upcoming elections, he apologized for the intrusion, but this potentially disastrous development required immediate action. Yet again, the forces of good and evil were as clearly defined as in a Last Judgment: "It is *revolting* to annihilate the immediate approaches to Chandigarh by an industrial city, and this at the very moment when the theory of the 'Industrial Linear City' appears as my social, political, geographical, demographical solution, responding at last to the modern conjuncture. . . . I am speaking to you as seriously, as profoundly as I know how. At the moment when Chandigarh appears as a site created for the good of mankind, here comes the devil to meddle with it, instituting this hideous canker on the flanks of this city!" Le Corbusier then tried his familiar tactic of false humility: "I am boring you. I am assailing you with complex arguments, each linked to all the others. And you are in the midst of elections at this very moment. I am embarrassed."[16]

At the end of the year, the architect wrote a letter to K. S. Narang, the secretary to the government of Punjab, which he copied to Nehru with a cover letter. Le Corbusier's contract as architectural advisor to Chandigarh had just been renewed, for the upcoming two years. "I accept this," he wrote, "but I must tell you that I shall do so *gratis:* without honorarium and without vacations. I am happy to offer this to India, a country I love."[17] He would come at least once a year to give advice and oversee and correct work; they would need to pay only for his round-trip transportation with Air India.

At the same time, he meticulously listed all the expenses that had not been covered for work to date. He had received nothing for his twenty-first and twenty-second trips to the new city, the last that June, and was now owed a total of 27,200 rupees. The accounting recalled Georges Jeanneret's diaries about cheese prices, but the conclusion was quite unlike anything Le Corbusier's father would have written: "I am pleased, then, to make you a gift of all these expenses incurred for Chandigarh and which are now added to my *gratis* service as Government Architectural Advisor. Perhaps you will be grateful for this gesture."[18]

In his cover letter to Nehru, Le Corbusier wrote, "I am making an important gift to India. Believe me, dear Mr. Nehru, I am making it with all my heart and in total sympathy with you. I am happy to contribute my *obol* to the financial appeal made to India at this difficult epoch for your country."[19] How like Le Corbusier to refer to the ancient Greek coin—worth one sixth of a drachma—as if he were building another Parthenon.

Nehru's response was cool. To begin with, the prime minister wrote that he would have answered sooner if Le Corbusier's office had not dispatched the letter written in December almost a month later. Nehru continued: "I appreciate your offer and gift to India."[20] But he said nothing more; there probably was another side to the story.

Perhaps the signature of a head of state was sufficient recompense for Le Corbusier. His weakness for the highest levels of officialdom was never ending. When another *Expo Le Corbusier* opened at Le Musée National d'Art Moderne in Paris, Le Corbusier was aware of the contrast to the opening of his previous show there: "Père Le Corbusier is respected now," he observed.[21] Not only were André Malraux and a bevy of other government ministers in evidence, but they actually looked at the work, with the esteemed minister of culture commenting specifically on the precision of the early Purist paintings.

Yet the architect was painfully aware that there was not even a small Unité d'Habitation in Paris—although he had now built a substantial one in Firminy, near the city of Saint-Etienne. Success in the capital still eluded him.

5

For the opening of the General Assembly at Chandigarh, Le Corbusier made another enormous enameled door, the size of a wall, that swung on its middle axis. With Jean Petit's help, he spent a dozen days in the factory in Luynes fabricating 110 square meters of enamel plaques—a substantial leap over the eighteen square meters for Ronchamp. They were baked at a temperature of eight hundred degrees Celsius—a fact that thrilled Le Corbusier.

He and Jean Petit presented those enamel plaques as a further gift to Jawaharlal Nehru specifically. The gesture testified to the architect's profound appreciation for what the Indian leader had had him do—with, he pointed out, one fifth of the means available in other places.

At the same time, as always, a further quest mattered more than the victory in hand. Knowing that Nehru himself would be present at the opening, Le Corbusier wanted to use the occasion to lay the foundation stone for the Open Hand. Le Corbusier had determined exactly where it would stand—near the assembly and the other buildings, with the Himalayas in profile behind it.

Even more than previously, Le Corbusier saw his monument as having unparalleled value to the world at large. It was his last hope of saving human civilization. Writing Nehru on June 26, 1963, at a time of heightened cold-war tension, the architect declared, "The modern world is torn between the U.S.A. and the U.S.S.R. The Asiatic East is gathering together." He believed that the location of the Open Hand, facing the Himalayas, was pivotal. *"At this precise moment there could not be a more significant place."*[22]

The sculpture was a gesture of welcome that signified an open heart on the part of all people to all people. He concluded his entreaty, "Dear Mr. Nehru, the symbol of the 'Open Hand' has a particular significance for me in the management of my life devoted up to now to the equipment of the machinist civilization. I feel with a deep instinct that India is the country where this sign must be dressed—India, which is for us Occidentals since four thousand years, the place of the highest trend of thought."[23]

6

Le Corbusier had almost resumed his former pace. He was no longer creating architecture with the same verve as when Yvonne and his mother had been alive, but again he had a purpose. He made urban plans for Venice and went to Brasília to plan the French embassy there. He found this capital city by his colleagues Lucio Costa and Oscar Niemeyer inventive, courageous, and optimistic. "It speaks to the heart," he said.[24] Le Corbusier's endorsement and generosity gave Niemeyer a boost, which the hundred-year-old architect still prizes.[25]

In 1962, Le Corbusier was asked to show his paintings in Barcelona. Since all of his major paintings had been commandeered for his retrospective at the Musée National d'Art Moderne de Paris, he declined. But he proposed an alternative, again writing about himself in the third person: "He doesn't feel that he's a jack-of-all-trades, but quite simply a free man, never having recognized the academy and having opposed the academy." He reminded the Barcelona architects who had invited him that the first lecture he had given in their city, in 1929, was called "To Liberate Oneself from the Academic Spirit."[26] To celebrate this liberation, Le Corbusier decided to assemble fifty photographic documents—selected from twenty thousand—that showed enlarged details of his work.

For the scale of these images, the architect had chosen "the measurement of 2 m 26, fruit of the double square '113 × 113' bearing certain proportions discovered one day and baptized 'The Modulor.' The 'Modulor' is a tool offered *gratis,* the patent having been placed in the public domain. . . . Such a resource, in the globalization which has seized the world at present, is a factor of peace—while leaving undisturbed the various systems of assigning dimension such as inch/foot, meter, etc."

He continued in a rampage. This device he had given to the world free of expense and that would have assured universal peace had been rejected by fools: "But the numbskulls and naughty boys, and those who are always ready and willing to say 'no!' (in this instance, they are idiots), declare that this is a strictly personal and arbitrary point of view. Upon the invention of the Modulor, this capacity for globalization was regarded as stateless, as antinational, and rejected with horror by those who have no notion what is involved."[27] His idea for a grand-summation photo mural at the Swiss Pavilion had also been mercilessly attacked, he pointed out. The *Gazette de Lausanne* had laced into the mural and called it a "corruption of minors" before Hitler's minions had destroyed it during the occupation—a detail he provided without mention of where he had been at the time.

Now, at last, Barcelona had accorded him the opportunity of righting these setbacks. He was extremely grateful. Le Corbusier relished putting together all these oversized photos of his urban schemes, architecture, paintings, murals, and drawings and having them go on public view.

The mural was in black and white. Thus, like some television in that same era, it demanded that viewers imagine the nonexistent hues. That necessity appealed to Le Corbusier. He cherished the ability of the human mind to transpose what it saw: "Color is the sign of life, the bearer of life. The world that opens before us today is becoming polychrome, has become polychrome. Open your eyes to the many colors of the automobiles, which not so long ago were all black."[28] To look at a black-and-white mural and mentally conjure vibrant hues required viewers to make a worthy leap. And it realized one of Le Corbusier's main goals: to get people engaged by using their eyes and imagination.

7

In 1963, the Carpenter Center for the Visual Arts was inaugurated at Harvard University. It was the first building credited to Le Corbusier in America and his last major structure. The intention of the building was the integration of the arts into general education at Harvard; the Carpenter Center was meant to beckon students from every discipline, with "the sole purpose to convey to present generations the desire and the need to conjugate the labor of hands and head, which is Le Corbusier's most important social virtue."[29]

Le Corbusier's longtime colleague José Luis Sert was the project supervisor. Le Corbusier himself spent only three days on location in the course of the entire design and construction, on a trip that had a shaky start. When, in June 1960, the architect had gone to the American embassy on avenue Gabriel in Paris to get his visa, he was asked if he had ever been a member of the Communist Party. He had not, but he deemed the question unseemly and proposed a meeting with the ambassador. The request was granted, and Le Corbusier asked Jean Petit to accompany him. Petit described the encounter: "Le Corbusier announces straight off that he is unwilling to answer any question about his opinions and his private life. He is a world-renowned architect, that is the sole useful answer to useless questions. The ambassador is charming and amiably accepts the architect's unmannerly bluntness."[30]

Le Corbusier then made the trip. He flew first-class on Pan Am, taking with him the maquette his office had already prepared, although he had not seen the site firsthand. When he arrived in Cambridge, he realized that, relative to the other structures, the small site Harvard had allotted showed how far the university really was from wanting the arts to have parity with law and history.

Nonetheless, what Le Corbusier achieved on the compressed lot in the middle of a rectangular block of neo-Classical buildings has considerable impact. The bold ramps, cantilevered ovoids, and deep *brises-soleil* are a strong statement of imagination and newness in contrast to the traditionalist red bricks and brownstone of the rest of the university.

Yet the Carpenter Center suffers from some of the shortcomings that often befell Le Corbusier's presence in America: a certain discomfort, a look of struggle, even confusion. For the building's opening in May 1963, Le Corbusier wrote Harvard president Nathan Pusey that his doctor would not permit him to attend. He neglected to say that he followed the doctor's orders only when it suited him. On one level, the architect had reconciled his relationship to the country that had once fueled his greatest optimism. On another, he deliberately kept his distance from the place where he had incurred some of his deepest wounds, and where he felt slighted still.

THE YEAR the Carpenter Center opened, Le Corbusier had good reasons to have his sights focused elsewhere. As minister of cultural affairs, Malraux was becoming more and more powerful and also increasingly loyal to the architect. He now asked Le Corbusier to design a museum of the twentieth century, to be constructed at the Rond-Point de la Défense, a forty-five-hectare parcel on the outskirts of Paris.

Le Corbusier again took up the museum idea he had realized in compromised forms in Tokyo, Ahmedabad, and Chandigarh. His excitement was palpable. He compared the idea of bringing it into existence to what he considered the ultimate act of creation: "Before giving birth, a woman doesn't know the color of her child's hair."[31]

But soon Le Corbusier and his staff came to the conclusion that the site was "devoid of all landscape charm" and proposed a different location in Saint-Germain-en-Laye. Le Corbusier also recommended that the city consider destroying both the Grand Palais and the Petit Palais—buildings he had never liked—to fulfill Malraux's request for a new museum. When he did not succeed in shifting the site to either true countryside or the city center, he abandoned the project.

STILL, LE CORBUSIER'S life had its sweet moments. In the spring of 1963, when he was offered a doctorate *honoris causa* by the University of Geneva, he was convinced that the main reason was that he was owed credit for the "prime" project for the League of Nations thirty years earlier. The architect wrote "Bravo!" on the letter that announced this redress of an old wrong.[32] While explaining that every day he turned down requests to travel, in this instance he accepted. His one stipulation was that he had to wear a suit, rather than evening clothes, at the celebratory banquet. The former Charles-Edouard Jeanneret enjoyed returning to Switzerland on his own terms. He stayed at the elegant Hotel Richmond—a distinction, given his many defeats at the hands of some of the League of Nations officials who had once been at home there.

Then the city of Florence organized a large Le Corbusier exhibition and gave him the gold medal of the city, declaring him the "greatest urbanist architect of our epoch."[33] The University of Florence was yet another institution to offer him a degree. In response, Le Corbusier wrote the French consul to the Italian city explaining that he had not requested the degree and had already received many such honors—he attached a list—but that, nonetheless, he would gladly be present at a ceremony if it could take place in Paris. The event occurred that December at the Italian embassy in the French capital: the mountain came to Mohammed.

That August, in Roquebrune-Cap-Martin, where he lived mostly in solitude even with the Rebutatos next door, Le Corbusier again reread *Don Quixote.* In his copy of the book, covered with the hide of his beloved Pinceau, he found a penciled note he had written nearly forty years earlier. It recorded a dialogue between himself and the young woman who had recently moved into his apartment: "Greatness. Von: 'And that time I walked from Montmartre to the rue Jacob?' Le Corbusier: 'But why did you walk all that way?' Von: 'Because I didn't have money for the Métro.' "[34]

12

With the people he still enjoyed, such as Jacques Hindermeyer and the Rebutatos, Le Corbusier was warm and outgoing; with those who annoyed him, he had become increasingly cantankerous. It was standard fare when Le Corbusier said to the Italian architect Giancarlo De Carlo, "I've been listening to you, and for a long while I wondered if I was dealing with an imbecile—yes, I was dealing with an imbecile."[35]

Those who met Le Corbusier's brother were struck by the contrast.

Albert was "much more affable and agreeable than Le Corbusier, much sweeter" than the "boorish" Edouard.[36] When Le Corbusier felt himself contradicted, he would explode, "I'm right! I'm right! I'm right!" The conversation stopped there.

He was despotic at the office. It had long been Le Corbusier's practice, after returning from his travels, to be furious at what the others had done in his absence, often requiring them to remove their own detailing and restore where a project had been before he left. On one occasion, when a range of buildings and urban plans were in process, he summarily dismissed all his draftsmen.

In February 1960, he sent a letter to his employees: "I have been quite dissatisfied lately with the slow progress of our work. I've already spoken to you about this. *And I am specifically requesting that you do not begin your tea breaks during the afternoon.* You are not to leave the studio. I am making this a specific request, for otherwise bad habits will be established. . . . Once again, there is a lapse in the production of drawings. What is the reason for this? I am astonished that it has not occurred to grown men like yourselves to establish a program for your work involving the numbering of the presumable plans to be drawn and the indication of the scale. . . . I am here to give you overall ideas concerning the creation of the work. You are sufficiently adult to take all the necessary initiatives within the parameters of the ideas I have given to you or that you have helped me discover. You are fortunate to be working in a studio characterized by a calm atmosphere. You must understand that I am overwhelmed by work every day including Sunday. Do not ask me to be a studio manager as well. The studio is reduced to a small number of persons. You are individuals, and we do not want to be organized here *à l'américaine* (a form of organization that does not correspond to the objectives I have in mind). . . . You will be good enough to take note of these instructions. I have written them out so that there can be no ambiguity."[37]

If someone was up to standards, however, Le Corbusier was exceedingly generous. When Roger Aujame, the young architect who had demonstrated the backstroke to him nearly twenty years earlier in the river near Vézelay, needed a letter of recommendation, the master interviewed him at length and then spent an hour and a half writing it.

Nonetheless, a firsthand account of Le Corbusier written that same year opens with a sentence that reads like a clinical impression of mild autism: "He does not have the open expression and the easy smile of those who readily inspire sympathy; admiration and grace are lacking; the eyes are dull, the voice is flat and uneven." The author was Maurice Jardot, in his introduction to the architect's autobiographical *My Work.* Jardot's description of Le Corbusier's "porcupine manner" and his "expostulations, abruptness . . .

aggressiveness, egoism, complacency and . . . somewhat bleak attitude" was published with the subject's approval and tacit endorsement.[38] Le Corbusier did not mind being seen as difficult so long as he achieved his purposes.

To many people, Le Corbusier seemed "distant; not very smiling or making people at ease . . . and always in a big hat"; he did not waste time or suffer fools, for his sole remaining objective in life was to get buildings and cities made the right way.[39] Effectiveness was the imperative. This was why he took the Métro between the office and the rue Nungesser-et-Coli; it was more efficient than a taxi. Similarly, he collected seashells and stones because they succeeded at being what they were.

9

The conclusion of Le Corbusier's relations with India was not a happy one. On October 26, 1963, the architect sent a telegram to Jawaharlal Nehru: "URGENT stop Dangerous intrigue at Chandigarh against Corbusier and Jeanneret stop Hostility of Secretary Capital Project stop Letter following. LE CORBUSIER."[40]

The letter sent that same day explained that Le Corbusier felt he had been slighted. Four days earlier, there had been an opening ceremony for the Bhakra Dam, which he and Pierre had helped design. He had not been invited. Pierre Jeanneret, on the scene in Chandigarh, was reporting "violent hostility" on the part of the new local administration. K. S. Narang, now in charge, was annoyed that Le Corbusier was remaining as a government advisor, even if unpaid. Le Corbusier went on to state his achievements to the prime minister in the same manner with which he had touted his virtues to his mother when she complained of her leaking roof.

> Dear Mr Nehru, since twelve years I have made an enormous effort for yourself and Chandigarh. I have created an important "Plan of the City" (town planning) and I have made the plans of the four palaces of the Capitol: High Court, Secretariat, Assembly and Museum of Knowledge. Moreover my intervention in the construction of the Bahkra Dam has been considerable (Power Plant and top of the Dam). This intervention of mine has given Chandigarh a world-wide reputation.
>
> My architecture has universal value (and signification) . . . but it is not appreciated in certain departments. (There has been considerable criticism in the Legislature on "Le Corbusier and his buildings.")

> You are aware of my deepest respect and friendship for you; since twelve years you are present in my preoccupations. Chandigarh and my other works have placed me at the head of the architectural evolution in the world without leaving my office 35 rue de Sèvres. I have transformed architecture all over the world. It is modest to write in this way!! I am very sorry, please excuse me, but it is a fact.[41]

The stilted English was a result of the translation someone in his office had made from his French. The errors had been relatively minor thus far. But the translator made a truly unfortunate mistake in Le Corbusier's conclusion: "I wish to (and I must) complete my work at Chandigarh. I have written that my work would be gratuitous [*sic*], without any fees (I had informed you of this in my letter dated the 17th December, 1962.) I ask to remain beside you so that Chandigarh should be an Indian landmark."[42]

For Nehru's review, Le Corbusier attached correspondence from Narang and Pierre Jeanneret that made clear the gravity of the situation. Pierre's letter explained precisely how the Punjab government had terminated Le Corbusier's role on October 18, 1963. At a time when there were fourteen works still under consideration, both Pierre and Le Corbusier deemed it urgent that Le Corbusier return to Chandigarh—even if the new regime did nothing more than pay for his airplane ticket and accept his continuation of the role he had had for twelve years.

There is no indication that Nehru answered. On November 4, Le Corbusier again wrote the prime minister, this time too impatient to have his letter translated from the French, which, after all, he had discovered Nehru spoke at their very first marvelous meeting, under much happier circumstances: "Dear Mr. Nehru, Forgive me for disturbing you once again. I enclose a photograph of the project for the monument accepted by the Bahkra Dam Committee. This project is unbelievably stupid and horrible. Life is difficult!!! Believe me, dear Mr. Nehru, you have my profound friendship. P.S. If this project reaches the stage of execution, I shall make certain it is published the world over and in all periodicals of the highest reputation. And the world will be dismayed."[43]

Again, there was no answer.

With an old man's trembling hands, the seventy-six-year-old Le Corbusier wrote a last letter to Nehru in March 1964. Even to a distinguished prime minister, he did not bother with a full sentence to start. The message was urgent enough to warrant his telegraphic style: "Dear Monsieur Nehru, troubles and tempests at Chandigarh. Actions have been taken in opposition to us," he began. Then—treating himself, as he often did, as a subject to be observed—he continued, "Le Corbusier has created a work at Chandigarh that is admired the world over. Pierre Jeanneret as well." He then reverted to the first person: "I am government advisor. My ideas and plans must be respected."

Le Corbusier was devastated. As he told the man who had defended him so assiduously in the past, the Indians he had come to know over the previous decade were of "the highest value, morally and professionally."[44] He begged for Nehru's help.

He never received a response. Today, the world deems Chandigarh among Le Corbusier's greatest triumphs—for India as well as for the architect personally. To Le Corbusier, it was, in the end, another bitter defeat.

LX

> Drowning, of course, drowning is strange, I mean strange for those on shore. It all seems done so discreetly. The onlooker, attention caught by a distant feathery cry, peers out intently but sees nothing of the struggle, the helpless silencing, the awful slow-motion thrashing, the last, long fall into the bottomless and ever-blackening blue. No. All that is to be seen is a moment of white water, and a hand, languidly sinking.
>
> —JOHN BANVILLE, *Eclipse*

1

In 1955, Le Corbusier had taken Hilary Harris, Marguerite Tjader Harris's son, into the office at 35 rue de Sèvres as an intern. Twenty years earlier, Hilary had been the six-year-old Toutou who had joined his mother and the architect in driving around New York. In the thirties, whenever Le Corbusier wrote to his American mistress, he almost always included a message to her affable son. Now the boy had become a young man who wanted to study the connections between cinema and architecture. Especially with the Philips Pavilion being planned, there was no better place to explore that relationship, from both an aesthetic and a technical point of view, than the office of his mother's lover.

Harris returned to America following the internship, but he and Le Corbusier remained in touch. In April 1960, on a trip to Paris, Harris eagerly tried to visit, and he telephoned the studio repeatedly. On the day they were finally supposed to talk, Le Corbusier had a meeting at the Ministry of Construction that lasted longer than anticipated, prompting an explanatory letter from his secretary to "Madame Tjader Harris" in Darien apologizing for the missed encounter with her son.

In the spring of 1961, Marguerite Tjader Harris sent a note to Le Corbusier's office saying that she had missed seeing him in New York and now was at the Lutétia, half a block from 35 rue de Sèvres. She instructed him to phone on the morning of Tuesday, May 30, to see if they could schedule a rendezvous either at the hotel or somewhere else. She said she wanted to show him photos of her son's work.

At the bottom of Tjader Harris's letter, Le Corbusier wrote, "Lunch 24 N-C Friday June 2 1961."[1] Now that Yvonne was no longer alive, the coast was clear.

The following April, Hilary Harris, whose film company had an office on Eighth Avenue in Greenwich Village, wrote Le Corbusier urging him to come by on his next trip to New York so he could show the architect his films and a machine for drawing he was trying to make. Le Corbusier was in India at the time and never made the visit.

Then, at the start of 1963, Marguerite Tjader Harris, on behalf of her son, wrote Le Corbusier about an architectural project far grander, even, than the Gare d'Orsay proposal. Its location was in the middle of Manhattan. The liaison that had begun thirty years earlier now seemed to be leading to one of the greatest projects of Le Corbusier's life.

Tjader Harris explained it very simply. It was her pleasant duty to offer the seventy-five-year-old Le Corbusier an enormous architectural commission. The site was thirty-five acres on the west side of Manhattan, between Fifty-seventh and Seventy-second streets, along the Hudson River. Le Corbusier would design an entire neighborhood adjacent to Lincoln Center. The powerful Amalgamated Lithographers' Union was in charge. They had a budget of two hundred and fifty million dollars and wanted to build on 8 percent of the acreage, leaving the rest for parks and "banksides" next to new docks on the river. Apartment buildings, an international student center, stores, a library, and recreational facilities, including a swimming pool and playing fields, were envisaged for the site.

Le Corbusier could thus transform a large part of New York City. The situation was different from his proposals for Paris; little destruction would be required since at that time there were mainly railroad yards on the site.

Le Corbusier made some calculations. On his lover's typewritten letter, he penciled in the upper left-hand corner

1 are = 100 m^2
1 acre = 50 ares = 5000 m^2
35 acres = 35 × 5000 = 175 000

In the left-hand margin, he wrote,

250,000,000 × 500 = 1,250,000,000 00
A $ = 490

490 ou 500
725,000 000 000 000[2]

This is how his aging mind worked: in mathematical sequences, feeling the sheer excitement of large numbers when they demarcated land mass and money. Converting dollars into francs, this, at long last, was the chance for victory in America.

2

Tjader Harris reported that the union president, Edward Swayduck, had been speaking with Hilary about a film on which they hoped to work together. In the course of their conversation, he had raised the subject of this urban center and said he wanted to find an architect. Swayduck greatly admired Le Corbusier already and told Hilary he would love to approach the renowned Swiss but had no idea how to find him.

Swayduck was thrilled when Hilary Harris offered to make the connection. Now the only question was how, when, and where Swayduck and the architect could meet—assuming Le Corbusier had the time and interest for such an encounter.

Tjader Harris provided enticing details. President John F. Kennedy was supposed to visit New York that coming summer to launch the project. Hilary, now a successful filmmaker, was working day and night, which is why his mother had written on his behalf. The son's dream, beyond negotiating this commission, was to make a film about Le Corbusier's work in India. In the meantime, he would send Le Corbusier a photo of the site in Manhattan.

Tjader Harris asked Le Corbusier how Swayduck should make his approach and under what conditions the architect would accept an invitation to New York. It was urgent. But after three decades of scheduling trysts, she knew the system. If he couldn't answer, could his secretary please do so? "From what I understand, you'll be quite free to do as you like. In friendship, ever, Marguerite."[3]

HILARY HARRIS sent Le Corbusier the photo and his own letter the following day to reiterate the seriousness of the offer. The panoramic picture, taken from a low-flying aircraft, showed what was mainly a wasteland a few blocks from Central Park and the skyscrapers of Gotham that Le Corbusier had first discovered in 1935. "Airview Number 60-741" from the Fairchild Aerial Survey included, among other things, the RCA Building—which Le Corbusier had visited with Marguerite Tjader Harris when Toutou was six years old. One never knew what would lead to what.

3

It took Le Corbusier only a few days to answer:

> My dear Hilary,
>
> I was glad to have your news; what a long time it's been! I received your letter of January 26, 1963, accompanying your mother's of January 25, discussing the great project between 57th Street and 72nd Street along the Hudson.
>
> I've thought the matter over, and reason has convinced me that I cannot concern myself with this business. It is a matter of too great importance for me to follow it in all its technological and administrative details. I'm 75 years old and still in perfect health, but I'm no longer at an age when one can take such enterprises in hand. Add to that the difficulty of the language (English) and American pronunciation, and add further the divergence of conceptions of life and work in general between Americans and Frenchmen. You must find the right man for such a situation. I am not he, or I am no longer he.
>
> The UN building appears in the upper-right corner of your photograph—a bitter memory for me. I worked in New York for 18 months, and my plans were not borrowed but stolen! I am the opposite of a man engaged in financial speculations. I am an artist (an architect and something else besides), and my whole life consists of work, hard, modest, continuous, persevering, and uncomprising work. I've never compromised in my entire career. Only the Americans have done so with my UN plans, making them into a demihorror.
>
> Please don't regard my refusal as a manifestation of ill humor, but let me repeat the factors involved:
>
> My age
> The speculative nature of the enterprise
> The intervention of "architecture."
>
> With regard to this last factor: my entire life and the books I have

written have manifested it, have entered public opinion, have indeed entered the public domain. Others can utilize it without any objection from me.

It is to this factor that I think you should turn your attention: find a second or third or fourth Le Corbusier. Good luck!

It was generous of you to think of me in this business. I am grateful to you, and you have my thanks.

I hope that you are doing extraordinary things with your film work.

I have the fondest memories of you, and I send you my friendliest sympathies.

Le Corbusier[4]

THAT SAME DAY, the aging architect wrote his longtime lover at Vikingsborg:

Dearest Friend

You send astonishing news! I thank you for thinking of me with regard to an enterprise of this importance. I have answered your son, Hilary, and enclose a copy of my letter to him.

I am hardly a pessimist, but at my age I am an old pine or an old palm, the choice is yours. (I cite two trees that habitually grow straight.)

You have certainly become what people call one of the great women of the USA: fortune, consideration, and exalted sentiments as a "right-thinking American." It gives me great pleasure to think of you.

I dream of being able to be armed with my two hands and working at things I am passionately concerned about, but life is too hard for me, and I am compelled to adopt an imperative discipline.

Greet New York for me, whisper that it has kicked me out of the United Nations with a frightful brutality, a gesture it repeated to wrest me away from UNESCO in Paris and reject me by veto. Say what one may and do what one may, there are certain things that cannot be digested! You may think I've become a grumbler; the fact is quite the contrary, I maintain the best humor at all times, but it cannot be detected by the naked eye.

With all my friendship.

Le Corbusier[5]

4

Marguerite Tjader Harris gave Le Corbusier what must have been his dream response. She wrote that he had already changed the world with his work, that he was still "the pioneer." She spoke to him in his sort of language: he no longer needed to "crack his skull with a mountain of details." She also stood up to him: "But Le Corbusier, I don't like your way of referring to me. I am not a 'right-thinking' and 'respectable' American woman. . . . Quite the contrary. What fortune I have I have expended and dispensed in many directions, thus liberating myself from this great burden. I now concentrate on writing and traveling." She went on to explain that she knew interesting people, not socialites, and assured him that work mattered deeply to her. Finally, she let Le Corbusier know that she would see him again in Paris, "*domino volente.*"[6]

A MONTH LATER, Hilary Harris wrote Le Corbusier that the people in charge of the lithographers' union hoped the architect would reconsider. No one else could realize their dream and do justice to their idealism. Wanting to serve the future of humankind and facilitate world peace, the union officials realized that a central plaza was essential. They wondered if Le Corbusier would at least come up with a master plan—even if he delegated the details of the buildings to others. Again, President Kennedy's name was invoked. His support, as well as that of the mayor of New York and other city officials, was assured. Le Corbusier would be respected in every way: "The leaders of this enterprise respect and greatly admire your need to work without compromise of any kind. . . . Is it really too late to expunge your bad memories of New York by making this project achievable in complete independence? The directors have asked me to tell you that they would consider this a supreme gift you could give to New York, to the youth of America and to the youth of all the nations who come here."[7] Harris further suggested that if Le Corbusier still rejected the proposal of his flying across the Atlantic to study the site, then Swayduck would gladly dispatch a delegate to Paris.

Although Swayduck himself then made the trip, the New York project never even reached the stage of sketches, but one can imagine what it might have been. Here Le Corbusier could perhaps have realized one of the inventive cityscapes he had designed for a myriad of locations: his ideal of proud skyscrapers standing on pilotis, joyous buildings for sport and human assembly—the type of structure he had first designed for Moscow—and capacious parks. The architecture would have a look of sheer triumph, and the green spaces would have brought a large public into a natural paradise and offered, inevitably, a sequence of splendid framed vistas.

But Le Corbusier never answered. After March 1963, there was no further communication with either Marguerite Tjader Harris or her son.

5

In 1964, big plans were afloat. Le Corbusier completed the design of the French embassy for which he had visited Brasília. He conceived of the ambassador's house as an exceptionally handsome elaboration of the Pavilion de L'Esprit Nouveau, with a graceful seven-story circular office building nearby. He also resumed work on the Olivetti calculator plant at Rho, near Milan; it was to be a floating rectangular slab and a longer bowed slab linked by a thin bridge: a futuristic vision that combined the geometric and the organic. In addition, he began the design of a long hospital complex in Venice, and was working on a large congress hall in Strasbourg, where the mayor seemed a perfect client: "Under such favorable conditions, the architect may say that he labors like the Good Lord: total responsibility, integrity, loyalty. It will then be understood that architecture belongs to the realm of passion."[8] And he was designing the pavilion in Zurich.

More proposed commissions sparked interest even if they came to nothing. Fidel Castro asked Le Corbusier to construct a "press building" in Cuba. Jean Martin, with whom the architect had made the enamel door plaques in Luynes, asked him to create "Corbusier" toilets and bidets. Le Corbusier declined with the explanation that "human legs and behinds will not acquire the habit, for over the last 50 years they have become accustomed to the English porcelain shape (Water-Closet)," but he liked the idea, and so would have Yvonne.[9]

Honors were coming in a flood. There was a large show of his work in Zurich. An exhibition opened in La Chaux-de-Fonds called "De Léopold-Robert à Le Corbusier," thus linking him with the artist for whom his childhood street had been named. Like many who disparage the power structure, he was happy enough when it applauded him. The architect was now proud to rise yet another notch in French officialdom and be named Grand Officer of the Legion of Honor. If his mother had been alive, perhaps she would have attended the ceremony; at least he would have sent her piles of newspaper clippings.

This time, Le Corbusier was even willing to wear his evening clothes. A photograph in the December 20 *France-Soir* shows him with President Charles de Gaulle—both in their elegant, wide-lapeled dinner jackets leaning toward each other, as a man who opposed Vichy congratulated one who had tried to work within Pétain's ranks. André Malraux declared, "France pays homage to the world's greatest architect."[10]

But even if the masters of ceremony touted him, endorsement overall was short of what Le Corbusier really wanted. Of all the projects in the office, the only one that was built was the pavilion in Zurich—three years too late for Le Corbusier to see it. When the architect's friend and colleague Paul Ducret died in September, Le Corbusier wrote, "I do not mourn those who die, death is a beautiful thing when one has lived an active life."[11]

6

For a little while longer, however, Le Corbusier trudged along. The office had the usual number of potential projects in 1964—even if none were realized—and, with the start of 1965, the architect devoted himself to the Venice hospital. He had taken it on, he said, out of love for the location; no other city addressed the issues of urban living in the same way as Venice, a place he had adored since 1907.

Le Corbusier designed a sprawling horizontal complex that meandered around and over canals. Most of it was only one story high. It provided rooms and care for 1,200 emergency cases and acutely ill patients. Its complex roof structure equipped every one of the rooms, while windowless, with side skylights that would enable patients to control both the temperature and the amount of sunlight coming in and also give these ill people "the feeling of being pleasantly isolated."[12] How the hospital would really have turned out is another matter. These cell-like rooms without windows at eye level might have felt confining.

Beyond that, as with the Gare d'Orsay cultural center, Le Corbusier wished to impose a building concept that looks as if it has descended from another planet. Extending into the water with its gondola port and laboratories and operating rooms, this behemoth would have borne little relationship to the palazzi and canals and old neighborhoods around it. The architect was better off building in locations like Ronchamp and La Tourette and Chandigarh, where the relationship was between Le Corbusier's work and nature. When the pairing was between Le Corbusier's ideas and an existing city, it often became a rivalry the architect had to win. Most people are glad he lost.

7

On July 27, two days before he was to leave for the south of France for his annual holiday, Le Corbusier worked at 35 rue de Sèvres throughout the morning. It was a reversal of his previous routine, but he now found himself too tired to make architecture in the afternoons.

He and his former staff architect Jerzy Soltan visited that day, and they took a taxi to the rue Nungesser-et-Coli to have lunch there. Soltan recalled: "Le Corbusier offered me a drink. The sun was resplendent on the terraces. All sorts of plants were in bloom. Far away, Mount Valerian was vibrating in the summer heat; nearby, bees and flies buzzed around their heads. What will you have? Something light. Perhaps a Dubonnet. And you? Le Corbusier poured himself a double pastis, hardly taking any water. It is a deadly beverage, and I protested mildly. Le Corbusier dismissed my grumbling. He was smiling but serious. As long as he was alive he would not allow himself to be pampered. As long as you live, live with gusto! After luncheon, however, he weakened visibly. Yes, he thought he would lie down. A Mediterranean siesta—nothing more. Kindly, but firmly, he saw me off."[13] It was the following day that the architect took off his shirt in Dr. Hindermeyer's dining room because of what he described as rats in the plumbing.

A day later, Le Corbusier took a Paris–Nice flight. The air journey was a remarkable improvement over the long treks by car or train of years ago. When he arrived at Roquebrune-Cap-Martin, he wrote Albert, "My fatigues are those of a man of fifty." He described a life in which, without exception, he was at the office at nine every morning—which would have been true if the studio counted as the office. "So, dear friends, brothers, comrades or near relations, let me and my fatigue get the hell out of here."[14]

Again, Edouard announced his beliefs to his older brother: "My morality: in life, to be doing. This means, to act in all modesty with exactitude, with precision; an atmosphere favoring the creation of art = modest regularity, continuity, perseverance."[15] Le Corbusier told Albert how happy he was to be at l'Etoile de Mer and how wonderful Thomas Rebutato and his wife were.

Summing things up, the architect voiced his confidence in Albert's musical talent and assured Albert that his future would be full of successes. As for himself, Le Corbusier had other ambitions: "Myself, I have one hope for life, expressed by a crude phrase: everyone has to croak some day. . . . Yet it is a hopeful phrase, one which commits a man to choosing life, the one worthwhile choice on this earth (for oneself, for one's conscience), and with it the choice of laughter, good spirits, without donning the gloomy mask of the offstage actor. Greetings, old man. As you see, the physical and the moral are naturally good; I shake my brother's hand."[16]

A YOUNG PHOTOGRAPHER took some shots of the seventy-seven-year-old architect walking into the sea in his black swim trunks. Le Corbusier turned to the man with his camera and said, "Don't take the trouble with an ugly old man like me. It would be better for you to take pictures of Princess Grace, just behind that rock, or Brigitte Bardot at Saint Tropez."[17]

8

Charles-Edouard Jeanneret wrote one last time to the companion with whom he had braved winter winds on Alpine peaks when they were both under the age of ten and had their mother and father at their sides. On August 24, responding to his brother's concern about him, he assured Albert that the Rebutatos were being attentive to his need for a healthy diet and for ample rest and relaxation. "They treat me as if I were a stick of

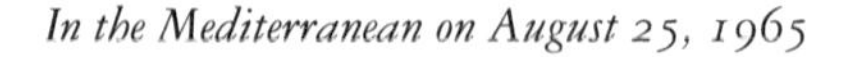

In the Mediterranean on August 25, 1965

barley-sugar." Le Corbusier told Albert, "I've never felt better." He chided his older sibling for having taken on the role of nurse. "I'm feeling fine!" he insisted.[18]

Meanwhile, Le Corbusier was correcting the manuscript of Jean Petit's book about him—in truth, his own book about himself. He praised its preface for saying "that I'm a simple guy. Which is the truth."[19] He probably did not know that this was the same adjective Josephine Baker had used to describe him more than thirty-five years earlier.

Concluding that letter, Charles-Edouard Jeanneret did something rare in his life. He turned his attention completely to the other person. This was not a time to say anything about himself—his beliefs, his achievements. Rather, it was an occasion only to bolster spirits and encourage confidence.

He focused not on art but on music: the passion of their mother, the lifeblood of the household. "Dear old man, go on with your sharps and flats for the delight of our ears. Your music's in fine shape. You're eighty and I'm 78. . . . Greetings, older brother."[20]

It was one of his distortions for the sake of poetry. Three days later, more than a month before Le Corbusier would have reached his seventy-eighth birthday, his body was brought in by the tide under a lustrous sun.

We live in an old chaos of the sun,
Or old dependency of day and night,
Or island solitude, unsponsored, free,
Of that wide water, inescapable.

—WALLACE STEVENS, *"Sunday Morning"*

ACKNOWLEDGMENTS

The idea of my writing a biography of Le Corbusier was initially proposed by Rebecca Wilson, then an editor at Weidenfeld and Nicolson in London, where we had worked together on my biography of Balthus. Rebecca knew that no one else had written a book about Le Corbusier's entire life, and I am extraordinarily grateful for her suggestion that I should undertake the task.

The project would not have proceeded without the endorsement of my remarkable editor at Alfred A. Knopf, Victoria Wilson. Her support, patience, and understanding for more than two decades have become a mainstay of my existence, and the guidance she has given for the nine years I have been working on Le Corbusier has been of inestimable value. Vicky's overarching intelligence and powerfully incisive mind, combined with her rare integrity and spectacular sense of humor, are unfailing. Moreover, she has in spades the rare quality that Le Corbusier himself considered the most important of all—genuine heart. It is a privilege to know her.

I owe my acquaintance with Vicky to the greatest of literary matchmakers, the marvelous Gloria Loomis. Merriam-Webster defines the word "agent" as "a power that acts . . . a moving force . . . in which a mind or a governing intelligence executes its intentions"; that's only the half of it. Gloria is also a friend in the truest sense, and her combination of consummate professionalism with abiding warmth is a boon not just to my life but to that of my entire family. She is one of the most understanding and perceptive people I have ever met, and she makes other people's existences better.

WITH THESE THREE fine people there from the beginning, I faced a thrilling, but initially daunting, task in trying to know who Le Corbusier really was. During the first few months of research, I felt as if I were trying to gain entry to the most private of Swiss bank vaults. I could not imagine how I could unlock the dense steel door that guarded my subject's personality. The first individual who came to my aid, and who has played a role of immeasurable value to this book ever since, was Stéphane Potelle. When we met, he was librarian at the Fondation Le Corbusier in Paris; subsequently, he worked full-time on the project. In guiding me to far-ranging sources, in tracking down a plethora of details, and in helping me organize the vast amount of information I needed to distill in an effort to know Le Corbusier as a human being, Stéphane has done a prodigious amount of work with grace and intelligence. Equally important, his deep personal engagement with our subject, his tireless interest in Le Corbusier's fascinating personality, his eschewal of the clichés with which people have thought about the architect, and his deep knowledge of French history have made him a true ally and an ideal tutor.

This book would not have been possible without the extreme generosity and graciousness of the two directors of the Fondation le Corbusier during whose tenures I have done my research and writing. Evelyn Tréhin accorded me every opportunity a scholar could desire. In 1999 and 2000, I regularly haunted her establishment, where I was treated with utmost graciousness. Then, when Mme. Tréhin knew I had gleaned almost all that was possible from Le Corbusier's letters to William Ritter and his mother, and from all the literature on the architect, she invited me for what was a biographer's dream: a chance to read previously unstudied letters between Le Corbusier and his great, secret inamorata. That correspondence with Marguerite Tjader Harris was like an epistolary novel, one of passion and romance, except that there was nothing fictive about it. Mme. Tréhin's successor, the insightful and refreshingly independent Michel Richard, has been nothing other than wonderful in his support of this book. A true man of letters—open-minded, full of humor, and erudite—he has been spectacularly giving of his time and energy, and true to both the professionalism and the gift for laughter that Le Corbusier cherished. The trust he evinced in according me blanket permission to quote freely from Le Corbusier's letters and other writings showed an open-mindedness, selflessness, and generosity that had unequaled impact on this text.

My friend Eve Tribouillet-Rozenczweig has been not just, as always, a true sustainer of my morale, but she has shown, time and again, an intellectual perspicacity of the highest order. Her complete bilinguality combined with her real psychological understanding allowed me to see, in some of Le Corbusier's more obscure ramblings, aspects of the architect that otherwise would have eluded me.

Philippe Corfa has been amazing in the work he has done by putting my text in order at each of its many stages of revision. It has been my good fortune to work with someone of such patience, meticulousness, and overriding intelligence, and I am immensely grateful. It is not an overstatement to say that without him I cannot imagine how I would have completed the book.

Daphne Warburg Astor has been the exemplar of friendship and sage advice. Always there in the rough patches, offering encouragement whenever it was needed, boosting my spirits on countless occasions, she has been a fine presence in both my life and that of my entire family.

There are few people more pleasurable to talk to about human relationships, and in particular those of parents and children, than Sophie Dumas, a vibrant human being whose input on this book has had great meaning. Pierre-Alexis Dumas, in addition to being a wonderful friend, is one of the most knowledgeable people on this earth when it comes to the issues of aesthetics and color, and the meaning of real dedication to art; I am grateful for the impact of many of our conversations on this book.

From the time I began this project, my spectacular friend Nick Ohly, a gifted architect and passionate enthusiast of great buildings, was a true soul mate. Time and again I bounced ideas off of him, and had the benefit of responses from someone in Le Corbusier's own profession who understood a range of issues from an insider's point of view. At the same time, Nick was a warm and encouraging presence, as well as an ideal companion for frequent games of tennis and squash, always a boost to my spirits. On the day of his untimely death in November 2007, we had discussed yet another nuance of Le Corbusier's work, and I like to picture Nick as he was at that moment: smiling, interested, in love with beauty, and full of insight.

At the Fondation Le Corbusier in Paris, the following people have been both extremely professional and consistently kind: Isabelle Godineau, manager of the archives, who has helped unstintingly with the images and documents for this book; Delphine Studer, specialist in documents, who also tracked down material and assisted with the images; and Arnaud Dercelles, librarian, who helped with research materials.

The following Le Corbusier experts, all remarkable scholars, have imparted their knowledge in a way that has been of the utmost value to this publication: Tim Benton, whose specialty is Le Corbusier's villas; Caroline Maniaque, who knows more than anyone else about the Maisons Jaoul; Jean-Louis Cohen, a versatile scholar with a particular expertise about Le Corbusier and the Soviet Union; Stanislaus Von Moos, a specialist in Charles-Edouard Jeanneret's early years as well as a fine architectural historian in general; Kiran Joshi, a professor at the Chandigarh College of Architecture, Chandigarh; Alejandro Lapunzina, an expert on Le Corbusier's work in Latin America; Sven Sterken, a specialist in the life and work of Iannis Xenakis; Flora Samuel, a professor interested in Le Corbusier's relationship to women; and Mardges Bacon, an expert on Le Corbusier and America.

I am also very grateful to the colleagues of Le Corbusier who were generous with their time and willingness to tell anecdotes: Roger Aujame, Jean-Louis Véret, Lucien Hervé, M. Sharma, and Robert Rebutato. Balkrishna Doshi, in particular, was exceptionally helpful in shedding light on the spiritual Le Corbusier, in a long discussion we had in dramatic circumstances immediately following the Ahmedabad earthquake that, earlier that same morning, had killed ten thousand people within a five-kilometer radius of where we sat—adding unanticipated significance to our discussion of Le Corbusier's views on mortality as well as on construction standards.

Oscar Niemeyer, just shy of his hundredth birthday when he and I spent several hours together discussing Le Corbusier, abetted my quest significantly, and I am grateful to Victor Tamm for setting up our meeting in Rio.

Ivan Zaknic's helpfulness and enthusiasm for this project have been a particular boon. His translation of *Voyage to the Orient* and his *The Final Testament of Père Corbu* are both masterful; this fine professor of architecture and architecture historian has been exceptionally kind. Dr. Jacques Hindermeyer, whom I initially met thanks to Ivan, has been a source of information and insights central to my understanding of Le Corbusier, and I thank this charming and energetic man for his willingness to make his friend "Corbu" come alive.

Joan Davidson of the J. M. Kaplan Fund helped make possible the marvelous translations by Richard Howard that play such a vital role in this book. I thank her, and of course I thank Richard himself. The energy and commitment this splendid poet and linguist devoted to understanding Le Corbusier's idiosyncratic language, the inventiveness with which he put that autodidact's French into an English equivalent, have been extraordinary. Since one of my main goals has been to present Le Corbusier as he really was, even if that meant revealing his confused and confusing use of language, Richard's attentiveness to the nuances of translation has been indispensable.

Charles Kingsley, one of the finest people I know, as well as one of the most talented photographers, has helped this book by his perpetual good humor and friendship, his wonderful companionship on the tennis and squash courts, and by the splendid support he has offered as a director of the Josef and Anni Albers Foundation.

John Eastman—so bright, warm, and generous—has been there in a myriad of ways. A perpetually stimulating friend and warmhearted ally, he is one of those rare individuals who combine a profound intellect and penetrating mind with a spectacular sense of fun. His abiding humanity in our conversations pertaining directly or indirectly to Le Corbusier have had a significant impact on this narrative. John, too, is a director of the Albers Foundation, and has been exceptionally wise and generous in that capacity.

When Josef and Anni Albers created the foundation that bears their names, they stated as its goal "the revelation and evocation of vision through art." In the range of ways that the foundation has helped this book, it has, I believe, furthered that goal. Josef and Anni often voiced the most profound admiration for Le Corbusier, as well as a particular fascination with Ronchamp, and I hope they would be pleased with this undertaking. I owe so much to the Alberses as people—they were the real thing, totally committed to what mattered in art, entirely uncorrupted by the art world—and I am immensely honored to work to preserve their legacy and to try to perpetuate their values. The biography of Le Corbusier addresses many of the issues that both Josef and Anni held most dear.

Oliver Barker, one of the splendid people at the Albers Foundation, has devoted himself to one aspect after another of this project, maintaining his grace and professionalism in every situation, always making life easier. I also want to thank everyone else at the Albers Foundation who has helped: Anne Barker, Jessica Csoma, Brenda Danilowitz, Andres Garces, Fritz Horstman, Jeannette Redensek, Tyler Sage, and Molly Wheeler.

John Young and Joan Frankel of the Florence Gould Foundation have been incredibly generous and supportive and encouraging; I thank them profusely.

Harriet Shapiro gave unsparingly of her time and energy to help this project at a pivotal moment. With her elegant use of language as well as her noble sense of values, she offered significant guidance for which I am more than grateful.

The guidance I have received from Brigitte Lozerec'h—a gifted linguist, splendid writer, and spirited and stylish individual of great intellect—has been a blessing. And Veronique Wallace, such a generous and caring friend, provided me with a haven in which to write at a crucial moment, doing so with the charm and wisdom and graciousness that are her hallmarks.

George Gibson, a superb and immensely kind human being, has, as has been true for over thirty years, been wonderfully supportive. Laura Mattioli, so passionate for beauty, so understanding of the priorities of a real art lover, has, as always, asked the right questions and set a superb example of dedication to the primacy of visual experience that mattered to Le Corbusier himself. Brigitte Degois offered sustenance both moral and culinary; I am intensely grateful to her and her husband, Gilles Degois, himself possessed by some of the same energy and daring as my subject. Nicholas Marang has been a boon to this book from the start, most especially by leading me on skis to the snowcapped mountain peaks so essential to the existence of the Jeannerets. Kenneth Marcus has been, as always, understanding, encouraging, good-humored, compassionate, and exceedingly generous with his time and energy. Mickey Cartin has been the exemplar of Corbusean qualities: straightforward, warm, consumed by his love for great art, and always good for a laugh. What a pleasure it is to have him as a friend. Sean O'Riordain has helped this project along in many ways as we have bicycled through downpours in County Cork or kayaked off to islands at sea; a superb friend and companion, he savors life with Corbusean robustness. Anne Peretz, generous, knowledgeable, and immensely kind, has been yet another source of inspiration. Alan Riding, a relatively new friend, has come to feel like someone I have known forever, blessedly, and has offered important insights, counsel, and leads to important details about Le Corbusier during the occupation of Paris.

Leslie Waddington has believed in this book from its inception and has been, as always, an immensely perceptive and sustaining friend; Clodagh Waddington, so bright and witty and intelligent, has been a marvelous ally. The visit that they, along with my wife and Eve Tribouillet-Rozenczweig, made to 24 rue Nungesser-et-Coli was a pivotal event for me.

I owe profuse thanks to Carmen Johnson at Alfred A. Knopf; she has been the epitome of graciousness and professionalism while addressing a myriad of complex details. Timothy Mennel has my appreciation for the great care with which he reviewed the manuscript. I am also extremely grateful to Ellen Feldman for her acuity and patience throughout the production process. Peter Mendelsund designed a cover for this book that reflects a visual brillance I am sure Le Corbusier would have admired; it captures the subject's liveliness, his wish both to be public and to be hidden, his monocular vision, and his ability to use color and form to evoke the rhythm of great jazz.

I am grateful to the following people for their constant encouragement and, in many instances, impact on this book: Michael Adler, Julie Agoos, Micky Astor, John Banville, Barry Bergdoll, Rosamond Bernier, Bim Bissell, Claire Bloom, Adam Brophy, Jerome Bruner, Laurent de Brunhoff, Anne Chambreaux, Lo-Yi Chan, Diana Cooper, Peter Cooper, Peter Deasy, Jodie Eastman, Marion Ettlinger, Martin Filler, Samual Gaube, Allen Grossman, Jane Grossman, Pankaj Gupta, Carlotta Hadley, Margaret Jay, Raffi Kaiser, Louise Kennedy, Gretchen Kingsley, Sylvia Kohler, Joan J. Kohn, Nancy Lewis, Ellen Weber Libby, Heinz Liesbrock, Ruth Lord, Patrick Marrioti, Susie and Marc and Maxime Martin, David Melchinger, Eskandar Nabavi, Michel Navarra, Carole Obedin, Mary O'Reilly, Seamus O'Reilly, Pierre Otolo, Emilie Pelaez, Amanda Pennelly, Martha Peterson, Sam Peterson, Elena Prentice, Tim Prentice, John Read, Jane Reynolds, Phyllis Rose, Didier Royer, Barbara Ryden, John Ryden, Jane Fearer Safer, Morley Safer, Sanford Schwartz, Mark Simon, Henry Singer, Paul Spike, Gustav de Staël, Jerl Surratt, Mami Mafuta Sira Sylla, Terry Tabaka, Philippe Tribouillet, Sandrine Vallé-Potelle, Ruth Agoos Villalovos, James Wallace, Joan Warburg, Helen Ward, Katinka Weber, Russ Weigel, Frank Williams, and Jeanette Zwingenberger. I also want to thank, for their time and interest in this project, Gae Aulenti, Linda Benglas, Olivier Betourné, Sophie de Closets, Claude Durand, Barbara Findeisen, Francine du Plessix Gray, Jim Grissom, Arthur Lubow, Toshiko Mori, Denise René, John Richardson, Anand Sarabhai, Vincent Scully, Ronald Steel, Vikas Thapar, and Bijan Yar.

And there are certain individuals who, while no longer alive, have been present in my thoughts, intensely, as I considered one aspect or another of Le Corbusier's work and life. Herbert Agoos, Leland Bell, Lee V. Eastman, Hans Farman, Rosalie Fox, James Hadley, Jack Kenney, R. W. B. Lewis, Louisa Matthiasdottir, Clara Nell McIntee, Jackie Onassis, Justine Peterson, Albert J. Solnit, Edward M. M. Warburg, King-Lui Wu, and Warren Zimmerman all helped me better grasp what I believe to be the priorities of human existence, and thus nurtured this project. I have also often thought of the interview about Le Corbusier I had with the late Philip Johnson, although his only answer to my various questions was always the same refrain: "He's a shit, a shit, a shit, a shit."

When I was at the Loomis School in the early 1960s, two utterly splendid teachers had an impact on me that has caused me to think of them continually while writing about Le Corbusier. Allan Lundie Wise, who taught English, made Robert Browning's words "A man's reach must exceed his grasp, or what's a heaven for?" come alive, and his emphasis on the rules of Strunk and White had, I hope, the desired effect. Joseph Savoie Stookins introduced me to the magnificence of the French language and, in 1964, gave a lecture on the Gothic cathedral that catapulted me into new realms of interest that connect directly with the writing of this book.

Like Georges Jeanneret, my marvelous father, Saul Weber, encouraged to the hilt the appreciation of nature and the miracles of the earth, and my dynamic mother, Caroline Fox Weber, was not unlike Marie in her abiding passion for music. The parallels stop there, fortunately. Both of my parents always encouraged me warmly; moreover, they had a verve for life and panache and originality—as well as a profound political consciousness—that graced my life from the start. I hope I have done justice to their wonderful values in my presentation of Le Corbusier in all of his complexity.

The late Dr. Pearl A. Weber, Ph.D., C.A.T., was a guiding light, especially in regard to Le Corbusier's more spiritual side and Yvonne's mix of tenderness and ferocity. And Lester Weber kept me perpetually alert to Le Corbusier's humor and grounding in the earthy realities of existence, as well as the value the architect placed on charm and dapper appearance.

MY TWO DAUGHTERS, independent and extraordinary women in very different ways, have both provided loving encouragement as I have written this book. Lucy Swift Weber has been particularly helpful in calling my attention to the connections of Le Corbusier and his work to the design world today, leading me to intriguing examples of the way that the architect's vision has penetrated multiple realms; at the same time, she has, as always, been the exemplar of human warmth. Charlotte Fox Weber has, with her astonishing acuity, played more of a role in this project than she can have imagined, not just by providing, usually at precisely the right moment, an apt statement by Goethe or Plato or Nietzsche, as if she knew just what I needed to understand, but by being, perpetually, an incredible ally. Charlotte is as alive to the wonders of existence and the reaches of the human mind as anyone I know, and she is the exemplar of family devotedness. It is impossible to imagine these years of thinking about Le Corbusier and his life without having both Lucy and Charlotte in mine.

The mother of these two exceptional human beings, my wife, Katharine, is everything one could ask for in a true life companion: intensely bright, deeply funny, profoundly humane, and extraordinarily strong. She has shown an abiding understanding of all that the pursuit of Le Corbusier has meant in our mutual existence, and her unique alertness and wit, and a competence beyond the norm, have been mainstays. Whether I was at the epicenter of that earthquake in Ahmedabad or fleeing a burning hotel in Japan in her absence, or watching rain flow through the downspouts at Ronchamp and exploring the hidden spaces of Le Corbusier and Yvonne's apartment with her at my side, she has been a source of balance and joy in my quest to grasp Le Corbusier. How lucky I am to have the love and support of this amazing woman whom I love so deeply.

IN 1973, my older sister, Nancy, and I made an impromptu trip to Europe together when we were both emotionally at somewhat loose ends. Our itinerary revolved around the wish to go to Venice, look at Paul Klee's paintings in Bern, and visit Ronchamp—three destinations which we sensed would offer balm and pleasure. Like the children of Georges and Marie Jeanneret, we depended on the closeness of sibling ties and believed in the healing powers of art.

I will never forget our first glimpse of Ronchamp. It was on a crystal clear November evening, and, following a wonderful inexpensive meal at the local village inn, where we were staying in cheap but pleasant rooms, we drove and then walked toward the looming bell-clapper form of Le Corbusier's spectacular church.

Neither of us could believe what we saw. Our remarkable parents had brought us up to love life, to prize art, and to worship independent minds; we were both delirious with joy. Ronchamp was closed for the night, but the moonlight on its ever-changing surfaces brought us such a surfeit of pleasure that to have gone inside would have been too much.

The next day, in brilliant autumn sunlight, we spent hours inside, marveling at Corbu's vibrant windows and the spectacular flow of space. How fortunate I am to have a sibling who understands, and has encouraged for six decades, that sense of wonder. It is an honor to be able to dedicate this book to her.

NFW, Bethany, Connecticut, April 2008

NOTES

Unless otherwise noted, all archival sources are from the Fondation Le Corbusier, Paris. The code numbers provided identify individual letters according to their organization at the Fondation.

PREFACE

1. Quoted in Richard Jenkyns, "The Pleasures of Melodrama," *The New York Review of Books,* July 11, 1996, p. 10.
2. R2-2-46, letter to mother, June 11, 1951, Paris (on Bogotá stationery).
3. Ibid.
4. R2-4-55, letter to mother, March 28, 1942, Vichy, Queen's Hotel.
5. Michael Burleigh, *The Third Reich: A New History* (New York: Hill & Wang, 2001), p. 4.

CHAPTER 1

1. *Parisien libéré,* September 1965.
2. Jean Petit, *Le Corbusier lui-même* (Geneva: Editions Rousseau, 1970). (Written in 1964, this book was published six years later.)
3. Interview at Robert Rebutato's studio, October 5, 2000.
4. *Midi libre,* August 28, 1965.
5. R1-12-27, letter to Yvonne Gallis, September 22, 1927, Vevey, Villa Le Lac.
6. *La Nouvelle république des Pyrénées,* August 28, 1965.
7. Interview with Jean Louis Véret, one of the architects in Le Corbusier's office, January 2000.
8. R1-6-148, letter to mother, January 10, 1927, Paris.
9. Conversation among Jacques Hindermeyer, Ivan Zaknic, and Nicholas Fox Weber (NFW), Paris, November 4, 2000.
10. Ivan Zaknic, *The Final Testament of Père Corbu: A Translation and Interpretation of* Mise au point (New Haven: Yale University Press, 1997), p. 67. According to Kenneth Frampton, Le Corbusier made the comment to Jerzy Soltan, but Soltan told Zaknic that the architect said it to André Maisonnier. Ivan Zaknic said that Roger Aujame reported Le Corbusier saying the same thing to him (interview, October 12, 2000).
11. Hindermeyer interviews, February 11 and November 19, 2001.
12. Ibid.
13. Ibid.
14. "Malraux disait 'C'est le plus grand architecte du monde.' Et pourtant Le Corbusier croyait avoir 'raté' sa vie," *L'Union. Grand quotidien d'information issue de la résistance,* August 28, 1965.
15. Ibid.
16. *Feuille d'avis de Lausanne,* September 28–29, 1965.
17. Hindermeyer interview, December 2, 2002.
18. Le Corbusier, *Mise au point* (Paris: Editions Forces Vives, 1966).
19. Zaknic, *Final Testament,* p. 67.
20. R2-2-42, letter to mother, May 2, 1951, Paris.
21. *RIBA Journal* (Royal Institute of British Architects), April 1953, p. 218.
22. Le Corbusier, *Oeuvre complète,* vol. 8: *The Last Works* (Zurich: Les Editions d'Architecture, 1995), p. 186.
23. Ibid.
24. The quotations and the entire anecdote come from Olivier Todd's excellent *Malraux: A Life* (New York: Alfred A. Knopf, 2005), p. 394.
25. *Le Monde,* September 3, 1965.

26. Interview with Stanislaus Von Moos, September 26, 2000, Paris; the anecdote was told to him by Sigfried Giedion.
27. Robert Doisneau and Jean Petit, *Bonjour Monsieur Le Corbusier* (Zurich: H. Grieshaber, 1988).
28. Interview with Roger Aujame, October 6, 2000.
29. Interview with Dr. Hindermeyer, November 19, 2001.
30. Ibid.
31. Ibid.
32. Interview with Roger Aujame, October 6, 2000; the story was reported to him by Charlotte Perriand.
33. Interview with Dr. Hindermeyer, November 19, 2001.
34. Interviews with Denise René, May 11 and May 15, 2000.
35. Robert Rebutato reports that after the body was incinerated, Le Corbusier was given a rolled-up newspaper containing pieces of Yvonne's bones, which he took to the repast at Mme. Ducret's following the ceremony. It was there that he said, "Voici tout qui me reste de ma belle [not "chère"] Yvonne." Interview, October 5, 2000.
36. Pierre Joffroy, "Pourquoi le plus grand architecte fut-il le plus mal aimé?" *Paris Match,* September 11, 1965.
37. R1-6-149, letter to mother, February 3, 1927, Paris.
38. R1-6-118, letter to mother, April 19, 1926, Paris.
39. R1-6-120, letter to mother, April 22, 1926, Paris.

CHAPTER II

1. H. Allen Brooks, *Le Corbusier's Formative Years: Charles-Edouard Jeanneret at La Chaux-de-Fonds* (Chicago: University of Chicago Press, 1997), p. 9. While there have been no previous biographies that take Le Corbusier through his entire life, this impressive and scholarly work thoroughly charts the architect's beginnings.
2. R3-18-12 to 22, letter to Ritter, October 6, 1910, Munich.
3. R3-18-127, letter to Ritter, December 12, 1911, La Chaux-de-Fonds.
4. R3-18-128 to 143, letter to Ritter, November 1, 1911, Pisa, mailed from La Chaux-de-Fonds.
5. R3-18-144, letter to Ritter, December 15, 1911, La Chaux-de-Fonds, Le Couvent.
6. Maximilien Gauthier, *Le Corbusier ou l'architecture au service de l'homme* (Paris: Editions Denoël, 1944).
7. Ibid., p. 11.
8. Petit, *Le Corbusier lui-même,* p. 24.
9. In *La Chaux-de-Fonds, son passé et son présent. Notes et souvenirs historiques publiés à l'occasion du centième anniversaire de l'incendie du 5 mai 1794* (La Chaux-de-Fonds: Imprimerie Nationale Suisse, 1894).
10. Petit, *Le Corbusier lui-même,* p. 24.
11. Ibid., p. 23.
12. Gauthier, *Le Corbusier ou l'architecture au service de l'homme,* p. 16.
13. Petit, *Le Corbusier lui-même,* p. 23.
14. R1-07-176, death announcement for Le Corbusier's mother, February 15, 1960.
15. Petit, *Le Corbusier lui-même,* p. 24.
16. Gauthier, *Le Corbusier ou l'architecture au service de l'homme,* p. 17.
17. Ibid., pp. 17–18.
18. Le Corbusier, "Confession," in *L'Art décoratif d'aujourd'hui* (Paris: Authod, 1981), p. 198.
19. Petit, *Le Corbusier lui-même,* p. 24.
20. Ibid., p. 198.
21. Gauthier, *Le Corbusier ou l'architecture au service de l'homme,* p. 16.
22. Ibid., p. 17.
23. Brooks, *Le Corbusier's Formative Years,* p. 12.
24. Ibid., p. 13.
25. Gauthier, *Le Corbusier ou l'architecture au service de l'homme,* p. 17.
26. Brooks, *Le Corbusier's Formative Years,* p. 15.
27. Ibid., p. 21.
28. Gauthier, *Le Corbusier ou l'architecture au service de l'homme,* p. 18.
29. Petit, *Le Corbusier lui-même,* p. 24.
30. Ibid., p. 25.
31. Ibid., pp. 25, 28.
32. Owen Jones, *The Grammar of Ornament* (London: Day and Son, 1856).
33. Ibid., p. 156.
34. Petit, *Le Corbusier lui-même,* p. 135.
35. Jean Petit, *Le Corbusier parle* (Lugano: Jean Petit et Fidia Edizione d'Arte, 1996), p. 11.

36. Brooks, *Le Corbusier's Formative Years,* p. 18.
37. Petit, *Le Corbusier lui-même,* p. 28.
38. Le Corbusier, *Oeuvre complète,* vol. 8, p. 134.
39. John Ruskin, *The Seven Lamps of Architecture* (Boston: Frederick J. Quinby Company, n.d.), p. 14.
40. Ibid., p. 15.
41. Ibid., p. 190.
42. R1-2-118, journal of Georges Edouard Jeanneret.
43. Brooks, *Le Corbusier's Formative Years,* p. 91.

CHAPTER III

1. Petit, *Le Corbusier lui-même,* p. 28.
2. John Ruskin, *Les matins à Florence, simple étude d'art chrétien* (Paris: H. Laurens, 1906).
3. R1-4-1, letter to parents, September 5, 1907, Florence.
4. Ibid.
5. E-2-12-6 to 9, letter to L'Eplattenier, September 19, 1907, Florence.
6. Ibid.
7. R1-4-1, letter to parents, September 5, 1907, Florence.
8. Ibid.
9. E2-2-6 to 9, letter to L'Eplattenier, September 19, 1907, Florence.
10. R1-4-14 to 17, letter to parents, September 23, 1907, Florence.
11. R1-4-23 to 24, letter to parents, October 8, 1907, Florence.
12. Ibid.
13. R1-4-2, letter to parents, September 14, 1907, Florence.
14. R1-4-14 to 17, letter to parents, September 23, 1907, Florence.
15. E2-12-8, letter to L'Eplattenier, September 19, 1907, Florence.
16. E2-12-10, letter to L'Eplattenier, September 21, 1907, Florence.
17. Ibid.
18. R1-4-14 to 17, letter to parents, September 23, 1907, Florence.
19. R1-4-18 to 25, letter to parents, October 8, 1907, Florence.
20. R1-4-17, letter to parents, September 23, 1907, Florence.
21. E2-12-9, letter to L'Eplattenier, September 19, 1907, Florence.
22. Ibid.
23. R1-4-14, letter to parents, September 23, 1907, Florence.
24. Ibid.
25. Ibid.
26. E2-12-9, letter to L'Eplattenier, September 19, 1907, Florence.
27. Ibid.
28. Le Corbusier, "Une cellule à l'échelle humaine," in *Précisions sur un état présent de l'architecture et de l'urbanisme* (Paris: Crès, 1930), pp. 91–92.
29. Le Corbusier, *Le Modulor, Essai sur une mesure harmonique à l'échelle humaine applicable universellement à l'architecture et à la mécanique* (Boulogne-sur-Seine: Editions de l'Architecture d'Aujourd'hui, 1950), p. 27.
30. "Atelier de bâtisseurs Le Corbusier. L'unité d'Habitation de Marseille," *Le Point* 38, November 1950, p. 30, fig. 37: "Une résurrection: Croquis de jeunesse de L.-C en 1907 à la Chartreuse d'Ema (Toscane)."
31. R1-4-10 to 13, letter to parents, September 14, 1907, Florence.
32. R1-4-2, postcard to parents, September 14, 1907, Florence.
33. R1-4-3, letter to parents, September 24, 1907, Florence.
34. R1-4-10 to 13, letter to parents, September 14, 1907, Florence.
35. Ibid.
36. R1-4-26 to 31, letter to parents, October 24, 1907, Padua, mailed in Venice.
37. Ibid.
38. E2-12-12, letter to L'Eplattenier, November 1, 1907, Venice.
39. Ibid.
40. R1-4-34 to 36, letter to parents, November 16, 1907, Vienna.
41. Ibid.
42. R1-4-26 to 31, letter to parents, October 24, 1907, Venice.
43. R1-4-7, letter to parents, November 1, 1907, Venice.
44. Ibid.

CHAPTER IV

1. R1-4-35, letter to parents, November 17, 1907, Vienna.
2. Ibid.
3. E2-12-17, postcard to L'Eplattenier, November 17, 1907, Vienna.
4. E2-12-26, letter to L'Eplattenier, February 29, 1908, Vienna.
5. R1-4-35, letter to parents, November 17, 1907, Vienna.

6. Ibid.
7. Ibid.
8. R1-4-98 to 109, letter to parents, March 8, 1908, Vienna.
9. R-4-42 to 51, letter to parents, December 5, 1907, Vienna.
10. Ibid.
11. R1-4-98 to 109, letter to parents, March 8, 1908, Vienna.
12. Ibid.
13. R1-4-63 to 74, letter to parents, January 7, 1908, Vienna.
14. Ibid.
15. Ibid.
16. Ibid.
17. Ibid.
18. Ibid.
19. R1-4-98 to 109, letter to parents, March 8, 1908, Vienna.
20. R1-4-42 to 51, letter to parents, December 5, 1907, Vienna.
21. R1-4-98 to 109, letter to parents, March 8, 1908, Vienna.
24. Ibid.
25. Ibid.
26. E2-12-51 to 52, letter to L'Eplattenier, July 22, 1908, Paris.
27. Ernest Renan, *Vie de Jésus* (Paris: Calman-Lévy, 1906), from Le Corbusier's personal library.
28. Paul V. Turner, *La Formation de Le Corbusier: Idéalisme et mouvement moderne* (Paris: Macula, 1987).
29. Renan, *Vie de Jésus,* pp. 132, 123, 127.
30. Ibid., pp. 126, 301.
31. Diary of Georges-Edouard Jeanneret, May 12, 1908.
32. Ibid., January 9, 1909.
33. Ibid.
34. R1-4-129 to 136, letter to parents from Albert and Charles-Edouard, September 9, 1909, Paris.
35. Ibid.
36. R1-4-137 to 144, letter to parents, November 8, 1909, Paris.

CHAPTER V

1. E2-12-28, letter to L'Eplattenier, February 19, 1908, Vienna.
2. E2-12-29, letter to L'Eplattenier, March 1, 1908, Vienna.
3. R1-4-98 to 109, letter to parents, August 3, 1908, Vienna.
4. Ibid.
5. Ibid.
6. Gauthier, *Le Corbusier ou l'architecture au service de l'homme,* p. 24.
7. Ibid.
8. Ibid., p. 25.
9. Ibid.
10. Ibid., p. 27.
11. Ibid., p. 28.
12. Petit, *Le Corbusier lui-même,* p. 30.
13. Ibid., pp. 30–31.
14. Ibid., p. 32.
15. E2-12-34 to 36, letter to L'Eplattenier, July 3, 1908, Paris.
16. Ibid.
17. Ibid.
18. Ibid.
19. E2-12-38 to 50, letter to L'Eplattenier, November 22 and 25, 1908, Paris.
20. Ibid.
21. Petit, *Le Corbusier lui-même,* p. 33.
22. E2-12-38 to 50, letter to L'Eplattenier, November 22 and 25, 1908, Paris.
23. Ibid.

CHAPTER VI

1. R1-5-8 to 11, letter to parents, April 10, 1910, Munich.
2. R1-5-12 to 17, letter to parents, May 16, 1910, Munich.
3. Ibid.
4. Charles-Edouard Jeanneret, *Etude sur le mouvement d'art décoratif en Allemagne* (La Chaux-de-Fonds: Hac Fli & Cie, 1912; rpt. New York: Da Capo Press, 1968).
5. I am grateful to H. A. Brooks's careful discussion of this manuscript in *Le Corbusier's Formative Years.*
6. Le Corbusier, *Urbanisme* (Paris: Crès, 1924).
7. R1-5-68, letter to parents, October 20, 1910, Berlin.
8. R3-18-1 to 3, letter to Ritter, June 17, 1910, Berlin.
9. R1-5-38 to 49, letter to parents, November 11, 1910, Berlin–Neu-Babelsberg.
10. Ibid.
11. Ibid.
12. E2-12-54 to 59, letter to L'Eplattenier, January 16, 1911, Berlin.
13. R1-5-38 to 49, letter to parents, November 11, 1910, Berlin–Neu-Babelsberg.
14. R1-5-50 to 57, letter to parents, December 2, 1910, Berlin.

15. R3-18-28 to 40, letter to Ritter, December 28, 1910, Berlin–Neu-Babelsberg.
16. Ibid.
17. R1-5-38 to 49, letter to parents, November 11, 1910, Berlin–Neu-Babelsberg.
18. R3-18-27, postcard to Ritter, December 14, 1910, Berlin–Neu-Babelsberg.
19. Ibid.
20. R3-18-28 to 40, letter to Ritter, December 28, 1910, Berlin–Neu-Babelsberg.
21. R3-18-52 to 56, letter to Ritter, December 17, 1910, Berlin–Neu-Babelsberg.
22. Ibid.
23. Petit, *Le Corbusier lui-même,* p. 38 (January 4, 1911, Berlin).
24. R3-18-28 to 40, letter to Ritter, January 1, 1911, Berlin–Neu-Babelsberg.
25. E2-12-57, letter to L'Eplattenier, January 16, 1911, Berlin.
26. R3-18-4 to 7, letter to Ritter, June 21, 1910, Berlin.
27. E2-12-57, letter to L'Eplattenier, January 16, 1911, Berlin.
28. R3-18-59 to 69, letter to Ritter, March 1, 1911, Berlin–Neu-Babelsberg.
29. Ibid.
30. Ibid.
31. Ibid.

CHAPTER VII

1. Le Corbusier, *Journey to the East,* edited and annotated by Ivan Zaknic, translated by Ivan Zaknic in collaboration with Nicole Pertuiset (Cambridge, Mass.: MIT Press, 1987), p. 26.
2. Ibid., pp. 36–39.
3. Balkrishna Doshi, "Le Corbusier's Work: A Personal Reading," paper presented at conference celebrating Chandigarh, January 1999, p. 5.
4. R3-18-82 to 92, letter to Ritter, May 30, 1911, boat to Belgrade.
5. Le Corbusier, *Journey to the East,* p. 23.
6. Ibid.
7. R3-18-93 to 102, letter to Ritter, July 5, 1911, Pera.
8. Ibid.
9. Ibid.
10. I am grateful to Eve Tribouillet-Rosenczweig for this idea.
11. R3-18-93 to 102, letter to Ritter, July 5, 1911, Pera.
12. Ibid.
13. Ibid.
14. Ibid.
15. Brooks, *Le Corbusier's Formative Years,* p. 262.
16. Ibid.
17. R1-5-82, postcard to father, August 12, 1911, Constantinople.
18. Le Corbusier, *Journey to the East,* p. 153.
19. Ibid., p. 154.
20. Ibid., p. 156.
21. Ibid., p. 157.
22. Ibid.

CHAPTER VIII

1. Edith Wharton, *The Cruise of the Vanadis,* excerpted in "A Pilgrim's Progress," *The Guardian,* August 7, 1904.
2. Le Corbusier, *Journey to the East,* pp. 173, 174.
3. Ibid., p. 174.
4. Ibid., pp. 176–77.
5. Ibid., p. 179.
6. Ibid., p. 180.
7. Ibid., p. 184.
8. R3-18-106 to 115, letter to Ritter, September 10, 1911, Athens–Mount Athos.
9. Le Corbusier, *Journey to the East,* pp. 192, 193.
10. Ibid., p. 193.
11. Ibid., p. 195.
12. Ibid., p. 208.
13. R1-18-107, letter to Ritter, September 10, 1911, St. Giorgio.
14. Ibid.
15. Petit, *Le Corbusier parle,* p. 10.
16. Le Corbusier, *Journey to the East,* p. 216.
17. Ibid.
18. Ibid., p. 220.
19. Ibid., pp. 211–12.
20. Ibid., pp. 236, 235.
21. E2-12-96, letter to L'Eplattenier, October 15, 1911, Rome.
22. R1-5-85, letter to parents, September 27, 1911, Athens.
23. Ibid.
24. R1-5-88 to 91, letter to parents, October 15, 1911, Rome.
25. R1-5-87, letter to parents, October 15, 1911, Rome.
26. E2-12-96, letter to L'Eplattenier, October 15, 1911, Rome.

CHAPTER IX

1. R3-18-120 to 121, letter to Ritter, October 25, 1911, Florence.
2. R3-18-128 to 143, letter to Ritter, November 1, 1911, written in Pisa and on train back to Switzerland, subsequently mailed from La Chaux-de-Fonds.
3. R3-18-145 to 160, letter to Ritter, December 15, 1911, La Chaux-de Fonds.
4. Ibid.
5. Ibid.
6. Ibid.
7. R3-18-120 to 121, letter to Ritter, November 25, 1911, Florence.
8. Ibid.
9. R3-18-161 to 162, letter to Ritter, February 2, 1912, La Chaux-de-Fonds.
10. R3-18-145 to 160, letter to Ritter, December 15, 1911, La Chaux-de-Fonds.
11. R3-18-163 to 170, letter to Ritter, March 8, 1912, written on board train to Zurich and mailed from La Chaux-de-Fonds.
12. Ibid.
13. R3-18-186 to 188, letter to Ritter, May 27, 1912, La Chaux-de-Fonds.
14. R3-18-192 to 196, letter to Ritter, June 24, 1912, La Chaux-de-Fonds.
15. R3-18-197 to 205, letter to Ritter, August 4, 1912, La Chaux-de-Fonds.
16. Ibid.
17. Ibid.
18. Ibid.
19. Ibid.
20. Ibid.
21. Ibid.
22. R3-18-210 to 217, letter to Ritter, October 15, 1912, La Chaux-de-Fonds.
23. Ibid.
24. R3-18-197 to 205, letter to Ritter, August 4, 1912, La Chaux-de-Fonds.
25. E2-6-152 to 153, letter to Auguste Klipstein, August 20, 1912, La Chaux-de-Fonds.
26. Jeanneret, *Etude sur le mouvement d'art décoratif en Allemagne.* See also Petit, *Le Corbusier lui-même,* p. 44.
27. R3-18-220 to 232, letter to Ritter, November 17, 1912, La Chaux-de-Fonds.
28. Ibid.
29. Ibid.
30. Ibid.
31. R3-18-241, letter to Ritter, January 2, 1913, La Chaux-de-Fonds.
32. R3-18-265 to 273, letter to Ritter, May 9, 1913, La Chaux-de-Fonds.
33. Ibid.
34. Brooks, *Le Corbusier's Formative Years,* p. 311.

CHAPTER X

1. R3-18-357 to 361, letter to Ritter, September 22, 1914, La Chaux-de-Fonds.
2. Ibid.
3. Ibid.
4. Paul V. Turner deserves credit for pointing this out. See his *La Formation de Le Corbusier,* p. 124.
5. R3-18-368 to 372, letter to Ritter, October 9, 1914, La Chaux-de-Fonds.
6. R3-18-376, letter to Ritter, November 12, 1914, La Chaux-de-Fonds.
7. R3-18-378, postcard to Ritter, November 28, 1914, La Chaux-de-Fonds.
8. R3-18-380 to 381, postcard to Ritter, December 9, 1914, La Chaux-de-Fonds.
9. R3-18-426 to 430, letter to Ritter, June 8, 1915, La Chaux-de-Fonds.
10. "Premier pas dans une demeure," ibid.
11. R3-18-431 to 459, letter to Ritter, June 9, 1915, La Chaux-de-Fonds.
12. Ibid.
13. R3-18-243 to 251, letter to Ritter, January 14, 1913, La Chaux-de-Fonds.
14. R3-18-431 to 459, letter to Ritter, June 9, 1915, La Chaux-de-Fonds.
15. Ibid.
16. Ibid.
17. Ibid.
18. Ibid.
19. Ibid.
20. Ibid.
21. Ibid.
22. R3-18-474 to 475, letter to Ritter, July 28, 1915, La Chaux-de-Fonds.
23. R3-18-476 to 478, postcard to Ritter, August 12, 1915, Paris.
24. R3-18-479, postcard to Ritter, August 21, 1915, Paris.
25. R3-18-480 to 481, postcard to Ritter, September 7, 1915, Paris.
26. Ibid.

CHAPTER XI

1. R3-19-103 to 112, letter to Ritter, January 13, 1917, sent from Bern, written aboard a train to Paris and describing events from August 1915.
2. Ibid.
3. Ibid.
4. Ibid.
5. Ibid.
6. Ibid.
7. Ibid.
8. Ibid.
9. Ibid.
10. Ibid.
11. R3-19-18 to 21, letter to Ritter, March 22, 1916, La Chaux-de-Fonds.
12. Ibid.
13. Ibid.
14. R3-19-26 to 30, letter to Ritter, April 29, 1916, La Chaux-de-Fonds.
15. Ibid.
16. Ibid.
17. Ibid.
18. Ibid.
19. Ibid.
20. Ibid.
21. Ibid.
22. Ibid.
23. Ibid.
24. Ibid.
25. R3-19-57 to 59, letter to Ritter, August 16, 1916, La Chaux-de-Fonds.
26. Ibid.

CHAPTER XII

1. Gauthier, *Le Corbusier ou l'architecture au service de l'homme,* p. 39.
2. R3-19-113, letter to Ritter, January 26, 1917, Paris.
3. R3-19-122, letter to Ritter, February 19, 1917, Paris.
4. Joyce Lowman, "Le Corbusier, 1910–1925: The Years of Transition," Ph.D. diss., University of London, 1981, p. 92. Lowman acquired this information from a 1975 interview with Max Du Bois.
5. R3-19-122, letter to Ritter, February 19, 1917, Paris.
6. Ibid.
7. R3-19-153 to 159, letter to Ritter, July 1, 1917, Paris.
8. R3-19-145 to 150, letter to Ritter, May 3, 1917, Paris.
9. R3-19-214 to 218, letter to Ritter, March 14, 1918, Paris.
10. R3-19-194 to 213, letter to Ritter, January 27, 1918, Paris.
11. R3-19-214 to 219, letter to Ritter, March 14, 1918, Paris; diary for March 7, 1918.
12. R3-19-214 to 218, letter to Ritter, March 14, 1918, Paris.
13. R1-6-19 to 21, letter to parents, March 16, 1918, Paris.
14. R3-19-231 to 244, letter to Ritter, April 30, 1918, Paris; diary for Easter Monday, April 1, 1918.
15. Ibid.
16. R3-19-143 to 144, postcard to Ritter, April 30, 1917, Chartres.
17. Ibid.
18. R3-19-145 to 150, letter to Ritter, May 3, 1917, Paris.
19. R3-19-153 to 159, July 1, 1917, Paris.
20. R3-19-195 to 213, letter and diary to Ritter, January 31, 1918, Paris; diary of October 16, 1917.
21. Ibid.
22. Ibid.
23. Ibid.
24. R3-19-185 to 188, letter to Ritter, October 31, 1917, Paris.
25. Ibid.

CHAPTER XIII

1. R3-19-195 to 213, letter to Ritter, January 31, 1918, Paris.
2. Ibid.
3. Ibid.
4. Ibid.
5. Ibid.
6. Ibid.
7. Ibid.

CHAPTER XIV

1. Amédée Ozenfant, *Mémoires, 1886–1962* (Paris: Seghers, 1968), p. 101.
2. *L'Elan,* 1915–1916, ten issues.
3. Ozenfant, *Mémoires,* p. 97.
4. Art et Liberté, under the presidency of Auguste Perret.
5. The body of Le Corbusier literature, including most of the published chronologies and all of the texts for which the architect himself was

directly responsible, gives 1918 as the year of his meeting with Amédée Ozenfant. Not that it is a definitive source, but Ozenfant's autobiography gives May 1917 as the occasion of that pivotal encounter—as Paul V. Turner, in a footnote to p. 138 of *La formation de Le Corbusier,* pointed out. If indeed this was so—although nothing in Jeanneret's diarylike letters corroborates it—then it is possible that it was Ozenfant who took Jeanneret to the performance of the Ballets Russes. Ozenfant also wrote that, when they first met, Jeanneret was blind to the merits of Cubism. In any event, the 1917 date seems certain. In a letter of May 6, 1917, Jeanneret proposes various times when Ozenfant might come spend time with him. Françoise Ducros's *Amédée Ozenfant* (Paris: Cercle d'Art, 2001), p. 44, points out: "Traces of the rapprochement between the two artists appear in a letter dated May 5 1917, then in a second letter addressed by LC to Oz on May 23 1917." The first letter, apparently from Ozenfant, seems to show that Le Corbusier is trying to see him ("my time has been much taken up recently. Now there's a free moment & I'd be delighted to have a visit. I'm never free afternoons, and you say that you yourself prefer mornings: all for the best. Would you like to come Friday morning? I'm at work at 8, and I'll expect you then"). Ozenfant is therefore not in error when he writes, "In May 1917 I finally met Charles-Edouard Jeanneret" (*Mémoires,* p. 101). Yet their success in seeing each other—following that lunch—probably occurred only later in 1917, since Jeanneret did not mention Ozenfant in letters to either Ritter or his parents until the start of 1918.

6. Gauthier, *Le Corbusier ou l'architecture au service de l'homme,* p. 41.
7. Amédée Ozenfant, *Foundations of Modern Art* (New York: Brewer, Warren & Putnam, 1931), p. 325.
8. Amédée Ozenfant, "Notes sur le cubisme," in *L'Elan* 10, December 1916, quoted in *Le Corbusier, une encyclopédie* (Paris: Centre Georges Pompidou, 1987), p. 280.
9. R3-19-214 to 219, letter and diary to Ritter, March 14, 1918, Paris.
10. R1-6-13 to 15, letter to parents, February 17, 1918, Paris.
11. R3-19-214 to 219, letter and diary to Ritter, March 14, 1918, Paris.
12. Ibid.
13. Ibid.
14. R1-6-18, letter to parents, March 12, 1918, Paris.
15. R1-6-19 to 21, letter to parents, March 16, 1918, Paris.
16. Ibid.
17. Ibid.
18. Ibid.
19. Ibid.
20. Ibid.
21. Ibid.
22. Ibid.
23. R3-19-222 to 230, letter to Ritter, March 23, 1918, Paris.
24. Ibid.
25. Ibid.
26. R3-19-233 to 244, letter to Ritter, December 5, 1918, Paris.
27. R1-6-13 to 15, letter to parents, February 17, 1918, Paris.
28. Ibid.
29. Ibid.
30. Ibid.
31. R3-19-249 to 266, letter and diary to Ritter, June 18, 1918, Paris.
32. Ibid.
33. Ibid.
34. Ibid.
35. Ibid.
36. Ibid.
37. Brooks, *Le Corbusier's Formative Years,* chap. 9, pt. III.
38. R1-10-414, letter to Albert Jeanneret, June 16, 1918, Paris.
39. Ibid.
40. R1-6-29 to 31, letter to parents, June 16, 1918, Paris.
41. Ibid.
42. Ibid.
43. R3-19-249 to 266, letter and diary to Ritter, June 18, 1918, Paris.
44. Ibid.
45. Ibid.

CHAPTER XV

1. R3-19-268 to 283, letter and diary to Ritter, August 2, 1918, Paris.
2. Ibid.

3. Ibid.
4. Ibid.
5. Ibid.
6. Ibid.
7. Ibid.
8. Ibid.
9. Ibid.
10. Ibid.
11. R3-19-288 to 291, letter to Ritter, October 1, 1918, Paris.
12. R3-19-284 to 285, postcard to Ritter, September 3, 1918, Paris.
13. R3-19-322 to 332, letter to Ritter, January 20, 1919, Saint-Nazaire; diary for October 23, 1918.
14. Ibid.
15. Amédée Ozenfant and Charles-Edouard Jeanneret, *Après le Cubisme,* Commentaires sur l'art et la vie moderne, vol. 1 (Paris: Editions des Commentaires, 1918).
16. R3-19-288 to 291, letter to Ritter, October 1, 1918, Paris.
17. R3-19-322 to 332, letter to Ritter, January 20, 1919, Paris.
18. Ibid.
19. R1-6-44, letter to parents, November 21, 1918, Paris.

CHAPTER XVI

1. Ozenfant and Jeanneret, *Après le Cubisme,* pp. 11, 27.
2. Ibid., p. 147.
3. Ibid., pp. 152, 157, 158, 161, 163.
4. R3-19-322 to 332, letter and diary to Ritter, January 20, 1919, Paris; diary of November 12, 1918.
5. R3-19-312 to 314, letter to Ritter, November 20, 1918, Paris.
6. R3-19-315 to 317, letter to Ritter, December 19, 1918, Saint-Nazaire.
7. R1-6-19 to 21, letter to parents, March 16, 1918, Paris.
8. R3-19-315 to 317, letter to Ritter, December 19, 1918, Saint-Nazaire.
9. Ozenfant, *Mémoires,* p. 103.
10. R3-19-322 to 332, letter and diary to Ritter, January 20, 1919, Paris; diary of January 1, 1919.
11. R1-6-49 to 51, letter to parents, January 9, 1919, Paris.
12. Ibid.
13. R1-6-52, letter to father, January 25, 1919, Paris. Various books claim that Jeanneret renounced architecture between 1918 and 1922 to pursue painting. Statements of this sort more than disprove the point, even if there was a hiatus in the completion of his buildings.
14. Ibid.
15. R3-19-322 to 332, letter and diary to Ritter, January 20, 1919, Paris.
16. Gauthier, *Le Corbusier ou l'architecture au service de l'homme,* pp. 61–63.
17. R1-6-56 to 58, letter to parents, March 10, 1919, Paris.
18. Ibid.
19. R3-19-335 to 339, letter to Ritter, April 10, 1919, Paris.
20. R1-6-61 to 62, letter to parents, May 9, 1919, Paris.

CHAPTER XVII

1. G1-6-164 to 167, letter to Ozenfant, June 9, 1919, Paris.
2. Ibid.
3. R1-6-76, letter to parents, November 5, 1919, Paris.
4. R1-6-83 to 84, letter to parents, January 24, 1920, Paris.
5. R1-6-89, letter to parents, April 20, 1920, Paris.
6. R3-19-365 to 367, letter to Ritter, June 19, 1920, Paris.
7. Ibid.
8. Quoted in Carlos S. Eliel, ed., *L'Esprit Nouveau, Purism in Paris, 1918–1925* (Los Angeles: LACMA, 2001), p. 25.
9. Ibid., p. 24.
10. R3-19-372 to 374, letter to Ritter, January 30, 1921, Paris.
11. Ibid.

CHAPTER XVIII

1. Le Corbusier, *Le Modulor,* p. 27.
2. R3-19-372 to 374, letter to Ritter, January 30, 1921, Paris.
3. Ibid.
4. R3-19-375 to 378, letter to Ritter, March 11, 1921, Paris.
5. Le Corbusier, *The Decorative Art of Today,* trans. James I. Dunnett (London: Architectural Press, 1987/1998), p. 111.
6. R3-19-375 to 378, letter to Ritter, March 11, 1921, Paris.
7. Gauthier, *Le Corbusier ou l'architecture au service de l'homme,* p. 45.

8. R3-19-375 to 378, letter to Ritter, March 11, 1921, Paris.

CHAPTER XIX

1. Gauthier, *Le Corbusier ou l'architecture au service de l'homme,* p. 47.
2. Le Corbusier–Saugnier, "Maisons en série," *L'Esprit Nouveau* 13, December 1921, p. 1538.
3. Le Corbusier and Pierre Jeanneret, *Oeuvre complète,* vol. 1: *1910–1929* (Zurich: Les Editions d'Architecture, 1974), p. 31.
4. R3-19-385 to 386, letter to Ritter, July 30, 1921, Paris.
5. Ibid.
6. Petit, *Le Corbusier lui-même,* p. 34.
7. From *Bulletin,* quoted in Le Corbusier and Jeanneret, *Oeuvre complète,* vol. 1, p. 34.
8. William J. R. Curtis, *Le Corbusier: Ideas and Form* (Oxford: Phaidon, 1986), p. 61.
9. Norma Evenson, *Le Corbusier: The Machine and the Grand Design* (New York: Braziller, 1969), p. 17.
10. Ibid.
11. Ibid.
12. Interview with Vincent Scully, August 28, 2002.
13. R3-19-389 to 392, letter to Ritter, April 7, 1922, Paris.
14. Ibid.
15. Ibid.
16. Ibid.
17. R3-19-395 to 396, letter to Ritter, June 21, 1922, Paris.
18. R3-19-397 to 398, postcard to Ritter, September 16, 1922, Venice.
19. R3-19-399 to 400, postcard to Ritter, September 22, 1922, Venice.

CHAPTER XX

1. Petit, *Le Corbusier lui-même,* pp. 55, 56.
2. Petit, *Le Corbusier parle,* p. 12.
3. R1-12-5, letter to Yvonne, September 27, 1922, Brent-sur-Montreux.
4. R1-12-2, letter to Yvonne, August 23, 1922, Vevey.
5. Ibid.
6. R1-12-3, letter to Yvonne, September 21, 1922, Vincenne.
7. Ibid.
8. R1-12-6, letter to Yvonne, August 27, 1923, Blonay, Les Chábles.
9. R1-12-6, letter to Yvonne, August 27, 1923, Blonay, Les Chábles.
10. R1-12-8, letter to Yvonne, December 24, 1923, Blonay, Les Chables.

CHAPTER XXI

1. R1-6-188, letter to parents, November 27, 1921, Paris.
2. Tim Benton, *The Villas of Le Corbusier, 1920–1930* (New Haven: Yale University Press, 1987), p. 69.
3. Ibid.
4. Ibid.
5. Ibid., p. 63.
6. Interview with Violaine de Montmollin, February 19, 2000.
7. Le Corbusier and Jeanneret, *Oeuvre complète,* vol. 1, p. 60.
8. Ibid., vol. 1, p. 65.
9. Ibid., vol. 1, p. 64.
10. Le Corbusier, *Toward a New Architecture,* p. 1.
11. Ibid., p. 3.

CHAPTER XXII

1. R3-19-401, letter to Ritter, March 10, 1924, Paris.
2. Jerzy Soltan, "Working with Le Corbusier," in *Le Corbusier,* ed. H. Allen Brooks (Princeton: Princeton University Press, 1987), p. 1.
3. Ibid.
4. Ibid., p. 2.
5. R1-6-99, letter to parents, June 25, 1924, Avignon.
6. R1-12-9, letter to Yvonne, December 28, 1923, Les Chables.
7. R1-12-13, letter to Yvonne, September 11, 1924, business trip to Brittany.
8. R3-19-405 to 407, letter to Ritter, February 24, 1925, Prague.
9. Ibid.
10. Ibid.
11. Le Corbusier, *The City of To-morrow and Its Planning,* trans. John Rooker (London: Architectural Press, 1929), p. xxiii.
12. Ibid.
13. Ibid., p. xxiii, xxiv.
14. A2-14-305, letter to M. Vaneck, March 2, 1925, Brno.
15. Le Corbusier, *The City of To-morrow and Its Planning,* p. 231, n. 2.
16. Ibid., p. 287.

17. Ibid., p. 288.
18. Le Corbusier and Jeanneret, *Oeuvre complète,* vol. 1, p. 104.
19. Petit, *Le Corbusier lui-même,* p. 59.
20. Ibid., p. 61.
21. Eliel, ed., *L'Esprit Nouveau,* p. 55.
22. Le Corbusier and Jeanneret, *Oeuvre complète,* vol. 1, p. 97.
23. Le Corbusier, *The Decorative Art of Today,* p. 16.
24. Ibid., p. 17.
25. Ibid., p. 163.
26. T2-20/412, letter from Paul Valéry, 1925.
27. Le Corbusier, *The Decorative Art of Today,* p. 214.

CHAPTER XXIII

1. R1-6-107 to 108, letter to father, November 29, 1925, Paris.
2. Ibid.
3. Ibid.
4. R1-12-20, letter to Yvonne, December 24, 1925, Vevey.
5. R1-6-109 to 110, letter to parents, December 31, 1925, Paris.
6. R1-6-111 to 112, letter to mother, January 4, 1925, Paris.
7. R3-19-408 to 411, letter to Ritter, January 18, 1926, Paris.
8. Ibid.
9. R1-12-21, letter to Yvonne, January 11, 1926, Vevey.
10. R3-19-408 to 411, letter to Ritter, January 14, 1926, Paris.
11. Ibid.
12. Ibid.
13. Ibid.
14. Ibid.
15. Ibid.
16. Ibid.
17. R1-6-113, letter to mother, January 26, 1926, Paris.
18. Brian Brace Taylor, *Le Corbusier et Pessac, 1914–1928* (Paris: Fondation Le Corbusier, 1972), p. 37.
19. Ibid., p. 38.
20. E1-13-11, Blaise Cendrars to Le Corbusier, November 15, 1926, n.p.
21. Le Corbusier and Jeanneret, *Oeuvre complète,* vol. 1, p. 128.
22. Ibid.
23. Ibid.
24. Ibid.
25. Ibid., vol. 1, pp. 129, 130.
26. R1-12-22, letter to Yvonne, March 31, 1926, Paris.
27. R1-6-114, letter to mother, March 29, 1926, Paris.
28. R1-6-116, postcard to mother, April 10, 1926, Paris.
29. R1-6-117, letter to mother, April 13, 1926, Paris.
30. Ibid.
31. Ibid.
32. Ibid.
33. R1-6-120, letter to mother, April 22, 1926, Paris.
34. R1-6-121, letter to mother, May 1, 1926, Paris.
35. R1-6-125 to 126, letter to mother, May 26, 1926, Paris.
36. R1-6-122, letter to mother, May 5, 1926, Brussels.
37. Ibid.
38. Ibid.
39. Ibid.
40. R1-6-125 to 126, letter to mother, May 26, 1926, Paris.
41. Ibid.
42. R1-6-145 to 146, letter to mother, n.d., n.p.
43. Ibid.
44. Ibid.
45. Ibid.
46. R1-12-23, letter to Yvonne, July 2, 1926, Vevey.
47. R1-6-130 to 131, letter to mother, July 20, 1926, Paris.
48. Ibid.
49. R1-6-135, letter to mother, August 4, 1926, Le Piquey.
50. Ibid.
51. Ibid.
52. R1-6-133 to 134, letter to mother, August 18, 1926, Paris.
53. Ibid.
54. Ibid.
55. R1-6-136, letter to mother, October 9, 1926, Paris.
56. Ibid.
57. R1-6-137, letter to mother, October 25, 1926, Paris.
58. Ibid.
59. R1-6-138, postcard to mother, October 31, 1926, Zurich.
60. R1-6-139, letter to mother, November 29, 1926, Paris.
61. R1-6-142, letter to mother, December 17, 1926, Paris.
62. R1-6-139, letter to mother, November 29, 1926, Paris.

CHAPTER XXIV

1. R1-6-148, letter to mother, January 10, 1927, Paris.
2. Ibid.
3. R1-6-49, letter to mother, February 3, 1927, Paris.
4. R1-6-161 to 162, letter to mother, May 8, 1927, Paris.
5. Ibid.
6. R1-7-42, letter from mother, June 16, 1927, Vevey.
7. Ibid.
8. Ibid.
9. Ibid.
10. R1-7-51, letter from mother, September 5, 1927, Vevey.
11. R1-6-165, letter to mother, July 12, 1927, Paris.
12. R1-6-167 to 168, letter to mother, July 29, 1927, Paris.
13. R1-6-154 to 155, letter to mother, March 17, 1927, Paris.
14. R1-6-167 to 168, letter to mother, July 29, 1927, Paris.
15. R1-6-170, letter to mother, August 18, 1927, Le Piquey.
16. R1-6-171, letter to mother, August 26, 1927, Paris.
17. R1-12-27, letter to Yvonne, September 22, 1927, Villa Le Lac, Corseaux, via Vevey.
18. Ibid.
19. R1-6-172 to 173, letter to mother, October 6, 1927, Paris.
20. Ibid.
21. Ibid.
22. R1-12-412 to 416, letter to Ritter, October 13, 1927, Paris.
23. Ibid.
24. Ibid.
25. Ibid.
26. Ibid.
27. Ibid.
28. Ibid.
29. Files of League of Nations 32/62683/28594 and files of the Geneva State, B.13, November 16, 1927.
30. R1-6-177, letter to mother, December 1, 1927, Paris.
31. Ibid.
32. R1-6-178 to 179, letter to mother, December 16, 1927, Paris.
33. Le Corbusier and Jeanneret, *Oeuvre complète,* vol. 1, p. 161.

CHAPTER XXV

1. Charlotte Perriand, *Une vie de création* (Paris: Odile Jacob, 1998), p. 23.
2. Ibid., p. 25.
3. Ibid., pp. 26, 27.
4. Ibid., p. 33.
5. R1-6-151 to 153, letter to mother, March 5, 1927, Paris.
6. Ibid.
7. Ibid.
8. Ibid.
9. R1-6-150, letter to mother, February 16, 1927, Paris.
10. R1-6-151 to 153, letter to mother, March 5, 1927, Paris.
11. Ibid.
12. Ibid.
13. R1-6-156 to 157, letter to mother, March 29, 1927, Paris.
14. R1-6-151 to 153, letter to mother, March 5, 1927, Paris.
15. Ibid.
16. R1-6-154 to 155, letter to mother, March 17, 1927, Paris.
17. R1-6-156 to 157, letter to mother, March 29, 1927, Paris.
18. R1-6-176, letter to mother, November 21, 1927, Paris.
19. Ibid.
20. Ibid.
21. R1-7-40, letter from mother, November 25, 1927, Vevey.
22. R1-6-177, letter to mother, December 1, 1927, Paris.
23. Ibid.
24. R2-1-2, letter to mother, February 7, 1928, Paris.
25. R2-1-4, letter to mother, February 19, 1928, Paris.
26. R2-1-5, letter to mother, March 3, 1928, Paris.
27. X1-6-25, Paul Bourquin, "Les Idées de M. Le Corbusier. Maisons et cités de demain," *L'Impartial,* February 21, 1928, La Chaux-de-Fonds.
28. X1-6-28, Alexandre de Senger, "La Crise dans l'architecture," *Le Bulletin technique de la Suisse romande,* February 1928.
29. R2-1-5, letter to mother, March 3, 1928, Paris.
30. R1-7-52, letter from Marie Jeanneret to Albert and Lotti Jeanneret, February 24, 1928, Vevey.

31. Gauthier, *Le Corbusier ou l'architecture au service de l'homme,* p. 139.

CHAPTER XXVI

1. R2-1-12, letter to mother, September 4, 1928, Paris.
2. Ibid.
3. Petit, *Le Corbusier lui-même,* p. 67.
4. Ibid., pp. 66–67.
5. Petit, *Le Corbusier parle,* p. 95.
6. Jean-Louis Cohen, *Le Corbusier and the Mystique of the USSR: Theories and Projects for Moscow, 1928–1936* (Princeton: Princeton University Press, 1992), p. 37. I am grateful to Cohen's excellent book for much of the information concerning Le Corbusier and the Soviet Union.
7. Ibid., p. 29.
8. R2-1-18, postcard to Marie C. A. Jeanneret, October 13, 1928, Moscow.
9. Cohen, *Le Corbusier and the Mystique of the USSR,* p. 42.
10. Mogues, "La ville future, la conférence fait par l'architecte Le Corbusier au Musée Polytechnique sur l'architecture et l'urbanisme," Moscow, October 26, 1928. This document consists of handwritten notes made by Mogues about the lecture Le Corbusier gave in Moscow; cited ibid.
11. Cohen, *Le Corbusier and the Mystique of the USSR,* p. 44.
12. Ibid., p. 48.
13. Ibid.
14. Ibid., p. 54.
15. R1-7-56, letter from mother, October 10, 1928, Vevey.
16. Ibid.
17. R2-1-19, letter to mother, October 16, 1928, Moscow.
18. R1-7-60, letter from mother, October 20, 1928, Vevey.
19. Ibid.
20. Ibid.
21. El Lissitzky, "Idoli I idolopokonniki," *Stroitelnaia Promyshlennost* 7, nos. 11–12, 1929, in Cohen, *Le Corbusier and the Mystique of the USSR,* p. 108.
22. Ibid.
23. Ibid., p. 109.
24. Ibid.
25. Ibid., p. 112.
26. Ibid., p. 115.
27. Ibid., pp. 116–17.

CHAPTER XXVII

1. R2-1-23, letter to mother, November 11, 1928, Paris.
2. Ibid.
3. R3-19-417 to 420, letter to Ritter, December 16, 1928, Prague.

CHAPTER XXVIII

1. Le Corbusier and Jeanneret, *Oeuvre complète,* vol. 1, p. 186.
2. Ibid., vol. 1, p. 187.
3. R1-7-62, letter from Marie Jeanneret to Albert Jeanneret, February 11, 1929, Vevey.
4. Ibid.
5. R2-1-37, letter to mother, April 10, 1929, Paris.
6. R1-7-62, letter from Marie Jeanneret to Albert Jeanneret, February 11, 1929, Vevey.
7. R2-1-39, letter to mother, May 22, 1929, Bordeaux. Here "D.D." stands for *dodo,* the French word for "nap."
8. R1-12-30, letter to Yvonne, n.d., n.p. (written on trip to give lecture in Zurich and Stuttgart).
9. R1-12-32, letter to Yvonne, June 3, 1929, Moscow.
10. R2-1-43, letter to mother, June 20, 1929, Paris.
11. Ibid.
12. R1-7-66, letter from mother to Le Corbusier and Yvonne, June 20, 1929, Vevey.
13. R1-7-193, letter from Yvonne Gallis to Marie Jeanneret, July 3, 1929, Paris.
14. R2-1-48, letter to mother, August 10, 1929, Paris.
15. Ibid.
16. R2-1-49, letter to mother, August 22, 1929, Paris.
17. R2-1-51, letter to mother, September 12, 1929, Paris.
18. R1-7-194, letter from Yvonne Gallis to Marie Jeanneret, September 3, 1929, Paris.

CHAPTER XXIX

1. R2-1-51, letter from Le Corbusier and Yvonne to mother, September 12, 1929, Paris.
2. R1-12-35, postcard to Yvonne, September 14, 1929, Bordeaux.

3. Ibid.
4. R2-1-54, letter to mother, September 15, 1929, aboard the *Massilia.*
5. R2-1-55, letter to mother, September 25, 1929, aboard the *Massilia.*
6. R2-1-58, letter to mother, October 9, 1929, Majestic Hotel, Buenos Aires.
7. Ibid.
8. R2-1-60, letter to mother, October 27, 1929, Majestic Hotel, Buenos Aires.
9. R2-1-63, letter to mother, October 29, 1929, Majestic Hotel, Buenos Aires.
10. Ibid.
11. R2-1-52, letter to mother, November 14, 1929, written aboard the *Giulio Cesare.* (Garrono is also discussed in R2-1-63, letter to mother, October 29, 1929, Majestic Hotel, Buenos Aires.)
12. R2-1-63, letter to mother, October 29, 1929, Majestic Hotel, Buenos Aires.
13. R2-1-66 to 68, letter to mother, November 2–4, 1929, Buenos Aires.
14. R1-7-68, letter from mother, October 15, 1929, Vevey.
15. Ibid.
16. Alistair Horne, *Seven Ages of Paris* (New York: Alfred A. Knopf, 2002), p. 334.
17. Ibid., p. 335.
18. All of the Baker biographies say that Baker and Le Corbusier first met on board the *Lutétia* when they were sailing from Rio to France on a crossing that began on December 9. In fact, they met more than a month earlier. Le Corbusier first wrote his mother about Baker on November 2.
19. R2-1-66 to 68, letter to mother, November 2–4, 1929, Buenos Aires.
20. Ibid.
21. Ibid.
22. Ibid.
23. Ibid.
24. Ibid.
25. Ibid.
26. R2-1-52 to 53, letter to mother, November 14, 1929, aboard the *Giulio Cesare.* N.b. This letter is incorrectly dated in the transcript of the Fondation Le Corbusier, where the date is given as September 14.
27. Ibid.
28. Ibid.
29. Le Corbusier and Jeanneret, *Oeuvre complète,* vol. 1, p. 32.
30. R2-1-52 to 53, letter to mother, November 14, 1929, aboard the *Giulio Cesare.*
31. R2-1-69 to 70, letter to mother, November 22, 1929, São Paulo.
32. Ibid.
33. Petit, *Le Corbusier lui-même,* p. 68.
34. Ibid.
35. Joséphine Baker and Jo Bouillon, *Joséphine* (Paris: Editions Robert Laffont, 1976), p. 109.
36. Interview with Jean-Claude Baker, March 12, 2003.
37. R1-7-198, Yvonne Gallis to Mme. Jeanneret, November 29, 1929, Paris.
38. R1-7-200, Yvonne Gallis to Mme. Jeanneret, December 10, 1929, Paris.
39. Perriand, *Une vie de création,* p. 38.

CHAPTER XXX

1. John Richardson, *Sacred Monsters, Sacred Masters* (New York: Random House, 2001), p. 5. I am grateful to Richardson for additional information on the Errázurizes.
2. Ibid., pp. 5, 4.
3. Ibid., p. 11.
4. Ibid.
5. Le Corbusier and Jeanneret, *Oeuvre complète,* vol. 2: *1929–1934* (Zurich: Les Editions d'Architecture, 1977), p. 52.
6. E. B. White, "Dusk in Fierce Pajamas," *The New Yorker,* January 27, 1934.
7. Le Corbusier and Jeanneret, *Oeuvre complète,* vol. 2, p. 52.
8. Le Corbusier, *Précisions sur un état présent de l'architecture et de l'urbanisme* (Paris: Crès, 1930).
9. R2-1-80, letter to mother, March 1930, Moscow.
10. R2-1-81, letter to mother, April 25, 1930, Paris.
11. R2-1-79, letter to mother, March 30, 1930, Paris.
12. R2-1-83, letter to mother, May 15, 1930, Paris.
13. Ibid.
14. R2-1-86, letter to mother, July 18, 1930, Paris.
15. R2-1-92 to 93, letter to mother, September 28, 1930, Paris.

16. Ibid.
17. Ibid.
18. Ibid.
19. R2-1-97, letter to mother, October 12, 1930, Paris.
20. Ibid.
21. Le Corbusier and Jeanneret, *Oeuvre complète,* vol. 2, p. 161.
22. Le Corbusier to M. Titulescu, September 18, 1930, in *Schweizerische Bauzeitung* 23, December 6, 1930.
23. R2-1-97, letter to mother, October 12, 1930, Paris.
24. R2-1-99, letter to mother, October 29, 1930, Paris.
25. R2-1-97, letter to mother, October 12, 1930, Paris.
26. Ibid.
27. R2-1-100, letter to mother, November 9, 1930, Paris.
28. Ibid.

CHAPTER XXXI

1. Alice Goldfarb Marquis, *Alfred H. Barr, Jr.: Missionary for the Modern* (Chicago: Contemporary Books, 1989), p. 107.
2. Petit, *Le Corbusier lui-même,* p. 74.
3. Cohen, *Le Corbusier and the Mystique of the USSR,* p. 184.
4. R2-1-138, letter to mother, December 15, 1931, Paris.
5. E2-12-400, letter to Hélène de Mandrot, June 28, 1930, Paris.
6. R2-1-112 to 113, letter to mother, n.d. (ca. April 4, 1931), Toulon.
7. Ibid.
8. R2-1-117, letter to mother, April 19, 1931, Paris.
9. Interview with Lucien Hervé, May 29, 2002; my thanks to Agnès B. for setting this up.
10. Ibid.
11. R2-1-117, letter to mother, April 19, 1931, Paris.
12. R2-1-115, letter to mother, April 2, 1931, Algiers.
13. R2-1-117, letter to mother, April 19, 1931, Paris.
14. Le Corbusier and Jeanneret, *Oeuvre complète,* vol. 2, p. 73.
15. Ibid., vol. 2, p. 67.
16. R2-1-108, letter to mother, February 25, 1931, Paris.
17. Alexandre de Senger, *Le Cheval de Troie du Bolchévisme* (Bienne: Editions du Chandelier, 1931). This book was in Le Corbusier's personal library.
18. Gauthier, *Le Corbusier ou l'architecture au service de l'homme,* p. 183.
19. Ibid., p. 187.
20. Ibid., p. 190.
21. Ibid., p. 174.
22. R2-1-140, letter to mother, March 29, 1931, Hotel St. Georges, Algiers.
23. R2-1-118, letter to mother, n.d. (ca. April 26, 1931), Paris.
24. Ibid.
25. R2-1-122, letter to mother, July 30, 1931, Paris.
26. Ibid.
27. R2-1-123, letter to mother, July 1931, Paris.
28. R2-1-130, letter to mother, August 10, 1931, between Taragonne and Valencia.
29. R2-1-128, postcard to mother, August 30, 1931, Ghardaïa.
30. R2-1-131, letter to mother, September 1, 1931, Algiers.
31. R2-1-132, letter to mother, October 7, 1931, Paris.
32. Ibid.
33. Ibid.
34. R2-1-134, letter to mother, October 21, 1931, Paris.
35. R2-1-139, letter to mother, December 25, 1931, Paris.
36. Cohen, *Le Corbusier and the Mystique of the USSR,* p. 188.
37. Ibid., p. 192.
38. Ibid., pp. 193–94.
39. Ibid., p. 195.
40. Ibid., p. 199.
41. Perriand, *Une vie de création,* p. 54.
42. Ibid.
43. Le Corbusier and Jeanneret, *Oeuvre complète,* vol. 2, p. 75.
44. Petit, *Le Corbusier lui-même,* p. 75.
45. Petit, *Le Corbusier parle,* p. 83.
46. Le Corbusier and Jeanneret, *Oeuvre complète,* vol. 2, p. 144.
47. Ibid., vol. 2, p. 146.
48. Petit, *Le Corbusier lui-même,* p. 78.
49. Ibid.
50. Sylvia Kahan, *Une Muse de la musique moderne: Une Vie de Winnaretta Singer, princess de Polignac (1865–1943)* (Paris: Les Presses de Réel, 2007), p. 150.
51. Ibid., p. 223.
52. Brian Brace Taylor, *Le Corbusier: The*

City of Refuge, Paris, 1929–1933 (Chicago: University of Chicago Press, 1987), p. 111.

53. Ibid., p. 107.
54. Le Corbusier, *My Work* (London: Architectural Press, 1960), p. 106.
55. T1-18-14, Le Corbusier to M. Jourdain, December 8, 1933, Paris.
56. T1-18-16, Le Corbusier to Anatole de Monzie, December 16, 1933, Paris.

CHAPTER XXXII

1. Mardges Bacon, *Le Corbusier in America: Travels in the Land of the Timid* (Cambridge, Mass.: MIT Press, 2001), p. 32. Here, as throughout, for details concerning Le Corbusier in America, I am extremely grateful to Bacon's thorough and excellent book.
2. *New York Herald Tribune,* October 22, 1935.
3. *New York Times,* October 22, 1935.
4. Le Corbusier, *Quand les cathédrales étaient blanches, voyage au pays des timides* (Paris: Plon, 1937), p. 77.
5. Bacon, *Le Corbusier in America,* p. 40.
6. Le Corbusier, *Quand les cathédrales étaient blanches,* p. 84.
7. Ibid.
8. Bacon, *Le Corbusier in America,* p. 37.
9. Le Corbusier, *Quand les cathédrales étaient blanches,* p. 49.
10. Ibid.
11. Ibid.
12. Ibid.
13. Ibid., p. 50.
14. Ibid.
15. E3-10-4, Mrs. Harris to Le Corbusier, April 25, 1932, Blonay.
16. Ibid.
17. Bacon, *Le Corbusier in America,* p. 52.
18. Ibid.
19. Le Corbusier, *Quand les cathédrales étaient blanches,* p. 105.
20. Ibid., pp. 59–60.
21. Bacon, *Le Corbusier in America,* p. 72.
22. Ibid.
23. Le Corbusier, *Quand les cathédrales étaient blanches,* p. 203.
24. Ibid.
25. Ibid.
26. Ibid., p. 205.
27. Ibid.
28. Ibid.
29. Ibid.
30. Ibid., p. 206.
31. Ibid.
32. Ibid.
33. Ibid., pp. 206–7.
34. Ibid., p. 207.
35. Ibid., p. 266.
36. Bacon, *Le Corbusier in America,* pp. 95, 96.
37. Le Corbusier, *Quand les cathédrales étaient blanches,* p. 155.
38. Ibid., pp. 155–56.
39. Ibid., p. 156.
40. Ibid., p. 157.
41. Ibid., p. 248.
42. Bacon, *Le Corbusier in America,* p. 73.
43. E2-9-12, Frank Lloyd Wright to Leo Weissenborg, November 8, 1935.
44. Le Corbusier, *Quand les cathédrales étaient blanches,* p. 223.
45. Ibid., p. 215.
46. Ibid., pp. 217–19.
47. Ibid., p. 220.
48. Ibid., p. 308.
49. Ibid., pp. 232, 233.
50. Ibid., p. 234.
51. Ibid., p. 235.
52. Ibid., pp. 235–37.
53. Petit, *Le Corbusier lui-même,* p. 79.
54. E3-10-12, letter to Mrs. Harris, December 14, 1935, aboard the *Lafayette.*
55. Ibid.
56. Ibid.
57. Ibid.
58. Ibid.
59. Bacon, *Le Corbusier in America,* p. 56.
60. Ibid.
61. Le Corbusier, *Quand les cathédrales étaient blanches,* p. 309.

CHAPTER XXXIII

1. Le Corbusier and Jeanneret, *Oeuvre complète,* vol. 3: *1934–1938* (Zurich: Les Editions d'Architecture, 1977), p. 42.
2. E3-10-15, letter to Mrs. Harris, July 31, 1936, Rio de Janeiro, Collection CCA Montréal DR 1984–1904.
3. Ibid.
4. E3-10-16, letter to Mrs. Harris, August 4, 1936, Rio de Janeiro.
5. Ibid.
6. Petit, *Le Corbusier lui-même,* p. 82.
7. Le Corbusier, "Des canons, des munitions? Merci, des logis . . . SVP," (Boulogne sur Seine: Architecture d'Aujourd'hui, 1938), p. 128.

8. Ibid.
9. R2-1-150, letter to mother, April 20, 1937, Paris.
10. Ibid.
11. Le Corbusier, "Des canons, des munitions?," p. 129.
12. Ibid., p. 131.
13. Interview with Balthus, January 14, 1991.
14. Le Corbusier, "Des canons, des munitions?," p. 135.
15. E3-10-26, letter to Mrs. Harris, December 8, 1937, Paris.
16. Ibid.
17. Ibid.
18. E3-10-29, letter to Mrs. Harris, January 25, 1938, Paris.
19. Petit, *Le Corbusier lui-même,* p. 84.
20. Le Corbusier, letter to Dr. Valensi, secretary of 19 Juin, June 11, 1938.
21. Petit, *Le Corbusier lui-même,* p. 84.
22. Ibid.
23. Peter Adam, *Eileen Gray, Architect/Designer* (New York: Harry N. Abrams, 1987), p. 174.
24. Ibid., pp. 309–10.
25. Ibid., p. 311.
26. Ibid.
27. R2-1-264, letter to mother, September 21, 1938, Saint-Tropez.
28. Ibid.
29. E3-10-33, letter to Mrs. Harris, December 8, 1938, Paris.
30. R2-1-264, letter to mother, September 21, 1938, Saint-Tropez.
31. R2-1-263, letter to mother, August 23, 1938, Saint-Tropez.
32. Petit, *Le Corbusier lui-même,* p. 84.
33. R1-7-84, letter from mother, September 11, 1938, Villa Le Lac, Vevey.
34. Ibid.
35. Ibid.
36. R1-7-86, letter from Albert and mother, September 28, 1938, Vevey.
37. Ibid.
38. E3-10-34, letter to Mrs. Harris, March 21, 1939, Paris.
39. Ibid.
40. E3-10-35, letter from Mrs. Harris to Le Corbusier, March 21, 1939, Paris.
41. R2-1-185, letter to mother, March 8, 1939, Paris.
42. R2-1-152, letter to mother, March 26, 1930, Paris.
43. R2-1-153, letter to mother, June 3, 1939, London.
44. R2-1-156, letter to mother, September 3, 1939, Paris.
45. R2-1-157, letter to mother, September 9, 1939, Vézelay.
46. R2-1-158 to 159, letter to mother and brother, September 27, 1939, Vézelay.
47. Ibid.
48. Quoted in Julian Jackson, *France: The Dark Years, 1940–1944* (Oxford: Oxford University Press, 2001), p. 95.
49. R1-1-165, letter to mother, December 18, 1939, Vézelay.
50. R2-1-160, letter to mother, October 14, 1939, Vézelay.
51. Ibid.
52. Ibid.
53. Ibid.
54. Quoted in Jackson, *France,* p. 111.
55. Ibid.
56. R2-1-165, letter to mother, December 18, 1939, Vézelay.
57. R2-1-163 to 164, letter to mother, November 20, 1939, Vézelay.
58. Ibid.
59. E3-10-37, letter to Mrs. Tjader Harris, November 22, 1939, Vézelay.
60. R2-1-165, letter to mother, December 18, 1939, Vézelay.
61. Alexis Carrel, *Man, the Unknown* (New York and London: Harper & Brothers, 1935), pp. 314, 315.

CHAPTER XXXIV

1. R2-4-3, letter to mother, January 29, 1940, Paris.
2. Jackson, *France,* p. 95.
3. R2-4-4, letter to mother, February 14, 1940, Paris.
4. Ibid.
5. R2-4-5, letter to mother, March 19, 1940, Paris.
6. R2-4-8T, letter to mother, May 10, 1940, Paris.
7. Ibid.
8. Ibid.
9. R2-4-9, letter to mother, May 21, 1940, Paris.
10. R2-1-161, letter to mother, October 28, 1939, Vézelay.
11. R2-4-9, letter to mother, May 21, 1940, Paris.
12. Jackson, *France,* p. 126.
13. Petit, *Le Corbusier lui-même,* p. 86.
14. Roger Price, *A Concise History of France* (Cambridge: Cambridge University Press, 2005), pp. 253, 254.

15. R2-4-10, letter to mother, July 3, 1940, Vichy.
16. Ibid.
17. Jackson, *France,* pp. 178, 179.
18. R2-4-10, letter to mother, July 3, 1940, Vichy.
19. R2-4-11, letter to mother, August 2, 1940, Ozon.
20. Ibid.
21. Ibid.
22. Ibid.
23. R1-7-88, letter from mother, August 22, 1940, Vevey.
24. Ibid.
25. R2-4-13 to 14, letter to mother, August 18, 1940, Ozon via Tournay.
26. R1-7-89, letter from mother, September 27, 1940, Vevey.
27. R2-4-15, letter to mother, August 27, 1940, Ozon.
28. R1-12/51T, letter to Yvonne, September 18, 1940, Vichy.
29. Ibid.
30. Ibid.
31. R1-7-89, letter from mother, September 27, 1940, Vevey.
32. Ibid.
33. Georges Valois, "La nouvelle étape du Fascisme," *Le Nouveau Siècle,* May 23, 1927.
34. D2-3-271, letter to Pierre Winter, September 8, 1930, Paris.
35. R2-4-16, letter to mother, October 1, 1940, Ozon.
36. Price, *A Concise History of France,* p. 260.
37. R1-7-89, letter from mother, September 27, 1940, Vevey.
38. Ibid.
39. Ibid.
40. Price, *A Concise History of France,* p. 259.
41. R2-4-17, letter to mother, October 31, 1940, Ozon.
42. Ibid.
43. Ibid.
44. R2-4-18 to 20, letter to mother, November 16, 1940, Ozon.
45. Ibid.
46. Ibid.
47. Ibid.
48. R1-7-93, letter from mother, December 1, 1940, Vevey.
49. Ibid.
50. Ibid.
51. R2-4-24, letter to mother, January 17, 1940, Vichy.
52. Jackson, *France,* p. 263.
53. R2-4-22, letter to mother, December 18, 1940, Ozon.
54. R2-4-24, letter to mother, January 17, 1941, Vichy.
55. R1-7-95, letter from mother, January 18, 1941, Vevey.
56. R2-4-25, letter to mother, January 31, 1941, Vichy.
57. Ibid.
58. R2-4-26, letter to mother, February 17, 1941, Hotel Albert Ier, Vichy.
59. Ibid.
60. R1-7-96, letter from mother, March 12, 1941, Vevey.
61. R2-4-28 to 29, letter to mother, March 27, 1941, Queen's Hotel, Vichy.
62. Ibid.
63. Ibid.
64. Ibid.
65. Ibid.
66. Ibid.
67. Le Corbusier, *Les maisons "Murondins"* (Paris–Clermont-Ferrand: E. Chiron, 1942).
68. R2-4-30, letter to mother, April 22, 1941, Vichy.
69. R1-7-97, letter from mother, May 18, 1941, Vevey.
70. Petit, *Le Corbusier lui-même,* p. 87.
71. Ibid.
72. R2-4-33, letter to mother, June 2, 1941, Vichy.
73. Ibid.
74. A2-17-239, Demande de dérogation, June 2, 1941, Vichy.
75. Ibid.
76. R1-7-98, letter from mother, June 4, 1941, Vevey.
77. R1-7-100, letter from mother, July 29, 1941, Vevey.
78. R1-7-103, letter from mother, September 14, 1941, Geneva.
79. R1-7-104, letter from mother, September 30, 1941, Vevey.
80. Ibid.
81. R2-4-38, letter to mother, October 6, 1941, Vichy.
82. R2-4-39, letter to mother, October 17, 1941, Vichy.
83. R2-4-40, letter to mother, October 23, 1941, Vichy.
84. R2-4-44, telegram to mother, November 8, 1941, Geneva.
85. R2-4-43, postcard to mother, November 6, 1941, Vichy.

86. R2-4-46 to 47, letter to mother, November 30, 1941, Vichy.
87. Ibid.
88. Ibid.
89. Ibid.
90. R2-4-48, letter to mother, December 15, 1941, Vichy.
91. Ibid.
92. R2-4-49, letter to mother, December 27, 1941, Vichy.
93. E2-13-38, letter from Pierre Jeanneret, December 29, 1941, Grenoble.
94. Ibid.
95. Ibid.
96. Ibid.

CHAPTER XXXV

1. R2-4-51, letter to mother, January 31, 1942, Vichy.
2. R1-7-106, letter from mother, February 5, 1942, Vevey.
3. R2-4-52, letter to mother, February 12, 1942, Vichy.
4. Ibid.
5. Le Corbusier to M. Berthelot, February 14, 1942, Vichy.
6. R2-4-53, letter to mother, March 19, 1942, Vichy.
7. Ibid.
8. Jackson, *France,* p. 143.
9. Ibid., pp. 327, 328.
10. Andrés Horacio Reggiani, "Alexis Carrel, the Unknown: Eugenics and Population Research Under Vichy," *French Historical Studies* 25, no. 2 (Spring 2002): 339.
11. B3-12-219, letter from Alexis Carrel, February 19, 1942, Paris.
12. A2-17-17, letter to Alexis Carrel, March 7, 1942, Hotel du Cheval Blanc, Vézelay.
13. R2-4-55, letter to mother, March 28, 1942, Vichy.
14. Ibid.
15. Jackson, *France,* p. 350.
16. R2-4-55, letter to mother, March 28, 1942, Vichy.
17. Ibid.
18. R1-7-104, letter from mother, March 25, 1942, Vevey.
19. R2-4-56, letter to mother, April 15, 1942, Hotel Aletti, Algiers.
20. Ibid.
21. A2-17-53, letter from François de Pierrefeu, April 18, 1942, Vichy.
22. Ibid.
23. Ibid.
24. Ibid.
25. R2-4-54, letter to mother, May 26, 1942, Vichy.
26. Petit, *Le Corbusier lui-même,* p. 92.
27. Interview with Roger Aujame, October 5, 2000.
28. A2-17-57, letter from François de Pierrefeu, October 3, 1942, Vichy.
29. Jackson, *France,* p. 447.

CHAPTER XXXVI

1. R2-4-59, letter to mother, December 22, 1942, Paris.
2. Note from Le Corbusier to M. Lallemant, January 8, 1943, Paris.
3. Letter from Le Chef du Cabinet Civil to M. le Ministre Secrétaire d'Etat à l'Education Nationale (Secrétaire général des Beaux Arts), 7/O.M., January 19, 1943, Vichy.
4. Letter from Le Conseiller d'Etat Secrétaire Général des Beaux Arts, Etat Français Paris, L. Hautecoeur, to Monsieur le Chef du Cabinet Civil de M. le Maréchal Pétain at the Hotel du Parc, February 12, 1943.
5. R2-4-60, postcard to mother, January 6, 1943, Paris.
6. R2-4-61, letter to mother, March 23, 1943, Paris.
7. Interview with Roger Aujame, October 5, 2000.
8. R2-4-61, letter to mother, March 23, 1943, Paris.
9. Hervé Le Boteuf, *La Vie Parisienne sous l'Occupation* (Paris: Editions France-Empire, 1997), p. 342; with thanks to Alan Riding.
10. R2-4-64, letter to mother, June 15, 1943, Paris.
11. R2-4-65, letter to mother, July 21, 1943, Paris.
12. Ibid.
13. R2-4-66, letter to mother, October 12, 1943, Paris.
14. R2-4-67, letter to mother, November 6, 1943, Paris.
15. R2-4-66, letter to mother, October 12, 1943, Paris.
16. R2-4-67, letter to mother, November 6, 1943, Paris.
17. The Internet Encyclopedia of Philosophy, http://www.utm.edu/research/iep/p/protagor.htm.

18. F2-14-109, letter from J. Merlet, December 3, 1943, Vichy.

CHAPTER XXXVII

1. R2-4-68, letter to mother, February 7, 1944, Paris.
2. Ibid.
3. R2-4-69, letter to mother, March 22, 1944, Paris.
4. R2-4-71, letter to mother, May 28, 1944, Paris.
5. R2-4-73 to 74, letter to mother, November 7, 1944, Paris.
6. Ibid.
7. Ibid.
8. R2-4-77, postcard to mother, April 28, 1945, Nancy.
9. Ibid.
10. Le Corbusier and Jeanneret, *Oeuvre complète,* vol. 4: *1938–1946* (Zurich: Les Editions d'Architecture, 1977), p. 132.
11. Petit, *Le Corbusier lui-même,* p. 94.
12. R2-4-78, postcard to mother, May 8, 1945, Paris.
13. A2-17-236, letter from Jean Balleuf, May 25, 1945.
14. Petit, *Le Corbusier parle,* pp. 102, 103.
15. Petit, *Le Corbusier lui-même,* p. 92.
16. Janet Flanner, *Paris Journal, 1944–1965* (New York: Atheneum, 1965), p. 40.
17. Petit, *Le Corbusier lui-même,* p. 87.

CHAPTER XXXVIII

1. R2-04-81, letter to mother, August 3, 1945, Paris.
2. R2-04-82, letter to mother, August 28, 1945, Paris.
3. Petit, *Le Corbusier lui-même,* p. 94.
4. Ibid., p. 96.
5. Le Corbusier, *Les trois établissements humains* (Paris: Denoël, 1945).
6. Petit, *Le Corbusier lui-même,* p. 95.
7. R1-9-9, cable from Yvonne Le Corbusier, December 6, 1935, Paris.
8. Petit, *Le Corbusier lui-même,* p. 96.
9. Ibid.
10. Le Corbusier and Jeanneret, *Oeuvre complète,* vol. 5: *1946–1952,* (Zurich: Les Editions d' Architecture, 1977), p. 179.
11. Jerzy Soltan, "Working with Le Corbusier," in H. Allen Brooks, ed., *Le Corbusier: The Garland Essays* (New York: Garland, 1987), p. 11.
12. Petit, *Le Corbusier parle,* p. 13.

CHAPTER XXXIX

1. R2-4-83 to 84, letter to mother, March 24, 1946, Paris.
2. Ibid.
3. Ibid.
4. Ibid.
5. R2-4-85, letter to mother, April 14, 1946, Paris.
6. Ibid.
7. Ibid.
8. R2-4-87, letter to mother, May 3, 1946, Paris.
9. George A. Dudley, *A Workshop for Peace: Designing the United Nations Headquarters, New York* (Cambridge, Mass.: Architectural History Foundation, MIT Press, 1994), p. 43.
10. E3-10-42, letter to Mrs. Harris, May 17, 1946, Roosevelt Hotel, New York.
11. Ibid.
12. Ibid.
13. Ibid.
14. Ibid.
15. Ibid.
16. E3-10-43, letter to Mrs. Harris, May 27, 1946, Roosevelt Hotel, New York.
17. Ibid.
18. R2-4-88, letter to mother, July 21, 1946, New York, sent from Paris.
19. Ibid.
20. Ibid.
21. Ibid.
22. R1-12-58, letter to Yvonne, September 5, 1946, New York.
23. Ibid.
24. R2-04-90, letter to mother, November 6, 1946, Grosvenor Hotel, New York.
25. Dudley, *A Workshop for Peace,* pp. 15, 16.
26. R1-12-64, letter to Yvonne, November 18, 1946, New York.
27. D1-18/213, letter from J. D. Rockefeller Jr. to Dr. E. Zuleta Angel, December 10, 1946, New York.
28. E3-10-45, letter to Mrs. Harris, December 3, 1946, Grosvenor Hotel, New York.
29. R1-12-64, letter to Yvonne, November 18, 1946, New York.
30. R2-4-96, letter to mother, December 29, 1946, Paris.

31. Ibid.
32. Petit, *Le Corbusier lui-même,* p. 98.
33. R2-04-99, letter to mother, February 20, 1947, Hotel Grosvenor, New York.
34. Ibid.
35. Ibid.
36. R2-04-100 to 101, letter to mother, March 16, 1947, Paris.
37. Soltan, "Working with Le Corbusier," p. 5.
38. Petit, *Le Corbusier parle,* p. 104.
39. R2-04-100 to 101, letter to mother, March 16, 1947, Paris.
40. Ibid.
41. Ibid.
42. R2-4-102, letter to mother, March 22, 1947, Paris.
43. Ibid.
44. R1-12-66, letter to Yvonne, March 24, 1947, Grosvenor Hotel, New York.
45. R2-4-103, letter to mother, March 27, 1947, New York.
46. Bacon, *Le Corbusier in America,* p. 392.
47. Geoffrey T. Hellman, "Profiles, from Within to Without," *The New Yorker,* April 26 and May 3, 1947.
48. Ibid.
49. R1-12-60, letter to Yvonne, April 22, 1947, Grosvenor Hotel, New York.
50. Dudley, *A Workshop for Peace,* pp. viii, 236.
51. R1-12-60, letter to Yvonne, April 22, 1947, Grosvenor Hotel, New York.
52. Ibid.
53. Ibid.
54. Hellman, "Profiles, from Within to Without."
55. Ibid.
56. Ibid.
57. Ibid.
58. Ibid.
59. Ibid.
60. D1-18-240 to 241, letter to Geoffrey Hellman, May 13, 1947, Grosvenor Hotel, New York.
61. Ibid.
62. R2-04-104 to 105, letter to mother, May 6, 1947, New York.
63. Ibid.
64. R1-04-113, letter to mother, July 19, 1947, Paris.
65. Bacon, *Le Corbusier in America,* and Dudley, *A Workshop for Peace* are excellent sources on the subject.
66. Dudley, *A Workshop for Peace,* p. 340.
67. R2-04-114, letter to mother, August 1, 1947, Paris.
68. R2-04-115, letter to mother, September 6, 1947, Paris.
69. R2-04-116 to 117, letter to mother, November 14, 1947, Paris.
70. Ibid.
71. Ibid.
72. Ibid.

CHAPTER XL

1. E2-7-268, letter to Luis Miro Quesada, May 12, 1947, Grosvenor Hotel, New York.
2. E2-7-269, letter to Hedwig Lauber, July 17, 1947, Paris.
3. Le Corbusier and Jeanneret, *Oeuvre complète,* vol. 5, p. 24.
4. Ibid.
5. Ibid.
6. R2-04-118 to 119, letter to mother, January 10 and 12, 1948, Paris.
7. Ibid.
8. Ibid.
9. Ibid.
10. Ibid.
11. Ibid.
12. R2-4-120, letter to mother, January 2, 1948, Paris.
13. R2-04-121, letter to mother, April 4, 1948, Paris.
14. R2-04-122, postcard to mother, June 11, 1948, Marseille.
15. R2-04-123 to 125, letter to mother, August 18, 1948, Paris.
16. Ibid.
17. Ibid.
18. Ibid.
19. Ibid.
20. E3-10-47, letter to Mrs. Harris, October 7, 1948, Smyrna.
21. Le Corbusier, "De Divino Proportione," lecture given at Milan Triennale, September 1951.

CHAPTER XLI

1. E3-10-48, letter to Mrs. Harris, February 23, 1949, written while flying over New York, mailed from Bogotá.
2. E3-10-49, letter to Mrs. Harris, June 17, 1949, New York.
3. R2-2-1, letter to mother, February 19, 1949, Paris.
4. R2-2-3 to 4, letter from Dr. Curutchet

to Le Corbusier and letter from Le Corbusier to his mother, July 9, 1949, Paris.
5. R2-2-6, letter to mother, August 20, 1949, Hotel Majestic, Menton.
6. R1-12-67, letter to Yvonne, August 1, 1949, Venice.
7. Ibid.
8. R2-2-7, letter to mother, August 30, 1949, Roquebrune-Cap-Martin.
9. E2-19-30, letter to Picasso, August 23, 1949, Roquebrune-Cap-Martin.
10. R2-2-8, letter to mother, September 7, 1949, Paris.
11. Ibid.
12. Ibid.
13. Ibid.
14. R2-2-9 to 10, letter to mother, October 23, 1949, Paris.
15. R2-2-11, letter to mother, November 16, 1949, Paris.
16. Ibid.
17. R2-2-12 to 13, letter to mother, December 11, 1949, Paris.
18. Interview with Lucien Hervé, May 29, 2002.
19. Ibid.
20. R2-2-14, letter to mother, December 23, 1949, Paris.
21. Ibid.
22. E1-5-96, letter from Badovici, December 30, 1949, n.p.
23. E1-5-104, letter to Badovici, August 23, 1950, Paris.
24. E1-6-176 to 178, letter to André Bauchant, October 31, 1949, Paris.
25. Ibid.
26. R2-2-16, letter to mother, February 24, 1950, Bogotá.
27. R1-12-73, letter to Yvonne, February 17, 1950, Bogotá.
28. R2-2-16, letter to mother, February 24, 1950, Bogotá.
29. R1-12-73, letter to Yvonne, February 17, 1950, Bogotá.
30. R2-2-17, letter to mother, April 13, 1950, Paris; written by Le Corbusier but including entries by Albert.
31. R2-2-19, letter to mother, May 30, 1950, Paris.
32. R2-2-20, letter to mother, June 9, 1950, Paris.
33. R2-2-22, letter to mother, August 26, 1950, Paris.
34. R1-12-77, letter to Yvonne, August 30, 1950, New York.
35. Ibid.
36. R1-12-78, letter to Yvonne, September 2, 1950, Bogotá.
37. R1-12-79, letter to Yvonne, September 4, 1950, Bogotá.
38. R1-12-82, letter to Yvonne, September 19, 1950, Hotel Continental, Bogotá.
39. R1-12-83, letter to Yvonne, September 28, 1950, New York.
40. Ibid.
41. E2-7-274T, letter to H. Lauber, October 20, 1950, Paris.
42. E2-07/283, letter to H. Lauber, September 25, 1951, Paris.
43. E2-7/300, letter from H. Lauber, June 6, 1957, Zurich.
44. R2-2-24, letter to mother, November 28, 1950, Paris.
45. R2-2-25, letter to mother, December 5, 1950, Paris.

CHAPTER XLII

1. Ravi Kalia, *Chandigarh: The Making of an Indian City* (Oxford: Oxford University Press, 1990), p. 42.
2. Ibid., p. 12.
3. Ibid., p. 87.
4. Ibid., p. 88.
5. R2-2-26, letter to mother, December 10, 1950, Paris.
6. R2-2-27, letter to mother, December 21, 1950, Paris.
7. Petit, *Le Corbusier lui-même,* p. 103.
8. Le Corbusier, *Poésie sur Alger* (Paris: Falaize, 1950).
9. Le Corbusier, *Une petite maison* (Zurich: Girsberger, 1954).
10. R2-2-34, letter to mother, January 21, 1951, Paris.
11. Ibid.
12. R2-2-37, letter to Albert and mother, February 5, 1951, Paris.
13. Ibid.
14. Mike Lebowitz, "French Landmark Housed Prisoners During WWII," *Jerusalem Post,* June 3, 2004.
15. R2-2-38, letter to mother, February 18, 1951, Paris.

CHAPTER XLIII

1. R1-12-96, letter to Yvonne, February 25, 1951, Chandigarh.
2. Ibid.
3. Ibid.

4. Ibid.
5. Petit, *Le Corbusier lui-même,* pp. 104, 105.
6. R1-12-87, letter to Yvonne, February 27, 1951, Chandigarh.
7. Petit, *Le Corbusier lui-même,* p. 103.
8. Ibid., p. 104.
9. Petit, *Le Corbusier parle,* p. 15.
10. Petit, *Le Corbusier lui-même,* p. 104.
11. Ibid.
12. R1-12-87, letter to Yvonne, February 26, 1951, Chandigarh.
13. Ibid.
14. Ibid.
15. R1-12-89, letter to Yvonne, March 4, 1951, Chandigarh.
16. R1-12-90, letter to Yvonne, March 7, 1951, Chandigarh.
17. Ibid.
18. R2-2-39, letter to mother, March 12, 1951, Simla.
19. Ibid.
20. Balkrishna V. Doshi, *Le Corbusier and Louis I. Kahn: The Acrobat and the Yogi of Architecture* (Ahmedabad: Vastu-Shilpa Foundation, 1990), p. 3.
21. Ibid.
22. Ibid., p. 5.
23. Ibid., p. 8.
24. Petit, *Le Corbusier lui-même,* pp. 110, 111.
25. Ibid.
26. R2-2-42, letter to mother, May 2, 1951, Paris.
27. R2-2-43, letter to mother, May 6, 1951, New York.
28. Petit, *Le Corbusier lui-même,* p. 110.
29. R2-2-44, letter to mother, May 20, 1951, Bogotá.
30. R2-2-46, letter to mother, June 11, 1951, Paris, on Bogotá stationery.
31. Ibid.
32. Le Corbusier and Jeanneret, *Oeuvre complète,* vol. 5, pp. 112–13.
33. Ibid., vol. 5, p. 112.
34. Ibid., vol. 5, p. 113.
35. R1-12-87, letter to Yvonne, February 27, 1951, Chandigarh.
36. Ibid.

CHAPTER XLIV

1. Petit, *Le Corbusier parle,* pp. 8, 9.
2. Hilary Spurling, *Matisse the Master* (London: Hamish Hamilton, 2005), p. 450.
3. E2-15-164, letter to Matisse, August 24, 1951, Roquebrune-Cap-Martin.
4. R2-2-48, letter to mother, August 27, 1951, Roquebrune-Cap-Martin.
5. R2-2-49, letter to mother, September 9, 1951, Paris.
6. Ibid.
7. Ibid.
8. Ibid.
9. Ibid.
10. R2-2-51, letter to mother, November 9, 1951, Simla.
11. Ibid.
12. Petit, *Le Corbusier lui-même,* p. 105.
13. Ibid.
14. Ibid.
15. Ibid.
16. R2-2-52, letter to mother, December 12, 1951, Marseille.
17. Ibid.
18. Ibid.
19. Petit, *Le Corbusier lui-même,* p. 112.
20. R2-2-54, letter to mother, January 14, 1952, Paris.
21. Ibid.
22. R1-12-95, letter to Yvonne, January 22, 1952, Chandigarh.
23. Ibid.
24. R2-2-55 to 56, letter to mother, enclosing copy of a letter from Nehru, April 5, 1952, Simla.
25. Ibid.
26. Petit, *Le Corbusier parle,* p. 68.
27. Le Corbusier, *When the Cathedrals Were White* (New York: Reynal and Hitchcock, 1947), p. 108.
28. Ibid.
29. *Le Corbusier Talks with Students* (New York: Princeton Architectural Press, 1999), p. 67.
30. E2-04-74, letter to Van Ameringen, February 25, 1952, Paris.
31. Ibid.
32. Ibid.
33. R2-2-31, letter from Yvonne to mother, December 31, 1950, Paris.
34. Petit, *Le Corbusier parle,* p. 105.
35. G2-12-337, letter to M. T. Harris, April 17, 1952, Paris.
36. M2-6-143, letter from M. T. Harris, June 12, 1952, Darien, Connecticut.
37. G2-12-337, letter to M. T. Harris, April 17, 1952, Paris.
38. M2-6-145, letter from M. T. Harris, June 25, 1952, Scott's Cove, Darien, Connecticut.
39. Ibid.

40. G2-12-518, letter to M. T. Harris, June 27, 1952, Paris.
41. R2-2-58, letter to mother, June 12, 1952, Paris.
42. R1-12-99, letter to Yvonne, July 18, 1952, Grand Hotel Continental, Ajaccio.
43. Ibid.
44. R2-2-60, letter to mother, August 20, 1952, Paris.
45. Ibid.
46. R2-2-97, letter to mother, August 4, 1954, l'Etoile de Mer, Roquebrune-Cap-Martin.
47. Petit, *Le Corbusier parle,* p. 53.
48. Ibid., p. 55.
49. Brassaï, *The Artists of My Life* (New York: Viking Press, 1982), pp. 84, 85.
50. Ibid.
51. Ibid., p. 85.
52. Ibid., p. 86.
53. Ibid.
54. Ibid., pp. 86, 87.
55. Ibid., p. 87.
56. Ibid., p. 90.
57. Ibid.

CHAPTER XLV

1. Quotation provided by Jim Grissom, author of a forthcoming book on Le Corbusier's women. During the French production of *A Streetcar Named Desire,* starring Jean Marais as Stanley, Williams was introduced to Le Corbusier's work by Jean Cocteau.
2. R2-2-63 to 64, letter to mother, October 2, 1952, Roquebrune-Cap-Martin.
3. Ibid.
4. Le Corbusier et son atelier, rue de Sèvres 35, *Oeuvre complète,* vol. 6: *1952–1957* (Zurich: Les Editions d'Architecture, 1977), p. 90.
5. Ibid.
6. Ibid., vol. 6, pp. 90, 91.
7. Ibid., vol. 6, p. 91.
8. Ibid., vol. 6, pp. 91, 92.
9. Ibid., vol. 6, p. 92.
10. Doshi, *Le Corbusier and Louis I. Kahn,* p. 1.
11. Petit, *Le Corbusier lui-même,* p. 112.
12. Interview with Gisèle Gambu-Moreau, April 11, 2000.
13. "Happy Hive," *Time,* February 2, 1948.
14. "What's Luxurious," *Time,* June 12, 1950.
15. "The Trouble with Stilts," *Time,* January 22, 1951.
16. Ibid.
17. R2-2-65, letter to mother, October 15, 1952, Paris.
18. Ibid.
19. Ibid.
20. Ibid.
21. Ibid.
22. Petit, *Le Corbusier lui-même,* p. 112.
23. Ibid.

CHAPTER XLVI

1. R1-12-102, letter to Yvonne, November 26, 1952, Chandigarh.
2. Ibid.
3. R2-2-66, letter to mother, November 30, 1952, Chandigarh.
4. R1-12-102, letter to Yvonne, November 26, 1952, Chandigarh.
5. Ibid.
6. Ibid.
7. R2-2-66, letter to mother, November 30, 1952, Chandigarh.
8. Ibid.
9. R2-2-70, letter to mother, December 15, 1952, Chandigarh.
10. Ibid.
11. R2-2-68, letter from Royal Institute of British Architects, December 11, 1952, London.
12. Petit, *Le Corbusier parle,* p. 109.
13. R2-2-72, letter to mother, February 1, 1953, Paris.
14. R2-2-73, letter to mother, March 1, 1953, Paris.
15. R2-2-75, letter from Jeanne Heilbuth to Mrs. Jeanneret, March 19, 1953, Paris.
16. R2-2-77, letter to mother, March 30, 1953, Paris.
17. R2-2-78, letter to mother, May 17, 1953, Paris.
18. Ibid.
19. R2-2-79, letter to mother, June 2, 1953, Chandigarh.
20. Ibid.
21. R2-2-80, letter to mother, July 1, 1953, Paris.
22. R2-2-83, letter to mother, September 8, 1953, Paris.
23. E2-176 to 177, letter to Nehru, September 22, 1953, Paris.
24. R2-2-86, letter to mother, October 30, 1953, Paris.
25. Ibid.

26. Ibid.
27. "Nehru's Call to End Communalism," *The Sunday Tribune* (Ambala), November 8, 1953.
28. Ibid.
29. Ibid.
30. Ibid.
31. R2-2-87, letter to mother, November 29, 1953, Paris.
32. Ibid.
33. Ibid.
34. R2-2-90 to 91, letter to mother, January 27, 1954, Chandigarh.
35. Ibid.
36. Ibid.
37. R2-2-92, letter to mother, March 1, 1954.
38. Ibid.
39. Ibid.

CHAPTER XLVII

1. Le Corbusier et son atelier, rue de Sèvres 35, *Oeuvre complète,* vol. 6, p. 144.
2. Ibid.
3. Interview with Balkrishna Doshi, Ahmedabad, January 26, 2001.
4. Ibid.
5. Ibid.
6. Ibid.
7. R2-2-98, letter to mother, August 8, 1954, Roquebrune-Cap-Martin.
8. R2-2-99, letter to mother, September 26, 1954, Paris.
9. R2-2-100, letter to mother, October 24, 1954, Paris.
10. R2-2-103, letter to mother, November 17, 1954, Chandigarh.
11. Ibid.
12. R2-2-104 to 107, letter to mother, December 16–17, 1954, Cairo.
13. R2-2-111, letter to mother, February 17, 1955, Roquebrune-Cap-Martin.
14. Ibid.
15. Ibid.

CHAPTER XLVIII

1. M2-9-182, letter from Th. Rebutato, December 22, 1960, Roquebrune-Cap-Martin.
2. E3-10-53T, letter to Marguerite Tjader Harris, February 15, 1955, Etoile de Mer, Roquebrune-Cap-Martin.
3. Ibid.
4. Ibid.
5. Ibid.
6. G2-18-24, letter to Marguerite Tjader Harris, March 13, 1955, Paris.

CHAPTER XLIX

1. "Nehru Opens New Punjab High Court Building," unidentified paper, May 19, 1955.
2. Ibid.
3. Interview with M.S. Sharma, Chandigarh, January 29, 2001.
4. Petit, *Le Corbusier lui-même,* p. 116.
5. Doshi, *Le Corbusier and Louis I. Kahn,* p. 10.
6. Ibid.
7. Ibid.
8. Ibid., p. 14.
9. Ibid.
10. Ibid., p. 16.
11. Ibid., p. 17.
12. Ibid.
13. Ibid., p. 18.
14. Ibid., p. 19.

CHAPTER L

1. Interview with Anand Sarabhai, Ahmedabad, January 25, 2001.
2. G2-15-431, letter from A. P. Ducret to Mrs. Sarabhai, July 7, 1953, Paris.
3. G2-18-142, letter to Mrs. Manorama Sarabhai, February 7, 1955, Paris.
4. P3-5-223, letter to Mrs. Manorama Sarabhai, May 1, 1956, Ahmedabad.
5. Taya Zinkin, "No Compromise with Le Corbusier," *Manchester Guardian Weekly,* September 16, 1965, p. 14.
6. Ibid.
7. Ibid.
8. Interview with M. S. Sharma, Chandigarh, January 29, 2001.
9. Ibid.
10. Ibid.
11. Petit, *Le Corbusier lui-même,* pp. 116, 117.
12. Ibid.
13. From typescript from Main Ouverte book, November 26–27, 1954 statement, p. 12, FLC Code B 53.

CHAPTER LI

1. Le Corbusier et son atelier, rue de Sèvres 35, *Oeuvre complète,* vol. 6, p. 94.
2. Ibid.
3. Peter Serenyi, "Timeless but of Its

Time: Le Corbusier in India," in *The Le Corbusier Archive,* ed. H. Allen Brooks, vol. 26: *Ahmedabad 1953–1960* (New York: Garland, 1983), pp. 176–77. This is a particularly astute and helpful narrative.

4. Ibid.
5. Doshi, *Le Corbusier and Louis I. Kahn,* p. 11.
6. Ibid.
7. Ibid.
8. Le Corbusier et son atelier, rue de Sèvres 35, *Oeuvre complète,* vol. 6, p. 78.
9. Quoted to NFW by Anni Albers.
10. Doshi, *Le Corbusier and Louis I. Kahn,* pp. 11, 12.
11. Charles Correa, *Chandigarh: The View from Benares,* in H. Allen Brooks, ed., *The Le Corbusier Archive,* vol. 20 (New York: Garland, 1983), p. 198.
12. Deborah Gans, *The Le Corbusier Guide* (Princeton: Princeton Architectural Press, 1987), p. 232.
13. Correa, *Chandigarh,* p. 197.
14. Kalia, *Chandigarh,* p. 29.
15. Interviews with residents of Chandigarh, January 2001.

CHAPTER LII

1. Jim Grissom provided this quotation as well.
2. Danièle Pauly, *Le Corbusier: The Chapel of Ronchamp,* bilingual ed. (Paris: Fondation Le Corbusier, 1997), p. 59.
3. A. M. Cocagnac and M. R. Capellades, *Les chapelles du Rosaire à Vence par Matisse et de Notre-Dame-du-Haut à Ronchamp par Le Corbusier* (Paris: Cerf, 1955), p. 107.
4. Le Corbusier, *Ronchamp, les carnets de la recherche patiente 2* (Stuttgart: Les Editions Girsberger, 1957), p. 89.
5. Le Corbusier, *Textes et dessins pour Ronchamp* (Ronchamp: Association Oeuvre Notre-Dame-du-Haut, 1981), unpaginated.
6. Profuse thanks to Pauly, *Le Corbusier,* for this observation.
7. Le Corbusier, *L'Architecture d'aujourd'hui,* special issue on Le Corbusier, April 1948, p. 44.
8. Cocagnac and Capellades, *Les chapelles,* p. 107.
9. Le Corbusier, *Textes et dessins pour Ronchamp.*
10. Pauly, *Le Corbusier,* p. 87.
11. Ibid.
12. Ibid., p. 97.
13. Abbé Bolle-Redat, "Mieltes," *Journal de Notre Dame du Haut,* December 1971, p. 4.
14. Le Corbusier, *Le Livre de Ronchamp* (Paris: Les Cahiers Forces Vives/Editec, 1961), p. 18.

CHAPTER LIII

1. Philippe Potié, *Le Corbusier: le couvent Sainte Marie de la Tourette* (Paris: Fondation Le Corbusier, 2001), p. 62.
2. Ibid., p. 60.
3. Ibid., p. 7.
4. E1-17-79, letter to Le Révérend Père Couturier, May 11, 1953, Paris.
5. Letter from R. P. Couturier to Le Corbusier, July 28, 1953, Paris, in Jean Petit and Le Corbusier, *Un Couvent de Le Corbusier* (Paris: Les Cahiers Forces Vives/Editec, 1961), p. 23.
6. Ibid., p. 26.
7. Ibid., p. 28.
8. Fr. M.-A. Couturier, "Le Corbusier," *L'Art Sacré* 7–8 (March–April 1959).
9. Statement from Le Corbusier, February 15, 1954, Chandigarh.

CHAPTER LIV

1. Le Corbusier et son atelier, rue de Sèvres 35, *Oeuvre complète,* vol. 7: *1957–1965* (Zurich: Les Editions d'Architecture, 1977), p. 16.
2. Pauly, *Le Corbusier,* p. 103.
3. R1-12-104, letter to Yvonne, December 9, 1953, n.p.
4. Ibid.
5. Interview with Jacques Hindermeyer, November 4, 2000.
6. E3-10-53, letter to Mrs. Tjader Harris, February 15, 1955, Roquebrune-Cap-Martin.
7. Ibid.
8. Ibid.
9. R2-2-112 to 114, letter to mother, March 4, 1955, Paris.
10. R2-2-117 to 119, letter to mother, April 17, 1955, Roquebrune-Cap-Martin.
11. Ibid.
12. Ibid.
13. R2-2-120 to 121, letter to mother, May 15, 1955, Paris.

14. Ibid.
15. R2-2-122 to 123, letter to mother, June 5, 1955, Paris.
16. R2-2-124, letter to mother, June 23, 1955, Paris.
17. Ibid.
29. Ibid.
30. Petit, *Le Corbusier lui-même,* p. 116.
31. X1-18-151, Jean Petit, "Consécration de Marseille. Voici la Maison Radieuse de Nantes-Rezé," *Combat* (France), July 5, 1955.

CHAPTER LV

1. *Le Figaro,* June 27, 1955.
2. "Notre-Dame-du-Haut officiellement et solennellement réinstallée par son S. Exc. Mgr Dubois dans son domaine à Ronchamp," *Le Courrier de Belfort et du Territoire,* June 25, 1955.
3. Ibid.
4. Ibid.
5. Jean Petit and Pino Musi, *Ronchamp Le Corbusier* (Lugano: Fidia Edizioni d'Arte, Association Oeuvre de Notre Dame du Haut à Ronchamp, René Bolle Redat, 1997), n.p.
6. *Le Courrier de Belfort et du Territoire,* June 25, 1955.
7. Petit and Musi, *Ronchamp Le Corbusier,* n.p.
8. *Le Courrier de Belfort et du Territoire,* June 25, 1955.
9. In *L'Art Sacré,* special issue on Ronchamp, September–October 1955, p. 23.
10. Ibid., pp. 24–25.
11. *Le Courrier de Belfort et du Territoire,* June 25, 1955.
12. Ibid.
13. Ibid.
14. Ibid.
15. Petit and Musi, *Ronchamp Le Corbusier,* n.p.
16. Ibid.
17. Ibid.
18. Petit, *Le Corbusier parle,* p. 48.
19. R2-2-125 to 126, letter to mother, June 27, 1955, Ronchamp.
20. Ibid.
21. Ibid.
22. Ibid.
23. Ibid.
24. M. A. Couturier, "Le Corbusier/Ronchamp," in *L'Art Sacré,* July–August 1953, pp. 29, 31.
25. Petit, *Le Corbusier parle,* p. 49.
26. Petit and Musi, *Ronchamp Le Corbusier,* n.p.
27. Ibid.
28. G2-19-108, letter to M. Tjader Harris, June 24, 1955, Paris.

CHAPTER LVI

1. R2-2-129, letter to mother, August 9, 1955, Roquebrune-Cap-Martin.
2. Ibid.
3. R1-7-248, postcard from mother, July 11, 1955, Le Lac, Vevey.
4. E1-13-16, letter from Blaise Cendrars, September 5, 1955, n.p.
5. R2-2-131, letter to mother, September 23, 1955, Paris.
6. R2-2-132 to 135, letter to mother, October 9, 1955, Paris.
7. R2-2-136, letter to mother, November 10, 1955, Bangkok. (Plane travel on Air France from Tokyo to Ahmedabad.)
8. Ibid.
9. Ibid.
10. Petit, *Le Corbusier lui-même,* pp. 117, 118.
11. Interview with Caroline Maniaque, January 22, 2003.
12. "Le Corbusier vu par Marie Jaoul," in *Corbu vu par* (Liège: P. Mardaga, 1987), p. 67.
13. Ibid., p. 68.
14. U3-08/56-57, Le Corbusier, personal memo (notes for an unpublished article), January 4, 1956.
15. Petit, *Le Corbusier lui-même,* p. 118.
16. Ibid.
17. Ibid., p. 119.
18. Ibid.
19. Ibid.
20. Le Corbusier, "Jean Prouvé a élevé . . . ," February 29, 1956, in *Jean Prouvé et Paris* (Paris: Editions du Pavillon de l'Arsenal, Picard Editeur, 2001), p. 284.
21. R1-12/125T, letter to Yvonne, September 15, 1956, n.p.
22. R1-12-347, letter to Yvonne, April 4, 1957, Orly Airport (en route to India).
23. R1-12-348, letter to Yvonne, April 29, 1957, Chandigarh.
24. Petit, *Le Corbusier parle,* p. 9.
25. Petit, *Le Corbusier lui-même,* p. 120.
26. Ibid., p. 121.
27. Ibid.

CHAPTER LVII

1. Le Corbusier, *Le Poème Electronique,* ed. Jean Petit (Paris: Les Editions de Minuit, 1958), n.p.
2. Marc Treib, *Space Calculated in Seconds: The Philips Pavilion, Le Corbusier, Edgard Varèse* (Princeton: Princeton University Press, 1996), pp. 6, 7.
3. Ibid., p. 193.
4. Ibid., p. 218.
5. Ibid., pp. 87, 88.
6. Ibid.
7. Ibid.
8. J2-19-173, letter to Kalff, July 22, 1958, Paris.
9. Le Corbusier, *Le Poème Electronique,* n.p.
10. Treib, *Space Calculated in Seconds,* p. 211.
11. Ibid., p. 252.
12. R2-2-137, letter to mother, June 17, 1958, Paris.
13. Ibid.
14. R2-2-139, letter to mother, August 23, 1958, Roquebrune-Cap-Martin.
15. Ibid.
16. Ibid.
17. Le Corbusier et son atelier, rue de Sèvres 35, *Oeuvre complète,* vol. 7, p. 187.
18. Petit, *Le Corbusier parle,* p. 19.
19. Petit, *Le Corbusier lui-même,* p. 124.
20. Ibid.
21. Le Corbusier, *Les Trois établissements humains,* ed. Jean Petit (Paris: Editions de Minuit, 1997). This book was originally printed in 1945 (Paris: Denoël, Collection Ascoral) without this statement, which is not from Le Corbusier but from Charles Péguy. See Catherine de Smet, "Le Livre comme synthèse des Arts. Editions et design graphique chez Le Corbusier, 1945–1965," Ph.D. diss., EHESS, Paris, 2002, p. 383.
22. Le Corbusier, *Les Trois établissements humains,* pp. 11, 13.
23. Ibid., p. 45.
24. X1-20-138, J. M. Nussbaum, "Mme. Marie Jeanneret-Perret, mère de Le Corbusier," *L'Impartial* (Switzerland), September 1959.
25. R1-10 246T, letter to Albert Jeanneret, February 18, 1960, n.p.
26. Ibid.

CHAPTER LVIII

1. G1-10-194, letter to Marguerite Tjader Harris, September 2, 1956, Paris.
2. E3-10-55, letter to Marguerite Tjader Harris, October 6, 1956, Paris.
3. E3-10-56, letter from Marguerite Tjader Harris, October 9, 1956, Darien, Conn.
4. G1-16-110 to 111, letter to Marguerite Tjader Harris, July 22, 1959, Paris.
5. Ibid.
6. Ibid.
7. E3-10-59, letter from Marguerite Tjader Harris, December 10, 1959, Darien, Conn.
8. Ibid.
9. E3-10-61, Secretary of Le Corbusier to Marguerite Tjader Harris, April 15, 1960, Paris.
10. Interview with Brother Roland Ducret, April 25, 2001.
11. Ibid.
12. Ibid.
13. Petit and Le Corbusier, *Un Couvent de Le Corbusier,* p. 131.
14. Ibid., pp. 130, 131.
15. Ibid., pp. 132, 20.
16. Ibid., p. 29.
17. Ibid.
18. Ibid., p. 132.
19. Interview with Brother Roland Ducret, April 25, 2001.
20. Petit and Le Corbusier, *Un Couvent de Le Corbusier,* p. 20.
21. X2-1-73, René Deroudille, "Inauguration du couvent des dominicains," *Derrnière heure Lyonnaise,* October 20, 1960.
22. Ibid.
23. Petit and Le Corbusier, *Un Couvent de Le Corbusier,* p. 28.
24. Ibid., pp. 28, 29.
25. *Paris Match,* September 11, 1965, pp. 44–58.

CHAPTER LIX

1. Petit, *Le Corbusier lui-même,* p. 124.
2. Ibid.
3. Ibid., p. 123.
4. Interview with Denise René, Paris, March 11, 2002.
5. Petit, *Le Corbusier lui-même,* p. 125.
6. Ibid.

7. Ibid., p. 126.
8. Ibid.
9. Ibid.
10. Ibid.
11. Ibid.
12. Le Corbusier et son atelier, rue de Sèvres 35, *Oeuvre complète,* vol. 7, p. 220.
13. T2-18/131, Charles Colbert to J. W. Rankin, March 21, 1961, New York.
14. T2-18-152, letter from Charles Colbert, April 17, 1961, New York.
15. Grayson Kirk, President, Columbia University, New York City, April 28, 1961.
16. Le Corbusier to Nehru, February 14, 1962, in Petit, *Le Corbusier lui-même,* p. 127.
17. G3-3-9, letter to Narang, December 14, 1962, n.p.
18. Ibid.
19. G3-3-11, letter to Nehru, December 17, 1962, sent January 4, 1963, n.p.
20. P2-19-93, letter from Nehru, February 9, 1963, New Delhi.
21. Petit, *Le Corbusier lui-même,* p. 128.
22. G3-3-397 to 398, letter to Nehru, June 26, 1963, New Delhi.
23. Ibid.
24. Petit, *Le Corbusier lui-même,* p. 129.
25. Interview with Oscar Niemeyer, Rio de Janeiro, July 12, 2007.
26. Letter to the architects of Barcelona, October 8, 1962, quoted in Petit, *Le Corbusier lui-même,* p. 130.
27. Ibid.
28. Ibid., pp. 130, 131.
29. Le Corbusier et son atelier, rue de Sèvres 35, *Oeuvre complète,* vol. 7, p. 54.
30. Petit, *Le Corbusier parle,* p. 47.
31. Petit, *Le Corbusier lui-même,* p. 132.
32. T2-18-268, letter from Jean Graven, rector of University of Geneva, May 11, 1963, Geneva.
33. Petit, *Le Corbusier lui-même,* p. 132.
34. Ibid., p. 131.
35. Interview with Roger Aujame, Paris, October 5, 2000.
36. Ibid.
37. Letter from Le Corbusier to his staff, February 24, 1960, in Robert Doisneau and Jean Petit, *Bonjour M. Le Corbusier* (Zurich: Hans Grieshaber, n.d.), p. 92.
38. Le Corbusier, *My Work* (London: Architectural Press, 1960), pp. 9, 10, 11.
39. Interview with Françoise Jollant Kneebone, Paris, November 3, 2000.
40. P2-13-94, telegram to Nehru, October 26, 1963, Paris.
41. P2-13-98, letter to Nehru, October 26, 1963, Paris.
42. Ibid.
43. G3-4-94, letter to Nehru, November 4, 1963, Paris.
44. P2-13-100, letter to Nehru, March 30, 1964, Paris.

CHAPTER LX

1. E3-10-62, letter from Mrs. Tjader Harris, May 29, 1961, Hotel Lutétia, Paris.
2. E3-10-65, letter from Mrs. Tjader Harris, January 25, 1963, Vikingsborg, Darien, Conn.
3. Ibid.
4. G3-03-103 to 104, letter to Hilary Harris, February 2, 1963, Paris.
5. G3-03-102, letter to Marguerite Tjader Harris, February 2, 1963, Paris.
6. E3-10-69, letter from Marguerite Tjader Harris, February 11, 1963, Darien, Conn.
7. E3-10-70, letter from Hilary T. Harris, March 29, 1963, New York.
8. Petit, *Le Corbusier lui-même,* p. 132.
9. Ibid.
10. X2-3-116, "De Gaulle a félicité Le Corbusier, Grand Officier de la Légion d'honneur," *France-Soir,* December 20, 1963.
11. Petit, *Le Corbusier lui-même,* p. 132.
12. Ibid.
13. Soltan, "Working with Le Corbusier," p. 16.
14. Letter to Albert Jeanneret, July 29, 1965, Roquebrune-Cap-Martin, in Petit, *Le Corbusier lui-même,* pp. 139, 140.
15. Ibid.
16. Ibid.
17. Zaknic, *The Final Testament of Père Corbu,* p. 73.
18. Letter to Albert Jeanneret, August 24, 1965, Roquebrune-Cap-Martin, in Petit, *Le Corbusier lui-même,* p. 140.
19. Ibid.
20. Ibid.

INDEX

Page numbers in *italics* refer to illustrations.

A NOTE ON THE TYPE

The text of this book was set in Garamond No. 3. It is not a true copy of any of the designs of Claude Garamond (ca. 1480–1561), but an adaptation of his types, which set the European standard for two centuries. It probably owes as much to the designs of Jean Jannon, a Protestant printer working in Sedan in the early seventeenth century, who had worked with Garamond's romans earlier, in Paris, but who was denied their use because of Catholic censorship. This particular version is based on an adaptation by Morris Fuller Benton.

COMPOSED BY

North Market Street Graphics, Lancaster, Pennsylvania

PRINTED AND BOUND BY

Berryville Graphics, Berryville, Virginia

DESIGNED BY

Iris Weinstein